Ross M

With Shi

Kevin E. Kline

Microsoft®
SQL Server
2012

Management and Administration

SAMS | 800 East 96th Street, Indianapolis, Indiana 46240 USA

Microsoft® SQL Server 2012 Management and Administration

Copyright © 2013 by Pearson Education, Inc.

ISBN-13: 978-0-672-33600-3
ISBN-10: 0-672-33600-6

The Library of Congress cataloging-in-publication data is on file.

Printed in the United States of America

First Printing September 2012

Trademarks

All terms mentioned in this book that are known to be trademarks or service marks have been appropriately capitalized. Sams Publishing cannot attest to the accuracy of this information. Use of a term in this book should not be regarded as affecting the validity of any trademark or service mark.

Warning and Disclaimer

Every effort has been made to make this book as complete and as accurate as possible, but no warranty or fitness is implied. The information provided is on an "as is" basis. The author and the publisher shall have neither liability nor responsibility to any person or entity with respect to any loss or damages arising from the information contained in this book.

Bulk Sales

Sams Publishing offers excellent discounts on this book when ordered in quantity for bulk purchases or special sales. For more information, please contact

U.S. Corporate and Government Sales
1-800-382-3419
corpsales@pearsontechgroup.com

For sales outside of the U.S., please contact

International Sales
international@pearsoned.com

Editor-in-Chief
Greg Wiegand

Acquisition Editor
Neil Rowe

Development Editor
Mark Renfrow

Managing Editor
Kristy Hart

Project Editors
Monika Grzesiak
Jovana Shirley

Copy Editor
Barbara Hacha

Indexer
Lisa Stumpf

Proofreaders
Chrissy White
Sarah Kearns

Technical Editors
J. Boyd Nolan
Alex T. Silverstein

Editorial Assistant
Cindy Teeters

Cover Designer
Anne Jones

Compositor
Nonie Ratcliff

Contributing Writer
Saleem Hakani

Contents at a Glance

Introduction 1

Part I: SQL Server 2012 Database Engine Administration and Management Topics

1 Installing or Upgrading the Database Engine to
   SQL Server 2012 13
2 Administering and Configuring the Database Engine Settings 67
3 Administering Storage, I/O, and Partitioning 127
4 Creating Packages and Transferring Data On-Premise
   and to the Cloud 179
5 Managing and Optimizing SQL Server 2012 Indexes 229
6 Backing Up and Restoring SQL Server 2012 Databases 283

Part II: Hardening, Auditing, and Securing SQL Server 2012

7 Hardening and Auditing a SQL Server 2012 Implementation 335
8 Administering SQL Server 2012 Security and Authorization 383
9 Encrypting SQL Server 2012 Data and Communications 429

Part III: SQL Server 2012 AlwaysOn High-Availability and Disaster Recovery Alternatives

10 Implementing and Managing AlwaysOn Availability Groups 483
11 Implementing and Managing AlwaysOn Failover
    Clustering Instances 527
12 Implementing and Managing Database Mirroring 587
13 Implementing and Managing Replication 621

Part IV: Performance Tuning, Monitoring, Troubleshooting, and Maintenance

14 Performance Tuning and Troubleshooting SQL Server 2012 677
15 Monitoring SQL Server 2012 729
16 SQL Server 2012 Maintenance Practices 779

Part V: Multi-Instance Management, Consolidation, and Private Clouds

17 Implementing and Managing Policy-Based Management............811

18 Managing Workloads with Resource Governor...........................839

19 Consolidation, Virtualization, and Private Clouds.....................869

    Index..909

Table of Contents

Introduction 1

**Part I: SQL Server 2012 Database Engine Administration and
          Management Topics**

**1 Installing or Upgrading the Database Engine to
   SQL Server 2012** **13**

What's New for Installation with SQL Server 2012? 14

Preplanning and Preparing a SQL Server 2012
Server Database Engine Installation 16

Gathering Additional Information Necessary to Proceed 25

Installing a New Installation of SQL Server 2012 31

Upgrading the Database Engine to SQL Server 2012 40

Finalizing the SQL Server 2012 Installation or Upgrade 51

Installing SQL Server 2012 on Windows Server Core 53

Managing SQL Server 2012 Installations 62

Summary 64

Best Practices 64

**2 Administering and Configuring the Database
   Engine Settings** **67**

What's New for DBAs When Administering the
Database Engine on SQL Server 2012 68

Administering SQL Server 2012 Server Properties 68

Administering the SQL Server Database Engine Folders 87

Administering Database Properties 98

SQL Server Database Engine Management Tasks 114

Administering the SQL Server Agent 119

Summary 123

Best Practices 124

3 Administering Storage, I/O, and Partitioning **127**

What's New for DBAs When Administering Storage
on SQL Server 2012 128

Storage Hardware Overview 129

Designing and Administering Storage on SQL
   Server 2012 140
Designing for BLOB Storage 158
Designing and Administrating Partitions in
   SQL Server 2012 164
Data Compression in SQL Server 2012 172
Summary 175
Best Practices 175

4 Creating Packages and Transferring Data On-Premise
   and to the Cloud **179**
What's New in Integration Services for SQL Server 2012 180
Options for Creating Packages 181
Integration Services Packages 182
Developing Packages 189
Enhancing Packages 199
Deploying and Running IntegrationServices Packages 212
Transferring Data with Integration Services 221
Moving Data to the Cloud 224
Summary 228
Best Practices 228

5 Managing and Optimizing SQL Server 2012 Indexes **229**
What's New for Indexes with SQL Server 2012 229
The Importance of Indexes 230
How Indexes Work 230
General Index Characteristics 238
Index Design and Strategy 242
Administering Indexes 247
Configuring Indexes for Maximum Performance 268
Summary 280
Best Practices 280

6 Backing Up and Restoring SQL Server 2012 Databases **283**
What's New for Backup and Recovery with SQL
   Server 2012? 283
The Importance of Backups 285
Backing Up and Recovering the Database Engine 289

Backup and Recovery Impact on Other Database
  Engine Features 324
Summary 330
Best Practices 330

Part II: Hardening, Auditing, and Securing SQL Server 2012

7 Hardening and Auditing a SQL Server 2012 Implementation   335
  What's New for Hardening and Auditing
    SQL Server 2012 Implementation? 336
  Windows and SQL Server Authentication 337
  Using Configuration Tools to Harden the Installation 343
  Hardening SQL Server Service Accounts 350
  Installing Service Packs and Critical Fixes 355
  Leveraging SQL Server Auditing Strategies 357
  Monitoring Events with SQL Server Audit 359
  Additional SQL Server Hardening Recommendations 373
  Summary 379
  Best Practices 380

8 Administering SQL Server 2012 Security and Authorization   383
  What's New for Security and Authorization with
    SQL Server 2012? 383
  SQL Server Security 385
  Security Management DDL 398
  Administering SQL Server Security 404
  Contained Database Authentication 421
  Summary 427
  Best Practices 427

9 Encrypting SQL Server 2012 Data and Communications   429
  What's New for Encryption with SQL Server 2012? 430
  Encryption in SQL 431
  Column Encryption 432
  Securing the Data Storage 435
  Extensible Key Management 444
  Transparent Data Encryption 446
  Securing Connections 452

Using Certificates 456
SQL Server and BitLocker Drive Encryption 465
Configuring BitLocker Drive Encryption on a
  SQL Server System 469
Summary 478
Best Practices 478

Part III: SQL Server 2012 AlwaysOn High-Availability and Disaster Recovery Alternatives

10 Implementing and Managing AlwaysOn Availability Groups   483

SQL Server 2012 AlwaysOn Availability Groups Overview 484
Implementing AlwaysOn Availability Groups 490
Managing AlwaysOn Availability Groups 509
Monitoring and Troubleshooting AlwaysOn
  Availability Groups 520
Summary 525
Best Practices 526

11 Implementing and Managing AlwaysOn Failover Cluster Instances   527

SQL Server 2012 AlwaysOn Failover Cluster
  Instances Overview 527
What's New for SQL Server 2012 AlwaysOn
  Failover Cluster Instances? 528
Additional Elements of AlwaysOn Failover
  Cluster Instances 537
Implementing a Single-Instance SQL Server 2012
  Failover Cluster 544
Implementing a Multiple-Instance SQL Server 2012
  Failover Cluster 564
Multi-subnet SQL Server 2012 Failover Cluster Overview 568
Implementing Multi-subnet SQL Server 2012
  Failover Cluster 571
Managing Failover Clusters from a SQL Server 2012
  Perspective 574
Verifying the Status of Clustered Service and
  Applications, Nodes, Storage, and Networks 574
Managing Failover Clusters from a Windows Server
  2008 R2 Perspective 580

Summary 583
Best Practices 583

12 Implementing and Managing Database Mirroring **587**

SQL Server 2012 Database Mirroring Overview 588
Combining Database Mirroring with Other SQL
Server 2012 Technologies 596
Implementing a Database Mirroring Session 599
Managing a Database Mirroring Session 607
Monitoring and Troubleshooting a Database
Mirroring Session 614
Summary 618
Best Practices 619

13 Implementing and Managing Replication **621**

SQL Server 2012 Replication Essentials 622
Implementing SQL Server Replication 639
Managing SQL Server 2012 Replication 667
Monitoring and Troubleshooting SQL Server Replication 670
Summary 672
Best Practices 672

**Part IV: Performance Tuning, Monitoring, Troubleshooting, and
Maintenance**

14 Performance Tuning and Troubleshooting SQL Server 2012 ... **677**

Platform Troubleshooting and Optimization 680
Database Troubleshooting and Optimization 691
Application Optimization and Troubleshooting 714
Introducing Extended Events to Troubleshoot SQL Server ... 718
Summary 726
Best Practices 726

15 Monitoring SQL Server 2012 .... **729**

What's New for Monitoring in SQL Server 2012? 730
Gaining Quick Insight into a SQL Server System 731
The Data Collector and the Management Data Warehouse 744
SQL Server Utilities 757

Creating Operators and Sending Email Alerts..................763
Using the Windows Server 2008 R2 Performance
  Monitoring Tools...769
Additional Tools to Monitor SQL Server 2012................776
Summary...777
Best Practices..777

16 SQL Server 2012 Maintenance Practices....................**779**
What's New for Maintenance with SQL Server 2012?.........779
Establishing a SQL Server Maintenance Plan....................780
Creating a Maintenance Plan...792
Establishing Maintenance Schedules for SQL Server........805
Summary...807
Best Practices..807

Part V: Multi-Instance Management, Consolidation, and Private Clouds

17 Implementing and Managing Policy-Based Management.....**811**
Introduction to Policy-Based Management.........................811
Policy-Based Management Concepts..................................813
Implementing Policy-Based Management..........................819
Monitoring and Enforcing Best Practices by Using
  Policy-Based Management...830
Summary...836
Best Practices..836

18 Managing Workloads with Resource Governor............**839**
What's New for Resource Governor in SQL Server 2012.......840
Overview of Resource Governor Concepts, Workflow, and
  Scenarios..841
Implementing and Configuring Resource Governor...........845
Creating a Workload Group..852
Understanding Default Transact-SQL Syntax with
  Resource Governor...858
Managing Resource Governor...860
Monitoring Resource Governor...862
Summary...867
Best Practices..868

19 Consolidation, Virtualization, and Private Clouds **869**

Understanding Consolidation, Virtualization,
and Private Cloud Strategies 870

Planning Your Implementation of Hyper-V 878

Installation of the Microsoft Hyper-V Server Role 883

Becoming Familiar with the Hyper-V Administrative
Console 886

Installing a SQL Server 2012 Guest Operating
System Session 889

Modifying SQL Server 2012 Guest Session
Configuration Settings 893

Launching a Hyper-V Guest Session 898

Using Snapshots of Guest Operating System Sessions 900

Optimizing SQL Server 2012 for Private Cloud 903

Summary 905

Best Practices 905

Index **909**

About the Author

Ross Mistry is an author, public speaker, principal enterprise architect, and veteran in the Silicon Valley. He has published numerous books and articles and frequently speaks at conferences worldwide.

With more than 15 years of experience, Ross has been a trusted advisor providing strategic guidance for many C-level executives and has been responsible for planning and implementing technology solutions for some of the largest companies in the world. He has taken on the lead architect role for many Silicon Valley internet startups and Fortune 100 organizations, including Network Appliance, McAfee, The Sharper Image, Visa, CIBC, Levi's, Wells Fargo, and Intel. He specializes in data platform, business productivity, unified communications, core infrastructure, and private cloud.

At Microsoft, Ross is a director and principal enterprise architect at the Microsoft Technology Centers (MTCs). The MTCs are collaborative environments that provide access to innovative technologies and world-class expertise, giving organizations the ability to envision, design, and deploy solutions to meet their exact needs. He is currently in the process of launching and leading the first MTC in Canada.

Ross is an active participant in the SQL Server community. He co-managed the main Microsoft SQL Server Twitter account @SQLServer and frequently speaks at technology conferences around the world. He has recently spoken at TechEd, PASS Summit, SQL Connections, and SQL BITS. He is a series author and has formulated many best practices and written many whitepapers and articles for Microsoft, *SQL Server Magazine*, and Techtarget.com.

You can follow Ross on Twitter at @RossMistry or contact him at http://www.rossmistry.com.

Contributing Authors

Shirmattie Seenairne is a seasoned and successful author, technical writer, and editor with over ten years of experience in the technology field. She has contributed to many books, including *Introducing SQL Server 2012*, *Windows Server 2008 R2 Unleashed*, *SQL Server 2008 Management and Administration*, *Exchange Server 2007 Unleashed*, and *SharePoint Server 2007 Unleashed*.

As a technical writer, Shirmattie has written many whitepapers, design documents, and operational procedures for Fortune 100 organizations such as Microsoft, Network Appliance, Solectron, and Gilead Sciences Inc. Shirmattie also writes articles for TechTarget on various subjects.

Kevin E. Kline is a renowned database expert and software industry veteran currently serving as the Director of Engineering Services at SQL Sentry, a leading vendor of database and business intelligence tools. A Microsoft SQL Server MVP since 2004, Kevin was a founding board member and former president of PASS. He has written or co-written eleven books including the best-selling *SQL in a Nutshell*. Kevin contributes monthly columns to *SQL Server Pro* and *DBTA* magazines. He is a noted trainer and thought leader on IT leadership skills, database management technology and practices, and SQL Server performance tuning and optimization. Kevin is a top-rated speaker at conferences worldwide such as Microsoft TechEd, the PASS Summit, DevTeach, Oracle OpenWorld, and SQL Connections. He tweets at @kekline and blogs at http://KevinEKline.com.

Dedication

I dedicate this book to my children. One day your life will flash before your eyes—make sure it's worth watching. And to the conclusion and next chapter in the game of life: Retire with the Crown *and* Return of the King—*October 1, 2012.*

Acknowledgments

Firstly, I would like to thank my wife and children for their patience while I was working on my latest title. Your unwavering support and inspiration is what keeps me motivated and on the right track. I am very proud of my family and looking forward to building greater memories in the years to come.

I would also like to acknowledge my contributing authors: Shirmattie Seenarine and Kevin Kline. Thank you for sharing SQL Server best practices and putting together great content in a short timeframe. Shirmattie, your attention to detail, hard work, and dedication is very much appreciated. Kevin, I have followed your work for years, and I am very proud to have you on the author team. I look forward to working with both of you on future engagements.

To my friends at Sams Publishing: I would like to thank Neil Rowe for providing me with this excellent writing opportunity and the whole production team who worked on making this book another successful title: Monika Grzesiak, Barbara Hacha, Mark Renfrow, Stephane Nakib, Jovana Shirley, Chrissy White, Sarah Kearns, Cindy Teeters, Anne Jones, and Nonie Ratcliff. Special thanks to Monika for being very meticulous and managing the production lifecycle.

Lastly, I can't forget J. Boyd Nolan for doing an excellent job on technical editing, Saleem Hakani, principal architect at Microsoft, for providing best practices and notes from the field, my colleagues on the SQL Server product group, and the folks at Fusion-io for providing me with the storage memory platform for my SQL Server private cloud, which was used to create the book.

—Ross Mistry

I would like to thank Ross Mistry for the opportunity to write with him on this book and for taking the time to mentor me even when it seemed impossible for him to take on yet another task. His drive for excellence, know-how, and passion for technology is nothing short of admirable.

To my parents, it is my greatest wish is to be an outstanding parent like the both of you. You taught me the importance of hard work, family, and unconditional love. I am forever grateful to the both of you for always being ready to help in my time of need. I love you both.

In addition, a big thanks must be given to the publication team for all their hard work. This book has evolved into a fantastic piece because of all you.

—Shirmattie Seenarine

I'd like to begin by thanking Ross Mistry for bringing me in on this project. I've always enjoyed Ross's work, so it was especially enjoyable to get to work directly with Ross on the newest edition of the book. I'm amazed by Ross's energy and incredible alacrity. I learned a lot from him during this project and hope to work with him again. His patience and guidance ensured that I got the work done on time and with top quality. Barbara Hacha, copy editor, deserves a medal for all of the format fixes she had to put in to make my content meet the standards. And technical editor J. Boyd Nolan did an outstanding job driving for clear and rich content.

In addition, I'd like to thank Richard Douglas for performing an additional early technical edit on four of my chapters in this book. Richard's contribution helped me get the content delivered on time and elevated the quality of content enormously. Finally, no technical author can ever adequately thank his family enough for the sacrifice of time and attention that a book project entails. Rachel, thank you for being my encourager, supporter, and touchstone. Working from home, with you by my side, is my greatest blessing. To my horde of girls—Anna, Katie, Savannah, Kaylee, and Ava—thank you for being a help in the house and a bright spot during the long days and nights of toil!

—Kevin E. Kline

We Want to Hear from You!

As the reader of this book, *you* are our most important critic and commentator. We value your opinion and want to know what we're doing right, what we could do better, what areas you'd like to see us publish in, and any other words of wisdom you're willing to pass our way.

We welcome your comments. You can email or write to let us know what you did or didn't like about this book—as well as what we can do to make our books better.

Please note that we cannot help you with technical problems related to the topic of this book.

When you write, please be sure to include this book's title and author as well as your name and email address. We will carefully review your comments and share them with the author and editors who worked on the book.

Email: consumer@samspublishing.com

Mail: Sams Publishing
            ATTN: Reader Feedback
            800 East 96th Street
            Indianapolis, IN 46240 USA

Reader Services

Visit our website and register this book at informit.com/register for convenient access to any updates, downloads, or errata that might be available for this book.

Introduction

SQL Server 2012 is Microsoft's latest cloud-ready information platform providing Database Administrators (DBAs) the ability to efficiently protect, unlock, and scale the power of their data across the desktop, device, datacenter, and private or public cloud.

Although similar to the previous versions of SQL Server, SQL Server 2012 offers a tremendous number of new capabilities enabling mission-critical performance, breakthrough insights, and a flexible hybrid IT environment that can span across on-premise servers, private or public clouds.

This book is designed to be the ultimate SQL Server 2012 guide for DBAs because it provides detailed strategic guidance in the areas of planning and implementation, management, administration, security, high availability, disaster recovery, monitoring, and performance tuning.

Moreover, this book includes industry best practices, tips, and step-by-step instructions based on real-world examples from the industry's best SQL Server experts who have developed, influenced, and worked with the product several years before it shipped.

Some of the new features covered in this book include AlwaysOn Availability Groups for achieving mission-critical availability, installing SQL Server 2012 on Windows Server Core, which is a new deployment option, implementing ColumnStore Indexes to achieve blazing fast query performance, migrating data to public clouds, and optimizing SQL Server in a Private Cloud deployment.

The book is based on the Microsoft Windows Server 2008 R2 operating system. As a result, not only will readers gain knowledge about SQL Server 2012, but they will also have the opportunity to understand the advantages of running and installing SQL Server 2012 on Windows Server 2008 R2.

What Is in This Book?

This book is organized into five parts, with each part made up of several chapters focusing on core SQL Server 2012 management and administration topics. The parts and chapters of the book are detailed in the following sections.

Part I—SQL Server 2012 Database Engine Administration and Management Topics

The first part of the book begins by providing an overview of SQL Server 2012, including planning and installing the new cloud–ready information platform. After you get SQL Server 2012 installed, the majority of your time will be spent managing and administering the new SQL Server infrastructure. Therefore, the remainder of Part I consists of chapters dedicated to SQL Server 2012 administration and management.

Chapter 1: Installing or Upgrading the Database Engine to SQL Server 2012

With the recent release of SQL Server 2012, organizations are eager to migrate to the new and improved cloud-ready information data platform. However, many organizations feel challenged when trying to establish the best strategies for moving forward. This chapter focuses on the various SQL Server 2012 installation, deployment, and migration strategies. It answers the question once and for all whether organizations should upgrade from a previous version or perform a new SQL Server 2012 installation from scratch and then conduct a migration.

Other topics highlighted in this chapter include hardware and software requirements, supported migration strategies, new deployment features, such how to install SQL Server 2012 on Windows Server Core, and automating the installation. Moreover, this chapter describes the benefits associated with running SQL Server on Windows Server 2008 R2 and showcases the different tools to utilize to achieve a successful installation or migration.

Chapter 2: Administering and Configuring the Database Engine Settings

After SQL Server 2012 is installed, it is necessary to configure and administer the server. This chapter focuses on administering and configuring the core features and components associated with the Database Engine. Topics include administering and configuring the SQL Server Properties pages,

Database Properties pages, Database Engine folders, and the SQL Server Agent. Managing server and database configuration settings, such as memory, processor performance, and many other settings, are also covered in depth.

Chapter 3: Administering Storage, I/O, and Partitioning

This chapter, which is a new edition to the book, focuses on all topics related to SQL Server storage. It starts off by introducing the fundamental concepts around SQL Server storage, IO configurations, and hardware-related topics, such as hard disks, RAID, SAN, and SSDs. The chapter then includes step-by-step configurations based on best practices on database file placement, creating filegroups, data compression, and partitioning.

Chapter 4: Creating Packages and Transferring Data On-Premise and to the Cloud

A common DBA task is transferring data or databases between source and target environments. This chapter focuses on importing, exporting, and transforming data and databases via SQL Server Management Studio and Integration Services. The chapter also covers how packages are created, saved, and executed as well as the management of the Integration Services component. Finally, this chapter also showcases how to deploy a database from on-premise instances of SQL Server to Windows Azure SQL Database, which is the Microsoft public cloud offering.

Chapter 5: Managing and Optimizing SQL Server 2012 Indexes

Similar to an index found in a book, an index in SQL Server is utilized for fast retrieval of data from tables. This chapter covers planning, designing, implementing, and managing indexes within the Database Engine. This chapter also includes how to achieve blazing-fast query performance with SQL Server 2012's new ColumnStore Index.

Chapter 6: Backing Up and Restoring SQL Server 2012 Databases

Backing up and restoring databases is one of the most critical duties of a DBA. It is important that DBAs understand the concepts associated with SQL Server backups and recovery so that in the event of a disaster, they can restore the database to the point of failure. This chapter covers the concepts and step-by-step procedures on creating backups and how to conduct restores with SQL Server Management Studio and Transact-SQL.

The chapter also includes other backup and recovery items that are important for DBAs, such as backup compression, backing up full-text catalogs, creating snapshots, and how to back up databases partaking in SQL Server 2012's new feature known as AlwaysOn availability groups.

Part II—Hardening, Auditing, and Securing SQL Server 2012

Part II of SQL Server 2012 Management and Administration is dedicated to topics pertaining to SQL Server 2012 security and achieving compliance within your environment. The security chapters cover hardening, auditing, authorization, securing, and encryption in its entirety.

Chapter 7: Hardening and Auditing a SQL Server 2012 Implementation

SQL Server is regularly targeted by hackers because it is a repository of sensitive data for organizations. If an organization's system is breached, hackers can gain access to confidential information including credit card numbers, Social Security numbers, and marketing information. As such, it is imperative that DBAs secure and audit the SQL Server implementation and the data residing in it. This chapter provides an overview of how to harden a SQL Server implementation based on industry best practices so that vulnerabilities and security breaches are minimized. After the implementing is hardened and secured, the chapter discusses auditing concepts and administrative tasks.

Chapter 8: Administering SQL Server Security and Authorization

After the SQL Server installation is hardened, the next step involves administering security and granting authorization to the SQL Server environment. Chapter 8 is all about security administration topics: creating logons, granting access and authorization, understanding SQL Server roles, administering password policies, endpoint authentication, SQL Server and database principals, role-based security, and user and schema separation.

Chapter 9: Encrypting SQL Server 2012 Data and Communications

Organizations and DBAs are facing excessive pressure from regulatory agencies to ensure that mission-critical data stored within SQL Server is encrypted. Not only is it important to ensure that data stored within SQL Server is encrypted, but it is equally important to ensure that data in transit and at rest is also encrypted.

Chapter 9 shares many strategies, tips, and best practices on how to leverage the encryption-based technologies included in SQL Server 2012 and Windows Server 2008 R2 for end-to-end data protection. Among these strategies are leveraging transparent data encryption, integrating security with a Hardware Security Module (HSM), using certificates to encrypt data in transit, and encrypting SQL Server volumes with BitLocker.

Part III—SQL Server 2012 AlwaysOn High-Availability and Disaster Recovery Alternatives

DBAs typically feel compelled to choose just the right technologies to achieve high availability and disaster recovery when designing a SQL Server infrastructure. Some of the challenges they face are illustrated in their questions: Should I use availability groups, failover cluster instances, database mirroring, peer-to-peer replication, or live migration? Which alternative provides the best protection? How does Windows Server 2008 R2 impact my decision? This part of the book will alleviate pressure and concerns by providing DBAs with best practices and tips on how to design and choose the right SQL Server 2012 high-availability alternative to meet their organization's needs.

In this part, the chapters showcase SQL Server 2012's new AlwaysOn features to protect databases in the enterprise from both planned and unplanned downtime.

Chapter 10: Implementing and Managing AlwaysOn Availability Groups

AlwaysOn Availability Groups is a brand-new high-availability and disaster-recovery capability introduced in SQL Server 2012 that provides greater uptime, improved productivity, and greater hardware utilization. This chapter first provides an overview of the new AlwaysOn capability, and then teaches the reader how to deploy and manage AlwaysOn availability groups to protect a group of databases. Finally, the chapter covers how to deploy active secondaries and virtual network names and how to offload backups for maximum performance.

Chapter 11: Implementing and Managing AlwaysOn Failover Clustering Instances

AlwaysOn Failover Cluster Instances (FCI) is another high availability and disaster recovery capability under the new AlwaysOn brand of technologies. The main focus of Chapter 11 is to teach readers how to design, implement, and manage a failover cluster instance with SQL Server 2012.

The chapter is also based on Windows Server 2008 R2. As a result, it includes step-by-step procedures for both the Windows Server 2008 R2 and SQL Server 2012 failover cluster instance.

Finally, the chapter also includes coverage of the new failover cluster instance enhancements, such as native support for multi-site and multi-subnet clustering, configuring failure conditions with the flexible failover policy, and leveraging local tempdb for deployments.

Chapter 12: Implementing and Managing Database Mirroring
Chapter 12 deals with configuring and managing database mirroring so that organizations can enhance the availability of their SQL Server databases, increase business continuity, and maintain a hot standby of their database in another geographic location. The chapter includes detailed step-by-step instructions for configurations of all three database mirroring modes: high availability, high protection, and high performance.

This chapter also includes best practices from the field, case studies, and discussions of how to integrate database mirroring with other high-availability alternatives, such as failover clustering, and how to recover from a failed server.

Chapter 13: Implementing and Managing Replication
SQL Server Replication is another way of distributing data from a source instance of SQL Server to other instances of SQL Server. This chapter focuses on replication components and provides a prelude to the different types of replication scenarios that a database administrator can manage, such as snapshot, merge, and transactional replication. Step-by-step replication configurations, including the peer-to-peer replication scenario, a form of high availability, are also presented.

Part IV—Performance Turning, Monitoring, Troubleshooting, and Maintenance
Part IV of this book covers performance turning, monitoring, troubleshooting, and maintenance techniques to ensure that SQL Server 2012 is optimized and performing at the highest possible levels.

Chapter 14: Performance Tuning and Troubleshooting
SQL Server 2012
After SQL Server 2012 is placed in operation and is being monitored, it is important to take action on the findings. It is often difficult to anticipate

real-world loads during the development phase of application deployment; thus, it is critical to adjust the parameters of the SQL Server 2012 platform to optimize the performance after it is deployed. Frequently, DBAs need to troubleshoot the performance of SQL Server 2012 to address problems that are uncovered by monitoring.

This chapter focuses on how to tune, optimize, and troubleshoot the performance of an instance of SQL Server 2012. Specific tools and components include Windows Server 2008 R2 performance monitor, performance thresholds, SQL Server Profiler, Database Engine Tuning Advisor, Query Analysis, and Extended Events.

Chapter 15: Monitoring SQL Server 2012

SQL Server 2012 includes a tremendous number of native tools that should be leveraged to monitor databases and the SQL Server instance. This chapter first teaches a DBA how to use native tools to gain quick insight into a SQL Server system. The latter part of the chapter covers data collection gathering with Data Collector, which now includes Utility Control Point, and explains how to conduct performance monitoring with the Windows Server 2008 R2 Performance Monitor tools. The chapter ends with coverage of configuring SQL Server alerts, operators, and emails.

Chapter 16: SQL Server 2012 Maintenance Practices

For SQL Server to perform at optimal levels, a DBA should conduct routine maintenance on each database. This chapter focuses on best practices associated with maintaining databases within the SQL Server Database Engine.

The discussion includes creating maintenance plans to check database integrity, shrink databases, reorganize indexes, and update statistics. Additionally, this chapter provides recommendations on daily, weekly, monthly, and quarterly maintenance practices to be conducted on SQL Server.

Part V—Multi-Instance Management, Consolidation, and Private Clouds

Chapter 17: Implementing and Managing Policy-Based Management

Enforcing best practices and standardization on many instances of SQL Server is an extremely difficult task for DBAs in large organizations. To ensure standardization, a DBA should define policies that can be applied to one or more instances of SQL Server instances, databases, and objects with Policy-Based Management.

New concepts, components, terminology, and reporting with Policy-Based Management as well as best practices are discussed in this chapter. Readers' attention is then turned to real-world step-by-step examples of how to implement Policy-Based Management in their environments.

Chapter 18: Managing Workloads with Resource Governor

SQL Server 2012 provides Resource Governor, a feature that DBAs can use to manage SQL Server workloads and system resource consumption. This chapter focuses on concepts and step-by-step procedures on how to implement Resource Governor by specifying limits on the amount of CPU and memory that incoming application requests can use.

Chapter 19: Consolidation, Virtualization, and Private Clouds

Consolidation, virtualization and private clouds are the hottest trends in the database industry in order for organizations to reduce total cost of ownership (TOC), pool IT resources, provide self-service capabilities, and deliver SQL Server as an infrastructure as a service. This chapter covers the following: understanding consolidation, virtualization, and private cloud strategies; planning and virtualizing SQL Server on Hyper-V; and how to optimize SQL Server in a private cloud.

Sample Databases

To facilitate running the steps throughout the book, all the examples are based on the AdventureWorks2012 sample OLTP database, the AdventureWorks2012 data warehouse sample database, or the Customer sample database.

All these sample databases can be downloaded directly from CodePlex, which is Microsoft's free open source project-hosting site. The website and downloads provide the step-by-step instructions on how to install the sample databases on SQL Server 2012.

The exact link to the OLTP and data warehouse Adventureworks2012 sample can be found at http://msftdbprodsamples.codeplex.com/releases/view/55330.

Be sure to choose the correct MSI file based on the schema and the processor type of your system.

The Customer database can be downloaded from the sample Integration Services Product Samples website at http://msftisprodsamples.codeplex.com. The package sample name is "Execute SQL Statements in a Loop Sample Package" and the customer data, which needs to be imported into a newly created Customer database, is located in Customer.txt file.

In addition, the book is based on SQL Server 2012 Enterprise Edition running on Windows Server 2008 R2 Enterprise Edition. The following elements were used for the scenarios of the book:

Element	Description
Domain	Companyabc.com
Domain Controller	TOR-DC01.companyabc.com
Sites	Toronto, New York, and San Francisco
SQL Server Names	SQLServer01\Instance01
	SQLServer02\Instance01
	SQLServer03\Instance01

PART I

SQL Server 2012 Database Engine Administration and Management Topics

IN THIS PART

CHAPTER 1   Installing or Upgrading the Database Engine to SQL Server 2012

CHAPTER 2   Administering and Configuring the Database Engine Settings

CHAPTER 3   Administering Storage, I/O, and Partitioning

CHAPTER 4   Creating Packages and Transferring Data On-Premise and to the Cloud

CHAPTER 5   Managing and Optimizing SQL Server 2012 Indexes

CHAPTER 6   Backing Up and Restoring SQL Server 2012 Databases

CHAPTER 1

Installing or Upgrading the Database Engine to SQL Server 2012

The Database Engine in SQL Server 2012 is the nucleus of SQL Server 2012. Its features are nothing short of impressive. Many organizations today run complex data applications that command the use of a feature like SQL Server's Database Engine, which is Microsoft's first cloud-enabled database platform. From a transactional perspective, it is used to store, process, and secure data for the most demanding data-consuming applications within your enterprise. Moreover, the Database Engine offers many other benefits and advantages for organizations. It controls authorization to SQL Server objects, provides high-availability functionality, and includes subfeatures such as SQL Server Replication, Full-Text and Semantic Extractions for Search, and Data Quality Services. This chapter describes the step-by-step process for installing a new installation of SQL Server 2012 Database Engine and/or upgrading an existing SQL Server Database Engine implementation to SQL Server 2012. In addition, this chapter covers how to leverage the planning tools to ensure a successful installation, upgrade, or transition.

Even though the SQL Server 2012 installation process is very intuitive and has been simplified, a DBA must make several key decisions to ensure that the completed installation or upgrade will meet the needs of the organization. For example, is it beneficial to upgrade an existing SQL Server implementation to SQL Server 2012, or is it preferred to conduct a new installation from scratch? What are the ramifications of these alternatives? Will you lose your existing SQL Server settings, databases, and configurations? This chapter covers these prerequisite planning tasks to address the questions and concerns of DBAs.

In addition, this chapter also covers the hardware and software prerequisites, supported SQL Server 2012 upgrade paths, supported Windows operating systems for running SQL Server 2012, and how to install SQL Server 2012 on Windows Server 2008 R2 Server Core, which is a new SQL Server 2012 deployment option.

What's New for Installation with SQL Server 2012?

SQL Server continues to deliver a robust experience when installing or upgrading to SQL Server 2012. Moreover, SQL Server 2012 introduces significant enhancements to make the installation or upgrade process even more simple and seamless compared to its predecessors. The new installation features for SQL Server 2012 consist of the following:

- **Business Intelligence Edition**—SQL Server 2012 introduces a brand-new edition called Business Intelligence. As the name suggests, this edition provides all of the business intelligence features to provide organizations with premium self-service and business intelligence capabilities.

- **Server Core**—For the first time, SQL Server 2012 supports Server Core as an installation option. Server Core is a scaled-down version of Windows Server 2008 R2 operating system, which can be used to increase availability and minimizes the server's security, serviceability, and resource footprints.

- **Product Update**—When installing SQL Server, you will be prompted to install the latest product updates from the Internet to ensure that the installation has the latest updates to enhance your SQL Server security and performance.

- **Data Quality Services (DQS)**—DQS enables a data steward for a DBA to maintain the quality of the organization's data. This is a new Database Engine subfeature that can be separately installed.

- **SQL Server Data Tools**—These new tools were formerly known as Business Intelligence Studio. The tools can be used to build solutions based on business intelligence features, such as Analysis Services, Reporting Services, and Integration Services.

- **SQL Server Multi-subnet Clustering**—SQL Server 2012's AlwaysOn Failover Clustering Instances supports multi-subnet clustering where each node in the failover cluster can reside on different subnets. The failover clustering installation wizard supports this configuration out-of-the-box.

- **Local TembDB Support with Failover Clustering**—Another installation option new to SQL Server 2012 is the ability to deploy tempdb onto local storage when deploying failover clusters. Previously, the tempdb database was required to be installed on shared storage.

- **SMB Support**—User and System Databases affiliated with the Database Engine can be installed on a file share on an SMB Server. SMB file shares can be leveraged when installing a standalone version of SQL Server or an AlwaysOn Failover Cluster Instance.

Deprecated SQL Server 2012 Database Engine Elements

Not only is it essential to understand the new features and functionality associated with the Database Engine, but it is equally important to understand older elements that have been deprecated in SQL Server 2012. Let's examine the list of deprecated elements that are no longer supported or associated with the Database Engine.

- The following backup and restore commands are discontinued:
  - RESTORE { DATABASE | LOG } WITH [MEDIA] PASSWORD
  - BACKUP { DATABASE | LOG } WITH MEDIAPASSWORD.
  - BACKUP {DATABASE | LOG} WITH MEDIAPASSWORD

- The preferred encryption algorithm is AES, because RC4 or RC4_128 is deprecated.

- Linked Server should replace remote servers.

- SQL Server 90 compatibility levels are no longer supported. Databases must at least maintain a compatibility level of 100.

- The SET ROWCOUNT for INSERT, UPDATE AND DELETE statements have been deprecated and should be replaced with the TOP keyword.

- The HOLDLOCK table hit without parentheses has been replaced with HOLDLOCK with parenthesis.

- The SQL Server Maintenance Plan feature should replace the tool sqlmaint utility.

Note

The preceding bullets itemize the main features deprecated with the Database Engine. However, for a full list of each item, review the topic "Deprecated Database Engine Features and Discontinued Database Engine Functionality in SQL Server 2012" in SQL Server Books Online (BOL).

Preplanning and Preparing a SQL Server 2012 Server Database Engine Installation

Before you begin the actual installation of SQL Server 2012 Database Engine, you must make several decisions concerning preliminary tasks. How well you plan these steps will determine how successful your installation is because many of these decisions cannot be changed after the installation is complete.

Verifying Minimum Hardware Requirements

Whether you are installing SQL Server 2012 in a lab or production environment, you need to ensure that the hardware chosen meets the minimum system requirements. In most situations, the minimum hardware requirements presented will not suffice; therefore, Table 1.1 provides not only the minimum requirements, but also the recommended and optimal system requirements for the hardware components.

> **Note**
>
> This book is tailored toward the Standard and Enterprise Editions associated with the Database Engine. As such, the minimum hardware and software requirements documented in Table 1.1 and Table 1.2 of this chapter cover only the Standard and Enterprise Editions of SQL Server 2012. To review the hardware and software requirements for the Business Intelligence Edition and other specialized editions, such as Express, Express with Tools, and Express with Advanced Services, refer to the section "Hardware and Software Requirements for Installing SQL Server 2012" in SQL Server 2012 Books Online (BOL).

Table 1.1 **SQL Server 2012 Processor and Memory System Requirements**

SQL Server 2012 Enterprise, and Standard Edition (64-bit) x64

Component	Minimum Requirements	Recommended Requirements
Processor	AMD Opteron, AMD Athlon 64, Intel Xeon EM64T, and AMD Athlon 64, Intel Intel Pentium IV EM64T	AMD Opteron, Xeon EM64T, and Intel Pentium IV EM64T
Processor Speed	1.4GHz	2.0GHz or above
Memory	1GB	4GB or above

SQL Server 2012 Enterprise and Standard Edition (32-bit) x64

Component	Minimum Requirements	Recommended Requirements
Processor	Pentium III	Pentium III
Processor Speed	1.0GHz	2GHz or higher
Memory	512MB	2.048GB or above

The minimum disk space requirements differ depending on which SQL Server 2012 feature will be installed. Table 1.2 depicts these minimum disk space specifications itemized by feature.

Table 1.2 **SQL Server 2012 Minimum Disk Requirements**

SQL Server 2012 Feature	Minimum Disk Space Required in MB
Database Engine and Data Files, Replication, Full-Text Search, and Data Quality Services	811
Analysis Services and Data Files	345
Reporting Services and Report Manager	304
Integration Services	591
Master Data Services	243
Client Components	1823
SQL Server Books Online (BOL)	200

Tip

When designing and selecting the system specifications for a SQL Server implementation, even the optimal system requirements recommendations from Microsoft might not suffice. It is a best practice to assess the SQL Server workloads that will be hosted on the server during the time of production implementation, which should also include future growth. For example, a SQL Server 2012 system running 50 instances of the Database Engine for consolidation will require much more than the recommended specification of 2GB of RAM to run adequately. In addition, if you plan to deploy SQL Server's Fast Track reference architecture to accelerate your data warehouse workloads, you may require 64 cores and 2TB of RAM. Therefore, size the system accordingly and test the load before going live into production; otherwise, you may experience a production outage.

Examining SQL Server 2012 Software Prerequisites

Before installing SQL Server 2012, it is also important to get acquainted with the software prerequisites, because many of these prerequisites outline best practices. As such, you should take the time to review the prerequisites before implementation to ensure installation or upgrade success. The SQL Server 2012 software prerequisites include

- .NET Framework 3.5 SP1 or later.
- .NET Framework 4.0 or later.
- Windows Installer 4.5 or later.
- SQL Server Native Client.
- SQL Server Setup Support Files.
- Internet Explorer 7 or later.
- At least Windows PowerShell 2.0.
- Latest Windows Server hot fixes are recommended.
- If SQL Server 2012 will be virtualized, Hyper-V is required and supported.

> **Note**
>
> For more information and consolidating and virtualizing SQL Server 2012 on Windows Server Hyper-V, refer to Chapter 19, "Consolidation, Virtualization, and Private Clouds."

The SQL Server installation wizard will first verify whether these software prerequisites are installed. If they are not, don't panic—the SQL Server 2012 installation wizard is very intuitive and will most likely prompt and then install these software prerequisites automatically. Therefore, you won't have to spend hours conducting Internet-based searches trying to nail down the appropriate downloads, including versions. This is especially true if using Windows Server 2008 R2 with Server Pack 1 or later.

Choosing the Appropriate SQL Server Edition

SQL Server 2012 comes in a variety of editions that are tailored to suit the needs and requirements of different organizations and applications. The SQL Server 2012 Editions include the Enterprise, Standard, Business Intelligence, Web, Express with Advanced Services, Express with Tools, Express, and Developer Editions, as described in the following sections.

SQL Server 2012 Enterprise Edition

The SQL Server 2012 Enterprise Edition is the complete feature set of the product and is designed to support the needs of the largest enterprises. It includes all the features for scalability, performance, high availability, enterprise security, organization compliance, data warehousing, business intelligence, and enterprise manageability. The Enterprise Edition is fully 64-bit capable and can support the maximum processors and memory found in the Windows Server 2008 and Windows Server 2008 R2 operating systems.

Some other features found only in the Enterprise Edition include AlwaysOn Availability Groups, Active Secondaries, Multi-Subnet Clustering, Database Snapshots, Connection Director, Online Page and Fire Restore, Online Schema Change, Fast Recovery, Mirrored Backups, Hot Add CPU and Memory, Table and Index Partitioning, Data Compression, Resource Governor, Partitioned Table Parallelism, Multiple FILESTREAM Containers, SQL Server Audit, Transparent Data Encryption (TDE), Extensible Key Management, enhanced database mirroring features, Resource Governor, Backup Compression, online operations, Hot Add CPU, Performance Data Collector, Extensible Key Management, Failover Clustering, Transparent Data Encryption, Peer-to-Peer Replication, SQL Server Utility Control Point, Integration Services Advanced Adapters and Advanced Transforms, Master Data Services, Change Data Capture, and Scalable Shared Databases.

SQL Server 2012 Business Intelligence Edition

The SQL Server 2012 Business Intelligence Edition is a new offering and makes its debut in the SQL Server 2012 release. It includes the Business Intelligence features found in SQL Server 2012 and offers premium self-service and business intelligence capabilities for large organizations, rapid data discovery with Power View, Analysis Services, Reporting Services, Data Quality Services, and Master Data Services. Its maximum compute capacity includes the lesser of 4 sockets or 16 cores and 64GB of RAM. It is worth noting that Analysis Services and Reporting Services can leverage the operating system maximum.

SQL Server 2012 Standard Edition

The SQL Server 2012 Standard Edition includes the core set of functionality needed to support departmental applications, small data warehouses, and line-of-business applications. It is designed for the needs of small- to medium-sized organizations. The Standard Edition is fully 64-bit capable, can be deployed on Server Core, and can support the lesser of 4 sockets or 16 cores and 64GB of RAM. It is worth mentioning that two nodes of Failover Clustering, Database Mirroring (Safety Full Only), and Backup Compression are also supported within the Standard Edition.

SQL Server 2012 Web Edition

The SQL Server 2012 Web Edition is designed for organizations that are looking to reduce their total cost of ownership for web hosting. Web Edition can support the lesser of 4 sockets or 16 cores and 64GB of RAM.

SQL Server 2012 Express Edition

The SQL Server 2012 Express Edition is the free entry-level edition that is designed to support small or targeted data-driven applications with a core set of secure database requirements. This edition is limited to lesser of 1 socket or 4 cores and 1GB of RAM. The maximum relational database size is 10GB.

SQL Server 2012 Developer Edition

The SQL Server 2012 Developer Edition provides all the same features and functionality as the Enterprise Edition but is licensed only for development purposes.

The following link includes the full list of features supported based on the Editions of SQL Server 2012:

http://msdn.microsoft.com/en-us/library/cc645993(v=sql.110).aspx

Choosing the Appropriate Windows Operating System Version and Edition

SQL Server 2012 can run on a number of Windows operating systems. The SQL Server 2012 Enterprise Edition, Business Intelligence Edition, and Standard Editions run on Windows Server 2008 R2 SP1 "Datacenter, Enterprise, Standard, and Web Editions" or Windows Server 2008 SP2 "Datacenter, Enterprise, Standard, and Web Editions." SQL Server 2012 can no longer be deployed on Windows Server 2003 and Windows 2000. The Standard and Specialized editions support Windows Server 2008 R2 SP1, Windows 7 SP1, Windows Server 2008 SP2, and Windows Vista SP2. Finally, SQL Server 2012 now supports deployment on Windows Server Core to increase security, reduces surface attack, and increases availability via fewer operating system patches. If SQL Server 2012 is deployed on

Server Core, only the Server Core deployment option on Windows Server 2008 R2 SP1 Datacenter, Enterprise, Standard, or Web is supported.

Benefits of Running SQL Server 2012 on Windows Server 2008 R2

Hands down, the Windows Server 2008 R2 family of operating systems is the best choice for running SQL Server 2012. By combining the two products, the highest level of security, scalability, reliability, high availability, and compliance can be achieved. Some of the major benefits of running SQL Server 2012 on Windows Server 2008 R2 include the following:

- **Maximum Scalability**—Windows Server 2008 R2 allows SQL Server to achieve maximum scalability from a processor and memory perspective. Windows Server 2008 R2 offers SQL Server 2012 up to 256 logical processors and up to 2 terabytes of RAM to take on the largest workloads.

- **Server Core**—Server Core is a minimal server installation option for servers running on the Windows Server 2008 or Windows Server 2008 R2 operating system. Server Core provides a scaled-down, low-maintenance server environment to help reduce maintenance, attack surface, management, and significantly reduce OS patching. SQL Server 2012 supports only Server Core when deployed on Windows Server 2008 R2 SP1 or later.

- **Authentication**—The Windows Server 2008 R2 authentication mechanism provides the highest level of security for authorization when running Active Directory Domain Services. SQL Server can leverage the following: Active Directory role-based security for authorization and administration, two-factor authentication with SmartCard-based certificates and biometric devices, and integration with certificate services. Finally, Kerberos can be used for all SQL Server protocols.

- **Encryption**—By combining the encryption technologies included in both SQL Server 2012 and Windows Server 2008 R2, it is possible to achieve encryption from an end-to-end perspective.

- **Minimized Footprint**—Both Windows Server 2008 R2 and SQL Server 2012 provide a modularized installation process that is very granular. Therefore, you install only what you need. This strategy minimizes the attack surface, which in turn, mitigates breaches and compromises.

- **Compliance**—Features and functionality such as integrating Audit and Audit Specifications directly with the Windows Server 2008 R2 event and security logs allows for stronger auditing functionality, which is a requirement for many organizations striving to achieve organizational compliance.

- **High Availability Clustering**—Windows Server 2008 R2 supports up to 16 nodes within a SQL Server 2012 AlwaysOn Failover Cluster Instance. In addition, the requirement of having all nodes within the same subnet has been alleviated. Consequently, with the new quorum model and no subnet restriction, it is easier to achieve geographically dispersed clusters.

- **PowerShell**—The latest scripting technology geared toward effectively managing Windows Server and Microsoft applications has extended to SQL Server 2012. DBAs can use the powerful command-line scripting technologies to automate administrator tasks for both Windows Server and SQL Server 2012.

- **Consolidation and Virtualization**—Hyper-V with Windows Server 2008 R2 can be used to consolidate SQL Server into a Private Cloud virtualized environment, which in turn reduces SQL Server hardware and total cost of ownership within the infrastructure.

- **Live Migration**—When using Hyper-V with Windows Server 2008 R2, an organization can achieve high availability for SQL Server Guest Operating Systems because it is possible to move a SQL Server Virtual Machine from one Hyper-V host to another without any perceived SQL Server downtime.

Understanding the Windows Server 2008 R2 Family of Operating Systems

In the Windows 2008 R2 family of operating systems are four main editions, and SQL Server 2012 can run on any of them. These editions include Windows Server 2008 R2 Standard, Windows Server R2 2008 Enterprise Edition, Windows Server 2008 R2 Datacenter Edition, and Windows Web Server 2008 R2.

Organizations and DBAs must understand their workload needs and requirements when selecting the appropriate Windows Server 2008 R2 operating system edition to utilize. In addition, the Windows Server edition selected must also coincide with requirements pertaining to the edition of SQL Server 2012 selected. For example, the Windows Server 2008 R2

Enterprise Edition might be selected if there is a need to implement AlwaysOn Availability Groups or the need to sustain an eight-node SQL Server AlwaysOn Failover Cluster Instance. The Standard Edition may be selected to save on licensing costs; or Windows Server 2008 R2 Datacenter Edition with Hyper-V may be selected if there is a need to provide unlimited virtualization for a SQL Server Private Cloud implementation. Windows Server 2008 R2 supports only 64-bit processor architectures, and the Standard, Enterprise, and Datacenter Editions ship with or without Hyper-V. Hyper-V is Microsoft hypervisor technology providing virtualization based on Windows Server 2008 R2. As mentioned earlier, each of these editions also supports a Server Core installation alternative.

Finally, when running SQL Server 2012 on Windows Server 2008 R2, the maximum amount of RAM supported by the operating system when running the Standard Edition is 32GB and 2TB when running the Enterprise and Datacenter Editions. Hence, it is strongly recommended to use the x64 versions of the operating system whenever possible because it allows for greater flexibility and upgradability.

New Installation, Upgrade, or Transition?

Organizations that have conducted a SQL Server implementation in the past may need to perform a new SQL Server 2012 installation, a side-by-side installation, or upgrade their existing SQL Server system, which is commonly referred to as an *in-place* upgrade. Moreover, organizations may choose to transition to SQL Server 2012 by first installing a new installation and then migrating SQL Server databases and objects from the legacy environment. There are benefits to each of these options. The next two sections detail the benefits.

Should You Perform a New SQL Server 2012 Installation?

The primary benefit of a new installation is that by installing the operating system from scratch, you are starting with a known good server and a brand-new SQL Server 2012 implementation. You can avoid migrating problems that might have existed on your previous server—whether due to corrupt software, incorrect configuration settings, or improperly installed applications. Moreover, a new installation provides an opportunity for housecleaning because legacy SQL Server elements are not carried over.

For example, it is common for an old SQL Server system to have many outdated databases, packages, user accounts, and stored procedures that have not been touched in more than 10 years. Keep in mind, however, that you will also lose all configuration settings from your previous installation.

In addition, all SQL Server elements, such as databases, user accounts, packages, and so on, will need to be migrated and/or transitioned. Furthermore, required applications on the legacy server will need to be reinstalled after the installation of the new operating system and the SQL Server 2012 implementation are complete. Make sure you document your server configuration information and back up any data that you want to keep.

When running SQL Server 2012, situations may exist where installing a new installation from scratch is the only option. For example, it is not possible to upgrade a legacy SQL Server Failover Cluster from SQL Server 2005 running on Windows Server 2003 to SQL Server 2012 AlwaysOn Failover Cluster Instance running on Windows Server 2008 R2. In addition, SQL Server 7.0 and SQL Server 2000 upgrades to SQL Server 2012 are no longer supported.

Note

When performing a new installation of SQL Server 2012, it is possible to install a new SQL Server 2012 instance on an existing system with a previous version of SQL Server, such as SQL Server 2008 R2. This is known as a side-by-side installation, which is supported, and a migration of existing data from SQL Server 2008 R2 Instance to SQL Server 2012 Instance can be achieved within the same server.

Should You Upgrade an Existing SQL Server System to SQL Server 2012?

Upgrading, on the other hand, replaces your current SQL Server binaries but keeps existing databases, components, features, packages, users, settings, groups, rights, and permissions intact. In this scenario, you don't have to reinstall applications or restore data. Before choosing this option, keep in mind that you should test your applications and databases for compatibility before migration. Just because they worked on previous versions of SQL Server does not mean they will work on SQL Server 2012.

As always, before performing any type of server maintenance such as a SQL Server or Windows Server in-place upgrade, you should perform a complete backup of the SQL Server environment, any applications residing on the server, and data that you want to preserve. Do not forget to include the System State when backing up the SQL Server system. It is required when performing a restore if you want to maintain the existing Windows settings.

Table 1.3 lists the upgrade paths for SQL Server 2012.

Table 1.3 **SQL Server 2012 Upgrade Paths**

Previous SQL Server System	Upgrade to SQL Server 2012
SQL Server 2012	SQL Server version upgrades supported
SQL Server 2008 R2 SP1	Yes, fully supported to like edition
SQL Server 2008 SP2	Yes, fully supported to like edition
SQL Server 2005 SP4	Yes, fully supported to like edition
SQL Server 2000	Not supported
SQL Server 7.0	Not supported
SQL Server 6.5	Not supported

Tip

In-place upgrades can be accomplished only when using the same edition. For example, an upgrade from SQL Server 2008 R2 Standard to SQL Server 2012 Enterprise cannot be achieved. Nevertheless, there is a way around this situation. It is possible to upgrade from SQL Server 2008 R2 Standard to SQL Server 2012 Standard and then conduct an edition upgrade from SQL Server 2012 Standard to SQL Server 2012 Enterprise. On the other hand, many organizations running legacy versions of SQL Server use a Physical to Virtual (P2V) tool to convert their physical servers to virtual servers.

Gathering Additional Information Necessary to Proceed

During the installation of SQL Server 2012, you will have to tell the setup wizard how you want your server configured. The wizard will take the information you provide and configure the server settings to meet your specifications.

Taking the time to gather the information described in the following sections before starting your installation or upgrade will likely make your SQL Server 2012 installation go faster, smoother, and easier.

New SQL Server 2012 Installation or In-Place Upgrade

The first and most major decision when moving toward SQL Server 2012 is determining whether to implement a brand-new SQL Server installation from scratch or conduct an in-place upgrade. If you don't already have SQL Server in your existing infrastructure, it is a "no-brainer," and a new installation is warranted. However, if a legacy version of SQL Server resides in the infrastructure, the organization must decide between an in-place upgrade or a new installation. If a new installation is chosen, it is necessary to transition existing SQL Server data from the legacy system to the newly established SQL Server 2012 system. As mentioned earlier, each alternative has benefits and disadvantages.

New SQL Server 2012 Standalone Installation or AlwaysOn

Another major decision needs to be made in the planning phases: Should SQL Server 2012 be installed in a standalone system, or should AlwaysOn be utilized? AlwaysOn Failover Clustering Instance (FCI) provides high availability for a SQL Server instance and AlwaysOn Availability Groups provides protection at the database level. A standalone installation is also sufficient because it is cheaper, easier to administer, and does not require specific failover clustering hardware.

> **Note**
>
> To install SQL Server 2012 AlwaysOn Availability Groups, review Chapter 10, "Implementing and Managing AlwaysOn Availability Groups." To install AlwaysOn Failover Cluster Instances, review Chapter 11, "Implementing and Managing AlwayOn Failover Clustering Instances."

Physical or Virtual Installation

Another decision that many customers face is whether to virtualize SQL Server. SQL Server virtualization or Private Cloud deployments are very common deployment alternatives for organizations looking to archive a dynamic datacenter with self-service capabilities. If you virtualize SQL Server, you need to ensure that the SQL Server workload fits within the hypervisor of choice. Many large-scale SQL Server workloads will not be virtualized because they may demand 128 cores or 2TB of RAM, which typically exceeds the guest operating system maximum capacity. None-theless, understand your workload before making a decision.

Full Edition with the Graphical User Interface or Server Core

With the new Server Core deployment option, DBAs may be plagued with the decision to install SQL Server on the traditional GUI-based installation of Windows or on the Server Core deployment option. As mentioned earlier, Server Core is a better alternative for DBAs who want to bolster security and availability during planned Windows maintenance. However, not all DBAs are familiar with scripting and using a command shell. In addition, all features of SQL Server are not supported on Server Core, too.

Single-Instance or Multiple-Instance Installation

For years now, discussions on the topic of single-instance versus multiple-installation have both engulfed and engaged the SQL Server community. Should you install a single-instance SQL Server installation and place all databases on one instance or scale up and create a multiple-instance SQL Server installation and spread databases across each of these instances? This question continues to echo through every organization. Here are some best practices to assist in making such an arduous decision.

One of the main drawbacks of placing all databases on a single-instance installation involves the tempdb database. The tempdb database is a shared resource among all databases contained within the same SQL Server instance. Performance degradation may occur because the tempdb database is the single point of contention for all temporary database workloads. In multiple-instance installations, a tempdb database is created for each instance, minimizing contention and performance degradation.

Many DBAs implement multiple instances for other reasons, including regulatory compliance, administrator autonomy, different global security policies, global server settings, and compatibility requirements.

Note

Only one instance within the installation can maintain the default instance name. Therefore, if a default instance already exists, SQL Server 2012 must be installed as a named instance.

Side-by-Side Installations with Previous Versions of SQL Server

Organizations also have the option to install a brand-new installation of SQL Server 2012 on a server that is already running a legacy instance of SQL Server such as 2005, 2008, or 2008 R2. Based on this methodology, more than one version of SQL Server will reside on the system.

Typically, the preference is to either conduct an in-place upgrade or install SQL Server 2012 on new hardware to minimize hardware contention and performance degradation. However, side-by-side installations are sometimes warranted. Let's look at the situations that support this installation. SQL Server 2012 will coexist with SQL Server 2008 R2 and SQL Server 2005. Unfortunately, SQL Server 2000 is not supported, but hopefully the majority of the organizations out there have already transitioned off of SQL Server 2000 because it is no longer supported by Microsoft.

Determining Which SQL Server 2012 Features to Install

Give serious thought to the SQL Server 2012 features before installing them. The modular setup of SQL Server 2012 is made up of many independent features, also referred to as components, allowing for complete customization by organizations. This typically results in minimal surface area and more granularity compared with older editions of SQL Server. This improved modular installation process is said to be "slim and efficient," like other Microsoft products such as Windows Server, Exchange, and System Center.

The following items describe the modular installation, including shared features that can be selected during the installation of SQL Server 2012:

- **Database Engine Services**—This is the core service for storing, processing, and securing data. It is designed to provide a scalable, fast, and high-availability platform for access and the other components. Three subfeatures within the Database Engine are

  - **SQL Server Replication**—Replication allows DBAs to copy databases to different locations and keep the copies synchronized. This can be used for data distribution, synchronization, fault tolerance, disaster recovery, load balancing, or testing. The Replication component manages database replication and interacts primarily with the Database Engine features.

  - **Full-Text and Semantic Extractions for Search**—The Full-Text Search engine populates and manages the full-text catalogs. The Full-Text engine also makes full-text searches easier by maintaining indexes, a thesaurus, noise words, and linguistic analysis of the full-text indexes. It also includes Semantic Extraction for key phrases and similarity search on content stored within the Database Engine.

  - **Data Quality Services**—Select this new option to include Data Quality database objects with the installation.

- **Analysis Services**—The SQL Server 2012 Analysis Services (SSAS) feature provides online analytical processing (OLAP) and data mining. OLAP is a modification of the original database concept of online transaction processing (OLTP). OLAP is designed to provide immediate answers to analytical and ad hoc queries from a multidimensional cube known as an OLAP cube. Data mining is the process of searching large volumes of data for patterns and trends. SSAS allows SQL Server 2012 to provide both these capabilities and is the core feature of business intelligence.

- **Reporting Services**—The Microsoft SQL Server 2012 Reporting Services (SSRS) feature allows for the presentation and delivery of data in a variety of ways. The reports can include tables, matrices, and free-form data. The source data for the reports can be provided by the Database Engine component, the Analysis Services component, or any Microsoft .NET data provider such as ODBC or OLE DB to access data sources such as Oracle or file-based data.

- **Shared Features**—Features designated as "Shared Features" or "Management Tools" include

  - **Integration Services**—The SQL Server 2012 Integration Services (SSIS) feature integrates data from different sources. This integration includes importing, exporting, and transforming data from disparate sources. The data can be copied, merged, restructured, and cleaned as part of the integration processing, which makes the integration services a powerful tool in the development of data warehouses. It is imperative to mention that the Integration Services component fills an important gap in the extract.

  - **Master Data Services**—MDS was first introduced in SQL Server 2008 R2. It is the SQL Server solution for master data management to ensure the integrity and consistency of information and that there is a single version of the truth within an organization.

  - **SQL Server Data Tools**—This feature installs the SQL Server development environment, including tools formerly known as Business Intelligence Development Studio. It is essentially Microsoft Visual Studio with some additional SQL Server 2012 business intelligence project types. It is an application development environment that allows developers to build business intelligence-related applications that include Analysis Services, Integration Services, and Reporting Services.

- **Reporting Services - SharePoint**—This feature includes the Reporting Services component and integrates it directly into SharePoint.

- **Reporting Services Add-in for SharePoint Products**—This feature includes the management and user interface components to integrate a SharePoint product with an SSRS report server in SharePoint integrated mode.

- **Data Quality Client**—Provides a graphical user interface to connect to the DQS Server. It also allows a DBA to centrally monitor data-cleansing tasks.

- **Client Tools Connectivity**—This feature includes the installation of communication components between clients and servers.

- **Client Tools Backward Compatibility**—This feature was heavily requested by the SQL Server community. When Client Tools Backward Compatibility is installed, a DBA can manage legacy SQL Server systems.

- **Client Tools SDK**—This feature includes the Software Development Kit containing resources for developers.

- **SQL Server Books Online**—SQL Server Books Online (BOL) is Microsoft's documentation for SQL Server 2012.

- **Management Tools Complete**—When installed, SQL Server 2012 will possess all the management tools, including Management Studio, support for Reporting Services, Analysis Services, Integration Services, SQL Server Profiler, and Database Tuning Advisor.

- **Management Tools Basic**—This refers to the scaled-down version of the management toolset. It includes management studio support only for the Database Engine, SQL Server Express, SQL Server Command-Line Utility, and PowerShell.

- **SQL Client Connectivity SDK**—This feature includes the Software Development Kit containing connectivity resources for developers.

- **Distributed Replay Controller**—This feature provides the orchestration layer for actions between distributed replay clients.

- **Distributed Replay Client**—When installed, this feature includes the Distributed Replay Client.

When installing the SQL Server 2012 Database Engine, the typical sub-features to install include the following:

- Replication
- Full-Text and Semantic Extractions for Search
- Integration Services
- Client Connectivity Components
- Management Tools
- Management Studio
- SQL Server Books Online

Installing a New Installation of SQL Server 2012

The following sections depict the step-by-step instructions for installing a new installation of the SQL Server 2012 Database Engine feature, including supplementary subfeatures such as SQL Server Replication, Full-Text and Semantic Extractions for Search, Integration Services, and Shared Components.

1. Log in to the server with administrative privileges and insert the SQL Server 2012 media. Autorun should launch the SQL Server 2012 Installation Center landing page; otherwise, click Setup.exe.

2. On the SQL Server Installation Center landing page, select the Installation page, and then click the New SQL Server Stand-alone Installation or Add Features to an Existing Installation link, as displayed in Figure 1.1.

> **Note**
>
> If SQL Server's setup software prerequisites have not been met, the installation wizard will prompt and then install the prerequisites. After the prerequisites have been installed, the SQL Server installation process will resume. SQL Server 2012 software prerequisites may include hot fixes, .NET Framework, and the latest Windows Installer. In addition, system restarts may be required after SQL Server's setup software prerequisites are installed. If so, rerun setup after the reboot to continue with the SQL Server installation.

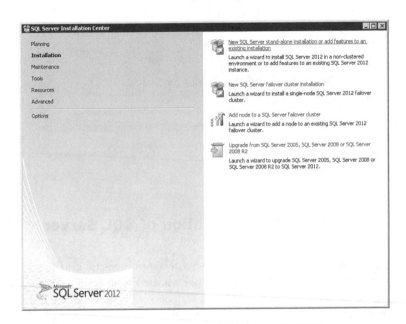

FIGURE 1.1
Performing a new SQL Server standalone installation.

3. On the Setup Support Rules page, review the outcome of the System Configuration Checker. Ensure that all tests associated with the operation passed without any failures, warnings, or skipped elements. Alternatively, you can review a standard or comprehensive report by selecting the Show Details button or View Detailed Report. To continue with the installation, click OK, as illustrated in Figure 1.2.

4. On the Product Key page, enter the SQL Server Product Key and click Next.

5. On the License Agreement page, accept the licensing terms. Alternatively, choose whether you want to participate in improving the product by sending feature usage to Microsoft, and then click Next.

6. On the Setup Support Files page, the wizard prompts whether additional setup support files are required for the installation. In addition, with SQL Server 2012, the installation wizard scans for product updates. If additional files or product updates are required, review the status of the files required, and then click Install.

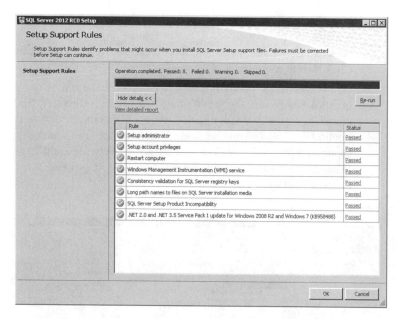

FIGURE 1.2
Reviewing potential problems identified with the Setup Support Rules.

7. The Setup Support Rules page will be displayed again and will identify any outstanding items that may hinder the installation process
associated with the SQL Server installation. Review and correct failures and warnings before commencing the installation. If failures are
not displayed, click Next to start the installation. After any outstanding installations are complete, review the details and then click Next.

Note

Some of the items that will be tested for in step 7 are the Fusion Active
Template Library, Previous Release of SQL Server 2008 Business
Intelligence Development Studio, Unsupported SQL Server products,
whether the server is a Domain Controller, the version of Windows
PowerShell, Edition WOW64 Platform, and Windows Firewall Settings.

8. On the Setup Role page, specify the type of installation to conduct.
The options include SQL Server Feature Installation, SQL Server

PowerPivot for SharePoint, or All Features with Defaults. For this example, the first option—SQL Server Feature Installation—has been chosen because we want to specify the exact features to install. Click Next to continue.

9. On the Feature Selection page, select the desired features to be installed, and provide the path for the Shared Feature Directory. For this example, the Database Engine Services, SQL Server Replication, Full-Text and Semantic Extractions for Search, and appropriate Shared Features such as Integration Services and the Management Tools have been selected. Click Next to proceed, as illustrated in Figure 1.3.

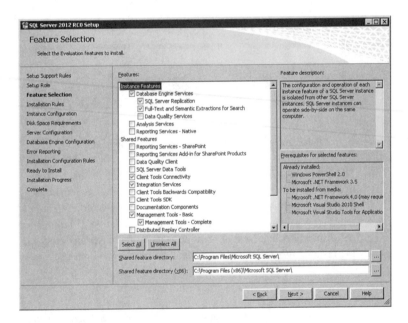

FIGURE 1.3
Specifying the SQL Server features to be installed.

10. On the Installation Rules page, setup will run additional rules to ensure the installation will not be blocked. Ensure all operations passed and then click Next to continue. If an element failed, correct and continue with the installation. Click the Show Details button or View Detailed Report if you need to review each rule checked and its correlating status.

11. On the Instance Configuration page, specify the Name and Instance ID for the SQL Server installation. The options include either the Default Instance name, which is MSSQLServer, or a Named Instance. In addition, click the ellipsis button in the Instance Root Directory area and specify the path for the installation. Click Next as displayed in Figure 1.4.

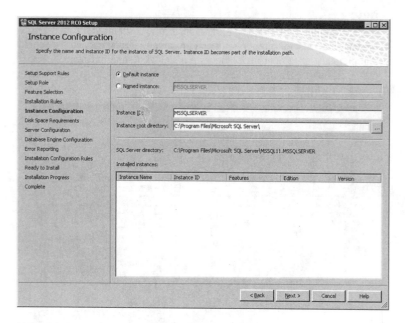

FIGURE 1.4
Configuring the SQL Server instance.

Note

Each instance name provided must be unique, and there can be only one default instance per SQL Server system.

---

12. The next page is the Disk Space Requirements. Review the disk space summary for the SQL Server components and features selected to be installed and then click Next.

13. The Server Configuration page includes configuration settings for both Service Accounts and Collation. On the Service Accounts tab, enter a valid low-privilege service account name and password for each service account. Next, specify the Startup Type for each service account listed, as illustrated in Figure 1.5. Options include Automatic, Manual, or Disabled. Before proceeding to the next step, click the Collation tab.

Note

Review Chapter 7, "Hardening and Auditing a SQL Server 2012 Implementation," for more information on understanding service accounts and choosing an account based on the principal of least privilege.

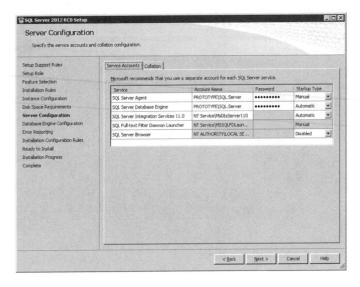

FIGURE 1.5
Specifying the SQL Server service accounts.

Tip

From a hardening perspective, Microsoft recommends entering a separate service account for each SQL Server component and feature being installed. In addition, the account specified should follow the principle of least privilege. For more information on selecting the desired service account and hardening a SQL Server implementation, see Chapter 7.

14. On the Collation tab, enter the desired collation option for the Database Engine. It is possible to change default collation settings used by the Database Engine and Analysis Services for language and sorting by selecting Customize. Click Next to continue.

15. The Database Engine Configuration page consists of three tabs: Account Provisioning, Data Directories, and FILESTREAM. On the first tab, in the Account Provisioning section, specify the Authentication Mode, which consists of either Windows Authentication Mode or Mixed Mode (SQL Server authentication and Windows authentication). If Mixed Mode is selected, enter and confirm the password for the Built-in SQL Server Administrator account. The next step is to provision a SQL Server Administrator by either selecting the option Add Current User or clicking Add and specifying a SQL Server administrator account.

Note

SQL Server 2012 offers the opportunity to rename the SA account during installation. Renaming the SA account increases security because the account name is well known in the industry.

---

16. The second tab, Data Directories, located still within the Database Engine Configuration page, is used for specifying the location of the default directories associated with the installation of this SQL Server instance. The directories include Data Root Directory, System Database Directory, User Database Directory, User Database Log Directory, tempdb Directory, tempdb Log Directory, and Backup Directory. Either maintain the default directories or specify a new directory for performance and availability.

Tip

Because I/O to log files is sequential and I/O to database files is random, for increased performance, it is a best practice to place log files on a separate disk from database files. In addition, placing the tempdb on its own disk with multiple data files also bolsters performance and reduces file contention.

---

17. The final tab on the Database Engine Configuration page is FILESTREAM. Here, decide whether you want to enable FILESTREAM. If FILESTREAM is enabled, additional parameters must be entered, such as Enable FILESTREAM for File I/O Streaming Access, Windows Share Name, and whether to allow remote clients to have streaming access to FILESTREAM data. Click Next to proceed.

18. On the Error and Usage Reporting page, help Microsoft improve SQL Server features and services by sending error reports and feature usage to Microsoft. Specify the level of participation and then click Next.

19. The final check will take place to ensure that the installation process will not be blocked. On the Installation Rules page, review for any outstanding errors or warnings and then click Next to continue.

20. Before commencing the SQL Server 2012 Installation, review the features to be installed on the Ready to Install page and then click Install. Take note of the Configuration File path location because the ConfigurationFile.ini file can be used to automate a similar installation.

21. When the installation process starts, you can monitor its progress accordingly. When the installation setup completes, review the success status based on each SQL Server feature and then click Next.

22. On the Complete page, review the location of the SQL Server summary upgrade log file and additional items, which can be found in the supplemental information section. Click Close to finalize the installation.

23. To conduct post-installation tasks, review the upcoming section "Finalizing the SQL Server 2012 Installation or Upgrade" in this chapter.

Notes from the Field: Automating the Installation of SQL Server 2012 Using a Configuration File

In today's IT organizations, DBAs are responsible for installing, managing and maintaining multiple instances of SQL Servers in the enterprise, especially with the wide adoption of virtualization and private cloud deployments. Automating the installation of SQL Server 2012 would not only help reduce the workload of a DBA but would also help ensure that consistent and standard installations across the enterprise can be achieved while satisfying the organization's requirements of rapid provisioning.

There are different ways DBAs can automate the installation of SQL Server 2012. Here we will show you two simple ways of automating the installation of SQL Server 2012 using a configuration file that can be called by passing a parameter to the SQL Server 2012 Setup.exe program from the command prompt. The two ways to generate the .INI file are as follows:

- Generate a .INI file by launching Setup.exe.
- Create a .INI file that can be used with Setup.exe.

Generate an .ini file by launching Setup.exe

To autogenerate an .INI file, which is the easier method of the two alternatives, follow these instructions:

1. Launch Setup.exe from your installation folder.

2. Follow the setup wizard to go through the installation options up to the Ready to Install page. At the bottom of the Ready to Install page, you'll notice Configuration File Path with a link to a file called ConfigurationFile.ini. This file contains all the options and their values you selected during the setup process.

3. Make a note of the location of the Configuration File Path and click Cancel to exit out of the Setup.exe.

4. You can now install SQL Server 2012 on other computers using the recorded options and values by calling the following from the command prompt:

   Setup.exe /ConfigurationFile=ConfigurationFile.INI

Create a .INI file that can be used with Setup.exe

Creating an unattended installation using an .INI file is a fairly simple process. First, create the .INI file using a notepad or any text editor, and then add SQL Server installation options using [Options].

Here's an example of a sample .INI file that you can follow to create your own:

```
;SQL Server "2012" Configuration File
[OPTIONS]
ACTION="Install"
QUIET="True"
QUIETSIMPLE="False"
UpdateEnabled="True"
FEATURES=SQLENGINE,REPLICATION,FULLTEXT,DQ
```

```
INSTALLSHAREDDIR="D:\Program Files\Microsoft SQL
Server"
INSTANCENAME="SQLTEST"
INSTANCEID="SQLTEST"
INSTANCEDIR="C:\Program Files\Microsoft SQL Server"
AGTSVCACCOUNT="NT AUTHORITY\NETWORK SERVICE"
AGTSVCSTARTUPTYPE="Manual"
SQLSVCSTARTUPTYPE="Automatic"
FILESTREAMLEVEL="0"
SQLCOLLATION="SQL_Latin1_General_CP1_CI_AS"
SQLSVCACCOUNT="NT AUTHORITY\NETWORK SERVICE"
SQLSYSADMINACCOUNTS="REDMOND\shakani"
SECURITYMODE="SQL"
ADDCURRENTUSERASSQLADMIN="False"
TCPENABLED="1"
NPENABLED="0"
BROWSERSVCSTARTUPTYPE="Automatic"
FTSVCACCOUNT="NT Service\MSSQLFDLauncher$SQLTEST"
```

After the ConfigurationFile.ini is ready, you can use this file across multiple machines to install SQL Server 2012.

It is also possible to specify passwords at the command prompt instead of putting them in a configuration file by passing the following parameters when calling Setup.exe:

```
Setup.exe /SQLSVCPASSWORD="*********"
/AGTSVCPASSWORD="*********"
/ConfigurationFile=ConfigurationFile.INI
```

Upgrading the Database Engine to SQL Server 2012

When upgrading an existing SQL Server system to SQL Server 2012, all SQL Server databases, configuration settings, security settings, and programs are retained from the previous installation. However, you need to perform several important prerequisite tasks before the upgrade, as discussed in the following sections.

> **Tip**
>
> It is not possible to change the installation path when upgrading a system to SQL Server 2012. In addition, there must be enough free space on the system and SQL Server partition to support the upgrade; otherwise, the upgrade will come to a halt.

Creating a SQL Server Feature Discovery Report

One of the first tasks a DBA should conduct when upgrading an existing SQL Server system to SQL Server 2012 is to create a discovery report. A SQL Server discovery report, ultimately, is an inventory of the SQL Server components and features installed on an existing SQL Server installation. SQL Server 2012 comes with a tool called the SQL Server Feature Discovery Report, which will generate a list of features and products. This report can automatically be generated for SQL Server 2012, SQL Server 2008 R2, SQL Server 2008, SQL Server 2005, and SQL Server 2000 by selecting Installed SQL Server Features Discovery Report, on the Tools page, located on the SQL Server Installation Center landing page.

Microsoft Assessment and Planning (MAP) Toolkit for SQL Server

Because the SQL Server Feature Discovery Report focuses only on the local installation, the MAP toolkit can be used to discover SQL Server instances across the enterprise. The tool provides a complete network inventory of SQL Server, Oracle, MySQL and Sybase installations. In addition, the tool can be used to discover SQL Server Instances, Databases, and Features, and the reports are very comprehensive for planning, migrating, virtualizing, and consolidating SQL Server. Some of the additional hardware and platform characteristics the tool offers that DBAs will find handy include performance characteristic collection, how many cores are allocated to each server, what is the underlying operating system, and whether SQL Server is clustered or virtualized. The tool can be launched by selecting Microsoft Assessment and Planning (MAP) Toolkit for SQL Server, on the Tools page, located on the SQL Server Installation Center landing page, or it can be downloaded directly from Microsoft's website.

Backing Up the Server

Whenever you are making a major change on a server, something could go wrong. A complete backup of the SQL Server environment, including the SQL Server system databases and Windows Server System State, can make the difference between confidently telling the boss you had a setback, so you conducted a rollback, or quivering while you try to find a way to tell your boss a complete disaster has taken place.

Verifying System Compatibility

The first action when upgrading an existing SQL Server system to SQL Server 2012 is running the System Configuration Checker. Launch the System Configuration Checker by first selecting Planning and then System Configuration Checker via the SQL Server 2012 Installation Center landing page.

The System Configuration Checker is an informative tool that conducts a scan on the existing system and indicates problems that might occur when the SQL Server support files are installed. After the scan is completed, a detailed report is presented that indicates the operations that passed, failed, were skipped, or that presented warnings. View the detailed report, correct any issues, and rerun the scan to ensure absolute success. Then move on to the next prerequisite task, which is running the SQL Server 2012 Upgrade Advisor.

Running the SQL Server Upgrade Advisor

Make it a prerequisite task to test the existing SQL Server system that you plan to upgrade for compatibility issues. Accomplish this by running the SQL Server Upgrade Advisor. The SQL Server Upgrade Advisor is an intuitive tool included with the SQL Server 2012 installation media.

When invoked, the wizard will first analyze previously installed SQL Server components and then produce a detailed report indicating possible upgrade anomalies even at the database level. In addition, the report provides links to information on how to resolve the issues identified—how convenient!

Caution

Before conducting an in-place upgrade, it is imperative to acknowledge and fix all anomalies. If anomalies go unresolved, the upgrade is sure to fail, resulting in a production outage.

It is important to mention that the Upgrade Advisor can be installed on a remote system and still analyze the following SQL Server components: the Database Engine, Analysis Services, Reporting Services, and Integration Services.

Installing the SQL Server Upgrade Advisor

Follow the steps to install the SQL Server Upgrade Advisor:

1. Launch the SQL Server Installation Center.

2. Select the Planning link and then click Install Upgrade Advisor.

3. Click Next on the SQL Server 2012 Upgrade Advisor Setup Welcome screen.

4. Accept the License Agreement, and then click Next.

5. Provide the installation path on the Feature Selection page. Click Next to continue.

6. Click Install to initiate the installation and then click Finish to finalize.

Performing a Compatibility Test with SQL Server Upgrade Advisor

When running the SQL Server 2012 Upgrade Advisor, the high-level steps include identifying SQL Server components to analyze, providing credentials for authentication, providing additional parameters, executing analysis, and finally, reviewing the results. Conduct the following steps to perform a compatibility test using the SQL Server 2012 Upgrade Advisor on the SQL Server system you plan to upgrade:

1. Click Start, All Programs, SQL Server 2012, SQL Server 2012 Upgrade Advisor.

2. On the Welcome to SQL Server 2012 Upgrade Advisor page, select the link Launch Upgrade Advisor Analysis Wizard and then click Next. If you are prompted with another Welcome Screen, Click Next.

3. On the SQL Server Components page, provide the name of the SQL Server and then specify the components that will be analyzed. Click Next, as shown in Figure 1.6.

4. Provide the Instance name and the authentication mechanism for the SQL Server instance and then click Next.

5. On the SQL Server Parameters page, indicate what additional elements should be analyzed. Options include databases, trace files, and SQL Server batch files. Click Next to continue.

6. The Reporting Services Parameters page is an optional step. If a Reporting Services scan was selected, enter the name of the Reporting Services instance and then choose the authentication mechanism that will be used. Click Next.

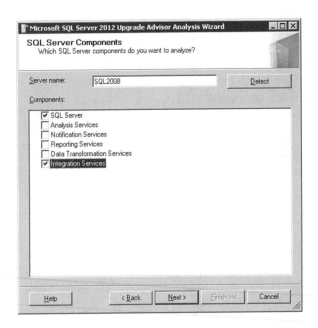

FIGURE 1.6
Specifying the SQL Server Components to analyze.

7. The Analysis Services Parameters page is another optional step. If an Analysis Services scan was selected, enter the name of the Analysis Services instance. Next, choose the authentication mechanism that will be used. Click Next.

8. The next optional screen focuses on SSIS parameters for SSIS packages. Select either the Analyze SSIS Packages on Server option or the Analyze SSIS Package Files option. If the second option is selected, specify the path to the SSIS packages. In addition, if the packages are password protected, enter a password. Click Next to continue.

9. Confirm the Upgrade Advisor Settings and then click Run to commence the analysis.

10. The Upgrade Advisor Progress page provides progress messages for each component being analyzed. The status message includes any of the words error, failure, or success. View the status messages in the details pane or, alternatively, launch the report. Click Close as indicated in Figure 1.7.

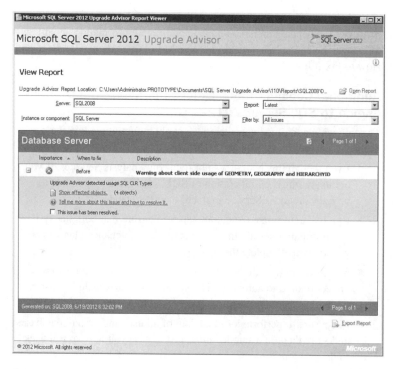

FIGURE 1.7
Reviewing the Upgrade Advisor Analysis Complete Report.

> **Note**
>
> The analysis output is written to a file; therefore, the report can be viewed from the Upgrade Advisor Progress page or at a later date. To review the report at another time, launch the Upgrade Advisor Report Viewer from the Upgrade Advisor start page.

The report can be viewed by server and then by instance or component. Moreover, the report can be filtered by All Issues, All Upgrade Issues, Pre-Upgrade Issues, All Migration Issues, Resolved Issues, or Unresolved Issues. The output report also indicates when issues should be addressed. For instance, the report may indicate that the issue should be addressed before the upgrade or after the upgrade. It is beneficial to review each message to ensure no issues exist when upgrading the existing SQL Server system to SQL Server 2012. When drilling through each message, it is possible to expand on an issue and gain additional information about how to resolve the anomaly by clicking the Tell Me More About This Issue and How to Fix It link.

Additional Considerations Before Upgrading the Database Engine to SQL Server 2012

The following additional considerations apply before upgrading the Database Engine to SQL Server 2012:

- Even though this book does not focus on Analysis Services, if you are upgrading a 64-bit edition of SQL Server, it is imperative to upgrade Analysis Service first and then the Database Engine.

- Run the appropriate DBCC commands to ensure that both the system and user databases are in good health. A maintenance plan can be generated to complete these tasks.

- Make certain that all databases, specifically the system databases, are configured to autogrow. The system databases include master, model, msdb, and tempdb.

- Make sure to perform a full backup of all user and system databases and store them in a safe location, just in case you have to roll back to the previous version.

- Ensure that you have administrative access to all user and system databases and that each database has logon information in the master system database.

- Review the list of retired or deprecated commands and update stored procedures and objects in your database appropriately. For example, ServerpropertyEx() has been retired and no longer works in SQL Server 2012. Instead, a DBA will need to use ServerProperty().

- Configure the Max Worker Threads setting to a value of 0.

- Disable all startup stored procedures because the upgrade process may restart the server.

- Remove any startup options from SQL Server service properties before initiating the upgrade process.

- If Replication is enabled, stop replication during the upgrade process.

- Conduct a rolling upgrade if database mirroring is used. First upgrade the mirrored instance, failover services, and then upgrade the principal instance (which is now the mirror). It is also recommended to remove the witness and change the operation mode to high safety during the upgrade.

- In SQL Server 2000, Log Shipping was established with a Database Maintenance Plan. Because the installation in SQL Server 2005 and SQL Server 2012 no longer uses a maintenance plan to implement Log Shipping, it is not possible to upgrade a SQL Server 2000 system running Log Shipping to SQL Server 2012.

Performing the SQL Server 2012 Upgrade

At this point, you have accomplished quite a few tasks. Let's review: Your data is backed up, you have read the release notes, you ran the SQL Server System Configuration Checker and the SQL Server Upgrade Advisor, and you addressed the issues or warnings identified. It is now time to upgrade to SQL Server 2012. This example focuses on upgrading the Database Engine associated with SQL Server 2008 R2 to SQL Server 2012.

1. Log in to the server and insert the SQL Server 2012 media. Autorun should launch the SQL Server 2012 Installation Center landing page; otherwise, click Setup.exe.

2. On the SQL Server Installation Center landing page, first select the Installation link and then Upgrade from SQL Server 2005, SQL Server 2008, or SQL Server 2008 R2.

3. On the Setup Support Rules page, review the outcome of the System Configuration Checker. Ensure that all tests associated with the operation passed without any failures, warnings, or skipped elements. Alternatively, you can review a standard or comprehensive report by selecting the Show Details button or View Detailed Report. Click OK to continue with the installation.

4. On the Product Key page, enter the SQL Server Product Key and click Next.

5. On the License Agreement page, accept the Licensing Terms. Alternatively, choose whether you want to participate in improving the product by sending feature usage to Microsoft and then click Next.

6. On the Setup Support Rules page, the wizard will prompt whether additional setup support files are required for the installation. In addition, with SQL Server 2012, the installation wizard will scan for

product updates. If additional files or Product Files are required, review the status of the files required and then click Install.

7. On the Select Instance page, use the drop-down menu and specify a SQL Server instance to upgrade. Click Next, as displayed in Figure 1.8.

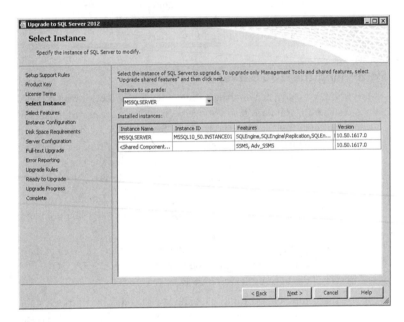

FIGURE 1.8
Specify the SQL Server instance to upgrade.

Note

The Installed Instances section displays all the instances installed on the system. In addition, to upgrade only SQL Server Management Tools, choose the option Upgrade Shared Features Only in the Instance to Upgrade drop-down list.

---

8. Review the features to be upgraded in the Select Features page and then Click Next.

> **Note**
>
> It is not possible to modify the SQL Server features being released during an upgrade.

9. Review the name and InstanceID for the SQL Server instance being upgraded and click Next.

10. The next page is the Disk Space Requirements. Review the disk space summary for the SQL Server components and features selected to be upgraded and then click Next.

11. If prompted, specify the service accounts and collation configuration on the Server Configuration page and then click Next.

12. On the Full-Text Upgrade page, specify an option of how the existing Full-Text catalogs will be processed after the upgrade. Click Next, as displayed in Figure 1.9.

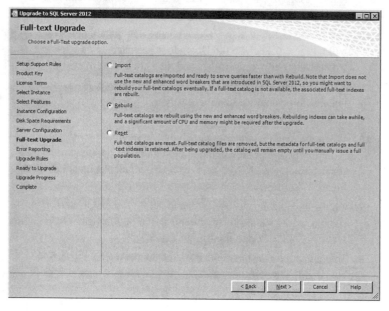

FIGURE 1.9
Specifying the Full-Text Upgrade option.

- **Import**—Full-Text catalogs are imported "as is" and are ready to serve queries. This process is much faster than rebuilding the Full-Text catalogs; however, the import does not leverage the new Full-Text features and functionality associated with SQL Server 2012.

- **Rebuild**—When this option is selected, the Full-Text catalogs are rebuilt using the new and enhanced word breakers associated with SQL Server 2012. This process is typically slower, and a significant amount of processor and memory is required to tackle this operation.

- **Reset**—The final option is Reset. The Full-Text catalogs will be removed; therefore, after the upgrade is complete, the catalogs will remain empty until they are manually processed with a full population.

13. On the Error and Usage Reporting page, help Microsoft improve SQL Server features and services by sending error reports and feature usage to Microsoft. Specify the level of participation and then click Next.

14. The final check will take place to ensure that the upgrade process will not be blocked. On the Upgrade Rules page, review for any outstanding errors or warnings and then click Next to continue.

15. Before commencing the SQL Server 2012 upgrade, review the features to be upgraded on the Ready to Upgrade page and then click Upgrade.

16. When the upgrade process starts, you can monitor its progress accordingly. When the upgrade setup completes, review the success status based on each SQL Server feature. Click Next, as shown in Figure 1.10.

17. On the Complete page, review the location of the SQL Server summary upgrade log file and items in the Supplemental Information section. Click Close to finalize the upgrade.

18. To conduct post-installation tasks, review the upcoming section "Finalizing the SQL Server 2012 Installation or Upgrade."

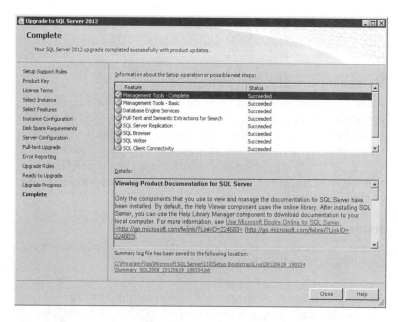

FIGURE 1.10
Reviewing the results of the SQL Server 2012 upgrade.

Finalizing the SQL Server 2012 Installation or Upgrade

After the installation or upgrade of SQL Server 2012 is complete, it is beneficial to review the following tasks to finalize the installation.

Reviewing SQL Server 2012 Logs

When the installation or upgrade is complete, it is a best practice to review the setup log file, review the Windows application log, and review SQL Server logs for any issues or warnings. As noted earlier, the location to the SQL Server 2012 installation setup file can be found on the Complete page during the final stages of the installation or upgrade.

Downloading and Installing Updates

Even though the Windows Server system may be configured to automatically obtain server updates, it is still a best practice to check for missing SQL Server 2012 and Windows Server service packs and critical fixes.

These outstanding service packs and critical fixes can be installed with Microsoft Update or a software distribution tool such as System Center Configuration Manager.

Hardening the SQL Server Installation

Another important step to finalize the SQL Server 2012 installation or upgrade is hardening the SQL Server implementation. A number of tasks should be completed to harden the SQL Server installation. Some of these tasks include using Policy Based Management to reduce the surface attack area, enabling a Windows Server advanced firewall, and leveraging the SQL Server Configuration Manager Tool to disable unnecessary protocols and features.

Items to Consider After an Upgrade

This section describes additional items to take into consideration after an upgrade to SQL Server 2012 is complete.

Running SQL Server Management Studio for the First Time

After the upgrade is complete and you launch SQL Server Management Studio for the first time, you will be prompted to import customized user settings from the previous version of SQL Server Management Studio. Click Yes or No and be aware that some SQL Server 2012 default settings might be changed after you import your customized settings.

Choosing the Database Compatibility Level After the Upgrade

When SQL Server systems are upgraded to SQL Server 2012, it is beneficial to understand how compatibility level settings affect databases. The compatibility levels include the following:

- SQL Server 2012—Version 110
- SQL Server 2008 and SQL Server 2008 R2—Version 100
- SQL Server 2005—Version 90

If you select one of these options, the database behaviors are to be compatible with that specified version of SQL Server. This setting affects only a specific database and not all databases associated with a SQL Server instance.

> **Note**
>
> After the upgrade, SQL Server automatically sets the compatibility level to the earlier version of SQL Server.

> **Tip**
>
> Keep in mind that after you upgrade the databases by detaching and attaching from a previous version of SQL Server to SQL Server 2012, it is not possible to reattach the database to the older version of SQL Server, even if the database compatibility is set to the older version. Therefore, it is recommended that you take a full backup of all the databases prior to the upgrade process and keep it in a safe and secure location in case it is required.

The settings can be changed by right-clicking a database and specifying the compatibility level on the Database Options page or by using the ALTER DATABASE command. The following Transact-SQL sample illustrates how to change the compatibility level:

```
Alter Database <database name>
Set Compatibility_Level =<90 | 100 | 110>
```

From a best-practice perspective, you should change the database to single-user mode before changing the database compatibility settings. This prevents inconsistent results if active queries are executed.

Additional Post-Upgrade Tasks

- Update Statistics on all users and system databases.
- Execute DBCC_UPDATEUSAGE on all databases to ensure that all databases have the correct row and page counts.
- With SQL Server 2012, queries on partitioned tables and indexes are processed differently. Therefore, it is recommended to remove the USE PLAN hint from the query.

Installing SQL Server 2012 on Windows Server Core

Windows Server Core, an installation option, was one of the most innovative and anticipated features introduced with Windows Server 2008. The Windows Server Core installation provides a minimal environment for running a specific server role, including a domain controller, web server, or DHCP server. In this situation, only a subset of the Windows Server binaries is utilized. The Server Core installation is so stripped that traditional installation components, such as a desktop shell, graphical user interface, Windows Explorer, Microsoft Internet Explorer, and the MMC, are not included. Therefore, the server must be fully managed and configured via the command prompt or by using remote administration tools from another server. Unfortunately, the previous versions of SQL Server were not supported on Server Core. However, SQL Server 2012 now supports Server Core, provided that the operating system you are using is Windows Server 2008 R2 SP1 and later.

By maintaining a minimized installation footprint by stripping out only the typical components and only supporting specific roles, the Server Core installation reduces maintenance, attack surface, management, and reduces operating system patching for SQL Server 2012.

The next sections will provide the step-by-step procedures for installing Windows Server Core from scratch, the basic Server Core configurations settings, and then how to deploy SQL Server 2012 on Server Core.

Installing Windows Server 2008 R2 Server Core

Let's start by installing Windows Server Core, which is very similar to a regular server install. To recap, an administrator agrees to the licensing terms, supplies configuration responses, and the Windows Server 2008 R2 Installation Wizard copies the files and configures the server. However, unlike a traditional installation of Windows, when the installation is complete and you log on, there isn't a GUI to configure the server. The server can be configured and managed only via the command line.

The Server Core installation reboots your machine or virtual server a couple of times when device detection and the installation takes place. Eventually, you'll be presented with the logon screen. Follow these steps to conduct a Windows Server 2008 R2 SP1 Server Core installation:

1. Insert the Windows Server 2008 R2 SP1 media. The Install Windows page automatically launches; otherwise, click Setup.exe.

2. Specify the Language to Install, Time and Currency Format, and Keyboard or Input Method and then click Next.

3. Click Install Now to begin the installation process.

4. On the Select the Operating System You Want to Install page, select the Windows Server 2008 R2 SP1 (Server Core Installation). Click Next to continue.

5. Review the license terms and select the I Accept the License Terms option and then click Next.

6. On the Which Type of Installation Do You Want page, select Custom (Advanced) and then Click Next.

7. On the Where Do You Want to Install Windows page, select the disk where you plan to install the Windows system files. Alternatively, you can click the Drive (Options) to create, delete, extend, or format partitions. In addition, click Load Driver to install drivers for the Windows Server 2008 R2 SP1 installation that are not available on the media.

> **Note**
>
> If the only drive available is Unallocated Space, Windows Server 2008 R2 automatically creates a partition based on the largest size and formats the partition with NTFS.

The installation process will commence by copying the files, installing the Windows operating system, and configuring features. After this process is complete, the server will automatically reboot itself and require the installer to change the administrator password for the system. Enter and confirm the new administrator password, and then use the new password to log on to Server Core. You will now be presented with a Command Prompt window.

Configuring and Managing a Windows Server Core Installation

All the tasks affiliated with configuring and managing server core must be conducted via the command prompt or with scripts. As you can imagine, this became challenging for IT Professionals or DBAs who were not familiar with command line and scripting. Thankfully, the SCONFIG utility was introduced in the Server Core deployment options when using Windows Server 2008 R2. Its purpose was to dramatically ease the initial server configuration of server core deployments for IT Professionals or DBAs who are familiar with GUI-based tools and not comfortable with commands or scripting.

The following sections cover general tasks associated with configuring and managing a Server Core system after the installation is complete via SCONFIG. As an alternative, an administrator can use the command prompt to configure the server.

Launching the Command Prompt in a Windows Server Core Installation

Remember, with Server Core, the Start menu does not exist. Because of this, one of the most important tasks an administrator must understand when managing a Server Core installation is how to launch the command prompt. It is worth noting that the command prompt will be presented when the server starts up, however, it is fairly common that a DBA may close the command prompt window. The following steps will assist you:

1. Press Ctrl+Alt+Delete.

2. Select Start Task Manager.

3. On the Windows Task Manager screen, select File, then New Task (Run).

4. In the Create New Task dialog box, type **cmd.exe** and then click OK.

Using SCONFIG to Configure Windows Server Core

Now that you have a command prompt, let's use SCONFIG to configure the server and prepare for the installation of SQL Server 2012. You can launch the utility menu, as illustrated in Figure 1.11, by typing **SCONFIG** at the command prompt. The following steps articulate the basic configuration settings required to deploy SQL Server 2012.

FIGURE 1.11
Leveraging SCONFIG to configure a Windows Server Core Installation.

1. On the SCONFIG console, select option 8 to configure the network settings associated with the server. Network settings such as IP Address, Subnet Mask, Default Gateway, and DNS should be configured for each available network adapter. When complete, return to the SCONFIG main menu.

2. On the SCONFIG console, select option 1 to configure the domain-based settings for this server. Select Yes when prompted to change the computer name before restarting the computer.

3. In the menu, specify a computer name. When prompted, reboot the server and then return to the main menu in SCONFIG.

Tip

Although not required, it is beneficial to configure Remote Management, Remote Desktop, and Download and Install Updates before commencing. All these tasks can be easily conducted via the SCONFIG utility using menus 4, 6, and 7.

Installing SQL Server 2012 on Windows Server Core

Now that Windows Server Core has been installed and configured, it is time to implement SQL Server 2012. Because the general GUI does not exist on a Windows Server Core installation, the traditional SQL Server setup installation wizard does not work. Therefore, you must install SQL Server from the command prompt by using the /Q parameter, which represents an installation using a quite simple mode. Alternatively, it is also possible to install SQL Server 2012 on Server Core by using a configuration file. Before installing SQL Server, let's understand which features are supported.

SQL Server 2012 Supported Features on Windows Server Core

To install specific features such as the Database Engine or Analysis Services, the /FEATURES parameters must be utilized. Table 1.4 outlines the Feature Parameters including a description of the feature. Table 1.5 shows the DBA how to pass values for a specific feature.

Table 1.4 **Feature Parameters**

Feature Parameters	Description
SQLENGINE	Parameter required to install the Database Engine.
REPLICATION	Installs the Replication feature along with Database Engine.
FULLTEXT	Installs the FullText feature along with Database Engine.
AS	Installs all Analysis Services feature.
IS	Installs all Integration Services feature.
CONN	Installs the connectivity components.

Table 1.5 **Parameter and Values**

Parameter and Values	Description
/FEATURES=SQLEngine	Installs only the Database Engine.
/FEATURES=SQLEngine, FullText	Installs the Database Engine and Full-Text and Semantic Extractions for Search.
/FEATURES=SQLEngine, Conn	Installs the Database Engine and the connectivity components.
/FEATURES=SQLEngine, AS, IS, Conn	Installs the Database Engine, Analysis Services, Integration Services, and the connectivity components.

> **Note**
>
> Not all of the SQL Server features are supported on Server Core. The features not supported include Reporting Services, SQL Server Data Tools, Client Tools Backward Compatibility, Client Tools SDK, SQL Server Books Online, Distributed Replay Controller, SQL Client Connectivity SDK, Master Data Services, and Data Quality Services.

Installing SQL Server 2012 via the Command Prompt in Windows Server Core

Now that the Server Core system is prepared and added to the network, you can begin the SQL Server 2012 installation. The following script is an example of a typical SQL Server 2012 installation on Server Core using the feature parameters outlined earlier. It includes the installation of the SQL Server 2012's Database Engine feature, including the Replication subcomponent. You will need to pass the following parameters: SQL

Server Service Account, including password, and the account you plan to use for the Systems Administrator.

```
Setup.exe /qs /ACTION=Install /FEATURES=SQLEngine,Replication
/INSTANCENAME=MSSQLSERVER
/SQLSVCACCOUNT="<Domain\ServiceAccount>"
/SQLSVCPASSWORD="<EnterComplexPassword>"
/SQLSYSADMINACCOUNTS="<Domain\ServiceAccount>"
/AGTSVCACCOUNT="NT AUTHORITY\Network Service"
/IACCEPTSQLSERVERLICENSETERMS
```

> **Note**
>
> For more information on installing SQL Server 2012 from a command prompt, including all the installation parameters, review the article "Install SQL Server 2012 from the Command Prompt" in SQL Server 2012 Books Online.

Finalizing the SQL Server 2012 Server Core Installation

We have now successfully installed SQL Server 2012 on Windows Server Core. Because a GUI does not exist on the Server Core installation, let's review best practices on how to administer Windows Server Core and SQL Server 2012 with remote tools. The best approach to managing the Windows portion of Server Core is to connect to Server Core with Server Manager and Computer Management MMC Snap-in from another Windows Server 2008 R2 SP1 system running the full installation. By connecting with Server Manager, a DBA can manage roles, features, firewall rules, diagnostics, services, and storage. When using Computer Management Snap-in, it is possible to configure services, protocols, and remote access for SQL Server via SQL Server Configuration Manager. For SQL Server management, you should install and use SQL Server Management Studio on a remote server to connect to the instance of SQL Server running on Server Core. The following tasks illustrate some of the Server Core management tasks that can come in handy.

Enabling Server Core Remote Management via SCONFIG

Before connecting with Server Manager, you must ensure remote management for the Server Core system has been enabled. This can be done with SCONFIG. This can be achieved by using the following steps:

1. Log on to the Server Core system where you have installed SQL Server 2012.

2. At the command prompt, type in **SCONFIG**.

3. Select option 4 to Configure Remote Management.

4. In the Configure Remote Management menu, conduct the following tasks:

   ■ Select option 1 to Allow MMC Remote Management.

   ■ Select option 2 to enable Windows PowerShell.

   ■ Select option 3, Allow Server Manager Remote Management.

5. Based on your organization's policy, you may have to enable, disable, or configure SQL Server Ports for the Windows Firewall. Configurations can be conducted via Server Manager, Powershell, or Windows Group Policies.

Manage Server Core Roles, Features, and Firewall Settings by Using Server Manager

If necessary, perform the following steps to configure roles, features, and firewall settings on a remote machine that is running the full edition of Windows Server 2008 R2 SP1:

1. Click Start, Administrator Tools, and then Server Manager.

2. In the tree pane of the MMC, right-click the top node of a Server Manager snap-in and then click Connect to Another Computer.

3. In the Connect to Another Computer dialog box, enter the name or IP address of the SQL Server system running Windows Server 2008 R2 SP1 Server Core computer in the Another computer string box, or browse for another server on the network. Click OK.

4. After you connect to a remote computer, notice that the name of the computer changes in the Server Manager node of the tree pane.

5. Conduct any management tasks required, such as configuring firewall settings.

Manage SQL Server Configuration Manager Settings via Computer Management

You should now be able to connect to SQL Server 2012 running on the Server Core installation by using SQL Server Management Studio tools from another Windows Server system. You will need to provide the SQL Server 2012 Server Core computer name and instance when connecting remotely via SQL Server Management Studio. If you cannot connect, and you have already configured Server Core for remote access and configured the firewall, you may have to enable remote connections, enable client protocols, or configure services on the instance of SQL Server residing on Server Core. This can be achieved by using Computer Management MMC Snap-In or by using Transact-SQL Script.

1. From a remote machine, click Start and then type `compmgmt.msc` at the run command.

2. In the tree pane of the MMC, right-click the top node of a Computer Management snap-in and then click Connect to Another Computer.

3. In the Connect to Another Computer dialog box, enter the name or IP address of the SQL Server system running Windows Server 2008 R2 SP1 Server Core computer in the Another computer string box or browse for another server on the network. Click OK.

4. After you connect to a remote computer, notice that the name of the computer changes in the Computer Management node of the tree pane.

5. Expand Services and Applications.

6. Expand SQL Server Configuration Manager, as illustrated in Figure 1.12, to view or configure SQL Server services, client protocols, and remote access.

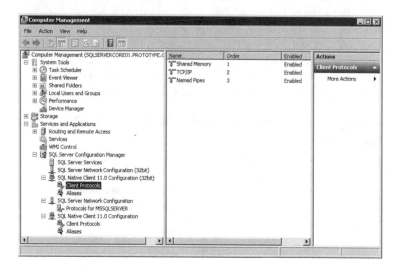

FIGURE 1.12

Configuring SQL Server Configuration settings remotely with Computer Management MMC Snap-in.

Alternatively, you can use the following Transact-SQL statement to enable remote access:

```
EXEC sys.sp_configure N'remote access', N'1'
GO
RECONFIGURE WITH OVERRIDE
GO
```

Managing SQL Server 2012 Installations

The following sections explain how to manage SQL Server 2012 installations.

Employing Additional SQL Server 2012 Instances

As mentioned earlier, many organizations decide on scaling up their SQL Server infrastructure by creating consolidated SQL Server systems with multiple-instance installations. To achieve the goal of installing additional instances on an existing system, a DBA must relaunch the SQL Server 2012 installation utility and then select the option New SQL Server Stand-alone Installation or Add Features to an Existing Installation.

When the new SQL Server installation wizard begins, follow the steps in the earlier section "Installing a New Installation of SQL Server 2012"; however, on the Installation Type page, select the option Perform a New Installation of SQL Server 2012, as displayed in Figure 1.13. Then on the Feature Selection page, select the desired features to be installed for the new instance. Finally, on the Instance Configuration page, provide the instance with a unique name and proceed with the installation.

Adding Features to an Existing SQL Server 2012 Installation

The process for adding and removing SQL Server features to an existing Installation is similar to the steps involved when adding additional SQL Server instances. The DBA must select New SQL Server Stand-alone Installation or Add Features to an Existing Installation from the SQL Server 2012 Installation Center's Installation page. However, on the Installation Type screen, the option Add Features to an Existing Instance of SQL Server 2012 must be selected. Then on the Feature Selection page, select the features to be added and continue through the wizard.

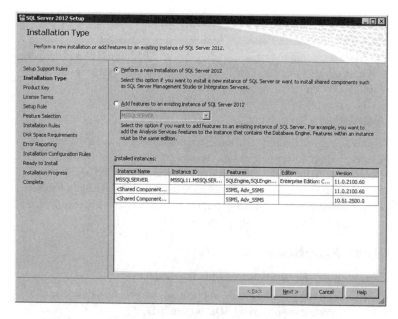

FIGURE 1.13
Adding additional SQL Server instances to an existing installation.

> **Note**
>
> It is not possible to add features when upgrading to SQL Server 2012;
> therefore, this strategy should be used for adding features after the SQL
> Server upgrade is complete.

Changing SQL Server 2012 Editions

Another feature included with SQL Server 2012 is the potential to conduct
an edition upgrade after SQL Server 2012 has been installed. For example,
if an organization is running the Standard Edition and decides that it wants
to leverage the features and functionality associated with the Enterprise
Edition, the organization can conduct an edition upgrade instead of formatting and reinstalling from scratch. Another advantageous scenario includes
moving from SQL Server 2008 R2 Standard to SQL Server 2012
Enterprise Edition. This objective is achieved by first upgrading the SQL
Server system from SQL Server 2008 R2 Standard to SQL Server 2012

Standard and then running the Edition Upgrade to upgrade the installation Enterprise Edition of SQL Server 2012.

To conduct an edition upgrade on SQL Server 2012, the Edition Upgrade must be selected from the Maintenance page on the SQL Server 2012 Installation Center landing screen.

Summary

The SQL Server 2012 installation process and deployment tools bear similarities to those found in previous versions of SQL Server. However, feature and performance enhancements associated with the new SQL Server 2012 Installation Center tool have improved the installation experience, whether you are installing a single SQL Server implementation from scratch or upgrading an existing system to SQL Server 2012.

Best Practices

The following are best practices from this chapter:

- Verify that your databases, applications, hardware, devices, and drivers are supported by SQL Server 2012.

- Stick to using the recommended or optimal hardware and software requirements when installing or upgrading to SQL Server 2012.

- Leverage the planning tools and documentation associated with the SQL Server Installation Center when installing or upgrading to SQL Server 2012.

- Run the System Configuration Checker tool as a prerequisite task when either installing or upgrading to SQL Server 2012.

- Install and run the Upgrade Advisor to identify any upgrade anomalies when upgrading a system to SQL Server 2012.

- When performing an upgrade, make sure you document your SQL Server system and database configuration information and perform a backup of any SQL Server data and objects that you want to keep.

- Leverage Windows Server 2008 R2 as the operating system when running SQL Server 2012.

- Leverage Windows Server 2008 R2 Server Core for maximum security and availability.

- Finalize a SQL Server implementation by hardening the system based on the best practices listed in Chapter 7.

- Utilize Policy Based Management to configure the surface area of one or many SQL Server systems.

- The Windows Server 2008 R2 Advanced Firewall is enabled by default; therefore, review Chapter 7 to understand how to configure the firewall for SQL Server access.

- Review Books Online if you need to upgrade other SQL Server 2012 features above and beyond the Database Engine.

- Data, log, and tempdb directories should be on separate physical disks or Logical Unit Numbers (LUNs) for performance whenever possible.

CHAPTER 2

Administering and Configuring the Database Engine Settings

Although SQL Server 2012 is composed of numerous components, one component is often considered the foundation of the product. The Database Engine is the core service for storing, processing, and securing data for the most challenging data systems. Note that the Database Engine is also referred to as Database Engine Services. Likewise, it provides the foundation and fundamentals for the majority of the core database administration tasks. As a result of its important role in SQL Server 2012, it is no wonder that the Database Engine is designed to provide a scalable, fast, secure, and highly available platform for data access and other components. In addition, SQL Server 2012 is Microsoft's first cloud-ready information platform that has tight integration with private cloud and public cloud deployments, such as SQL Azure.

This chapter focuses on administering the Database Engine component, also referred to as a feature in SQL Server 2012. Administration tasks include managing SQL Server properties, database properties, folders within SQL Server Management Studio, and the SQL Server Agent based on SQL Server 2012. In addition, Database Engine configuration and management tasks are also covered.

Even though the chapter introduces and explains all the management areas within the Database Engine, you are directed to other chapters for additional information. This is a result of the Database Engine feature being so large and intricately connected to other features.

What's New for DBAs When Administering the Database Engine on SQL Server 2012

SQL Server 2012 introduces a tremendous number of new features, in addition to new functionality, that DBAs need to be aware of. The following are some of the important Database Engine management enhancements within SQL Server Management Studio:

- AlwaysOn Availability Groups, which provides a single integrated solution for databases to achieve both high availability and disaster recovery. The management associated with AlwaysOn is conducted via the new AlwaysOn High Availability folder in Object Explorer.

- AlwaysOn Availability Groups offer a new capability for read-only access to a secondary for reporting, backup operations, and some management tasks. The capability is known as Active Secondary Replicas.

- AlwayOn Failover Cluster Instances (FCI) provides multi-subnet support where each failover cluster node can be connected to a different subnet or set of subnets.

- A new wizard that allows you to seamlessly deploy a database to SQL Azure.

- FILESTREAM supports multiple containers to achieve higher performance and scalability when supporting unstructured data.

- Contained Databases simplifies a DBA's task when moving databases from one instance of SQL Server to another because users in a contained database are no longer associated with logins on the instance of SQL Server.

- Blazing fast performance can be achieved on data warehouse workloads with a new Columnstore Index.

Administering SQL Server 2012 Server Properties

The SQL Server Properties dialog box is the main place where you, as a database administrator (DBA), configure server settings specifically tailored toward a SQL Server 2012 Database Engine installation.

You can invoke the Server Properties dialog box for the Database Engine by following these steps:

1. Choose Start, All Programs, Microsoft SQL Server 2012, SQL Server Management Studio.

2. Connect to the Database Engine.

3. In Object Explorer, right-click a SQL Server Instance and then select Properties.

The Server Properties dialog box includes eight pages of Database Engine settings that you can view, manage, and configure. The eight Server Properties pages are similar to what was found in SQL Server 2008 R2 and include the following:

- General
- Memory
- Processors
- Security
- Connections
- Database Settings
- Advanced
- Permissions

Note

Each of the SQL Server Properties settings can be easily scripted by clicking the Script button. The Script button is available on each Server Properties page. The Script output options available include Script Action to New Query Window, Script Action to a File, Script Action to Clipboard, and Script Action to a Job.

Note

In addition, it is possible to obtain a listing of all the SQL Server configuration settings associated with a Database Engine installation by executing the following query in Query Editor:

```
SELECT * FROM sys.configurations
ORDER BY name ;
GO
```

The following sections provide examples and explanations for each page in the SQL Server Properties dialog box.

Administering the General Page

The first Server Properties page, General, includes mostly information pertaining to the SQL Server 2012 installation, as illustrated in Figure 2.1. Here you can view the following items: SQL Server name; product version, such as Standard, Enterprise, or 64-bit; Windows platform, such as Windows 2008 R2 or Windows 2008; SQL Server version number; language settings; total memory in the server; number of processors; Root Directory; Server Collation; and whether the installation is clustered. With SQL Server 2012, there is also a new property called Is HADR Enabled, which represents whether or not AlwaysOn Availability Groups is enabled for this instance of SQL Server.

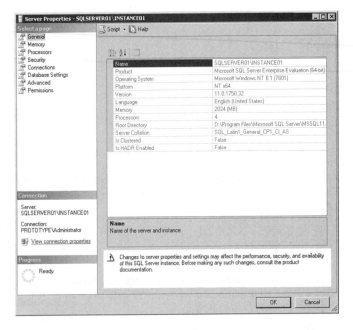

FIGURE 2.1
Administering the Server Properties General page.

Administering the Memory Page

Memory is the second page within the Server Properties dialog box. As shown in Figure 2.2, this page is broken into two sections: Server Memory Options and Other Memory Options. Each section has additional items to configure to manage memory; they are described in the following sections.

Administering the Server Memory Options

The Server Memory options are as follows:

- **Minimum Server Memory and Maximum Server Memory—** These items within Memory Options are for inputting the minimum and maximum amount of memory allocated to a SQL Server instance. The memory settings inputted are calculated in megabytes.

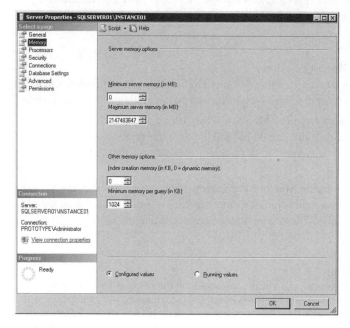

FIGURE 2.2
Administering the Server Properties Memory page.

The following Transact-SQL code can be used to configure Server Memory Options:

```
sp_configure 'awe enabled', 1
RECONFIGURE
GO
sp_configure 'min server memory', ,<MIN AMOUNT IN MB>
RECONFIGURE
GO
sp_configure 'max server memory', <MAX AMOUNT IN MB>
RECONFIGURE
GO
```

> **Note**
>
> The information enclosed in angle brackets < > needs to be replaced with a value specific to this example. This applies to this Transact-SQL example and subsequent ones to follow in this chapter and book.

Other Memory Options

The second section, Other Memory Options, has two additional memory settings tailored toward index creation and minimum memory per query:

- **Index Creation Memory**—This setting allocates the amount of memory that should be used during index creation operations. The default value is 0, which represents dynamic allocation by SQL Server.
- **Minimum Memory Per Query**—This setting specifies the minimum amount of memory in kilobytes that should be allocated to a query. The default setting is configured to the value of 1024KB.

> **Note**
>
> SQL Server can dynamically manage both the memory associated with index creation and the memory for queries. However, you can specify values for index creation if you're creating many indexes in parallel. You should tweak the minimum memory setting per query if many queries are occurring over multiple connections in a busy environment. Also, keep in mind that the Min Memory Per Query option always has precedence over Index Create Memory option. If you are making changes to both the options, and if you leave Index Create Memory to less than the Min Memory Per Query, you may receive a warning message, but the value will be set. However, you will encounter the same warnings during the execution of the query.

Use the following Transact-SQL statements to configure Other Memory Options:

```
sp_configure 'index create memory, <NUMBER IN KB>
RECONFIGURE
GO
sp_configure 'min memory per query, <NUMBER IN KB>
RECONFIGURE
GO
```

Administering the Processors Page

The Processors page, shown in Figure 2.3, should be used to administer or manage any processor-related options for the SQL Server 2012 Database Engine. Options include threads, processor performance, affinity, and parallel or symmetric processing.

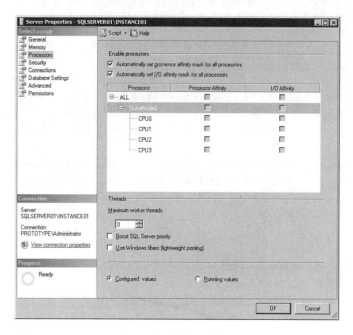

FIGURE 2.3
Administering the Server Properties Processor page.

Enabling Processors

Similar to a DBA, the operating system is constantly multitasking. Therefore, the operating system moves threads between different processors to maximize processing efficiency. You should use the Processors page to administer or manage any processor-related options, such as parallel or symmetric processing. The processor options include the following:

- **Enable Processors**—The two processor options in this section include Processor Affinity and I/O Affinity. Processor Affinity allows SQL Server to manage the processors; therefore, processors are assigned to specific threads during execution. Similar to Processor Affinity, the I/O Affinity setting informs SQL Server about which processors can manage I/O disk operations.

Tip

SQL Server 2012 does a great job of dynamically managing and optimizing processor and I/O affinity settings. If you need to manage these settings manually, you should reserve some processors for threading and others for I/O operations. A processor should not be configured to do both.

- **Automatically Set Processor Affinity Mask for All Processors**—If this option is enabled, SQL Server dynamically manages the Processor Affinity Mask and overwrites the existing Affinity Mask settings.

- **Automatically Set I/O Affinity Mask for All Processors**—Same thing as the preceding option: If this option is enabled, SQL Server dynamically manages the I/O Affinity Mask and overwrites the existing Affinity Mask settings.

Threads

The following Threads items can be individually managed to assist processor performance:

- **Maximum Worker Threads**—The Maximum Worker Threads setting governs the optimization of SQL Server performance by controlling thread pooling. Typically, this setting is adjusted for a server hosting many client connections. By default, this value is set to 0. The 0 value represents dynamic configuration because SQL Server determines the number of worker threads to utilize. If this setting will be statically managed, a higher value is recommended for a busy server with a high number of connections. Subsequently, a lower number is recommended for a server that is not being heavily utilized and has a small number of user connections. The values to be entered range from 10 to 32,767.

Tip

Microsoft recommends maintaining the Maximum Worker Threads setting at 0 to negate thread starvation. Thread starvation occurs when incoming client requests are not served in a timely manner because of a small value for this setting. Subsequently, a large value can waste address space because each active thread consumes 512KB.

- **Boost SQL Server Priority**—Preferably, SQL Server should be the only application running on the server; therefore, it is recommended to enable this check box. This setting tags the SQL Server threads with a higher priority value of 13 instead of the default 7 for better performance. If other applications are running on the server, performance of those applications could degrade if this option is enabled, because those threads have a lower priority. If enabled, it is also possible that resources from essential operating system and network functions may be drained.

- **Use Windows Fibers (Lightweight Pooling)**—This setting offers a means of decreasing the system overhead associated with extreme context switching seen in symmetric multiprocessing environments. Enabling this option provides better throughput by executing the context switching inline.

Note

Enabling fibers is tricky because it has its advantages and disadvantages for performance. This is derived from how many processors are running on the server. Typically, performance gains occur if the system is running a lot of CPUs, such as more than 16, whereas performance may decrease if there are only 1 or 2 processors. To ensure the new settings are optimized, it is a best practice to monitor performance counters after changes are made.

These Transact-SQL statements should be used to set processor settings:

```
sp_configure 'affinity mask', <VALUE>;
RECONFIGURE;
GO


sp_configure 'affinity I/O mask', :<VALUE>;
RECONFIGURE;
GO
sp_configure 'lightweight pooling', <0 or 1>;
RECONFIGURE;
GO


sp_configure 'max worker threads', :<INTEGER VALUE>;
RECONFIGURE;
GO


sp_configure 'priority boost', <0 or 1>;
RECONFIGURE;
GO
```

Administering the Security Page

The Security page, shown in Figure 2.4, maintains serverwide security configuration settings. These SQL Server settings include Server Authentication, Login Auditing, Server Proxy Account, and Options.

Server Authentication

The first section in the Security page focuses on server authentication. At present, SQL Server 2012 continues to support two modes for validating connections and authenticating access to database resources: Windows Authentication Mode and SQL Server and Windows Authentication Mode. Both of these authentication methods provide access to SQL Server and its resources. SQL Server and Windows Authentication Mode is regularly referred to as *mixed mode authentication.*

Note

During installation, the default authentication mode is Windows Authentication. The authentication mode can be changed after the installation.

FIGURE 2.4
Administering the Server Properties Security page.

The Windows Authentication Mode setting is the default Authentication setting and is the recommended authentication mode. It leverages Active Directory user accounts or groups when granting access to SQL Server. In this mode, you are given the opportunity to grant domain or local server users access to the database server without creating and managing a separate SQL Server account. It's worth mentioning that when Windows Authentication Mode is active, user accounts are subject to enterprisewide policies enforced by the Active Directory domain or the local Windows Server, such as complex passwords, password history, account lockouts, minimum password length, maximum password length, and the Kerberos protocol. These enhanced and well-defined policies are always a plus to have in place.

The second authentication option is SQL Server and Windows Authentication (Mixed) Mode. This setting uses either Active Directory user accounts or SQL Server accounts when validating access to SQL Server. Starting with SQL Server 2005, Microsoft introduced a means to enforce password and lockout policies for SQL Server login accounts when using SQL Server Authentication.

> **Note**
>
> Review the authentication sections in Chapter 7, "Hardening and Auditing a SQL Server 2012 Implementation," for more information on authentication modes and which mode should be used as a best practice.

Login Auditing

Login Auditing is the focal point on the second section on the Security page. You can choose from one of the four Login Auditing options available: None, Failed Logins Only, Successful Logins Only, and Both Failed and Successful Logins.

> **Tip**
>
> When you're configuring auditing, it is a best practice to configure auditing to capture both failed and successful logins. Therefore, in the case of a system breach or an audit, you have all the logins captured in an audit file. The drawback to this option is that the log file will grow quickly and will require adequate disk space. If this is not possible, only failed logins, which is the default setting, should be captured as the bare minimum.

Server Proxy Account

You can enable a server proxy account in the Server Proxy section of the Security page. The proxy account permits the security context to execute operating system commands by the impersonation of logins, server roles, and database roles. If you're using a proxy account, you should configure the account with the least number of privileges to perform the task. This bolsters security and reduces the amount of damage if the account is compromised.

Additional Security Options

Additional security options available in the Options section of the Security page are as follows:

- **Enable Common Criteria Compliance**—When this setting is enabled, it manages database security. Specifically, it manages features such as Residual Information Protection (RIP), controls access to login statistics, and enforces restrictions where, for example, the column titled GRANT cannot override the table titled DENY.

■ **Enable C2 Audit Tracing**—When this setting is enabled, SQL
Server allows the largest number of the success and failure objects to
be audited. The drawback to capturing for audit data is that it can
degrade performance and take up disk space. The files are stored in
the Data directory associated with the instance of the SQL Server
installation.

■ **Cross-Database Ownership Chaining**—Enabling this setting
allows cross-database ownership chaining at a global level for all
databases. Cross-database ownership chaining governs whether the
database can be accessed by external resources. As a result, this
setting should be enabled only when the situation is closely managed
because several serious security holes would be opened.

Administering the Connections Page

The Connections page, as shown in Figure 2.5, is the place where you
examine and configure any SQL Server settings relevant to connections.
The Connections page is broken up into two sections: Connections and
Remote Server Connections.

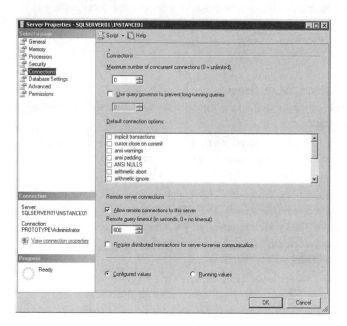

FIGURE 2.5
Administering the Server Properties Connections page.

Connections

The Connections section includes the following settings:

- **Maximum Number of Concurrent Connections**—The first setting determines the maximum number of concurrent connections allowed to the SQL Server Database Engine. The default value is 0, which represents an unlimited number of connections. The value used when configuring this setting is really dictated by the SQL Server hardware, such as the processor, RAM, and disk speed.

- **Use Query Governor to Prevent Long-Running Queries**—This setting creates a stipulation based on an upper-limit criteria specified for the time period in which a query can run. The default value is 0, which represents an unlimited amount of time.

- **Default Connection Options**—For the final setting, you can choose from approximately 16 advanced connection options that can be either enabled or disabled, as shown in Figure 2.5.

> **Note**
>
> For more information on each of the default Connection Option settings, refer to SQL Server 2012 Books Online. Search for the topic "Server Properties Connections Page."

Remote Server Connections

The second section located on the Connections page focuses on Remote Server settings:

- **Allow Remote Connections to This Server**—If enabled, the first option allows remote connections to the specified SQL Server. With SQL Server 2012, this option is enabled by default.

- **Remote Query Timeout**—The second setting is available only if Allow Remote Connections is enabled. This setting governs how long it will take for a remote query to terminate. The default value is 600; however, the values that can be configured range from 0 to 2,147,483,647. Zero represents infinite.

- **Require Distributed Transactions for Server-to-Server Communication**—The final setting controls the behavior and protects the transactions between systems by using the Microsoft Distributed Transaction Coordinator (MS DTC).

> **Note**
>
> When using Windows Server 2008 and later, MS DTC is referred to as DTC.

Administering the Database Settings Page

The Database Settings page, shown in Figure 2.6, contains configuration settings that each database within the SQL Server instance will inherit. The choices available on this page are broken out by Fill Factor, Backup and Restore, Recovery, and Database Default Locations.

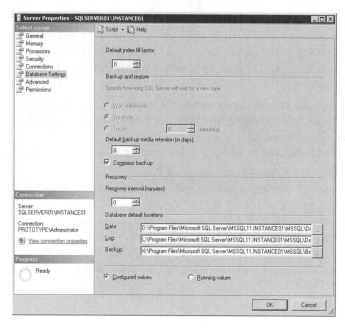

FIGURE 2.6
Administering the Server Properties Database Settings page.

Default Index Fill Factor

The Default Index Fill Factor setting specifies how full SQL Server should configure each page when a new index is created. The default setting is 0, and the ranges are between 0 and 100. The 0 value represents a table with room for growth, whereas a value of 100 represents no space for subsequent insertions without requiring page splits. A table with all reads typically has a higher fill factor, and a table that is meant for heavy inserts typically has a low fill factor. The value 50 is ideal when a table has a balanced load of reads and writes. This setting is global to all tables within the Database Engine.

For more information on fill factors, refer to Chapter 5, "Managing and Optimizing SQL Server 2012 Indexes," and Chapter 16, "SQL Server 2012 Maintenance Practices."

Backup and Restore

The Backup and Restore section of the Database Settings page includes the following settings:

- **Specify How Long SQL Server Will Wait for a New Tape**—The first setting governs the time interval SQL Server will wait for a new tape during a database backup process. The options available are Wait Indefinitely, Try Once, or Try for a Specific Number of Minutes.

- **Default Backup Media Retention (In Days)**—This setting is a systemwide configuration that affects all database backups, including the translation logs. You enter values for this setting in days, and it dictates the time to maintain and/or retain each backup medium.

- **Compress Backup**—If the Compress Backup systemwide setting is enabled, all new backups associated with the SQL Server instance will be compressed. Keep in mind there is a trade-off when compressing backups. Space associated with the backup on disk is significantly reduced; however, processor usage increases during the backup compression process. For more information on compressed backups, refer to Chapter 6, "Backing Up and Restoring SQL Server 2012 Databases."

Note

It is possible to leverage Resource Governor in order to manage the amount of workload associated with the processor when conducting compressed backups. This will ensure that the server does not suffer from excessive processor resource consumption, which eventually leads to performance degradation of the server. For more information on Resource Governor, refer to Chapter 18, "Managing Workloads with Resource Governor."

Recovery

The Recovery section of the Database Settings page consists of one setting:

- **Recovery Interval (Minutes)**—Only one Recovery setting is available. This setting influences the amount of time, in minutes, SQL Server will take to recover a database. Recovering a database takes place every time SQL Server is started. Uncommitted transactions are either committed or rolled back.

Database Default Locations

Options available in the Database Default Locations section are as follows:

- **Data, Log, and Backup**—The three folder paths for Data, Log, and Backup placement specify the default location for these files. Click the ellipsis button on the right side to change the default folder and specify a new location.

Administering the Advanced Page

The Advanced Page, shown in Figure 2.7, contains the SQL Server general settings that can be configured.

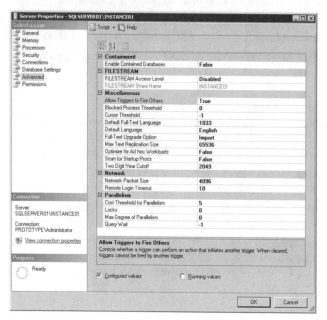

FIGURE 2.7
Administering the Server Properties Advanced Settings page.

Containment

Contained Database is a brand-new feature in SQL Server 2012. It is a concept in which a database includes all the settings and metadata required to define the database and has no configuration dependencies on the instance of the SQL Server Database Engine where the database is installed. Isolation between the users and database is achieved because users can connect to the database without authenticating a login at the Database Engine level. The Containment section includes the global configuration setting to determine whether contained databases will be enabled for an instance of SQL Server. The options include True or False.

FILESTREAM

FILESTREAM is a new storage methodology in SQL Server 2012. Only one item can be configured via the Advanced page.

- **Filestream Access Level**—FILESTREAM allows for the storage of unstructured data. The global server options associated with FILESTREAM configuration include the following:

  - **Disabled**—The Disabled setting does not allow Binary Large Object (BLOB) data to be stored in the file system.

  - **Transact-SQL Access Enabled**—FILESTREAM data is accessed only by Transact-SQL and not by the file system.

  - **Full Access Enabled**—FILESTREAM data is accessed by both Transact-SQL and the file system.

Miscellaneous Settings

Options available in the Miscellaneous section of the Advanced page are as follows:

- **Allow Triggers to Fire Others**—If this setting is configured to True, triggers can execute other triggers. In addition, the nesting level can be up to 32 levels. The values are either True or False.

- **Blocked Process Threshold**—The threshold at which blocked process reports are generated. Settings include 0 to 86,400.

- **Cursor Threshold**—This setting dictates the number of rows in the cursor that will be returned for a result set. A value of 0 represents that cursor keysets are generated asynchronously.

■ **Default Full-Text Language**—This setting specifies the language to be used for full-text columns. The default language is based on the language specified during the SQL Server instance installation.

■ **Default Language**—This setting is also inherited based on the language used during the installation of SQL. The setting controls the default language behavior for new logins.

■ **Full-Text Upgrade Option**—Controls the behavior of how full-text indexes are migrated when upgrading a database. The options include Import, Rebuild, or Reset.

■ **Max Text Replication Size**—This global setting dictates the maximum size of text and image data that can be inserted into columns. The measurement is in bytes.

■ **Optimize for Ad Hoc Workloads**—This setting is set to False by default. If set to True, this setting will improve the efficiency of the plan cache for ad hoc workloads.

■ **Scan for Startup Procs**—The configuration values are either True or False. If the setting is configured to True, SQL Server allows stored procedures that are configured to run at startup to fire.

■ **Two Digit Year Cutoff**—This setting indicates the uppermost year that can be specified as a two-digit year. Additional years must be entered as a four-digit number.

Network Settings

Options available in the Network section of the Advanced page are as follows:

■ **Network Packet Size**—This setting dictates the size of packets being transmitted over the network. The default size is 4096 bytes and is sufficient for most SQL Server network operations.

■ **Remote Login Timeout**—This setting determines the amount of time SQL Server will wait before timing out a remote login. The default time is 30 seconds, and a value of 0 represents an infinite wait before timing out. The default setting is 20.

Parallelism Settings

Options available in the Parallelism section of the Advanced page are as follows:

- **Cost Threshold for Parallelism**—This setting specifies the threshold above which SQL Server creates and runs parallel plans for queries. The cost refers to an estimated elapsed time in seconds required to run the serial plan on a specific hardware configuration. Set this option only on symmetric multiprocessors. For more information, search for "cost threshold for parallelism option" in SQL Server Books Online.

- **Locks**—The default for this setting is 0, which indicates that SQL Server is dynamically managing locking. Otherwise, you can enter a numeric value that sets the utmost number of locks to occur.

- **Max Degree of Parallelism**—This setting limits the number of processors (up to a maximum of 64) that can be used in a parallel plan execution. The default value of 0 uses all available processors, whereas a value of 1 suppresses parallel plan generation altogether. A number greater than 1 prevents the maximum number of processors from being used by a single-query execution. If a value greater than the number of available processors is specified, however, the actual number of available processors is used. For more information, search for "max degree of parallelism option" in SQL Server Books Online.

- **Query Wait**—This setting indicates the time in seconds a query will wait for resources before timing out.

Administering the Permissions Page

The Permissions page, as shown in Figure 2.8, includes all the authorization logins and permissions for the SQL Server instance. You can create and manage logins and/or roles within the first section. The second portion of this page displays the Explicit and Effective permissions based on the login or role.

For more information on permissions and authorization to the SQL Server 2012 Database Engine, refer to Chapter 8, "Administering SQL Server Security and Authorization."

FIGURE 2.8
Administering the Server Properties Permissions page.

Administering the SQL Server Database Engine Folders

After you configure the SQL Server properties, you must manage the SQL Server Database Engine folders and understand how the settings should be configured. The SQL Server folders contain an abundant number of configuration settings that need to be managed on an ongoing basis. The main SQL Server Database Engine top-level folders, as shown in Figure 2.9, are as follows:

- Databases
- Security
- Server Objects
- Replication
- AlwaysOn High Availability
- Management
- Integration Services Catalogs

Each folder can be expanded, which leads to more subfolders and thus more management of settings. The following sections discuss the folders within the SQL Server tree, starting with the Databases folder.

FIGURE 2.9
Viewing the Database Engine folders.

Administering the Databases Folder

The Databases folder is the main location for administering system and user databases. Management tasks that can be conducted by right-clicking the Database folder consist of creating new databases, attaching databases, restoring databases, deploying Data-tier Applications, importing Data-tier Applications, and creating custom reports.

The Databases folder contains subfolders as a repository for items such as system databases, database snapshots, and user databases. When a Database folder is expanded, each database has a predefined subfolder structure that includes configuration settings for that specific database. The database structure is as follows: Database Diagrams, Tables, Views, Synonyms, Programmability, Service Broker, Storage, and Security.

Let's start by examining the top-level folders and then the subfolders in subsequent sections.

Administering the System Databases Subfolder

The System Databases subfolder is the first folder within the Database tree. It consists of all the system databases that make up SQL Server 2012. The system databases consist of

- **Master Database**—The master database is an important system database in SQL Server 2012. It houses all system-level data, including system configuration settings, login information, disk space, stored procedures, linked servers, and the existence of other databases, along with other crucial information.

- **Model Database**—The model database serves as a template for creating new databases in SQL Server 2012. The data residing in the model database is commonly applied to a new database with the Create Database command. In addition, the tempdb database is re-created with the help of the model database every time SQL Server 2012 is started.

- **Msdb Database**—Used mostly by the SQL Server Agent, the msdb database stores alerts, scheduled jobs, and operators. In addition, it stores historical information on backups and restores, SQL Mail, and Service Broker.

- **Tempdb**—The tempdb database holds temporary information, including tables, stored procedures, objects, and intermediate result sets. Each time SQL Server is started, the tempdb database starts with a clean copy.

Tip

It is a best practice to conduct regular backups on the system databases. In addition, if you want to increase performance and response times, it is recommended to place the tempdb data and transaction log files on different volumes from the operating system drive. Finally, if you don't need to restore the system databases to a point in failure, you can set all recovery models for the system databases to Simple.

Notes from the Field: Best Practices for Configuring Tempdb Database

The tempdb database is usually one of the busiest databases on your SQL Server instance because it has a high rate of create/drop object activity. This would mean that the system metadata related to object creation/deletion is heavily used. The size and physical placement of the tempdb database can adversely affect the overall performance of your SQL Server instance. For example, if the size of tempdb database is too small, part of the system-processing load may be taken up with autogrowing tempdb to the size required to support the workload. You can potentially avoid this overhead by sizing the data and log file of tempdb database appropriately. Therefore, optimizing tempdb database is critically important for the overall performance of your SQL Server instance.

Here are some of the best practices from the field on configuring tempdb database to achieve optimum performance. Please note that though these best practices may work just fine in a production SQL Server environment, it is important that these items be tested in a prototype environment before applying the changes in production.

- Create additional tempdb data files based on the number of CPUs to maximize disk bandwidth. Using multiple files reduces tempdb storage contention and yields significantly better scalability. However, do not create too many files because this can reduce performance and increase management overhead. The best practice is to create one data file for each CPU on the server. Keep in mind that the dual-core CPU is considered to be two CPUs; therefore, it is recommended that you create two data files on a dual-core CPU system.

- Configure database to autogrow as required. This allows the data and log files of tempdb to grow until the disk is full. If your SQL Server 2012 production environment cannot tolerate the potential for application timeouts occurring during the autogrow operations, you should preallocate file space to allow for the expected workload.

- Set the tempdb file growth increment to a reasonable size to avoid the files from growing by too small of a value. If the file growth value is too small, compared to the amount of data that is being written to tempdb, tempdb database may have to constantly expand. This will affect the overall performance of tempdb operations.

Here's the guidance on how tempdb database file size and file growth can be configured:

- If the initial size of tempdb is > 0MB and < 100MB, you can set the file growth value to 10MB.

- If the initial size of tempdb is > 100MB and < 500MB, you can set the file growth value to 20 or 25MB.

- If the initial size of tempdb is > 500MB, you can set the file growth value to 10% or 20%.

You may have to adjust the percentage value based on the speed of the I/O subsystem on which the tempdb files would be residing. Changing tempdb file size will have an immediate effect, which means if you increase the size of the tempdb data file to 20MB and increase the file growth increment to 15%, the new values immediately take effect.

- Make sure each tempdb file is configured with the same size and allows for optimal proportional-fill performance.
- Place the tempdb database on a fast I/O subsystem and use disk striping if there are many directly attached disks. Keep the tempdb database on a separate disk and not with the disk used by other user and system databases.

Administering the Database Snapshots Subfolder

The second top-level folder under Databases is Database Snapshots. A *snapshot* allows you to create a point-in-time read-only static view of a database. Typical scenarios for which organizations use snapshots consist of running reporting queries, reverting databases to state when the snapshot was created in the event of an error, and safeguarding data by creating a snapshot before large bulk inserts occur. All database snapshots are created via Transact-SQL syntax and not with SQL Server Management Studio.

For more information on creating and restoring a database snapshot, view the database snapshot sections in Chapter 6.

Administering a User Databases Subfolder

The rest of the subfolders under the top-level Database folder are all the user databases. The user database is a repository for all aspects of a database, including administration, management, and programming. Each user database running within the Database Engine shows up as a separate subfolder. From within the User Database folder, you can conduct the following tasks: back up, restore, take offline, manage database storage, manage properties, manage database authorization, encryption, shrink, create policies, and configure log shipping or database mirroring. In addition, from within this folder, programmers can create the database schema, including tables, views, constraints, and stored procedures by clicking generate scripts.

Note

Database development tasks such as creating a new database, views, or stored procedures are beyond the scope of this book, because this book focuses only on administration and management tasks affiliated with the Database Engine.

Administering the Security Folder

The second top-level folder in the SQL Server instance tree, Security, is a repository for all the Database Engine securable items meant for managing security, specifically authorization. The sublevel Security Folders consist of

- **Logins**—This subfolder is used for creating and managing access to the SQL Server Database Engine. A login can be created based on a Windows or SQL Server account. In addition, it is possible to configure password policies, server role and user mapping access, and permission settings.

- **Server Roles**—SQL Server 2012 leverages the role-based model for granting authorization to the SQL Server 2012 Database Engine. Predefined SQL Server Roles already exist when SQL Server is deployed. These predefined roles should be leveraged when granting access to SQL Server and databases.

- **Credentials**—Credentials are used when there is a need to provide SQL Server authentication users an identity outside SQL Server. The principal rationale is for creating credentials to execute code in assemblies and for providing SQL Server access to a domain resource.

- **Cryptographic Providers**—The Cryptographic Providers subfolder is used for managing encryption keys associated with encrypting elements within SQL Server 2012. For more information on Cryptographic Providers and SQL Server 2012 encryption, see Chapter 9, "Encrypting SQL Server Data and Communications."

- **Audits and Server Audit Specifications**—SQL Server 2012 introduces enhanced auditing mechanisms, which make it possible to create customized audits of events residing in the Database Engine. These subfolders are used for creating, managing, storing, and viewing audits in SQL Server 2012. For more information on creating and managing audits including server audit specifications, refer to Chapter 7.

Administering the Server Objects Folder

The third top-level folder located in Object Explorer is called Server Objects. Here you create backup devices, endpoints, linked servers, and triggers.

Backup Devices

Backup devices are a component of the backup and restore process you use when working with user databases. Unlike the earlier versions of SQL Server, backup devices are not needed; however, they provide a great way to manage all the backup data and transaction log files for a database under one file and location.

To create a backup device, follow these steps:

1. Choose Start, All Programs, Microsoft SQL Server 2012, SQL Server Management Studio.

2. In Object Explorer, connect to the Database Engine, expand the desired server, and then expand the Server Objects folder.

3. Right-click the Backup Devices folder and select New Backup Device.

4. In the Backup Device dialog box, specify a Device Name and enter the destination file path, as shown in Figure 2.10. Click OK to complete this task.

This Transact-SQL syntax can also be used to create the backup device:

```
USE [master]
GO
EXEC master.dbo.sp_addumpdevice @devtype = N'disk',
@logicalname = N'Rustom''s Backup Device',
@physicalname = N'C:\Rustom''s Backup Device.bak'
GO
```

For more information on using backup devices and step-by-step instructions on backing up and restoring the Database Engine, refer to Chapter 7.

Endpoints

To connect to a SQL Server instance, applications must use a specific port that SQL Server has been configured to listen on. In the past, the authentication process and handshake agreement were challenged by the security industry as not being robust or secure. Therefore, SQL Server uses a concept called *endpoints* to strengthen the communication security process. As a side note, endpoints have been around since SQL Server 2005.

The Endpoint folder residing under the Server Objects folder is a repository for all the endpoints created within a SQL Server instance. The endpoints are broken out by system endpoints, database mirroring, service broker, Simple Object Access Protocol (SOAP), and Transact-SQL.

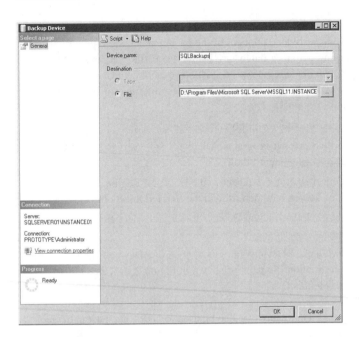

FIGURE 2.10
Creating a backup device with SQL Server Management Studio.

Linked Servers

As the enterprise scales, more and more SQL Server 2012 servers are introduced into an organization's infrastructure. As this occurs, you are challenged to provide a means to allow distributed transactions and queries between different SQL Server instances. Linked servers provide a way for organizations to overcome these hurdles by providing the means of distributed transactions, remote queries, and remote stored procedure calls between separate SQL Server instances or non–SQL Server sources such as Microsoft Access.

Follow these steps to create a linked server with SQL Server Management Studio (SSMS):

1. In Object Explorer, first connect to the Database Engine, expand the desired server, and then expand the Server Objects Folder.

2. Right-click the Linked Servers folder and select New Linked Server.

3. The New Linked Server dialog box contains three pages of configuration settings: General, Security, and Server Options. On the

General Page, specify a linked server name, and select the type of server to connect to. For example, the remote server could be a SQL Server or another data source. For this example, select SQL Server.

4. The next page focuses on security and includes configuration settings for the security context mapping between the local and remote SQL Server instances. On the Security page, first click Add and enter the local login user account to be used. Second, either impersonate the local account, which will pass the username and password to the remote server, or enter a remote user and password.

5. Still within the Security page, enter an option for a security context pertaining to the external login that is not defined in the previous list. The following options are available:

   ▪ **Not Be Made**—Indicates that a login will not be created for user accounts that are not already listed.

   ▪ **Be Made Without a User's Security Context**—Indicates that a connection will be made without using a user's security context for connections.

   ▪ **Be Made Using the Login's Current Security Context**— Indicates that a connection will be made by using the current security context of the user who is logged on.

   ▪ **Be Made Using This Security Context**—Indicates that a connection will be made by providing the login and password security context.

6. On the Server Options page, you can configure additional connection settings. Make any desired server option changes and click OK.

Note

Impersonating the Windows local credentials is the most secure authentication mechanism, provided that the remote server supports Windows authentication.

Triggers

The final folder in the Server Objects tree is Triggers. It is a repository for all the triggers configured within the SQL Server instance. Because creating triggers is a development and admin task, it is not covered in this book.

Administering the Replication Folder

Replication is a means of distributing data among SQL Server instances. In addition, peer-to-peer replication can also be used as a form of high availability and for offloading reporting queries from a production server to a second instance of SQL Server. When administering and managing replication, you conduct all the replication tasks from within this Replication folder. Tasks include configuring the distributor, creating publications, creating local subscriptions, and launching the Replication Monitor for troubleshooting and monitoring.

Administering, managing, and monitoring replication can be reviewed in Chapter 13, "Implementing and Managing Replication."

AlwaysOn High Availability

As mentioned earlier, AlwaysOn availability groups is most likely the highest desired capability for DBAs because it provides a single integrated solution to achieve both high availability and disaster recovery for mission critical databases. This new folder is where you implement, administer, and manage availability groups. Common tasks include the following:

- Use the wizard to create an availability group.
- Create and manage replicas.
- Add databases to availability groups.
- Create and manage availability group listeners.
- Launch the Availability Groups Dashboard.

This is the most highly anticipated feature, which is covered in Chapter 10, "Implementing and Managing AlwaysOn Availability Groups."

Administering the Management Folder

The Management folder contains a plethora of old and new elements used to administer SQL Server management tasks. The majority of the topics in the upcoming bullets are covered in dedicated chapters, as the topics and content are very large. The subfolders found in the Management folder consist of the following:

- **Data-tier Applications (DAC)**—A Data-tier Application, a new feature introduced with SQL Server 2008 R2, is an entity that contains all the database and instance objects used by an application. A DAC provides a single unit for authoring, deploying, and managing the data-tier objects instead of having to manage them separately. Deploying Data-tier Applications can be achieved by right-clicking the Data-tier Application folder and selecting Deploy Data-tier Application. To effectively create and deploy Data-tier Applications for a SQL Server instance, review Chapter 15, "Monitoring SQL Server 2012."

- **Policy Management**—Policy Management allows DBAs to create policies to control and manage the behavior and settings associated with one or more SQL Server instances. Policy-Based Management ensures that a system conforms to usage and security practices of an organization and its industry by constantly monitoring the surface area of a SQL Server system, database, and/or objects. To effectively establish and monitor policies for a SQL Server environment, review Chapter 17, "Implementing and Managing Policy-Based Management."

- **Data Collection**—Data Collection is the third element in the Management folder. It is the main place for DBAs to manage all aspects associated with the new SQL Server 2012 feature, Performance Studio. Performance Studio is an integrated framework that allows DBAs the opportunity for end-to-end collection of data from one or more SQL Server systems into a centralized data warehouse. The collected data can be used to analyze, troubleshoot, and store SQL Server diagnostic information. To further understand how to administer Performance Studio, data collections, and the central repository and management reports, review Chapter 15.

- **Resource Governor**—Resource Governor can be used in a variety of ways to monitor resource consumption and manage the workloads of a SQL Server system. By leveraging Resource Governor and defining the number of resources a workload can use, it is possible to establish a SQL Server environment that allows many workloads to run on a server, without the fear of one specific workload cannibalizing the system. For more information on managing Resource Governor, refer to Chapter 18.

- **Extended Events**—SQL Server Extended Events is a general event-handling system for server systems. The Extended Events infrastructure supports the correlation of data from SQL Server, and under certain conditions, the correlation of data from the operating system and database applications. This folder is used to create, manage, and monitor Extended Events for a specific instance of SQL Server.

- **Maintenance Plans**—The Maintenance Plan subfolder includes an arsenal of tools tailored toward automatically sustaining a SQL Server implementation. DBAs can conduct routine maintenance on one or more databases by creating a maintenance plan either manually or by using a wizard. Some of these routine database tasks involve rebuilding indexes, checking database integrity, updating index statistics, and performing internal consistency checks and backups. For more information on conducting routine maintenance, review Chapter 16.

- **SQL Server Logs**—The SQL Server Logs subfolder is typically the first line of defense when analyzing issues associated with a SQL Server instance. From within this subfolder, it is possible to configure logs, view SQL Server logs, and view Windows logs. By right-clicking the SQL Server Log folder, you have the option to limit the number of error logs before they are recycled. The default value is 6; however, you can select a value from 6 to 99. The logs are displayed in a hierarchical fashion with the Current log listed first.

- **Database Mail**—The Database Mail folder should be leveraged to configure SQL Server email messages using the SMTP protocol. Management tasks include configuring mail system parameters, creating mail accounts, administering profiles, and mail security. For more information on managing Database Mail, see Chapter 15.

- **Distributed Transaction Coordinator**—There isn't much to manage; however, the Distributed Transaction Coordinator (DTC) provides status on the DTC service from within SSMS. Although status is presented, such as running or stopped, the DTC service must be managed with the Services snap-in included with Windows Server 2008 R2.

- **Legacy**—The Legacy subfolder includes a means of managing legacy SQL Server 2012 elements that are still supported and not yet decommissioned. Typically, these elements are pre–SQL Server 2005 and include Database Maintenance Plans, Data Transformation Services, and SQL Mail.

Integration Services Catalogs Folder

The Integration Services catalog is created on your instance of SQL Server, and it is now what stores all the objects associated with your project after the project is deployed. A major improvement is that after you deploy your project, all the packages are organized into folders in the catalog.

Administering Database Properties

The Database Properties dialog box is the place where you manage the configuration options and values of a user or system database. You can execute additional tasks from within these pages, such as database mirroring and transaction log shipping. The configuration pages in the Database Properties dialog box include the following:

- General
- Files
- Filegroups
- Options
- Change Tracking
- Permissions
- Extended Properties
- Mirroring
- Transaction Log Shipping

The upcoming sections describe each page and setting in its entirety. To invoke the Database Properties dialog box, perform the following steps:

1. Choose Start, All Programs, Microsoft SQL Server 2012, SQL Server Management Studio.

2. In Object Explorer, first connect to the Database Engine, expand the desired server, and then expand the Databases folder.

3. Select a desired database such as AdventureWorks2012, right-click, and select Properties. The Database Properties dialog box, including all the pages, is displayed in the left pane.

Administering the Database Properties General Page

General, the first page in the Database Properties dialog box, displays information exclusive to backups, database settings, and collation settings. Specific information displayed includes the following:

- Last Database Backup
- Last Database Log Backup
- Database Name
- State of the Database Status
- Database Owner
- Date Database Was Created
- Size of the Database
- Space Available

- Number of Users Currently Connected to the Database
- Collation Settings

You should use this page for obtaining information about a database, as displayed in Figure 2.11.

FIGURE 2.11
Viewing the General page in the Database Properties dialog box.

Administering the Database Properties Files Page

The second Database Properties page is called Files. Here you can change the owner of the database, enable full-text indexing, and manage the database files, as shown in Figure 2.12.

Managing Database Files

The Files page is used to configure settings pertaining to database files, transaction logs, and FILESTREAM data. You will spend time working in the Files page when initially rolling out a database and conducting capacity planning. Following are the settings you'll see:

- **Data and Log File Types**—A SQL Server 2012 database is composed of two types of files: data and log. Each database has at least one data file and one log file. When you're scaling a database, it is possible to create more than one data and one log file. If multiple data files exist, the first data file in the database has the extension *.mdf, and subsequent data files maintain the extension *.ndf. In addition, all log files use the extension *.ldf.

- **FILESTREAM Data File Types**—FILESTREAM data is another file type available within SQL Server 2012. It is available only if FILESTREAM is enabled on the SQL Server Instance. Enabling FILESTREAM data was discussed earlier in this chapter.

FIGURE 2.12
Configuring the database files settings from within the Files page.

> **Tip**
>
> To reduce disk contention, many database experts recommend creating multiple data files. The database catalog and system tables should be stored in the primary data file, and all other data, objects, and indexes should be stored in secondary files. In addition, the data files should be spread across multiple disk systems or Logical Unit Number (LUN) to increase I/O performance.

- **Filegroups**—When you're working with multiple data files, it is possible to create filegroups. A filegroup allows you to logically group database objects and files. The default filegroup, known as the Primary Filegroup, maintains all the system tables and data files not assigned to other filegroups. Subsequent filegroups need to be created and named explicitly.

- **Initial Size in MB**—This setting indicates the preliminary size of a database or transaction log file. You can increase the size of a file by modifying this value to a higher number in megabytes.

- **Autogrowth**—This feature enables you to manage the file growth of both the data and transaction log files. When you click the ellipsis button, a Change Autogrowth dialog box appears. The configurable settings include whether to enable autogrowth, and if autogrowth is selected, whether autogrowth should occur based on a percentage or in a specified number of megabytes. The final setting is whether to choose a maximum file size for each file. The two options available are Restricted File Growth (MB) or Unrestricted File Growth.

> **Tip**
>
> When you're allocating space for the first time to both data files and transaction log files, it is a best practice to conduct capacity planning, estimate the amount of space required for the operation, and allocate a specific amount of disk space from the beginning. It is not a recommended practice to rely on the autogrowth feature because constantly growing and shrinking the files typically leads to excessive fragmentation, including performance degradation.

> **Note**
>
> Database files should reside only on RAID sets to provide fault tolerance and availability while at the same time increasing performance. If cost is not an issue, data files and transaction logs should be placed on RAID 1+0 volumes. RAID 1+0 provides the best availability and performance because it combines mirroring with striping. However, if this is not a possibility due to budget constraints, data files should be placed on RAID 5 and transaction logs on RAID 1. For more information pertaining to administering database files, such as increasing the initial size of a database file, creating additional filegroups, and configuring autogrowth on a file, see Chapter 3, "Administering Storage, I/O, and Partitioning."

Managing FILESTREAM Data

Until SQL Server 2008, organizations have been creatively inventing their own mechanisms to store unstructured data. Now SQL Server 2012 introduces a new file type that can assist organizations by allowing them to store unstructured data such as bitmap images, music files, text files, videos, and audio files in a single data type, which is more secure and manageable.

From an internal perspective, FILESTREAM creates a bridge between the Database Engine and the NTFS file system included with Windows Server. It stores varbinary(max) binary large object (BLOB) data as files on the file system, and Transact-SQL can be leveraged to interact with the file system by supporting inserts, updates, queries, search, and backup of FILESTREAM data. FILESTREAM is covered in Chapter 3.

Administering the Database Properties Filegroups Page

As stated previously, filegroups are a great way to organize data objects, address performance issues, and minimize backup times. The Filegroup page is best used for viewing existing filegroups and FILESTREAM data, creating new ones, marking filegroups and FILESTREAM data as read-only, and configuring which filegroup or FILEGROUP will be the default.

To improve performance, you can create subsequent filegroups and place database files, transaction log files, FILESTREAM data, and indexes onto them. In addition, if there isn't enough physical storage available on a volume, you can create a new filegroup or FILESTREAM file and physically place all files on a different volume or LUN if Storage Area Network (SAN) is being used.

Finally, if a database has static data, it is possible to move this data to a specified filegroup or FILESTREAM and mark this filegroup or FILESTREAM as read-only. This minimizes backup times; because the data does not change, SQL Server marks this filegroup and FILESTREAM and skips it.

Administering the Database Properties Options Page

The Options page, shown in Figure 2.13, includes configuration settings on Collation, Recovery Model, and other options such as Automatic, Cursor, and Miscellaneous. The following sections explain these settings.

FIGURE 2.13
Viewing and configuring the Database Properties Options page settings.

Collation

The Collation setting located on the Database Properties Options page specifies the policies for how strings of character data are sorted and compared, for a specific database, based on the industry standards of particular languages and locales. Unlike SQL Server collation, the database collation setting can be changed by selecting the appropriate setting from the Collation drop-down box.

Recovery Model

The second setting within the Options page is Recovery Model. This is an important setting because it dictates how much data can be retained, which ultimately affects the outcome of a restore.

Understanding and Effectively Using Recovery Models

Each recovery model handles recovery differently. Specifically, each model differs in how it manages logging, which results in whether an organization's database can be recovered to the point of failure. The three recovery models associated with a database in the Database Engine are as follows:

- **Full**—This recovery model captures and logs all transactions, making it possible to restore a database to a determined point in time or up to the minute. Based on this model, you must conduct maintenance on the transaction log to prevent logs from growing too large and disks becoming full. For example, a database in full recovery mode might also have a SQL Agent job to perform a transaction log backup every 15 minutes, ensuring the database never loses more than 15 minutes of data in the event of a crash. When you perform a transaction log backup, unused space is made available again and can be reused until the next planned backup. Organizations may notice that maintaining a transaction log slightly degrades SQL Server performance when the transaction log file resides on the same disk, RAID, or SAN LUN as the data files because IO is split between to two devices.

- **Simple**—This model provides organizations with the least number of options for recovering data. The Simple recovery model truncates the transaction log after each backup. This means a database can be recovered only up to the last successful full or differential database backup. This recovery model also provides the least amount of administration because transaction log backups are not permitted. In addition, data entered into the database after a successful full or differential database backup is unrecoverable. Organizations that store data they do not consider mission-critical may choose to use this model.

- **Bulk-Logged**—This recovery model maintains a transaction log and is similar to the Full recovery model. The main difference is that transaction logging is minimal during bulk operations to maximize database performance and reduce the log size when large amounts of data are inserted into the database. Bulk import operations such as BCP, BULK INSERT, SELECT INTO, CREATE INDEX, ALTER INDEX REBUILD, and DROP INDEX are minimally logged.

Because the Bulk-Logged recovery model provides only minimal logging of bulk operations, you cannot restore the database to the point of failure if a disaster occurs during a bulk-logged operation. In most situations, an organization will have to restore the database, including the latest transaction log, and rerun the Bulk-Logged operation.

This model is typically used if organizations need to run large bulk operations that degrade system performance and do not require point-in-time recovery.

Note

When a new database is created, it inherits the recovery settings based on the Model database. The default recovery model is set to Full.

Next, you need to determine which model best suits your organization's needs. The following section is designed to help you choose the appropriate model.

Selecting the Appropriate Recovery Model

It is important to select the appropriate recovery model because doing so affects an organization's ability to recover, manage, and maintain data.

For enterprise production systems, the Full recovery model is the best model for preventing critical data loss and restoring data to a specific point in time. As long as the transaction log is available, it is possible to even get up-to-the-minute recovery and point-in-time restore if the end of the transaction log is backed up and restored. The trade-off for the Full recovery model is its impact on other operations.

Organizations leverage the Simple recovery model if the data backed up is not critical, if data is static or does not change often, or if loss is not a concern for the organization. In this situation, the organization loses all transactions since the last full or last differential backup. This model is typical for test environments or production databases that are not mission-critical.

Finally, organizations that typically select the Bulk-Logged recovery model have critical data, but logging large amounts of data degrades system performance, or these bulk operations are conducted after hours and do not interfere with normal transaction processing. In addition, there isn't a need for point-in-time or up-to-the-minute restores.

> **Note**
>
> It is possible to switch the recovery model of a production database and switch it back. This would not break the continuity of the log; however, there could be negative ramifications to the restore process. For example, a production database can use the Full recovery model, and immediately before a large data load, the recovery model can be changed to Bulk-Logged to minimize logging and increase performance. The only caveat is that the organization must understand that it lost the potential for point-in-time and up-to-the-minute restores during the switch.

Switching the Database Recovery Model with SQL Server Management Studio

To set the recovery model on a SQL Server 2012 database using SSMS, perform the following steps:

1. In Object Explorer, first connect to the Database Engine, expand the desired server, and then expand the database folder.
2. Select the desired SQL Server database, right-click the database, and select Properties.
3. In the Database Properties dialog box, select the Options page.
4. In Recovery Model, select either Full, Bulk-Logged, or Simple from the drop-down list and click OK.

Switching the Database Recovery Model with Transact-SQL

It is possible not only to change the recovery model of a database with SQL Server Management Studio, but also to make changes to the database recovery model using Transact-SQL commands such as ALTER DATABASE. You can use the following Transact-SQL syntax to change the recovery model for the AdventureWorks2012 Database from Simple to Full:

```
--Switching the Database Recovery model
Use Master
ALTER DATABASE AdventureWorks2012 SET RECOVERY FULL
GO
```

Compatibility Level

The Compatibility Level setting located on the Database Properties Options page is meant for interoperability and backward compatibility of previous versions of SQL Server. The options available are SQL Server 2012 (110), SQL Server 2008 (100), and SQL Server 2005 (90).

> **Note**
>
> Unlike SQL Server 2008 R2, SQL Server 2012 does not support SQL Server 2000 (80) compatibility mode or earlier.

Containment Type

A new setting in SQL Server 2012 represents the type of containment to use on the database. The options available are none and partial.

Other Options (Automatic)

Also available on the Database Properties Options page are these options:

- **Auto Close**—When the last user exits the database, the database is shut down cleanly, and resources are freed. The values to be entered are either True or False.

- **Auto Create Statistics**—This setting specifies whether the database will automatically update statistics to optimize a database. The default setting is True, and this value is recommended.

- **Auto Shrink**—Similar to the shrink task in a maintenance plan or Integration Services, if this setting is set to True, SQL Server removes unused space from the database on a periodic basis. For production databases, it is not recommended to enable this setting.

- **Auto Update Statistics**—Similar to the Auto Create Statistics settings, this setting automatically updates any out-of-date statistics for the database. The default setting is True, and this value is recommended.

- **Auto Update Statistics Asynchronously**—If the statistics are out of date, this setting dictates whether a query should be updated first before being fired.

Other Options (Containment)

The following options pertain to the settings associated with the Containment section for a database.

- **Default Full-Text Language LCID**—The language of the data in the columns based on a full text index. The value of 1033 is the default that represents English.

- **Default Language**—This setting represents the default language term that will be used with Full-Text search if no value is specified.

- **Nested Triggers Enabled**—This option dictates whether an AFTER trigger can cascade or perform an action that initiates another trigger. The value of 1 represents AFTER triggers that can cascade to as many as 32 levels. The value of 0 represents AFTER triggers that cannot cascade.

- **Transform Noise Words**—This configuration setting is used to suppress an error message if noise words cause a Boolean operation on a Full-Text query to return zero rows.

- **Two Digit Year Cutoff**—Specifies the two-digit year cutoff. The default value is 2049.

Other Options (Cursor)

The following options are also available on the Database Properties Options page:

- **Close Cursor on Commit Enabled**—This setting dictates whether cursors should be closed after a transaction is committed. If the value is True, cursors are closed when the transaction is committed, and if the value is False, cursors remain open. The default value is False.

- **Default Cursor**—The values available include Global and Local. The Global setting indicates that the cursor name is global to the connection based on the Declare statement. In the Declare Cursor statement, the Local setting specifies that the cursor name is Local to the stored procedure, trigger, or batch.

FILESTREAM

The following options pertain to the containment settings for the database:

- **FILESTREAM Directory Name**—When you enable nontransactional access to files at the database level, you can optionally provide a directory name at the same time by using the DIRECTORY_NAME option. This setting specifies the name of the directory name used for FILESTREAM.

- **FILESTREAM Non-Transacted Access**—FileTables let Windows applications obtain a Windows file handle to FILESTREAM data without requiring a transaction. To allow this nontransactional access to files stored in SQL Server, a DBA must specify the desired level of nontransactional access at the database level for each database that will contain FileTables. The values include Full, Off, and ReadOnly.

Other Options (Miscellaneous)

The following options are also available on the Database Properties Options page:

- **Allow Snapshot Isolation**—This value should be set to True in order to enhance concurrency for OLTP applications.

- **ANSI NULL Default**—The value to be entered is either True or False. When set to False, the setting controls the behavior to supersede the default nullability of new columns.

- **ANSI NULLS Enabled**—This setting controls the behavior of the comparison operators when used with null values. The comparison operators consist of Equals (=) and Not Equal To (<>).

- **ANSI Padding Enabled**—This setting controls whether padding should be enabled or disabled. Padding dictates how the column stores values shorter than the defined size of the column.

- **ANSI Warnings Enabled**—If this option is set to True, a warning message is displayed if null values appear in aggregate functions.

- **Arithmetic Abort Enabled**—If this option is set to True, an error is returned, and the transaction is rolled back if an overflow or divide-by-zero error occurs. If the value False is used, an error is displayed; however, the transaction is not rolled back.

- **Concatenate Null Yields Null**—This setting specifies how null values are concatenated. True indicates that string + NULL returns NULL. When this setting is False, the result is string.

- **Cross-Database Ownership Chaining Enabled**—Settings include either True or False. True represents that the database allows cross-database ownership chaining, whereas False indicates that this option is disabled.

- **Date Correlation Optimization Enabled**—If this option is set to True, SQL Server maintains correlation optimization statistics on the date columns of tables that are joined by a foreign key.

- **Is Read Committed Snapshot On**—Toggle this setting in order to control whether or not Read Committed Snapshots should be on or off.

- **Numeric Round-Abort**—This setting indicates how the database will handle rounding errors.

- **Parameterization**—This setting controls whether queries are parameterized. The two options available are Simple and Forced. When you use Simple, queries are parameterized based on the default behavior of the database, whereas when you use Forced, all queries are parameterized.

- **Quoted Identifiers Enabled**—This setting determines whether SQL Server keywords can be used as identifiers when enclosed in quotation marks.

- **Recursive Triggers Enabled**—When this setting is enabled by setting the value to True, SQL Server allows recursive triggers to be fired.

- **Trustworthy**—This setting allows SQL Server to grant access to the database by the impersonation context. A value of True enables this setting.

- **VarDecimal Storage Format Enabled**—When this option is set to True, the database is enabled for the VarDecimal storage format. When using SQL Server 2012, True is the default setting. In addition, it is not possible to disable this feature if tables within the database are using the VarDecimal storage format.

Other Options (Recovery)

Also available on the Database Properties Options page is page verification:

- **Page Verify**—This option controls how SQL Server handles incomplete transactions based on disk I/O errors. The available options include Checksum, Torn Page Detection, and None.

Other Options (Service Broker)

The Service Broker section includes the following settings:

- **Broker Enabled**—This is a database-level setting indicating whether Service Broker is enabled or disabled.

- **Honor Broker Priority**—The second setting controls the Honor Broker Priority behavior. The options available are True and False.

- **Service Broker Identifier**—The third setting displays the identifier associated with the Service Broker.

Other Options (State)

The following options are available on the Database Properties Options page:

- **Database Read Only**—Setting the database value to True makes the database read-only.

  The default syntax for managing the read-only state of a database is as follows:

```
ALTER DATABASE database_name
<db_update_option> ::=
  { READ_ONLY | READ_WRITE }
```

- **Database State**—This field cannot be edited; it informs you of the state of the database. Possible states include Online, Offline, Restoring, Recovering, Recovery Pending, Suspect, and Emergency.

  To change the state of a database with Transact-SQL, use the default syntax:

```
ALTER DATABASE database_name
<db_state_option> ::=
{ ONLINE | OFFLINE | EMERGENCY }
```

- **Encryption Enabled**—This field indicates whether encryption is enabled for a specific database. The options include True and False.
- **Restrict Access**—This setting manages which users can connect to the database. Possible values include Multiple, Single, and Restricted. The Multiple setting is the default state, which allows all users and applications to connect to the database. Single-user mode is meant for only one user to access the database. This is typically used for emergency administration. The final setting, Restricted, allows only members of the db_owner, dbcreator, or sysadmin accounts to access the database.

  The Transact-SQL code for setting the Restrict Access value is as follows:

```
ALTER DATABASE database_name
<db_user_access_option> ::=
    { SINGLE_USER | RESTRICTED_USER | MULTI_USER }
```

Administering the Change Tracking Page

The Change Tracking page is another feature associated with SQL Server 2012. This page is used to administer change tracking settings for a particular database. Four configurable change tracking settings are provided:

- **Enable or Disable Change Tracking** by configuring the first setting to either True or False.

- **Retention Period** indicates the number of days to maintain change tracking information. The default value is set to 2.

- **Retention Period Units** is the third setting. When selecting options associated with this setting, a DBA can choose from Days, Hours, and Minutes. Typically, organizations choose Days unless there is an unexpected breach and tracking is required for a smaller increment of time.

- **Auto Cleanup** is the final setting. The default setting is True, which indicates that it is enabled. When this setting is enabled, change tracking information will automatically be removed after the retention period entered has expired.

The basic Transact-SQL syntax to enable Change Tracking for a specific database is as follows:

```
Use [Master]
Go
Alter Database [Desired Database] Set CHANGE_TRACKING = ON
GO
```

Administering the Database Properties Permissions Page

The Database Properties Permissions page is used to administer database authorization and role-based access and to control permissions on the database. Chapter 8 covers these topics in their entirety.

Administering the Database Properties Extended Permissions Page

The Database Properties Extended Permissions page is used for managing extended properties on database objects, such as descriptive text, input masks, and formatting rules. The extended properties can be applied to schema, schema view, or column view.

Administering the Database Properties Mirroring Page

Database mirroring is a SQL Server high-availability alternative for increasing availability of a desired database. Database mirroring transmits transaction log records directly from one SQL Server instance to another SQL Server instance. In addition, if the primary SQL Server instance becomes unavailable, the services and clients automatically fail over to the mirrored server. Automatic failover is contingent on the settings and versions used.

The Database Properties Mirroring page is the primary tool for configuring, managing, and monitoring database mirroring for a database. The Mirroring page includes configuration settings for security; mirroring operating mode; and the principal, mirror, and witness server network addresses. For more information on configuring database mirroring, review Chapter 12, "Implementing and Managing Database Mirroring."

Administering the Database Properties Transaction Log Shipping Page

The final Database Properties page is Transaction Log Shipping. Transaction log shipping is one of the SQL Server 2012 high-availability options. Similar to database mirroring, in log shipping, transactions are sent from a primary server to the standby secondary server on an incremental basis. However, unlike with database mirroring, automatic failover is not a supported feature.

The configuration settings located on the Transaction Log Shipping page in the Database Properties dialog box are the primary place for you to configure, manage, and monitor transaction log shipping.

SQL Server Database Engine Management Tasks

The following sections cover additional tasks associated with managing the SQL Server Database Engine.

Changing SQL Server Configuration Settings

Presently, most of the configuration settings can be changed from within SQL Server Management Studio. These settings can also be changed using the SP_CONFIGURE Transact-SQL command. The syntax to change configuration settings is as follows:

```
SP_CONFIGURE ['configuration name'], [configuration
setting, value]
GO
```

```
RECONFIGURE WITH OVERRIDE
GO
```

The `configuration name` represents the name of the setting to be changed, and the `configuration setting value` is the new value to be changed. Before you can change settings, however, you must use the `SP_CONFIGURE` command. You must enable advanced settings by first executing the following script:

```
SP_CONFIGURE 'show advanced options', 1
GO
RECONFIGURE
GO
```

For a full list of configuration options, see SQL Server 2012 Books Online.

Managing Database Engine Informational Reports

To succeed in today's competitive IT industry, you must be armed with information pertaining to SQL Server 2012. SQL Server 2012 continues to deliver a tremendous number of canned reports that can be opened directly from within SQL Server Management Studio. These reports provide information that allows you to maximize efficiency when conducting administration and management duties.

You can open these canned reports by right-clicking a SQL Server instance in Management Studio, selecting Reports, and then Standard Reports. The standard server reports include the following:

- Server Dashboard
- Configuration Changes History
- Schema Changes History
- Scheduler Health
- Memory Consumption
- Activity—All Blocking Transactions
- Activity—All Cursors
- Activity—Top Cursors
- Activity—All Sessions
- Activity—Top Sessions
- Activity—Dormant Sessions
- Activity—Top Connections
- Top Transactions by Age

- Top Transactions by Blocked Transactions Count
- Top Transactions by Locks Count
- Performance—Batch Execution Statistics
- Performance—Object Execution Statistics
- Performance—Top Queries by Average CPU Time
- Performance—Top Queries by Average IO
- Performance—Top Queries by Total CPU Time
- Performance—Top Queries by Total IO
- Server Broker Statistics
- Transaction Log Shipping Status

The standard report titled Server Dashboard is a great overall report that provides an overview of a SQL Server instance, including activity and configuration settings. However, if a standard report does not suffice, a DBA can also create a custom report.

You can also open canned reports for a specific database by right-clicking a database in Object Explorer, selecting Reports, and then Standard Reports. The standard database reports include the following:

- Disk Usage
- Disk Usage by Top Tables
- Disk Usage by Tables
- Disk Usage by Partition
- Backup and Restore Events
- All Transactions
- All Blocking Transactions
- Top Transactions by Age
- Top Transactions by Blocked Transaction Count
- Top Transactions by Locks Count
- Resource Locking Statistics by Object
- Object Execution Statistics
- Database Consistency History
- Index Usage Statistics
- Index Physical Statistics
- Schema Changes History
- User Statistics

Detaching and Attaching Databases

Another common task you must conduct is attaching and detaching databases. This is covered in Chapter 4, "Creating Packages and Transferring Data On-Premise and to the Cloud."

Scripting Database Objects

SQL Server 2012 has two levels of scripting functionality that assist you in automatically transforming a SQL Server task or action into a Transact-SQL script. The scripting functionality is a great way to automate redundant administration responsibilities or settings. Moreover, you don't have to be a Transact-SQL scripting expert to create solid scripts.

You can generate a script from within a majority of the SQL Server dialog boxes or pages. For example, if you make changes to the SQL Server Processor Properties page, such as enabling the options Boost SQL Server Priority or User Windows Fibers, you can click the Script button at the top of the screen to convert these changes to a script. In addition, this script can be fired on other SQL Servers to make the configuration automatically consistent across similar SQL Servers Instances.

When you click the Script button, the options available are Script Action to New Query Window, Script Action to File, Script Action to Clipboard, and Script Action to Job.

Another alternative to creating scripts is right-clicking a specific folder within Object Explorer and selecting Script As or right-clicking a database, selecting Tasks, and then selecting Generate Script to invoke the Script Wizard. Some of these tasks include scripting database schemas, jobs, tables, stored procedures, and just about any object within SQL Server Management Studio. Additional scripting statements include Create, Alter, Drop, Select, Insert, and Delete.

Managing SQL Server with PowerShell

PowerShell is integrated and supported in SQL Server 2012. PowerShell is a command-line shell and scripting language that bolsters administrators' management experiences as they achieve greater control and productivity by leveraging a new standardized admin-focused scripting language, which includes more than 130 standard cmdlets and consistent syntax and utilities. PowerShell is a prerequisite for installing SQL Server 2012, and it is included with the Windows Server 2008 R2 operating system as an optional feature that can be installed. For an overview of PowerShell with SQL Server 2012, including the PowerShell components, provider, cmdlets, and most common DBA tasks with PowerShell, refer to

SQL Server PowerShell in SQL Server 2012 Books Online at
http://msdn.microsoft.com/en-us/library/hh245198(v=sql.110).aspx.

Backing Up and Restoring the Database

Creating a backup and recovery strategy is probably the most important
task you have on your plate. When you're creating backups, it is imperative that you understand the recovery models associated with each database, such as Full, Simple, and Bulk-Logged, and understand the impact of
each model on the transaction log and the recovery process. In addition, it
is a best practice to back up the user databases, but to restore a full SQL
Server environment, the system database should be included in the backup
strategy.

For more information on recovery models and backing up and restoring the
Database Engine, see Chapter 6.

Transferring SQL Server Data

There are many ways to transfer data or databases from within SQL Server
Management Studio. There are tasks associated with importing and exporting data and copying and/or moving a full database with the Copy
Database Wizard. To use the transferring tasks, right-click a database,
select Tasks, and then select Import Data, Export Data, or Copy Database.

Each of these ways to move data is discussed in its entirety in Chapter 4.

Taking a SQL Server Database Offline

As a DBA, you may sometimes need to take a database offline. When the
database is offline, users, applications, and administrators do not have
access to the database until it has been brought back online.

Perform the following steps to take a database offline and then bring it
back online:

1. Right-click a desired database, such as AdventureWorks2012, select
    Tasks, and then select Take Offline.

2. In the Task Database Offline screen, verify that the status represents
    that the database has been successfully taken offline and then select
    Close.

Within Object Explorer, a red arrow pointing downward is displayed on the
Database folder, indicating that the database is offline. To bring the database back online, repeat the preceding steps but select Online instead.

In addition, you can use the following Transact-SQL syntax to change the state of a database from Online, Offline, or Emergency:

```
ALTER DATABASE database_name
<db_state_option> ::=
    { ONLINE | OFFLINE | EMERGENCY }
```

> **Note**
>
> When the database option is configured to an Emergency state, the database is considered to be in single-user mode; the database is marked as read-only. This mode is meant for addressing crisis situations.

Renaming a Database

The following steps illustrate how to change the name of a database by using SQL Server Management Studio:

1. In Object Explorer, right-click the name of the database and select Rename.

2. Type the new name for the database and press Enter.

Administering the SQL Server Agent

The SQL Server Agent is a Microsoft Windows Service that executes scheduled tasks configured as SQL Server jobs. Ultimately, in SQL Server 2012, any task can be transformed into a job; therefore, the task can be scheduled to reduce the amount of time wasted on manual database administration. The SQL Server Agent can be managed from within SQL Server Management Studio.

> **Note**
>
> The SQL Server Agent service must be running to execute jobs and tasks. This is the first level of investigation when you're troubleshooting why agent jobs are not firing.

Administering the SQL Server Agent Properties

Before utilizing the SQL Server Agent, you should first verify and configure the Agent properties to ensure that everything is copacetic. The SQL Server Agent Properties dialog box is invoked by right-clicking the

SQL Server Agent in SSMS and selecting Properties. The SQL Server Agent Properties dialog box has six pages of configuration settings, described in the following sections.

The General Page

The SQL Server Agent page maintains configurable settings such as Auto Restart SQL Server If It Stops Unexpectedly and Auto Restart SQL Server Agent If It Stops Unexpectedly.

From a best-practice perspective, both the restart settings should be enabled on mission-critical databases. This prevents downtime in the event of a server outage because the service will restart if failure is inevitable.

You can change the error log path if preferred and configure a send receipt via the Net send command. In addition, you can include execution trace messages to provide meticulous information on SQL Server Agent operations.

The Advanced Page

The Advanced page controls the behavior of SQL Server Event Forwarding and Idle CPU conditions. It is possible to forward unhandled events, all events, or events based on predefined severity levels selected in the drop-down list to a different server. The target server must be specified in the server drop-down list. The differences between unhandled and handled events are that unhandled events forward only events that no alert responds to, whereas handled events forward both the event and the alert. The final section is tailored toward SQL Server Agent and CPU settings. These settings define the conditions when jobs will run based on values such as average CPU usage falling below a certain percentage and whether or not it remains below the specified level for a period of time in seconds.

> **Note**
>
> In enterprise production environments, a SQL Server instance should have enough processing power so that these CPU condition settings are not required.

The Alert System Page

The Alert System page includes all the SQL Server settings for sending messages from agent alerts. The mail session settings are based on the prerequisite task of configuring SQL Server Database Mail. These topics are discussed in Chapter 15.

The Job System Page

The Job System page controls the SQL Server Agent shutdown settings. You can enter a numeric value based on a time increment that governs how long a job can run before automatically being shut down. It is also possible to specify a nonadministrator Job Step Proxy Account to control the security context of the agent; however, this option is available only when you're managing earlier SQL Server Agent versions.

The Connections Page

The Connections page should be used to configure a SQL Server alias for the SQL Server Agent. An alias is required only if a connection to the Database Engine will be made without using the default network transport or an alternate named pipe.

The History Page

You should use the final page, History, for configuring the limit size of a job history log setting. The options include setting maximum job history log size in rows and maximum job history rows per job.

Administering SQL Server Agent Jobs

The first subfolder located under the SQL Server Agent is the Job folder. Here, you create new jobs, manage schedules, manage job categories, and view the history of a job.

Follow these steps to create a new job:

1. In Object Explorer, first connect to the Database Engine, expand the desired server, and then expand the SQL Server Agent folder.

2. Right-click the Jobs folder and select New Job.

3. On the General page in the New Job dialog box, enter a name, owner, category, and description for the new job.

4. Ensure that the Enabled check box is set to True.

5. Click New on the Steps page. When the New Job Steps page is invoked, type a name for the step and enter the type of job this will be. The options range from Transact-SQL, which is the most common, to other items such as stored procedures, Integrations Services packages, and replication. For this example, select Transact-SQL Type and enter the following Transact-SQL syntax in the command window:

```
BACKUP DATABASE [AdventureWorks2012] TO  DISK =
N'C:\Program Files\Microsoft SQL Server
```

```
\MSSQL.1\MSSQL\Backup\AdventureWorks2012.bak'
WITH NOFORMAT, NOINIT,
NAME = N'AdventureWorks2012-Full Database Backup',
SKIP, NOREWIND, NOUNLOAD,  STATS = 10
GO
```

6. From within the General page, parse the command to verify that the syntax is operational and click the Advanced page.

7. The Advanced page includes a set of superior configuration settings. For example, you can specify actions on successful completion of this job, retry attempts including intervals, and specify what to do if the job fails. This page also includes Output File, Log to Table, History, and the potential to run the job under a different security context. Click OK to continue.

8. Within the New Job dialog box, you can use the Schedules page to view and organize schedules for the job. Here you can create a new schedule or select one from an existing schedule.

9. Click OK to finalize the creation of the job.

Enabling or Disabling a SQL Server Agent Job

Each SQL Server Agent job can be either enabled or disabled by right-clicking the job and selecting either Enable or Disable.

Viewing SQL Server Agent Job History

From a management perspective, you need to understand whether a SQL Server Agent job was fired properly, completed successfully, or just outright failed. The Job History tool, which is a subcomponent of the Log File Viewer, provides thorough diagnostics and status of job history. Perform the following steps to review job history for a SQL Server Agent job from within SQL Server Management Studio:

1. In Object Explorer, first expand the SQL Server Agent and then the Jobs folder.

2. Right-click a desired job and select View Job History.

3. In the Log File Viewer, review the log file summary for any job from within the center pane.

4. Choose from additional options such as loading saved logs, exporting logs, creating a filter, parsing through logs with the search feature, and deleting logs.

Administering SQL Server Alerts and Operators

The SQL Server Alerts and Operators folders are used for monitoring the SQL Server infrastructure by creating alerts and then sending out notifications to operators. For more information on creating alerts and operators, review Chapter 15.

Administering SQL Server Proxies

The Proxies Folder found within the SQL Server Agent enables you to view or modify the properties of the SQL Server Agent Proxy account. You enter a proxy name and credentials and select the subsystem the proxy account has access to.

Administering SQL Server Error Logs

The final folder in the SQL Server is Error Logs. You can configure the Error Logs folder by right-clicking the folder and selecting Configure. The configuration options include modifying the error log file location, reducing the amount of disk space utilized by enabling the option Write OEM Error Log, and changing the Agent Log Level settings. These settings include enabling Error, Warnings, and/or Information.

Perform the following steps to view SQL Server Agent Error Logs:

1. In Object Explorer, first expand the SQL Server Agent and then the Error Logs folder.

2. When all the error logs are listed under the Error Logs folder, double-click any of the error logs to view them.

Summary

The Database Engine is the core component within SQL Server; it provides a key service for storing, processing, and securing data. SQL Server 2012 introduces many new features that improve your success at administering and managing this core component. In addition, reading this chapter will help you to fully understand how to manage and administer a SQL Server instance server properties, configuration settings, Database Engine folders, database properties, and SQL Server Agent.

Review the other break-out chapters in the book for more information on items such as hardening a SQL Server infrastructure, encryption, Policy Based Management, Resource Governor, backups, and maintenance plans.

Best Practices

The following list is a summary of some of the best practices from the chapter:

- Leverage the scripting utility within SQL Server Management Studio to transform administration tasks into Transact-SQL syntax.

- Unless there is a specific need to do otherwise, it is a best practice to allow SQL Server to dynamically manage the minimum and maximum amount of memory allocated to SQL Server. However, if multiple applications are running on SQL Server, it is recommended to specify minimum and maximum values for SQL Server memory. Then the application cannot starve SQL Server by depriving it of memory.

- The preferred authentication mode is Windows Authentication over SQL Server Authentication because it provides a more robust authorization mechanism.

- Use Change Tracking to ensure accountability and compliance on databases and database objects. However, it is equally important to test the performance of using Change Tracking in the test environment before enabling it in the production environment.

- Leverage the SQL Server Database compression technologies to reduce storage utilization.

- Configuring SQL auditing is recommended to capture both failed and successful logins.

- Do not set the database to automatically shrink on a regular basis because this leads to performance degradation and excessive fragmentation over time.

- The first Database Engine administration task after a successful SQL installation should involve tuning and configuring the server properties. If you have several SQL Server 2012 instances that need to be configured, use the SQL Server Central Management Server feature, which will help reduce a lot of your time and will help maintain configuration standards and uniformity of SQL Server instances.

- Configure the recovery model for each database accordingly and implement a backup and restore strategy. This should also include the system databases.

- Database files, transaction log files, and operating system files should be located on separate volumes for performance and availability.

- When multiple database files and transaction log files exist, organize them through the use of filegroups.

- Create basic reports in Management Studio to better understand the SQL Server environment.

- Automate administration tasks by using SQL Server 2012 Agent jobs.

- Implement object, database, and server level policies using SQL Server 2012 Policy Based Management System.

CHAPTER 3

Administering Storage, I/O, and Partitioning

This chapter focuses on the use and most effective configuration of storage components within a Database Engine instance of SQL Server 2012. Storage and I/O (input/output) within SQL Server 2012 requires special attention because it is perhaps the most likely subsystem to experience suboptimal performance when left to the default settings. As a consequence, the well-prepared DBA will want to spend a bit of extra time in planning, configuring, and tuning SQL Server's storage and I/O settings.

This chapter introduces the fundamental concepts around SQL Server storage and I/O configuration and tuning. This overview includes hardware-related topics, such as hard disks, RAID, and SAN. Going beyond overview, this chapter will delve into the best practices and industry standards for SQL Server administrator activities, such as the number and placement of database and transaction log files, partitions, and tempdb configuration.

Most features related to SQL Server storage and I/O are configured and administered at the database level. That means that administrative tasks in SQL Server Management Studio will typically focus on database-level objects in the Object Explorer, as well as on database properties. Toward the end of this chapter, an important I/O performance-enhancing feature, data compression, is also discussed.

Even though the chapter introduces and explains all the administration and configuration principles of the SQL Server 2012 Storage Engine, you will occasionally be directed to other chapters for additional information. This is a result of the Storage Engine feature being so large and intricately connected to other features.

What's New for DBAs When Administering Storage on SQL Server 2012

SQL Server 2012 enhances the functionality and scalability of the Storage Engine in several significant ways. The following are some of the important Storage Engine enhancements:

- SQL Server 2012 introduces a powerful new way to accelerate data warehouse workloads using a new type of index called a columnstore index, also known as a memory-optimized xVelocity index. Columnstore indexes can improve read performance on read-only tables by hundreds to thousands of time, with a typical performance improvement of around tenfold. Refer to Chapter 5, "Managing and Optimizing SQL Server 2012 Indexes," for more details on this new type of index.

- SQL Server has long supported creation, dropping, and rebuilding indexes while online and in use by users, with a few limitations. SQL Server 2012 eliminates some of those restrictions, such that indexes containing XML, varchar(max), nvarchar(max), and varbinary(max) columns may be handled while the index is still online and in use.

- Partitioning in SQL Server 2012 has been enhanced, allowing up to 15,000 partitions by default, whereas older versions were limited to 1,000 partitions by default.

- SQL Server's storage methodology for storing unstructured data, FILESTREAM, has been improved. FILESTREAM allows large binary data, such as JPEGs and MPEGs, to be stored in the file system, yet it remains an integral part of the database with full transactional consistency. FILESTREAM now allows the use of more than one filegroup containing more than one file to improve I/O performance and scalability.

- The Database Engine Query Editor now supports IntelliSense. IntelliSense is an autocomplete function that speeds up programming and ensures accuracy.

To properly maximize the capabilities of SQL Server storage and I/O, it is important to understand the fundamentals about storage hardware. The following section introduces you to most important concepts involving storage and I/O hardware and how to optimize them for database applications.

Storage Hardware Overview

A basic understanding of server storage hardware is essential for any DBA who wants to effectively configure and administer the Database Engine of an instance of SQL Server 2012. The most elementary metric of hardware storage performance is IOPS, meaning input/output operations per second. Any elementary metric of performance is "throughput," which is the amount of megabytes per second that an I/O subsystem can read or write in a sustained fashion.

This section discusses the fundamental server hardware components used for storage and I/O and how those components affect SQL Server performance, scalability, and cost. Storage performance and scalability is usually balanced against what the budget allows. There are always trade-offs between what is best and what is the best that the checkbook can afford.

The hardware storage subsystem is based on these fundamental components:

- Hard Disks
- RAID (Redundant Arrays of Inexpensive Disks)
- Disk Controllers and Host Bust Adapters (HBA)
- Network Attached Storage (NAS), Storage Area Networks (SAN), and Logical Units (LUN)
- Solid State Drives (SSD)

The following section addresses the highlights concerning each of the preceding concepts:

Understanding Hard Disks

Hard disks have been with us for many decades and are familiar to most readers. Disks, also known as *spindles*, have natural limitations on their performance. Disks are essentially a mechanical spinning platter with a moving armature and read/write head that moves over the surface of the platter as needed to read and write data. Naturally, physics limits the speed that a mechanical device like this can perform reads and writes. Plus, the further apart the needed data might be on the surface of the disk, the further the armature has to travel, the longer it takes to perform the I/O operation. That's why defragmentation, or the process of putting related data back together in contiguous disk sectors, is so important for hard disk-based I/O subsystems.

Depending on the speed of rotation on the platter and the "seek" speed of the armature, a hard disk is rated for the number of I/Os it can perform per second, called IOPS. For example, a modern, current generation hard disk might sustain ~200 IOPS with a seek speed of ~ 3.5ms. A bit of math quickly reveals that a SQL Server with a single hard disk would be over-whelmed by an application that needed to do any more than a couple hundred transactions per second. (And don't forget that Windows needs to do I/O of its own!) So, the typical solution for high-performance database applications is to add more hard disks.

Time spent waiting for an I/O operation to complete is known as *latency*. Latency is usually very low for *sequential operations*—that is, an I/O that starts at one sector on the platter and moves directly to the next sector on the platter. Latency is usually higher for random operations—that is, an operation where the I/O starts at one sector but then must proceed to a random location elsewhere on the platter. Microsoft provides a lot of guid-ance about acceptable latency for a SQL Server I/O subsystem, with trans-action log latency recommended to be 10ms or less and database file latency recommended to be 20ms or less. These are very fast I/O response times, so doubling those recommendations is likely to be acceptable for most business applications.

Tip

To find out the latency sustained by the transaction log files for all of the databases on a given instance of SQL Server 2012, use the DMV `sys.dm_io_virtual_file_states`, like the following example:

```
SELECT DB_NAME(database_id) AS 'Database Name',
 io_stall_read_ms / num_of_reads AS 'Avg Read
Latency/ms',
 io_stall_write_ms / num_of_writes AS 'Avg Write
Latency/ms'
FROM sys.dm_io_virtual_file_stats(null, 2);
```

`Sys.dm_io_virtual_file_stats`, a Dynamic Management Function (DMF), accepts two parameters, the first being the specific database ID desired (or null for all database) and the second for the specific file of the database (with a value of 2 always being the transaction log file).

Although latency and IOPS are the most important characteristics of a hard disk for OLTP applications, business intelligence (BI) applications are typically heavy on read operations. Consequently, BI applications usually seek to maximize "disk throughput" because they make frequent use of large, serial reads culling through many gigabytes of data. A typical, current-generation hard disk today has a throughput ~125MB/second at 15,000 RPM. In BI applications, DBAs frequently monitor disk throughput along with disk latency. Refer to Chapter 15, "Monitoring SQL Server 2012," for more details on monitoring SQL Server 2012's performance.

Tip

To find out how much disk space is available on the hard disk volumes of a SQL Server instance, query the DMV sys.dm_os_volume_stats. For example, to find out the drive name, how much space is used, and how much is available on the disk where the tempdb database data resides use the following code:

```
SELECT volume_mount_point, total_bytes, available_bytes
FROM sys.dm_os_volume_stats(2,1)
```

The next section tells the best way to combine multiple disks for greater I/O performance, the redundant array of inexpensive disks (RAID).

Understanding RAID Technologies

If a single hard disk is insufficient for the I/O needs of the SQL Server instance, the usual approach is to add more hard disks. It is possible to add more spindles and then place specific SQL Server objects, such as tempdb, onto a single, additional hard disk and thereby see an improvement in I/O performance by segregating the I/O. Bad idea! Hard disks are prone to failure and, when they fail, a single hard disk failure can crash SQL Server. Instead, DBAs use redundant arrays of inexpensive disks (RAID) to add more hard disks while providing greater fault tolerance.

RAID is described in terms of many "levels." But with database technology, the most commonly used types of RAID are RAID1, RAID5, and RAID10. RAID0 is also described but not recommended for databases. These are described a bit more in the following sections.

RAID0

RAID0, called *striping*, spreads IOPS evenly across two disks. RAID0 is very fast for reads and writes, but if any one disk in the array fails, the whole array crashes.

Figure 3.1 Shows two disks in RAID0 configuration.

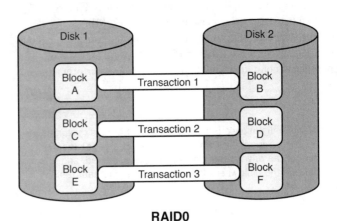

RAID0

FIGURE 3.1
RAID Level 0, striped array of disks.

In this example, assume we have three transactions of two blocks each. So, Transaction1 needs to write two blocks to disk: Block A and Block B. Transaction2 needs to write Blocks C and D. Finally, Transaction3 needs to write Blocks E and F.

Each transaction takes only half the time to write to the RAID0 set as it would with a single disk because each of the two blocks are written simultaneously on Disk 1 and Disk 2, instead of writing the two blocks serially on a single disk. Of course, the downside is that if either drive fails, you lose the whole set, given that half of the data is on Disk 1 and the other half is on Disk 2.

RAID1
RAID1, called *mirroring*, is essentially a set of two disks in which every read and every write operation is performed on both disks simultaneously. Fault tolerance is improved because either disk can fail without crashing the array, allowing SQL Server to continue operating. The DBA or server administrator can then replace the failed drive without an emergency drill. RAID1 is essentially as fast as a single hard disk, but it is fault tolerant whenever a single disk in the array fails.

Figure 3.2 represents two disks in RAID1 configuration.

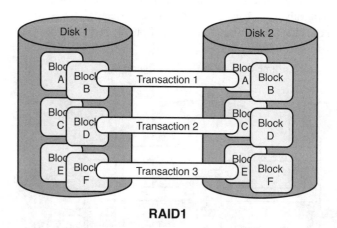

RAID1

FIGURE 3.2
RAID Level 1, mirrored array of disks.

In this example, assume as before that we have three transactions of two blocks each, this time written to a RAID1 set. So, Transaction1 needs to write two blocks to disk: Block A and Block B. Transaction2 needs to write Blocks C and D. Finally, Transaction3 needs to write Blocks E and F.

Each transaction takes about the same to write to the RAID1 set as it would with a single disk because each of the two blocks are written sere-ally on Disk 1 and Disk 2, just like on a single disk. The big benefit here is that if either drive fails, you still have a full and complete copy of the data on both Disk 1 and Disk 2. And since there is no parity bit calculation, write speed is superior to that of RAID5.

RAID5

RAID5 is a group of at least three disks in which every read is striped across all the disks in the array. This means that read-centric IOPS are faster than with a single disk because the required data can be pulled from more than one disk simultaneously. Write performance, however, is slower than read performance on RAID5 because every write IOP also includes one additional parity write. This parity bit enables the array to reassemble any lost data should one of the drives in the array fail. That means a RAID5 can survive a single drive failure, but not more than one drive failure at a time.

It also means that RAID5 is good for read-heavy applications, but is not as good for write-heavy applications. RAID5 can be expanded beyond three disks, but is typically never bigger than seven disks because of the considerable time needed to reconstruct a failed drive from the parity bits written across all those other drives.

Figure 3.3 represents three disks in RAID5 configuration.

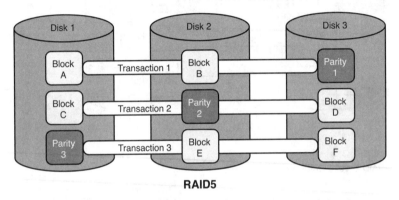

RAID5

FIGURE 3.3
RAID Level 5, striped array of disks with parity.

In this example, assume as before that we have three transactions of two blocks each, this time written to a RAID5 set. So, Transaction1 needs to write two blocks to disk: Block A and Block B. Transaction2 needs to write Blocks C and D. Finally, Transaction3 needs to write Blocks E and F.

The first difference you'll notice is that RAID5 requires a minimum of three disks. Each transaction takes longer to write to the RAID5 set as it would with a single disk because each of the two blocks are written as a stripe across two of the disks while the third disk has a calculated parity bit written to it. The calculation and extra block write takes more time. A transaction that reads two blocks off of the RAID5 set would be faster than a single disk read, because the blocks are striped and could be read simultaneously. The benefit here is that if any single drive fails, you have enough information to recalculate the missing data using the parity blocks. The other benefit is that it is cheaper than other kinds of RAID sets.

But RAID5 has drawbacks too. First, write operations are a lot slower than on DASD or the other RAID configurations described here. Second, even though RAID5 provides inexpensive fault tolerance, should a drive fail, the process of calculating the values of the missing data from the parity blocks can be time consuming. So a full recovery, while easy to do, can be slower than on RAID1 or RAID10.

RAID10

RAID10 is also called RAID1+0. RAID10 is a group of at least four disks in which a RAID1 pair of disks are also striped, RAID0 style, to another pairs of RAID1 disks. This approach uses twice as many disks as RAID1. But it means that the array can sustain *two* failed drives simultaneously without crashing, as long as the failed disks are not in a single RAID1 pair. RAID10 has both fast read and write speeds, but is more expensive and consumes more space than RAID1 and RAID5.

Figure 3.4 represents four disks in RAID10 configuration.

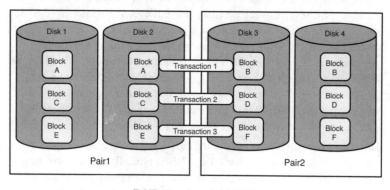

RAID10, a.k.a. RAID1+0

FIGURE 3.4
RAID Level 10, mirrored plus striping.

In this example, assume as before that we have three transactions of two blocks each, this time written to a RAID10 set. So, Transaction1 needs to write two blocks to disk: Block A and Block B. Transaction2 needs to write Blocks C and D. Finally, Transaction3 needs to write Blocks E and F.

The first difference you'll notice is that RAID10 requires a minimum of four disks. Each transaction is faster to write to the RAID10 set as it would with a single disk because each of the two blocks are written as a stripe across each pair of mirrored disks. A transaction that reads two blocks off of the RAID 10 set would be much faster than a single disk read, because the blocks are striped and could be read simultaneously. So, both writes and reads are typically faster than any other option presented here.

In addition to speed of both read and write operations, RAID10 sets are more fault tolerant than any other configuration. That is because each mirrored pair within the RAID10 set can sustain a single disk failure, meaning that *more* than one disk can fail without causing the array to crash.

But RAID10 most obvious and dramatic drawback is the cost of requiring at least four disks. The disks themselves are costly, but they also consume plenty of space and energy as well. If you can afford them, RAID10 arrays are certainly the best option. But they constitute a much greater expense than DASD.

Disk Controllers and Host Bus Adapters (HBA)

Disks are typically configured and controlled using one of two popular standards: SCSI (pronounced "scuzzy") and IDE/ATA (usually "A-T-A" for short). SCSI is by far the most popular standard for servers, whereas ATA (usually labeled as SATA) is the most popular standard for home and personal use. Servers using hard disks that adhere to these standards can be directly cabled to the disks, resulting in the acronym DASD, for Direct Attached Storage Device. DASD can also be cabled using standard network protocols like IP over Ethernet cable or Fibre Channel. Note that Fibre Channel and iSCSI are seen primarily on SANs.

Host bus adapters (HBAs) control the movement of data between the server motherboard and the hard disks. HBAs typically include performance options, such as a built-in cache, which can improve performance by buffering writes to the hard disk and then sending them in a burst.

> **Note**
>
> HBAs with write-cache controllers are not always safe for use with databases. How so? If a write-cache ever sustains a power failure, any write IOPS stored in the write-cache will vanish and be lost. As a precaution, many HBAs include a built-in battery backup. But the battery backup is not always be able to recharge or lose its ability to hold a charge without disabling the write-cache. Therefore, it's important for DBAs to ensure that their HBA has a battery backup that automatically disables itself if the battery fails.

HBAs are important in storage and I/O discussions because it is possible, with enough active processes, to saturate a single HBA. For example, imagine a scheduled job attempts to back up all databases simultaneously on a SQL Server with multiple TBs of data while other I/O heavy operations were also processing. A situation like that could attempt to push through more I/O than the HBA can sustain. HBAs are also important because their firmware may need to be independently updated and maintained when faced with updates to Windows or other hardware components. Remember to stay apprised of vendor recommendations and updates when using high-end HBAs.

Network Attached Storage (NAS), Storage Area Networks (SAN), and Logical Units (LUN)

The Internet is full of information about digital storage. However, some of it is old, outdated, or simply not useful. With SQL Server and storage, consider Network Attached Storage (NAS) as one such area where DBAs should steer clear. Think of NAS servers as more of a file-and-print server technology, not suitable for SQL Server database files, transaction log files, or backup files. NAS may be useful in some Extract-Transform-Load (ETL) applications, but only when their use and potential failure won't crash the production SQL Server database.

Storage Area Networks (SAN) are usually slightly slower than DASD, if only because they are more heavily used by a variety of applications than DASD. SAN is typically expensive and also has a degree of management overhead in that it should be set up, configured, and administrated only by a dedicated IT professional. But what it loses in speed, it makes up in flexibility, redundant components, and manageability.

For example, it is very easy to extend, reduce, or reconfigure storage on a SAN in Logical Units (LUNs) without stopping important Windows services, like SQL Server. These LUNs can be made available to Windows servers as if they were regular disk drives, when in fact they are usually RAID volumes or even just portions of RAID volumes. In fact, it is easy for SAN administrators to virtualize storage so that it can be quickly moved around on-the-fly.

This is great for SAN administrators, but it can be bad for DBAs if the storage the application has been depending upon is shared with another application in the enterprise. For example, it is possible to configure a large RAID10 volume as two LUNs. These two LUNs share the same underlying disks and, if both LUNS are busy, contend with one another for IOPS on the underlying RAID volume. It's not good, but certainly a possibility.

Depending on the SAN in use, enormous amounts of cache may also be available to help speed I/O processing. These caches can also be quickly and easily configured (and reconfigured) by SAN administrators to better balance and tune applications that use the SAN.

Unfortunately, many if not most SAN administrators think about storage only as measured by volume, not IOPS or disk throughput. Consequently, it is up to DBAs to know how much I/O performance their applications need and to monitor I/O performance within SQL Server to ensure that they are achieving adequate I/O performance. Many a SAN administrator has been startled to find out that the SQL Server DBA is better informed about the I/O speed (or lack thereof) on the LUNs assigned to them than they are, usually due to a misconfigured setting somewhere on the SAN.

The bottom line for DBAs when administrating storage on a SAN is to follow the SAN vendor's recommendations wherever possible, and then to monitor and performance tune the SQL Server instance as if the LUN(s) are normal disks.

Solid State Disks (SSD)

The new kids on the block for storage and I/O subsystems are several kinds of solid state disks (SSDs). SSDs are treated just like hard disks when configured, as individual devices or in RAID volumes. Because they are entirely electronic in nature, they offer significant savings in power consumption, speed, and resistance to damage from impact compared to hard disks. SSDs are becoming increasingly popular in the database administration community because they are remarkably faster than hard disks, especially for random I/O operations.

From a hardware perspective, a variety of different types of memory chips might be used within the SSD. But the two most common types of memory in SSDs are DRAM, which usually has volatile memory, and NAND flash memory, which is slower but nonvolatile. Volatile memory loses data when it loses power, whereas nonvolatile memory does not lose data when there is no power. When assessing flash memory-based SSDs, multilevel cell (MLC) flash memory is slower and less reliable than single-level cell (SLC) flash memory.

SSDs, however, have a few special considerations. First, the memory blocks within an SSD can be erased and rewritten a limited number of times. (DRAM-based SSD does not have this limitation.) Enterprise-quality flash drives work around this limitation by overprovisioning the amount of storage on the SSD through algorithms called *wear leveling*, thus ensuring that the SSD will last for the same duration as a similarly priced hard disk. Second, SSDs require a lot of free memory blocks to perform write operations. Whereas hard disks simply overwrite an unused sector, SSDs must clear out a previously written block using an algorithm called TRIM.

Finally, whereas SQL Server indexes residing on hard disks need frequent defragmentation, indexes residing on SSDs have no such requirement. Because all memory blocks on the SSD are only a few electrons away, all read access is pretty much the same speed whether the index pages are contiguous or not.

Now that you understand the most important aspects of storage hardware, let's discuss the principles and management tasks that correlate the storage and I/O elements of SQL Server back to the system hardware.

The following "Notes from the Field" section introduces the one of the most commonly used methods of improving I/O performance: segregation of workload.

Notes from the Field: Segregating I/O for Better Performance and Reliability

One trick for improving storage performance, scalability, and fault tolerance is simply a process of segregating the I/O workload across the optimum number of I/O subcomponents—while balancing all those components against the cost of what the organization can afford. That is because hard disks have only one armature and read-write head per spinning disk, also known as a *spindle*.

Each spindle can only do one activity at a time. But we very often ask spindles to do contradictory work in a database application, such as performing a long serial read at the same time other users are asking it to do a lot of small, randomized writes. Any time a spindle is asked to do contradictory work, it simply takes much longer to finish the requests. On the other hand, when we ask disks to perform complementary work and segregate the contrary work off to a separate set of disks, performance improves dramatically.

For example, a SQL Server database will always have at least two files: a database file and a transaction log file. The I/O workload of the database file, many random reads and writes, stands in stark contrast to the I/O workload of the transaction log file, a series of sequential writes, one immediately after the other. Because the typical transactional database I/O workload is at odds with the transaction log I/O workload, the first step of segregation most DBAs perform is to put the database file(s) and the transaction log file on entirely separate disk, whether a single disk or RAID array or LUN on a SAN.

Similarly, if I/O performance is still underperforming, the DBA might then choose to segregate the tempdb workload onto an entirely separate disk array, because its workload is likely conflicting with or at least sapping the I/O performance of the main production database. As I/O needs grow, the DBA may choose a variety of other methods available to segregate I/O. SQL Server offers a variety of options to increase I/O performance entirely within SQL Server. However, DBAs also have a big bag of tricks, at the hardware level, available to improve I/O performance.

For example, when attempting to improve I/O performance within SQL Server, many DBAs will place all system databases (such as Master, MSDB, distribution, and the like) onto their own disk arrays, segregated away from the main production database(s). They may choose to add more files to the database's filegroup and either explicitly place certain partitions, tables, and indexes onto the other files or allow SQL Server to automatically grow partitions, tables, and indexes onto the newly added file, thus further segregating I/O across more disk arrays. It is not uncommon to see very busy production databases with a lot of files, each on a different disk array. They might take the single busiest table in a database, which happens to generate 50% of the I/O on that instance, and split it into two partitions: one containing transactions under one week old (where most of the I/O occurs) and those over a week old, which are less frequently accessed as they age. The options abound.

On the hardware side of the equation, DBAs might reconfigure a specific drive (for instance, the F: drive) from a single disk to multiple disks in a RAID array with much higher I/O speed and capacity; for example, from 7,000 RPM disks to 15,000 RPM disks. They might upgrade a slower RAID 5 array to a faster RAID 10 array with a larger number of disks. They might increase the amount of read and write cache available on the hard disk controller(s) or SAN. They might add an additional hard disk controller to open more channels between the backplane and the I/O subsystem. In some cases, I/O problems are resolved by adding memory, when the I/O bottleneck is caused by constantly refreshing the buffer cache from disk. Again, a DBA can speed up the I/O subsystem in many ways.

But the fundamental principle applied in each of the previous examples is that the DBA is looking for an opportunity to take areas within SQL Server that are "bottlenecked" and segregate them to their own separate I/O component. Refer to and Chapter 14, "Performance Tuning and Troubleshooting SQL Server 2012," and Chapter 15 for more details on monitoring SQL Server I/O and tuning performance storage and troubleshooting errors on SQL Server, respectively.

Designing and Administering Storage on SQL Server 2012

The following section is topical in approach. Rather than describe all the administrative functions and capabilities of a certain screen, such as the

Database Settings page in the SSMS Object Explorer, this section provides a top-down view of the most important considerations when designing the storage for an instance of SQL Server 2012 and how to achieve maximum performance, scalability, and reliability.

This section begins with an overview of database files and their importance to overall I/O performance, in "Designing and Administering Database Files in SQL Server 2012," followed by information on how to perform important step-by-step tasks and management operations. SQL Server storage is centered on databases, although a few settings are adjustable at the instance-level. So, great importance is placed on proper design and management of database files.

The next section, titled "Designing and Administering Filegroups in SQL Server 2012," provides an overview of filegroups as well as details on important tasks. Prescriptive guidance also tells important ways to optimize the use of filegroups in SQL Server 2012.

Next, FILESTREAM functionality and administration are discussed, along with step-by-step tasks and management operations in the section "Designing for BLOB Storage." This section also provides a brief introduction and overview to another supported method storage called Remote Blob Store (RBS).

Finally, an overview of partitioning details how and when to use partitions in SQL Server 2012, their most effective application, common step-by-step tasks, and common use-cases, such as a "sliding window" partition. Partitioning may be used for both tables and indexes, as detailed in the upcoming section "Designing and Administrating Partitions in SQL Server 2012."

Designing and Administrating Database Files in SQL Server 2012

Whenever a database is created on an instance of SQL Server 2012, a minimum of two database files are required: one for the database file and one for the transaction log. By default, SQL Server will create a single database file and transaction log file on the same default destination disk. Under this configuration, the data file is called the Primary data file and has the .mdf file extension, by default. The log file has a file extension of .ldf, by default. When databases need more I/O performance, it's typical to add more data files to the user database that needs added performance. These added data files are called Secondary files and typically use the .ndf file extension.

As mentioned in the earlier "Notes from the Field" section, adding multiple files to a database is an effective way to increase I/O performance, especially when those additional files are used to segregate and offload a portion of I/O. We will provide additional guidance on using multiple database files in the later section titled "Designing and Administrating Multiple Data Files."

When you have an instance of SQL Server 2012 that does not have a high performance requirement, a single disk probably provides adequate performance. But in most cases, especially an important production database, optimal I/O performance is crucial to meeting the goals of the organization.

The following sections address important proscriptive guidance concerning data files. First, design tips and recommendations are provided for where on disk to place database files, as well as the optimal number of database files to use for a particular production database. Other guidance is provided to describe the I/O impact of certain database-level options.

Placing Data Files onto Disks

At this stage of the design process, imagine that you have a user database that has only one data file and one log file. Where those individual files are placed on the I/O subsystem can have an enormous impact on their overall performance, typically because they must share I/O with other files and executables stored on the same disks. So, if we can place the user data file(s) and log files onto separate disks, where is the best place to put them?

Note

Database files should reside only on RAID volumes to provide fault tolerance and availability while increasing performance. If cost is not an issue, data files and transaction logs should be placed on RAID1+0 volumes. RAID1+0 provides the best availability and performance because it combines mirroring with striping. However, if this is not a possibility due to budget, data files should be placed on RAID5 and transaction logs on RAID1. Refer to the earlier "Storage Hardware Overview" section in this chapter for more information.

When designing and segregating I/O by workload on SQL Server database files, there are certain predictable payoffs in terms of improved performance. When separating workload on to separate disks, it is implied that by "disks" we mean a single disk, a RAID1, -5, or -10 array, or a volume mount point on a SAN. The following list ranks the best payoff, in terms of providing improved I/O performance, for a transaction processing workload with a single major database:

1. Separate the user log file from all other user and system data files and log files. The server now has two disks:

   ■ Disk A:\ is for randomized reads and writes. It houses the Windows OS files, the SQL Server executables, the SQL Server system databases, and the production database file(s).

   ■ Disk B:\ is solely for serial writes (and very occasionally for writes) of the user database log file. This single change can often provide a 30% or greater improvement in I/O performance compared to a system where all data files and log files are on the same disk.

Figure 3.5 shows what this configuration might look like.

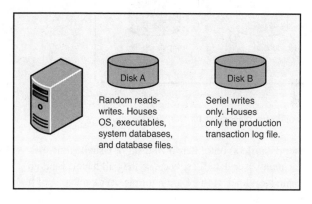

FIGURE 3.5
Example of basic file placement for OLTP workloads.

2. Separate tempdb, both data file and log file onto a separate disk. Even better is to put the data file(s) and the log file onto their own disks. The server now has three or four disks:

   ■ Disk A:\ is for randomized reads and writes. It houses the Windows OS files, the SQL Server executables, the SQL Server system databases, and the user database file(s).

   ■ Disk B:\ is solely for serial reads and writes of the user database log file.

■ Disk C:\ for tempd data file(s) and log file. Separating tempdb onto its own disk provides varying amounts of improvement to I/O performance, but it is often in the mid-teens, with 14–17% improvement common for OLTP workloads.

■ Optionally, Disk D:\ to separate the tempdb transaction log file from the tempdb database file.

Figure 3.6 shows an example of intermediate file placement for OLTP workloads.

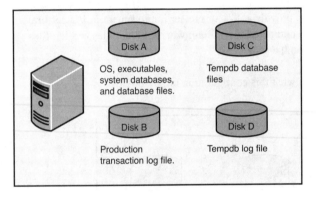

FIGURE 3.6
Example of intermediate file placement for OLTP workloads.

3. Separate user data file(s) onto their own disk(s). Usually, one disk is sufficient for many user data files, because they all have a randomized read-write workload. If there are multiple user databases of high importance, make sure to separate the log files of other user databases, in order of business, onto their own disks. The server now has many disks, with an additional disk for the important user data file and, where needed, many disks for log files of the user databases on the server:

■ Disk A:\ is for randomized reads and writes. It houses the Windows OS files, the SQL Server executables, and the SQL Server system databases.

■ Disk B:\ is solely for serial reads and writes of the user database log file.

■ Disk C:\ is for tempd data file(s) and log file.

- Disk E:\ is for randomized reads and writes for all the user database files.

- Drive F:\ and greater are for the log files of other important user databases, one drive per log file.

Figure 3.7 shows and example of advanced file placement for OLTP workloads.

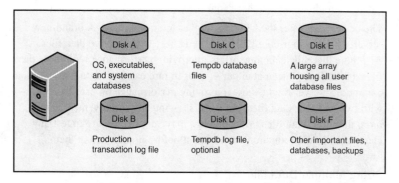

FIGURE 3.7
Example of advanced file placement for OLTP workloads.

4. Repeat step 3 as needed to further segregate database files and transaction log files whose activity creates contention on the I/O subsystem. And remember—the figures only illustrate the concept of a *logical* disk. So, Disk E in Figure 3.7 might easily be a RAID10 array containing twelve actual physical hard disks.

Utilizing Multiple Data Files

As mentioned earlier, SQL Server defaults to the creation of a single primary data file and a single primary log file when creating a new database. The log file contains the information needed to make transactions and databases fully recoverable. Because its I/O workload is serial, writing one transaction after the next, the disk read-write head rarely moves. In fact, we don't want it to move. Also, for this reason, adding additional files to a transaction log almost never improves performance. Conversely, data files contain the tables (along with the data they contain), indexes, views, constraints, stored procedures, and so on. Naturally, if the data files reside on segregated disks, I/O performance improves because the data files no longer contend with one another for the I/O of that specific disk.

Less well known, though, is that SQL Server is able to provide better I/O performance when you add secondary data files to a database, even when the secondary data files are on the same disk, because the Database Engine can use multiple I/O threads on a database that has multiple data files. The general rule for this technique is to create one data file for every two to four logical processors available on the server. So, a server with a single one-core CPU can't really take advantage of this technique. If a server had two four-core CPUs, for a total of eight logical CPUs, an important user database might do well to have four data files.

The newer and faster the CPU, the higher the ratio to use. A brand-new server with two four-core CPUs might do best with just two data files. Also note that this technique offers improving performance with more data files, but it does plateau at either 4, 8, or in rare cases 16 data files. Thus, a commodity server might show improving performance on user databases with two and four data files, but stops showing any improvement using more than four data files. Your mileage may vary, so be sure to test any changes in a nonproduction environment before implementing them.

Sizing Multiple Data Files

Suppose we have a new database application, called BossData, coming online that is a very important production application. It is the only production database on the server, and according to the guidance provided earlier, we have configured the disks and database files like this:

1. Drive C:\ is a RAID1 pair of disks acting as the boot drive housing the Windows Server OS, the SQL Server executables, and the system databases of Master, MSDB, and Model.

2. Drive D:\ is the DVD drive.

3. Drive E:\ is a RAID1 pair of high-speed SSDs housing tempdb data files and the log file.

4. DRIVE F:\ in RAID10 configuration with lots of disks houses the random I/O workload of the eight BossData data files: one primary file and seven secondary files.

5. DRIVE G:\ is a RAID1 pair of disks housing the BossData log file.

Most of the time, BossData has fantastic I/O performance. However, it occasionally slows down for no immediately evident reason. Why would that be?

As it turns out, the size of multiple data files is also important. Whenever a database has one file larger than another, SQL Server will send more I/O to the large file because of an algorithm called *round-robin, proportional fill*. "Round-robin" means that SQL Server will send I/O to one data file at a time, one right after the other. So for the BossData database, the SQL Server Database Engine would send one I/O first to the primary data file, the next I/O would go to the first secondary data file in line, the next I/O to the next secondary data file, and so on. So far, so good.

However, the "proportional fill" part of the algorithm means that SQL Server will focus its I/Os on each data file in turn until it is as full, in proportion, to all the other data files. So, if all but two of the data files in the BossData database are 50Gb, but two are 200Gb, SQL Server would send four times as many I/Os to the two bigger data files in an effort to keep them as proportionately full as all the others.

In a situation where BossData needs a total of 800Gb of storage, it would be much better to have eight 100Gb data files than to have six 50Gb data files and two 200Gb data files.

Tip

To see the latency of all of the data files, the log file, and the disks they reside on, use this query:

```
SELECT physical_name AS drive,
  CAST(SUM(io_stall_read_ms) / (1.0 + SUM(num_of_reads))
AS NUMERIC(10, 1)) AS 'Avg Read Latency/ms',
  CAST(SUM(io_stall_write_ms) / (1.0 +
SUM(num_of_writes)) AS NUMERIC(10, 1)) AS 'Avg Write
Latency/ms',
  CAST((SUM(io_stall)) / (1.0 + SUM(num_of_reads +
num_of_writes)) AS NUMERIC(10, 1)) AS 'Avg Disk
Latency/ms'
FROM sys.dm_io_virtual_file_stats(NULL, NULL) AS d
  JOIN sys.master_files AS m
        ON m.database_id = d.database_id
        AND m.file_id = d.file_id
GROUP BY physical_name
ORDER BY physical_name DESC;
```

Remember, Microsoft's recommendation is that data file latency should not exceed 20ms, and log file latency should not exceed 10ms. But in practice, a latency that is twice as high as the recommendations is often acceptable to most users.

Autogrowth and I/O Performance

When you're allocating space for the first time to both data files and log files, it is a best practice to plan for future I/O and storage needs, which is also known as *capacity planning*.

In this situation, estimate the amount of space required not only for operating the database in the near future, but estimate its total storage needs well into the future. After you've arrived at the amount of I/O and storage needed at a reasonable point in the future, say one year hence, you should preallocate the specific amount of disk space and I/O capacity from the beginning.

Over-relying on the default autogrowth features causes two significant problems. First, growing a data file causes database operations to slow down while the new space is allocated and can lead to data files with widely varying sizes for a single database. (Refer to the earlier section "Sizing Multiple Data Files.") Growing a log file causes write activity to stop until the new space is allocated. Second, constantly growing the data and log files typically leads to more logical fragmentation within the database and, in turn, performance degradation.

Most experienced DBAs will also set the autogrow settings sufficiently high to avoid frequent autogrowths. For example, data file autogrow defaults to a meager 25Mb, which is certainly a very small amount of space for a busy OLTP database. It is recommended to set these autogrow values to a considerable percentage size of the file expected at the one-year mark. So, for a database with 100Gb data file and 25GB log file expected at the one-year mark, you might set the autogrowth values to 10Gb and 2.5Gb, respectively.

Note

We still recommend leaving the Autogrowth option enabled. You certainly do not want to ever have a data file and especially a log file run out of space during regular daily use. However, our recommendation is that you do not rely on the Autogrowth option to ensure the data files and log files have enough open space. Preallocating the necessary space is a much better approach.

Additionally, log files that have been subjected to many tiny, incremental autogrowths have been shown to underperform compared to log files with fewer, larger file growths. This phenomena occurs because each time the log file is grown, SQL Server creates a new VLF, or virtual log file. The

VLFs connect to one another using pointers to show SQL Server where one VLF ends and the next begins. This chaining works seamlessly behind the scenes. But it's simple common sense that the more often SQL Server has to read the VLF chaining metadata, the more overhead is incurred. So a 20Gb log file containing four VLFs of 5Gb each will outperform the same 20Gb log file containing 2000 VLFs.

Configuring Autogrowth on a Database File

To configure autogrowth on a database file (as shown in Figure 3.8), follow these steps:

1. From within the File page on the Database Properties dialog box, click the ellipsis button located in the Autogrowth column on a desired database file to configure it.

2. In the Change Autogrowth dialog box, configure the File Growth and Maximum File Size settings and click OK.

3. Click OK in the Database Properties dialog box to complete the task.

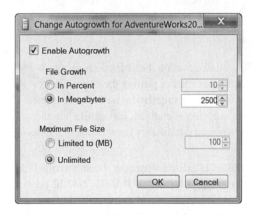

FIGURE 3.8
Configure Autogrowth on database files.

You can alternately use the following Transact-SQL syntax to modify the Autogrowth settings for a database file based on a growth rate of 10Gb and an unlimited maximum file size:

```
USE [master]
GO
ALTER DATABASE [AdventureWorks2012]
MODIFY FILE ( NAME = N'AdventureWorks2012_Data',
```

```
MAXSIZE = UNLIMITED , FILEGROWTH = 10240KB
)
GO
```

> **Tip**
>
> The prevailing best practice for autogrowth is to use an absolute number, such as 100Mb, rather than a percentage, because most DBAs prefer a very predictable growth rate on their data and transaction log files.

Data File Initialization

Anytime SQL Server has to initialize a data or log file, it overwrites any residual data on the disk sectors that might be hanging around because of previously deleted files. This process fills the files with zeros and occurs whenever SQL Server creates a database, adds files to a database, expands the size of an existing log or data file through autogrow or a manual growth process, or due to a database or filegroup restore. This isn't a particularly time-consuming operation unless the files involved are large, such as over 100Gbs. But when the files are large, file initialization can take quite a long time.

It is possible to avoid full file initialization on data files through a technique call instant file initialization. Instead of writing the entire file to zeros, SQL Server will overwrite any existing data as new data is written to the file when instant file initialization is enabled. Instant file initialization does not work on log files, nor on databases where transparent data encryption is enabled.

SQL Server will use instant file initialization whenever it can, provided the SQL Server service account has SE_MANAGE_VOLUME_NAME privileges. This is a Windows-level permission granted to members of the Windows Administrator group and to users with the Perform Volume Maintenance Task security policy.

For more information, refer to the SQL Server Books Online documentation.

Shrinking Databases, Files, and I/O Performance

The Shrink Database task reduces the physical database and log files to a specific size. This operation removes excess space in the database based on a percentage value. In addition, you can enter thresholds in megabytes, indicating the amount of shrinkage that needs to take place when the database reaches a certain size and the amount of free space that must remain after the excess space is removed. Free space can be retained in the database or released back to the operating system.

It is a best practice not to shrink the database. First, when shrinking the database, SQL Server moves full pages at the end of data file(s) to the first open space it can find at the beginning of the file, allowing the end of the files to be truncated and the file to be shrunk. This process can increase the log file size because all moves are logged. Second, if the database is heavily used and there are many inserts, the data files may have to grow again.

SQL 2005 and later addresses slow autogrowth with instant file initialization; therefore, the growth process is not as slow as it was in the past. However, sometimes autogrow does not catch up with the space requirements, causing a performance degradation. Finally, simply shrinking the database leads to excessive fragmentation. If you absolutely must shrink the database, you should do it manually when the server is not being heavily utilized.

You can shrink a database by right-clicking a database and selecting Tasks, Shrink, and then Database or File.

Alternatively, you can use Transact-SQL to shrink a database or file. The following Transact=SQL syntax shrinks the AdventureWorks2012 database, returns freed space to the operating system, and allows for 15% of free space to remain after the shrink:

```
USE [AdventureWorks2012]
GO
DBCC SHRINKDATABASE(N'AdventureWorks2012', 15, TRUNCATEONLY)
GO
```

Note

Although it is possible to shrink a log file, SQL Server is not able to shrink the log file past the oldest, active transaction. For example, imagine a 10Gb transaction log that has been growing at an alarming rate with the potential to fill up the disk soon. If the last open transaction was written to the log file at the 7Gb mark, even if the space prior to that mark is essentially unused, the shrink process will not be able to shrink the log file to anything smaller than 7Gb. To see if there are any open transactions in a given database, use the Transact-SQL command DBCC OPENTRAN.

Tip

It is best practice not to select the option to shrink the database. First, when shrinking the database, SQL Server moves pages toward the beginning of the file, allowing the end of the files to be shrunk. This process can increase the transaction log size because all moves are logged. Second, if the database is heavily used and there are many inserts, the database files will have to grow again. SQL 2005 and above addresses slow autogrowth with instant file initialization; therefore, the growth process is not as slow as it was in the past. However, sometimes auto-grow does not catch up with the space requirements, causing perform-ance degradation. Finally, constant shrinking and growing of the database leads to excessive fragmentation. If you need to shrink the database size, you should do it manually when the server is not being heavily utilized.

Administering Database Files

The Database Properties dialog box is where you manage the configuration options and values of a user or system database. You can execute additional tasks from within these pages, such as database mirroring and trans-action log shipping. The configuration pages in the Database Properties dialog box that affect I/O performance include the following:

- Files
- Filegroups
- Options
- Change Tracking

The upcoming sections describe each page and setting in its entirety. To invoke the Database Properties dialog box, perform the following steps:

1. Choose Start, All Programs, Microsoft SQL Server 2012, SQL Server Management Studio.

2. In Object Explorer, first connect to the Database Engine, expand the desired instance, and then expand the Databases folder.

3. Select a desired database, such as AdventureWorks2012, right-click, and select Properties. The Database Properties dialog box is displayed.

Administering the Database Properties Files Page

The second Database Properties page is called Files. Here you can change the owner of the database, enable full-text indexing, and manage the database files, as shown in Figure 3.9.

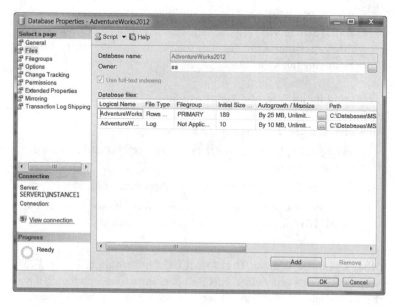

FIGURE 3.9
Configuring the database files settings from within the Files page.

Administrating Database Files

Use the Files page to configure settings pertaining to database files and transaction logs. You will spend time working in the Files page when initially rolling out a database and conducting capacity planning. Following are the settings you'll see:

- **Data and Log File Types**—A SQL Server 2012 database is composed of two types of files: data and log. Each database has at least one data file and one log file. When you're scaling a database, it is possible to create more than one data and one log file. If multiple data files exist, the first data file in the database has the extension `*.mdf` and subsequent data files maintain the extension `*.ndf`. In addition, all log files use the extension `*.ldf`.

- **Filegroups**—When you're working with multiple data files, it is possible to create filegroups. A filegroup allows you to logically group database objects and files together. The default filegroup, known as the Primary Filegroup, maintains all the system tables and data files not assigned to other filegroups. Subsequent filegroups need to be created and named explicitly.

- **Initial Size in MB**—This setting indicates the preliminary size of a database or transaction log file. You can increase the size of a file by modifying this value to a higher number in megabytes.

Increasing Initial Size of a Database File

Perform the following steps to increase the data file for the AdventureWorks2012 database using SSMS:

1. In Object Explorer, right-click the AdventureWorks2012 database and select Properties.

2. Select the Files page in the Database Properties dialog box.

3. Enter the new numerical value for the desired file size in the Initial Size (MB) column for a data or log file and click OK.

Other Database Options That Affect I/O Performance

Keep in mind that many other database options can have a profound, if not at least a nominal, impact on I/O performance. To look at these options, right-click the database name in the SSMS Object Explorer, and then select Properties. The Database Properties page appears, allowing you to select Options or Change Tracking. A few things on the Options and Change Tracking tabs to keep in mind include the following:

- **Options: Recovery Model**—SQL Server offers three recovery models: Simple, Bulk Logged, and Full. These settings can have a huge impact on how much logging, and thus I/O, is incurred on the log file. Refer to Chapter 6, "Backing Up and Restoring SQL Server 2012 Databases," for more information on backup settings.

- **Options: Auto**—SQL Server can be set to automatically create and automatically update index statistics. Keep in mind that, although typically a nominal hit on I/O, these processes incur overhead and are unpredictable as to when they may be invoked. Consequently, many DBAs use automated SQL Agent jobs to routinely create and update statistics on very high-performance systems to avoid contention for I/O resources.

- **Options: State: Read-Only**—Although not frequent for OLTP systems, placing a database into the read-only state enormously reduces the locking and I/O on that database. For high reporting systems, some DBAs place the database into the read-only state during regular working hours, and then place the database into read-write state to update and load data.

- **Options: State: Encryption**—Transparent data encryption adds a nominal amount of added I/O overhead.

- **Change Tracking**—Options within SQL Server that increase the amount of system auditing, such as change tracking and change data capture, significantly increase the overall system I/O because SQL Server must record all the auditing information showing the system activity.

Designing and Administering Filegroups in SQL Server 2012

Filegroups are used to house data files. Log files are never housed in filegroups. Every database has a primary filegroup, and additional secondary filegroups may be created at any time. The primary filegroup is also the default filegroup, although the default file group can be changed after the fact. Whenever a table or index is created, it will be allocated to the default filegroup unless another filegroup is specified.

Filegroups are typically used to place tables and indexes into groups and, frequently, onto specific disks. Filegroups can be used to stripe data files across multiple disks in situations where the server does not have RAID available to it. (However, placing data and log files directly on RAID is a superior solution using filegroups to stripe data and log files.) Filegroups are also used as the logical container for special purpose data management features like partitions and FILESTREAM, both discussed later in this chapter. But they provide other benefits as well. For example, it is possible to back up and recover individual filegroups. (Refer to Chapter 6 for more information on recovering a specific filegroup.)

To perform standard administrative tasks on a filegroup, read the following sections.

Creating Additional Filegroups for a Database

Perform the following steps to create a new filegroup and files using the AdventureWorks2012 database with both SSMS and Transact-SQL:

1. In Object Explorer, right-click the AdventureWorks2012 database and select Properties.

2. Select the Filegroups page in the Database Properties dialog box.

3. Click the Add button to create a new filegroup.

4. When a new row appears, enter the name of the new filegroup and enable the option Default.

Alternately, you may create a new filegroup as a set of adding a new file to a database, as shown in Figure 3.10. In this case, perform the following steps:

1. In Object Explorer, right-click the AdventureWorks2012 database and select Properties.

2. Select the Files page in the Database Properties dialog box.

3. Click the Add button to create a new file. Enter the name of the new file in the Logical Name field.

4. Click in the Filegroup field and select <new filegroup>.

5. When the New Filegroup page appears, enter the name of the new filegroup, specify any important options, and then click OK.

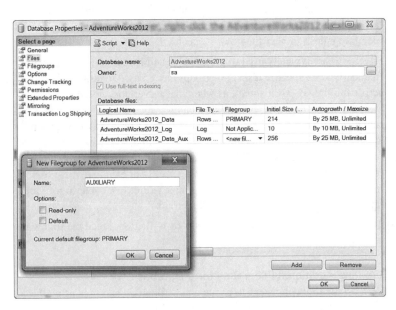

FIGURE 3.10
Creating a New Filegroup from the Files page.

Alternatively, you can use the following Transact-SQL script to create the new filegroup for the AdventureWorks2012 database:

```
USE [master]
GO
ALTER DATABASE [AdventureWorks2012] ADD FILEGROUP
[SecondFileGroup]
GO
```

Creating New Data Files for a Database and Placing Them in Different Filegroups

Now that you've created a new filegroup, you can create two additional data files for the AdventureWorks2012 database and place them in the newly created filegroup:

1. In Object Explorer, right-click the AdventureWorks2012 database and select Properties.

2. Select the Files page in the Database Properties dialog box.

3. Click the Add button to create new data files.

4. In the Database Files section, enter the following information in the appropriate columns:

Columns	Value
Logical Name	AdventureWorks2012_Data2
File Type	Data
FileGroup	SecondFileGroup
Size	10MB
Path	C:\
File Name	AdventureWorks2012_Data2.ndf

5. Click OK.

> **Note**
>
> For simplicity in the preceding example, the File page for the new database file is located in the root of the C: drive for this example. In production environments, however, you should place additional database files on separate volumes to maximize performance.

The earlier image, in Figure 3.10, showed the basic elements of the Database Files page. Alternatively, use the following Transact-SQL syntax to create a new data file:

```
USE [master]
GO
ALTER DATABASE [AdventureWorks2012]
ADD FILE (NAME = N'AdventureWorks2012_Data2',
FILENAME = N'C:\AdventureWorks2012_Data2.ndf',
SIZE = 10240KB , FILEGROWTH = 1024KB )
TO FILEGROUP [SecondFileGroup]
GO
```

Administering the Database Properties Filegroups Page

As stated previously, filegroups are a great way to organize data objects, address performance issues, and minimize backup times. The Filegroup page is best used for viewing existing filegroups, creating new ones, marking filegroups as read-only, and configuring which filegroup will be the default.

To improve performance, you can create subsequent filegroups and place database files, FILESTREAM data, and indexes onto them. In addition, if there isn't enough physical storage available on a volume, you can create a new filegroup and physically place all files on a different volume or LUN if a SAN is used.

Finally, if a database has static data such as that found in an archive, it is possible to move this data to a specific filegroup and mark that filegroup as read-only. Read-only filegroups are extremely fast for queries. Read-only filegroups are also easy to back up because the data rarely if ever changes.

> **Note**
>
> Alternatively, you can create a new filegroup directly in the Files page by adding a new data file and selecting New Filegroup from the Filegroup drop-down list.

Designing for BLOB Storage

As mentioned in the earlier section on filegroups, special purpose I/O technologies are available for those use-cases where standard approaches to I/O management are less optimized. A very common situation is found in handling BLOB (binary large object) files. Suppose you are building an application to correlate terrain maps with overlays of data about all the objects that are noteworthy on the map. Your database has data describing all the roads, railroads, electricity, infrastructure, towns, buildings, and so forth. The database also has tables for the metadata and geospatial data types that correlate all of the important objects to exact positions on the maps. The maps themselves, however, are huge multigigabyte image files.

Now the problem arises: Should we store the map image file into a varbinary(max) column within the database, or should we store only a pointer in the database linking the metadata to the map image file on the Windows file system? If we choose the first option, the database will be enormously bloated and take a very long time to back up, restore, and perform other preventative maintenance tasks. If we choose the second option, we have to deal with a much more complex backup and recovery scenario, and we risk having a situation where transactions involving both the map files and the database data may not fully commit or rollback depending on the responsiveness of the Windows file system. What's a person to do?

The good news is that Microsoft has implemented FILESTREAM data storage specifically for this scenario.

Managing FILESTREAM Data

In previous years, organizations had to invent and maintain their own mechanisms to store unstructured data. Now SQL Server supports a file type that enables organizations to store unstructured data such as bitmap images, music files, text files, videos, and audio files in a single data type, which is more secure and manageable.

From an internal perspective, FILESTREAM creates a bridge between the Database Engine and the NTFS file system of the Windows Server. It stores varbinary(max) binary large object (BLOB) data as files on the file system, while enabling the database engine to interact with the file system through Transact-SQL inserts, updates, queries, as well as full backup and recovery of FILESTREAM data.

In other words, you get all the benefits of a full, transactional database with all the benefits of storing the BLOBs on the file system. FILESTREAM can be enabled at the instance-level and the database-level.

Enabling FILESTREAM Data at the Instance-Level

The first step for managing FILESTREAM data is to enable it on the instance of SQL Server. The following steps indicate how to enable FILESTREAM data:

1. Choose, Start, All Programs, Microsoft SQL Server 2012, Configuration Tools, and then select SQL Server Configuration Manager.

2. In SQL Server Configuration Manager, highlight SQL Server Services, and then double-click the SQL Server Instance for which you want to enable FILESTREAM. The SQL Server Instance is located in the right pane.

3. In the SQL Server Properties dialog box, select the FileStream tab.

4. Enable the desired FILESTREAM settings, and then click OK. The options include Enable FILESTREAM for Transact-SQL Access, Enable FILESTREAM for File I/O Streaming Access, and Allow Remote Clients to Have Streaming Access to FILESTREAM Data.

5. The final step is to fire the following Transact-SQL code in Query Editor:

```
Exec sp_configure_filestream_access_level, 2
RECONFIGURE
```

Using the Database Properties Option Page to Enable FILESTREAM

The following options are also available in the SSMS Object Explorer by right-clicking a specific database name, selecting Properties, and then selecting the Database Properties Option page:

- **FILESTREAM Directory Name**—The directory name for FILESTREAM data in the specified database.

- **FILESTREAM Nontransacted Access**—The value to be entered may be OFF, READ_ONLY, or FULL. OFF is the setting when FILESTREAM is disabled for the instance. READ_ONLY and FULL are used to enable FileTables. FileTables are a way to programmatically interact with BLOBs on the Windows Server file system. FileTables are configured independently of FILESTREAM. Because they are programming constructs, they are beyond the scope of this book. Refer to the SQL Server Books Online for more information.

Following is an example using Transact-SQL. To set the AdventureWorks2012 database to enable nontransaction access, you can use this ALTER DATABASE syntax:

```
USE [master]
GO
ALTER DATABASE [AdventureWorks2012]
  SET FILESTREAM
    ( NON_TRANSACTED_ACCESS = FULL,
    DIRECTORY_NAME= N'AdventureWorksFST' )
WITH NO_WAIT
GO
```

Administering the FILESTREAM from the Advanced Page of the Server Properties Dialog

The Advanced Page, shown in Figure 3.11, contains the SQL Server general settings that can be configured. The only important settings on this page, in terms of I/O, are the FILESTREAM settings.

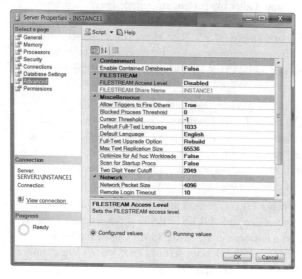

FIGURE 3.11
Administering the Server Properties Advanced Settings page.

Two items can be configured via the Advanced page:

- **Filestream Access Level**—This setting displays how the SQL Server instance will support FILESTREAM. FILESTREAM allows for the storage of unstructured data. The global server options associated with FILESTREAM configuration include the following:

- **Disabled**—The Disabled setting does not allow Binary Large Object (BLOB) data to be stored in the file system.
- **Transact-SQL Access Enabled**—FILESTREAM data is accessed only by Transact-SQL and not by the file system.
- **Full Access Enabled**—FILESTREAM data is accessed by both Transact-SQL and the file system.
- **FILESTREAM Share Name**—This setting displays the read-only share name configured during installation and setup of the SQL Server instance.

Enhancements to FILESTREAM in SQL Server 2012

Previous versions of SQL Server allowed only one FILESTREAM container per filegroup. This limitation hampered I/O performance and scalability. SQL Server 2012 now supports multiple FILESTREAM containers per filegroup. Other improvements include the ability to set a maximum size for the container, a DBCC SHRINKFILE EMPTYFILE command to shrink and empty FILESTREAM containers, support for multiple storage drives and multiple disks, and enhancements to the CREATE DATABASE and ALTER DATABASE to support the new features.

Just as database performance improves with multiple data files, FILESTREAM I/O scalability and performance improve with multiple disks. Many users are reporting a doubling in I/O performance for write speed and as much as a fivefold improvement in read speed, when writing and reading 1Mb BLOB files in a test environment, compared to SQL Server 2008 R2. Of course, your mileage may vary.

Not only can you enable FILESTREAM at the server level, as shown in Figure 3.11, you may also enable FILESTREAM at the database level. To do so, right-click on a database name in the SSMS Object Explorer and select Properties; then click the Options setting. The Options Page, similar to that shown in Figure 3.12, will appear:

Refer to the earlier descriptions associated with Figure 3.11, since the options are identical in meaning.

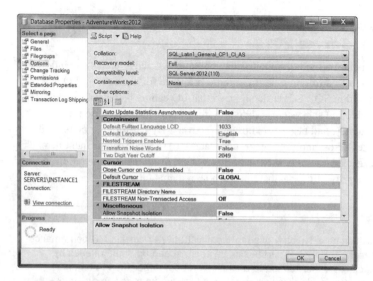

FIGURE 3.12
Administering FILESTREAM on the Database Options page.

Overview of Remote BLOB Store (RBS)

The Remote BLOB Store, or RBS, is an optional add-on component to manage and store BLOBs on cheap, commodity storage. It is frequently used with SQL Servers that support SharePoint and is not, by default, installed with SQL Server. You can find RBS online on the SQL Server 2008 R2 Feature Pack page at http://go.microsoft.com/fwlink/?LinkID=210168.

RBS provides similar benefits as FILESTREAM by moving BLOB files to cheaper storage. RBS provides a number of programmatic means of manipulating the data. RBS also supplies a FILESTREAM provider to store the BLOB data within SQL Server, but also offers the flexibility to use different storage solutions other than SQL Server. RBS provides an API so that you can write your own providers, such as another database platform, and includes a sample provider to the Windows NTFS file system, complete with source code. RBS can be found on Codeplex at http://sqlrbs.codeplex.com/.

Designing and Administrating Partitions in SQL Server 2012

A popular method of better managing large and active tables and indexes is the use of partitioning. Partitioning is a feature for segregating I/O workload within SQL Server database so that I/O can be better balanced against available I/O subsystems while providing better user response time, lower I/O latency, and faster backups and recovery. By partitioning tables and indexes across multiple filegroups, data retrieval and management is much quicker because only subsets of the data are used, meanwhile ensuring that the integrity of the database as a whole remains intact.

Tip

Partitioning is typically used for administrative or certain I/O performance scenarios. However, partitioning can also speed up some queries by enabling lock escalation to a single partition, rather than to an entire table. You must allow lock escalation to move up to the partition level by setting it with either the Lock Escalation option of Database Options page in SSMS or by using the LOCK_ESCALATION option of the ALTER TABLE statement.

After a table or index is partitioned, data is stored horizontally across multiple filegroups, so groups of data are mapped to individual partitions. Typical scenarios for partitioning include large tables that become very difficult to manage, tables that are suffering performance degradation because of excessive I/O or blocking locks, table-centric maintenance processes that exceed the available time for maintenance, and moving historical data from the active portion of a table to a partition with less activity.

Partitioning tables and indexes warrants a bit of planning before putting them into production. The usual approach to partitioning a table or index follows these steps:

1. Create the filegroup(s) and file(s) used to hold the partitions defined by the partitioning scheme.

2. Create a partition function to map the rows of the table or index to specific partitions based on the values in a specified column. A very common partitioning function is based on the creation date of the record.

3. Create a partitioning scheme to map the partitions of the partitioned table to the specified filegroup(s) and, thereby, to specific locations on the Windows file system.

4. Create the table or index (or ALTER an existing table or index) by specifying the partition scheme as the storage location for the partitioned object.

Although Transact-SQL commands are available to perform every step described earlier, the Create Partition Wizard makes the entire process quick and easy through an intuitive point-and-click interface. The next section provides an overview of using the Create Partition Wizard in SQL Server 2012, and an example later in this section shows the Transact-SQL commands.

Leveraging the Create Partition Wizard to Create Table and Index Partitions

The Create Partition Wizard can be used to divide data in large tables across multiple filegroups to increase performance and can be invoked by right-clicking any table or index, selecting Storage, and then selecting Create Partition. The first step is to identify which columns to partition by reviewing all the columns available in the Available Partitioning Columns section located on the Select a Partitioning Column dialog box, as displayed in Figure 3.13. This screen also includes additional options such as the following:

- **Collocate to an Available Partitioned Table**—Displays related data to join with the column being partitioned.

- **Storage Align Non Unique Indexes and Unique Indexes with an Indexed Partition Column**—Aligns all indexes of the table being partitioned with the same partition scheme. If you do not select this option, you may place indexes independently of the columns they point to.

The next screen is called Select a Partition Function. This page is used for specifying the partition function where the data will be partitioned. The options include using an existing partition or creating a new partition. The subsequent page is called New Partition Scheme. Here a DBA will conduct a mapping of the rows selected of tables being partitioned to a desired filegroup. Either a new partition scheme should be used or a new one needs to be created. The final screen is used for doing the actual mapping. On the Map Partitions page, specify the partitions to be used for each partition and then enter a range for the values of the partitions. The ranges and settings on the grid include the following:

- **Filegroup**—Enter the desired filegroup for the partition.

- **Left and Right Boundary**—Used for entering range values up to a specified value. Left boundary is based on Value <= Boundary and Right boundary is based on Value < Boundary.

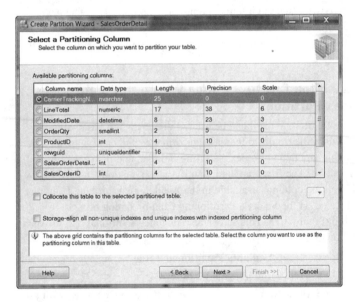

FIGURE 3.13
Selecting a partitioning column.

> **Note**
>
> By opening the Set Boundary Values dialog box, a DBA can set boundary values based on dates (for example, partition everything in a column after a specific date). The data types are based on dates.

- **RowCount**—Read-only columns that display required space and are determined only when the Estimate Storage button is clicked.

- **Required Space**—Read-only columns that display required space and are determined only when the Estimate Storage button is clicked.

- **Available Space**—Read-only columns that display available space and are determined only when the Estimate Storage button is clicked.

- **Estimate Storage**—When selected, this option determines the rowcount, required, and available space.

Designing table and index partitions is a DBA task that typically requires a joint effort with the database development team. The DBA must have a strong understanding of the database, tables, and columns to make the correct choices for partitioning. For more information on partitioning, review Books Online.

Enhancements to Partitioning in SQL Server 2012

SQL Server 2012 now supports as many as 15,000 partitions. When using more than 1,000 partitions, Microsoft recommends that the instance of SQL Server have at least 16Gb of available memory. This recommendation particularly applies to partitioned indexes, especially those that are not aligned with the base table or with the clustered index of the table. Other Data Manipulation Language statements (DML) and Data Definition Language statements (DDL) may also run short of memory when processing on a large number of partitions.

Certain DBCC commands may take longer to execute when processing a large number of partitions. On the other hand, a few DBCC commands can be scoped to the partition level and, if so, can be used to perform their function on a subset of data in the partitioned table.

Queries may also benefit from a new query engine enhancement called partition elimination. SQL Server uses partition enhancement automatically if it is available. Here's how it works. Assume a table has four partitions, with all the data for customers whose names begin with R, S, or T in the third partition. If a query's WHERE clause filters on customer name looking for 'System%', the query engine knows that it needs only to partition three to answer the request. Thus, it might greatly reduce I/O for that query. On the other hand, some queries might take longer if there are more than 1,000 partitions and the query is not able to perform partition elimination.

Finally, SQL Server 2012 introduces some changes and improvements to the algorithms used to calculate partitioned index statistics. Primarily, SQL Server 2012 samples rows in a partitioned index when it is created or rebuilt, rather than scanning all available rows. This may sometimes result in somewhat different query behavior compared to the same queries running on SQL Server 2012.

Administrating Data Using Partition Switching

Partitioning is useful to access and manage a subset of data while losing none of the integrity of the entire data set. There is one limitation, though. When a partition is created on an existing table, new data is added to a specific partition or to the default partition if none is specified. That means the default partition might grow unwieldy if it is left unmanaged. (This concept is similar to how a clustered index needs to be rebuilt from time to time to reestablish its fill factor setting.)

Switching partitions is a fast operation because no physical movement of data takes place. Instead, only the metadata pointers to the physical data are altered.

You can alter partitions using SQL Server Management Studio or with the ALTER TABLE…SWITCH Transact-SQL statement. Both options enable you to ensure partitions are well maintained. For example, you can transfer subsets of data between partitions, move tables between partitions, or combine partitions together. Because the ALTER TABLE…SWITCH statement does not actually move the data, a few prerequisites must be in place:

- Partitions must use the same column when switching between two partitions.
- The source and target table must exist prior to the switch and must be on the same filegroup, along with their corresponding indexes, index partitions, and indexed view partitions.
- The target partition must exist prior to the switch, and it must be empty, whether adding a table to an existing partitioned table or moving a partition from one table to another. The same holds true when moving a partitioned table to a nonpartitioned table structure.
- The source and target tables must have the same columns in identical order with the same names, data types, and data type attributes (length, precision, scale, and nullability). Computed columns must have identical syntax, as well as primary key constraints. The tables

must also have the same settings for ANSI_NULLS and QUOTED_
IDENTIFIER properties. Clustered and nonclustered indexes must be
identical. ROWGUID properties and XML schemas must match.
Finally, settings for in-row data storage must also be the same.

■ The source and target tables must have matching nullability on the
partitioning column. Although both NULL and NOT NULL are
supported, NOT NULL is strongly recommended.

Likewise, the ALTER TABLE...SWITCH statement will not work under certain
circumstances:

■ Full-text indexes, XML indexes, and old-fashioned SQL Server rules
are not allowed (though CHECK constraints are allowed).

■ Tables in a merge replication scheme are not allowed. Tables in a
transactional replication scheme are allowed with special caveats.
Triggers are allowed on tables but must not fire during the switch.

■ Indexes on the source and target table must reside on the same partition as the tables themselves.

■ Indexed views make partition switching difficult and have a lot of
extra rules about how and when they can be switched. Refer to the
SQL Server Books Online if you want to perform partition switching
on tables containing indexed views.

■ Referential integrity can impact the use of partition switching. First,
foreign keys on other tables cannot reference the source table. If the
source table holds the primary key, it cannot have a primary or
foreign key relationship with the target table. If the target table holds
the foreign key, it cannot have a primary or foreign key relationship
with the source table.

In summary, simple tables can easily accommodate partition switching.
The more complexity a source or target table exhibits, the more likely that
careful planning and extra work will be required to even make partition
switching possible, let alone efficient.

Here's an example where we create a partitioned table using a previously
created partition scheme, called Date_Range_PartScheme1. We then create
a new, nonpartitioned table identical to the partitioned table residing on the
same filegroup. We finish up switching the data from the partitioned table
into the nonpartitioned table:

```
CREATE TABLE TransactionHistory_Partn1 (Xn_Hst_ID int, Xn_Type
char(10))
ON Date_Range_PartScheme1 (Xn_Hst_ID) ;
GO
CREATE TABLE TransactionHistory_No_Partn (Xn_Hst_ID int,
Xn_Type char(10))
ON main_filegroup ;
GO
ALTER TABLE TransactionHistory_Partn1 SWITCH partition1 TO
TransactionHistory_No_Partn;
GO
```

The next section shows how to use a more sophisticated, but very popular, approach to partition switching called a *sliding window partition*.

Example and Best Practices for Managing Sliding Window Partitions

Assume that our AdventureWorks business is booming. The sales staff, and by extension the AdventureWorks2012 database, is very busy. We noticed over time that the TransactionHistory table is very active as sales transactions are first entered and are still very active over their first month in the database. But the older the transactions are, the less activity they see. Consequently, we'd like to automatically group transactions into four partitions per year, basically containing one quarter of the year's data each, in a rolling partitioning. Any transaction older than one year will be purged or archived.

The answer to a scenario like the preceding one is called a *sliding window partition* because we are constantly loading new data in and sliding old data over, eventually to be purged or archived. Before you begin, you must choose either a LEFT partition function window or a RIGHT partition function window:

1. How data is handled varies according to the choice of LEFT or RIGHT partition function window:

   ■ With a LEFT strategy, partition1 holds the oldest data (Q4 data), partition2 holds data that is 6- to 9-months old (Q3), partition3 holds data that is 3- to 6-months old (Q2), and partition4 holds recent data less than 3-months old.

   ■ With a RIGHT strategy, partition4 holds the holds data (Q4), partition3 holds Q3 data, partition2 holds Q2 data, and partition1 holds recent data.

- Following the best practice, make sure there are empty partitions on both the leading edge (partition0) and trailing edge (partition5) of the partition.

  - RIGHT range functions usually make more sense to most people because it is natural for most people to to start ranges at their lowest value and work upward from there.

2. Assuming that a RIGHT partition function windows is used, we first use the SPLIT subclause of the ALTER PARTITION FUNCTION statement to split empty partition5 into two empty partitions, 5 and 6.

3. We use the SWITCH subclause of ALTER TABLE to switch out partition4 to a staging table for archiving or simply to drop and purge the data. Partition4 is now empty.

4. We can then use MERGE to combine the empty partitions 4 and 5, so that we're back to the same number of partitions as when we started. This way, partition3 becomes the new partition4, partition2 becomes the new partition3, and partition1 becomes the new partition2.

5. We can use SWITCH to push the new quarter's data into the spot of partition1.

Tip

Use the $PARTITION system function to determine where a partition function places values within a range of partitions.

Some best practices to consider for using a slide window partition include the following:

- Load newest data into a heap, and then add indexes after the load is finished. Delete oldest data or, when working with very large data sets, drop the partition with the oldest data.

- Keep an empty staging partition at the leftmost and rightmost ends of the partition range to ensure that the partitions split when loading in new data, and merge, after unloading old data, do not cause data movement.

- Do not split or merge a partition already populated with data because this can cause severe locking and explosive log growth.

- Create the load staging table in the same filegroup as the partition you are loading.

- Create the unload staging table in the same filegroup as the partition you are deleting.
- Don't load a partition until its range boundary is met. For example, don't create and load a partition meant to hold data that is one to two months older before the current data has aged one month. Instead, continue to allow the latest partition to accumulate data until the data is ready for a new, full partition.
- Unload one partition at a time.
- The ALTER TABLE...SWITCH statement issues a schema lock on the entire table. Keep this in mind if regular transactional activity is still going on while a table is being partitioned.

Data Compression in SQL Server 2012

With data explosion occurring in the industry and enterprise, more and more data is being stored within SQL Server. However, the databases are no longer averaging 100GB in size as they were 10 years ago. Now databases are becoming larger than ever, with sizes from 10 to 50TB now being common. In addition, it is often only a select few tables within the database that are growing to these record-breaking sizes. To combat this, even though storage is getting cheaper, Microsoft has introduced data compression and tools, namely the Data Compression Wizard and specific Transact-SQL statements, to facilitate data compression. Therefore, a DBA can compress tables and indexes to conserve storage space at a slight CPU cost. One of the main design goals of data compression was to shrink data warehouse fact tables. Fact tables are typically the largest tables within a data warehouse because they contain the majority of the data associated with a database.

Note

Compression is available only in the Enterprise Edition of SQL Server. To get an idea of how much space, and potentially I/O as well, use the `sp_estimate_data_compression_savings` system stored procedure to calculate the storage savings associated with a compressed object.

SQL Server provides two methods, Page and Row compression, to reduce data storage on disk and speed I/O performance by reducing the amount of I/O required for transaction processing. Page and row compression work in different, yet complementary, ways and are worth further discussion.

Page compression uses an algorithm called "deduplication." When dedupli-cating, as the name implies, SQL Server looks for duplicate values that appear again and again within the data page. For example, the table HumanResources.Employee in the AdventureWorks2012 database contains an nvarchar(50) column called JobTitle. This column contains many dupli-cate values—things like "Design Engineer" and Research and Develop-ment Manager." These values might appear many times on a single data page. Using page compression, SQL Server can remove such duplicate values within a data page by replacing each duplicate value with a tiny pointer to a single appearance of the full value. (Incidentally, this is known as "dictionary-based compression.")

By comparison, row compression does not actually use a compression algorithm per se. Instead, when row compression is enabled, SQL Server simply removes any extra, unused bytes in a fixed data type column, such as a CHAR(50) column.

Page and row compression are not compatible, but by enabling page compression SQL Server automatically includes row compression. You can also specify compression per partition, so partitioned tables could have multiple compression specifications at once.

Using the Data Compression Wizard to Compress Space

The Data Compression Wizard can be used to analyze and compress space associated with a table stored in a heap or clustered index structure. In addition, it can also support compression tables using nonclustered index and index views. Finally, if the table is partitioned, a DBA can compress portions of the tables, and various partitions do not have to maintain the same compressed settings.

The Data Compression Wizard can be invoked by right-clicking any table or index and selecting Storage and then Manage Compression. The first step is to select the compression type based on a partition number, or you can choose to use the same compression for all partitions. The compres-sion options include Row, Page, or None, indicating no compression.

The next step is to click the Calculate button to review the disk cost savings. The cost savings will be displayed in the Requested Compressed Space column based on a partition number. This is displayed in Figure 3.14. The final step includes selecting an output option. It is possible to create a script, run immediately, or schedule the task to commence at a later time.

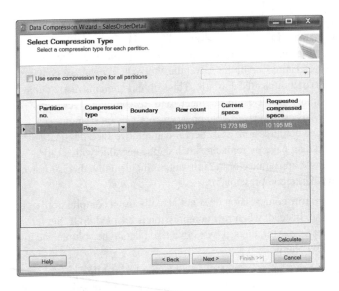

FIGURE 3.14
Specifying the compression type with the Data Compression Wizard.

Data Compression with Transact SQL

For those of you who do not like using a GUI, the following examples outline the default syntax for compressing data with Transact-SQL.

Creating a Table with Row Compression Enabled

```
CREATE TABLE <Table Name>
(<Column 1. int, <Column 2> nvarchar(50) )
WITH (DATA_COMPRESSION = ROW);
GO
```

Creating a Table with Page Compression Enabled

```
CREATE TABLE <Table Name>
(<Column 1. int, <Column 2> nvarchar(50) )
WITH (DATA_COMPRESSION = PAGE);
GO
```

The following Transact-SQL syntax illustrates compressing the Sales Order Detail table in the AdventureWorks2012 database by the page compression setting:

```
USE [AdventureWorks2012]
ALTER TABLE [Sales].[SalesOrderDetail]
REBUILD PARTITION = ALL
WITH
(DATA_COMPRESSION = PAGE
)
```

You can monitor compression activity with the performance counters Page Compression Attempts/sec and Page Compressed/sec found in the SQL Server Access Methods Object. For example, this Transact-SQL code will query both counters:

```
SELECT cntr_value
FROM sys.dm_os_performance_counters
WHERE counter_name LIKE 'Page Compression%'
```

As mentioned earlier, compression is included only in the Enterprise Edition of SQL Server. Compression technologies dramatically cut I/O requests and storage; however, the storage gained is typically at the cost of added CPU activity. Therefore, it is strongly advised that you test before implementing data compression in a production workload scenario. In most transaction processing scenarios, SQL Server has CPU to spare and sorely needs more I/O throughput. However, occasionally the improvement to I/O performance is not big enough to warrant the lost CPU. Test to ensure that performance is not negatively impacted.

Summary

The Database Engine is the core component within SQL Server; it provides a key service for storing, processing, and securing data. SQL Server 2012 introduces many new features that improve your success at administering and managing this core component. In addition, reading this chapter will help you to fully understand how to manage and administer SQL Server instance server properties, configuration settings, Database Engine folders, database properties, and SQL Server Agent.

Best Practices

This chapter focused on optimizing storage and I/O. Best practices directly related to storage and I/O are the following:

- The default configuration of filegroups and files is adequate only for small and/or lightly used databases. High-performance databases will require a lot of tuning and modification from the defaults. Be sure to document your changes.

■ When creating filegroups and files for a database, preconfigure their size for what they need to be a year or more from today. Set the autogrow parameter to a specific, absolute value of sufficient size so that autogrowth will not happen frequently. Better yet, avoid autogrowth altogether by enlarging data files and transaction log files during preventative maintenance hours.

■ Ensure that database files and the transaction log file for all databases reside in RAID volumes. RAID1+0 is the best, but more costly. RAID5 is good for read-heavy applications. If cost is an issue, RAID1 is an inexpensive option for write-heavy databases, such as tempdb.

■ SSD is a game-changer. It is exceedingly fast compared to hard disks, especially for applications that are heavy on randomized I/O. However, SSD has its own set of special management issues.

■ Monitor and tune storage and I/O for tempdb just as you would for a business-critical production database. On SQL Server instances with many active databases, tempdb is frequently the busiest database on the entire instance.

■ Do not create multiple files and filegroups for the transaction log file.

■ Database files, the transaction log file, and operating system files should be located on physically separate volumes for performance and availability. By "physically separate," understand that this means completely separate from other I/O intensive processes. It will do no good, for example, to put all transaction logs together onto the same RAID. In business-critical applications, each database file should be separate from other database files, while the transaction log file should be completely isolated.

■ Create additional database files on physically separate volumes to speed I/O. Make sure that all database files are of identical size and organize them through the use of filegroups.

■ If the following steps have not sped up I/O enough to meet the needs of the application, consider creating partitions on the most heavily used table(s) and/or index(es) to further segregate I/O onto physically separate volumes.

- SANs are often black boxes to DBAs. Make sure that I/O performance is at least comparable to direct-attached storage (DASD) and that SAN administrators are held accountable not only for storage volume but also for I/O throughput.

In addition, the following list is a summary of some other of the best practices from this chapter:

- Leverage data compression to reduce disk space consumed by data files and to speed I/O by reducing the overall amount of I/O occurring.

- Do not set the database to automatically shrink because this leads to performance degradation and excessive fragmentation over time.

- Configure the recovery model for each database accordingly and implement a backup and restore strategy. This should also include the system databases and should be tested regularly. Having a backup doesn't mean you can recover a database, and only a test recovery will reveal that.

- Review the other break-out chapters in the book for more information on items such as hardening a SQL Server, encryption, Policy-Based Management, Resource Governor, and SQL Agent jobs like backups, DBCC corruption checks, and maintenance activities.

CHAPTER 4

Creating Packages and Transferring Data On-Premise and to the Cloud

SQL Server 2012 Integration Services (SSIS) provides data movement and transformation capabilities for SQL Server. Since SQL Server 2005, SSIS replaced SQL Server 2000 Data Transformation Services (DTS). SSIS provides for the following data services:

- Extraction
- Transformation
- Loading

This triumvirate of data services is frequently referred to as ETL. The process encapsulates the extraction of data from a source, the transformation of the data to suit the requirements of the application, and the loading of the data into a destination. The transformations can include normalizing, sanitizing, merging, aggregating, and copying the data. The sources and destinations for the data can be SQL databases, third-party ODBC data, flat files, or any number of other data locations.

SSIS delivers high-performance ETL services with a rich set of tools for designing, testing, executing, and monitoring these integrations. SSIS consists of packages that define the logic for the extraction, transformation, and loading steps and an engine that performs the steps defined in the package. A service allows administration and monitoring of the packages on the server and a development environment for creating and debugging the package definitions.

Note

Support for migrating or running Data Transformation Services (DTS) packages has been discontinued in this release of SQL Server. Migrating DTS packages to SSIS is strongly considered.

What's New in Integration Services for SQL Server 2012

SSIS showcases a number of new features and enhancements in SQL Server 2012. Become familiar with the principal changes and how they relate to creating packages and transforming data on-premise and to the cloud:

- SQL Server 2012 introduces a new deployment model that allows a DBA to deploy projects to an Integration Services server in a centralized fashion. The Integration Services server enables better management of packages by introducing a new concept of server environments.

- The Integration Services catalogs in Management Studio are used to create server environments for specifying runtime values for packages contained in a project deployed to the Integration Services server. These variable values are mapped to the project parameters.

- The latest release of SSIS delivers extra views, stored procedures, and stored functions for troubleshooting both performance and data anomalies.

- A number of areas have seen significant enhancements pertaining to deployment. These deployment enhancements include sharing connection managers, parsing flat files with embedded qualifiers, assigning values to properties within packages, the capability to easily compare packages, undo and redo up to 20 actions in SSIS Designer, and smarter capabilities pertaining to mapping columns.

- The Integration Services Merge and Merge Join transformations have been optimized to reduce memory operations when in use.

- To achieve better data quality, Integration Services now includes DQS Cleansing transformation.

> **Note**
>
> If you installed a new instance of SQL Server 2012, the packages, tools, and wizards included in this chapter provide a way to migrate data and databases from older versions of SQL Server.

Options for Creating Packages

There are several options for creating SSIS packages and transferring data in SQL Server 2012. Some of the options do not require in-depth knowledge of SSIS and are appropriate for simple importing and exporting of data. Other options require a more detailed understanding, but offer more flexibility and capability for transforming and manipulating data.

Import and Export Wizard

The Import and Export Wizard is useful for quickly importing or exporting data from SQL Server when there is little need for manipulation of the data. Behind the scenes, the wizard produces an SSIS package. The package can be run once and discarded, or it can be saved to a file or in the MSDB database for later use. The wizard will handle basic data type conversions but will not address more complex cleansing of data, such as reformatting telephone numbers. The wizard can be launched from SQL Server Management Studio by right-clicking a database and selecting Tasks, Import Data, or Tasks, Export Data.

The packages produced by the Import and Export Wizard can provide a useful starting point for developing new packages. The wizard will create the basic structure of the package. The package can then be opened and edited in SQL Server Data Tools. This can make it easier to add additional transformations to the package. An example of the Import and Export Wizard will be covered in the "Creating a Package" section later in this chapter.

Copy Database Wizard

The Copy Database Wizard is used to copy databases from an instance of SQL Server 2000 or later to SQL Server 2012. The wizard produces an SSIS package, like the Import and Export Wizard. Unlike the packages produced by the Import and Export Wizard, the package created is useful only for copying databases. It can be edited in SQL Server Data Tools. The package will be stored in the MSDB database and is located in the

<SERVERNAME>\DTS Packages\Copy Database Wizard Packages folder, which you can browse to using the Integration Services Object Explorer in SQL Server Management Studio. This wizard will be covered in the "Using the Copy Database Wizard" section later in the chapter.

SQL Server Data Tools

SQL Server Data Tools, formerly known as Business Intelligence Development Studio (BIDS) offers the most flexibility in creating SSIS packages. It offers complete access to all the tasks, transformations, and connectivity options available in SSIS. It can be used to create new packages or edit existing packages. This flexibility also requires more understanding of how SSIS works. The next section covers the features and options available in SSIS in more detail.

A package can be created directly in SQL Server Data Tools by using the Import and Export Wizard to add the package to the project and then editing it using the full set of design tools available. The Integration Services Connection Project template will present a wizard for configuring your source and destination connections and create a basic package as a starting point for moving data.

Note

You can install SQL Server Data Tools during SQL Server installation by choosing SQL Server Data Tools on the Feature Selection.

Integration Services Packages

Packages allow you to control not only the transfer of data in and out of the SQL Server 2012 server (commonly referred to as extraction, transformation, and loading, or ETL for short), but also to automate a variety of maintenance and administrative functions. This can all be done through a graphical development environment that provides debugging and troubleshooting support.

The types of tasks you are likely to want to automate include the following:

- Importing and exporting data from SQL Server
- Maintaining databases, rebuilding indexes, and other administrative tasks
- Running commands and coordinating multiple steps of a process

The package model gives you access to intensive scriptlike control and power, but in an easy-to-use and modular interface. Similar capabilities exist in scripting, batch files, or programming languages such as Visual Basic. However, Integration Services packages bring those capabilities to a model that is built around the database architecture and a data integration toolset. It has predefined tasks that are database oriented and geared toward a DBA.

Throughout this chapter, the optional SQL Server 2012 sample files will be used. This allows you to do the procedures shown in the chapter with the same data and follow the steps exactly.

Note

The SQL Server 2012 Integration Services provide a complex and rich set of development tools for integrating and processing information. These tools allow sophisticated programmatic solutions to be developed to meet complex business needs.

However, the administration and maintenance requirements of DBAs are usually more straightforward and simple, and require less development effort. The SQL Server 2012 Integration Services tools also simplify the process of developing administration and maintenance solutions. This chapter focuses on the needs of the DBAs rather than those of a developer.

Packages consist of control flows and control flow tasks, data flows and data flow components, connections, and various supporting structures such as event handlers, variables, and logging. Although each package is self-contained, packages are organized into projects for ease of development and distribution.

Understanding how these various pieces fit together is the key to being able to use packages to automate administrative and maintenance tasks.

Projects and Solutions

Packages are organized into projects and solutions. Projects are containers for packages. Each project can contain multiple packages. In addition to the packages, a project contains the definitions for data sources and data source views that are used by the packages.

A *solution* is a container for organizing projects that are related or that compose a business solution. When a project is created, the SQL Server Data Tools automatically create a solution for the project if one does not already exist.

DBAs rarely use solutions or projects, because most packages used by DBAs are standalone packages. However, a package must be part of a project in order to debug it in SQL Server Data Tools.

Control Flow

The control flow is the organizing element of the package. Control flows contain a series of tasks that determine what the package will do, including data flows to orchestrate data movement. Each package has one primary control flow. There can be additional control flows associated with event handlers, as discussed in the "Event Handlers" section in this chapter. Each control flow can contain nested control flows in the form of containers. Containers allow package developers to organize tasks and set up repeating tasks, such as conditional loops. Containers can contain tasks and other containers, allowing for sophisticated nested logic and processing.

The available types of containers are listed in Table 4.1.

Table 4.1   **Container Types**

Container	Description
For Each Loop and For Loop	Repeats the tasks contained in the container until the end of the collection or test condition is reached.
Sequence	Used to sequence and isolate tasks into smaller control flows.

Note

SSIS also uses an internal container called the TaskHost that can contain a single task. Every task is automatically hosted in this container. This is transparent when developing packages, but it can be helpful to remember that every task is essentially a container that holds only one task.

Tasks

Tasks are the individual units of work in a package. You can use tasks to do such things as execute a SQL statement, import data, copy a database, send mail, or initiate a data flow. Each task has a set of properties associated with it that control its behavior at runtime. A multitude of different tasks provide a rich set of tools to automate work. Table 4.2 shows several of the commonly used control flow tasks. There is a complete list of control flow tasks in the Books Online topic "Integration Services Tasks."

Table 4.2 **Control Flow Tasks**

Task	Description
Data Flow Task	Runs data flows to extract data, apply column-level transformations, and load data.
File System Task	Performs common operations on files and directories.
Execute Package Task	Allows one package to execute another.
Execute SQL Task	Executes a SQL statement against a relation database.
Data Profiling Task	Task that profiles the data in SQL Server databases for statistical information, correlation of data, and patterns in the data.
Transfer Database Tasks	These tasks move SQL Server Task and Transfer databases or SQL Server Objects objects in those databases from one instance to another.

Data Flow

The data flow determines how data is moved, which is the main goal of any data integration process. This is the nuts and bolts of the extraction, transformation, and loading of the data. Data flows are also referred to as *pipelines* because data flows from one location to another within them. Individual units of work in a data flow are known as *components*. Data flow components are organized into sources, transformations, and destinations. These control where data comes from, how it is changed, and where it goes, respectively. Depending on the function of the component, it may have several inputs and outputs. Components can be connected by joining the output from one component to the input on another component. This connection is a *data flow path*, and it shows how data will move through the pipeline.

A variety of sources and destinations are available in the data flow components. Most sources have an equivalent destination. For example, there is an ADO.NET source and an ADO.NET destination. The XML Source, however, does not have an equivalent destination, and there are several destinations (such as the Data Reader destination) that do not have equivalent sources. The common sources and destinations are listed in Table 4.3. The complete list can be found in the Books Online topics "Integration Services Sources" and "Integration Services Destinations."

Table 4.3   **Common Source and Destination Components**

Source or Destination	Description
ADO.NET Source	Consumes data from a .NET Framework data provider
Excel Source	Extracts data from an Excel file
Flat File Source	Extracts data from a flat file
OLE DB Source	Consumes data from an OLE DB provider
ADO.NET Destination	Loads data using a .NET Framework data provider
Excel Destination	Writes data to an Excel Workbook
Flat File Destination	Writes data to a flat file
OLE DB Destination	Loads data using an OLE DB provider

The possible transformations are where the data flow really shows its versatility. There are transformations that operate on individual rows and on sets of rows. There are transformations that can join rows, split rows, or even do lookups into another table for references. This gives you a multitude of options for what to do with the data that is being moved between a source and a destination.

The transformations can also be executed sequentially to allow more than one transformation to be done on the data, and different flow paths can be taken dependent on the data as well, allowing decisions to be made for each row of data.

Row transformations are the most commonly used data-flow transformation elements. They can transform column values or create new columns. Typical uses are to change the data type of a column, manipulate text (such as splitting a name field into first and last names), or create a copy of a column for future manipulation.

The rowset transformations output a new set of rows based on the input rows. Typical uses include sorting a rowset through the Sort transform or averaging columns in a rowset using the Aggregate transform.

A set of transformations allow data to be split, joined, or used as a lookup reference. Frequently, rowsets must be split into separate groups. For example, a table of customers may need to be cleaned by removing those below a certain age. The conditional split would be used to separate the data on the basis of that condition.

There are also transformations that allow data to move in and out of the data flow. For example, the import and export transformations allow data to be brought into and out of the data flow via files. The audit transformation allows data from the running environment to be brought into the data flow, for example, by allowing the login name of the user to be put into a column.

Table 4.4 lists the commonly used data-flow components. The complete list can be found in the Books Online topic "Integration Services Transformations."

Table 4.4   **Data Flow Transformation Components**

Transformation	Description
Data Conversion Transformation	The transformation that converts the data type of a column to a different data type
Derived Column Transformation	The transformation that populates columns with the results of expressions
Script Component	The transformation that uses .NET script to extract, transform, or load data
OLE DB Command Transformation	The transformation that runs SQL commands for each row in a data flow
Aggregate Transformation	The transformation that performs aggregations such as AVERAGE, SUM, and COUNT
Sort Transformation	The transformation that sorts data
Conditional Split Transformation	The transformation that routes data rows to different outputs
Union All Transformation	The transformation that merges multiple data sets
Lookup Transformation	The transformation that looks up values in a reference table using an exact match
Row Count Transformation	The transformation that counts rows as they move through it and stores the final count in a variable

Connections

Connections allow the package to connect to a variety of sources, destinations, and services. Connections include databases, flat files, Excel spreadsheets, FTP services, and others. Table 4.5 contains a list of the commonly used connection types. A complete list is in Books Online under the topic "Connection Managers."

Table 4.5   **Connection Types**

Connection Managers	Description
ADO.NET Connection Manager	For connecting to relational data sources by using ADO.NET
Excel Connection Manager	For connecting to Excel workbooks
Flat File Connection Manager	For accessing data in a single flat file
ODBC Connection Manager	For connecting to data sources by using ODBC
OLE DB Connection Manager	For connecting to data sources by using OLE DB

Connections are instantiated through connection managers, which are logical representations of the connections. The connection managers contain all the properties needed for the connection. A single connection manager can be reused throughout a package, such as a connection to a database, or a connection to an SMTP mail server. In addition, there can be more than one connection manager of the same type, such as when connections to multiple flat files are needed.

Event Handlers

Event handlers trigger when the package or tasks raise events. These events are raised when significant conditions occur, including errors (OnError), warnings (OnWarning), information messages (OnInformation), or when the package or task completes (OnPostExecute). The complete list of events can be found in Books Online under the topic "Integration Services Event Handlers."

Event handlers launch control flows, which can include all the same tasks as the package control flow. In effect, the event handlers are containers with control and data flows that execute only when their trigger condition is encountered.

Variables

Variables are used to store values that the package can use at runtime. For example, a variable can be used to store the count of rows processed by a Row Count Transformation in the data flow. Or it can be used to store the value for a parameterized SQL statement to be run from an Execute SQL Task. Variables can be defined at the package level, or they can be scoped to a container or individual task.

A number of system variables provide additional information about the package execution. These include `StartTime`, which indicates the start time of the package or task, and `ExecutionInstanceGUID`, which provides a unique identifier each time the package is executed. A complete list of system variables can be found in Books Online under the topic "System Variables."

Log Providers and Logging

When packages execute, detailed information is generated about the execution of the package. This information is very useful for troubleshooting and auditing the package. By default, this information is displayed in the console but not stored anywhere. This information can be captured in logs for later review and analysis.

SSIS can log to a number of destinations, including text files, SQL Server, or the Windows Event Log, through the use of log providers. Custom log providers can be created as well. Log providers abstract the actual mechanics of writing log information to a specific destination away from the package.

The package can log to more than one provider at a time—for example, to both the Windows Event Log and to the SQL Server. The same events will be logged to both providers.

Developing Packages

As stated earlier, packages are the core of the Integration Services. Packages are developed in the SQL Server Data Tools, which is a sophisticated development environment with extensive development and debugging features. The specific tool used for Integration Services is the SSIS Designer, which is the graphical tool to develop and maintain the SSIS packages. The SSIS Designer allows you to:

- Build control and data flows
- Configure event handlers
- Execute and debug packages
- Graphically follow the package execution

This section will cover using the SSIS Designer in creating a package, reviewing the package, and running the package.

Creating a Project

To start this sample, a project needs to be created to contain the packages. This project can contain multiple packages that are related for ease of maintenance and organization. A solution will be created automatically for any new project.

To create a project, follow these steps:

1. Launch SQL Server Data Tools, by specifying Start, All Programs, Microsoft SQL Server 2012 and then SQL Server Data Tools.

2. If this is the first time launching SQL Server Data Tools, choose Business Intelligence Settings as the default environment, and then click Start Visual Studio.

3. Select File, New, Project.

4. Select the Integration Services Project template.

5. Change the name—in this case, Customer Project.

6. Select a location to store the project, such as `c:\projects\`.

7. Leave the Solution Name as is—in this case, Customer Project. A directory will be created for the new solution. Click OK to create the project.

The project will be opened with a default package name, `Package.dtsx`.

Creating a Package

A simple package will now be created. This package will import the `Customers.txt` sample file (available in the Integration Services samples from CodePlex at http://msftisprodsamples.codeplex.com/), which contains customer records for more than 2,000 customers. The data contains name, birth date, yearly income, occupation, and other key data.

To create the import package, follow these steps:

1. If necessary, launch the SQL Server SQL Server Data Tools.

2. Open the Customer Project created in the previous section.

3. Click Project, SSIS Import, and Export Wizard. Click Next on the first page of the wizard.

4. In the Data Source drop-down list, select Flat File Source.

5. In the File Name field, click Browse to browse for the file to import.

6. Navigate to C:\Program Files\Microsoft SQL Server\100\Samples\Integration Services\Package Samples\ExecuteSQLStatementsInLoop Sample\Data Files\.

7. Select the Customers.txt file and click Open.

8. Check the box Column Names in the first data row, and click Next.

9. Review the columns, and data the wizard will import, and click Next.

10. Select SQL Server Native Client 11.0 in the Data Source drop-down list. In the Server Name field, select SQLServer01\Instance01. Select AdventureWorks2012 in the Database field, and click Next.

11. Ensure that the Destination table name is [dbo].[Customers]. Click Preview to review the columns and data. Click Close to close the preview window, and click Next.

12. Review the summary. Note the location where the package will be saved and that the package will not be run immediately.

13. Click Finish to build and save the package. A new package name, CustomerImport.dtsx, will be created.

14. Click Close to exit the wizard, and select File, Save All to save the project.

The project now has a package that will import the `Customers.txt` source file into a Customers table in the AdventureWorks2012 database.

Walkthrough of a Package

To better familiarize you with the SSIS Designer package development user interface in SQL Server Data Tools, this section will explore the interface using the newly created customer import package.

The Solution Explorer shows the view of the Customer project with the packages, as shown in Figure 4.1. This view is located in the SSIS Designer in the upper-right pane. The package that was created in the previous section can be seen.

Selecting the `CustomerImport.dtsx` package will show the properties of the package in the Properties window in the lower-right pane. This is true of the interface in general; selecting an object will show its properties.

The name of the package can be changed here to something more appropriate, such as Import Customers.

To do this, follow these steps:

1. Select the `CustomerImport.dtsx` package in the Solution Explorer.

2. In the Properties pane, change the filename to `CustomerImport.dtsx`.

3. The interface asks whether the package object name should be changed as well. Click Yes to accept the change.

4. Select File, Save All to save the changes.

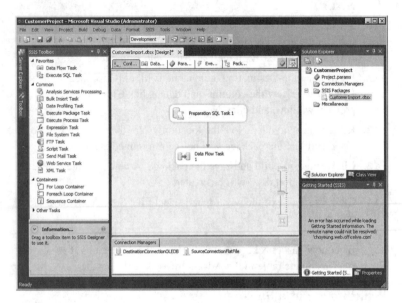

FIGURE 4.1
The Customer Import project.

The SSIS Packages folder in the Solution Explorer will show the updated name. The default package Package.dtsx can be deleted in the Solution Explorer window as well by right-clicking the package and selecting Delete. After the changes, only one package, named CustomerImport.dtsx, should be visible in the Solution Explorer.

The Error List window is located below the Connection Managers window and shows any errors, warnings, or messages that the package generates. This window is active and will show messages as soon as they are detected by the interface during the design of the package. The Error List may be hidden or minimized and can be displayed by selecting View, Error List from the menu.

Walkthrough of the Control Flow

In the Control Flow window are the control steps of the CustomerImport package. These steps are instances of control flow tasks. There are only

two tasks in this particular package: the Preparation SQL Task 1 and the
Data Flow Task 1. Clicking the Preparation SQL Task 1 will change the
focus of the Properties pane and show the properties of the task. These
properties can be difficult to interpret until you are familiar with the tasks.

An alternative method of reviewing the configuration of a task is to use the
edit function. This can be accessed by selecting the task in the designer
pane and right-clicking to select Edit. Doing this for the CustomerImport
package Preparation SQL Task shows the configuration shown in Figure
4.2. The figure shows that the task is an Execute SQL Task type, and the
SQLStatement parameters can be seen in the SQLStatement field, although
the statement scrolls off the window. Selecting the SQLStatement field will
display an ellipsis button (...) that you can click to view the SQL statement
in a larger window. This task will execute the SQL statement to create the
Customers table in the AdventureWorks2012 database in preparation for
the import. Click Cancel to close the Execute SQL Task Editor.

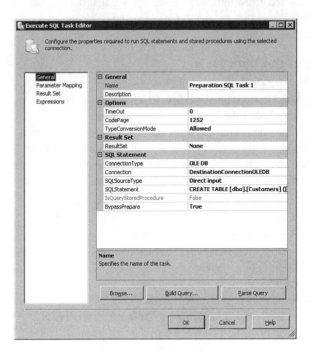

FIGURE 4.2
The Task Editor window.

The Task Editor window will change depending on the specific task being edited. The left side of the SQL Server Data Tools interface contains the Toolbox window. If the window is not visible, it can be displayed by selecting View, Toolbox from the menu. This window shows all the control flow tasks that are available. These range from the Execute SQL Task to Send Mail Task to maintenance tasks such as the Back Up Database Task. When the Control Flow designer window is open, the Toolbox window will show only control flow tasks.

The tasks in the control flow are connected by arrows. These arrows are precedence constraints, and they control the flow of execution between tasks. Preparation SQL Task 1 has a green arrow that connects to Data Flow Task 1. This indicates that Preparation SQL Task 1 must complete before Data Flow Task 1 can begin executing. The fact that the arrow is green indicates that it is a Success precedence constraint, meaning that Preparation SQL Task 1 must complete successfully before Data Flow Task 1 can begin. A red arrow indicates that the preceding task must fail, and a blue arrow indicates that as long as the preceding task completes (regardless of success or failure), the subsequent task can begin.

Walkthrough of the Data Flow

The Data Flow Task shown in the Control Flow designer window is expanded in the Data Flow designer window, which can be accessed by editing the Data Flow Task or by clicking the Data Flow tab in the designer window. The steps in the data flow are called components, which helps differentiate them from control flow tasks. The Data Flow designer window for the CustomerImport package shows two items: the Source-Customers_txt component and the Destination-Customers component.

These two items are shown in Figure 4.3. The overall architecture of the data flow is to take data from a source, transform it in some manner if needed, and put the transformed data into a destination.

Right-clicking the Source-Customers_txt item and selecting Edit shows the configuration of the source. The item in this case is a Flat File Source, as indicated by the title of the window. Clicking the Connection Managers option shows the name of the connection manager, which will be examined in "Walkthrough of the Connection Managers," later in this section. Clicking the Preview button shows a preview of the first 200 rows that will be imported from the source. Selecting the Columns option on the left shows the columns that are available from the source (the external columns) and also how the columns are mapped into the output. Columns can easily be renamed in this area. As an example of this, change

EmailAddress to SMTP in the Output Column. Finally, selecting the Error Output option on the left allows you to indicate what to do, on a column-by-column basis, in response to errors. In the case of either errors in or truncation of the column data, the choices are to fail the component (the default behavior), ignore the failure, or redirect the row. Clicking OK saves the changes to the item.

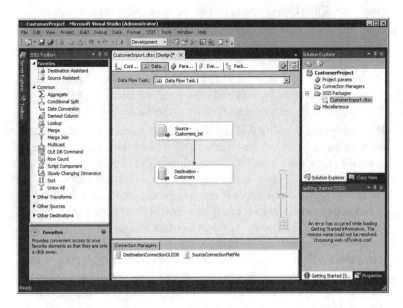

FIGURE 4.3
The Data Flow designer window.

Right-clicking the Destination–Customers item and selecting Edit shows the configuration properties of the OLE DB Destination. Selecting the Connection Managers option shows the destination connection. The OLE DB Connection Manager setting specifies the destination connection manager, which will be discussed in the next section, "Walkthrough of the Connection Managers." The Data Access mode shows how the data will be inserted into the destination, and the table or view within the database can also be selected. Various other options exist on this screen, as well, such as whether to lock the table when inserting.

Selecting the Mappings option on the left results in an error because the Customers table does not exist in the AdventureWorks2012 database. Click OK to clear the error, and then click the New button next to the Name of the table or the view field. This creates a SQL script to create the table. The name of the table will default to the name of the data flow component (Destination–Customers), so change the name in the script to dbo.Customers.

Select the Mappings options in the OLE DB Destination Editor again to show the mappings of the columns. The mappings can be adjusted here if needed.

Finally, the Error Output option on the left shows what happens if errors occur during the insertion of the data. Unlike the Flat File Source, the OLE DB Destination does not allow column-specific error handling. Either the entire row is inserted, or the entire row fails.

Much like the control flow, the Data Flow designer window has associated Toolbox items that can be accessed via the vertical tab on the left pane. The Toolbox is organized by sources, transformations, and destinations.

The components in a data flow are connected with data flow paths, which are represented by arrows, just like with the control flow tasks. However, in the data flow, the arrows indicate the flow of data from one component to another, rather than the flow of execution. Data flow paths show the connection of one component's output to another component's input. Green arrows indicate the successful data output from a component, and red arrows indicate an output that contains data with errors. Different components offer different numbers of inputs and outputs, depending on their purpose. For example, Source components do not have inputs, as they are the starting point for data entering the data flow. Destination components may have no outputs, or they may have only an error output because they are endpoints for data in a data flow.

Walkthrough of the Connection Managers

The Connection Managers window, located below the designer window, shows the source and destination connections. Right-click the SourceConnectionFlatFile connection manager and select Edit to see the properties of the source. In the General options, the filename and the format of the file are specified. Selecting the Columns option to the left will display the columns of the source, with the first 100 rows for verification. In the Advanced options window, you can adjust the details for each column, including the data type, the name of the column, and the length. You can click the Suggest Types button to scan the data and adjust the data type. Finally, use the Preview option window to preview the first 200 rows to ensure that the data is being read properly.

Editing the DestinationConnectionOLEDB connection shows the configuration setting of the destination. In this case, under the Connection options, the provider is shown as Native OLE DB\SQL Native Client 11.0. The server name is specified, as well as the form of authentication to use and the database to connect to. A Test Connection button lets you verify whether the connection is configured successfully. The All options window allows you to set the configuration at a very detailed level, such as encryption or timeout settings.

Interestingly, the specific table within the database is not specified in the destination connection manager. The connection is to the database rather than the table. The table into which the data will be inserted is specified at the item level in the data flow.

Running a Package

One of the nice features of the SQL Server Data Tools interface is the capability to run the package in the UI. This allows you to test and debug packages in a controlled environment before unleashing them on production.

The Control Flow and Data Flow windows of the package show the graphical view of the tasks in the package. In the graphical view of the flows, the status of the box is reflected in the color of the box:

- **Green**—Task Successful
- **Yellow**—Task in Progress
- **Red**—Task Failed

The Progress tab of the package shows the detailed progress, including useful information such as phase start and end, the percentage complete, and key diagnostic information. Within this window, it is easy to copy any message to paste it into a search or documentation. This information will be available even after ending debugging of the package, on the Execution Results tab.

Caution

The shortcut for running the debugger is the F5 key. This key conflicts with the standard Refresh key, which is also F5. This means if you attempt to refresh the screen using the standard shortcut key, the package may unexpectedly execute.

Be careful when refreshing in the SQL Server Data Tools.

The package in the designer runs in debugging mode. To start debugging the package, follow these steps:

1. Launch the SQL Server Data Tools.

2. Open the Customer Project created earlier.

3. Click the `CustomerImport.dtsx` in the Solution Explorer.

4. Select Debug, Start Debugging to run the package.

5. The CustomerImport package control flow Preparation SQL Task 1 will change to yellow and then to red, indicating a problem in the execution of the package.

6. Review the messages in the Output window in the lower-right corner. In particular, note the message "There is already an object named 'Customers' in the database."

7. Select the Data Flow tab and note that the data flow items have not executed; they are still white (rather than yellow, green, or red).

8. From the menu, select Debug, Stop Debugging to halt the execution.

The problem is that the Customers table was already created earlier. This table could be manually deleted, but maybe it should be dropped as part of the package execution on a normal basis. To do this, the control flow of the CustomerImport package will be adjusted to drop the Customers table. To add this task to the control flow, follow these steps:

1. With the CustomerImport package Control Flow tab selected, click the Toolbox tab.

2. Select the Execute SQL Task control flow item and drag it to the Control Flow window. Position the task above the Preparation SQL Task 1.

> **Note**
>
> Two errors will come up immediately in the Error List, which are validation errors. One indicates that no connection manager is specified, and the other indicates that validation errors exist.
>
> These errors are normal and will be resolved as the task is configured.

3. Edit the newly created task by right-clicking it and selecting Edit.

4. In the Name field, enter **Drop Customers Table SQL Task**. Enter this same text into the Description field.

5. In the Connection drop–down list, select the DestinationConnection OLEDB connection manager.

6. In the SQLStatement field, click the button to expand the field and enter the text: `drop table[dbo].[Customers]`

7. Click OK to close the SQLStatement window. Click OK again to close the Task Editor.

8. On the Drop Customers Table SQL Task, there is a green arrow. Click the arrow and drag it to the top of the Preparation SQL Task. Click to attach the arrow.

9. Save the project.

The control flow for the package should now have the Drop Customers SQL Task connected to the Preparation SQL Task 1, and the Preparation SQL Task 1 should be connected to the Data Flow Task 1 by green arrows. There should be no errors in the Error List.

Now the CustomerImport package can be run again using the menu command Debug, Start Debugging. The control flow status indicators will indicate green checkmarks indicating that the tasks completed successfully.

Enhancing Packages

This section will discuss various ways that SSIS packages can be modified to include additional functionality. This will include performing additional transformations on the data, logging messages from the package, and enabling packages to run on multiple servers without modification to the package files.

Transforming Data

In the CustomerImport package, the data was transferred without any transformation. This section will examine how the data can be transformed while being transferred.

Suppose there is a request to import the Customer data into the AdventureWorks2012 database, but the data owner wants the customers partitioned into two separate tables. One table (HighIncomeCustomers) will contain the customers with a yearly income of $100,000 or more, and the other table (ModerateIncomeCustomers) will contain customers with a yearly income of less than $100,000.

The CustomerImport package will need to be modified to support this. This requires a conditional split, which is essentially a case statement based on the yearly income.

The first step is to adjust the control flow. In the Control Flow designer of the CustomerImport package, do the following:

1. Copy and paste the Execute SQL Task to Drop the Customers Table.

2. Edit the Drop Customers Table SQL Task, changing the Name and Description to `Drop HighIncomeCustomers Table SQL Task`.

3. Edit the SQLStatement to change the `[dbo].[Customers]` to `[dbo].[HighIncomeCustomers]`.

4. Edit the second Drop Customers Table SQL Task (named Drop Customers Table SQL Task 1), changing the Name and Description to `Drop ModerateIncomeCustomers Table SQL Task`.

5. Edit the SQLStatement to change the `[dbo].[Customers]` to `[dbo].[ModerateIncomeCustomers]`.

6. Copy and paste the Preparation SQL Task 1.

7. Edit the first Preparation SQL Task 1, changing the Name and Description to `HighIncomeCustomers Preparation SQL Task`.

8. Edit the SQLStatement to change the `[dbo].[Customers]` to `[dbo].[HighIncomeCustomers]`.

9. Edit the second Preparation SQL Task 1 (named Preparation SQL Task 1 1), changing the Name and Description to `ModerateIncomeCustomers Preparation SQL Task`.

10. Edit the SQLStatement to change the `[dbo].[Customers]` to `[dbo].[ModerateIncomeCustomers]`.

11. Remove the existing arrows between the tasks by highlighting them and pressing Delete.

12. Drag the tasks into order with the drop tasks first, the preparation tasks next, and finally, the Data Flow Task.

13. Select each task starting at the top, and then drag the green arrow on the task to make them sequential.

14. Save the package as `CustomerImport2.dtsx` by selecting File, Save `CustomerImport.dtsx As`. When prompted to rename the object, choose Yes.

The control flow should now look like the control flow shown in Figure 4.4. The boxes in the figure have been adjusted to improve the readability.

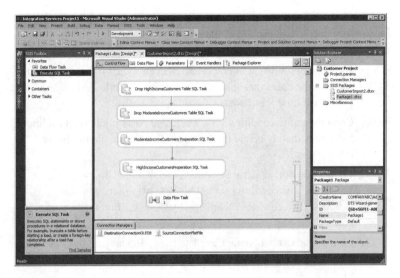

FIGURE 4.4
The CustomerImport2 package control flow.

The next adjustment to the package is to change the data flow. This is where the actual work of splitting the customers takes place.

In the Data Flow designer of the CustomerImport2 package, do the following to set up the conditional split:

1. Drag the Conditional Split item from the Toolbox.

2. Rename the Conditional Split to Conditional Split on Yearly Income. This can be done from the Properties window by setting the Name property or by selecting the Conditional Split and pressing F2.

3. Remove the existing arrow between the `Source Customers_txt` source and the destination by highlighting it and pressing Delete.

4. Select the `Source Customers_txt source`, and then click the blue arrow. Drag the arrow to the Conditional Split component.

5. Edit the Conditional Split item.

6. Expand the Type Casts folder on the right and drag the (DT_I4) type cast to the first Condition Field. The Output Name will automatically be labeled Case 1.

7. Expand the Columns folder and drag the Yearly Income column to the end of the condition for Case 1.

8. Expand the Operators folder and drag the Greater Than or Equal To (>=) operator to the end of the condition for Case 1.

9. Enter **100000** after the >= operator. Click the Output Name column, and the Condition should be black, indicating that it parsed correctly and that the data types match. The condition should be (DT_I4) [YearlyIncome]>=100000.

10. Copy the entire condition for Case 1, and paste it into the Condition field immediately below the first one. The Output Name will be labeled Case 2.

11. Change the operator from Greater Than or Equal To (>=) to Less Than (<). The condition should be (DT_I4)[YearlyIncome] <100000. The condition should be black, indicating that it parsed correctly.

12. Change the Output Name Case 1 to High Income and the Case 2 to Moderate Income. Click OK to save the changes.

The Conditional Split item is now ready to split the customers between high income and moderate income. The next step is to set up the destinations and link them to the conditional split to complete the flow.

To set up the destinations, follow these steps:

1. Copy and paste the Destination–Customers item to create a second one.

2. Rename the first Destination–Customers to Destination - High Income Customers.

3. Select the Conditional Split component, and drag the blue line to Destination–High Income Customers. Select High Income from the Output Selection dialog, and click OK.

4. Edit the Destination–High Income Customers destination, and click the New button next to the name of the table or view the drop-down list.

5. On the first line, change the text [Destination–High Income Customers] to [HighIncomeCustomers] and click OK; then click OK again to save the item.

6. Rename the second Destination–Customers 1 to Destination - Moderate Income Customers.

7. Select the Conditional Split component, and drag the blue line to Destination - Moderate Income Customers. Select Moderate Income from the Output Selection dialog, and click OK.

8. Edit the Destination–Moderate Income Customers and click the New button next to the Name of the table or view the drop-down list.

9. On the first line, change the text [Destination - Moderate Income Customers] to [ModerateIncomeCustomers] and click OK; then click OK again to save the item.

10. Drag the tasks into order with the Source-Customers_txt item first, followed by the Conditional Split, and finally, the two Destinations next to each other on the same line.

11. Save the package.

The data flow should now look like the flow in Figure 4.5. Again, the boxes have been adjusted to improve the readability of the flow.

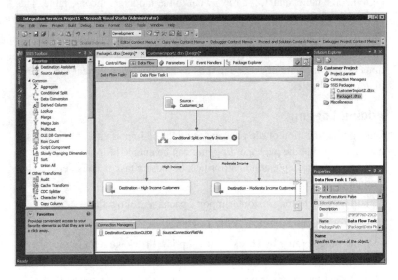

FIGURE 4.5
The CustomerImport2 package data flow.

The CustomerImport2 package is now ready to execute. Clicking Debug, Start Debugging executes the package. The package executes and shows the following messages in the Output window:

```
SSIS package "CustomerImport2.dtsx" starting.
....
Information: 0x4004300B at Data Flow Task 1,SSIS.Pipeline:
"component "Destination - High Income Customers" (94)" wrote
210 rows.
```

```
Information: 0x4004300B at Data Flow Task 1,SSIS.Pipeline:
"component "Destination - Moderate Income Customers" (252)"
wrote 1848 rows.
Information: 0x40043009 at Data Flow Task 1,SSIS.Pipeline:
Cleanup phase is beginning.
SSIS package "CustomerImport2.dtsx" finished: Success.
```

The results of the execution can also be viewed graphically in the Data Flow design window when you are debugging the package in the SQL Server Data Tools. This view is a color-coded representation of the data flow, as discussed before. In this instance, the graphic also shows the count of rows output at each step. In the figure, the number of rows from the source is 2,058. At the output of the conditional split, 210 rows went to the high income table, and 1,848 rows went to the moderate income table. This information matches the results in the Output window.

This example illustrates how easy it is to transform and manipulate the data during the data flow. A multitude of different data flow transformations exist, which are discussed in the "Data Flow" section near the beginning of the chapter.

Adding Logging

During the execution of the package, it might be important to log what is happening inside the package. Logging can be enabled for an entire package or for a single container or task because a task is considered to be a container by SSIS.

To add logging to the CustomerImport2 package, follow these steps:

1. From the menu, select SSIS, Logging.

2. Enable logging by checking the top-level package item in the Containers window—in this case, the CustomerImport2.

3. Select the Provider type for the log. In this case, use the SSIS log provider for Text files.

4. Click Add. A row will be added to the list of logs. Ensure that the check box under the Name column on the new row is checked.

5. In the window, click Configuration and use the drop-down list to select New Connection.

6. In the File Connection Manager Editor, from the Usage Type drop-down list, select Create File.

7. Enter the filename into the File field, in this case **c:\data**
   CustomerImport2.txt. If c:\data does not exist, it will need to be
   created before the package is executed. Then click OK.

8. Click the Details tab to select the events to log.

9. Select the check box next to the Events column to select all the
   events.

10. Click OK to save the logging configuration.

11. Save the package.

To test the logging, debug the package. After the package has executed,
review the log file CustomerImport2.txt. It should contain complete
details of the package execution. Logging all events does incur some overhead, however, so in real-world implementations, a subset of events should
be used. The most important events for troubleshooting are the OnError,
OnWarning, OnPreExecute, and OnPostExecute events. In many scenarios,
these provide enough information to identify the source of a problem.

Using Expressions

Expressions are a very powerful feature of SSIS that allows packages to
adjust their properties at runtime. They are a key element in developing
flexible packages that do not require manual intervention each time they
are run.

For an example of using expressions, consider the logging that was added
to the CustomerImport2 package. If the package is executed again, the log
entries for the new execution will be appended to the existing file. In a
production environment, where the package may be executed nightly or
multiple times a day, this can result in very large and difficult-to-read log
files. However, expressions can be used to start a new log file each day that
the package is run. To modify the CustomerImport2 package to use an
expression, follow these steps:

1. Select the CustomerImport2.txt connection manager in the
   Connection Managers window. Press F4 to ensure that the Properties
   window is open.

2. Locate the Expressions item in the list of properties. Select it, and
   click the ellipsis button (...) to open the Property Expressions Editor.

3. Under Property, select ConnectionString. The ConnectionString
   property holds the filename for File connection managers.

4. Click the ellipsis button next to the Expressions column.

5. In the Expression Builder dialog, type the following into the
Expression field:

```
"C:\\data\\CustomerImport2_" +
((DT_WSTR,5)YEAR(GETDATE())) + "-" +
((DT_WSTR,5)MONTH(GETDATE())) + "-" +
((DT_WSTR,5)DAY(GETDATE())) + ".txt".
```

The backslashes need to be doubled because they are escape characters in the SSIS expression language.

6. Click the Evaluate Expression button to see the results of the expression. It should appear similar to `c:\data\CustomerImport2_2008-
7-31.txt`, but with the current date.

7. Click OK to close the Expression Builder, and click OK again to
close the Property Expressions Editor.

If the package is executed again, a new log file will be created in the data
directory, with the current date appended to the filename. This is a simple
example of using expressions to make a package more dynamic. Because
they can be applied to task properties, selected data flow component properties, and variables, they offer a great deal of power in developing the
package.

Sending Email

It can be useful to have the package notify someone when it completes.
For example, it might be desirable to send an email message when the
CustomerImport2 package completes.

Follow these steps:

1. Select the Control Flow tab in the designer window of the
CustomerImport2 package.

2. Drag the Send Mail Task from the Toolbox to the Control Flow
designer window.

3. Select the Data Flow Task.

4. Select the green arrow and drag it to the Send Mail Task.

5. Edit the Send Mail Task and select the Mail options.

6. From the SmtpConnection drop-down list, select New Connection.

7. In the SMTP Server field, enter the fully qualified domain name
(FQDN) of the SMTP server, such as smtphost.companyabc.com.
Then click OK.

8. In the From field, enter the From email address.

9. In the To field, enter the destination email address.

10. In the Subject field, enter a subject, such as `CustomerImport2 Completed`.

11. In the MessageSource field, enter a message body.

12. Click OK to save the settings and then save the package.

The modified CustomerImport2 should have the Data Flow Task 1 task connected to the Send Mail Task by a green arrow. The package will send an email after the Data Flow Task completes. Notice in the Connection Manager window that there is a new SMTP Connection Manager.

The feature could be used to send an email when the control flow starts, ends, or even in intermediate stages as required.

Adding Error Handling

In spite of the best-laid plans, errors will occur during the execution of packages. However, errors in the package can be handled through the use of events.

To notify someone if the CustomerImport2 package experiences an error, execute the following steps:

1. Open the CustomerImport2 package created previously.

2. Select the Event Handler tab.

3. The CustomerImport2 executable (the package) and the `OnError` event handler are selected by default. The drop–down list shows other event handler types.

4. Click the link in the middle of the pane, which reads "Click here to create an 'OnError' event handler for executable 'CustomerImport2.'"

5. Drag the Send Mail Task from the Toolbox to the Event Handler window.

6. Edit the Send Mail Task and select the Mail options.

7. From the SmtpConnection drop-down list, select the SMTP Connection Manager. This is the same one created previously, which will be reused for this task.

8. In the From field, enter the From email address.

9. In the To field, enter the destination email address.

10. In the Subject field, enter a subject, such as CustomerImport2 Error.

11. In the MessageSource, enter a message body.

12. Click OK to save the settings, and then save the package.

To introduce an error to test the error handling, rename the source file Customers.txt in the directory C:\Program Files\Microsoft SQL Server\100\Samples\Integration Services\Package Samples\ExecuteSQL StatementsInLoop Sample\Data Files\ to Customers.tst. This will cause an error when the package attempts to import the data.

After renaming the source data file, running the package will cause an error, and the OnError event handler will trigger and execute the Send Mail Task. Interestingly, the task color will show the execution status as with any other task. If no errors exist, the event handler tasks remain white. If an error occurs, the event handler tasks will change color to reflect the execution (yellow) and their completion (green).

Restore the original filename for the source data file Customers.txt to run the package. The package should now generate the successful completion email message and not the error email message.

Although this example is a single simple task, more complex control and data flows can be created to handle error events in a more sophisticated fashion. All the tasks that are available in the Control Flow designer are also available in the event handler, including the capability to add data flows to the event handler.

Adding Configurations

Many of the configuration settings in packages are static, meaning they don't need to change between environments. But the servers to which the package will be deployed may have different configurations and settings, which can cause the package to fail. A different package could be created with different settings for each server, but this would become a maintenance headache. Package configurations are a feature in SSIS that help make packages portable, meaning that they can be moved between environments without having to modify the package itself. Package configurations allow you to store some settings for the package outside of the package itself, creating a package with dynamic settings that make it adaptable to the local conditions.

Package configurations can come from the following sources:

- Environment variables
- Registry entries
- SQL Server
- Parent package variables
- XML configuration file

An example of a static setting is the CustomerImport2 package using the SQL Server 2012 instance SQLServer01\Instance01. Perhaps this is the development instance of the database. After the package has developed to a sufficient point, it needs to be moved to a QA environment for additional testing. This QA environment is in a second instance of SQL Server 2012, SQLServer01\Instance02. To address this problem, the server name can be stored in an XML configuration file. This allows the package to be deployed to different servers easily by updating the configuration file without having to customize the package for each environment.

The steps needed to accomplish this are as follows:

1. Launch the SSIS Designer and open the Customer project.
2. Open the CustomerImport2 package.
3. Select SSIS, Package Configurations.
4. Check the Enable Package Configurations check box.

Note

You can also access the Package Configuration Organizer by clicking the ellipsis button next to the Configuration property. The Configuration property appears in the properties window for the package.

---

5. Click the Add button. Click Next.
6. From the Configuration Type drop-down list, select the XML Configuration file type.
7. Enter **c:\projects\Customer Project\Customer Project\ CustomerImport2.dtsconfig** into the Configuration filename field. Then click Next.

> **Note**
>
> SSIS does not have full support for relative paths. Instead, the full path to the configuration file should be entered here. The path to the configuration file can be modified when the package is deployed or executed.

8. In the Objects window, locate and expand the DestinationConnection OLEDB connection manager in the Connection Managers folder. Expand the Properties folder that appears under it.

9. Select the ConnectionString property.

10. Click Next.

11. Enter **Destination Connection Configuration** for the Configuration name.

12. Click Finish.

13. Click Close to close the Package Configurations Organizer.

14. Save the project.

The package configuration will now dynamically replace the destination database connection string with the contents of the XML configuration file at runtime.

Before deploying the package, it is important to test that the configuration works in the SSIS Designer. Configurations are loaded in the design environment, as well as at runtime. To test it, follow these steps:

1. Open the configuration file (c:\projects\Customer Project\Customer Project\CustomerImport2.dtsconfig) in a text editor, such as Notepad, or in SQL Server Data Tools.

> **Tip**
>
> The XML syntax for the configuration can be a little confusing, but SQL Server Data Tools makes it much easier to understand. Not only does it have syntax highlighting, but it includes an autoformatting feature that makes the XML much more readable. To use it, open the XML document, click inside it, and press Crtl+K, then Ctrl+D.

2. Locate the `<ConfiguredValue>` and `</ConfiguredValue>` tags within the XML. The connection string is contained between these two tags.

3. Update the text in the connection string that reads `Data Source=`
   `SQLServer01\Instance01;` to `Data Source=SQLServer01\`
   `Instance02;`.

4. Save the configuration file. Now close and reopen the Customer
   Import2 package in the SSIS Designer.

5. Select the DestinationConnectionOLEDB connection manager,
   and edit it. The Server Name field should show `SQLServer01\`
   `Instance02`.

6. Now open the configuration file again, and change the server
   instance back to the original value.

The fact that SQL Server Data Tools applies the configurations at design
time makes it easy to verify that they are working correctly. The package's
destination server can now be modified by altering the configuration file.
When executing the package outside of the SQL Server Data Tools environment, a command-line switch can be applied that allows the package to
use a different configuration file at runtime. This will be discussed further
in the section "Running Packages."

Tip

A common problem encountered with configurations is related to passwords. For security reasons, SSIS will not save passwords in any type of
configuration. For example, if a configuration is created for a connection
string, and the connection string uses a password instead of Windows
Authentication, the password will be removed from the connection string
that is stored in the configuration.

The workaround for this is to open the configuration directly, using the
appropriate tool for the configuration type (Notepad for XML, SQL Server
Management Studio for SQL Server, and so on) and add the password
into the connection string directly. Be aware that the configuration should
be stored securely if it will contain passwords.

Adding Maintenance Tasks

Packages are not just for extraction, transformation, and loading
(ETL). Packages are very useful in the maintenance of SQL Server 2012.
You can execute maintenance tasks such as backing up a database, rebuilding indexes, or shrinking a database. These tasks can be executed in a
series and include conditional elements to control the execution.

Note

Many of the maintenance tasks can be executed in a maintenance plan in SQL Server Management Studio. This provides a rich wizard-driven interface to create and modify maintenance plans to back up, reindex, shrink, and perform all the other maintenance tasks. These are the same SSIS maintenance tasks available in the SQL Server Data Tools environment.

SQL Server Management Studio is the preferred method of running maintenance in SQL Server 2012. However, when specific maintenance tasks need to be executed in line with control flows in a package or in response to errors in a package, SQL Server Data Tools can be used to add the appropriate tasks to the package.

Deploying and Running Integration Services Packages

After a package is designed and tested, the package will need to be deployed to an instance of SQL Server Integration Services. You can run the packages from the SSIS Designer, but they will not perform as quickly and can't be scheduled from that interface. Running packages on the server will be discussed in the "Running Packages" section later in this chapter.

Two factors are involved in deploying packages. The first is choosing a storage location for the packages. The second is how to deploy the packages to the chosen storage location.

Storing Packages

Packages can be stored in the SQL Server MSDB database, SSIS package storage, or the file system:

- **MSDB**—Packages stored in the MSDB database are stored in the sysssispackages table. Folders can be created in MSDB to help organize the packages.

Note

In SQL Server 2005, SSIS packages were stored in the sysdtspackages90 table.

- **Package Store**—Packages stored in the Package Store database are stored by default in the %Program Files%\Microsoft SQL Server\100\DTS\Packages\ directory. Folders can be created in the Package Store to help organize the packages.

- **File System**—Packages stored in the file system can be located on any accessible drive and path. File system storage is not managed by the SSIS service. The administrator simply copies .dtsx files to the designated folder.

Both MSDB storage and the Package Store can be managed from SQL Server Management Studio by connecting the Integration Services instance. Folders can be used to organize the packages in both, and packages can be imported and exported from both locations through SQL Server Management Studio. The export features allow administrators to save packages to other SSIS instances or to a file with a .dtsx extension. The exported file can be edited in SQL Server Data Tools. The Import feature can be used to import .dtsx files or packages from another SSIS instance to the local instance.

> ### Note
>
> Unfortunately, packages cannot be dragged and dropped within the folder structure of the SSIS storage. You must use the Export and Import feature to move the packages around.
>
> However, you can drag and drop files within the native Windows file system. When you do, the changes are reflected in the SSIS file system folder.

Deploying Packages

Packages can be deployed in three ways:

- Manually
- Using a Package Manifest
- Using DTUTIL.exe

Each method has its advantages and disadvantages. Manual deployment requires little preparation, but does not scale well if deploying to many servers. Packaged deployments are very customizable and can adapt to different server configurations, but require effort to create the deployment packages.

Manual Deployment

Manual deployment is straightforward and consists of importing the package into the SSIS, either to the File System storage or the SQL Server storage (MSDB).

To import a package in SQL Server Management Studio, follow these steps:

1. Choose Start, All Programs, Microsoft SQL Server 2012, SQL Server Management Studio, and then connect to an instance of SQL Server.

2. In Object Explorer, Select Integration Services from the Server Type drop-down list, and click Connect.

3. Expand the Stored Packages folder and right-click the File System folder. Select Import Package.

4. Select the location of the package—in this case, File System. Enter the path and filename for the package. Alternatively, click the button next to the Package path field to browse for a package. Browse to the locations of the CustomerImport2 package, which is in C:\Projects\Customer Projects\Customer Project\, and select the CustomerImport2.dtsx file. Click Open.

5. Click in the Package Name field. The package name CustomerImport2 will be filled in automatically, but can be changed if needed. Click OK to import the package.

The package will be displayed in the File System folder and can now be run or scheduled from there.

Tip

An alternative to going through the import process described in the preceding steps is to copy the .dtsx file to the file system directory, by default %Program Files%\Microsoft SQL Server\100\DTS\Packages. This can be useful if you want to deploy an entire folder of packages at once. However, this method can't be used if you want to store the packages in MSDB.

Building a Package Deployment Utility

Deploying the package requires that a deployment utility be built. This utility is the executable that will install the package on a target server.

To build the deployment utility, execute the following steps:

1. Right-click the Customer Project in the Solution Explorer window, and select Properties.

2. Select the Deployment Utility option page.

3. Change the CreateDeploymentUtility value to True.

4. Note the DeploymentOutputPath option. This is the location where the utility will be built underneath the project directory structure. Click OK to save the settings.

5. Select Build, Build Customer Project. This will create the files needed to deploy the package to another server.

The build will have created three files: `Customer Project.SSISDeploymentManifest`, `CustomerImport2.dtsx`, and `CustomerImport2.dtsConfig`. These will be located in the project directory, specifically `C:\Projects\Customer Project\Customer Project\bin\Deployment\`.

Note

The deployment build is for the entire project, so all the packages in the project will be deployed to the destination server. This allows a set of packages that deliver a solution to be bound and installed together as a unit.

The next step is to install the package on the destination server.

1. Copy the files in `C:\Projects\Customer Project\Customer Project\bin\Deployment\` to the destination server—in this case, SQLServer02.

2. On the destination server—in this case, SQLServer02—double-click the `Customer Project.SSISDeploymentManifest` file. This launches the Package Installation Wizard. Click Next on the first page.

3. Leave the default File System deployment and click Next.

4. Ensure that the folder is C:\Program Files\Microsoft SQL Server\100\DTS\Packages\Customer Project, and click Next.

5. Click Next to install the package.

6. The package configuration file can be updated on this page. Expand the Properties item, and update the text under the Value column from `Data Source=SQLServer01\Instance01` in the connection string to `Data Source=SQLServer01\Instance02`. Then click Next.

7. Click Finish to close the Summary window.

The package installation can be verified by launching the SQL Server Management Studio. The Customer Project and the CustomerImport2 package should be visible in Stored Packages, File System. The package can now be run or scheduled as described in "Running Packages," later in this chapter.

Using DTUTIL

DTUTIL is a command-line utility that can be used to deploy packages, among other things. It has the ability to apply a password to the package when it is deployed, regenerate package identifiers (used to uniquely identify a package for logging purposes), and to digitally sign packages. Unlike the package manifest, it can be run without requiring user interaction, making it ideal for large-scale, automated deployments.

Securing SSIS Packages

SQL Server Integration Services supports a number of security features. These security features protect the packages from unauthorized execution, modification, sensitive information, and even protect the entire contents of the packages. This section describes the database roles and the protection levels for packages.

> ### Note
>
> In addition to the security that SSIS provides to packages, you must also be concerned with other areas of security with regard to packages. Packages frequently use data files, configuration files, and log files. These files are not protected by the security mechanisms within SSIS.
>
> To ensure that confidential information is not exposed, you must protect the locations of these files as well. Typically, you do this at the operating system level through Access Control List (ACL) controls and the Encrypting File System (EFS).

SSIS has three database roles for controlling access to packages. They roughly fall into the categories of administrator, user, and operator. If more granularity is needed in the rights assignment, you can create user-defined roles.

The fixed database level roles and their rights are listed in Table 4.6.

Table 4.6   **Fixed Security Roles**

Role	Description
db_ssisadmin or sysadmin	This role gives users all the available SSIS rights. This includes enumerating, viewing, executing, importing, exporting, and deleting any package.
db_ssisltduser	This role gives users the ability to enumerate all packages. However, the user is limited to viewing, executing, importing, exporting, and deleting only the user's own packages.
db_ssisoperator	This role gives users the ability to enumerate, view, execute, and export any package.
Windows Administrators	Windows Administrators can view all currently executing packages and stop the execution of any package.

Protection levels are set on packages when they are created in the SQL Server Data Tools or the wizards. These protection levels prevent the unauthorized execution or modification of packages. Protection levels can be updated on packages when they are imported into the SSIS package store.

The protection levels refer to sensitive information in what they protect. These are typically passwords in connection managers, but can include any task property or variable that is marked as sensitive.

The options for protection levels are listed in the following sections.

Do Not Save Sensitive (DontSaveSensitive)

The DontSaveSensitive option suppresses sensitive information in the package when it is saved. This protection level does not encrypt; instead, it prevents properties that are marked sensitive from being saved with the package, and therefore makes the sensitive data unavailable when the package is closed and reopened. This protection level is often combined with Package Configurations to store the secure information.

Caution

Configurations must have secure information manually entered because SSIS will not save sensitive data to a configuration. After sensitive information has been added, the configuration needs to be protected because the SSIS security mechanisms do not apply to configuration files.

Encrypt All/Sensitive with Password (`EncryptAllWithPassword`/
`EncryptSensitiveWithPassword`)
The `EncryptAllWithPassword` or `EncryptSensitiveWithPassword`
option encrypts the package by using a password the user supplies when
the package is created or exported. To open the package in SSIS Designer
or run the package by using the `DTEXEC` command-prompt utility, the user
must provide the package password. Using the `EncryptAll*` option encrypts
the entire package, and the `EncryptSensitive*` option will encrypt just the
items designated as sensitive.

Encrypt All/Sensitive with User Key (`EncryptAllWithUserKey`/
`EncryptSensitiveWithUserKey`)
The `EncryptSensitiveWithUserKey` option is the default setting for packages. The `EncryptAllWithUserKey` or `EncryptSensitiveWithUserKey`
option encrypts the package by using a key based on the user profile. Only
the user who created or exported the package can decrypt the information
in the package, preventing other users from using the package with the
sensitive information included. Using the `EncryptAll*` option encrypts the
entire package, and the `EncryptSensitive*` option encrypts just the items
designated as sensitive. This Protection Level option can create challenges
in real-world scenarios because only a single user can use or modify the
package.

Rely on Server Storage for Encryption (`ServerStorage`)
The `ServerStorage` option protects the whole package using SQL Server
database roles. This option is supported only when a package is saved to
the SQL Server MSDB database. It is not supported when a package is
saved to the file system from SQL Server Data Tools.

Running Packages

You can trigger the packages from within the SQL Server Management
Studio and monitor their execution progress in detail.

Using Management Studio to Run Packages
To run a package (using the CustomerImport2 package) within SSIS, do
the following:

1. Choose Start, All Programs, Microsoft SQL Server 2012, SQL
   Server Management Studio, and then connect to an instance of SQL
   Server.

2. Select Integration Services from the Server Type drop-down list and click Connect.

3. Expand the Stored Packages folder, and then the File System folder.

4. Right-click the CustomerImport package imported earlier and select Run Package. The Execute Package Utility runs.

5. In the General options page, you will see the package source, the server, the authentication, and the package name.

6. Click the Reporting options page to see the reporting options available.

7. Click the Set Values options page to see the options available. Using this page, properties on the package can be overridden at runtime. This is a useful feature for changing values that may need to be unique for each execution of the package.

8. Click the Command Line options page to see the command-line version of the execution. This capability is useful to automate the package execution in the future.

Note

You can add parameters to the command line by selecting the Edit the Command Line Manually option.

---

9. Click Execute to run the package.

10. The Package Execution Progress window opens, displaying the package progress and information. This is the same information displayed on the Progress tab in SQL Server Data Tools. The message should indicate that 210 rows were written to the HighIncomeCustomers table, and 1,848 rows were written to the ModerateIncomeCustomers table.

11. Click Close to close the Progress window.

12. Click Close to close the Execute Package utility.

Note

The Execute Package Utility can be opened without using SQL Server Management Studio. Run DTEXECUI at a command prompt, and it will open.

> **Caution**
>
> The Execute Package Utility is useful for setting up a package to execute. However, packages that report a large amount of information will run progressively slower when run from the Execute Package Utility. For this reason, it is better to execute large or long-running packages from DTEXEC (the command-line version of the Execute Package Utility) or from SQL Server Agent.
>
> Also, running a package from SQL Server Management Studio through the Execute Package Utility or DTEXEC uses the local machine's resources to execute the package. If SQL Server Management Studio is connected to a remote server, the package is executed using the resources of the local machine, not the remote server. To ensure that the server resources are used, run the package from SQL Server Agent.

Using DTEXEC to Run Packages

DTEXEC is a command-line utility for executing packages. It supports all the options of the Execute Package Utility, but does not use a GUI. This makes it ideal for automating package executions. It can be used from a CmdExec step in a SQL Agent job or from any tool capable of calling a command-line utility. The complete list of command-line switches for DTEXEC is available in Books Online.

Scheduling Packages

Packages can be scheduled to run automatically using the SQL Server Agent. The package needs to be accessible to the SQL Server Agent to be scheduled.

In this example, the CustomerImport2 package needs to be run every day at 6 a.m. to update the Customer table. To schedule a package for execution, follow these steps:

1. Choose Start, All Programs, Microsoft SQL Server 2012, SQL Server Management Studio, and then connect to an instance of SQL Server..

2. Connect to the Database Engine of the SQL Server.

3. Right-click SQL Server Agent and select New, Job.

4. In the General options page, enter the name of the job—in this example, Daily Customer Update.

5. Select the Steps option page, and click New to create a new step.

6. Enter the Step name—in the example, Update Customer.

7. In the Type drop-down list, select SQL Server Integration Services Package.

8. In the Package Source drop-down list, select the SSIS Package Store.

9. In the Server drop-down list, select SQLServer01 as the server name.

10. Click the Package selection button to the right of the Package field.

11. Browse the Select an SSIS Package window to find the CustomerImport2 package imported earlier. Then click OK.

12. Click OK to save the step.

13. Select the Schedules option page and click New to create a new job schedule.

14. In the Name field, enter **Daily at 6 AM**. In the Occurs drop-down list, select Daily. Change the Occurs Once at field to 6:00:00 AM.

15. Click OK to save the schedule, and click OK again to save the job.

The job will now run the SSIS package at 6 a.m. every day. The job is saved in the database and can be reviewed in the Jobs folder within the SQL Server Agent. You can test it by right-clicking the job and selecting Start Job.

Jobs can run a series of packages in a sequence of steps and even with conditional branches that depend on the output of the preceding packages. This allows packages to be chained together to complete a larger task.

By default, packages will be run under the permissions of the SQL Agent account. If the packages need additional privileges, a proxy account can be used for the SQL Server Agent job. See the topic "Creating SQL Server Agent Proxies" in Books Online.

Transferring Data with Integration Services

The Data Flow Task is the primary means of transferring data with SSIS. However, there are additional options for specific needs that DBAs face on a regular basis. Among the items available are the ability to copy databases and to perform bulk inserts of data.

Using the Copy Database Wizard

SSIS includes a Transfer Database Task that can be included in packages. This is useful if other tasks need to be performed in conjunction with the database transfer because the SSIS package can be used to coordinate them. In addition to the Transfer Database Task, a database can be copied using the SQL Server Management Studio Copy Database Wizard. This process is useful if the database will need to be copied only once or if the transfer of the database is all that needs to be accomplished. Follow these steps to copy the AdventureWorks2012 database from SQLServer01\Instance01 to SQLServer01\Instance02 using the Copy Database Wizard:

1. Choose Start, All Programs, Microsoft SQL Server 2012, SQL Server Management Studio, and then connect to an instance of SQL Server.

2. Connect to the source database server—in this case, SQLServer01\Instance01. Expand the Databases folder.

3. Right-click the AdventureWorks2012 database and select Tasks, Copy Database. Click Next at the first page of the wizard.

4. Select the Source server, which should be the SQLServer01\Instance01 server, and click Next.

5. Select the Destination server, which should be the SQLServer01\Instance02 server, and click Next.

6. The default Transfer Method is to use the detach and attach method, which will bring the source database offline. Because this would be disruptive, select Use the SQL Management Object Method. This will keep the source database online. Click Next to continue.

7. Verify that the AdventureWorks2012 database is selected, and click Next.

8. Change the option to drop the destination database if it already exists, which is the Drop Any Database option. This forces an overwrite of the database on the destination server. Click Next.

9. Don't select any additional objects to transfer. Ensure that Logins are not selected to transfer. Click Next.

10. Click Next to leave the package defaults. Then click Next to run immediately.

11. Review the choices and click Finish to execute the transfer.

Note

Depending on the security context that the SQL Agent account is run under, a proxy account may need to be specified that has access to both the source and destination databases.

This method is easy to use for a one-time copy of a database. Note that the wizard creates a package in the MSDB storage of the destination server, which can be seen by connecting to the SSIS on the destination server. This package can be run more than once if there is a need to copy the database on a regular basis.

Using the Bulk Insert Task

The Bulk Insert Task can be used to import text files into SQL Server tables. The Bulk Insert Task is very efficient at loading large amounts of data, but can't perform any data conversion or transformations. The text file to be imported must be delimited and can use a format file to define the rows and columns. To use it, follow these steps:

1. Launch the SSIS Designer and open the Customer project.

2. Create a new package by selecting Project, New SSIS Package.

3. Rename the package to `BulkInsertCustomer.dtsx` by right-clicking the package in the Solution Explorer and selecting Rename. When prompted, select Yes to rename the package object.

4. Drag the Bulk Insert Task from the Toolbox to the Control Flow designer. Edit the task by right-clicking and selecting Edit.

5. Select the Connection option. Click the Connection drop-down list and select New Connection. In the Configure OLE DB Connection Manager dialog box, click New to create a new connection. Specify the Server name as SQLServer01\Instance01 and the database as AdventureWorks2012. Click OK, and then click OK again to return to the Bulk Insert Task Editor.

6. In the Destination Table field, select the [AdventureWorks2012].[dbo].[Customers] table that was created in earlier samples.

7. Ensure that the ColumnDelimiter field is set to Tab.

8. Click the File drop-down list and select New Connection. Set the Usage Type to Existing File and browse to the C:\Program Files\Microsoft SQL Server\100\Samples\Integration Services\Package Samples\ExecuteSQLStatementsInLoop Sample\Data Files\Customers.txt file. Click Open, and then click OK to return to the Bulk Insert Task Editor.

9. Select the Options option to the left, and set the FirstRow field to 2, to skip the first row containing the column headers.

10. To see the package run, select Debug, Start Debugging. The package should run, and the Bulk Insert Task should turn green.

Caution

The Bulk Insert Task will append the rows to what already exists in the table. To delete the existing rows first, add an Execute SQL Task to truncate the table first.

Note

There is also the Bulk Copy utility (`bcp.exe`), which can be used to manually import or export data from a table. The bcp utility bulk copies data from or to a data file from an existing table in a database.

The Bulk Copy utility is less convenient than the wizards because it requires that the table be created in advance, and the command options are relatively obscure. However, it can be useful for getting information from older versions of SQL Server.

Moving Data to the Cloud

Many organizations interested in finding ways to reduce total cost of ownership are moving their data and managing it in the cloud with Windows Azure SQL Database, formerly known as SQL Azure Database. The next two sections introduce Windows Azure SQL Database and provides an example of how data is moved to the cloud.

Introducing Windows Azure SQL Database

SQL Database is Microsoft's public cloud relational database, which offers a large-scale multi-tenant database service hosted and managed in Microsoft datacenters throughout the world. With SQL Database, Microsoft provides enterprise class availability, scalability, security, and self-healing, while still allowing DBAs to create and manage databases, logins, users, and roles. This kind of flexibility resonates in SQL Server. For example, Microsoft SQL Server offers the cloud on your terms. As such, a hybrid IT environment can be built where there may be a mix of on-premise and off-premise platforms hosting your mission-critical databases. In addition, note the enhancements SQL Server 2012 brings to SQL Server Management Studio, which will easily allow DBAs to migrate databases from on-premises to SQL Database in the cloud. The Deploy Database to

SQL Database wizard allows a DBA to achieve the following cloud-based goals:

- Migrate a database from on-premise to SQL Database.
- Migrate a database from SQL Database to on-premise.
- Move a database from one instance of SQL Database to another.

Let's turn our attention to the actual step-by-steps to achieve this goal.

Migrating Databases to Windows Azure SQL Database

The following steps showcase how to migrate a database from an on-premise instance of SQL Server to SQL Database. The steps that follow use the Deploy Database Wizard to migrate a database.

> **Note**
>
> This example assumes you have a Windows Azure account and have already created a SQL Server instance. If not, obtain a trial account by clicking the Get the Free Trial link under Windows Azure on http://msdn.microsoft.com/en-us/. Use the Windows Azure Database Management tools to create the SQL Server instance. In addition, you may have to update the firewall rules with the IP address of the server you plan to use to connect to the SQL Server instance via SQL Server Management Studio.

1. In Object Explorer, right-click a desired instance of SQL Server and expand the Database folder.

2. Right-click the database you want to deploy to Windows Azure SQL Database, select Tasks, and then choose Deploy Database to SQL Azure to invoke the Deploy Database Wizard. For this example, a database called TestDatabase containing two tables was used.

3. On the Introduction page, review the welcome message and click Next.

4. Conduct the following steps on the Deployment Settings page, as illustrated in Figure 4.6:

   a. Click the Connect button and specify the name and login credentials of the SQL Azure server that will host the database you want deployed to the cloud.

   b. In the SQL Azure Database Settings, choose the appropriate edition of SQL Database from the drop-down menu, such as Business or Web.

   c. Choose the maximum database size (in GB) from the drop-down menu.

   d. Specify a local directory for the temporary file.

   e. Click Next to continue.

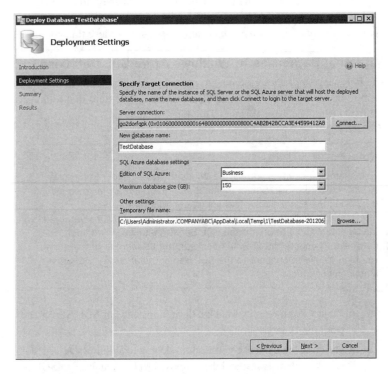

FIGURE 4.6
Deployment Settings on the Deploy Database to SQL Database Wizard.

   5. On the Summary page, review the specific source and target configurations selected for this operation, and then click Finish to commence the deployment.

   6. The progress page is invoked as illustrated in Figure 4.7. This page displays a progress bar that indicates the status for the following items:

     ■ Extracting schema from database

     ■ Resolving references in schema model

- Validating schema model
- Validating schema for data package
- Exporting data from database
- Processing database
- Creating database on target
- Importing database
- Creating deployment plan

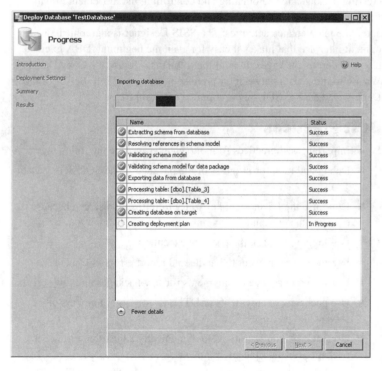

FIGURE 4.7
Viewing the Progress Report on the Deploy Database to SQL Database Wizard.

7. Review the Results page to ensure each operation was successful, and click Finish to close the wizard.

> **Note**
>
> View the new database using the Windows Azure SQL Database portal or connect to the SQL Server instance in Windows Azure with SQL Server Management Studio.

Summary

Packages and the SQL Server Data Tools provide a rich environment for creating packages for automating and controlling the movement of data. Packages are very useful, not only to import or export data but also to automate maintenance activities. The SSIS Designer is a graphical development interface that makes it easy for even the beginning DBA to create, test, and deploy packages. In addition, remember to use the Copy Database Wizard to move data between on-premise instances of SQL Server or the Deploy Database to SQL Azure to move data to the cloud.

Best Practices

Some important best practices from the chapter include the following:

- Debug and monitor progress of the package in the SQL Server Data Tools.
- Don't use the F5 shortcut key to try to refresh the screen because it executes the current package instead.
- Use logging to track the package execution.
- Use the OnError event to handle and report errors in packages.
- Use manual package deployments for few packages and few servers.
- Use packaged deployments or DTUTIL for larger numbers of servers and packages.
- Use package configurations to dynamically adjust the settings of packages for multiple environments.
- Use expressions to make packages more dynamic.
- Use maintenance plans to set up maintenance for databases, rather than packages.
- Use package tasks to include specific maintenance tasks within packages.
- Use the Copy Database Wizard for one-time database transfers.

CHAPTER 5

Managing and Optimizing SQL Server 2012 Indexes

SQL Server 2012 uses indexes to structure and optimize access to data found within the tables of a database. Index design, maintenance, and optimization are key factors that contribute to how well a database performs. Although the lack of indexes or the use of poorly designed indexes, along with inadequate maintenance, can lead to performance degradation, well-designed and maintained indexes can significantly improve the overall performance of a database by reducing the disk I/O cost associated with locating data.

When you are performing management and administrative tasks on indexes, it is important to understand the various options and tools that help DBAs make the right index management and optimization decisions.

What's New for Indexes with SQL Server 2012

- Columnstore indexes are a revolutionary new concept allowing blistering performance gains compared to traditional indexes in data warehouse and read-intensive environments.

- Query hints, although not strictly a change to how indexes are stored, now allow new behaviors for the FORCESEEK hint and provide a new hint called FORCESCAN, which alters the behavior of how the query optimizer uses only an index scan operation as the access path to the referenced table or view.

- Spatial indexes, introduced in SQL Server 2008, have many improvements. For further information, refer to the spatial index sections.

The Importance of Indexes

A well-planned indexing strategy allows fast and efficient access to the underlying data. Indexes can be created on tables (and views in Enterprise Edition) and allows SQL Server to locate and manage data requests more efficiently. When efficiency is improved, the amount of time each operation takes is reduced, along with the cost, in SQL Server resources associated with performing the operation.

Index design is best performed during development of the database application. The reason is that the ability to create effective indexes is based on understanding how application queries are coded and how the data is stored in the database. However, indexes also require management after the database application is deployed and as usage patterns emerge or change. You can see examples of how to achieve this later in the chapter.

Managing and optimizing indexes as an ongoing process allows potential performance improvements without requiring changes to the underlying schema. As data is queried, the SQL Server Query Optimizer automatically determines the best method to access the data based on the type of operation and the available indexes.

How Indexes Work

The data within a SQL Server 2012 database is logically stored within tables. The data within a table is grouped into allocation units based on the column data type. The data within each allocation unit is physically stored in 8KB pages.

Note

For efficiency, groups of eight pages are managed together in a physical unit. This 64KB group of pages is referred to as an *extent*.

Pages within a table store the actual data rows along with the different structures to facilitate locating the data. When the rows of data associated with a table are not logically sorted, the table is referred to as a *heap* structure.

When a clustered index is created, the data in the heap is rearranged and becomes part of the index. A nonclustered index is created as a separate structure that simply points to the location of the data in the heap or clustered index. The different types of indexes have advantages and disadvantages along with different characteristics that need to be considered as part of the ongoing indexing maintenance strategy.

Note

By default, an index with a single partition is comparable to the organizational structure of tables and indexes in previous versions of SQL Server as it is stored within a single filegroup. If multiple partitions are leveraged, the index will span the partitions horizontally and can ultimately be placed in multiple filegroups, which may lead to increased performance.

Heap Structures

Ultimately, a heap is a table without a clustered index where data is not stored in any particular order. A heap structure is often the least efficient method of querying data rows in a table because all rows in the table are scanned each time the data is queried, making it an extremely intensive process. For example, when a specific row of data is needed or when a range of data is needed, all pages in the table are scanned to ensure the correct result is returned. A simile may help further explain heap structures. Searching for data on the heap structure would be like looking up a word in a dictionary that wasn't presented in alphabetical order or looking for a particular topic in a book that didn't contain an index. In any dictionary or book, an individual can look up the words "SQL Server" by scanning the words under the letter S—simple. On the other hand, if all words in a dictionary were stored based on a heap structure, the words would not be stored in a logical order, forcing people to search the dictionary page by page—ouch!

There are a few situations when the heap structure may be an efficient structure when dealing with small tables, infrequently accessed tables, or when large amounts of data are frequently written to or deleted from the table. The index maintenance cost can often outweigh any potential performance improvement on these types of tables. It is often recommended to avoid creating indexes on tables that fall into these categories.

Clustered Indexes

Only one clustered index can be created for a table; because a table can have only one physical order, it is commonly placed on *key* columns or columns used frequently, such as the ones referenced by the WHERE clause. When a clustered index is created, the table is sorted into a *b-tree* structure, allowing SQL Server to quickly locate the correct data. Figure 5.1 shows an example of a clustered index based on b-tree storage structure.

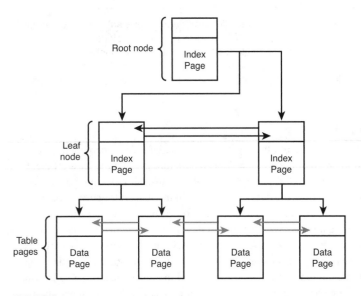

FIGURE 5.1
Clustered index b-tree structure.

The top of the index contains the root node, the starting position for the index. The intermediate level contains the index key data; the index data can point to other intermediate pages or the data in the leaf level. The leaf level nodes located at the bottom of the b-tree contain the actual table data. When the data in the table is queried, the Database Engine can quickly navigate the b-tree structure and locate specific data without having to scan each page.

> **Note**
>
> By default, primary keys are created using a clustered index, in turn creating an ordered table. It is possible to create, and is sometime advantageous to create a primary key using a nonclustered index. For example, it is common for developers to use the NEWID() function to populate a primary key instead of having to implement several round-trips fetching identity values for child records. The issue with this methodology is that the key is not ever increasing and so is highly susceptible to causing fragmentation because of its randomness in nature. This, in turn, leads to poor performance.

Nonclustered Indexes

Nonclustered indexes are implemented as a separate b-tree structure materializing the sorted data on new pages so that it does not affect the pages in the underlying table. Unlike a clustered index, more than one nonclustered index can be placed on columns within a table. Figure 5.2 shows an example of a nonclustered index b-tree.

The top of the index contains the root node, the starting position for the index. However, unlike clustered indexes, a nonclustered index does not contain any data pages and does not modify the data in the source table. The index pages on the leaf node contain a row locator that references the data in the associated table as well as any included columns.

If the underlying table is also clustered, the leaf node pages in the nonclustered index point to the corresponding clustered index key. If the underlying table does not have a clustered index, the leaf node pages in the nonclustered index point to the corresponding row in the heap using a row id.

Indexed Views

When a view is queried, the resulting data is materialized at runtime. Depending on the amount of data returned, a high cost can be associated with the materialization process. To reduce the cost of using complex views, you can create an index on a column in the view.

> **Note**
>
> The Query Optimizer may select a view index automatically, even if the view is not explicitly named in the FROM clause.

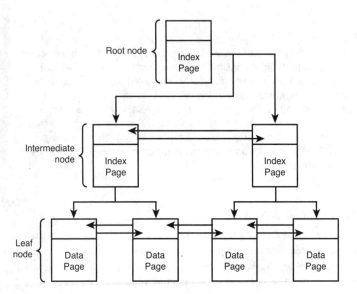

FIGURE 5.2
Nonclustered index b-tree structure.

The data that would normally be materialized during runtime is persisted as another physical copy in the database based on the same format as the columns referenced in the view. When the underlying data is changed, the related indexed views are automatically maintained just as clustered and nonclustered indexes are maintained.

Filtered Indexes

This feature can be described as an optimized nonclustered index that essentially behaves like a normal index with one exception: It covers only a well-defined subset of data found in a column. It might help to think of a filtered index as a regular index with a WHERE clause that identifies and indexes specific pieces of data in a column. Some advantages of using filtered indexes over traditional nonclustered indexes include smaller indexes, which in turn improve performance and reduce storage costs. Having a filter on the index may have a positive effect on statistics, which can lead to better estimations in query plans. In addition, filtered indexes reduce maintenance costs because a filter index needs to update only the subset of data when changes take place. It is a best practice to include a small number of keys or included columns in a filtered index definition and to incorporate only the columns that are necessary for the query optimizer to choose the filtered index for the query execution plan. The query optimizer can choose a filtered index for the query regardless of whether it does or does not cover the query. However, the query optimizer is more likely to choose a filtered index if it covers the query.

> **Note**
>
> Filtered indexes are the only indexes that do not contain one row per corresponding row in the base table. It is a common misconception that a null value in a table will not be in the index; this is not true. Because of this filter, a scan operation on a filtered index will not be as expensive as scans on other indexes against the base table.

Columnstore Indexes

With the release of SQL Server 2008, Microsoft introduced Star join optimization to improve the performance of Data Warehouse queries. This was joined by the very welcome addition of data compression in the form of page- and row-based compression algorithms.

SQL Server 2012 introduces some new technologies that push the current boundaries of data warehouses with Project Apollo, the codename for the latest set of advances that are all based around the column store structure, on which columnstore indexes can be created.

The terms column store and columnstore index are almost synonymous in SQL Server 2012 because the process of creating a columnstore index creates another copy of the data, but instead of being in the traditional row store format with a b-tree as per clustered and nonclustered indexes, they are stored in columns.

The example in Figure 5.3 shows a simplified definition of a single page of data with four attributes in each record that are often referred to as rows or slots. When a traditional data or index page is read, all attributes in the row are read if they are required or not. If unrequired attributes are read in, this is a waste of precious resources.

In contrast, as the name column store suggests, each attribute or column is stored on its own dedicated page or series of pages. This means that queries that run against column store structures read in only the necessary data. This reduces I/O, resulting in better performance. The fact that less data is read in means that less memory is being used when stored in the buffer cache. This may help keep pages in memory longer, meaning that physical disk reads happen less often, again resulting in better performance.

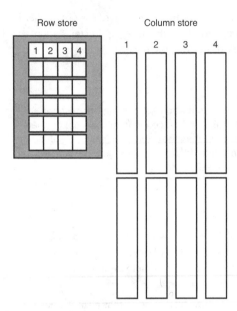

FIGURE 5.3
Row store versus column store storage comparison.

Columnstore indexes further improve performance by compressing the data using Run Length Encoding (RLE) and/or bit packing. This compression leads to further I/O savings because more data can be stored on a page. As mentioned in the previous paragraph, this will also lead to less need for memory and a higher page life expectancy. Page life expectancy is covered in Chapter 14, "Performance Tuning and Troubleshooting SQL Server 2012."

Compression works by finding values that are the same and replacing those subsequent identical values with other values that take up less space. This process is often referred to as bit rate reduction using lossless compression. SQL Server uses a very similar algorithm in its dictionary compression, which is part of page compression. Row compression is achieved by removing unnecessary spaces. In indexes, the data is sorted, which often leads to a low cardinality or highly redundant data; this type of data can be highly compressed. When using columnstores, each record is split across multiple pages. This could potentially lead to issues compressing data in composite indexes on the nonleading columns. To combat this, Microsoft uses a technology called VertiPaq, which was first introduced into PowerPivot and subsequently SQL Server Analysis Services in 2012.

The task of VertiPaq is to find the most efficient way of sorting multiple columns to compress them in the most efficient way possible. VertiPaq was first introduced to SQL Server in PowerPivot and has subsequently been added to SQL Server Analysis Services.

Batch Mode Processing

As the name suggests, batch mode processing processes a batch of data rather than a single row. This new method is highly optimized for the Nehalem/Opteron-style CPUs. The new algorithms used include benefits such as being able to process the compressed data in a number of cases, in contrast to traditional row and page compression, which would require each row on the page to be decompressed prior to processing. This results in much better use of parallelism and CPU cycles.

Spatial Indexes

The spatial data types include the geography data type for storing geodetic data and the geometry data type to store planar data. As more businesses seek applications and devices that deliver location intelligence, storing spatial data directly in SQL Server relational tables is becoming more popular and a regularly requested task. As such, DBAs need to become familiar with creating indexes for spatial data because a need now exists to enhance queries associated with this emerging type of data.

XML Indexes

XML indexes can be created on XML columns and should be considered when working with XML data types. The XML columns in a table are stored as binary large objects (BLOBs) and are subject to the 2GB limitation. Normally, when XML columns are queried, the data is shredded during runtime and placed into a relational table. The cost associated with this operation can be very high indeed, depending on the size of the XML column. An XML index shreds the data when the index is created, eliminating the cost of this operation during runtime. There is, however, a high cost associated with modification of indexed XML data; this may make it more suited to a relatively static data set.

A single primary index and three types of secondary indexes can exist on each XML column in a table for a total of 249 different XML indexes. Unlike traditional indexes, XML indexes cannot be created on views, table-valued variables, or computed XML columns.

General Index Characteristics

Whereas pages in a heap are not linked or related to each other, index pages are linked; this link type is typically referred to as a doubly linked list. This means one link points to the previous page, and one points to the next page. The doubly linked list effectively allows the Database Engine to quickly locate specific data or the starting and ending points of the range by moving through the index structure.

Both clustered and nonclustered indexes are stored as a b-tree structure. The b-tree structure logically sorts pages with the intention of reducing the amount of time needed to search for data. For example, when you're querying a heap, the entire table must be scanned because the data is not sorted. However, when you're querying a b-tree, the logical and physical organization of data allows the correct rows to be located quickly.

When creating an index, you must select one or more key columns. The index key can be any column with the exception of the varchar(max), nvarchar(max), varbinary(max), ntext, text, image, and XML data types. The combined length of the selected key column cannot exceed 900 bytes.

The effectiveness of an index is based on the key columns, so choosing the correct key columns is an important part of the clustered index design.

How Column Constraints Affect Indexes

Constraints can be defined on columns to ensure data integrity. For example, a constraint can be configured on a column that contains phone numbers to make sure that only valid phone numbers are entered in the correct format with the correct number of digits. When a unique constraint is created, a unique index is created behind the scenes. Likewise, when the primary key constraint is applied to a column, a unique clustered index is automatically created. In this scenario, if a clustered index already exists for the table, a nonclustered index is created instead.

How Computed Columns Affect Indexes

A computed column uses an expression to generate its value. Unless the computed column is marked as PERSISTED, the value of the computed column is not stored in the table like other columns; it is calculated when the data is queried.

Indexes can be created that include these columns. However, because of the complexity associated with computed columns, specific prerequisites must be met. Following are the prerequisites for indexes on computed columns:

- **Determinism**—The computed column expression must be deterministic. For example, the computed column expression can't use the SUM, AVG, or GETDATE functions because the result may change. On the other hand, the DATEADD and DATEDIFF functions are considered deterministic because they will always produce the same result based on the dates being calculated.

- **Precision**—The computed column expression must use precise data types. For example, the computed column expression can't normally use the float or real data types because the returned value may change slightly between queries. However, the float and real data types can be used if the column is also marked as PERSISTED because the imprecise data is calculated and stored in the table.

- **Data Type**—The computed column expression cannot evaluate to the text, ntext, or image data types. However, these columns can be included as nonkey columns in a nonclustered index.

- **Ownership**—The table and all functions referenced by the computed column must have the same owner.

- **Set Options**—The ANSI_NULLS option must be ON when using the CREATE TABLE and ALTER TABLE statements. When you're using the INSERT, UPDATE, and DELETE statements, the NUMERIC_ROUNDABORT option must be set to OFF, and the ANSI_NULLS, ANSI_PADDING, ANSI_WARNINGS, ARITHABORT, CONCAT_NULL_YIELDS_NULL, and QUOTED_IDENTIFIER options must be set to ON.

Clustered Index Characteristics

When a clustered index is created, the data in the table is sorted into the leaf nodes of a b-tree, essentially making the data in the table part of the index. Each table can contain only one clustered index because the data can be physically sorted one way.

Nonclustered Index Characteristics

When a nonclustered index is created, the data in the table is not modified. Instead, the leaf nodes of the b-tree contain a pointer to the original data. This pointer can either reference a row of data in a heap or a clustered index key, depending on the structure of the underlying table. For example, if the underlying table has a clustered and nonclustered index defined, the leaf nodes of the nonclustered index point to the key location in the clustered index. Conversely, if the underlying table is a heap, because it does not have a clustered index defined, the nonclustered index simply points to rows in the heap to locate the queried data.

Nonclustered Index Include Columns

Just as with clustered indexes, the combined length of the selected key columns cannot exceed 900 bytes. However, nonclustered indexes are able to "include" columns in the index that are not counted as part of the key. This feature is important because it allows indexes designed to cover all columns used by queries while maintaining a key length below the 900-byte limit.

Also like clustered indexes, the index key can be any column with the exception of the ntext, text, image, varchar(max), nvarchar(max), varbinary(max), and XML data types. However, the varchar(max), nvarchar(max), varbinary(max), and XML data types can be selected as included columns.

Nonclustered Columnstore Index Characteristics

Nonclustered columnstore indexes are suited to data warehouse and decision support systems. As with many new features, a number of limitations exist in the first major release. Microsoft has already stated that it is working on reducing the number of these for future releases. Current imitations with columnstore indexes in SQL Server 2012 include the following:

- Tables cannot be modified using DML commands. Using such commands on a table with a columnstore index will cause the statements to fail. To change data, the index must first be disabled; data can also be loaded in by switching partitions. After the change, the index will need to be rebuilt.

- Columnstore indexes cannot be created as filtered indexes.

- They cannot include computed or sparse columns.

- They cannot contain be created with the INCLUDE clause.

- Columnstore indexes can be created only on physical tables; they cannot be created on top of views or indexes views.

- The use of the UNION ALL statement can in some scenarios cause batch processing to be disregarded.

> **Note**
>
> A TechNet wiki article (http://social.technet.microsoft.com/wiki/contents/ articles/trickle-loading-with-columnstore-indexes.aspx) discusses a methodology called local-global aggregation. Local-global aggregation provides a way to insert data into a delta table, based upon a column-store index, while leaving it unchanged. This provides a functional means of writing to a columnstore index while retaining its outstanding performance characteristics.

XML Index Characteristics

An XML index should be used when dealing with XML column types. The first index on the XML column must be the primary index. The primary XML index shreds the XML data, allowing faster access to the data because the shredding operation does not need to be performed at runtime.

After a primary XML index is created, up to three secondary XML indexes can be created. Each secondary index is a different type and serves a different purpose. The different secondary indexes can be based on the path, value, or properties of the XML data.

Traditional indexes can be stored in different filegroups separate from the associated table. However, XML indexes are always stored in the same filegroup as the underlying table.

Filtered Index Characteristics

A filtered index may be useful when dealing with subsets of data. The storage format of a filtered index is not unlike the typical nonclustered indexes that are stored within the b-tree hierarchy. With a filtered index, however, only a subset of the data is indexed. When implementing filtered indexes, it is very important to understand the data stored within the table, including the desired column to be indexed, so that the appropriate WHERE clauses can be selected correctly.

A common scenario for implementing a filtered index usually includes queries that contain many null values within a column. Take, for example, a column such as column X with 10,000 rows of data, but only 700 rows contain data within column X. Therefore, a filtered index can be applied for the non-null data rows within the column, which equates to 700 rows of data. As a result of using a filtered index, the index is slimmer and more efficient from a cost perspective. Another scenario includes creating a filtered index on a data column and including only days after a specific date value, such as March 7, 2012, in the subset of data.

Spatial Index Characteristics

Using the new geography and geometry data types, organizations can store and manipulate both geodetic and planar spatial data directly in the relational database. DBAs will need to leverage spatial indexes to provide fast execution of queries involving spatial data. Fortunately, DBAs can make informed decisions when identifying the most suitable spatial index, because the Query Optimizer has been enhanced to include spatial data. When making these decisions, it is still beneficial to understand the internals and characteristics of how spatial data is stored in the database.

Similar to clustered and nonclustered indexes, spatial indexes use the same b-tree method for storing the indexed data. However, SQL Server breaks down the spatial data into a grid hierarchy; therefore, the data can be stored based on two-dimensional spatial data in linear order. The index construction process consists of breaking down the space into a grid hierarchy based on four levels. Level 1 is the top level.

In a multilevel grid hierarchy, each level of the index subdivides the grid sector that is defined in the level above it. For example, each successive level further breaks down the level above it, so each upper-level cell contains a complete grid at the next level. On a given level, all the grids have the same number of cells along both axes (for example, 4x4 or 8x8), and the cells are all one size.

In addition, because spatial data and indexes are stored directly in the SQL Server Database Engine, the SQL Server Query Optimizer can make cost-based decisions on which spatial indexes to use for a given query. This process is similar to any other index within SQL Server 2012.

Index Design and Strategy

Data in a SQL Server 2012 database can be accessed and managed through a variety of methods, depending on how the database application was developed. This can make the index design process relatively complicated because the optimal indexes must be created for the each data access scenario. The following sections provide guidance and strategy for the index design process.

Using Clustered Indexes

You should strive to create a clustered key that contains the smallest possible number of key columns within the 900-byte limit. The selected key column or columns should provide uniqueness that allows the data to be searched quickly. It is important to note that the clustered key is included in every nonclustered index, so the larger the clustered key, the larger each row in the nonclustered index will become.

Following are some general guidelines and best practices for creating clustered indexes:

- A clustered index should be small and ever increasing to reduce the possibility of fragmentation.

- A clustered index is often used when large amounts of data or a range of data is queried, such as the data spanning a single month from a table that contains data for an entire year.

- Queries that use the ORDER BY or GROUP BY clauses generally benefit from a clustered index because the data is already sorted and doesn't need to be re-sorted.

- A clustered index is effective when the data is accessed sequentially, the data is searched frequently, or the data would have to be sorted.

The data in the table is sorted as the clustered index is built. From this point, the index is automatically maintained. One downside of a clustered index is the potential cost of index maintenance. Specific operations such as frequent inserts into the middle of the table or many delete operations cause the entire table to shift because the order of the data is automatically maintained. These types of operations also cause nonclustered queries to be updated because the nonclustered index relies on the location of index data within the clustered index.

Using Nonclustered Indexes

Nonclustered indexes cover costly queries with the smallest number of key and included columns. Each nonclustered index introduces additional cost associated with maintaining the index; for this reason, it is important to select the key and include columns carefully. Following are some general guidelines and best practices for creating nonclustered indexes:

- A nonclustered index is often used when smaller data sets or exact matches are returned because the data page can be located quickly, and additional nonkey columns can be included to avoid exceeding the 900-byte key length limit.

- Nonclustered indexes should also be used to cover additional query scenarios the clustered index does not cover. As many as 999 nonclustered indexes can be created per table.

- When the underlying table has a clustered index defined, all nonclustered indexes on that table depend on the clustered index. If the clustered index is disabled, the nonclustered indexes are also automatically disabled.

Caution

If you see the "Key Lookup," operator or "RID Lookup" inside a query execution plan, the query is not covered by your index. In this scenarios you should consider adding the missing columns as part of the key or as included columns.

Using Columnstore Indexes

Because columnstore indexes only use the columns required by the query, it is recommended to include all columns in the table when creating a columnstore index. Incorporating each column in the index will require extra disk space, but due to the compression algorithms used, the amount of redundant data can be minimized.

Initial reports have indicated that the time to rebuild a columnstore index is longer than that of a normal nonclustered index. Developers and DBAs should note that this may lead to an increased period of time required for daily data-warehouse ETL processes. However, it has also been noted that a number of users have been able to forgo creating aggregation tables because of the increased performance that columnstore indexes can offer. The benefit of columnstore indexes over aggregation tables is that if a query were to change, all the columns would still be covered. This reduces development time, which has a fiscal savings for your company.

Using Unique Indexes and the Uniqueifier Column

When creating new indexes or altering existing indexes, you can enable the unique option to force unique values across the key column rows.
If the unique option is not selected, the SQL Server Database Engine appends a 4-byte uniqueifier column to the index key. The uniqueifier is stored in an area of the page called the variable block. If this block does not exist—that is, each key is of fixed length—this block must be created at the expense of a further 4 bytes per record: 2 bytes for the variable offset and 2 bytes for the end of row. This column is used to ensure uniqueness when nonunique data is included in the key. This column is maintained internally and cannot be changed.

Calculating Disk Space Requirements

When index creation and maintenance operations are performed, enough temporary space must exist in the filegroup the index will be created in; otherwise, the operation will fail.

When the index operation is performed, the sorting is done either in the same filegroup as the table or in the filegroup where the index is located. However, the sort operation can also be done in the tempdb to potentially improve performance at the expense of temporary disk space. For additional information on how to use the tempdb with indexes, see the section "Sorting Indexes in the tempdb" later in this chapter.

The sum of space needed for both the old and new structure is the starting point to determine the approximate amount of free space needed to perform the index operation. For example, if a heap has 64,000 rows and each row is 1000 bytes, approximately 61MB of free space is required for the source data. (Note that a wide variety of variables can influence the following calculations, such as nullable columns, variable length columns, bit data type columns, and so forth. The calculations that follow emphasize quick and simple calculations to provide a good, but less precise, space estimate. If you want a highly precise but very complex calculation, refer to Microsoft TechNet.)

This can be calculated with the following formula:

$$\text{Current Number of Rows} * \text{Average Row Length in Bytes} = \text{Source Structure Size}$$

or

$$64000 * 1000 \text{ Bytes} = 61.0351562 \text{ Megabytes}$$

The size estimate should be rounded up for the calculation. In this case, the 61MB heap size is rounded to 70MB. To create a clustered index on this heap, you need a total of 70MB free space. When the new index has been created, the space used by the old structure is reclaimed.

When a new index is created or an existing index is rebuilt, a fill factor can be defined. The target structure requires additional space if the fill factor setting is configured.

> **Note**
>
> The fill factor index option allocates additional space in each index page to anticipate growth. This reduces the chance of page splits and fragmentation as data is changed, but reduces the performance of the index by increasing the size of the index, there by causing somewhat more I/O reads than the same index without fill factor.

For example, if an 80% fill factor is specified, the 70MB heap requires approximately 88MB free space because 20% additional space is allocated for each page. You can use the following calculation to determine additional space needed because of the fill factor:

$$\text{Source Structure Size / Fill Factor Percentage}$$

or

$$70MB \: / \: 80\% = 87.5 \text{ Megabytes}$$

Existing nonclustered indexes also have to be worked into the formula. When a new clustered index is created, existing nonclustered indexes must be rebuilt because the leaf nodes must now use the clustered key instead of the heap row indicator to find data.

For example, if an existing nonclustered index has 64,000 rows and each row is 100 bytes, approximately 8MB is used for the existing nonclustered index. The following formula can be used to calculate the size of the existing nonclustered index:

$$\text{Rows in Index * Average Row Length in Bytes /}$$
$$\text{Current Fill Factor Percentage}$$

or

$$(64000 * 100 \text{ Bytes}) \: / \: (80\%) = 7.62939453 \text{ Megabytes}$$

The expected size of the nonclustered key can be estimated by adding the new clustered key size to the existing row length and then subtracting the existing 8-byte row indicator. For example, if the new clustered key size is 36 bytes, the expected space needed for the rebuilt nonclustered index is about 10MB. You can then use the following calculation to estimate the size of the new nonclustered index:

$$\text{Rows in Index * (Average Row Length in Bytes} - 8 +$$
$$\text{Clustered Key Size in Bytes) / Fill Factor Percentage}$$

or

$$(64000 * ((100 \text{ Bytes}) - (8 \text{ Bytes}) + (36 \text{ Bytes}))) \: / \: (80\%) = 9.765625 \text{ Megabytes}$$

The total source structure would then be 78MB (70MB heap + 8MB non-clustered index) and the total destination structure would be 98MB (88MB cluster + 10MB nonclustered index). A total of 98MB free space is required to complete the index operation, with 78MB space reclaimed after the operation has completed.

If the option to sort the index in the tempdb is enabled, the tempdb must have enough space to hold the equivalent of the source table. In this example, the source table is about 70MB. The sort in tempdb option is ignored if the sort operation can be performed in memory.

Administering Indexes

The administration of indexes can be performed either through the SQL Server Management Studio interface or through Transact-SQL code. When you are performing administration of SQL Server indexes, it is important to understand the different options available in the different versions of SQL Server.

The code examples provided in the following sections can be executed through the Query Editor window in SQL Server Management Studio.

Transact-SQL Index Syntax

Transact-SQL code can be used to manage indexes on tables in a SQL Server database. The CREATE INDEX statement can be used to create new indexes, the modification of existing indexes can be performed through the ALTER INDEX statement, and the removal of indexes can be performed through the DROP INDEX statement. Examples that use each of these index-related Transact-SQL statements are provided throughout this chapter.

Creating Relational Indexes with Transact-SQL

The following code shows the complete syntax of the CREATE INDEX Transact-SQL statement. You can use the CREATE INDEX statement to create a relational index on a table or view or an XML index on an XML column:

```
CREATE [ UNIQUE ] [ CLUSTERED I NONCLUSTERED ] INDEX index_name
    ON <object> ( column [ ASC I DESC ] [ ,...n ] )
    [ INCLUDE ( column_name [ ,...n ] ) ]
    [ WHERE <filter_predicate> ]
    [ WITH ( <relational_index_option> [ ,...n ] ) ]
    [ ON { partition_scheme_name ( column_name )
        I filegroup_name
```

```
        | default
        }
    ]
    [ FILESTREAM_ON { filestream_filegroup_name
| partition_scheme_name | "NULL" } ]
  [ ; ]
<object> ::=
{
    [ database_name. [ schema_name ] . | schema_name. ]
        table_or_view_name
}
<relational_index_option> ::=
{
    PAD_INDEX = { ON | OFF }
  | FILLFACTOR = fillfactor
  | SORT_IN_TEMPDB = { ON | OFF }
  | IGNORE_DUP_KEY = { ON | OFF }
  | STATISTICS_NORECOMPUTE = { ON | OFF }
  | DROP_EXISTING = { ON | OFF }
  | ONLINE = { ON | OFF }
  | ALLOW_ROW_LOCKS = { ON | OFF }
  | ALLOW_PAGE_LOCKS = { ON | OFF }
  | MAXDOP = max_degree_of_parallelism
  | DATA_COMPRESSION = { NONE | ROW | PAGE}
    [ ON PARTITIONS (
{ <partition_number_expression> | <range> }
    [ , ...n ] ) ]
}
<filter_predicate> ::=
    <conjunct> [ AND <conjunct> ]
<conjunct> ::=
    <disjunct> | <comparison>
<disjunct> ::=
        column_name IN (constant ,…)
<comparison> ::=
        column_name <comparison_op> constant
<comparison_op> ::=
    { IS | IS NOT | = | <> | != | > | >= | !> | < | <= | !< }
<range> ::=
<partition_number_expression> TO <partition_number_expression>
```

The following code shows the CREATE INDEX options used in previous versions of SQL Server. Backward compatibility is provided to allow easier transition to SQL Server 2012 from previous versions of SQL Server. You should not use these options when developing new code:

```
CREATE [ UNIQUE ] [ CLUSTERED I NONCLUSTERED ] INDEX index_name
    ON <object> ( column_name [ ASC I DESC ] [ ,...n ] )
    [ WITH <backward_compatible_index_option> [ ,...n ] ]
    [ ON { filegroup_name I "default" } ]
<object> ::=
{
    [ database_name. [ owner_name ] . I owner_name. ]
        table_or_view_name
}
<backward_compatible_index_option> ::=
{
    PAD_INDEX
  I FILLFACTOR = fillfactor
  I SORT_IN_TEMPDB
  I IGNORE_DUP_KEY
  I STATISTICS_NORECOMPUTE
  I DROP_EXISTING
}
```

Modifying Relational Indexes with Transact-SQL

The following example shows the complete syntax of the ALTER INDEX Transact-SQL statement. You can use this code to rebuild indexes, disable indexes, reorganize indexes, or modify or set options on existing relational indexes:

```
ALTER INDEX { index_name I ALL }
    ON <object>
    { REBUILD
        [ [PARTITION = ALL]
                    [ WITH ( <rebuild_index_option>
                        [ ,...n ] ) ]
            I [ PARTITION = partition_number
                [ WITH ( <single_partition_rebuild_index_option>
                    [ ,...n ] )
            ]
```

```
                ]
            ]
     | DISABLE
     | REORGANIZE
         [ PARTITION = partition_number ]
         [ WITH ( LOB_COMPACTION = { ON | OFF } ) ]
   | SET ( <set_index_option> [ ,...n ] )
     }
[ ; ]
<object> ::=
{
    [ database_name. [ schema_name ] . | schema_name. ]
        table_or_view_name
}
<rebuild_index_option > ::=
{
    PAD_INDEX = { ON | OFF }
  | FILLFACTOR = fillfactor
  | SORT_IN_TEMPDB = { ON | OFF }
  | IGNORE_DUP_KEY = { ON | OFF }
  | STATISTICS_NORECOMPUTE = { ON | OFF }
  | ONLINE = { ON | OFF }
  | ALLOW_ROW_LOCKS = { ON | OFF }
  | ALLOW_PAGE_LOCKS = { ON | OFF }
  | MAXDOP = max_degree_of_parallelism
  | DATA_COMPRESSION = { NONE | ROW | PAGE }
     [ ON PARTITIONS (
{ <partition_number_expression> | <range> }
     [ , ...n ] ) ]
}
<range> ::=
<partition_number_expression> TO <partition_number_expression>
}
<single_partition_rebuild_index_option> ::=
{
    SORT_IN_TEMPDB = { ON | OFF }
  | MAXDOP = max_degree_of_parallelism
  | DATA_COMPRESSION = { NONE | ROW | PAGE } }
}
```

```
<set_index_option>::=
{
    ALLOW_ROW_LOCKS = { ON | OFF }
  | ALLOW_PAGE_LOCKS = { ON | OFF }
  | IGNORE_DUP_KEY = { ON | OFF }
  | STATISTICS_NORECOMPUTE = { ON | OFF }
}
```

Removing Indexes with Transact-SQL

The following example shows the complete syntax of the DROP INDEX
Transact-SQL statement. You can use this code to remove a relational or
XML index:

```
DROP INDEX
{ <drop_relational_or_xml_or_spatial_index> [ ,...n ]
| <drop_backward_compatible_index> [ ,...n ]
}
<drop_relational_or_xml_or_spatial_index> ::=
        index_name ON <object>
    [ WITH ( <drop_clustered_index_option> [ ,...n ] ) ]
<drop_backward_compatible_index> ::=
    [ owner_name. ] table_or_view_name.index_name
<object> ::=
{
    [ database_name. [ schema_name ] . | schema_name. ]
        table_or_view_name
}
<drop_clustered_index_option> ::=
{
    MAXDOP = max_degree_of_parallelism
    | ONLINE = { ON | OFF }
  | MOVE TO { partition_scheme_name ( column_name )
             | filegroup_name
             | "default"
             }
  [ FILESTREAM_ON { partition_scheme_name
             | filestream_filegroup_name
             | "default" } ]
}
```

Creating Columnstore Indexes with Transact-SQL

The following code shows the complete syntax of the CREATE
NONCLUSTERED COLUMNSTORE INDEX Transact-SQL statement. You can
use the CREATE NONCLUSTERED COLUMNSTORE INDEX statement to create a
columnstore index on a fact table:

```
CREATE [ NONCLUSTERED ] COLUMNSTORE INDEX index_name
    ON <object> ( column  [ ,...n ] )
    [ WITH ( <column_index_option> [ ,...n ] ) ]
    [ ON {
            { partition_scheme_name ( column_name ) }
            | filegroup_name
            | "default"
          }
    ]
[ ; ]
<object> ::=
{
    [database_name. [schema_name ] . | schema_name . ]
     table_name
{
<column_index_option> ::=
{
      DROP_EXISTING = { ON | OFF }
    | MAXDOP = max_degree_of_parallelism
 }
```

Creating Spatial Indexes with Transact-SQL

The following code shows the complete syntax of the CREATE SPATIAL
INDEX Transact-SQL statement. You can use the CREATE SPATIAL INDEX
statement to create a spatial index on a spatial column:

```
Create Spatial Index
Create Spatial Index
CREATE SPATIAL INDEX index_name
  ON <object> ( spatial_column_name )
    {
        <geometry_tessellation> | <geography_tessellation>
    }
  [ ON { filegroup_name | "default" } ]
;
```

```
<object> ::=
    [ database_name. [ schema_name ] . | schema_name. ]
        table_name
<geometry_tessellation> ::=
{
  <geometry_automatic_grid_tessellation> |
<geometry_manual_grid_tessellation>
}
<geometry_automatic_grid_tessellation> ::=
{
    [ USING GEOMETRY_AUTO_GRID ]
          WITH   (
          <bounding_box>
               [ [,] <tessellation_cells_per_object> [ ,...n] ]
               [ [,] <spatial_index_option> [ ,...n] ]
    )
}
<geometry_manual_grid_tessellation> ::=
{
       [ USING GEOMETRY_GRID ]
          WITH (
                        <bounding_box>
                            [ [,]<tessellation_grid> [ ,...n] ]
                            [ [,]<tessellation_cells_per_object> [
,...n] ]
                            [ [,]<spatial_index_option> [ ,…■] ]
    )
}
<geography_tessellation> ::=
{
      <geography_automatic_grid_tessellation> |
<geography_manual_grid_tessellation>
}
<geography_automatic_grid_tessellation> ::=
{
    [ USING GEOGRAPHY_AUTO_GRID ]
    [ WITH (
        [ [,] <tessellation_cells_per_object> [ ,…■] ]
        [ [,] <spatial_index_option> ]
     ) ]
}
```

```
<geography_manual_grid_tessellation> ::=
{
    [ USING GEOGRAPHY_GRID ]
    [ WITH (
                [ <tessellation_grid> [ ,...n] ]
                [ [,] <tessellation_cells_per_object> [ ...n] ]
                [ [,] <spatial_index_option> [ ,...n] ]
                ) ]
}
<bounding_box> ::=
{
      BOUNDING_BOX = ( {
        xmin, ymin, xmax, ymax
        | <named_bb_coordinate>, <named_bb_coordinate>,
<named_bb_coordinate>, <named_bb_coordinate>
  } )
}
<named_bb_coordinate> ::= { XMIN = xmin | YMIN = ymin | XMAX =
xmax | YMAX=ymax }
<tesselation_grid> ::=
{
    GRIDS = ( { <grid_level> [ ,...n ] | <grid_size>,
<grid_size>, <grid_size>, <grid_size>  }
        )
}
<tesseallation_cells_per_object> ::=
{
   CELLS_PER_OBJECT = n
}
<grid_level> ::=
{
    LEVEL_1 = <grid_size>
  | LEVEL_2 = <grid_size>
  | LEVEL_3 = <grid_size>
  | LEVEL_4 = <grid_size>
}
<grid_size> ::= { LOW | MEDIUM | HIGH }
<spatial_index_option> ::=
```

```
{
    PAD_INDEX = { ON | OFF }
  | FILLFACTOR = fillfactor
  | SORT_IN_TEMPDB = { ON | OFF }
  | IGNORE_DUP_KEY = OFF
  | STATISTICS_NORECOMPUTE = { ON | OFF }
  | DROP_EXISTING = { ON | OFF }
  | ONLINE = OFF
  | ALLOW_ROW_LOCKS = { ON | OFF }
  | ALLOW_PAGE_LOCKS = { ON | OFF }
  | MAXDOP = max_degree_of_parallelism
    | DATA_COMPRESSION = { NONE | ROW | PAGE }
}
```

Creating Filtered Indexes with Transact-SQL

The following code shows examples of the CREATE FILTERED INDEX
Transact-SQL statement. You can use the CREATE FILTERED INDEX statement to create a filtered index on a subset of data residing in a column.
The first example displays a filtered index based on a subset of products
subcategories in the product table in the AdventureWorks2012 database:

```
CREATE NONCLUSTERED INDEX AK_ProductSubCategory
ON Production.Product(ProductSubCategoryID)
WHERE (ProductSubcategoryID = 17)
```

The next example illustrates creating a filtered index on ComponentID and
Start date columns in the Production.BillOfMaterials table in the
AdventureWorks2012 database. The filtered criteria is based on the
EndDate columns, which are not null:

```
CREATE NONCLUSTERED INDEX FIBillOfMaterialsWithEndDate
ON Production.BillOfMaterials (ComponentID, StartDate)
WHERE EndDate IS NOT NULL
```

Creating Indexes with SQL Server Management Studio

When working with indexes, not only is it possible to create indexes with
Transact-SQL, but indexes can also be created via SQL Server
Management Studio. Use the following steps to create either a clustered,

nonclustered, XML, spatial, or columnstore index with SQL Server Management Studio. This example shows how to create a new nonclustered index:

1. Choose Start, All Programs, Microsoft SQL Server 2012, SQL Server Management Studio, and then connect to an instance of SQL Server.

2. Expand the SQL Server instance, the Database folder, and then select the database that contains the table on which the index will be generated.

3. Expand the desired table, right-click the Indexes folder, and then select New Index.

4. Choose the type of index you want to create. Certain options may be ghosted out if they are not valid.

5. In the Index Name text box, enter a name for the new index. A default name is provided; however, it is a best practice to have a consistent naming structure.

6. To specify the index columns to be added, click Add.

7. Specify the column(s) to be indexed in the Select Columns From dialog box, and then click OK.

8. The order of columns can be altered by clicking an index key and clicking either Move Up or Move Down.

9. To add an included column, click the Included Columns tab, and click the Add button to add one or more columns. The advantages associated with creating Included Columns are as follows: The 900 byte size limit for the indexes does not apply because the columns defined in the include statement, called nonkey columns, are not counted in the number of columns by the Database Engine; also, the index maintenance overhead associated with the actual composite index columns is reduced.

10. Check the Unique box to make the index a unique index.

11. On the New Index screen, either click OK to finalize the creation of the index or proceed to the next steps to enter advanced configuration settings for the index being created. Figure 5.4 depicts the New Index screen.

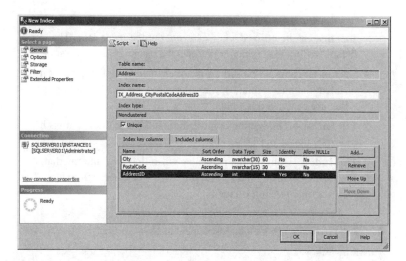

FIGURE 5.4
Creating a new nonclustered index in SQL Server Management Studio.

Options Page

Some additional options are available when creating indexes with SQL
Server Management Studio. The Options page includes the following
configurable settings, as displayed in Figure 5.5:

- **Auto Recompute Statistics**—Enabled by default, this option will
  automatically update index statistics when the index is being
  generated.

- **Ignore Duplicate Values**—This option will specify whether a duplicate key value can be inserted into the indexed column.

- **Allow Row Locks**—This setting performs row-level locking, which
  is also enabled by default. If this setting is cleared, index maintenance will be conducted faster; however, additional blocks on users
  may occur.

- **Allow Page Locks**—SQL Server uses page-level, row-level, or
  table-level locking. When this option is enabled, page locking is
  implemented.

- **Allow Online DML Processing**—If this option is enabled, the
  setting permits concurrent users access to the underlying clustered or
  nonclustered index data during the index operation.

■ **Maximum Degree of Parallelism**—Limits the number of processors that can be utilized when carrying out the index task. The default setting is 0, which represents the usage of all processors.

■ **Sort in tempdb**—This setting is not enabled by default, and if it is enabled, the intermediate sort results associated with building the index are conducted in tempdb.

■ **Fill Factor**—This setting controls how full the leaf level of each index should be during generation.

■ **Pad Index**—Controls the percentage of fullness for intermediate level pages by using the Fill Factor value—in other words, the fill factor setting for index pages.

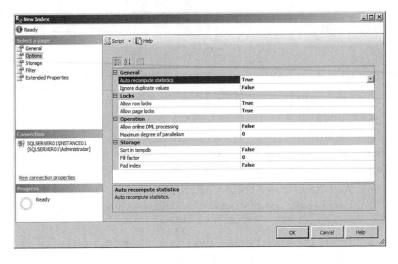

FIGURE 5.5
The Advanced New Index Settings on the Options page.

Storage Page

The Storage page, as illustrated in Figure 5.6, includes settings for the placement of the index. Indexes can be placed on additional or specified filegroups to maximize performance. Alternatively, placement can be assigned to a partition scheme. Compression options available in previous versions of the New Index have been removed. To create the index with row or page compression, script out the index and alter the Transact-SQL code to include the DATA_COMPRESSION clause, as shown in the section "Creating Relational Indexes with Transact-SQL."

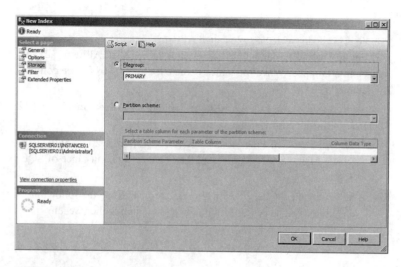

FIGURE 5.6
The Advanced New Index Settings on the Storage page.

Filter Page

In the Filter page, a DBA can create filter expressions for a new or existing index.

Note

Filtered indexes do not allow the IGNORE_DUP_KEY option; neither can they reference user-defined data type, spatial, or hierarchy data type columns.

Extended Properties

The Extended Properties page is used for managing extended properties on the index such as descriptive text. It is an often overlooked way of providing documentation of SQL Server solutions. For more information on understanding the options available on the Expended Properties page, review the topic Database Object (Extended Properties Page) in SQL Server Books Online.

Creating Clustered Indexes

The following procedure demonstrates the creation of a clustered index and shows the effect of creating a clustered index on a table. To begin the demonstration, run the following code within SQL Server Management Studio. This code creates a table called AllItems in the AdventureWorks2012 database. If an existing table called AllItems already exists, it is dropped. When the table is created, three rows of three columns of data are inserted.

Follow these steps to create the AllItems table in the AdventureWorks2012 database:

1. Choose Start, All Programs, Microsoft SQL Server 2012, SQL Server Management Studio, and then connect to an instance of SQL Server.

2. Select the New Query button from the toolbar. Type the following code into the Query Editor window and then click the Execute button:

```
USE AdventureWorks2012;
go
IF  EXISTS (SELECT * FROM sys.objects
WHERE object_id = OBJECT_ID(N'[dbo].[Allitems]')
 AND type in (N'U'))
DROP TABLE [dbo].[Allitems];
GO
USE [AdventureWorks2012];
GO
CREATE TABLE [dbo].[Allitems](
    [ID] [int] NOT NULL,
    [Item] [int] NOT NULL,
    [Value] [int] NOT NULL
) ON [PRIMARY];
GO

INSERT INTO [dbo].[Allitems]
VALUES
    (4, 23, 66),
    (2, 27, 28),
    (3, 28, 93);
GO

SELECT * FROM [dbo].[Allitems];
GO
```

When the code is executed, the results pane located below the Query
Editor window displays the following data:

```
ID     Item    Value
4      23      66
2      27      28
3      28      93
```

When a clustered index is added to the table, the data is sorted into the
clustered index b-tree. Follow these steps to add a clustered index to the
AllItems table:

1. In SQL Server Management Studio, expand the AdventureWorks2012
   database and then Tables.

2. Expand the dbo.AllItems table, which should be located near the top
   of the list. If the AllItems table is not displayed, click F5 to refresh
   the table list.

3. Right-click the Indexes folder located beneath the AllItems table and
   select New Index, Clustered Index from the menu. The New Index
   Properties dialog box opens.

4. In the Index Name field, type **IX_ID**. Click the Add button, select the
   ID column, and then click OK. Click OK to create the index.

5. Select the New Query button from the toolbar. Type the following
   code into the Query Editor window and then click the Execute
   button:

   ```
   SELECT * FROM dbo.AllItems
   ```

When the code is executed, the results pane located below the Query
Editor window displays the following data:

```
ID     Item    Value
2      27      28
3      28      93
4      23      66
```

The results show that the data has been sorted based on the ID column in
the table. The data has been sorted into a b-tree structure. The index nodes
contain the ID, and the leaf nodes contain the Item and Value columns.

You can easily create a clustered index through the CREATE INDEX statement. The following code looks for an existing index called IX_ID, and if
the index is found, it is dropped with the DROP INDEX statement. A new
clustered index using the ID column as the index key is then created:

```
USE [AdventureWorks2012]
IF EXISTS (SELECT name FROM sys.indexes WHERE name = 'IX_ID'
AND OBJECT_ID = OBJECT_ID(N'[dbo].[Allitems]'))
    DROP INDEX [IX_ID] ON [dbo].[AllItems]

USE [AdventureWorks2012]
GO
CREATE CLUSTERED INDEX [IX_ID] ON [dbo].[AllItems]
(
    [ID] ASC
) ON [PRIMARY]
GO
```

Notes from the Field: Choosing the Correct Clustered Index

The importance of choosing the correct clustered index is often overlooked. In the case of a GUID being chosen as the clustered key, especially when populated with the NEWID() function, the index will become heavily fragmented very quickly and also cause bloating in any nonclustered indexes.

Furthermore, using wide keys in a clustered index will result in many negative behaviors, including the following:

- Increase disk space consumed by data files due to the inclusion in every nonclustered index.

- Reduce the amount of records able to fit in the buffer pool.

- Reduce the page life expectancy.

- Creates larger log backup files when changes or maintenance to indexes are required.

- Larger log files lead to extra storage requirements on disk and possibly on tape.

- Larger log files may lead to longer recovery point objectives.

Ideally, a clustered index should meet most if not all of the following requirements:

- Ever increasing
- Unique
- Static
- Narrow
- Fixed width
- Non-nullable

Creating Nonclustered Indexes

The following procedure can be used to create a nonclustered index that includes the Item column as a nonkey column:

1. In SQL Server Management Studio, expand the AdventureWorks2012 database and then Tables.

2. Expand the dbo.AllItems table, right-click the Indexes folder located beneath the AllItems table, and select New Index from the menu. Select Nonclustered Index from the subsequent menu. The New Index Properties dialog box opens.

3. In the Index Name field, type **NX_ID_Item**. Click the Add button, select the ID column, and then click OK.

4. Select the Included Columns tab. Click the Add button, select the Item column, and then click OK. Click OK to create the index.

When you create a nonclustered index and include the Item column as a nonkey column, SQL Server can locate all the data required to support queries that include only the ID and Item columns. This can reduce the cost of executing queries that include these columns because all the data necessary to satisfy the query can be found in the index.

Creating Columnstore Indexes

The following procedure can be used to create a nonclustered columnstore index in SQL Server Management Studio. The AdventureWorks 2012 Data warehouse sample database will be used for the upcoming examples. The AdventureWorksDW2012 Data File can be downloaded from Codeplex at http://msftdbprodsamples.codeplex.com/ releases/view/55330:

1. In SQL Server Management Studio, expand the AdventureWorks DW2012 database and then Tables.

2. Expand the dbo.FactProductInventory table, right-click the Indexes folder located beneath the table, and select New Index from the menu. Select Nonclustered Columnstore Index from the subsequent menu. The New Index Properties dialog box opens.

3. In the Index Name field, type **IXCS_FactProductInventory**. Click the Add button, select all the columns, and then click OK.

4. Click OK to create the index.

When a query uses a nonclustered columnstore index, (see Figure 5.7) it reads only the pages from which it requires data. Unlike a row store index, a column store index can access just the data for the required columns. It can also benefit from segment elimination to further improve performance.

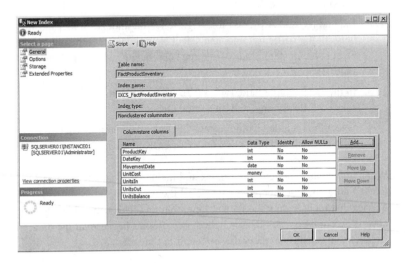

FIGURE 5.7
New Columnstore Index screen.

Disabling and Deleting Indexes

When a clustered index is disabled, the underlying data in the table is inaccessible. In addition, nonclustered indexes on the table are also disabled because nonclustered indexes rely on the clustered index key data to locate data in the table.

Follow these steps to disable the clustered index on the Person.Address table located in the AdventureWorks2012 database:

1. From within SQL Server Management Studio, expand a SQL Server instance, Databases, AdventureWorks2012, and then Tables. Expand the Person.Address table.

2. Expand the Indexes folder located beneath the Person.Address table. Right-click the PK_Address_AddressID index and select Disable.

3. When the Disable Index window opens, verify that the correct index is listed, and then click OK.

4. The Disable Index information dialog box is displayed as a reminder that disabling the index prevents access to the underlying table. Click Yes.

When the clustered index has been disabled, data in the table cannot be accessed. The following code demonstrates using the ALTER INDEX statement to disable the index:

```
USE [AdventureWorks2012]
GO
ALTER INDEX [PK_Address_AddressID] ON [Person].[Address]
DISABLE
GO
```

Use the following code to query the table. The results pane should state: "The query processor is unable to produce a plan because the index 'PK_Address_AddressID' on table or view 'Address' is disabled." This shows that the table is inaccessible when the index is disabled:

```
USE [AdventureWorks2012]
SELECT *
FROM [Person].[Address]
GO
```

Disabling nonclustered indexes and indexed views does not prevent access to the underlying data. Disabling this type of index simply prevents the Query Optimizer from potentially selecting the index as part of the execution plan.

With nonclustered and view indexes, the b-tree structure is physically deleted when the index is disabled; only the index metadata is kept. You can use the same procedure used to disable a clustered index to disable a nonclustered index.

If all indexes on a table are to be dropped, remove the clustered index last. If the clustered index is removed before nonclustered indexes, the nonclustered indexes have to be maintained when the clustered index is removed.

Enabling and Rebuilding Indexes

When an index is disabled, you can enable it by either rebuilding the index or re-creating the index. When a clustered index is disabled, nonclustered indexes for the table are automatically disabled, too. When the clustered index is rebuilt or re-created, the nonclustered indexes are not automatically enabled unless the option to rebuild all indexes is used.

Follow these steps to enable the clustered index on the Person.Address table located in the AdventureWorks2012 database:

1. From within SQL Server Management Studio, expand a SQL Server instance, Databases, AdventureWorks2012, and then Tables. Expand the Person.Address table.

2. Expand the Indexes folder located beneath the Person.Address table. Right-click the PK_Address_AddressID index and select Rebuild.

3. When the Rebuild Index window opens, verify that the correct index is listed, and then click OK.

When the clustered index has been rebuilt, the data can again be queried. However, the nonclustered indexes cannot be selected by the Query Optimizer because they need to be enabled individually. You can use the same procedure to enable each nonclustered index.

Alternatively, you can use the following code to rebuild all indexes on the table, effectively enabling each index as the rebuild is complete:

```
USE [AdventureWorks2012]
GO
ALTER INDEX ALL ON [Person].[Address] REBUILD
GO
```

To check the status of all indexes in the table, run the following code:

```
USE [AdventureWorks2012];
GO

SELECT
 name,
 type_desc,
 is_disabled
FROM Sys.Indexes
WHERE OBJECT_ID = OBJECT_ID(N'[Person].[Address]');
```

Implementing Index Maintenance and Maintenance Plans

A SQL Server 2012 maintenance plan allows different maintenance tasks to be performed automatically based on a customizable schedule. These tasks help reduce the administrative effort needed to keep the database healthy because the tasks are scheduled and executed automatically.

You can access maintenance plans through the SQL Server Management Studio by navigating to the Management\Maintenance Plans folder in the Object Explorer pane. You can create a new maintenance plan by right-clicking the Maintenance Plans folder and selecting New Maintenance Plan. You also can access the Maintenance Plan Wizard by right-clicking the Maintenance Plans folder and selecting Maintenance Plan Wizard.

Use the following code to enable the Agent XPs component:

```
sp_configure 'show advanced options', 1;
GO
RECONFIGURE;
GO
sp_configure 'Agent XPs', 1;
GO
RECONFIGURE
GO
```

When a maintenance plan is created either manually or through the Maintenance Plan Wizard, several tasks are available to maintain indexes. Following are the index-related maintenance plan options:

- **Check Database Integrity**—This task performs consistency checks on one or more databases. When you're configuring this task, an option is available to include the indexes in the integrity verification process.

- **Rebuild Index**—This task can be used to rebuild a specific index or all indexes in a database. This task can specify the fill factor and can sort the index results in tempdb to improve efficiency. This task can also use the online indexing option available in the SQL Server 2012 Enterprise and Developer Editions.

- **Reorganize Index**—This task can be used to reorganize a specific index or all indexes in a database. This task can also compact large objects during the reorganize process.

For additional information on how to administer SQL Server 2012 maintenance plans, see Chapter 16, "SQL Server 2012 Maintenance Practices."

SQL Server 2012 also provides the capability to back up indexes. For more information, see Chapter 6, "Backing Up and Restoring SQL Server 2012 Databases."

Configuring Indexes for Maximum Performance

When you are administering indexes, several options are available and should be considered to improve the overall performance of the indexes and index management operations.

Configuring Index Statistics

When an index is created, the option to recompute statistics is enabled by default. The Query Optimizer uses these statistics to determine the best method of accessing the data. Inaccurate statistics may cause the Query Optimizer to select a less-than-optimal execution plan.

The Database Engine periodically updates the statistics by testing them for accuracy. If necessary, the maintenance of statistics can be disabled. You can use the ALTER INDEX statement to disable collection of statistics. The following code demonstrates using the ALTER INDEX statement to disable statistics on the PK_Address_AddressID index on the Person.Address table:

```
USE [AdventureWorks2012]
GO
ALTER INDEX PK_Address_AddressID ON [Person].[Address]
SET(STATISTICS_NORECOMPUTE=ON);
GO
```

During the creation of an index through the SQL Server Management Studio, you can disable the collection of index statistics by deselecting the Auto Recompute Statistics option on the Option page.

> **Caution**
>
> Updating statistics directly after rebuilding an index can cause bad statistics. By default, when updating statistics a sample of the statistics is taken, whereas during the rebuild, the entire table is scanned, resulting in the statistics being completely up to date.

Examining Fragmentation Considerations

When a row is added to a full index page, a page split occurs, and about half the rows are moved to a new page. This is a costly operation because additional I/O operations are necessary to move the data. Additional I/O operations are then needed each time the data is accessed because the data is no longer contiguous. When an index is created or altered, the fill factor option can be used to help address fragmentation issues. This option can reduce the amount of fragmentation as the index grows by preallocating free space in the index data pages.

Follow these steps to determine the amount of fragmentation for an index:

1. From within SQL Server Management Studio, expand a SQL Server instance, Databases, AdventureWorks2012, and then Tables. Expand the Person.Address table.

2. Expand the Indexes folder located beneath the Person.Address table. Right-click the PK_Address_AddressID index and select Properties.

3. When the Index Properties dialog box opens, select the Fragmentation page to view the total fragmentation percentage for the index.

The DBCC SHOWCONTIG command can also be used to determine index fragmentation. However, this command has been marked for deprecation in a future release of SQL Server. It is recommended to use the management function sys.dm_db_index_physical_stats to replace the DBCC SHOWCONTIG command when checking index fragmentation. The following example illustrates the management function alternative for checking fragmentation. When this code is executed, the percentage of fragmentation for all indexes in the Person.Address table is returned:

```
USE AdventureWorks2012;
GO
SELECT
  a.index_id,
  b.name,
  a.avg_fragmentation_in_percent
FROM sys.dm_db_index_physical_stats (DB_ID(),
 OBJECT_ID(N'Person.Address'), NULL, NULL, NULL) AS a
  JOIN sys.indexes AS b
    ON a.object_id = b.object_id
      AND a.index_id = b.index_id;
GO
```

Implementing Fill Factor Administration

The fill factor can be configured so that each page in the leaf level allocates extra space for new rows. By default, the fill factor is set to 0, allowing only one additional row to be added to the page before a split operation is necessary. If the pages in the leaf level are expected to grow, you can use the Fill Factor setting to allocate extra space in each page. For example, set the Fill Factor setting to 80 percent to leave 20 percent room in each page for growth. The fill factor can be configured only when an index is created or rebuilt.

> **Note**
>
> Increasing the amount of free space in each page by implementing a fill factor results in a larger clustered index. A larger index increases the I/O cost when scanning the data and degrades read performance because more page reads are required. It may be necessary to set more space aside when using nonsequential keys to reduce the amount of page splits that can occur. Although read performance may be hampered, DML performance is often increased.

You can use the ALTER INDEX statement to set an 80 percent fill factor on the PK_Address_AddressID index located on the Person.Address table in the AdventureWorks2012 database:

```
USE [AdventureWorks2012]
GO
ALTER INDEX PK_Address_AddressID ON [Person].[Address]
REBUILD WITH(FILLFACTOR=80);
GO
```

The fill factor can also be configured through the SQL Server Management Studio. For example, to set the fill factor, create a new index by right-clicking the Indexes folder located beneath the Person.Address table and select New Index, then Nonclustered Index. In the New Index window, select the Options page and set the fill factor to the desired level.

Figure 5.8 shows the Set Fill Factor option set to 80 percent, allowing 20 percent free space within the leaf node of the index. The Pad Index option can also be configured to provide the intermediate level with additional free space.

> **Note**
>
> The free space allocated by the fill factor setting is not maintained; the space is allocated once when the clustered index is created. When the additional space is filled, a split operation occurs. To reallocate the space originally set aside under the fill factor setting during index creation, you must rebuild the index.

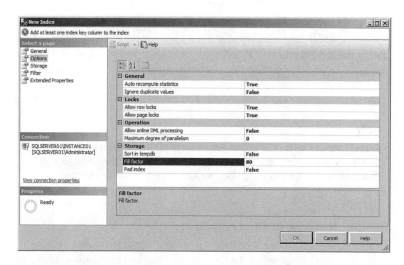

FIGURE 5.8
Fill factor options.

To view the fill factor value of one or more indexes, use the sys.indexes catalog view. You can use the following code to determine the fill factor on the PK_Address_AddressID index. The fill factor number is located in the fill_factor column:

```
USE AdventureWorks2012;
SELECT fill_factor FROM sys.indexes
WHERE name = 'PK_Address_AddressID';
```

Determining When to Rebuild or Reorganize an Index

When a split operation occurs, the data pages can become fragmented, and fragmentation can lead to performance-related issues. Two different options exist for dealing with fragmentation: The first is to reorganize the index, and the second is to rebuild the index.

When the level of fragmentation is greater than 5 percent but less than 30 percent, the reorganize option is recommended. When an index has 30 percent or greater fragmentation, a rebuild is recommended.

The reorganize process physically reorganizes the leaf nodes of the index, allowing more efficient access. The reorganize process is much lighter on the server and doesn't block queries or updates, essentially minimizing the impact on people using the database. In contrast, the rebuild process actually drops the existing index and re-creates it with the specified settings, such as fill factor. This option is more thorough but also uses more server resources, and if the Online option is not selected, the index is unavailable during the rebuild process. The sys.dm_db_index_physical_stats DMV is a great way for identifying size and fragmentation for data and indexes associated with a table or view.

> **Note**
>
> Online indexing is an Enterprise Engine feature that enables indexes to be rebuilt while users are active on the database. To take advantage of this feature, the Enterprise or Developer Editions must be installed.

Sorting Indexes in the tempdb

Normally, when an index is created, the sorting of the index data is done within the same filegroup as the table or the filegroup where the index is stored. However, when you are rebuilding existing indexes or creating new indexes, you can sort the data in the tempdb.

If the tempdb is physically located on a different set of disks, performance improvement can be achieved because the reading of data from one set of disks can be separated from the writing of data to the tempdb.

> **Note**
>
> To increase processing effectiveness, tempdb data files should be created at the ratio of one per two CPU cores, up to a maximum of eight files. This is recommended to reduce contention on internal allocation pages. (Note that this recommendation does *not* apply to log files, only to data files.)

You can use the ALTER INDEX statement to rebuild all indexes located on the Person.Address table in the AdventureWorks2012 database, using the tempdb to sort the data:

```
USE AdventureWorks2012;
GO
ALTER INDEX ALL ON Person.Address
REBUILD WITH (SORT_IN_TEMPDB = ON);
```

Using the Database Engine Tuning Advisor

The Database Engine Tuning Advisor is an effective tool to analyze and report the indexing potential. This tool allows the selection of a single table, a single database, or multiple databases for analysis. This is one of the key tools you should use when attempting to determine the appropriate indexes and the effect of indexes.

This tool works by placing a load on the selected objects. The results of this load are evaluated, and a recommendation is provided along with a potential improvement percentage. The recommended changes can then be implemented directly from within the tool.

This demonstration creates a sample workload file and then runs it against the Production.Product table in the AdventureWorks2012 database. Before you start, the existing clustered indexes on the table are dropped using the DROP INDEX statement. To drop the nonclustered indexes on the Production.Product table, run the following code:

```
USE [AdventureWorks2012]
GO
DROP INDEX [AK_Product_Name] ON [Production].[Product],
[AK_Product_ProductNumber]ON [Production].[Product],
[AK_Product_rowguid] ON [Production].[Product]
GO
```

After the nonclustered indexes have been deleted, the table can be more effectively analyzed for possible indexes. The next step is to create a work-load file; this is SQL code that will be used in the analysis process of the table. Follow these steps to create the workload file:

1. Choose Start, All Programs, Microsoft SQL Server 2012, SQL Server Management Studio.

2. Type the name of a SQL Server instance in the Server Name field, select Windows Authentication from the Authentication drop-down menu, and then click the Connect button.

3. Select the New Query button from the toolbar. Then type the following code into the Query Editor window:

```
USE [AdventureWorks2012];
GO
SELECT [Name],
  [ProductNumber],
  [StandardCost],
  [ListPrice]
```

```
FROM Production.Product
WHERE [ListPrice] - [StandardCost] > 50;
```

4. Select File, Save SQLQuery*N*.sql As. Then type **Workload.sql** into the File Name field and select a path to save the file.

After the workload file has been created, follow these steps to analyze a table for indexing purposes:

1. Choose Start, All Programs, Microsoft SQL Server 2012, Performance Tools, Database Engine Tuning Advisor. Alternatively, from Management Studio, click the Tools menu, and then select the option for Database Engine Tuning Advisor.

2. Type the name of a SQL Server instance into the Server Name field, select Windows Authentication from the Authentication drop-down menu, and then click the Connect button.

3. On the General tab, select the File option and then browse for the Workload.SQL file created in the previous steps. Select AdventureWorks2012 from the Database for Workload Analysis drop-down menu.

4. Click the down arrow next to the AdventureWorks2012 database and select the Product table from the list, as shown in Figure 5.9.

5. Select the Tuning Options tab and review the available options. Options include the ability to analyze different types of indexes and partitioning strategies. Click the Advanced button to specify space and online processing restrictions. The default options are acceptable for this demonstration.

6. The default options evaluate the table for nonclustered index potential and disable partitioning recommendations. Click the Start Analysis button.

The results, shown in Figure 5.10, show a nonclustered index with ListPrice as the key column and ProductNumber, Name, and StandardCost as included nonkey columns that would improve performance by 46 percent.

From within the Recommendation tab of the Database Engine Tuning Advisor, click the blue text in the Definition column to see the code necessary to create the recommended indexes. To apply all the recommendations, choose Actions, Apply Recommendation from the menu. The Apply Recommendations dialog box is displayed, allowing you to apply the recommendations immediately or schedule them for later.

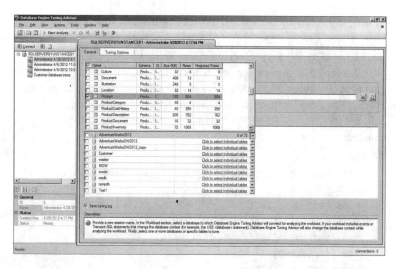

FIGURE 5.9
AdventureWorks2008 Index Tuning table selection.

This demonstration used a simple workload file to place a load on the database. This is often not appropriate or practical for large complex databases. As an alternative, you can use the information captured from the SQL Server profiler utility to place a more real-world load on the database.

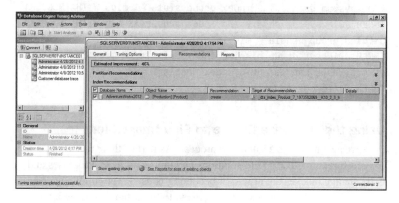

FIGURE 5.10
Database tuning recommendations.

Using System Information to Recommend Indexes

SQL Server provides DMVs that highlight missing indexes that, when added, could improve query performance. These DMVs, available since SQL Server 2008, provide missing index details within the actual execution plan of a query. The following query provides information on missing indexes since the last time the SQL Server service was restarted. To run this statement, the VIEW SERVER STATE permission must have been granted:

```
SELECT
    user_seeks * avg_total_user_cost * (avg_user_impact * 0.01)
[Index Advantage],
    migs.last_user_seek                 [Last User Seek],
    SUBSTRING(mid.[statement],2,CHARINDEX(
']',mid.[statement],1)-2)     [Database],
    mid.[statement]
[Database.Schema.Table],
    mid.equality_columns                [Equality lumns],
    mid.inequality_columns              [Inequality Columns],
    mid.included_columns                [Included Columns],
    migs.unique_compiles                [Unique Compiles],
    migs.user_seeks                     [User Seeks],
    migs.avg_total_user_cost            [Avg Total User Cost],
    migs.avg_user_impact                [Avg User Impact]
FROM sys.dm_db_missing_index_group_stats AS migs WITH (NOLOCK)
INNER JOIN sys.dm_db_missing_index_groups AS mig WITH (NOLOCK)
ON migs.group_handle = mig.index_group_handle
INNER JOIN sys.dm_db_missing_index_details AS mid WITH (NOLOCK)
ON mig.index_handle = mid.index_handle
ORDER BY [Index Advantage] DESC;
```

Using the Database Engine to Find Unused Indexes

Performance tuning is an iterative process. As part of this process, it is easy to forget to clear up old solutions and unused objects. Processes and code change indexes are at risk of becoming unused. The following code shows which indexes are causing overhead to the database engine by incurring more updates than reads:

```
SELECT
    Create_Date [UpSince],
    DATEDIFF(DD,Create_Date, GETDATE()) [UpTimeInDays]
FROM sys.databases WHERE name = 'tempdb';
```

```
go

DECLARE
    @Today DATETIME,
    @LastWeek DATETIME;

SELECT
    @Today = GETDATE(),
    @LastWeek = DATEADD(DD,-7,@Today);

SELECT
    DB_Name() [DBName],
    OBJECT_NAME(s.[object_id]) AS [Table Name],
    i.name AS [Index Name],
    i.index_id,
    user_updates AS [Total Writes],
    user_seeks + user_scans + user_lookups AS [Total Reads],
    user_updates - (user_seeks + user_scans + user_lookups) AS
[Difference],
    ISNULL((select 8192 * SUM(a.used_pages - CASE WHEN a.type
<> 1 THEN a.used_pages WHEN p.index_id < 2 THEN a.data_pages
ELSE 0 END)
        FROM sys.partitions as p
        JOIN sys.allocation_units as a ON a.container_id =
p.partition_id
        WHERE p.object_id = i.object_id
        AND p.index_id = i.index_id)/1024
    ,0.0) AS [SpaceUsed KB]
FROM sys.dm_db_index_usage_stats AS s WITH (NOLOCK)
INNER JOIN sys.indexes AS i WITH (NOLOCK)
ON s.[object_id] = i.[object_id]
AND i.index_id = s.index_id
WHERE OBJECTPROPERTY(s.[object_id],'IsUserTable') = 1
AND s.database_id = DB_ID()
AND user_updates > (user_seeks + user_scans + user_lookups)
AND i.index_id > 1
AND user_seeks + user_scans + user_lookups = 0
AND Last_User_Update BETWEEN @LastWeek AND @Today
AND Is_Primary_Key = 0
AND IS_Unique = 0
ORDER BY [Difference] DESC, [Total Writes] DESC, [Total Reads]
ASC;
```

> **Note**
>
> The preceding code was originally written by SQL Server MVP Glen Berry and has since been modified to remove primary and unique key constraints; the SpaceUsed KB attribute has also been added. Other modifications include adding a date range and a preceding query to show server uptime. The reason for including the server uptime is that the information gathered from these DMVs is transient. Remember that DMV data is lost whenever the SQL Server service is restarted. Therefore, ensure that the server has experienced a long period of uptime before choosing to drop any unused indexes. This recommendation is especially important on applications with both a data entry and a reporting component. Many reporting applications are run only on monthly, quarterly, or even yearly cycles. Consequently, it is possible that very important indexes are used quite infrequently. Take these considerations into account when choosing which indexes may be unnecessary.

Enterprise Indexing Features

The Enterprise Edition of SQL Server 2012 offers additional features not available in the Standard Edition. Note that these features are also available in the Developer Edition of SQL Server 2012.

Partitioning Indexes

The table that holds data and the index pages, along with standalone index structures, can be partitioned. This physically divides the data into partitions that can reside in different filegroups across different physical disks. This feature allows large tables and indexes to be physically managed as smaller sets of data while maintaining one logical table.

When you create an index through the SQL Server Management Studio or through Transact-SQL statements, you can set the partition scheme of the index. However, the partition scheme must already exist before the index can be configured to use the partition scheme.

If you create the index on a table that is already partitioned, the index automatically uses the same partition scheme as the parent table. Because of this, it is often easier to create the partition scheme for the underlying table first before creating the index. In this scenario, the table and index are "aligned" because they are using the same partition scheme.

However, if the index is stored away from the table in a different filegroup, the index partition scheme is not inherited from the underlying table and must be specified if necessary. In this scenario, the table and index can be "unaligned."

Online Indexing

When an index is created or rebuilt, the operation can be performed online. This allows the underlying table to be accessed during the operation. Use the following command to rebuild each of the indexes on the HumanResources.Shift table while keeping the data online:

```
USE [AdventureWorks2012]
GO
ALTER INDEX ALL ON HumanResources.Shift
REBUILD WITH(ONLINE = ON);
GO
```

You also can access the online indexing option through the SQL Server Management Studio as follows:

1. From within SQL Server Management Studio, expand a SQL Server instance, Databases, AdventureWorks2012, and then Tables. Expand the Production.Product table.

2. Right-click the Indexes folder located beneath this table and select New Index, then Nonclustered Index.

3. In the Name field, type **IX_SellStartDate_SellEndDate**. Click the Add button and choose the SellStartDate and SellEndDate columns. Then click the OK button.

4. Click the Options page. Set the option Allow Online DML Processing to true. Then click OK.

The index is then created online because the Allow Online DML Processing option was enabled.

Parallel Indexing

When an index is created, altered, or dropped, the number of processors used can be limited. Use the following command to rebuild each of the indexes on the Person.Address table in the AdventureWorks2012 database, specifying that the maximum number of processors to use is four:

```
USE [AdventureWorks2012]
GO
ALTER INDEX ALL ON [Person].[Address]
REBUILD WITH(MAXDOP=4);
GO
```

By default, the MAXDOP is set to 0, allowing the Database Engine to configure the number of processors based on how busy the server is. When the MAXDOP option is used, additional memory is used on the server.

> **Note**
> Although it is possible to set MAXDOP when creating a primary XML
> index, the option will be ignored, and only a single core is used.

Summary

Index design needs to be tested because different indexes are used for
different situations. Creating indexes on the correct key columns and
including appropriate nonkey data can significantly improve the efficiency
of database operations. Creating the wrong types of indexes, too many
indexes, or even setting the wrong indexing options can increase the overhead of the index along with the associated maintenance cost, resulting in
decreased database performance. For this reason, it is important to understand the characteristics of each type of index along with the limitations
and advantages of each.

In addition, it is also important to understand how to use the different SQL
Server 2012 tools available to assist with the index design and maintenance
process.

Best Practices

The following best practices were demonstrated and discussed in this
chapter:

- Managing and optimizing indexes is an ongoing process because
  performance can suffer both with the lack of indexes and poorly
  implemented and managed indexes.

- Create clustered indexes on columns that are frequently used and are
  lean data types. For example, the clustered index could be an identity column. However, it is not uncommon to create the clustered
  index on a column used in WHERE, ORDER BY, and GROUP BY clauses
  and in joins.

- Nonclustered indexes are used to speed queries. Therefore, try to
  create nonclustered indexes on frequently used search arguments,
  such as the columns using in WHERE clauses and JOIN clauses,
  columns using in ORDER BY and GROUP BY clauses, and HAVING
  clauses.

- Remember that indexes are most effective on columns with a large
  variety and distribution of values. Bad choices for an index might be
  a column that describes the gender of employees or that contains the

code for each of the 50 United States. In contrast, a column containing the hire date of employees in an organization with tens of thousands of workers would be a good column for a nonclustered index.

- Nonclustered indexes are dependent on the clustered index. Be careful when disabling a clustered index because the nonclustered indexes are also automatically disabled.

- A table can have only one clustered index. Take care to ensure that the key length of the clustered index doesn't exceed 900 bytes.

- Use nonclustered indexes to cover frequent or costly queries that are not covered by the clustered index. As many as 999 nonclustered indexes can be created on a table.

- Take care to ensure the key length of the nonclustered index doesn't exceed 900 bytes. Add columns as nonkey "include" columns to place additional data into the index.

- There are no statistics on a columnstore index; estimations are based on statistics taken from a b-tree index. Therefore, it is a best practice to update the statistics of traditional b-tree indexes prior to rebuilding a columnstore index and ensure that Auto Create Statistics is turned on.

- To alleviate performance degradation caused by fragmentation, maintain indexes by either updating or rebuilding indexes.

- If the tempdb is stored in a different filegroup or on a different set of physical disks, use the option to sort the index in the tempdb for a performance improvement.

- Leverage the Enterprise Edition's online indexing feature to eliminate downtime when removing fragmentation from indexes.

- When deleting all indexes on a table, remember to remove the clustered index last. If the clustered index is removed first, any nonclustered indexes are unnecessarily maintained as part of the removal process.

- Spatial indexes should be created to increase the response time of spatial queries.

- Leverage filtered indexes to improve performance and reduce maintenance costs on columns that have nulls.

CHAPTER 6

Backing Up and Restoring SQL Server 2012 Databases

One of the most important tasks of a DBA is to ensure that the new SQL Server infrastructure is being correctly backed up. Designing and implementing a proper backup strategy lends assurance that a successful recovery process can be initiated if an organization experiences problems with its databases, systems, servers, or sites.

This chapter covers the areas database administrators and organizations need to consider when conducting SQL Server backups and recoveries of databases associated with SQL Server 2012 Database Engine. Specifically, this chapter highlights how to back up and restore a database by using SQL Server Management Studio, maintenance plans, and Transact-SQL.

What's New for Backup and Recovery with SQL Server 2012?

With the tremendous amount of data being stored in our digital society, the size of databases used in organizations has increased exponentially over the past few years. This phenomenon in the database platform business is known as *data explosion*. As database sizes increase, so does the challenge of managing backups, including the administrative costs associated with the process. Fortunately, Microsoft addresses these concerns in SQL Server 2012 by introducing the Database Recovery Advisor, which can be used in conjunction with other fairly new features such as backup compression and Transparent Data Encryption.

Database Recovery Advisor

The Database Recovery Advisor allows a DBA to simplify the database restore process to the last backup taken or to a point of failure by creating a visual timeline based on all the backups taken from a database. The timeline helps differentiate between Full Database Backups, Differential Database Backups, Transaction Log Backups, and tail of the log because each type of backup is depicted with a different color in the timeline. Therefore, it is easy to locate and specify backups to restore a database to a point in time.

Backup from Multiple Secondaries When Using AlwaysOn Availability Groups

As discussed throughout the book, AlwaysOn Availability Groups is a brand-new high availability and disaster recovery solution that protects a group of databases by maintaining up to four secondary replicas. One of the value propositions of AlwaysOn Availability Groups is the potential to maximize hardware investments by offloading tasks such as backup operations from the primary replica to one or more of the secondary replicas. The ability to utilize secondaries offloads performance-related tasks from primary replica; therefore, the primary replica can focus on delivering mission-critical performance and availability. Backups can also be conducted on any of the secondaries, and the restore process is smart enough to stitch the Log Sequence Number (LSN) from different backups together to form a single restore.

AlwaysOn Replica Priority for Backups

AlwaysOn Availability Groups introduce a new concept known as backup preferences; therefore, SQL Server 2012 will automatically redirect backup jobs to preferred AlwaysOn Availability Group Replicas. For more information, review the "AlwaysOn Replica Priority for Backups" section toward the end of the chapter.

AlwaysOn Backup Support in Maintenance Plan Tasks

The Maintenance Plan Backup, Differential, and Transaction Log Tasks have a new option to support availability groups. The option impacts the way databases partaking in availability groups are handled. For availability databases, a DBA can choose the option to ignore replica priority for backup and backup on primary settings. This option is enabled only if the database is partaking in availability group. Moreover, the task could fail if the backup type is not supported on a secondary replica and the task runs on a secondary replica.

The Importance of Backups

Understanding how to back up the SQL Server 2012 Database Engine remains a big challenge for many organizations today, even for those organizations that make an effort to execute a backup strategy. Unfortunately, in many situations, it takes a disaster for them to realize that their backup strategy is inappropriate, or that specific SQL Server elements such as the transaction log or recovery model were overlooked. This awakening is far too late for those organizations, however, because they may have already experienced a horrific data loss.

Data loss is unacceptable in today's competitive economy. Losing mission-critical data residing in SQL Server can be particularly harmful to an organization's success because that data provides key information that ultimately gives an organization its competitive advantage. Organizations suffering catastrophic data loss are more susceptible to going out of business. Moreover, regulatory requirements, such as compliance with the Sarbanes-Oxley Act or PCI, place tremendous pressure on organizations to be more trustworthy and accountable for their data, especially financial information.

As more organizations begin to understand the value of their data, they also recognize that the backup and recovery operations of the SQL Server 2012 Database Engine are some of the most important SQL Server administrative tasks of DBAs. When you understand all the intricate details that make up SQL Server and the backup options available, you can better develop a database backup and restoration strategy that minimizes or eliminates data loss and corruption in your organization.

Suppose you're working with a full installation of SQL Server, which includes all its components. With the ability to identify all these parts and understand how they are associated, you can understand that your focus should be not only on backing up databases, but also on the other SQL Server components and items installed, such as Analysis Services, Reporting Services, Full-Text Catalogs, and Internet Information Services. You should take all these components into account to successfully back up and restore a SQL Server environment.

Note

To successfully back up and restore a complete SQL Server environment involves backing up not only databases, but all other SQL Server components and items installed. However, this chapter focuses strictly on backup and recovery tasks associated with the SQL Server 2012 Database Engine.

Items to Consider When Creating a Backup and Recovery Plan

The objective of all SQL Server 2012 backups is to restore a database to a known state. The most common need for backups is to recover data from accidental deletions due to human error. Other factors that might call for a recovery of data may include application errors, hardware failure, or the need to recover data to a prior state.

When organizations understand the objective and necessity for backups, they must attend to the business scope of their SQL Server backup and recovery plan. To help identify the scope, an organization needs to ask some of the following questions:

- Has a Service Level Agreement (SLA) already been defined?
- Is the data in each database considered to be mission-critical?
- Is there a clear statement of what should and shouldn't be backed up?
- What is the frequency of the backups?
- What standards are acceptable for offsite storage and retrieval?
- What is the escalation path for failed backups?
- What are the decision criteria for overrun jobs?
- Will the backups be password protected?
- How long will data be retained?
- How much data can the organization afford to lose at any given moment?
- What is the availability of resources governing the backup and restore process?
- What is the financial cost of downtime?
- Are there any regulatory requirements dictating how backups and restores should be conducted and managed?

After some of these questions are answered, the high-level scope of the desired backup starts to take shape. The organization then needs to address the technical aspects of the backup and recovery plan. Some of the technical questions may include the following:

- What SQL Server databases should be included in the backup and recovery plan?

- Should I back up the system databases?
- Which database recovery model should be used?
- How often should the backups occur?
- What type of media should be used?
- Should I leverage the Backup Compression feature? If so, do I have the Enterprise Edition?
- Which utilities, such as Transact-SQL (Transact-SQL), SQL Server Management Studio (SSMS), or third-party tools, should be leveraged when creating backups?

Backup Compression

Another item a DBA must consider is whether or not to leverage backup compression. Backup compression allows a DBA to compress database backups associated with the Database Engine, thus reducing the cost linked to backup storage. Backup compression is disabled by default and must be enabled at the server level to leverage this new rich feature. This can be achieved by enabling the Compress Backup option in the Database Settings page associated with the Server properties. Server properties can be accessed by right-clicking a desired SQL Server and selecting properties in SQL Server Management Studio. Alternatively, the following Transact-SQL syntax can be used to enable backup compression at the server level:

```
USE master;
GO
EXEC sp_configure 'backup compression default', '1';
RECONFIGURE WITH OVERRIDE;
```

There may be situations when backup compression at the server level is enabled; however, the compression feature is not required when backing up a specific database. Therefore, a DBA can override the backup compression default server setting when conducting a database backup on a specific database. The backup compression override option is available when creating backups with SQL Server Management Studio, Transact-SQL, Maintenance Plan Wizard, and the SQL Server 2012 Integration Services Back Up Database Task.

Note

Backup compression is a feature that used to be included only in the Enterprise and Developer editions of SQL Server; however, since SQL Server 2008 R2, backup compression has been included in the Standard Edition. It is straightforward to implement when using Transact-SQL because you can simply add COMPRESSION or NO COMPRESSION in the WITH options. In addition, it is also important to keep in mind that before you turn on database compression on your production SQL Server, make sure you evaluate the performance impact by running it on the test server that is similar to your production load.

Finally, database compression has great results. Obviously, compression results will vary and are indicative of what kind of data is stored in the database. However, compression ratios of 4-to-1 have been achieved. Unfortunately, with any compression technology, a performance trade-off always exists. Backup compression does not increase disk I/O because compressed data is smaller; however, CPU usage typically increases. It is beneficial to test backup compression before using it in production so that as a DBA, you are fully aware of the performance impact on the SQL Server system and associated SQL workload. Today this isn't a major concern because typical SQL Server installations have plenty of cores compared to a decade ago when processor power was very expensive and a limited commodity within the server.

Tip

The exact amount of compression you will get for your database depends primarily on the type of data. To evaluate backup compression savings, you can query the backup set table in MDSB database, as shown next:

```
SELECT Backup_Size/Compressed_Backup_Size
FROM MSDB..Backupset
GO;
```

Note

It is recommended to create a policy with Resource Governor that will govern the amount of CPU that can be consumed when conducting compressed backups. This will ensure that the compressed backups do not place excessive CPU pressure on the system, causing performance degradation. For more information on Resource Governor, refer to Chapter 18, "Managing Workloads with Resource Governor."

Database Backup Encryption

A final item many DBAs or organizations must take into consideration is organizational compliance associated with database backups and compression. SQL Server 2008 introduced a new and highly anticipated feature called backup encryption. When a database is encrypted with Transparent Data Encryption (TDE), all backups associated with the encrypted database are also encrypted. The certificate used to encrypt the database must be present to restore the database, or the data restore will fail and the data will be left in a decrypted, unusable state. Therefore, ensure that the certificates associated with TDE and the encrypted databases are stored safely. For more information on Transparent Data Encryption, see Chapter 9, "Encrypting SQL Server 2012 Data and Communications."

Backing Up and Recovering the Database Engine

The Database Engine is the heart of SQL Server. It is responsible for storing data, databases, stored procedures, security, and many more functions, such as full-text search, Database Mail, replication, and high availability. Because the Database Engine is one of the most vital components of the SQL Server database as a result of the crucial data it holds, it is essential for organizations to create a backup and recovery plan for the Database Engine.

The Storage Architecture

Executing a successful database backup and restore plan begins with understanding the Database Engine storage architecture. This involves having intimate knowledge of how SQL Server leverages database files, filegroups, transaction logs, and FILESTREAM.

SQL Server 2012 databases have three kinds of file types associated with them: database files, transaction log files, and FILESTREAM files. A SQL Server database is always made up of at least one data file and one transaction log file, and FILESTREAM data is optional. However, many large databases have multiple filegroups and many database files to address performance and scale—like SQL Server Fast Track relational data warehouse reference architecture implementations. The following sections elaborate on each of these files.

Database Files

The default database files reside within a primary filegroup. A *filegroup* is a logical structure for grouping data files and managing them as a logical unit. The primary filegroup contains the primary data file and any second-ary data files not stored in another filegroup. If you want to increase performance and the speed of the backup and recovery, it is recommended that you create additional files or filegroups and split database objects across these several filegroups to establish parallel processing.

The default extension for the database file within the primary filegroup is .mdf. Likewise, filegroups inherit the default extension .ndf. It is possible to create up to 32,767 user-defined filegroups per database, 32,767 files per database. Each database file can scale up to 16 terabytes. As you can imagine, an organization can have a tremendous amount of data, which would require a solid database backup and recovery plan.

Transaction Log Files

Every relational database has a transaction log to record database activity. Transaction logs are responsible for recording every modification made to the database. As such, these logs are a critical component of the database, especially during recovery because the log is counted on to restore the database to a point in time or the point of failure. The default extension for a transaction log is .ldf. As with database files, additional transaction log files can be added to increase performance, backups, and restore times; however, it is not a common practice. Each transaction log file can scale up to 2 terabytes.

FILESTREAM Files

Until SQL Server 2008, organizations have been creatively inventing their own mechanisms to store unstructured data. SQL Server 2008 introduced a new data type that can assist organizations by allowing them to store unstructured data such as bitmap images, music files, text files, videos, and audio files in a single data type, which is more secure and manageable. If FILESTREAM data is being leveraged, the DBAs must also take these files into consideration when backing up the database.

Tip

It is a best practice to place the database, transaction logs, and backups on separate disks. This will prevent catastrophic failure in the event that a single disk, volume, or LUN fails. In addition, this strategy also increases performance and allows a DBA to restore a database to the point of failure. It is also a good practice to ship your critical database backups offsite in case there's a natural disaster and your data is lost.

When you're confident that you understand the database, transaction log, and FILESTREAM files within the Database Engine, you should turn your attention to the various Database Engine recovery models in SQL Server. The level of understanding you have of each of these models significantly affects your database backup and restore strategy.

Using Recovery Models Effectively

Each model handles recovery differently. Specifically, each model differs in how it manages logging, which governs whether an organization's database can be recovered to the point of failure. The three recovery models associated with a database in the Database Engine are Full, Simple, and Bulk-Logged:

- **Full**—This model captures and logs all transactions, making it possible to restore a database to a given point in time or up to the minute. Based on this model, you must conduct maintenance on the transaction log to prevent logs from growing too large and disks from becoming full. When you perform backups, space is made available again and can be used until the next planned backup. Organizations may notice that maintaining a transaction log slightly degrades SQL Server performance because all transactions to the database are logged. Organizations that insist on preserving critical data often overlook this issue because they realize that this model offers them the highest level of recovery capabilities.

- **Simple**—This model provides organizations with the least number of options for recovering data. It truncates the transaction log after each backup. This means a database can be recovered only up to the last successful full or differential database backup. This recovery model also requires the least amount of administration because transaction log backups are not permitted. In addition, data entered into the database after a successful full or differential database backup is unrecoverable. Organizations that store data they do not deem to be mission-critical may choose to use this model.

- **Bulk-Logged**—This model maintains a transaction log and is similar to the Full recovery model. The main difference is that transaction logging is minimal during bulk operations to maximize database performance and reduce the log size when large amounts of data are inserted into the database. Bulk import operations such as BCP, BULK INSERT, SELECT INTO, CREATE INDEX, ALTER INDEX REBUILD, and DROP INDEX are minimally logged.

Because the Bulk-Logged recovery model provides only minimal logging of bulk operations, you cannot restore the database to the point of failure if a disaster occurs during a bulk-logged operation. In most situations, an organization has to restore the database, including the latest transaction log, and rerun the bulk-logged operation.

This model is typically used if organizations need to run large bulk operations that degrade system performance and do not require point-in-time recovery.

> **Note**
>
> When a new database is created, it inherits the recovery settings based on the model database. The default recovery model is set to Full.

Now that you're familiar with the three recovery models, you need to determine which model best suits your organization's needs. The next section is designed to help you choose the appropriate model.

Selecting the Appropriate Recovery Model

Selecting the appropriate recovery model affects an organization's ability to recover, manage, and maintain data.

For enterprise production systems, the Full recovery model is the best model for preventing critical data loss and restoring data to a specific point in time. As long as the transaction log is available, it is even possible to get up-to-the-minute recovery and point-in-time restore if the tail-end of the transaction log is backed up and restored. The trade-off for the Full recovery model is its impact on other operations.

Organizations leverage the Simple recovery model if the data backed up is not critical, if data is static and does not change often, or if loss is not a concern. In this situation, the organization loses all transactions since the last full or last differential backup. This model is typical for test environments or production databases that are not mission-critical.

Finally, organizations that typically select the Bulk-Logged recovery model have critical data but do not want to degrade system performance by logging large amounts of data, or they conduct these bulk operations such as data warehousing loads after hours so as not to interfere with normal transaction processing. In addition, such organizations do not need point-in-time or up-to-the-minute restores.

> **Note**
>
> You can switch the recovery model of a production database and switch it back. This does not break the continuity of the log; however, there could be negative ramifications to the restore process. For example, a production database can use the Full recovery model, and immediately before a large data load, the recovery model can be changed to Bulk-Logged to minimize logging and increase performance. The only caveat is that your organization must understand that it lost the potential for point-in-time and up-to-the-minute restores during the switch.

Switching the Database Recovery Model with SSMS

To set the recovery model on a SQL Server 2012 database using SSMS, perform the following steps:

1. Choose Start, All Programs, Microsoft SQL Server 2012, SQL Server Management Studio.

2. In Object Explorer, first connect to the Database Engine, expand the desired server, and then expand the database folder.

3. Select the desired SQL Server database, right-click the database, and select Properties.

4. In the Database Properties dialog box, select the Options page.

5. In the Recovery Model field, select either Full, Bulk-Logged, or Simple from the drop-down list, as shown in Figure 6.1, and click OK.

Switching the Database Recovery Model with Transact-SQL

Not only can you change the recovery model of a database with SSMS, but you can also make changes to the database recovery model using Transact-SQL commands such as ALTER DATABASE. You can use the following Transact-SQL script to change the recovery model for the Adventure Works2012 database from Simple to Full:

```
--Switching the Database Recovery model
Use Master
ALTER DATABASE AdventureWorks2012 SET RECOVERY FULL
GO
```

FIGURE 6.1
Selecting a database recovery model with SSMS.

SQL Server Backup Methods

Now that you've selected the appropriate recovery model, you should turn your attention to fully understanding the different backup methods available. This is the third step in successfully creating a backup and recovery solution for the Database Engine. The backup utility included in SQL Server offers several options for backing up databases. The following sections identify the following SQL Server backup methods:

- Full backups
- Differential backups
- Transaction log backups
- File and filegroup backups
- Partial backups
- Differential partial backups
- Copy-only backups
- Mirrored backups

Full Backup

The full backup is also commonly referred to as *full database backup*. Its main function is to back up the entire database as well as transaction logs, filegroups, and files. As a result, a full backup can be used to restore the entire database to its original state when the backup was completed.

Equally important, many people refer to the full database backup as the *baseline* for all other backups. The reason is that the full database backup must be restored before all other backups can be created or restored, such as differential backups, partial backups, and transaction logs.

The following script illustrates how to conduct a full database backup for the AdventureWorks2012 database.

Note

For this example and others in this chapter, the backup set is located on the C: drive in a folder called backups in proprietary backup file called SQLBackup. You should change the syntax in these examples to reflect the backup location and file of your choice based on your environment. If not, create a folder c:\backups and use the file SQLBackup.bak.

```
--SQL SERVER 2012 MANAGEMENT & ADMINISTRATION BY ROSS MISTRY
--FULL BACKUP EXAMPLE

BACKUP DATABASE [AdventureWorks2012]
TO DISK = N'c:\backups\SQLBackup.bak'
WITH NOFORMAT, NOINIT,
NAME = N'AdventureWorks2012-Full Database Backup',
SKIP, NOREWIND, NOUNLOAD, COMPRESSION, STATS = 10
GO
```

This example conducts a full database backup on the AdventureWorks2012 database. The additional options consist of Backup Set Will Not Expire, Backing Up to Disk, Append to the Existing Backup Set, and Compress Backup.

Differential Backups

Unlike a full database backup, a differential database backup backs up only data that changed after the last successful full database backup was conducted, resulting in a smaller backup.

The following script illustrates how to conduct a differential database backup for the AdventureWorks2012 database:

```
--SQL SERVER 2012 MANAGEMENT & ADMINISTRATION BY ROSS MISTRY
--DIFFERENTIAL BACKUP EXAMPLE

USE AdventureWorks2012
BACKUP DATABASE [AdventureWorks2012]
TO DISK = N'c:\backups\SQLBackup.bak'
WITH DIFFERENTIAL , NOFORMAT, NOINIT,
NAME = N'AdventureWorks2012-Differential Database Backup',
SKIP, NOREWIND, NOUNLOAD, COMPRESSION, STATS = 10
GO
```

This differential example creates a copy of all the pages in the database modified after the last successful full or differential AdventureWorks2012 database backup. The additional options consist of Backup Set Will Not Expire, Backing Up to Disk, Append to the Existing Backup Set, Verify Backups When Finished, Perform Checksum Before Writing to Media, Continue on Error, and Compress Backup.

Transaction Log Backup

Transaction log backups are useful only for those databases using a Full or Bulk-Logged recovery model. The transaction log backs up all data as of the last full backup or transaction log backup. As with a differential backup, it is worth remembering that a transaction log backup can be executed only after a full backup has been performed.

Additional options for backing up the transaction log include

- **Truncate the Transaction Log**—If log records were never truncated, they would constantly grow, eventually filling up the hard disk and causing SQL Server to crash. This option is the default transaction log behavior and truncates the inactive portion of the log.

- **Back Up the Tail of the Log**—This option is typically used as the first step when restoring SQL Server to a point in failure or point in time. Backing up the tail portion of the log captures the active log that has not been captured by a previous backup before a disaster occurs. This option allows you to recover the database and replay any transactions that have not been committed to the database or included in the backup sets already taken.

The following script illustrates how to create a transaction log backup for the AdventureWorks2012 database.

```
--SQL SERVER 2012 MANAGEMENT & ADMINISTRATION BY ROSS MISTRY
--TRANSACTION LOG BACKUP EXAMPLE
BACKUP LOG [AdventureWorks2012]
TO DISK = N'c:\backups\SQLBackup.bak'
WITH NOFORMAT, NOINIT,
NAME = N'AdventureWorks2012-Transaction Log Backup',
SKIP, NOREWIND, NOUNLOAD, COMPRESSION, STATS = 10
GO
```

This example conducts a transaction log database backup on the
AdventureWorks2012 database. The additional options consist of Backing
Up to Disk, Append to the Existing Backup Set, and Compress Backup.
The transaction log behavior truncates the transaction log when complete.

The following script illustrates how to create a transaction log (tail of the
log) backup for the AdventureWorks2012 database.

> **Note**
>
> It is a best practice to use the master database when performing the tail
> of the log transaction log backup with Transact-SQL.

```
--SQL SERVER 2012 MANAGEMENT & ADMINISTRATION BY ROSS MISTRY
--TRANSACTION LOG - TAIL LOG BACKUP EXAMPLE
BACKUP LOG [AdventureWorks2012]
TO DISK = N'c:\backups\SQLBackup.bak'
WITH NO_TRUNCATE , NOFORMAT, NOINIT,
NAME = N'AdventureWorks2012-Transaction Log Backup',
SKIP, NOREWIND, NOUNLOAD, NORECOVERY , COMPRESSION, STATS = 10
GO
```

This example conducts a backup of the tail of the transaction log on the
AdventureWorks2012 database and leaves the database in the restoring
state. The additional options consist of Back Up to Disk, Append to the
Existing Backup Set, and Compress Backup. The transaction log behavior
truncates the transaction log when complete.

File and Filegroup Backups
Instead of conducting a full backup, organizations can back up individual
files and filegroups. This backup method is often favorable to organizations
that can't consider backing up or restoring their databases because of size

and the time required for the task. When you use file and filegroup backups, backing up the transaction log is also necessary because the database must use the Full or Bulk-Logged recovery model.

The basic syntax for creating a file or filegroup backup is as follows:

```
BACKUP DATABASE { database_name | @database_name_var }
 <file_or_filegroup> [ ,...n ]
 TO <backup_device> [ ,...n ]
 [ <MIRROR TO clause> ] [ next-mirror-to ]
 [ WITH { DIFFERENTIAL | <general_WITH_options> [ ,...n ] } ]
 [;]
```

Following is a demonstration of a database that has two filegroups: Primary and Secondary. This backup conducts a full backup only on the Secondary Filegroup:

```
--SQL SERVER 2012 MANAGEMENT & ADMINISTRATION BY ROSS MISTRY
--FILEGROUP BACKUP
BACKUP DATABASE [Sample] FILEGROUP = N'Secondary'
TO DISK = N'C:\Backup\SQLBackup.bak'
WITH NOFORMAT, NOINIT, NAME = N'Sample-Full Filegroup Backup',
SKIP, NOREWIND, NOUNLOAD, COMPRESSION, STATS = 10
GO
```

Partial Backups

Partial backups were introduced as a new feature in SQL Server 2005. Primary filegroups and read/write filegroups are always backed up when a partial backup is executed. Any filegroups marked as read-only are skipped to save time and space. Partial backups should not be confused with differential backups. Unlike differential backups, partial backups are best used when read-only filegroups exist and you have chosen not to back up this data because it is static, such as a large data warehouse or table with archived partitions that never change. If you choose to back up a read-only filegroup, this choice must be identified in the BACKUP command. It is worth mentioning that a partial backup can be created only with Transact-SQL; this functionality is not included in SSMS.

The basic syntax for creating partial and differential backups is as follows:

```
--Creating a Partial Backup
BACKUP DATABASE { database_name | @database_name_var }
 READ_WRITE_FILEGROUPS [ , <read_only_filegroup> [ ,...n ] ]
  TO <backup_device> [ ,...n ]
```

```
[ <MIRROR TO clause> ] [ next-mirror-to ]
[ WITH { DIFFERENTIAL | <general_WITH_options> [ ,...n ] } ]
[;]
```

Differential Partial Backups

A differential partial backup has many of the features of a traditional
differential backup and a partial backup. Only data that has been modified
in the primary filegroups and read/write filegroups, and not marked as
read-only, is backed up since the last partial backup. As with partial
backups, this functionality is not included in SSMS and can be created
only with Transact-SQL. To use this functionality, you would have to
include the With Differential option, as indicated in the previous example.

Copy-Only Backups

The capability to make copy-only backups was introduced in SQL Server
2005 and continues to exist with SQL Server 2012. This backup type
provides an entire independent backup of a database without affecting the
sequence of the backup and restore process.

A common scenario for creating a copy-only backup is when you need to
refresh a staging database from production. You can create a copy-only
backup and restore it to the staging environment without affecting the
sequence of the conventional backup or restore process. SSMS supports
copy-only backups, too, if you check the Copy-Only option when using the
wizard. It is possible, however, to create copy-only backups on both the
database files and logs.

The basic syntax for creating a copy-only backup for a database file is as
follows:

```
BACKUP DATABASE database_name TO
 <backup_device> ... WITH COPY_ONLY …
```

The basic syntax for creating a copy-only backup for a transaction log file
is as follows:

```
BACKUP LOG database_name TO <backup_device>
.. WITH COPY_ONLY …
```

The following example demonstrates how to conduct a copy-only backup
on the AdventureWorks database. As you can see, the backup is similar to
a traditional backup; however, you need to insert the With Copy_Only
option.

```
--SQL SERVER 2012 MANAGEMENT & ADMINISTRATION BY ROSS MISTRY
--Copy Only Backup Example
BACKUP DATABASE [AdventureWorks2012]
TO DISK = N'c:\backups\SQLBackup.bak'
WITH COPY_ONLY, NOFORMAT, NOINIT,
NAME = N'AdventureWorks2012-Full Database Backup',
SKIP, NOREWIND, NOUNLOAD, COMPRESSION, STATS = 10
GO
```

> **Note**
>
> In SQL Server 2005, it was possible to create a copy-only backup only
> with Transact-SQL; however, in current releases, such as SQL Server
> 2012, this can be achieved with SSMS.

Mirrored Backups

Mirrored backups, also called *mirrored media sets*, is another new feature
that was introduced with SQL Server 2005 but continues to be delivered in
SQL Server 2012. Mirrored backups are a large timesaver. Unlike in the
past when you were given the arduous task of creating additional backup
copies in the event of a media failure, SQL Server 2012 can create a
maximum of four mirrors during a backup operation, which increases reliability and performance. Moreover, SQL Server 2012 also ensures the reliability of the media through database and backup checksums. The only
shortcoming to mirrored backups is that the media for each mirror must be
the same. For instance, if a backup is committed to tape, all mirrors must
also be committed to tape.

A mirrored backup is not necessarily a backup type, per se, but an optional
clause available when you're creating full, differential, or transaction log
backups.

The following Transact-SQL syntax creates a media set called Adventure
Works2012MediaSet using three tape drives as backup devices:

```
BACKUP DATABASE AdventureWorks2012 TO TAPE = '\\.\tape01',
➥TAPE = '\\.\tape02', TAPE = '\\.\tape03'
WITH
  FORMAT,
  MEDIANAME = 'AdventureWorks2012MediaSet'
```

Typically, the speed of a backup device is a bottleneck that causes backup performance degradation. To increase the speed of any type of backup, it is a best practice to use multiple backup devices or different volumes. When using multiple backup devices, or when different volumes are used, backups are written in parallel, thus increasing backup times and performance.

Note

For a complete listing of Transact-SQL syntax conventions on backups, including the arguments, options, and explanations, see "Backup Transact-SQL" in the SQL Server 2012 Books Online.

Backing Up Examples with SQL Server Management Studio

The following sections focus on SQL Server 2012 backup and restore strategies for databases within the Database Engine. The examples include backing up all user and system databases to disk with a maintenance plan, compressing backups, backing up the AdventureWorks2012 database using the Full recovery model, and restoring the AdventureWorks2012 database to the point of failure.

Understanding the Need to Back Up the System Databases

If you want to restore a SQL Server 2012 installation, it is imperative not only to back up SQL Server user databases, such as AdventureWorks2012, but also the system databases. The main SQL Server 2012 system databases are

- **Master Database**—The master database is an important system database in SQL Server 2012. It houses all system-level data, including system configuration settings, login information, disk space, stored procedures, linked servers, and the existence of other databases, along with other crucial information.

- **Model Database**—The model database serves as a template for creating new databases in SQL Server 2012. The data residing in the model database is commonly applied to a new database with the Create Database command. In addition, the tempdb database is re-created with the help of the model database every time SQL Server 2012 is started.

- **Msdb Database**—Used mostly by SQL Server Agent, the msdb database stores alerts, scheduled jobs, and operators. In addition, it also stores historical information on backups and restores, Mail, and Service Broker.

- **Tempdb**—The tempdb database holds temporary information, including tables, stored procedures, objects, and intermediate result-sets. Each time SQL Server is started, the tempdb database starts with a clean copy.

Additional system databases may be present under the System Databases folder if you install features such as Replication and Full-Text and Semantic Extractions for Search. It is also important to perform a backup of a hidden system database called Resource database. You will need to perform a file backup and file restore of this database because this database does not appear in SQL server management studio.

Note

By default, the master, msdb, and tempdb databases use the Simple recovery model, whereas the model database uses the Full recovery model by default.

It is a best practice to include the system databases with the existing user database backup strategy. At a minimum, the system databases should be backed up at the time a configuration is added, changed, or removed relative to a database, login, job, or operator.

Conducting a Full Backup Using SSMS

To perform a full SQL database backup on the AdventureWorks2012 database using SSMS, do the following:

1. In Object Explorer, first connect to the Database Engine, expand the desired server, and then expand the database folder.

2. Select the AdventureWorks2012 database.

3. Right-click the AdventureWorks2012 database, select Tasks, and then select Backup.

4. On the General page in the Back Up Database window, review the name of the database being backed up and validate that the Backup Type option is set to Full.

5. Type the desired name and description for the backup, and in the Backup Component section, choose Database, as shown in Figure 6.2.

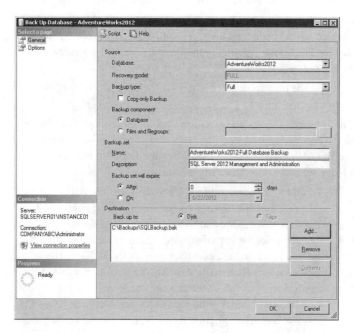

FIGURE 6.2
Viewing the SQL Server Back Up Database page.

The Destination section identifies the disk or tape media that will contain the backup. You can specify multiple destinations in this section by clicking the Add button. For disk media, a maximum of 64 disk devices can be specified. The same limit applies to tape media. If multiple devices are specified, the backup information is spread across those devices. All the devices must be present to restore the database. If no tape devices are attached to the database server, the Tape option is disabled.

6. In the Destination section, choose the backup to Disk option, as shown in Figure 6.2. Accept the default backup location or remove the existing path and click Add to select a new destination path for the backup.

7. In the Select Backup Destination window, type the path on the hard disk where the database backup will be created, including the backup filename, and then click OK. Alternatively, you can choose a backup device instead of storing the backup on hard disk.

   As mentioned earlier, the Copy-Only Backup option can now be enabled when conducting a backup with SQL Server Management Studio. The option is found in the Back Up Database window (see Figure 6.2).

8. Initialize the backup or enter advanced backup options by clicking Options in the Select a Page pane.

   The Overwrite Media section allows you to specify options relative to the destination media for the backup. The two options available are Back Up to the Existing Media Set and Back Up to A New Media Set and Erase All Existing Backup Sets.

   ■ When the first option, Back Up to the Existing Media Set, is selected, there are three potential settings to be configured. The first setting, Append to the Existing Backup Set, assumes that any prior backups that were contained on the media set are preserved and the new backup is added to them. The second setting, Overwrite All Existing Backup Sets, replaces any former backups on the existing media set with the current backup. An optional setting exists; Check Media Set Name and Backup Set Expiration forces SQL Server to verify the media set name and backup set expiration settings before a backup occurs on an existing media set by providing a media set name to be utilized.

   ■ The second option, Back Up to a New Media Set and Erase All Existing Backup Sets, allows you to create a new media set and erase previous backups sets by inputting a new media set name and description.

   Options in the Reliability section can be used to ensure that the backup that has been created can be used reliably in a restore situation. Verifying the Backup When Finished is highly recommended but causes the backup time to be extended during the backup verification. Similarly, the Perform Checksum Before Writing to Media option helps ensure that you have a sound backup but again causes the database backup to run longer. Finally, the backup process will fail if errors are found in the checksum analysis; therefore, indicate whether you want the backup process to proceed or stop by enabling the setting Continue on Error.

The options in the Transaction Log section are available for databases that are in the Full or Bulk-Logged recovery model. These options are disabled in the Simple recovery model and are available only if a Transaction Log backup is selected. The Truncate the Transaction Log option causes any inactive portion of the transaction log to be removed after the database backup is complete. This is the default option and helps keep the size of your transaction log manageable. The Backup the tail of the log option is related to point-in-time restores.

The options in the Tape Drive section are enabled only when you select Tape for the destination media. The Unload the Tape After Backup option rejects the media tape after the backup is complete. This feature can help identify the end of the backup and prevent the tape from being overwritten the next time the backup runs. The Rewind the Tape Before Unloading option is self-explanatory and causes the tape to be released and rewound prior to unloading the tape.

The last set of options is the compression settings to be used during the backup process. The options include Use the Default Server Settings, Compress Backup, and Do Not Compress Backup.

9. On the Options page, in the Overwrite Media section, maintain the default settings, Back Up to the Existing Media Set, and Append to the Existing Backup Set.

10. In the Reliability section, choose the options Verify Backup When Finished, Perform Checksum Before Writing Media, and Continue on Error.

11. In the Compression section, set the compression for this database backup to Compress Backup, as shown in Figure 6.3. Click OK to execute the backup.

12. Review the success or failure error message and click OK to finalize.

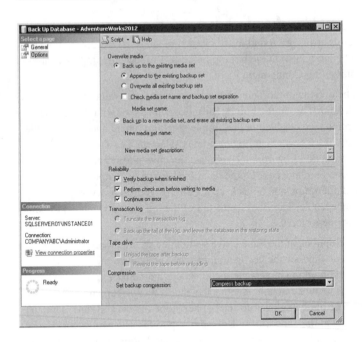

FIGURE 6.3
Setting SQL Server full backup advanced options.

Conducting a Differential Backup Using SSMS

To perform a differential SQL database backup on an individual database using SSMS, do the following:

1. Right-click the AdventureWorks2012 database, select Tasks, and then select Backup.

2. On the General page in the Back Up Database window, review the name of the database being backed up and validate that the Backup Type option is set to Differential.

3. Type the desired name and description for the backup, and in the Backup Component section, choose Database.

4. In the Destination section, choose the Disk option. Accept the default backup location or remove the existing path and click Add to select a new destination path for the backup.

5. In the Select Backup Destination window, type the path on the hard disk where the database backup will be created, including the

backup filename and then click OK. For this example, use the same destination path and filename used in the previous full backup steps.

6. On the Options page, in the Overwrite Media section, maintain the default settings, Back Up to the Existing Media Set and Append to the Existing Backup Set.

7. In the Reliability section, choose the options Verify Backup When Finished, Perform Checksum Before Writing to Media, and Continue on Error.

8. Set the desired backup compression settings. Then click OK to execute the backup.

9. Review the success or failure error message and click OK to finalize.

Conducting a Transaction Log Backup Using SSMS

To perform a transaction log SQL database backup on an individual database using SSMS, do the following:

1. In Object Explorer, first connect to the Database Engine, expand the desired server, and then expand the database folder.

2. Select the AdventureWorks2012 database.

3. Right-click the AdventureWorks2012 database, select Tasks, and then select Backup.

4. On the General page in the Back Up Database window, review the name of the database being backed up and validate that the Backup Type option is set to Transaction Log.

5. Type the desired name and description for the backup and in the Backup Component section, choose Database.

6. In the Destination section, choose the Disk option. Accept the default backup location or remove the existing path and click Add to select a new destination path for the backup.

7. In the Select Backup Destination window, type the path on the hard disk where the database backup will be created, including the backup filename, and click OK. For this example, use the same destination path and filename used in the previous full backup steps.

8. Initialize the backup or enter advanced backup options by clicking Options in the Select a Page pane.

The Transaction Log section allows you to specify options relative to how the transaction log should be handled during the backup. The two choices are as follows:

- Truncate the Transaction Log
- Back Up the tail of the log and Leave the Database in the Restoring State

After a checkpoint is performed, the inactive portion of the transaction log is marked as reusable. If the default option—Truncate the Transaction Log—is selected, the backup truncates the inactive portion of the transaction log, creating free space. The physical size of the transaction log still remains the same, but the usable space is reduced.

The second option—Back Up the tail of the log, and Leave the Database in the Restoring State—is typically used if a disaster occurs and you are restoring the database to a point in failure. Ultimately, this option backs up the active logs that were not already backed up. These active logs can then be used against the recently recovered database to a point in failure or point in time.

9. On the Options page, in the Overwrite Media section, maintain the default settings, Back Up to the Existing Media Set and Append to the Existing Backup Set.

10. In the Reliability section, choose the options Verify Backup When Finished, Perform Checksum Before Writing Media, and Continue on Error.

11. In the Transaction Log section, choose the option Truncate the Transaction Log.

12. In the Compression section, set the compression for this database backup to Compress Backup.

13. Review the settings, as shown in Figure 6.4, and click OK to execute the backup.

14. Review the success or failure error message and click OK to finalize.

Automating Backups with a Maintenance Plan

Instead of backing up a database and transaction logs individually with SSMS or Transact-SQL, you can automate and schedule this process by creating a maintenance plan. The Database Backup, Differential Backup, and Transaction Log maintenance plan tasks reduces the efforts required to create individual backups on all user and system databases. In addition, it is possible to create subtasks and schedule these items at separate times.

Maintenance plans are discussed further in Chapter 16, "SQL Server 2012 Maintenance Practices."

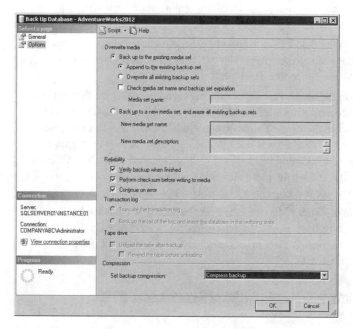

FIGURE 6.4
Selecting the option to truncate the Transaction Log on the Options page.

Note

In the real world, an organization will create multiple maintenance plans for both its system and user databases. In addition, transaction log backups and frequency of the backups would be determined based on their backup and recovery objects. The preceding example is strictly an example to help you get an understanding of the process.

Follow these steps to start the creation of a customized backup maintenance plan for all user and system databases by using the Maintenance Plan Wizard. We will create a full backup to occur daily at midnight, a differential backup to occur at noon, and a transaction log back up to occur every hour:

1. In Object Explorer, first connect to the Database Engine, expand the desired server, and then expand the Management folder.

2. Right-click Maintenance Plans and choose Maintenance Plan Wizard.

3. In the Welcome to the Database Maintenance Plan Wizard page, read the message and click Next.

4. On the Select Plan Properties page, enter a name and description for the maintenance plan, such as System and User Database Maintenance Plan Backups.

5. On the Select Plan Properties page, choose either the first option, Separate Schedules for Each Task, or the second option, Single Schedule for the Entire Plan or No Schedule. For this example, a single schedule was used for the entire plan; however, separate schedules could be specified if there is a need to create a different schedule for the Full (Midnight), Differential (Noon), and Transaction Log (Every Hour) backups. Then click Next.

6. In the Select Maintenance Tasks page, check the Back Up Database (Full), Back Up Database (Differential), and Back Up Database (Transaction Log) maintenance tasks, as shown in Figure 6.5, and click Next.

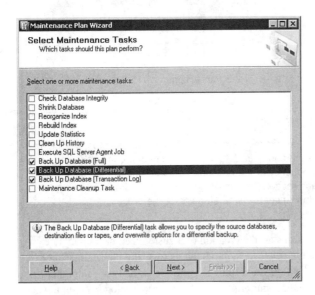

FIGURE 6.5
Selecting the backup tasks the maintenance plan should perform.

7. On the Select Maintenance Task Order page, review the order in which the tasks will be executed and click Next. For this example, the Back Up Database (Full) task should be listed first, then the Back Up Database (Differential), and then the Back Up Database (Transaction Log) task. Click Next to continue.

8. The Define Back Up Database (Full) Task screen will be invoked. The following backup options can be configured, as illustrated in Figure 6.6:

- **Backup Type**—Displays the type of backup being performed.

- **Database(s)**—Specify the databases affected by this mainte-nance plan task. The options include All Databases, System Databases, All User Databases (excluding system), and Individual databases.

- **Copy-Only Backup**—If selected, this option will conduct a copy-only backup and won't impact the recovery sequence.

- **For Availability Databases**—This option should be used if you only want to conduct a Copy-Only backup. As a reminder, a copy-only backup is independent of the sequence of conven-tional backups.

- **Backup Set Will Expire**—This option allows you to specify when the backup set will expire and can be overwritten by another backup based on number of days or a specific date.

- **Back Up To**—This option allows the backup to be written to a file or tape. A tape drive must be present on the system, and it is possible to write to a file residing on a network share.

- **Back Up Databases Across One or More Files**—For the backup destination, you can either add or remove one or more disk or tape locations. In addition, you can view the contents of a file and append to the backup file if it already exists.

- **Create a Backup File for Every Database**—Instead of selecting the option Back Up Databases Across One or More Files, you can let SQL Server automatically create a backup file for every database selected. In addition, it is also possible to automatically create a subdirectory for each database selected.

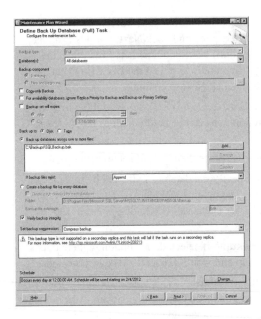

FIGURE 6.6
Configuring the Full Backup Settings on the Define Back Up Database (Full) Task.

Note

The subdirectory inherits permissions from the parent directory. Therefore, use NTFS permissions to secure this folder and restrict unauthorized access.

- **Verify Backup Integrity**—This option verifies the integrity of the backup when completed by firing a Transact-SQL command that verifies whether the backup was successful and accessible.

- **Set Backup Compression**—This option controls the compression settings associated with a database backup.

- **Schedule**—This option enables you to create a separate schedule for this specific task.

Now that you understand the options available when defining a backup database task, let's turn to our example. For our example, as illustrated in Figure 6.6, select All Databases, Backup to Disk and specify a location, if backup exists append, verify integrity, enable compression and set the schedule to occur every day at 12:00 am. Click Next to continue.

9. The next task in the maintenance plan is the Define Backup Database (Differential) Task. The potential options that can be configured are the same as in Define Back Up Database (Full) Task. However, the backup type will be a differential backup, not a full. For this example, use the following settings, and then click Next. Select All Databases, Backup to Disk and specify a location, if backup exists append, verify integrity, enable compression, and set the schedule to occur every day at 12:00 pm.

10. Next is the Back Up Database (Transaction Log) Task. Similar to the two tasks (Full and Differential), the options and configurations are very similar. However, the Backup Type is Transaction Log, and databases running the simple recovery model will be excluded. For this example, use the following settings, and then click Next. Select All Databases, Backup to Disk and specify a location, if backup exists append, verify integrity, enable compression, and set the schedule to occur every day and every hour. Click Next to continue.

Note

When you select the option to back up all databases, databases with the simple recovery model will be excluded because Transaction Log backups do not apply.

---

11. On the Select Report Options page, set the option to either write a report to a text file and enter a folder location, or email the report. If you want to email the report, Database Mail must be enabled and configured, and an Agent Operation with a valid email address must already exist. Click Next to continue.

12. The Complete the Wizard page summarizes the options selected in the Maintenance Plan Wizard. It is possible to drill down on a task to view advanced settings, as shown in Figure 6.7. Review the options selected and click Finish to close the summary page.

13. In the Maintenance Plan Wizard Progress page, review the creation status and click Close to end the Maintenance Plan Wizard.

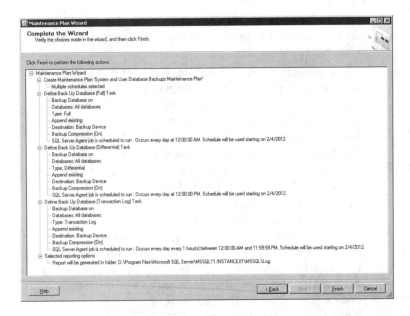

FIGURE 6.7
Configuring the Full Backup Settings on the Define Back Up Database (Full) Task.

14. The maintenance plan is then created and should be visible under the Maintenance Plan folder in SSMS. In addition, you can find the maintenance plan jobs in the Jobs folder within the SQL Server Agent. This is illustrated in Figure 6.8.

Note

For these backup examples, SQL Server is being backed up to disk. In production, backups should not be stored on the same disks as the database or transaction logs. For retention and recovery purposes, backups stored to disks should eventually be committed to tape and stored offsite. Recently, many organizations are moving toward cloud-based storage for backups, which is another alternative.

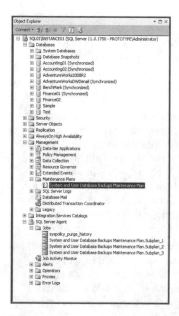

FIGURE 6.8
Viewing maintenance plans in SSMS.

Notes from the Field: Best Practices for Backing Up Large Mission-Critical Databases

Data explosion is occurring within the industry, and databases are becoming larger than ever before. As you can imagine, these large databases are putting a tremendous amount of pressure on DBAs because they must still meet their SLAs with regard to backup and recovery times. However, the backups and restores are taking much longer than before because of the size of these databases. Fortunately, organizations can take advantage of many features within SQL Server 2012 that alleviate these issues:

- **Use Multiple Backup Devices Simultaneously**—If you are performing a backup or restore on a large database, use multiple backup devices simultaneously to allow backups to be written to all the devices at the same time. Using multiple backup devices in SQL Server allows database backups to be written to all devices in parallel. One of the potential bottlenecks in backup throughput is the backup device speed. Using multiple backup devices can increase throughput in proportion to the number of devices used. Similarly, the backup can be restored from multiple devices in parallel.

- **Use Mirrored Media Set**—A total of four mirrors are possible per media set. With the mirrored media set, the backup operation writes to multiple groups of backup devices. Each group of backup devices makes up a single mirror in the mirrored media set. Each single mirror set must use the same quantity and type of physical backup devices and all must have the same properties.

- **Use Snapshot Backups (Fastest Backups)**—This is the fastest way to perform backups on databases. A snapshot backup is a specialized backup that is created almost instantaneously by using a split-mirror solution obtained from an independent hardware and software vendor. Snapshot backups minimize or eliminate the use of SQL Server resources to accomplish the backup. This is especially useful for moderate to very large databases in which availability is very important. In many cases, snapshot backups and restores can be performed in seconds with very little or zero effect on the server.

- **Use Low-Priority Backup Compression**—Backing up databases with the backup compression feature could increase CPU usage, and any additional CPU consumed by the compression process can adversely impact concurrent operations. Therefore, when possible, create a low-priority compressed backup whose CPU usage is limited by Resource Governor to prevent any CPU contention.

- **Use Full, Differential and Log Backups**—If the database recovery model is set to FULL, use a different combination of backups (FULL, DIFFERENTIAL, and LOG). This will help minimize the number of restores that need to be applied to bring the database to the point of failure.

- **Use File/Filegroup Backups**—Use file and filegroup backups and T-log backups. These allow for only those files that contain the relevant data, instead of the whole database, to be backed up or restored.

- **Use a Different Disk for Backups**—Do not use the same physical disk that holds database files or log files for backup purposes. Using the same physical disk not only affects the performance, but also may reduce the recoverability of the plan.

Conducting a Full Database Recovery

When database corruption or a disaster occurs, you need to restore the database to the point of failure or until a specific date and time. If the database is set to the Full recovery model during the backup, the high-level plan for restoring the database consists of the following sequential tasks: The first step, if possible, is to back up the active transactions (the tail of the log) and leave the database in a restoring state. The next step includes restoring the latest full backup and then the most recent differential backups, provided that differential database backups were taken. Finally, subsequent log files should be restored in sequence, with the final log being the tail of the log.

If the Simple recovery model is used, it is not possible to make transaction log backups; therefore, the restore process consists of restoring the last full backup and most recent differential backup.

Understanding the Database Recovery Options

When conducting a restore, a DBA should be aware of a number of recovery options. The following points outline these recovery options:

- **Restore Options**—When restoring the database, the following options could be utilized:

  - **Overwrite the Existing Database (With `Replace`)**—When used, this restore operation will overwrite the files of any database that is currently using the database name that will be restored.

  - **Preserve the Replication Settings (With `Keep_Replication`)**—Provided that replication was present before the backup was taken, this option will preserve the replication settings when restoring a published database to another instance of SQL Server.

  - **Restrict Access to the Restored Database (WITH `RESTRICTED_USER`)**—When this option is selected, the database will be restored and only restricted users such as db_owner, dbcreator, or sysadmin will have access to the database.

  - **Recovery State**—One of these three settings need to be selected to dictate the state of the database after the recovery operations are performed:

    - **RESTORE WITH RECOVERY**—This option recovers the database after the final backup within the restore process. The database will be ready to accept transactions and connectivity because uncommitted transactions will be rolled back; however, additional transaction logs cannot be restored.

    - **RESTORE WITH NO RECOVERY**—This option leaves the database in a recovery state with the intention additional restores can be conducted against the

database. If this option is selected, the Preserve
Replication Settings option is disabled, and you will
eventually have to restore the database using the WITH
RECOVERY option for users and applications to
connect. Uncommitted transactions will not be rolled
back; however, additional transaction logs can be
restored.

- **RESTORE WITH STANDBY**—This option leaves the
  database in a standby state. When the database is in a
  standby state, it can be used for limited read-only
  access. To use this option, a Standby file must be specified. Undo transactions will be saved to the standby file
  so recovery effected can eventually be reversed.

- **Tail of the Log Backup**—If a tail of the log backup has not already
  been conducted, select this option to designate that a tail of the log
  backup be performed along with the database restore.

- **Server Connections**—If specified, this option allows you to ensure
  that all active connections between Management Studio and the
  database are closed. If connections are not closed, restore operations
  may fail.

- **Prompt**—This option is self-explanatory. If selected, you will be
  prompted to continue after each database restore.

Understanding the Database Recovery Advisor

A new Database Recovery Advisor has been introduced in SQL Server
2012 to simplify the restore process for DBAs. By introducing a new
visual timeline, a DBA can quickly and easily restore a database to a point
in time. The visual timeline can be invoked by clicking the Timeline button
in the General page when using the Recovery task in SQL Server
Management Studio. Once invoked, the Backup Timeline, as illustrated in
Figure 6.9, illustrates a visual timeline of the backups. It is possible to
select an option to the last backup taken or to a specific date and time. The
time interval displays the options for the interval types viewable in the
timeline. The options are hour, six hours, day, or week. The timeline is
color coded based on the legends, which include Full Database Backup,
Differential Database Backup, Transaction Log Backup, and tail of the log.
If you are trying to restore to a specific date and time, use the scrollbar
beneath the timeline to move the cursor forward and backward to a desired
timeframe.

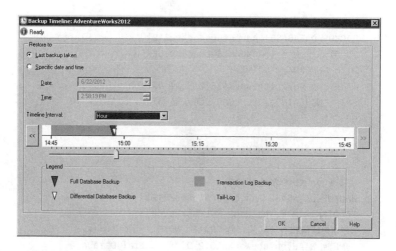

FIGURE 6.9
Leveraging the Backup Timeline in order to restore a database to a specific data and time.

Conducting a Recovery with SSMS

Now that you have an understanding of the recovery options and how to use the new Database Recovery Advisor, follow these steps to restore the AdventureWorks2012 database to the point of failure. To conduct this example, we require a Full Backup, Transaction Log Backup, and a tail of the log backup. You can use the backup examples earlier in the process or use the following Transact-SQL script to initialize the backups for this restore demonstration. The following example illustrates how to conduct a recovery with SSMS:

1. Choose Start, All Programs, Microsoft SQL Server 2012, SQL Server Management Studio.

2. In Object Explorer, first connect to the Database Engine, click New Query, and execute the following code to conduct full database, differential, and multiple transaction log backups, which can be utilized for the restore process:

    ```
    --SQL SERVER 2012 MANAGEMENT & ADMINISTRATION BY ROSS
    MISTRY
    --INITIALIZE BACKUPS FOR RECOVERY EXAMPLE
    ```

```
--PHASE 1 : FULL BACKUP
BACKUP DATABASE [AdventureWorks2012]
TO DISK = N'c:\backups\SQLBackup.bak'
WITH NOFORMAT, NOINIT,
NAME = N'AdventureWorks2012-Full Database Backup',
SKIP, NOREWIND, NOUNLOAD, COMPRESSION, STATS = 10
GO

--PHASE 2: DIFFERENTIAL BACKUP

USE AdventureWorks2012
BACKUP DATABASE [AdventureWorks2012]
TO DISK = N'c:\backups\SQLBackup.bak'
WITH DIFFERENTIAL , NOFORMAT, NOINIT,
NAME = N'AdventureWorks2012-Differential Database
Backup',
SKIP, NOREWIND, NOUNLOAD, COMPRESSION, STATS = 10
GO

--PHASE 3:TRANSACTION LOG BACKUP

BACKUP LOG [AdventureWorks2012]
TO DISK = N'c:\backups\SQLBackup.bak'
WITH NOFORMAT, NOINIT,
NAME = N'AdventureWorks2012-Transaction Log Backup',
SKIP, NOREWIND, NOUNLOAD, COMPRESSION, STATS = 10
GO

--PHASE 4: ANOTHER TRANSACTION LOG BACKUP

BACKUP LOG [AdventureWorks2012]
TO DISK = N'c:\backups\SQLBackup.bak'
WITH NOFORMAT, NOINIT,
NAME = N'AdventureWorks2012-Transaction Log Backup',
SKIP, NOREWIND, NOUNLOAD, COMPRESSION, STATS = 10
GO
```

3. To restore the database to the point of failure, first close any connections to the database, including any outstanding query windows, and
   then execute the following script to perform the tail of the log
   backup to begin disaster recovery. Close the query window before

moving on to the next step, which includes restoring full, differential, and transaction log backups taken in step 2 using SSMS. As an alternative, the Restore task in SSMS can also be used to create the tail of the log backup, as illustrated in Figure 6.10.

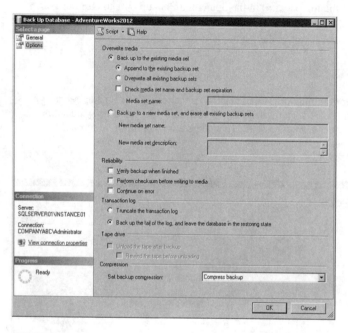

FIGURE 6.10
Using the SSMS to conduct a tail of the log backup.

```
--TRANSACTION TAIL LOG
Use Master
Go
BACKUP LOG [AdventureWorks2012]
TO DISK = N'c:\backups\SQLBackup.bak'
WITH NO_TRUNCATE , NOFORMAT, NOINIT,
NAME = N'AdventureWorks2012-Transaction Log Backup',
SKIP, NOREWIND, NOUNLOAD, NORECOVERY , COMPRESSION, STATS = 10
GO
```

4. In Object Explorer, right-click the AdventureWorks2012 database, select Tasks, Restore, and then select Database. (Notice that the

database is in a recovering state and is not operational. This is because we have conducted a tail of the log backup.)

5. On the General page in the Restore Database window, select all the database, differential, and transaction log backups (including the tail of the log backup) in the Select the Backup Sets to Restore grid, as shown in Figure 6.11. Notice that the tail of the log backup is the final backup in the list.

Note

It is worth noting that it is possible to click the Verify Backup Media button on the General page if you need to inspect and verify backup integrity or leverage the new Timeline command button to invoke the Database Recovery Advisor.

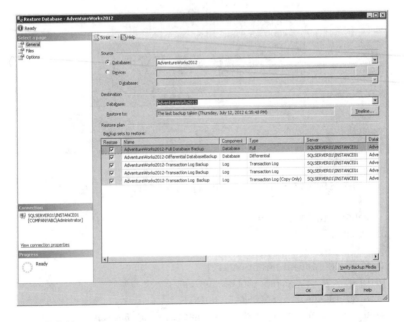

FIGURE 6.11
Specifying the Backup Sets to Restore when using the Restore Database Wizard with SSMS.

6. On the Options page in the Restore Database window, select the recovery options that meet your goals, based on the explanations in the previous Recovery Options section. For this example, we want to

restore the database to the point of failure, roll back uncommitted transactions, and leave the database in an operational state. The option, Overwrite the Existing Database (WITH REPLACE) RESTORE WITH RECOVERY, as shown in Figure 6.12, should be selected. For learning purposes, also enable the option to Prompt Before Restoring Each Backup and click OK.

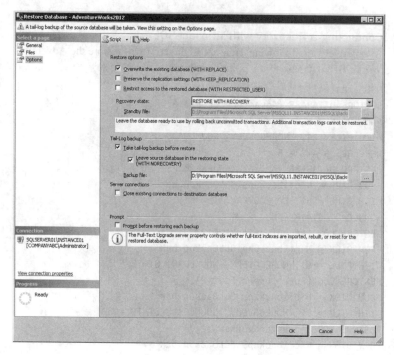

FIGURE 6.12
Reviewing the Restore Options page.

7. Because you have enabled the Prompt option, the Continue with Restore dialog box will prompt you to authorize each backup before proceeding to the next. Review each backup and click Yes. Notice how the wizard walks you through the process by first restoring the full backup, then the differential backup, and then all of the transaction logs, with the final being the tail of the log.

8. Review the restore success message and click OK.

> **Note**
>
> As indicated earlier, if you need to restore the database to a specific
> point in time, it is possible to use the new Database Recovery Advisor by
> clicking the Timeline button on the General page and then specifying a
> date and time to restore to. The process will stop rolling back any entries
> in the transaction log after this specified period.

Conducting a Recovery with Transact-SQL

Alternatively, the following Transact-SQL script will restore the Adventure
Works2012 database to the point of failure:

```
USE [master]
RESTORE DATABASE [AdventureWorks2012]
FROM DISK = N'c:\backups\SQLBackup.bak'
WITH FILE = 49, NORECOVERY, NOUNLOAD,
REPLACE, STATS = 5
RESTORE DATABASE [AdventureWorks2012]
FROM DISK = N'c:\backups\SQLBackup.bak'
WITH FILE = 50, NORECOVERY,
NOUNLOAD, STATS = 5
RESTORE LOG [AdventureWorks2012]
FROM DISK = N'c:\backups\SQLBackup.bak'
WITH FILE = 51, NORECOVERY, NOUNLOAD, STATS = 5
RESTORE LOG [AdventureWorks2012]
FROM DISK = N'c:\backups\SQLBackup.bak'
WITH FILE = 52, NORECOVERY, NOUNLOAD, STATS = 5
RESTORE LOG [AdventureWorks2012]
FROM DISK = N'c:\backups\SQLBackup.bak'
WITH FILE = 53, NOUNLOAD, STATS = 5
GO
```

Backup and Recovery Impact on Other Database Engine Features

The following sections outlines best practices and strategies on how to
back up and recover other features associated with the Database Engine.

AlwaysOn Replica Priority for Backups

AlwaysOn Availability Groups introduce a new concept known as *backup
preferences*; therefore, SQL Server 2012 will automatically redirect backup
jobs to preferred AlwaysOn Availability Group Replicas based on a backup

priority. It is possible to configure the Backup Preferences by right-clicking a desired availability group and selecting the Backup Preferences page in the Availability Group property dialog box. The Backup Preferences, as illustrated in Figure 6.13 include the following:

- **Prefer Secondary**—Select this option if you would like to automate the backups associated with databases partaking in an availability group to be conducted on a secondary replica. If a secondary replica is not available, the backup will occur on the primary replica.

- **Secondary Only**—This option indicates that all automated backups for the availability group must occur on the secondary replica.

- **Primary Only**—This option is used when you want to force all backups to occur only on the current primary replica.

- **Any Replica**—Backups can occur on any replica within the availability group.

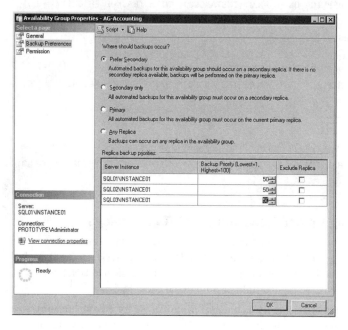

FIGURE 6.13
Configuring AlwaysOn Availability Groups backup preferences.

Understanding the AlwaysOn Backup Preference Page

Toward the bottom of the Backup Preference page is a grid that should be used to configure the backup priority settings for each replica. The options include specifying a backup priority for each replica and whether you want to exclude a replica from partaking in backups. For the backup priority, you can choose between priorities 1 to 100. The integer value of 1 represents the lowest priority, whereas 100 represents the highest priority. Obviously, the replica with the highest priority level will take precedence.

Alternatively, these settings can be configured with Transact-SQL, as in the following example, which changes the backup priority settings for three replicas partaking in an availability group called AG-Accounting. The values are 50, 75, and 100:

```
USE [master]
GO
ALTER AVAILABILITY GROUP [AG-Accounting]
MODIFY REPLICA ON N'SQL01\INSTANCE01' WITH (BACKUP_PRIORITY = 50)
GO
USE [master]
GO
ALTER AVAILABILITY GROUP [AG-Accounting]
MODIFY REPLICA ON N'SQL02\INSTANCE01' WITH (BACKUP_PRIORITY = 75)
GO
USE [master]
GO
ALTER AVAILABILITY GROUP [AG-Accounting]
MODIFY REPLICA ON N'SQL03\INSTANCE01' WITH (BACKUP_PRIORITY = 100)
GO
```

Backing Up and Recovering Full-Text Catalogs

The process of backing up and restoring full-text catalogs is similar to backing up and restoring database files. Unlike in SQL Server 2000, each full-text catalog in SQL Server 2012 is treated as a file and is automatically included in regular, full, or differential backups.

The catalog is essentially a container of properties for a group of full-text indexes. It exists in the database completely; it is no longer stored in the file system. When you back up your database, your full-text catalog and indexes are backed up with your database; you can't do more granular backups that contain only the full-text catalog. Nor is there a way to restore only the full-text catalog; database restores contain the database objects as well as any full-text indexes or catalogs that are in that database backup.

As a result, when backing up the full-text catalog, you should follow the full backup, differential backup, and transaction log backup and recovery procedures described earlier in the chapter.

Understanding and Creating Database Snapshots

Database snapshots provide a read-only copy of a SQL Server database at a specific point in time. This static view provides a comprehensive picture of the full database, tables, views, and stored procedures. Organizations can use a database snapshot to protect the state of a database at a specific time, to do offload reporting, or to maintain historical data. For instance, an organization can revert to a snapshot in the event it runs into problems. Keep in mind that this feature is available only with SQL Server 2012 Enterprise Edition.

When using database snapshots, some limitations exist, as follows:

- It is not possible to drop, detach, or restore a database if a snapshot already exists. The snapshot must be removed first.

- Snapshots of the system databases such as the model, master, or tempdb are not supported.

- Full-text indexing is not supported with database snapshots.

Caution

Database snapshots are a convenient feature, but they are not a replacement for maintaining a backup and restore plan. A backup and recovery plan is still necessary because changes made after the snapshot is taken are lost unless an organization also maintains regular and full backups that include the latest transaction log. This ensures that the most recent data is available for recovery. As a result, a snapshot should be viewed only as an extra layer of protection for preserving a database to a specific point in time.

Also remember to exclude any database snapshots when creating database backup jobs using Transact-SQL or via a maintenance plan. You can run the following query to identify any database snapshots on your local SQL Server instance that you can exclude:

```
Select
Name from Sys.Databases
Where Source_Database_ID IS NOT NULL
Go
```

If you want to fully use and manage snapshots, two tools are necessary. You must use Transact-SQL to create and revert to snapshots and SSMS to view snapshots. Both Transact-SQL and SSMS can be used to delete snapshots. The following sections show how to create, view, revert to, and delete database snapshots.

Creating a Database Snapshot with Transact-SQL

In the Query Analyzer, execute the following script to create a database snapshot for the AdventureWorks2012 database:

```
--Creating a database Snapshot with Transact-SQL
Use AdventureWorks2012
CREATE DATABASE AdventureWorks2012_Snapshot_1_SS ON
( NAME = AdventureWorks2012_Data, FILENAME =
'C:\Backups\AdventureWorks2012_Snapshot_1_SS.ss' )
AS SNAPSHOT OF AdventureWorks2012;
GO
```

Viewing a Database Snapshot with SSMS

After creating the database snapshot, you can view it using SSMS. Follow the steps in the preceding section to view the AdventureWorks2012 database snapshot and then follow these steps to view the snapshot:

1. In Object Explorer, first connect to the Database Engine, expand the desired server, expand the Database folder, and then expand the Database Snapshots folder.

2. Select the desired database snapshot to view (for this example, AdventureWorks2012_Snapshot_1_SS, as shown in Figure 6.14).

Reverting to a Database Snapshot with Transact-SQL

In Query Analyzer, execute the following script to revert the Adventure Works2012 database with the database snapshot created in the preceding steps:

```
USE Master
RESTORE DATABASE AdventureWorks2012
```

```
FROM DATABASE_SNAPSHOT = AdventureWorks2012_Snapshot_1_SS'
GO
```

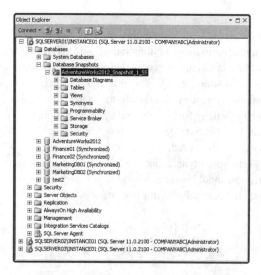

FIGURE 6.14
Viewing database snapshots with SSMS.

Dropping a Database Snapshot

You can drop a database snapshot by either right-clicking the snapshot in
SSMS and choosing Delete or by issuing a DROP statement that identifies
the name of the snapshot to be dropped.

The following script drops the AdventureWorks2012 snapshot created in
the preceding steps:

```
DROP DATABASE 'AdventureWorks2012_Snapshot_1_SS'
```

Tip

When naming snapshots, it is a best practice to first include the name of
the source database supplemented with the date and time of when the
snapshot was taken. For example: <DatabaseName>_snapshot_
<yyyy_mm_dd>_<hhmm>. Moreover, keep in mind that database snap-
shots are associated and dependent on the primary database. If the
primary database goes offline, the database snapshot will not be
accessible.

For more information on database snapshots, see the topic "Database Snapshots" in SQL Server 2012 Books Online.

Summary

Although you, as DBA, are charged with maintaining the SQL Server database, you can easily get caught up in daily administration and firefighting because your workload is often laborious. It is nonetheless imperative for you to develop and implement a strategic SQL Server backup and recovery plan. Currently, the backup maintenance task is likely the easiest tool available to implement the backup strategy for all user and system relational databases. In the event that Analysis Services, Reporting Services, or Internet Information Services is being used, it is important for each component to find its way into your organization's backup and restore plan. Finally, your organization should make it a habit to test and document your backup and recovery plan prior to implementation.

Best Practices

The following are best practices for backing up and restoring SQL Server 2012:

- Define and document an SLA relevant to the SQL Server 2012 environment.

- Test the backup and recovery plan on a periodic basis and also before production to validate that it is operational and the SLA can be met.

- Select the appropriate recovery model for all systems and user databases. Use the Full recovery model for mission-critical databases that need to be restored to the point of failure in the event of a disaster.

- Isolate database and transaction log files on separate spindles for recovery purposes.

- Save the backups locally on a redundant disk drive separate from the online databases and back up to tape on a regular basis.

- If database or transaction log backups are stored locally on disk, do *not* store them on the same volumes as the database and transaction log files. If a drive or volume failure occurs, both the files and backups could be lost.

- For retention and recovery purposes, the backups stored to disk should be committed to tape or a cloud-based provider.

- Commit to doing frequent backups if the system is an online transaction processing (OLTP) environment. An OLTP database is also known as the databases residing in the SQL Server Database Engine.

- To obtain a holistic overview of backup I/O performance, it is possible to isolate the backup I/O to and from devices by using the following counters:

  - The Device Throughput Bytes/sec counter of the SQLServer:Backup Device object

  - The Backup/Restore Throughput/sec counter of the SQLServer:Databases object

- Try to schedule backups when SQL Server is not in the process of being heavily updated.

- Use maintenance plans to streamline, automate, and schedule backups for all system and user databases.

- For large databases, consider introducing additional files or filegroups and include a combination of full, differential, filegroup, and transaction log backups to reduce backup and restore times.

- Speed up the backup process by selecting multiple backup devices.

- Leverage the new Backup Compression feature to minimize the backup footprint on disk. However, first test the impact in a dedicated lab before rolling out into production, and also evaluate how much disk savings you can gain by performing backup compression ratio.

- Use Resource Governor to limit CPU usage on compressed backups.

- When restoring the database to the point of failure, remember to first back up the tail of the log and then conduct the restore.

- For any high business impact data in the backup, make sure you encrypt the files before moving the backup tape or disk offsite. This will help protect unauthorized access to your business critical data if somebody gains physical access to backup files.

- Use the CHECKSUM option when performing database backups of critical data. This option helps verify that the pages in the database are reliable and are not corrupt. For more information, review "Database Backups" in Books Online.

PART II

Hardening, Auditing, and Securing SQL Server 2012

IN THIS PART

CHAPTER 7   Hardening and Auditing a SQL Server 2012 Implementation

CHAPTER 8   Administering SQL Server 2012 Security and Authorization

CHAPTER 9   Encrypting SQL Server 2012 Data and Communications

CHAPTER 7

Hardening and Auditing a SQL Server 2012 Implementation

SQL Server is regularly targeted by hackers because it is a repository of sensitive data for organizations. If the server is breached, hackers can gain access to confidential information, including credit cards, Social Security numbers, or sensitive customer data.

To prevent cybercrime or, at the very least, reduce it, Microsoft has been working very hard since 2002 to bring the community more secured products with the Microsoft Trustworthy Computing Initiative. Although Microsoft products are being transformed and are more secure by default and design because of Trustworthy Computing, the company is not delusional about where things stand today. Microsoft knows it must continue to invest in security to ensure the product continues to lead the database industry with the least amount of reported vulnerabilities. This is important for all DBAs to understand because it means that you should take additional steps to further harden your SQL Server implementation until you can rely fully on Trustworthy Computing. Moreover, it is equally important to audit your SQL Server infrastructure after it has been hardened.

This chapter shows how important it is to harden and audit the SQL Server implementation after SQL Server 2012 has been successfully deployed. The chapter explains how to manage a secure SQL Server implementation based on industry best practices so that vulnerabilities and security breaches are minimized. Moreover, the chapter also illustrates how to audit a SQL Server environment to ensure the highest form of organizational compliance. The following security topics are covered to harden and audit a SQL Server implementation: using configuration tools to minimize the attack surface, deciding which authentication method to use, enforcing strong passwords, using SQL Server security logs, choosing the appropriate service account, configuring advanced firewalls, creating server and database audits specifications, verifying security with Microsoft tools, and installing Windows and SQL Server Service Packs.

What's New for Hardening and Auditing SQL Server 2012 Implementation?

- SQL Server 2012 now supports the ability to be deployed on Windows Server 2008 R2 Server Core. The Server Core installation is so stripped down that traditional installation components, such as a desktop shell, graphical user interface, Windows Explorer, Microsoft Internet Explorer, and the MMC, are not included. Because the installation is so stripped down, the SQL Server installation is further hardened and much more secure.

- SQL Server accounts are following the principle of least privilege because they are better protected and now further isolated from the operating system. To further continue down the path of role separation, the local Windows Group BUILTIN\Administrators and Local System (NT Authority\System) are no longer automatically provisioned in the sysadmin fixed server role.

- Server auditing is now supported in all editions of SQL Server 2012. However, Database audits are limited to Enterprise, Datacenter, Developer, and Evaluation editions.

- The SQL Server Audit capability is now more resilient to failures when writing to an audit log—specifically on a remote share. In many cases, the target directory that hosts the audit log could reside on a remote share. If this remote share becomes unavailable, it could negatively impact auditing and in some cases shut down the server. If the target directory on a remote share goes down, SQL Server Audit will now be able to recover after the network connection is re-established.

- A new FAIL_OPERATION option for ON_FAILURE event has been introduced to fail an operation that would otherwise make an audit event to be written to a failed audit target. This option can be specified when creating a new Audit with SQL Server Management Studio or with the FAIL_OPERATION option for the ON_FAILURE event when using CREATE SERVER AUDIT Transact-SQL statement.

- Many organizations required the ability to control the amount of audit information collected without losing audit records. A new option has been introduced to limit the number of audit files without rolling over.

- A new WHERE clause has been introduced to allow SQL Server Audit the ability to filter audit events before they are written to the audit log.

> **Note**
>
> Policy-Based Management is a hardening technique; however, this book includes a dedicated chapter on this subject. For more information, see Chapter 17, "Implementing and Managing Policy-Based Management."

Windows and SQL Server Authentication

Authentication is commonly identified as a security measure designed to establish the validity of a user or application based on criteria such as an account, password, security token, or certificate. After a user or an application's validity is verified, authorization to access the desired object is granted.

At present, SQL Server 2012 continues to support two modes for validating connections and authenticating access to database resources: Windows Authentication mode and SQL Server and Windows Authentication mode. Both of these authentication methods provide access to SQL Server and its resources.

> **Note**
>
> During installation, the default authentication mode is Windows. However, the authentication mode can be changed after the installation.

Windows Authentication Mode

Windows Authentication mode is the default and recommended authentication mode. It leverages local accounts, Active Directory user accounts, and groups when granting access to SQL Server. In this mode, you, as the database administrator, are given the opportunity to grant domain or local server users access to the database server without creating and managing a separate SQL Server account.

When Windows Authentication mode is used, Active Directory user accounts are subject to enterprisewide policies enforced by the Active Directory domain, such as complex passwords, password history, account lockouts, minimum password length, maximum password length, and the Kerberos protocol. If the server is not partaking in a domain, the local security policies will govern the account's password and lockout behavior.

SQL Server and Windows Authentication Mode (Mixed)

SQL Server and Windows Authentication mode, which is regularly referred to as *mixed mode authentication*, uses either Active Directory user accounts or SQL Server accounts when validating access to SQL Server. Like the previous versions of SQL Server, SQL Server 2012 continues to support a means to enforce password and lockout policies for SQL Server login accounts when using SQL Server authentication. These SQL Server policies include enforcing password complexity, password expiration, and account lockouts. As a reminder, this functionality, which was introduced with SQL Server 2005, was not available in previous versions of SQL Server, and this was a major security concern for most organizations and DBAs. Essentially, this security concern played a role in helping define Windows authentication as the recommended practice for managing authentication in the past. Today, SQL Server and Windows Authentication mode (Mixed Mode) may be able to successfully compete with Windows Authentication mode; however, Windows Authentication specifically with Windows Server 2008 R2 Active Directory Domain Services is the breadwinner.

Which Mode Should Be Used to Harden Authentication?

When you are aware of the authentication methods, the next step is choosing one to manage SQL Server security. Although SQL Server 2012 now can enforce policies, Windows Authentication mode is still the recommended alternative for controlling access to SQL Server because this mode carries added advantages; Active Directory provides an additional level of protection with the Kerberos protocol. As a result, the authentication mechanism is more mature and robust. Therefore, administration can be reduced by leveraging Active Directory groups for role-based access to SQL Server. In addition, SQL Server 2012 continues to utilize Kerberos with all network protocols associated with the product. Network protocols include TCP, Named Pipes, Shared Memory, and Virtual Interface Adapter (VIA).

Nonetheless, this mode is not practical for everything out there. Mixed authentication is still required if a need exists to support legacy applications, if an application—or clients coming in from platforms other than Windows—requires it, and if a need for separation of duties exists.

It is common to find organizations where the SQL Server and Windows teams do not trust one another. Therefore, a clear separation of duties is required because SQL Server accounts are not managed via Active Directory.

Using Windows Authentication is a more secure choice. However, if mixed mode authentication is required, you must make sure to leverage complex passwords and the SQL Server 2012 password and lockout policies to further bolster security.

> **Note**
>
> The capability for SQL Server authentication in SQL Server 2012 to manage both password and lockout properties is available only if SQL Server is installed on Windows Server 2003 and later. The policies are enforced by the local security policy associated with the operating system

Configuring SQL Server 2012 Authentication Modes

To select or change the server authentication mode, follow these steps:

1. In SQL Server Management Studio, right-click a desired SQL Server and then click Properties.

2. On the Security page, as shown in Figure 7.1, select the desired server authentication mode under Server Authentication and then click OK.

3. In the SQL Server Management Studio dialog box, click OK to acknowledge the need to restart SQL Server.

4. In Object Explorer, right-click a desired server and then click Restart. If the SQL Server Agent is running, it requires a restart also.

> **Note**
>
> If Windows Authentication mode is selected during installation, the SA login is disabled by default. If the authentication mode is switched to SQL Server mixed mode after the installation, the SA account is still disabled and must be manually enabled. It is a best practice to reset the password when the mode is switched.

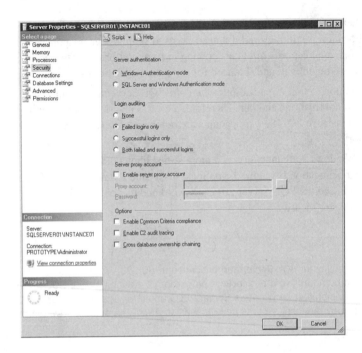

FIGURE 7.1
Configuring SQL Server 2012 authentication modes.

Security Ramifications of the SA Account

If SQL Server Authentication mode is used, a strong SA password should also be used. By default, the SA account has full administrative privileges over a SQL Server installation; therefore, in the event this account is compromised, the intruder will have full access to SQL Server and all databases.

In the past, it was common to find production SQL Server installations with a weak or blank SA password, which naturally increased the risk of security vulnerabilities and compromises. Microsoft introduced the idea of checking for blank SA passwords during the installation of Service Pack 4 on SQL Server 2000. Database administrators were further informed of the security vulnerabilities associated with maintaining a blank password; however, they were not forced to enter a password, which again left the account and server in a vulnerable state. This situation is no longer an issue since SQL Server 2005.

If you use SQL Server authentication, you must enter a strong SA password; otherwise, you cannot continue with the SQL Server installation. A strong password for SQL Server must contain at least six characters and satisfy at least three of the following four criteria:

- The password must contain uppercase letters.
- The password must contain lowercase letters.
- The password must contain numbers.
- The password must contain nonalphanumeric characters such as #, %, or ^.

In addition, a strong password cannot use typical or commonplace words that everyone in the IT field is accustomed to, such as *Password, Admin, Administrator, SA,* or *Sysadmin,* and cannot use either the name of the user logged on to the computer or the computer name. These are all considered weak passwords.

Not allowing a weak or blank password reinforces the fact that Microsoft is serious about its ongoing Trustworthy Computing Initiative. In the past few years, Microsoft has invested significant time and resources in enhancing the security of each of its products, including SQL Server 2012.

Tip

It is a best practice not to use the SA account for day-to-day administration, logging on to the server remotely, or having applications use it to connect to SQL.

Enforcing or Changing a Strong Password

If there is a need to change or assign a strong SA password because SQL Server and Windows Authentication mode is selected and the SA account is not disabled, do the following:

1. In Object Explorer, first expand the Security folder and then the Logins folder. Right-click the SA account and then click Properties.
2. On the General page in the Login Properties dialog box, as shown in Figure 7.2, enter a new complex SA password and confirm it.
3. Alternatively, enable the Enforce Password Policy and Enforce Password Expiration options and then click OK.
4. Restart Microsoft SQL Server Services, including SQL Server Agent.

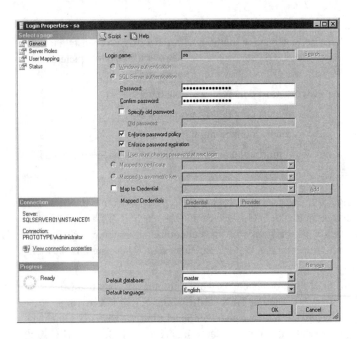

FIGURE 7.2
The SQL Server Login Properties dialog box for the SA account.

Disabling and Renaming the SA Account

When attackers want to compromise a SQL Server, they don't want to access the system as common users; they want complete control of the server so that they can gain access to all the data within it. Because most hackers already know the SA account exists, this makes hacking one step easier because this account would grant them complete control of the SQL Server if compromised. Similar to the way you use a Windows Administrator account, it is a best practice to rename and disable the SA account in SQL Server 2012 when running in mixed authentication mode. This technique increases security one step further because most hackers are familiar with the SA account and the rights associated with it.

> **Note**
>
> Don't forget that SQL Server 2012 now provides you with the option to rename the SA account during the installation of SQL Server 2012.

The following syntax first disables the SA account and then renames it to something not easily identified. This example uses the name Ross-Mistry:

```
USE MASTER
ALTER LOGIN sa DISABLE;
GO
ALTER LOGIN sa WITH NAME = [Ross-Mistry];
GO
```

> **Tip**
>
> Before renaming or disabling the SA account, make sure another account exists with administrator privileges; otherwise, you will not have access to the SQL Server. Also, it is a best practice to rename the account to something that is not related to an administrator, SA, or service, or is easily identifiable so that it's not so obvious that this account was previously SA.

Using Configuration Tools to Harden the Installation

After you've installed SQL Server 2012, you should run the SQL Server Configuration Manager to harden the SQL Server implementation.

Reducing the SQL Server 2012 Surface Area

It is beneficial to maintain a slim and efficient installation of SQL Server 2012 by minimizing its footprint. You can achieved this by reducing the SQL Server system's surface area by only installing necessary components and disabling unwanted services and features. These hardening techniques make SQL Server less susceptible to hackers and malicious attacks. This "slim and efficient" strategy also applies to the underlying Windows Server operating system. As a best practice, you should install only the required Windows role and features required to support the SQL Server 2012 features you plan to install.

> **Tip**
>
> The Policy-Based Management Surface Area Configuration facet should be used to harden a SQL Server infrastructure running the Database Engine. The Surface Area Configuration tool (SAC), which was included in SQL Server 2005, has been replaced with the Policy-Based Management framework; therefore, Policy-Based Management should be utilized to manage the SQL Server surface area. Policy-Based Management is covered in Chapter 17.

Using the SQL Server Configuration Manager Tool to Harden an Installation

You can use the SQL Server Configuration Manager tool when hardening a SQL Server implementation. This tool should be used to configure and lock down unwanted services and features associated with a SQL Server implementation. Elements that can be configured include services, network configurations, native client configurations, client protocols, and aliases installed on a server.

To launch this tool, choose Start, All Programs, Microsoft SQL Server 2012, Configuration Tools, SQL Server Configuration Manager. The SQL Server Configuration Manager window is shown in Figure 7.3. The following nodes appear in the tool:

- **SQL Server Services**—This node enables you to start, stop, pause, resume, or configure services. In addition, you should use the tool when changing service account names and passwords.

- **SQL Server Network Configuration**—This node is the place where you can configure, enable, or disable SQL Server network protocols for the SQL Server Services installed on a server. In addition, you can configure encryption and expose or hide a SQL Server database instance.

- **SQL Native Client Configuration**—This node enables you to lock down network protocols or make changes to settings associated with ports for client connections.

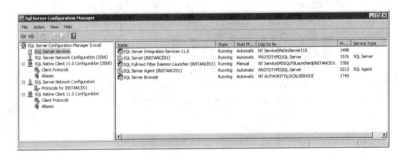

FIGURE 7.3

Managing services and connections and disabling unnecessary SQL services.

Hardening SQL Server Ports with SQL Configuration Manager

A default installation of SQL Server 2012 uses TCP port 1433 for client requests and communications. These ports are well known in the industry, which makes them a common target for hackers. Therefore, it is recommended to change the default ports associated with the SQL Server installation to put off hackers from port-scanning the default ports of the SQL Server installation. Unfortunately, SQL Server requires an open port for network communications. Therefore, this procedure prolongs the inevitable because the used port could eventually be found if the hacker is using sophisticated scanning tools.

Note

SQL Server 2012 does not automatically listen on port UDP 1434. Since SQL Server 2005, the task has been turned over to SQL Server Browser Services, which listens and resolves client connection requests made to the server. It also provides name and port resolution to clients when multiple instances are installed. During an installation of SQL Server 2012, the SQL Server Browser service startup mode is set to manual.

Follow these steps to change the default port using SQL Server Manager Configuration tools:

1. Choose Start, All Programs, Microsoft SQL Server 2012, Configuration Tools, SQL Server Configuration Manager.

2. Expand the SQL Server 2012 Network Configuration node and select Protocols for the SQL Server instance to be configured.

3. In the right pane, right-click the protocol name TCP/IP and choose Properties.

4. In the TCP/IP Properties dialog box, select the IP Addresses tab.

5. There is a corresponding entry for every IP address assigned to the server. Clear the values for both the TCP Dynamic Ports and TCP Port for each IP address except for the IP addresses under IPAll.

6. In the IPAll section for each instance, enter a new port that you want SQL Server 2012 to listen on, as shown in Figure 7.4.

7. Click Apply and restart the SQL Server Services.

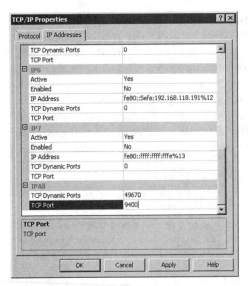

FIGURE 7.4
Changing the default SQL Server ports.

> **Note**
>
> The TCP Port for the default instance is automatically set to 1433, and the TCP Dynamic Ports setting is blank. The second and subsequent instances by default do not have the TCP Port set and have TCP Dynamic Ports set to 0. Using Dynamic Ports requires the use of the SQL Server Browser Service to direct incoming connections to the current port for that instance. This, however, makes it more difficult to set up firewalls and the like because the port can change each restart. Therefore it is recommended to use the SQL Server application name and not the port.

Hiding a SQL Server Instance from Broadcasting Information

It is possible for SQL Server clients to browse the current infrastructure and retrieve a list of running SQL Server instances. The SQL Server Browser service enumerates SQL Server information on the network. When the SQL Server is found, the client obtains the server name and can connect to it if it has the appropriate credentials. This can present a large security threat to organizations because sensitive production data can be compromised. Note that the SQL Server Browser service is required when running multiple instances on a single server. As indicated earlier, the Browser Service directs incoming connections to specific ports associated to an instance.

Organizations don't need to worry—there is help for this type of situation. The SQL Server Configuration Manager tool can be used to hide an instance of SQL Server. This is typically a best practice for mission-critical production database servers that host sensitive data because there is no need to broadcast this information. Clients and applications still can connect to SQL Server if needed; however, they need to know the SQL Server name, protocol, and which port the instance is using to connect.

To hide a SQL Server instance with SQL Server Configuration Manager, follow these steps:

1. Choose Start, All Programs, Microsoft SQL Server 2012, Configuration Tools, SQL Server Configuration Manager.

2. Expand the SQL Server 2012 Network Configuration node and select Protocols for the SQL Server instance to be configured.

3. Right-click Protocols for [Server\Instance Name] and then choose Properties.

4. In the Hide Instance box on the Protocols for [Server\Instance Name] Properties page, shown in Figure 7.5, select Yes.

5. Click OK and restart the services for the change to take effect.

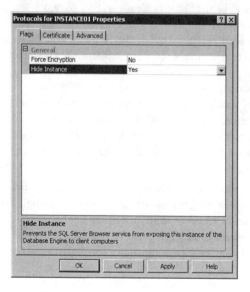

FIGURE 7.5
Hiding a SQL Server instance.

Hardening the SQL Server Installation with Windows Server Core

SQL Server 2012 now supports the ability to be deployed on Windows
Server 2008 R2 Server Core. The Server Core installation is so stripped
down that traditional installation components, such as a desktop shell,
graphical user interface, Windows Explorer, Microsoft Internet Explorer,
and the MMC, are not included. As such, the server must be fully managed
and configured by the command prompt, PowerShell CmdLets, or by using
remote administration tools such as Server Manager from another server.
By maintaining a minimized installation footprint by stripping out the
typical components and supporting only specific roles, the Server Core
installation reduces maintenance, attack surface, management, and disk
space required to support the installation. It is a recommended best practice to install SQL Server on Windows Server Core if a need exists to
harden the installation. Installing SQL Server 2012 on Windows Server
Core is covered in Chapter 1, "Installing or Upgrading the Database
Engine to SQL Server 2012."

Hardening a Server with the Security Configuration Wizard in Windows Server 2008 R2

The most impressive hardening tool and useful addition to the Windows
Server operating system has to be the Security Configuration Wizard
(SCW). SCW was first introduced as an add-in with Windows Server 2003
Service Pack 1; however, it is still included out-of-the-box with Windows
Server 2008 R2. SCW is an attack-surface reduction tool that allows you to
completely lock down a server, except for the particular services that it
requires to perform specific duties. The role-based security policies are
predefined and assist you by configuring services, network security, auditing, Registry settings, and more. This way, a WINS server responds only to
WINS requests, a DNS server has only DNS enabled, and a SQL Server
responds only to SQL requests. Windows Server 2008 R2 continues to
deliver this type of long-sought-after functionality.

SCW allows you to build custom role-based templates that can be exported
to additional servers, thus streamlining the security process when setting
up multiple systems. In addition, current security templates can be
imported into SCW so that existing intelligence can be maintained. The
SCW included with Windows Server 2008 R2 includes new improved
features and functionality, such as more server role configurations and
security settings out of the box, the possibility to disable unneeded services
based on the server role, the capability to establish restrictive audit policies, advanced firewall configurations, and the power to transform a SCW

policy into a Group Policy Object (GPO) and link it to an Organizational Unit (OU) for centralized SQL Server infrastructure management when using Active Directory Domain Services (ADDS).

The advantages to using the SCW service on SQL Server are immediately identifiable. SQL Server, because it houses sensitive data and is often indirectly exposed to the Internet by web service applications, is vulnerable to attack and therefore should have all unnecessary services and ports shut down. A properly configured firewall normally drops this type of activity, and although the preceding section focused on minimizing surface attacks, it is always a good idea to put in an additional layer of security for good measure.

The Security Configuration Wizard can be run to lock down SQL Server based on a SQL Server role-based template; therefore, only the bare necessities required will be operational. This includes SQL access, web and ASP-related web access, and any other access methods required for the server. In addition, network security, port configuration, and Registry settings can be configured. Each SQL Server implementation differs, so it is important to run the wizard on a prototype to determine what settings are right for each individual SQL Server.

> **Note**
>
> For best results, when you're locking down a server with the Security Configuration Wizard, it is a best practice to first harden the SQL Server installation with the configuration tools described in the previous sections and then run this tool.

To launch the Security Configuration Wizard, choose Start, All Programs, Administrative Tools, Security Configuration Wizard. Use the wizard to create a role-based SQL Server security policy that locks down unnecessary services, network security, ports, Registry settings, and audit policies.

Using the SQL Server Best Practice Analyzer (BPA) Tool to Harden an Installation

Another tool that is typically a database administrator's best friend is the SQL Server Best Practice Analyzer (BPA) tool. The BPA gathers data from Microsoft Windows and SQL Server configuration settings. The BPA is a database management tool that uses a predefined list of SQL Server recommendations and best practices to determine whether potential issues exist in the database environment. The BPA also covers security hardening best practices. A new BPA tool is released alongside new versions of SQL Server and can be downloaded directly from Microsoft.

Notes from the Field: Hardening and Reducing Attack Surface on Many SQL Server Instances

Reducing surface attacks and ensuring compliance are two of the most common issues brought up by customers at my architecture design sessions at the Microsoft Technology Center. Specifically, I receive a large number of questions on how to manage surface attacks when there are hundreds of SQL Server Instances running in an enterprise. By using Server Core and leveraging Policy-Based Management, it is possible to reduce surface attacks and achieve stronger compliance. For information on installing SQL Server 2012 on Server Core, review Chapter 1.

Furthermore, the Surface Area Configuration facet included in Policy-Based Management is a great way to manage surface area configuration on many instances of SQL Server from a centralized server. The surface area configuration facet includes the following expressions: AdHocRemoteQueriesEnabled, CLRIntegration, DatabaseMail, OleAutomation, RemoteDac, ServerBrokerEndpoint,SOAPEndPoints, SQLMail, WebAssistant, and XPCmdShell. If these features are not required, disable them on every instance of SQL Server with Policy-Based Management to reduce surface attack. For additional information, reference Chapter 17, "Implementing and Managing Policy-Based Management," chapter for steps on how to configure a policy.

Hardening SQL Server Service Accounts

You are prompted to enter a service account during the initial installation of SQL Server. Services can run under domain-based accounts, local service accounts, or built-in accounts such as Local System or Network Service. You can select to use a single service account for all instances and components being installed or to customize the installation by entering a dedicated service account for each instance and component.

The following SQL Server service accounts are available:

- **SQL Server Database Engine Service**—This account provides core database functionality by facilitating storage, processing, and controlled access of data and rapid transaction processing.

- **SQL Server Agent Service**—This account provides auxiliary functionality by executing jobs, monitoring SQL Server, creating alerts, and automating administrative tasks.

- **SQL Server Integration Services Service**—This account provides management support for SSIS package storage and execution.

- **SQL Server Analysis Services Service**—This account provides business intelligence applications by supplying online analytical processing (OLAP) and data mining functionality.

- **SQL Server Reporting Services**—This account acts as a liaison between Reporting Services and SQL Server by managing, executing, rendering, and delivering reports.

- **SQL Server Full-Text Filter Daemon Launcher**—This account manages full-text indexes on content and properties of structured and semistructured data to allow fast linguistic searches on this data.

- **SQL Server Browser**—This account acts as a liaison with client computers by enumerating SQL Server connection information.

- **SQL Server Active Directory Helper**—This account enables integration between SQL Server and Active Directory.

- **SQL Server VSS Writer**—This account provides the interface to back up and restore SQL Server via the Windows Server Volume Shadow Copy Service (VSS) infrastructure.

There aren't necessarily any hard-and-fast rules to follow when trying to determine the type of service account to use. The main objective is to understand the limitations and positive offerings of the service account being used. It is equally important to analyze the value of the data residing within SQL Server and the risks and amount of security exposure that would take place if the SQL Server database was compromised. Last, when hardening and choosing SQL Server service accounts, you should employ the principle of least privilege and isolation.

The Principle of Least Privilege

It is a best practice to configure a service account based on the principle of least privilege. According to the *principle of least privilege*, SQL Server service accounts should be granted the least number of rights and permissions to conduct a specific task. Based on this recommendation, you should *not* grant a service account unnecessary elevated privileges, such as domain administrator, enterprise administrator, or local administrator privileges. This enhances the protection of data and functionality from faults. Also, you should recognize that these highly elevated privileges are really not required. In fact, gone are the days when the SQL Server service accounts required domain administrator or local administrator privileges.

Service Account Isolation

For isolation purposes, a separate account should be created for each SQL Server instance and component being installed. Therefore, if the service account is compromised, only the one instance or component associated with the service account is breached. For example, suppose a bank is running 100 SQL Server instances and each instance maintains financial information. If one service account is used for all these instances, all 100 instances would be compromised in the event of a service account breach. This type of situation could be disastrous for a bank, especially with today's laws and regulatory requirements.

The need to create and manage more than one service account definitely increases administration and can be monotonous; however, it is a best practice to isolate each instance or component. One other notable benefit of isolation is witnessed with the amount of control organizations achieve through it. Organizations can grant specific permissions to one service account without elevating permissions to another service account that does not need elevated permissions.

The Types of Service Accounts Available

The following types of service accounts are available to choose from:

- **Local System Account**—This account grants full administrative rights to users on the local computer, which makes it a highly privileged account. As such, its use should be closely monitored. Note that this account does not grant network access rights.

- **Network Service Account**—This built-in account grants users the same level of access as members of the User group. This account allows services to interrelate with other services on the network infrastructure.

- **Domain User Account**—This account is used if the service will interrelate with other services on the network infrastructure.

- **Local Service Account**—Users of this built-in account have the same level of access that is designated to members of the User group. This limited access protects against service breaches.

Determining Which Type of Account to Use for SQL Server Services

The question that always surfaces regarding service accounts is, "Which service account should be used with implementing SQL Server 2012?" The answer depends on your intended use of the service account and the relationship it will have to the server and network.

Services that run as the local service account access network resources with no credentials. As a result, this account should not be used if you want the services to interact with other network resources. Moreover, it is a powerful account that has unrestricted access to all local system resources.

If you are looking for a service account that grants limited privileges like the local service account but also runs services that can interrelate with other services on the network infrastructure, you should consider using a network service account. This account uses the credentials of the computer account to gain access to the network. It is not recommended that you use this account for either the SQL Server service or the SQL Server Agent service account. Using the Network Service account for SQL Server Agent Service is not recommended. This is because multiple services can use the Network Service account; therefore, it is difficult to control which services have access to network resources, including SQL Server databases.

Consideration should also be given to the domain user account if its services will interact with other services on the network infrastructure. If you also want to perform certain activities including replication, remote procedure calls, or network drive backups, a domain user account is preferred over a network service account because only this account allows server-to-server activity. One point to keep in mind when using a domain account is that it must be authenticated on a domain controller.

The local system account is not recommended for use for the SQL Server service or SQL Server Agent services. The reason is that it is a best practice to configure a service so that it runs effectively with the least number of privileges granted. The local system account is a highly privileged account, which means it should be used very carefully. In addition, it probably has privileges that neither SQL Server Agent services nor SQL Server services actually require.

Tip

Microsoft recommends that you do not use a network service account if an account with lesser privileges is available. The reason is that the network service account is a shared account and can be utilized by other services running on the Windows Server system. Local User or Domain User accounts are preferred, specifically if they are not associated with highly privileged groups such as Domain Administrator.

Changing a SQL Server Service Account with SQL Server Configuration Manager

Typically, server administrators use the Services Snap-in component included with Windows Server called Server Manager or the Administrative tools to make changes to Windows Services. There are serious negative ramifications if SQL Server service accounts are changed using this tool. SQL Server service accounts require special Registry settings, NTFS file system permissions, and Windows user rights to be set, which the Windows tool does not address, thus causing a SQL Server outage. Fortunately, these additional permission requirements can be updated automatically if you use SQL Server native configuration tools such as the SQL Server Configuration Manager or SQL Server Surface Area Configuration. Therefore, it is a best practice to use the native SQL Server configuration tools when making changes to SQL Server service accounts; changes should not be made using the Windows Server Services tool.

Follow these steps to change the user account, including credentials for a SQL Server service such as the SQL Server Agent, using the SQL Server Configuration Manager:

1. Choose Start, All Programs, Microsoft SQL Server 2012, Configuration Tools, SQL Server Configuration Manager.

2. Select the SQL Server Services node.

3. In the right pane, double-click the SQL Server Agent Service.

4. In the SQL Server Agent box, enter a new service account name and password.

5. Confirm the password by retyping it, as shown in Figure 7.6, and click Apply.

6. Accept the message to restart the services and click OK.

The SQL Server Agent now uses the new service account credentials for authentication. In addition, Registry settings, NTFS permissions, and Windows rights are updated automatically.

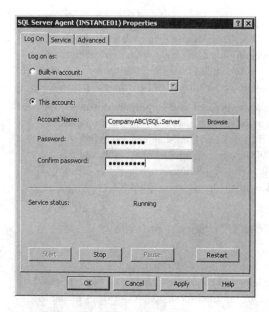

FIGURE 7.6
Changing the service account credentials.

Installing Service Packs and Critical Fixes

SQL Server 2012, like all other Microsoft applications and server products, is subject to periodic software updates. Interim updates can be downloaded and installed through the Windows Update option on the system or by visiting the Windows Update website (http://update.microsoft.com), which initiates the installer to check for the latest updates for Windows.

Likewise, major updates are essentially bundled as cumulative updates or service packs that roll up patches and updates into a single installation. Installation of cumulative updates and the latest service pack brings a server up to date, which means to the point in time when the service pack was issued. It is also worth noting that the future service packs for both SQL Server 2012 will most likely be cumulative. You can install a service pack update in one of three ways:

- **Windows Update**—The cumulative update or service pack can be downloaded and automatically installed as part of the normal update process. Ensure that Windows Updates has been configured to receive updates for Windows and other products from Microsoft Update, such as SQL Server.

- **Download and Install**—The cumulative update or service pack can be downloaded as a file. This file can then be launched to install the update. This is frequently done when a system is not connected to the Internet or when a scheduled installation is desired in contrast to an immediate installation after downloading from the Internet.

- **Automated Patch Management and Deployment Tools**—Software distribution tools can be used to install service pack updates. Systems Center 2012 Configuration Manager and Windows Software Update Services (WSUS) are examples of two tools you can use to accomplish the task. Windows Software Updates Services (WSUS) is a feature included in Windows Server 2008 R2.

Updating and Patching SQL Server and the Operating System

In addition to the patches that are installed as part of a SQL Server 2012 service pack, security updates and patches are constantly being released by Microsoft. It is advantageous to install these updates made available for SQL Server and the operating system. These patches can be manually downloaded and installed, or they can be automatically applied by using Windows Update.

It is a best practice to install critical fixes for both SQL Server and the operating system when they are released. In addition, major service packs and security rollups should be installed in a timely manner. All patches should be tested in a prototype lab before being deployed to production, and it is recommended that you conduct a full backup of the system prior to the installation of the patches.

Leveraging the Rolling Upgrade Strategy

Rolling upgrades is a strategy to deploy cumulative updates or service packs to SQL Server in a manner that minimizes SQL Server production downtime during the installations. To leverage this strategy, SQL Server high-availability alternatives such as AlwaysOn availability groups, AlwaysOn Failover Cluster Instances, or database mirroring must be employed. At a high level, a DBA would start off by patching the passive server, database replica, or database mirror. After the installation is complete on the passive server, database replica, or database mirror, a DBA would manually failover the SQL Server service from the active server, primary replica, or database principal, and then install the cumulative updates or service pack. This strategy also is applicable to the Windows Server Operating System.

Leveraging SQL Server Auditing Strategies

In the previous sections, you learned ways of minimizing security vulnerabilities on SQL Server. Now that SQL Server is hardened, it is beneficial to enable and leverage auditing. The following audit strategies will be covered:

- Understanding how SQL Server security logs play a part in security
- Configuring SQL Server security logs for auditing
- Enhanced auditing functionality included with SQL Server 2012
- Monitoring events with SQL Server Audit
- SQL Server 2012 Audit components
- Create the SQL Server Audit object with Transact-SQL
- Create SQL Server and Database audit specifications
- Viewing the newly created Audit Log

Understanding How SQL Server Security Logs Play a Part in Security

SQL Server security auditing monitors and tracks activity to log files that can be viewed through Windows application logs or SQL Server Management Studio. SQL Server offers the following four security levels for security auditing:

- **None**—Disables auditing so no events are logged.
- **Successful Logins Only**—Audits all successful login attempts.
- **Failed Logins Only**—Audits all failed login attempts.
- **Both Failed and Successful Logins**—Audits all login attempts.

At the very least, security auditing should be set to Failed Logins Only. As a result, failed logins can be saved, viewed, and acted on when necessary. Unless a change is made, security auditing is set, by default, to Failed Logins Only. On the other hand, it is a best practice to configure security auditing to capture Both Failed and Successful Logins. All logins are captured in this situation and can be analyzed when advanced forensics are required.

Configuring SQL Server Security Logs for Auditing

To configure security login auditing for both failed and successful logins, follow these steps:

1. In SQL Server Management Studio, right-click a desired SQL Server and then click Properties.

2. On the Security page, as shown in Figure 7.7, under Login Auditing, select the desired auditing criteria option button, such as Both Failed and Successful Logins, and then click OK.

3. Restart the SQL Server Database Engine and SQL Server Agent to make the auditing changes effective.

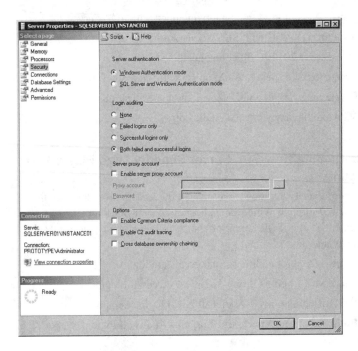

FIGURE 7.7
Configuring security auditing to both failed and successful logins.

Enhanced Auditing Functionality Included with SQL Server 2012

SQL Server systems are strong candidates to fall subject to the rules and regulations governed by regulatory requirements. SQL Server is typically a repository for organizations' and customers' data that tends to be both mission-critical and sensitive if it falls into the wrong hands.

One of the latest compliance rules some organizations are subject to includes the capability to successfully log events in a central repository and produce reports of all activity being captured. Microsoft understands the push toward better logging and auditing capabilities and has introduced new features and functionality in SQL Server 2012 that facilitate stronger auditing for compliance reasons.

The two objects, Audit object and Audit Specification object, organizations can now log every SQL Server action to the Windows Application Log, Windows Security Log, or to a file. In addition, when using Windows Server 2008 R2 or System Center 2012 Operations Manager, it is possible to create a central repository for all events collected across many SQL Server systems within the enterprise.

Monitoring Events with SQL Server Audit

Auditing has long been a part of corporate America, not to mention the rest of the world. But lately, with investor confidence falling and the economy's health deteriorating, discussions about auditing have taken center stage. One only has to think about the recent wave of corporate deception, including Fortune 500 companies like Enron and WorldCom or the big banks and the recent mortgage crisis, to understand why there was so much talk about the future of auditing. The actions of these corrupt corporate entities got the government to take notice and ultimately take back the integrity of the profession of auditing through the introduction of government requirements such as Sarbanes-Oxley (SOX), PCI Compliance, and FDA oversight of data.

With government regulations in place, organizations are now held more accountable for securing and auditing sensitive data. This has resulted in a strong marriage between databases and auditing in SQL Server 2012 because auditing logs are no longer an exception, but a norm today for most companies. Accordingly, SQL Server 2012 incorporates a new auditing functionality.

SQL Server 2012 introduced the Audit object and the Audit Specification object, which significantly enhanced the auditing capabilities compared to previous versions of SQL. It allowed organizations to audit all database and server events associated with the Database Engine. This was possible as the SQL Server Audit object leverages the new Extended Events framework coupled with DDL commands.

Note

Even if your organization is not governed by some form of regulatory compliance, it is still a best practice to leverage the new Audit object to increase awareness concerning log changes and access to sensitive company data.

In addition, by leveraging the logging improvements in Windows Server 2008 R2 and/or the Audit Collection Services component with System Center Operations Manager, organizations can easily centralize and consolidate server and database auditing events across the enterprise, which simplifies compliance, reduces total cost of ownership, and provides rich analysis based on auditing trends. This was inconceivable with the past versions of SQL Server.

SQL Server 2012 Audit Components

It is beneficial to first understand the terminology associated with the Audit components before implementing it. The upcoming sections will further examine the SQL Server Audit components and their associated terminology.

SQL Server Audit and Audit Destinations

To set up auditing, a DBA first creates a SQL Server Audit object and then specifies the location to which the audited events will be written. Audits can be saved to the Windows Security Log, the Windows Application Log, or to a file on the network infrastructure. The audit destination is also referred to as a *target*. Creating a SQL Server Audit object can be performed by using SSMS or Transact-SQL. Within a SQL Server instance, it is possible to generate more than one SQL Server Audit object; however, each Server Audit object would have its own audit destination.

Tip

In mission-critical environments where security and auditing are a major concern or requirement, it is a best practice to write auditing data to the Windows Security Log. The Windows Application Log is inferior compared to the Windows Security Log because it requests lower permissions, and any authenticated user can read or write to and from the log. In addition, files on the network are vulnerable to anyone who has access to the file system. Therefore, the Windows Security Log is the best choice because it offers the highest level of security, making audit data less subject to tampering.

Server Audit Specification

A Server Audit Specification object or type is associated with a SQL Server Audit object. It defines the server event that will be audited based on a predefined set of SQL Server Audit action types. Examples of Server Audit Action Groups include APPLICATION_ROLE_CHANGE_PASSWORD_ GROUP, SERVER_PERMISSION_CHANGE_GROUP, DATABASE_OWNERSHIP_ CHANGE_GROUP, and FAILED_LOGIN_GROUP. A DBA can choose from a plethora of Server Audit action types for auditing a SQL Server instance. Review the different Audit Action Types by right-clicking the Server Audit Specifications subfolder under Security in Object Explorer and select new Server Audit Specification. The Audit Action Type drop-down list will provide a full listing of Server-Level Audit Action Types available.

There is a one-to-one mapping between server audit specifications and server audits. Multiple server audit specifications can be created; however, they cannot be bound to the same server audit. Each specification requires its own server audit.

Database Audit Specification

A Database Audit Specification object is also associated with a server audit. It is similar to the Server Audit Specification object. In this case, however, the Database Audit Specification object defines the database event that will be audited based on a predefined set of Database-Level Audit Action Groups. Examples of Database-Level Audit Action Groups include DATABASE_ROLE_MEMBER_CHANGE_GROUP, DATABASE_OPERATION_ GROUP, and SCHEMA_OBJECT_CHANGE_GROUP. As with server audit specifications, there are many predefined Database-Level Audit Action Groups that are applicable to a database. In addition, database-level audits can be linked to a specific database action; for example, an event can be raised whenever a SELECT, UPDATE, INSERT, DELETE, EXECUTE, or RECEIVE statement is issued. Review the different Audit Action Types by right-clicking the Database Audit Specifications subfolder under a desired Database in Object Explorer and select new Database Audit Specification. The Audit Action Type drop-down list will provide a full listing of Database-Level Audit Action Types. It should be noted that there is a one-to-one mapping between database audit specifications and server audits. Multiple database audit specifications can be created; however, they cannot be bound to the same server audit. Each specification requires its own server audit.

> **Note**
>
> When creating and implementing server or database audit specifications, a server audit must already exist; it is a prerequisite task because a specification must be bound to the audit.

SQL Server Audit Failed Logon Attempt Example

The implementation of SQL Server Audit is relatively straightforward and involves four steps: The first step involves generating an audit and choosing a target. In the second step, the decision to create either a server audit specification or a database audit specification is required. The final two steps include enabling the audit and then reviewing the captured audit events on a periodic basis. The upcoming section will further examine the SQL Server Audit components and the terminology associated with this four-step installation process.

Before we dive into the step-by-step creation of an Audit object and audit specification with SQL Server Management Studio, let's first look at an example that captures failed logon attempts on a server via Transact-SQL. The example demonstrates the creation of a SQL Server audit with the target being a file on the file system with Transact-SQL.

Phase 1: Create the SQL Server Audit Object with Transact-SQL

The first step in this four-phase process is to create the Audit object. This example creates an audit called SQLServer01-Instance01-ServerAudit, which stores the audit logs to a file residing in a SQLServerAudit folder located on the C: drive. In addition, a default queue delay of 1000 is used. The default queue delay represents the amount of time in milliseconds that can elapse before audit actions are forced to be processed. Next, the Fail Operation alternative has been selected that represents the behavior in cases where the SQL Server Audit cannot write to the audit log. If SQL Server Audit cannot write to the log, all events associated with the Audit will fail. However, actions that do not require audit activity will still continue. A maximum of 10 files has been specified with the maximum file size of 5GB:

```
/* Create the SQL Server Audit. */
USE [master]
GO
CREATE SERVER AUDIT [SQLServer01-Instance01-ServerAudit ]
TO FILE
```

```
(FILEPATH = N'C:\SQLServerAudit'
,MAXSIZE = 5 GB
,MAX_FILES = 10
,RESERVE_DISK_SPACE = OFF)
WITH
(QUEUE_DELAY = 1000
,ON_FAILURE = FAIL_OPERATION)
GO
```

Phase 2: Enable the Newly Created Audit Object with Transact-SQL

Now that the audit has been created, the next step is to enable the audit. This can be done by executing the following Transact-SQL syntax:

```
/* Enable the SQL Server Audit. */
USE [master]
GO
ALTER SERVER AUDIT [SQLServer01-Instance01-ServerAudit]
WITH (STATE = ON) ;
GO
```

Phase 3: Create the SQL Server Audit Specification Object with Transact-SQL

The following Transact-SQL syntax illustrates how to create a server audit specification to capture failed logins based on our example. The Failed_Login_Group indicates that a principal tried to log on to SQL Server and failed:

```
/* Create the Audit Specification Object. */
USE [master]
GO
CREATE SERVER AUDIT SPECIFICATION
[ServerAuditSpecification-Failed-Login]
FOR SERVER AUDIT [SQLServer01-Instance01-ServerAudit]
ADD (FAILED_LOGIN_GROUP)
GO
```

Phase 4: Viewing the Newly Created Audit Log

The final phase in the process is to view the audit log for any irregularities or suspicious activity. Ironically, this is one of the most critical steps, which is too often overlooked. Before viewing the log, let's first generate some failed logon attempts on the server. This can be done by selecting File, Connect Object Explorer in SQL Server Management Studio. In the Connect to Server dialog box, ensure that the Server Type is set to the Database Engine, and enter the name of the SQL Server instance that is hosting the audits. Change the authentication to SQL Server Authentication. Enter the SA as the Login, type the incorrect password, and then click Connect. You should receive an Error 18456 message indicating that you cannot connect to the SQL Server because the login failed for user SA. Repeat the login attempt two more times so that a few more audit events are generated.

Follow these steps to review the audit log we generated in Phase 1:

1. In Object Explorer, expand a SQL Server instance, the Security folder, and then the Audits folder.

2. Right-click the audit, SQLServer01-Instance01-ServerAudit, and specify View Audit Logs.

3. The SQL Server Log File Viewer will be invoked as shown in Figure 7.8. Take note of the failed login attempts that were captured based on our audit specification. If you click an event where the Action ID states LOGIN FAILED, you will be able to review additional details, such as time, audit collection name, user account, and so on.

4. Click Close when you have finished reviewing the log.

Creating SQL Server Audits with SQL Server Management Studio

As mentioned earlier, the first step to monitoring changes on a SQL Server instance or database is to create the SQL Server Audit object. Follow these steps to create a SQL Server Audit object with SQL Server Management Studio:

1. In Object Explorer, expand a SQL Server instance, expand the Security folder, and then select the Audit folder.

2. Right-click the Audit folder and select New Audit, which will invoke the Create Audit dialog box, as illustrated in Figure 7.9.

3. On the General tab in the Create Audit dialog box, first specify a name for the audit in the Audit Name field.

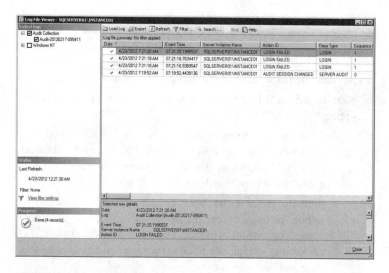

FIGURE 7.8

Viewing the Failed Login Group audit log.

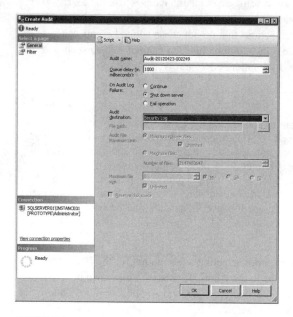

FIGURE 7.9

Creating an audit with SQL Server Management Studio.

4. Either maintain the Queue Delay default setting or enter a value in milliseconds between 0 and 2,147,483,647. The queue delay indicates the quantity of time that can elapse before audits are forced to be committed. The value of 0 indicates synchronous delivery.

5. Next, on the Audit Log Failure section, specify one of the following options:

    - **Continue**—This option indicates that the SQL Server operations will continue to operate even if SQL Server Audit cannot write to the audit logs. The audit continues to attempt to log events and will resume if the failure condition is resolved.

    - **Shut Down Server on Audit Failure**—When enabled, this setting forces the server to shut down if a SQL Server instance cannot successfully write audit events to a specified target. This setting is typically enabled for organizations dealing with strict auditing requirements.

    - **Fail Operation**—The Fail Operation is a brand-new option in SQL Server 2012. Basically, instead of shutting down the server and causing an outage in cases where the SQL Server Audit cannot write to the audit log, database actions will fail. However, actions that do not cause audited events can continue. The audit continues to attempt to log events and will resume if the failure condition is resolved.

Tip

Let's take a moment to understand the ramifications of enabling the Shut Down Server on Audit Log Failure option. When an event captured by the audit cannot be successfully written, the server will shut down. If this SQL Server instance is a mission-critical production server, a major outage will result and will continue to negatively impact the organization and users until the auditing functionality is fixed. So, tread carefully when making the decision to use this option because your decision will impact either security or functionality.

---

6. The next step includes selecting a destination for the audit from the predefined options in the Audit Destination drop-down box. The options include File, Security Log, and Application Log. Choose the appropriate destination.

7. If a file destination is selected, specify the additional options for the file based on the settings in the following list. If either the Security Log or Application Log was selected, the additional File options are

grayed out, so click OK to finalize the creation of the new audit. The additional File settings in the Create Audit dialog box consist of the following:

- **File Path**—Indicates the location of the file to which audit data will be written.

- **Audit File Maximum Limit**—Maximum Rollover option controls how many audit files should be maintained within the file system. The default option is set to Unlimited. This means that files will not be overwritten. A file restriction can be imposed by entering a number that represents the maximum number of files that can be maintained. The maximum number is 2,147,483,647.

- **Maximum Number of Files**—Indicates the maximum number of audit files. The options can be up to 2,147,483,647 files, which is the default setting.

- **Maximum File Size**—Indicates the maximum size for a file. Options include Unlimited or between 1024KB and 2,147,483,647 terabytes.

- **Reserve Disk Space**—The final option, Reserve Disk Space, guarantees that the maximum size allocated to the file in the previous setting is preallocated to the file system.

Enabling a SQL Server Audit with SQL Server Management Studio

The next step in the process is to enable the newly created audit. This can be done by expanding the Audits folder in Object Explorer, right-clicking the new audit, and then selecting Enable Audit. A red down arrow on the audit represents Disabled.

Create Server Audit Specification with SQL Server Management Studio

As mentioned earlier in the four-step example, after the SQL Server audit has been created and enabled, the next phase is to create the actual server or database audit specification. The following steps illustrate the creation of the server audit specification, which will monitor failed logins using SQL Server Management Studio:

1. In SQL Server Management Studio, connect to the Database Engine.

2. In Object Explorer, expand a SQL Server instance, expand the Security folder, and then select the Server Audit Specifications folder.

3. Right-click the Server Audit Specifications folder and select New Server Audit Specification to invoke the Create Server Audit Specification dialog box, as illustrated in Figure 7.10.

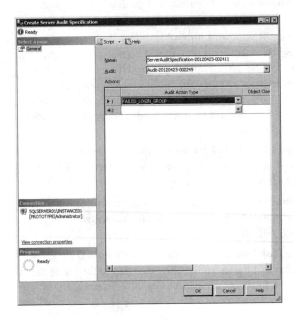

FIGURE 7.10
Creating a Server Audit Specification with SQL Server Management Studio.

4. On the General page in the Create Audit dialog box, first specify a name for the audit in the Name text box.

5. Select an audit from the drop-down list. An audit must already exist prior to this step.

6. In the Actions section, specify the desired server-level Audit Action Type from the drop-down list, such as FAILED_LOGIN_GROUP.

7. Click OK to finalize the creation of the Server Audit Specification.

8. Similar to the Audit Specification, the Server Audit Specification needs to be enabled by right-clicking the new Server Audit Specification and then selecting Enable Server Audit Specification.

9. When the logon attempt fails, close the dialog box and proceed to the steps in the previous section, "Viewing the Newly Created Audit Log."

Creating a Database Audit Specification with Transact-SQL

Instead of creating a server database audit specification, a DBA may choose to create an audit specification that is applicable to a user or system database. If a database audit specification is created, the Database Action Type will collect data on all databases within the SQL Server instance. On the other hand, if you want to audit only one database, that is possible by generating a database audit specification and applying it to one specific database.

Note

The steps for creating a database audit specification are the same as creating a Server Audit Specification, as illustrated in the previous example. However, in step 2, a DBA must expand a SQL Server Instance, expand a desired database, expand the Security Folder, and then select the Database Audit Specifications. Also ensure you have the appropriate permissions to write to the security log.

When working with database audit specifications, a DBA must still create the Server Audit object and enable it as a prerequisite task. The following steps demonstrate the creation of the database audit specification using Transact-SQL, which will monitor SELECT and INSERT statements on the AdventureWorks2012 database:

```
--STEP 1, Create the SQL Server audit
USE [master]
GO
CREATE SERVER AUDIT [AdventureWorks-Person-Password-Audit]
TO SECURITY_LOG
WITH
(       QUEUE_DELAY = 1000
        ,ON_FAILURE = SHUTDOWN
)
GO
--STEP 2, Enable the SQL Server audit
ALTER SERVER AUDIT [AdventureWorks-Person-Password-Audit]
WITH (STATE = ON) ;
GO
--STEP3 Create the Database Audit
  Specification on the AdventureWorks2012
```

```
USE AdventureWorks2012
GO
CREATE DATABASE AUDIT SPECIFICATION [Audit-Person-Password-
Table]
FOR SERVER AUDIT [AdventureWorks-Person-Password-Audit]
ADD (SELECT , INSERT
    ON Person.Password BY dbo )
WITH (STATE = ON)
GO
```

Let's generate a few audit events by running the following SELECT statements against the Person.Password table:

```
Use AdventureWorks2012
Select *
From Person.Password
Go
```

Now open the AdventureWorks-Person-Password-Audit log file by right-clicking the Audit folder in Object Explorer and choosing View Audit Logs. Notice how the SELECT statements against the Person.Password table have been captured in the log based on the ActiveID SELECT. The details of the log entry show the Session Server Principal Name and the Server Principal Name, including the user SID who accessed the table based on the SELECT statement.

Managing Audits and Audit Specifications

The next few sections include tasks associated with managing audits and audit specifications.

Using the Windows Server 2008 R2 Security Log as an Audit Target

Compared to other locations, the Windows Server 2008 R2 Security log is the best place to record audit object access, because it is the least likely to be tampered with. When using the Windows Server 2008 R2 Security log as an Audit target, two tasks must be initiated as prerequisites. First, the Audit Object Access setting must be configured on the Windows Server 2008 R2 system to allow audit events to be recorded. Second, the account used to generate audit events to the Security log, which is the SQL Server Agent, must be granted the Generate Security Audits permissions.

The following example illustrates how to conduct the first step by enabling Audit Object Access on a SQL Server 2012 system running Windows Server 2008 R2:

1. Log on to a Windows Server 2008 R2 system with administrative permissions.

2. Launch a command prompt with administrative privileges. This is achieved by choosing Start, All Programs, Accessories, right-clicking the Command Prompt, and then selecting Run as Administrator.

3. Execute the following code from the command prompt:

```
auditpol /set /subcategory:"application generated"
    /success:enable /failure:enable
```

4. Close down the command prompt. Note that the setting takes place immediately.

The next step is to open up the local security policy on the Windows Server 2008 R2 system that will be hosting the SQL Server Audit object and grant the account associated with the SQL Server Agent permission to record data to the Security Log. This can be accomplished by conducting the following steps:

1. Log on to a Windows Server 2008 R2 system with administrative permissions.

2. Click Start, Run, type **secpol.msc**, and then click OK to invoke the Windows Server 2008 R2 Local Security Policy.

3. In the Local Security Policy screen, first expand the Local Policies folder and then the User Rights Assignment.

4. In the right pane, double-click Generate Security Audits.

5. In the Generate Security Audits Properties dialog box, click Add User or Group.

6. In the Select Users, Computers, or Groups dialog box, enter the name of the security account of the SQL Server Agent, and then click OK.

7. Click Apply and then close the Local Security Policy tool.

8. Restart the SQL Server and SQL Server Agent Service.

> **Note**
>
> When more than one Windows Server 2008 R2 Security Log is being
> used to capture audits, a Windows Server 2008 R2 Active Directory
> Group Policy can be used to automatically grant and enforce the SQL
> Server Agent Account the appropriate permissions on the Security. It is a
> best practice to first create an Organizational Unit in Active Directory,
> place the desired SQL Server computers within the Organizational Unit,
> create the Group Policy, and then link the Group Policy to the Organizational
> Unit where the SQL Server computers reside.

Viewing Security Events from an Audit File via Transact-SQL

A new function can be leveraged to view security events associated with an
audit file residing on a SQL Server system. Here is the default syntax:

```
fn_get_audit_file ( file_pattern,
{default | initial_file_name | NULL },
{default | audit_file_offset | NULL } )
```

The DBA will need to specify the directory and path to the actual filename
that needs to be viewed. Here is an example based on an audit file called
Payrole_Security_Audit:

```
Select * From fn_get_audit_file
('C:\SQLServerAudit\*',null,null)
```

Dropping Audits and Audit Specifications

Using SQL Server Management Studio, right-click an audit, click Server
Audit Specification and/or Database Audit Specification, and select Delete.
It would be best to first delete the audit specification and then the audit
associated with the audit specification. The drop can also be achieved with
Transact-SQL. Here are the three basic syntaxes:

```
-- Drop Server Audit Specification
DROP SERVER AUDIT SPECIFICATION audit_specification_name
[ ; ]
--Drop Database Audit Specification
DROP DATABASE AUDIT SPECIFICATION audit_specification_name
[ ; ]
--Drop Server Audit
DROP SERVER AUDIT audit_name
  [ ; ]
```

Additional SQL Server Hardening Recommendations

The following sections focus on additional hardening techniques to further lock down SQL Server. The items include removing the BUILTIN\Administrators Windows group and using a firewall to filter out unwanted traffic.

Removing the BUILTIN\Administrators Windows Group

In the past, many DBAs in the industry were concerned about the BUILTIN\Administrators Windows group having sysadmin privileges by default over a SQL Server instance. Some people believe that this situation was one of the biggest out-of-the-box security flaws for SQL Server. The reason is that all local Windows administrators, including domain administrators, are given full control over SQL Server because they are part of the BUILTIN\Administrators Windows group. This led to a best practice to remove the BUILTIN\Administrators group to address this situation. Doing this hardens the SQL Server installation.

Because this was a major security flaw, Microsoft removed the group outright in SQL Server 2008 and later. Therefore, it is up to a DBA to decide whether a need still exists to add this group. At times this group may be present if you conduct an upgrade from a previous version of SQL Server.

In addition, with SQL Server 2012, additional protection to enhance role separation between BUILTIN\Administrators and Local System (NT Authority\System) has been achieved. This is because BUILTIN\Administrators and Local System (NT Authority\System) are not automatically provisioned in the sysadmin fixed server role. However, it is worth noting that local administrators can still access the Database Engine when in single-user mode.

Removing the BUILTIN\Administrators Windows Group with Transact-SQL

If the group existed from previous versions of SQL Server or using BETA code, the following Transact-SQL syntax removes the BUILTIN\Administrators Windows Group from a SQL Server instance. If you decide to run this syntax, you should execute it on each SQL Server instance installed in the organization:

```
Use Master
IF EXISTS (SELECT * FROM sys.server_principals
```

```
WHERE name = N'BUILTIN\Administrators')
DROP LOGIN [BUILTIN\Administrators]
GO
```

Using a Firewall to Filter Out Unwanted Traffic

Now that the default SQL Server ports have been changed according to the instructions in the previous section, the next step is to enable a firewall that will filter out unwanted traffic and allow connections only to the SQL Server designated from within the organization's infrastructure. The Windows firewall included with Windows Server 2008 R2 should be sufficient. However, if more advanced firewall features are sought, a full-fledged hardware-based firewall or software-based firewall should be used, such as Microsoft's Threat Management Gateway (TMG).

> **Note**
>
> A common problem in the past was that some organizations had their SQL Servers reside within the demilitarized zone (DMZ) or configured with public IP addresses. This made their SQL Server public-facing and, therefore, accessible from the outside world. As a general rule, when you're implementing SQL Server from within an infrastructure, it should never be Internet-facing, within the DMZ, or publicly accessible. Moreover, many organizations use a firewall within the infrastructure to filter unwanted traffic between internal networks. A common example where a firewall would be used to filter unwanted traffic is between the network hosting database servers and the network hosting applications that would communicate with the database network.

The following table summarizes the default ports utilized by common SQL Server components:

SQL Server Default Instance	1433
SQL Server Named Instance	Dynamic Port
Admin Connection	1434
Browser Service	1434
Default Instance running over HTTP Endpoint	80
Default Instance running over HTTPS Endpoint	443
Service Broker	4022
Analysis Services	2383

Reporting Services Web Services	80
Reporting Services Web Services HTTPS	443
Integration Services	135

Using the Integrated Windows Server 2008 R2 Firewall with Advanced Security

Windows Server 2008 R2 includes a vastly improved integrated firewall that is turned on by default in all installations of the product. The firewall, administered from a Microsoft Management Console (MMC) snap-in shown in Figure 7.11, gives unprecedented control and security to a server. It can be accessed by choosing Start, All Programs, Administrative Tools, Windows Firewall with Advanced Security.

The firewall is fully integrated with the Server Manager utility and the Server Roles Wizard. For example, if a DBA runs the Server Roles Wizard and chooses to make the server a file server or a domain controller, only then are those ports and protocols that are required for file server or domain controller access opened on the server. Unfortunately, this is not the case with SQL Server, and firewall rules must be created and configured manually.

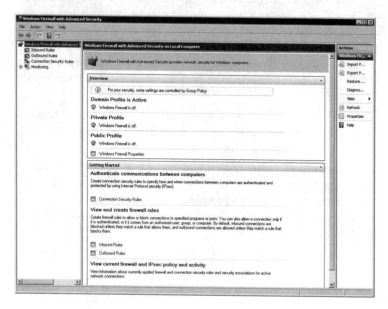

FIGURE 7.11
Using the integrated Windows Firewall with Advanced Security.

> **Note**
>
> It is instinctive for most DBAs or Windows administrators to disable software firewalls on servers, because they have caused problems with functionality in the past. This is not recommended in Windows Server 2008 R2, however, because the product is tightly integrated with its firewall, and the firewall provides for a much greater degree of security than previous versions of Windows Server provided.

Creating Rules for SQL Server 2012 on the Windows Server 2008 R2 Firewall

In certain cases, when a third-party application is not integrated with Server Manager, or when needing to open specific individual ports, it may become necessary to create firewall rules for individual services to run properly. This is the case when working with SQL Server 2012. Both inbound rules addressing traffic to the server, and outbound rules, addressing how the server can communicate out, can be created. Rules can be created based on the following factors:

- **Program**—A rule can be created that allows a specific program executable access. For example, you can specify that the C:\Program Files\Custom Program\myprogram.exe file has full outbound access when running. The Windows Firewall program will then allow any type of connections made by that program full access. This can be useful in scenarios when a specific application server uses multiple varied ports, but the overall security that the firewall provides is still desired.

- **Port**—Entering a traditional UDP or TCP port into the Add Rules Wizard is supported. This covers traditional scenarios such as, "We need to open port 1433 on the SQL Server system."

- **Predefined**—Windows Server also has built-in, predefined rules, such as those that allow AD DS, DFS, BITS, HTTP, and many more. The advantage to using a predefined rule is that Microsoft has done all the legwork in advance, and it becomes much easier to allow a specific service.

- **Custom**—The creation of custom rule types not covered in the other categories is also supported.

When configuring the Windows firewall, you can either create an exception for SQL Server based on the instance's port number or by adding the path to the SQL Server program. The default instance of SQL Server uses port 1433; however, ports are assigned dynamically when running more than one instance or even when creating AlwaysOn Availability Group Listeners. Therefore, it is a best practice to utilize the path of the program specifically when you are leveraging dynamic ports because the ports can constantly change.

Follow these steps to create a SQL Server exception on the Windows firewall by adding the path of the SQL Server program:

1. Open the Windows Firewall MMC Console (Start, All Programs, Administrative Tools, Windows Firewall with Advanced Security).

> **Note**
>
> A message box will be displayed if the Windows Firewall/Internet Connection Sharing (ICS) service is not running. Click Yes to activate the service and the firewall. In addition, another warning will appear, indicating that your computer is not protected and you must turn on Windows Firewall if the firewall setting is configured to Off.

2. Click on the Inbound Rules node in the node pane.

3. In the Action pane, click the link labeled New Rule.

4. In the Rule Type dialog box, shown in Figure 7.12, select to create a rule based on adding a program and click Next to continue.

5. Select the SQL Server instance from the program list. If the program is not available in the list, click Browse to search for it and provide the path for the appropriate SQL Server instance; for example, D:\Program Files\Microsoft SQL Server\MSSQL11.INSTANCE01\ MSSQL\Binn\sqlservr.exe, as illustrated in Figure 7.13. Then click Open.

> **Note**
>
> Microsoft SQL Server provides an instance ID for every SQL Server instance installed on a server. Typically, the ID is incremented by 1 when more than one instance is installed on a server. Use the SQL Server Configuration Manager tool to obtain the instance ID and installation path of a SQL Server instance. To find it, double-click the server name, and the Advanced tab displays the instance ID and installation path to the SQL Server instance.

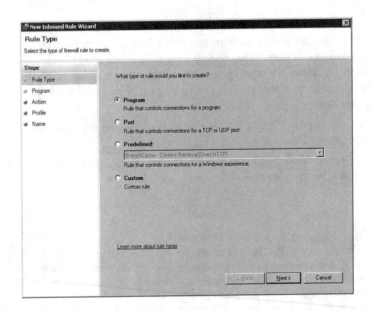

FIGURE 7.12
Setting Windows firewall options.

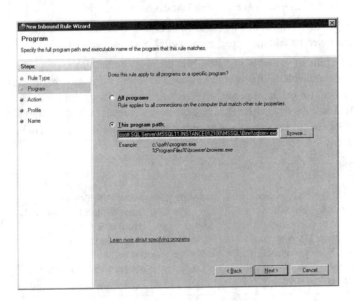

FIGURE 7.13
Setting the Windows firewall exception screen.

6. In the next window, on the Action tab, specify the action that should be taken when a connection matches the condition of the rule. The options are Allow the Connection, Allow the Connection If It Is Secure, and Block the Connection. Select Allow the Connection and then click Next.

7. On the Profile page, specify the desired profile box in which this rule will apply. This allows a DBA to specify that a rule applies only when connected to specific networks such as Domain. Click Next to continue.

8. Enter a descriptive name for the rule and click Finish.

9. Repeat these steps for every SQL Server instance or SQL component that requires an exception, such as Analysis Services, Integration Services, and so on.

10. Test the connection to the SQL Server from a desired client to validate both that the firewall is enabled and the appropriate exceptions were created.

Note

Create an exception for the SQL Server Browser service if there is a need to broadcast SQL Server information to clients over the network. Otherwise, SQL Server clients must know the names and ports of the clients when connecting.

Using the Integrated Windows Firewall is no longer just a good idea—it's a vital part of the security of the product. The addition of the capability to define rules based on factors such as scope, profile, IPsec status, and the like further positions the Server OS as one with high levels of integrated security.

Summary

One of the best features of SQL Server 2012 is that it's secure by default; however, when the SQL Server installation is complete, it is imperative that you harden the SQL Server implementation. You should understand all hardening techniques available so that you can determine which hardening strategies work best for your organization. Not every hardening technique works for everyone. Deploying SQL Server on Windows Server Core is another deployment strategy that many organizations are leveraging.

Finally, after the hardening is complete, don't forget to configure auditing and review security logs on a regular basis.

Additional security strategies such as encrypting SQL Server data and communications, Policy-Based Management, and administering SQL Server authorization and security are covered in the upcoming chapters.

Best Practices

Following is a summary of best practices for hardening and auditing a SQL Server environment:

- When the SQL Server installation is complete, harden the SQL Server environment.
- Install the most recent critical fixes and service packs for both Windows and SQL Server.
- When you're selecting authentication modes, Windows Authentication is a more secure choice. However, if mixed mode authentication is required, leverage complex passwords and SQL Server 2012 password and lockout policies to further bolster security.
- Do *not* use the SA account for day-to-day administration, logging on to the server remotely, or having applications use it to connect to SQL. It is best if the SA account is disabled and renamed.
- Create a role-based security policy with the Security Configuration Wizard tool.
- After SQL Server 2012 is installed, run the SQL Server Configuration Manager tool to disable unnecessary features and services and create policies with Policy-Based Management.
- Install only required components when installing SQL Server.
- After the server has been hardened, periodically assess the server's security using the MBSA and SQL Server BPA.
- For production SQL Servers running mission-critical databases, either hide the instance or disable the SQL Server Browser service.
- Change the default ports associated with the SQL Server installation to put off hackers from port-scanning the server.
- Use the new Audit Filtering capability to filter unnecessary audit events.

- Leverage the new ON_FAILURE = FAIL_Operation and MAX_FILES option to achieve audit resilience and the potential to automatically recovery from most file or network errors.
- Enable a firewall to filter unnecessary and unknown traffic.
- At the very least, set security auditing to failed login attempts; otherwise, both failed and successful logins should be captured and monitored.
- If upgrading previous versions of SQL Server, remove the BUILTIN\Administrators group from the SQL Server logins.

CHAPTER 8

Administering SQL Server Security and Authorization

By maintaining a strategy that is secure by design, secure by default, and secure in deployment, SQL Server 2012 allows for a much more effective method of design, implementation, and administration of security across resources and services provided by the SQL environment. Security permissions can be defined on a wide range of objects, from network endpoints that facilitate client communication, to execute permissions on a stored procedure, even down to the column level within a table. Complex security implementations can be efficiently controlled with granular role-based authorization and database schemas.

Administering SQL security is a key database administrator task that normally begins immediately following the hardening of the system. Understanding the different components related to security is essential to effective SQL security administration. This chapter discusses and demonstrates common administrative security tasks, incorporating best practices and new features introduced with SQL Server 2012.

What's New for Security and Authorization with SQL Server 2012?

The following list articulates the new SQL Server 2012 capabilities associated with security and authorization:

- SQL Server 2012 introduces 19 new permissions for the Database Engine. The following is a list of the new permissions that DBAs can take advantage of when securing the Database Engine:

- New GRANT, DENY, and REVOKE permissions to CONTROL/ VIEW DEFINTION/TAKE OWNERSHIP/REFERENCES/ALTER ON a search property list are available.

- New GRANT, DENY, and REVOKE permissions to ALTER ANY SERVER ROLE, CREATE SERVER ROLE, and CONTROL/VIEW DEFINTION/TAKE OWNERSHIP/ALTER ON a server role.

- New GRANT, DENY, and REVOKE permissions to ALTER ANY AVAILABILITY GROUP, CREATE AVAILABILITY GROUP, and CONTROL/VIEW DEFINTION/TAKE OWNERSHIP/ALTER ON an availability group.

- New GRANT, DENY, and REVOKE permissions to the CREATE SEQUENCE permission.

- New GRANT, DENY, and REVOKE permissions to the ALTER ANY EVENT SESSION permission.

> **Note**
>
> For those of you who are interested, the following Transact-SQL statement can be used to display a list of all the permissions within the SQL Server Database Engine. SELECT * FROM sys.fn_builtin_ permissions('');

- SQL Server 2012 now supports a default schema for Windows Groups for simplified security management. From a security management perspective, this was the number-one customer request because it caused many challenges for DBAs in the past. By supporting a default schema for Windows Groups, the schema is tied to a group rather than individual users, it prevents erroneous errors of assigning schema to the wrong users, prevents unnecessary implicit user and schema creation, and reduces the changes of wrong schema used in queries.

- Similar to how it was possible to create user-defined roles for databases in the past, SQL Server 2012 introduces the concept of creating user-defined server roles to increase flexibility, manageability, and better compliance. User-defined server roles provide better separation of duties and ultimately lock down administrator privileges. The CREATE SERVER ROLE, ALTER SERVER ROLE, and DROP SERVER ROLE can be used to manage server roles. Alternatively, the tasks can be achieved with SQL Server Management Studio.

- Contained Database Authentication—In the previous versions of SQL Server, authentication issues surfaced when moving databases between instances of SQL Server, because DBAs typically forgot to create logins on each instance of SQL Server that would host the database. Now with Contained Database Authentication, users can be authenticated and given access to a database without a login.

SQL Server Security

SQL Server 2012 continues to support two modes for validating connections and authenticating access to database resources: *Windows Authentication mode* and *SQL Server Authentication mode*. Both modes provide the ability for users to authenticate to SQL Server and access database resources.

> **Note**
>
> It is important to understand that security can be most effectively managed when the environment has been prepared and hardened. See Chapter 7, "Hardening and Auditing a SQL Server 2012 Implementation," for additional information.

When you're administering SQL Server security, it is important to follow the *principle of least privilege*. This basically means that only the permissions necessary to accomplish the task should be granted to the different user and service accounts. The principle of least privilege ensures that only the required resources are exposed to the client, while other resources are inaccessible and locked down. This improves the environment in multiple ways, including lowering the probability of accidental or intentional damage, increasing system scalability, and simplifying administration and deployment.

SQL Server 2012 facilitates flexible and scalable management of object permissions by allowing database users to be added to roles. Database roles serve a purpose similar to that of groups in the Windows operating system—they allow you to group accounts with common permission requirements and grant those permissions to a role instead of individual users. Figure 8.1 depicts at a high level how database objects are accessed by clients.

In Figure 8.1, the client communicates to SQL Server through an endpoint. The client provides credentials used for authentication either by explicitly entering them in SQL authentication mode or with pass-through Windows-based authentication. Server logins can be assigned permissions to server-level securable objects, including the SQL Server, endpoints, and other logins.

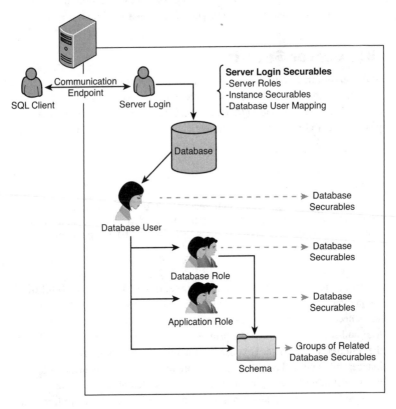

FIGURE 8.1
Overview of SQL Server security.

Note

A SQL Server login cannot be given permissions for database securable objects directly.

A login must be mapped to a database user; the database user then can be given permissions on database-scoped securable objects either directly or through database roles and schemas.

To grant permissions on database securable objects, you map the server login to a database user. Permissions for database objects can be granted directly to the database user; however, it is a best practice to add the database user to a database role or roles and then grant the appropriate permissions to those roles. See the section, "Role-Based Access," later on in this chapter, for best practices on granting access to SQL Server.

Endpoints and Communication

To communicate and access resources provided by a SQL Server, you must establish a connection to a server endpoint. In most cases, Tabular Data Stream (TDS) endpoints are used for communication with SQL Server. TDS packets sent by the client to the endpoint are encapsulated with a standard network protocol by way of the SQL Server Network Interface (SNI) protocol layer. The SNI layer used for TDS encapsulation is common to both the SQL Server and SQL client.

Endpoints for several common network protocols supported by SQL Server are created by default. In addition, an endpoint is created by default for the Dedicated Administrator Connection (DAC); this endpoint can be used only by members of the sysadmin fixed server role to establish an administrative connection to the server. Following are the default endpoints and protocols:

- Dedicated Administrator Connection (TCP)
- Transact-SQL Local Machine (Shared Memory)
- Transact-SQL Named Pipes (Named Pipes)
- Transact-SQL Default TCP (TCP)
- Transact-SQL Default VIA (VIA)

Default system endpoints cannot be dropped or disabled. However, they can be stopped and started, and the permissions for the endpoints can be altered as necessary. For each SQL Server instance, only a single named pipe and shared memory endpoint are supported. User-defined endpoints can have multiple instances per SQL Server instance; the protocol for user-defined endpoints is always HTTP or TCP.

The default system endpoints are all configured for the Transact-SQL payload type. This means they communicate with the endpoint using Transact-SQL. When a user defines an endpoint, the payload type can be configured as Transact-SQL, SOAP, Service Broker, database mirroring, or availability groups. For example, a database that is using database mirroring communicates with its partners through endpoints configured with the database mirroring payload type.

> **Note**
>
> The Dedicated Administrator Connection (DAC) allows you to connect to a server when the Database Engine does not respond to regular connections. By default, the DAC endpoint cannot be accessed remotely and is available only from the local computer. To allow remote access to DAC, you can enable the `remote admin connections` option through the `sp_configure` system stored procedure.

With the exception of HTTP, the protocols for each of the default endpoints are listed and can be configured in the SQL Server Configuration Manager. In addition, all endpoints are listed in Object Explorer in SQL Server Management Studio, under Server Objects, Endpoints.

When a protocol is disabled, the endpoint that implements the protocol cannot be used, although the endpoint may still be in the started state. In SQL Server 2012 Enterprise, Standard, and Workgroup Editions, only TCP/IP is enabled by default. In the Developer and Evaluation Editions, TCP/IP is disabled by default.

You can use the `sys.endpoints` catalog view to see the status of all endpoints on the server. The following query returns all the endpoints configured on the server:

```
USE MASTER
SELECT * FROM sys.endpoints
```

The `sys.http_endpoints`, `sys.soap_endpoints`, and `sys.endpoint_webmethods` catalog views can be used to get additional information about specific types of endpoints.

The `sys.server_permissions` catalog view can be used to see the permissions on server-level securable objects, including endpoints. You can use the `sys.server_principals` catalog view to retrieve the name of the server principal listed in the `grantee_principal_id` column.

For example, the following query returns the grantee permissions and grantee name for all endpoints on a server. Note that endpoints have a value of 105 in the `class` column:

```
USE MASTER
SELECT
  p.class_desc,
  p.major_id,
  p.minor_id,
  p.grantee_principal_id,
  sp.name as grantee_name,
  p.permission_name,
  p.state_desc
FROM sys.server_permissions p
  INNER JOIN sys.server_principals sp
  ON p.grantee_principal_id = sp.principal_id
WHERE class = 105
```

The resultset of the query shows that the principal public has been granted CONNECT permission on each of the endpoints by default. This essentially allows all logins to connect to any of the default endpoints, if the underlying protocol has also been enabled.

Note

It is a best practice to enable only communication protocols that are necessary and to allow only specific CONNECT permissions on endpoints.

You can administer existing protocols and endpoints through the SQL Server Configuration Manager Policy-Based Management, the AlwaysOn Availability Groups Wizard, the Database Mirroring Wizard, and by using Data Definition Language (DDL). However, you can also create new endpoints only through the CREATE ENDPOINT DDL.

Server Logins and Database Users

Server logins and database users are both principals. Logins are principals on the server level, and database users are principals on the database level. SQL Server permissions on securable objects can be granted to principals at the appropriate level. Logins can be granted permissions on server-level securable objects, and database users can be granted permissions on database-level securable objects, but logins cannot be granted permission to database-level objects and database users cannot be granted permissions to server-level objects.

Table 8.1 shows all the SQL Server principals.

Table 8.1 **SQL Server Principals**

Type	Description
Server	SQL Server login
Server	SQL Server login from Windows login
Server	SQL Server login from certificate
Server	SQL Server login from asymmetric key
Database	Database user
Database	Database role
Database	Database user mapped to Windows user
Database	Database user mapped to Windows group
Database	Database user mapped to certificate
Database	Database user with no login

> **Note**
>
> Principals are also securable objects; for example, users can be granted control permissions on other users, database roles, and so on.

Clients authenticate to the server using a login. The authentication used for the login can be either Windows-based or SQL-based. Windows authentication logins are recommended over SQL authentication logins because Windows logins can leverage Active Directory security, native authentication encryption, and pass-through (transparent) authentication.

When you're using Windows Authentication mode, the account can be either a local or domain-based user account or an account that is a member of a group (local or domain) that has been added as a login to SQL Server. When you're using SQL authentication, the account information, including hashed password, is stored in the master database of your SQL Server instance.

Both SQLServer and Windows-based logins provide access to server instance objects but not to database objects. The following securable objects can have permissions assigned to server logins:

- Servers
- Endpoints
- Logins
- Availability groups
- Server roles

SQL logins can be mapped to database users. Database users are then granted permissions on securable objects in the database. Following are database-level securable objects:

- Databases
- Stored procedures
- Tables
- Views
- Inline functions
- Scalar functions
- Table-valued functions
- Aggregate functions
- Application roles
- Assemblies
- Asymmetric keys
- Certificates
- Database roles
- Full-text catalogs
- Schemas
- Symmetric keys
- Synonyms
- Users
- User-defined data types
- XML schema collections
- Queues
- Sequences

Both SQL logins and users are considered securable objects and can have permissions assigned in the same fashion as any other object in the database.

Role-Based Access

Although database users can be granted permissions on objects directly, this is generally considered a bad practice when dealing with complex security scenarios. It is much more effective to create roles for each type of user, assign the correct permissions to the role, and make individual user accounts members of that role. Role-based access reduces the cost of ongoing security administration because users can be added and removed from roles without having to re-create complex permissions for each user.

Role-based access can be established at both the SQL Server level and in Active Directory. It is common to establish role-based access for all network services through Active Directory with the added benefit of organizationwide control of data services.

Using Active Directory for role-based access follows the standard of placing user accounts into domain global *role groups* and the role groups into domain local *access groups*. The access groups are then added to the SQL instance as logins and mapped to database users. The database users can then be added to the correct database role and/or security schemas. As a result, users added to role groups in Active Directory automatically obtain the correct permissions. Security management for the environment is transferred from SQL Server into Active Directory, where it can be controlled centrally.

Several server-level roles exist in each SQL Server instance. Server roles are used to grant administrative permissions on the server and are not used to grant permission to normal user accounts. Table 8.2 lists each server-level role and the permissions associated with each role.

Table 8.2   **Server-Level Roles**

Server Role	Default Permissions
bulkadmin	Granted: ADMINISTER BULK OPERATIONS
dbcreator	Granted: CREATE DATABASE
diskadmin	Granted: ALTER RESOURCES
processadmin	Granted: ALTER ANY CONNECTION, ALTER SERVER STATE
securityadmin	Granted: ALTER ANY LOGIN
serveradmin	Granted: ALTER ANY ENDPOINT, ALTER RESOURCES, ALTER SERVER STATE, ALTER SETTINGS, SHUTDOWN, VIEW SERVER STATE
setupadmin	Granted: ALTER ANY LINKED SERVER
sysadmin	Granted with GRANT option: CONTROL SERVER
public	Granted: VIEW ANY DATABASE

> **Note**
>
> All logins belong to the public server role by default. The public role is granted VIEW ANY DATABASE by default.

Several fixed database-level roles exist in each SQL Server database. Those predefined roles are used to grant a predefined set of permissions to database users and, with the exception of the public role, they are not used to assign permissions to individual objects. Table 8.3 lists each fixed database-level role and the permissions associated with each role.

Table 8.3 **Fixed Database-Level Roles**

Database Role	Default Permissions
db_accessadmin	Granted: ALTER ANY USER, CREATE SCHEMA
db_backupoperator	Granted: BACKUP DATABASE, BACKUP LOG, CHECKPOINT
db_datareader	Granted: SELECT
db_datawriter	Granted: DELETE, INSERT, UPDATE
db_ddladmin	Granted: ALTER ANY ASSEMBLY, ALTER ANY ASYMMET-RIC KEY, ALTER ANY CERTIFICATE, ALTER ANY CONTRACT, ALTER ANY DATABASE DDL TRIGGER, ALTER ANY DATABASE EVENT NOTIFICATION, ALTER ANY DATASPACE, ALTER ANY FULLTEXT CATALOG, ALTER ANY MESSAGE TYPE, ALTER ANY REMOTE SERVICE BINDING, ALTER ANY ROUTE, ALTER ANY SCHEMA, ALTER ANY SERVICE, ALTER ANY SYMMETRIC KEY, CHECKPOINT, CREATE AGGREGATE, CREATE DEFAULT, CREATE FUNCTION, CREATE PROCEDURE, CREATE QUEUE, CREATE RULE, CREATE SYNONYM, CREATE TABLE, CREATE TYPE, CREATE VIEW, CREATE XML SCHEMA COLLECTION, REFERENCES
db_denydatareader	Denied: SELECT
db_denydatawriter	Denied: DELETE, INSERT, UPDATE
db_owner	Granted with GRANT option: CONTROL
db_securityadmin	Granted: ALTER ANY APPLICATION ROLE, ALTER ANY ROLE, CREATE SCHEMA, VIEW DEFINITION
public	Granted: SELECT on system views

> **Note**
>
> All database users belong to the public database role by default. It is a best practice to avoid using the public database role when assigning permissions.

Database Schema

The database schemas were first introduced in SQL Server 2005 and provide several improvements when compared to previous versions of SQL Server. The schema is a key part of establishing flexible database security administration.

When objects are accessed in SQL Server 2005 or 2008, they are referenced by a four-part identifier, where parts have the following meaning:

[DatabaseServer].[DatabaseName].[DatabaseSchema].[DatabaseObject]

For example, the following query can be used to access the Employee table created as part of the HumanResources schema in the AdventureWorks2012 database. The AdventureWorks2012 database is hosted on Instance01 on the server SQLServer01.

```
SELECT *
FROM [SQLSERVER01\INSTANCE01].[AdventureWorks2012].
[HumanResources].[Employee]
```

The *database schema* is a namespace used to reference objects in the database. The schema provides a way to manage security on groups of objects as a unit. As new database objects are defined, they must be associated with a schema and automatically inherit the permissions granted on the schema.

The principal defined as the schema owner effectively owns all objects in the schema. When the owner of a schema is changed, all objects in the schema are owned by the new principal, with the exception of objects for which a different owner was explicitly defined.

> **Note**
>
> As mentioned earlier in the "What's New for Security and Authorization with SQL Server 2012" section, it is now possible to define a default schema for a Windows group rather than just individual users. Simply include the [WITH DEFAULT_SCHEMA = schema_name] when creating the group with Transact-SQL or use the User Mapping page when administering a Windows Group in SQL Server Management Studio.

Password Policies

Domain policies and local security policies provide the password and account lockout configuration that affects users' ability to authenticate and access SQL Server resources.

When Windows Authentication mode is used, these settings govern all users according to the defined password policy.

When SQL Server authentication is used, a SQL login can be configured to be subject to the password and lockout policies of the underlying local security or domain group policy. This functionality is supported only with the Windows Server 2003 or later operating systems, such as Windows Server 2008 R2.

Note

If SQL authentication is used, it is highly recommended to enable these options to enforce the local security policies to increase the level of security for SQL logins.

The following password policies can be used to help secure Windows and SQL Server authentication:

- **Enforce Password History**—This security setting determines the number of unique new passwords that have to be associated with a user account before an old password can be reused.

- **Maximum Password Age**—This security setting determines the period of time (in days) that a password can be used before the system requires the user to change it.

- **Minimum Password Age**—This security setting determines the period of time (in days) that a password must be used before the user can change it.

- **Minimum Password Length**—This security setting determines the least number of characters that a password for a user account may contain.

- **Password Must Meet Complexity Requirements**—This security setting determines whether passwords must meet complexity requirements. Complex passwords cannot contain the user's login name, must be at least six characters in length, and must contain characters from three of the four available character categories. Character categories include uppercase, lowercase, base 10 digits, and nonalphabetic characters.

- **Store Passwords Using Reversible Encryption**—This security setting determines whether the operating system stores passwords using reversible encryption. This setting affects only Windows authentication and has no effect on SQL Server logons.

Note

In Windows Server 2003, there can be only a single password policy for each Active Directory domain. Password policy settings for the domain must be defined in the root node for the domain.

This limitation was lifted in Windows Server 2008; password policies can be defined on a per-group and per-user basis.

These security policies can be accessed through the Windows Settings\ Security Settings\Account Policies\Password Policies node in the Default Domain Policy. Figure 8.2 shows the default Active Directory password policies.

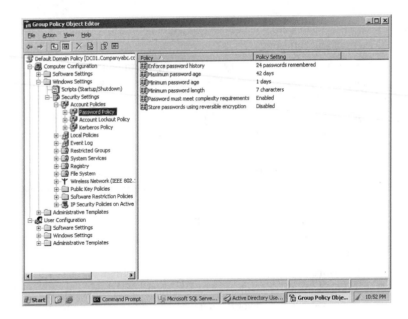

FIGURE 8.2
Windows password policies.

The following account lockout policies can be used to help secure Windows and SQL Server authentication:

- **Account Lockout Threshold**—This security setting determines the number of minutes a locked-out account remains locked out before automatically becoming unlocked. The available range is from 0 minutes to 99,999 minutes. If you set the account lockout duration to 0, the account is locked out until an administrator explicitly unlocks it.

- **Account Lockout Duration**—This security setting determines the number of failed logon attempts that causes a user account to be locked out. A locked-out account cannot be used until it is reset by an administrator or until the lockout duration for the account has expired. You can set a value between 0 and 999 failed logon attempts. If you set the value to 0, the account is never locked out.

- **Reset Lockout Counter After**—This security setting determines the number of minutes that must elapse after a failed logon attempt before the failed logon attempt counter is reset to 0 bad logon attempts. The available range is 1 minute to 99,999 minutes.

These security policies can be accessed through the Windows Settings\Security Settings\Account Policies\Account Lockout Policy node in the Default Domain Policy. Figure 8.3 shows the default Active Directory account lockout policies.

When these policies are configured, the resulting domain-level group policy or the local security policy helps secure the environment by preventing low-security passwords.

Logon Triggers

Logon triggers were first introduced in SQL Server 2005 Service Pack 2 and this functionality is also included in SQL Server 2012. Logon triggers allow you to handle logon events on the server and enforce your own authentication policies based on logic implemented in the trigger. This enables you to create flexible logon policies based on multiple criteria.

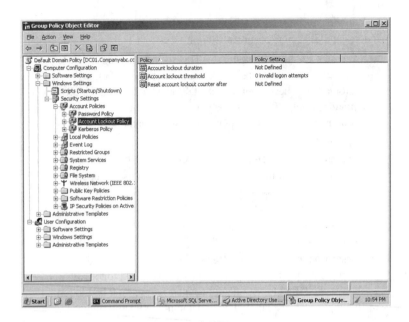

FIGURE 8.3
Windows account lockout policies.

The following Transact-SQL code gives an example of a trigger that disallows login attempts from user Bob between 6 p.m. and 6 a.m:

```
CREATE TRIGGER trg_after_hours_logins
ON ALL SERVER
FOR LOGON
AS
BEGIN
IF SUSER_SNAME()= 'Bob' AND
  ((SELECT DATEPART(hh, GETDATE())) >= 18
  OR (SELECT DATEPART(hh, GETDATE())) < 6)
  ROLLBACK;
END;
```

Security Management DDL

The data definition language (DDL) statements used to administer SQL Server 2012 security is provided in the following sections as a reference. The Transact-SQL (Transact-SQL) statements shown here are demonstrated in the section "Administering SQL Server Security" later in this chapter.

Managing Logins with DDL

The CREATE LOGIN statement can be used to define new SQL Server logins. The SQL Server login can be a Windows user account, a Windows security group, or a SQL Server account. The CREATE LOGIN statement replaces the sp_addlogin system stored procedure used in previous versions of SQL Server:

```
CREATE LOGIN login_name { WITH <option_list1> | FROM <sources> }

<sources> ::=
  WINDOWS [ WITH <windows_options> [ ,... ] ]
  | CERTIFICATE certname
  | ASYMMETRIC KEY asym_key_name

<option_list1> ::=
  PASSWORD = 'password' [ HASHED ] [ MUST_CHANGE ]
  [ , <option_list2> [ ,... ] ]

<option_list2> ::=
  SID = sid
  | DEFAULT_DATABASE = database
  | DEFAULT_LANGUAGE = language
  | CHECK_EXPIRATION = { ON | OFF}
  | CHECK_POLICY = { ON | OFF}
  | CREDENTIAL = credential_name

<windows_options> ::=
  DEFAULT_DATABASE = database
  | DEFAULT_LANGUAGE = language
```

The ALTER LOGIN statement can be used to modify existing SQL Server logins. For example, if the password policy of a SQL user causes the account to become locked out, the security administrator can use the ALTER LOGIN statement to unlock the account:

```
ALTER LOGIN login_name
  {
  <status_option>
  | WITH <set_option> [ ,... ]
  }
```

```
<status_option> ::=
   ENABLE | DISABLE

<set_option> ::=
  PASSWORD = 'password' [HASHED]
  [
   OLD_PASSWORD = 'oldpassword'
   | <password_option> [ <password_option> ]
  ]
  | DEFAULT_DATABASE = database
  | DEFAULT_LANGUAGE = language
  | NAME = login_name
  | CHECK_POLICY = { ON | OFF }
  | CHECK_EXPIRATION = { ON | OFF }
  | CREDENTIAL = credential_name
  | NO CREDENTIAL

<password_option> ::=
   MUST_CHANGE | UNLOCK
```

The DROP LOGIN statement can be used to remove logins from the server:

```
DROP LOGIN login_name
```

The preceding DDL statements replace their older counterparts in the form of system stored procedures. The following stored procedures are still available; however, these stored procedures are considered deprecated and should not be used:

- sp_addlogin
- sp_grantlogin
- sp_denylogin
- sp_revokelogin

Managing Users with DDL

The CREATE USER statement can be used to define a new database user. After the SQL Server login is created, the login can be mapped to a database as a user; from this point, permissions for the database can be assigned.

```
CREATE USER user_name
  [ { { FOR | FROM }
    {
     LOGIN login_name
     | CERTIFICATE cert_name
     | ASYMMETRIC KEY asym_key_name
    }
    | WITHOUT LOGIN
  ]
  [ WITH DEFAULT_SCHEMA = schema_name ]
```

The ALTER USER statement can be used to modify existing database users. For example, if you need to update the default schema for a user, you can use this statement:

```
ALTER USER user_name
   WITH <set_item> [ ,...n]

<set_item> ::=
   NAME = new_user_name
   | DEFAULT_SCHEMA = schema_name
```

Note

It is possible to create a database user without mapping it to a login. This allows you to create such a login, grant necessary permissions, and map it to a login at a later stage. Such logins can also be used inside the database to provide impersonated security context while executing code modules, such as stored procedures or functions.

The DROP USER statement can be used to remove a database user from a database. Removing a database user does not remove an associated login and, conversely, when the login is removed, the mapped database user account is not automatically removed; this step must be done manually to complete the removal:

```
DROP USER user_name
```

Managing Roles with DDL

The CREATE ROLE and ALTER ROLE statements can be used to define and modify database roles. Users should be assigned to database roles instead of being assigned to objects directly to get the appropriate permissions.

```
CREATE ROLE role_name [ AUTHORIZATION owner_name ]
ALTER ROLE role_name WITH NAME = new_name
```

The sp_addrolemember statement can be used to add principals to database roles. If a login is specified, a database user is automatically created for the login and added to the role:

```
sp_addrolemember [ @rolename = ] 'role',
  [ @membername = ] 'security_account'
```

The sp_droprolemember statement can be used to remove database users from database roles:

```
sp_droprolemember [ @rolename = ] 'role' ,
    [ @membername = ] 'security_account'
```

The sp_addsrvrolemember statement can be used to add logins to fixed server roles. Note that role membership for login sa and public server role cannot be changed:

```
sp_addsrvrolemember [ @loginame= ] 'login'
  , [ @rolename = ] 'role'
```

The sp_dropsrvrolemember statement can be used to remove logins from fixed server roles:

```
sp_dropsrvrolemember [ @loginame = ] 'login' ,
 [ @rolename = ] 'role'
```

Managing Schemas with DDL

The CREATE SCHEMA statement can be used to define a new database schema. Database roles and users can be granted permissions on a schema level. The schema is used to group database objects together, so permissions don't need to be assigned to individual objects:

```
CREATE SCHEMA schema_name_clause [ <schema_element> [ ...n ] ]

<schema_name_clause> ::=
  {
    schema_name
  | AUTHORIZATION owner_name
  | schema_name AUTHORIZATION owner_name
  }
```

```
<schema_element> ::=
  {
    table_definition | view_definition | grant_statement |
    revoke_statement | deny_statement
  }
```

The ALTER SCHEMA statement can be used to transfer ownership to another database user or role. This statement cannot be used to add or remove securable items from the schema. To add or remove securable objects from the schema, you use the ALTER SCHEMA statement:

```
ALTER SCHEMA schema_name TRANSFER securable_name
```

Managing Permissions with DDL

The statements shown in this section can be used to grant, deny, or revoke permissions on objects to principals. Only the basic syntax is shown; you can find additional object-specific syntax in SQL Server 2012 Books Online.

> **Note**
>
> Normally, deny permissions take precedence over grant permissions. However, for backward compatibility, column-level permissions take precedence over object permissions.

The GRANT statement gives principals such as database roles, users, and logins permissions to securable objects such as databases and tables. The WITH GRANT option essentially allows the grantee principal to give other principals the same permissions on the object:

```
GRANT { ALL [ PRIVILEGES ] }
  | permission [ ( column [ ,...n ] ) ] [ ,...n ]
  [ ON [ class :: ] securable ] TO principal [ ,...n ]
  [ WITH GRANT OPTION ] [ AS principal ]
```

The DENY statement prevents principals from accessing objects and inheriting permissions through membership in database roles:

```
DENY { ALL [ PRIVILEGES ] }
  | permission [ ( column [ ,...n ] ) ] [ ,...n ]
  [ ON [ class :: ] securable ] TO principal [ ,...n ]
  [ CASCADE] [ AS principal ]
```

The REVOKE statement removes any existing permissions, either granted or denied:

```
REVOKE [ GRANT OPTION FOR ]
    {
    [ ALL [ PRIVILEGES ] ]
    |
        permission [ ( column [ ,...n ] ) ] [ ,...n ]
    }
    [ ON [ class :: ] securable ]
    { TO | FROM } principal [ ,...n ]
    [ CASCADE] [ AS principal ]
```

Administering SQL Server Security

The following sections provide detailed instructions for administering SQL Server permissions and authorizing access to SQL Server resources. The demonstrations are shown using logins configured for either SQL Server or Windows Authentication mode because both can be added to roles and are given permissions the same way.

Note

Using Windows Authentication is considered a more secure choice and is recommended over SQL logins because Windows authentication protocols such as NT LAN Manager (NTLM) and Kerberos can be leveraged.

Using Windows Authentication provides several advantages over SQL Server authentication, including enterprisewide control of access accounts governed by domain security policies. In addition, Windows Authentication can leverage Active Directory authentication protocols such as NTLM and Kerberos when SQL Server is located in an Active Directory domain.

If SQL authentication is used, it is recommended that you leverage password and lockout policies in addition to login encryption to further bolster security.

The section "Password Policies" earlier in this chapter contains additional information on how to configure password policies.

Server Login Administration

The SQL login is the basic method of authenticating to the SQL Server. When Windows accounts are used, either NTLM or Kerberos authentication is used to authenticate the user. Kerberos will be the first preference, and then it will fall back to NTLM if Kerberos is not available. The user's credentials are sent in an encrypted form, making it difficult to discover them as they travel across the network.

Enabling Mixed Mode Authentication

SQL Server can be configured for Windows Authentication mode only or SQL Server and Windows Authentication mode. For simplicity, some of the demonstrations use SQL authentication and require the server to support both authentication modes.

Follow these steps to enable both Windows Authentication mode and SQL Server and Windows Authentication mode:

1. Choose Start, All Programs, Microsoft SQL Server 2012, SQL Server Management Studio, and then connect to an instance of SQL Server.

2. In Object Explorer, right-click a desired instance of SQL Server, and then click Properties.

3. On the Security page, under Server Authentication, select SQL Server and Windows Authentication mode, and then click OK.

4. In the SQL Server Management Studio dialog box, click OK to acknowledge the need to restart SQL Server.

5. In Object Explorer, right-click a desired server, and then click Restart. If the SQL Server Agent is running, it also requires a restart.

Note

If Windows Authentication mode is selected during installation, the sa login is disabled by default. If the authentication mode is switched to SQL Server mixed mode after the installation, the sa account is still disabled and must be manually enabled. It is a best practice to reset the password when the mode is switched.

Creating SQL Authentication Logins

The Logins node holds all the Windows and SQL logins for the server. From this node, the different server logins can be managed. The following

procedure can be used to create a new SQL login within SQL Server
Management Studio:

1. Choose Start, All Programs, Microsoft SQL Server 2012, SQL
   Server Management Studio, and then connect to an instance of SQL
   Server.

2. In Object Explorer, right-click a desired instance of SQL Server,
   expand Security, and select the Logins node.

3. Right-click the Logins node and select New Login. The Login –
   New window opens.

The following relevant login options are located on the General configuration page:

- **Login Name**—When Windows Authentication is used, this is the
  name of the existing Windows user or Windows security group.
  When SQL authentication is used, this is the name selected for the
  login.

- **Windows Authentication**—This option allows the selection of a
  Windows user account or security group for the logon. The Windows
  user account or security group can reside in Active Directory or the
  local server.

- **SQL Server Authentication**—This option allows the creation of an
  account where the account information, including the account password, is stored in the SQL database.

The following additional options are available on the General tab when
you use SQL Server authentication:

- **Enforce Password Policy**—This option configures the SQL Server
  to enforce domain or local server password policies. If SQL Server
  authentication is used, this option is highly recommended to help
  improve security.

- **Enforce Password Expiration**—This option configures the SQL
  Server to enforce domain or local server password expiration policies. This option should be enabled if the database application
  provides a way for the user to change the password.

- **User Must Change Password**—When this option is enabled, the
  user must change the password during the first authentication. This
  option should be enabled if the database application provides a way
  for the user to change the password.

Follow these steps to create the SQL Server login and complete the configuration page:

1. Enter Test.User1 in the Login Name field.
2. Select SQL Server authentication.
3. Enter the password.
4. Confirm the password.
5. Select Enforce Password Policy.
6. Select Enforce Password Expiration.
7. Select User Must Change Password at Next Login.
8. Leave Master as the Default database.
9. Leave <default> as the Default language.
10. Figure 8.4 shows how the Logon Properties window should look. Click OK to complete the page and create the login.

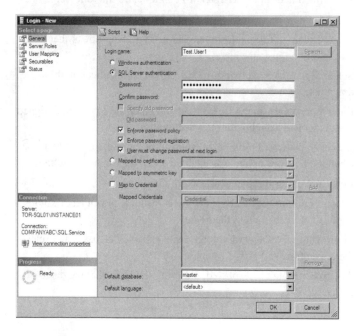

FIGURE 8.4
New SQL authentication logon properties.

The SQL login Test.User1 is created but currently has only a limited set of permissions. By default, all users are members of the public fixed server role.

You can use the following Transact-SQL code to accomplish the same task. This code creates a user called Test.User2 with `Password!!` set as the default password for the account:

```
USE [master]
GO
CREATE LOGIN [Test.User2] WITH
  PASSWORD=N'Password!!'
  MUST_CHANGE,
  DEFAULT_DATABASE=[master],
  CHECK_EXPIRATION=ON,
  CHECK_POLICY=ON
GO
```

After the logon account is created, the next step is to verify that the account can authenticate to the server. Configuring permissions for the login is described later in this chapter. To continue, do the following:

1. Launch a new instance of SQL Server Management Studio.

2. Select Database Engine from the Server Type drop-down; then enter the server and instance name.

3. Select SQL Server Authentication from the Authentication drop-down list.

4. Enter **Test.User1** in the Login field and enter the password assigned to the logon. Then click the Connect button.

5. A change password prompt is displayed because the User Must Change Password policy was enabled when the login was defined.

6. Enter and confirm the new password; then click OK.

7. A connection to the database engine is made. If the Object Explorer pane is not visible, press the F8 key.

8. From within the Object Explorer pane, expand Databases and select the AdventureWorks2012 database.

9. An error message is displayed, notifying the login that the database is inaccessible.

> **Note**
>
> When these steps are complete, ensure you log out and use a logon with the appropriate permissions to the instance of SQL Server so you can successfully conduct the additional steps within this chapter.

Although the account cannot access any of the databases, the authentication should be successful.

Creating Windows Authentication Logins

Creating a Windows login is similar to creating a SQL Server login. Another one of the many advantages to using Windows Authentication includes the ability to add domain security groups as the login instead of just the user account. Before you add a Windows account or security group as a SQL Server login, it must exist in Active Directory or on the local computer. Follow these steps to create a Windows user account in Active Directory:

1. On the SQL Server system, select Start, Run.

2. Type DSA.MSC, and then click OK.

3. Create a domain user account called Test.Domain1.

After creating the Active Directory user account, you can add the account as a login. Follow these steps:

1. In Object Explorer, expand the Security node.

2. Right-click the Logins node and select New Login.

3. Click the Search button.

4. Click Locations and select Entire Directory, and then click OK.

5. Type Test.Domain1 in the Object field.

6. Click the Check Name button to confirm the account name.

7. Click OK to return to the Login Properties window.

8. Select Master as the Default database.

9. Select <default> as the Default language.

10. Figure 8.5 shows how the Logon Properties window should look. Click OK to complete the page and create the login.

The user account is listed in the Logins folder. Perform the following steps to verify that the account can authenticate to the server. The SQL Server Management Studio can be executed as a different user account through the Run As command:

1. Add Choose, Start, All Programs, Microsoft SQL Server 2012. Then right-click SQL Server Management Studio and select Run As.

2. In the Run As window, enter COMPANYABC\Test.Domain1 in the User Name field.

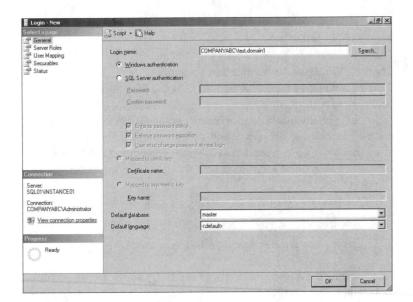

FIGURE 8.5
New Windows authentication logon properties.

Note

If you don't have the potential to leverage the Run As functionality, then log off and switch users. Logon in using CompanyABC\Test.Domain1.

---

3. Enter the associated account password and click OK. The SQL Server Management Studio opens under the Test.Domain1 account.

4. Select Database Engine from the Server Type drop-down list; then enter the server and instance name.

5. Select Windows Authentication from the Authentication drop-down list, and then click the Connect button.

6. A connection to the Database Engine is made. If the Object Explorer pane is not visible, press the F8 key.

7. From within the Object Explorer pane, expand Databases and select the AdventureWorks2012 database.

8. An error message is displayed, notifying the login that the database is inaccessible.

The authentication should be successful because the default database was set to Master and the login is a member of the public server role. The public role has limited access to the master database. If you set the default database to something else, such as AdventureWorks2012, the authentication would fail because the public role does not have access to this database by default.

You can use the following Transact-SQL code to add the Test.Domain1 user as a SQL login:

```
USE [master]
GO
CREATE LOGIN [COMPANYABC\Test.Domain1] FROM WINDOWS WITH
DEFAULT_DATABASE=[master]
GO
```

Database User Administration

After adding a login to the server, you can create a database user. The database user is essentially mapped back to the original login; this means the login is normally required before access to database resources can be authorized.

Follow these steps to manage database users. This procedure adds the login Test.User1 to the AdventureWorks2012 database in a SQL Server instance:

1. In Object Explorer, expand the AdventureWorks2012 Database folder, Security folder, and then select Users.

2. Right-click Users and select New User.

3. On the General page in the Database User – New dialog box, select one of the following user types from the User type list. The options include SQL user with login, SQL user without login, User mapped to a certificate, User mapped to an asymmetric key, or Windows user. For this example, the SQL user with Login was selected.

4. In the User name box, enter a name for the new user such as **Test.User1**.

5. Click the ellipsis button next to the Login Name field.

6. On the Select Login page, click Browse.

7. Select Test.User1, and then click OK.

8. Click OK to return to the General page.

9. Click the ellipsis button next to the Default Schema field.

10. On the Select Schema window, click Browse.

11. Select Human Resources, and then click OK.

12. The Database User properties window should look similar to Figure 8.6. Click OK to create the database user.

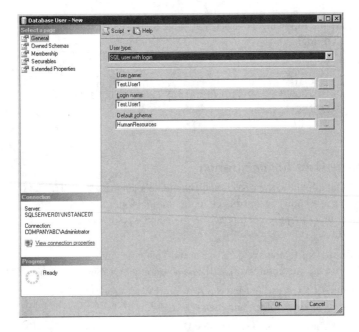

FIGURE 8.6
New database user properties.

For additional configurations, the following pages can be used:

- **Owned Schemas**—Should be used to configure owned schemas by this user.

- **Membership**—Should be used to assign database role membership such as db_owner or db_backupoperator to the user.

- **Securables**—This page is used to grant the login all possible securables and the permissions to those securables.

- **Extended Properties**—Add custom properties to the database user.

A user called Test.User1 is added to the database. You can use the following Transact-SQL code to add a login and an associated database user:

```
USE [AdventureWorks2012]
CREATE LOGIN [Test.User2]
 WITH PASSWORD=N'Password!'
 MUST_CHANGE,
 DEFAULT_DATABASE=[master],
 CHECK_EXPIRATION=ON, CHECK_POLICY=ON
GO
CREATE USER [Test.User2]
 FOR LOGIN [Test.User2]
 WITH DEFAULT_SCHEMA=[HumanResources]
GO
```

Now that you've added the login to the database, you can assign the correct permissions. Although permissions to objects can be assigned directly to users, it is recommended to create roles and database schemas to control access to database objects.

Windows-based logins can be mapped to database users using the same method. Database mapping for logins can also be configured on the Mapping Options page of the Login Properties window.

Database Role Administration

For efficient and effective management of data, users should be added to database roles. Each database role can be assigned permissions on a different object found in SQL Server.

The following procedure creates a new database role called Human Resources Reporting. The Test.User1 database user is added to this new role, and the role is given SELECT permissions to the HumanResources schema. Follow these steps:

1. In Object Explorer, expand AdventureWorks2012, Security, Roles, and select Database Roles.

2. Right-click Database Roles and select New Database Role.

3. Type **Human Resources Reporting** in the Name field.

4. Click the Add button.

5. On the Select Database User or Role page, click Browse.

6. Select Test.User1 and click OK.

7. Click OK to return to the Database Role properties window.

8. Select the Securables properties page.

9. Click the Search button.

10. Select All Objects of Type, and then click OK.

11. Select Schemas and click OK.

12. From the Securables list, select HumanResources.

13. In the Explicit Permissions list, enable Grant on the Select permission.

14. Click OK to complete the new role.

You can use the following Transact-SQL code to create and configure the Human Resources Reporting database role in the AdventureWorks2012 database:

```
USE [AdventureWorks2012]
GO
CREATE ROLE [Human Resources Reporting]
GO
USE [AdventureWorks2012]
GO
EXEC sp_addrolemember N'Human Resources Reporting',
 N'Test.User1'
GO
use [AdventureWorks2012]
GO
GRANT SELECT ON SCHEMA::[HumanResources]
TO [Human Resources Reporting]
GO
```

The code example first creates the database role, and then adds the user Test.User1 to the role. Finally, the role is given permissions to the schema object named HumanResources.

The sys.database_role_members and sys.database_principals catalog views can be used to display database roles.

Server Role Administration

As mentioned earlier, to provide stronger separation of duties and granular permissions at the server level, it is now possible to create user-defined server roles. For efficient and effective server-level management, a user-defined server role can be created, granular permissions can be applied to the securable, and members can be added to the newly created server role.

The following procedure creates a new server role called ServerRole AvailabilityGroupManagement. The server role is given explicit permissions to manage availability groups, and then the SQL Server group is added to the role. Just follow these steps:

1. In Object Explorer, expand the instance of SQL Server where you want to create the new server role.

2. Expand the Security folder.

3. Right-click the Server Roles folder and select New Server Role.

4. In the new Server Role dialog box, type **ServerRoleAvailabilityGroupManagement** into the Name field.

5. In the Owner box, enter the name of the server principal that will own the new role. It is also possible to click the ellipsis (...) to open the Select Server Login or Role dialog box.

6. Under the Securables section, select one or more securables for this server role, and then apply the appropriate explicit permissions in the Explicit box. For this example, the Availability Groups Securables are selected, and then the explicit permissions Alter, Control, and Take Ownership are applied, as illustrated in Figure 8.7.

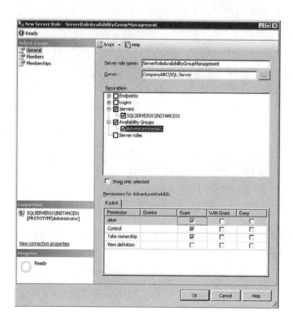

FIGURE 8.7
Assigning explicit permissions on securables for a new database role.

7. On the Members page, click the Add button to add logins or groups to the new server role.

8. A user-defined server role can be a member of another server role; therefore, as an optional step on the Memberships page, select a check box to make the current user-defined server role a member of a selected server role, such as DiskAdmin or Server Admin.

9. Click OK to complete the creation of the new server role.

Alternatively, you can use the following Transact-SQL code to create and configure the ServerRoleAvailabilityGroupManagement server role example from the previous steps:

```
USE [master]
GO
CREATE SERVER ROLE [ServerRole-AvailabilityGroup-Management]
AUTHORIZATION [CompanyABC\SQLServer]
GO
ALTER SERVER ROLE [ServerRole-AvailabilityGroup-Management]
ADD MEMBER [PROTOTYPE\SQL.Server]
GO
use [master]
GO
GRANT ALTER ON AVAILABILITY GROUP::[AdventureWorkAG]
TO [ServerRole-AvailabilityGroup-Management]
GO
use [master]
GO
GRANT CONTROL ON AVAILABILITY GROUP::[AdventureWorkAG]
TO [ServerRole-AvailabilityGroup-Management]
GO
use [master]
GO
GRANT TAKE OWNERSHIP ON AVAILABILITY GROUP::[AdventureWorkAG]
TO [ServerRole-AvailabilityGroup-Management]
GO
```

Security Schema Administration

The security schema for a database essentially provides a container for a group of objects in the database. Besides the default schemas found in all databases, the AdventureWorks2012 database has several schemas defined, including HumanResources, Person, Production, Purchasing, and Sales.

Follow these steps to establish a new schema called Test Schema for the AdventureWorks2012 database:

1. In Object Explorer, expand AdventureWorks2012, Security, and select Schemas.

2. Expand the Schemas node. Each of the default schemas for the AdventureWorks2012 database is listed.

3. Right-click the Schemas node and select New Schema. The new Schema Properties window opens.

4. In the Schema Name field, type `Test Schema`.

5. Click the Search button.

6. Click the Browse button.

7. Select Test.User1 and click OK.

8. Click OK to return to the Schema properties page.

On the Permissions page of the schema, you can define the permissions for each database user and role. These permissions can also be defined on the Database User or Role Property pages.

The permissions configured on the schema are applied to each object created in the schema for each principal given rights on the schema. This is very important when managing security because new objects can now inherit the correct permissions automatically.

Managing Application Roles

An application role is another type of principal that can be created in a SQL Server database. Like the database role, the application role is given permissions to database objects, can be added to other roles, and granted permissions through schemas. However, unlike the database role, the application role does not contain database users. The application role is designed to allow applications to obtain permissions on database objects.

When a user runs a database application, the application executes a specific stored procedure designed to activate the application role. The database application must be configured to provide the correct password for the role. If the authentication is successful, the user's security context changes completely to that of the application role. The only way to revert to the original context is through disconnecting and connecting again. The following syntax is used to define a new application role:

```
CREATE APPLICATION ROLE application_role_name
  WITH PASSWORD = 'password' [ , DEFAULT_SCHEMA = schema_name ]
```

You can also configure application roles through the SQL Server Management Studio by selecting the Application Roles node in the Security\Roles node of a database.

The sp_setapprole stored procedure must be executed by the application to activate the application role. Here's the syntax of the stored procedure:

```
sp_setapprole [ @rolename = ] 'role',
   [ @password = ] { encrypt N'password' }
 |
   'password' [ , [ @encrypt = ] { 'none' | 'odbc' } ]
   [ , [ @fCreateCookie = ] true | false ]
 [ , [ @cookie = ] @cookie OUTPUT ]
```

The sp_unsetapprole stored procedure must be executed by the application to change the user's context back to the original settings. Following is the syntax of this stored procedure. Note that the cookie option must be used in the sp_setapprole for this stored procedure to work:

```
sp_unsetapprole @cookie
```

As an alternative to application roles, database users can be created without explicit logins. Applications can then be configured to execute database code under the security context of this database user instead of the application role.

Server Endpoint Administration

Server endpoints allow communication with the SQL Server through one or more of the supported protocols. All endpoints for a SQL Server instance can be viewed through the SQL Server Management Studio. Follow these steps to view endpoints on a SQL Server instance:

1. In Object Explorer, expand Server Objects, Endpoints, Systems Endpoints, TSQL.

2. The default TSQL endpoints are listed.

If database mirroring or SOAP web services user-defined endpoints have been created, they are listed under the corresponding nodes within the Endpoints node.

The SQL Server Management Studio offers limited management of endpoints, allowing only the administration of permissions for endpoints and providing the ability to drop user-defined endpoints.

Note

System default endpoints cannot be dropped. However, you can start and stop these endpoints and change the permission on system default endpoints.

Endpoint security is important because it controls the different aspects of the endpoint, such as who can connect and who can administer an endpoint for a specific instance or application.

Follow these steps to change the permissions on the default system Transact-SQL Local Machine endpoint:

1. In Object Explorer, expand Security and select the Logins node.

2. Double-click the Test.User1 login created previously in the section "Creating SQL Authentication Logins."

3. Select the Securables page; then click the Search button.

4. Select All Objects of the Type; then click OK.

5. Enable Endpoints, and then click OK.

6. Select TSQL Local Machine from the Securables list.

7. Select the Deny column for the Connect permission.

8. Figure 8.8 shows how the Securables option page should look for the login. Click OK to change the permissions.

Open another instance of the SQL Server Management Studio from the test server SQLServer01 and attempt to authenticate as Test.User1. Because of the deny permission created, an attempt to authenticate as Test.User1 should fail even though the login is active.

Note

Endpoint permissions are associated with the actual name of the endpoint. This can be a problem when an endpoint is configured for dynamic ports because the name changes when the port changes. As a result, the security associated with the endpoint is lost.

As a best practice, avoid using endpoints with dynamic ports, specifically when endpoint permissions are used.

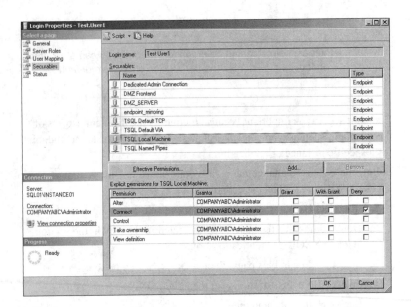

FIGURE 8.8
Login endpoint permissions.

You can create a new endpoint only through Transact-SQL statements. The CREATE, ALTER, and DROP ENDPOINT statements have many options; for additional information, see SQL Server 2012 Books Online.

The following code shows how to create a TCP endpoint called DMZ Frontend that listens on port 48620:

```
CREATE ENDPOINT [DMZ Frontend]
AS TCP (LISTENER_PORT=48620) FOR TRANSACT-SQL()
GO
```

The following warning message is displayed when the endpoint is created:

```
Creation of a Transact-SQL endpoint will result in the
revocation of any 'Public' connect permissions on the
'Transact-SQL Default TCP' endpoint. If 'Public' access is
desired on this endpoint, reapply this permission using 'GRANT
CONNECT ON ENDPOINT::[Transact-SQL Default TCP] to [public]'.
```

If necessary, you must add the public role to the default endpoint by running the command identified in the warning message.

You can use the following Transact-SQL statement to allow the user Test.User1 to connect to the newly created endpoint:

```
USE MASTER
GRANT CONNECT ON ENDPOINT::[DMZ Frontend] to [Test.User1]
GO
```

Contained Database Authentication

To further address security and compliance, SQL Server introduces a new capability known as contained database authentication. It allows users to be authenticated and to be given access directly to a database without a login on the instance of the SQL Server where the database resides. A fully contained database includes all the settings and metadata required and has no configuration dependencies. Contained Database Authentication provides organizations with the following benefits:

- Simplified deployment of database applications and increased manageability for database access

- Easier to deploy applications from different environments such as development to staging or staging to production because the databases are self-contained

- Tightly scoped security boundary because there is no longer the need to create unnecessary logins that caused management tracking issues in the past

- Better separation between administrators and users

- Fewer logins needed and less of a chance of orphaned or unused logins

Enabling Contained Database Authentication

The first step in using Contained Database Authentication is to enable it at the instance level of SQL Server. This can be done via the Server Properties Advanced page in SQL Server Management Studio or via Transact-SQL. Contained Databases are disabled by default.

> **Tip**
>
> Contained Database Authentication is a feature that must be first enabled or disabled at the instance level with an instance of SQL Server from a Database Engine perspective. Therefore, if you are working in an environment with multiple instances of SQL Server and want to use the feature, the Contained Database Authentication feature must enabled or disabled on each instance of SQL Server.

Follow these steps to enable Contained Database Authentication via SQL Server Management Studio:

1. In Object Explorer, connect to the instance of SQL Server in which you would like to configure Contained Database Authentication.

2. Right-click the instance of SQL Server and click Properties.

3. Click the Advanced page on the Server Properties dialog box.

4. In the Containment section, set the value to True, and then click OK, as illustrated in Figure 8.9. When the Contained Database Authentication option is set to True, contained databases can be created or attached to the Database Engine. On the flipside, if the option is set to False, contained databases cannot be created or attached to the Database Engine.

Alternatively, the following Transact-SQL statement can be used to enable or disable Contained Database Authentication:

```
sp_configure 'contained database authentication', 1 or 0;
GO
RECONFIGURE;
GO
```

When the Contained Database Authentication server option is set to (0), contained databases cannot be created or attached to the Database Engine. However, when Contained Database Authentication is set to (1), contained databases can be created or attached to the Database Engine.

> **Note**
>
> Contained databases have some unique threats that concern some organizations. To prevent any databases from being contained, set the Database Engine Contained Database Authentication option to 0.

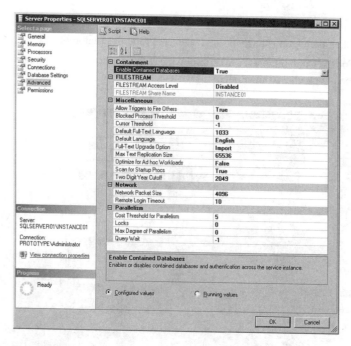

FIGURE 8.9
Enabling Contained Databases for an instance of SQL Server.

Enabling Partial Containment Within a Database

Remember that a contained element exists entirely within the database boundary, whereas an uncontained element crosses the database boundary, such as a login between a database and an instance of SQL Server. Now the confusing part: In SQL Server 2012, the contained database feature is currently availability only in a partially contained state. Therefore, after enabling the Contained Database Authentication option for an instance of SQL Server, the next step is to change the database configuration from uncontained to partially contained. This can be done via the Database Properties Options page or via the Alter Database Transact-SQL statement.

Follow these steps to enable Partial Containment for a specific database via SQL Server Management Studio:

1. In Object Explorer, connect to an instance of SQL Server that is hosting the database in which you would like to enable partial containment.

2. Right-click the desired database instance and click Properties.

3. Click the Options page on the Database Properties dialog box.

4. For the Containment Type drop-down, set the option to Partial, and then click OK, as illustrated in Figure 8.10.

FIGURE 8.10
Changing the Containment Type option for a database.

Alternatively, the following Transact-SQL statements can be used to enable partial containment for a database named Test:

```
USE [master]
Go
ALTER DATABASE [TEST] SET CONTAINMENT = PARTIAL WITH NO_WAIT
GO
```

Creating Contained Users

The next part of this process is to create a contained user that can be used for authentication within a contained or partially contained database. The process is similar to creating a traditional SQL Server login, and this task can be accomplished in SQL Server Management Studio or by using Transact-SQL.

Follow these steps to create a contained user login in SQL Server Management Studio:

1. In Object Explorer, connect to an instance of SQL Server that is hosting the database in which you would like to create a contained user.

2. Expand the desired database, and then expand the Security folder.

3. Right-click the Users folder, and then click New User.

4. In the New Database User dialog box, first select the user type. For this example, a SQL Server User with Password was selected; however, the options include:

   - SQL User with Login
   - SQL User without a Login
   - User Mapped to a Certificate
   - User Mapped to an Asymmetric Key
   - Windows User

5. Enter the User Name, Login Name, and Default Schema.

6. Use the additional pages, such as Owned Schemas, Membership, Securables, and Expanded Properties, to configure additional elements. For this example, the new SQL Server User has been granted the db_owner Owned Schema and Database Role Membership.

7. Click OK to finalize the creation of the new contained user.

Note

Because this newly created user is contained, it will exist only within the contained database. For additional proof, you will not see the user account if you expanded Security and then the Logins folder.

Connecting to a Database with a Contained User

The final step affiliated with this process is to test the contained user by connecting to the partially contained database with a contained user.

Follow these steps to connect to a contained database with a contained user:

1. In Object Explorer, launch the Connect to Server dialog box by clicking Connect.

2. On the Connect to Server dialog box, enter the server name of the instance of SQL Server that you want to connect to.

3. On the Authentication drop-down, select Windows Authentication or SQL Server Authentication. For this example, SQL Server Authentication is chosen.

4. Enter the SQL Server user account and password that was generated in the previous steps.

5. Click Options.

6. On the Connection Properties tab, type or select the name of the database for the connection. For this example, the test database was used.

7. Click Connect.

Note

When users connect to a contained database, they see only the databases they have access to; therefore, they will not see or have access to other databases, such as the master database.

Notes from the Field: Leveraging Partially Contained Databases in the Real World

Many large enterprise customers have started to leverage the Contained Database feature to alleviate downtime issues commonly experienced when moving databases from one instance of SQL Server to another. For example, in the past, many customers would use database mirroring, and when a database failover would occur from the primary database to the mirrored database, the application would fail because the logon required for the application to work did not exist on the instance of SQL Server hosting the database mirror copy. In addition, contained databases are being used in conjunction with SQL Server 2012 AlwaysOn Availability Groups when providing high availability and disaster recovery for mission-critical databases. Again, creating contained users reduces the ties to the instance of SQL Server and enables users and applications to connect directly to the contained database partaking in the availability group. Authentication is independent of which instance of SQL Server is hosting the failover replica copy of the database. Therefore, when you design your new implementation of AlwaysOn Availability Groups, don't forget to leverage the Contained Database feature to reduce downtime and ties to an instance of SQL Server.

Summary

Administering SQL Server security is a key task bestowed on database administrators. Understanding and leveraging the different security features associated with the SQL Server 2012 Database Engine and the different SQL Server 2012 components is essential to ensuring the integrity of the environment.

A properly implemented and well-maintained security model helps reduce the likelihood of sensitive data exposure, while increasing the overall scalability and reliability of the environment.

Best Practices

The following best practices can be taken from this chapter:

- To manage security most effectively, prepare and harden the environment. See Chapter 7 for additional information.

- When administering SQL Server security, follow the principle of least privilege. This basically means giving only the necessary permissions to the different user and service accounts needed to accomplish the task.

- Increase flexibility, manageability, and better compliance with user-defined server roles.

- Enable only communication protocols that are necessary, and allow only specific CONNECT permissions on endpoints.

- Decrease complexity of database schema management by using default schema for groups.

- Leverage Active Directory, specifically running Windows Server 2008 R2 to establish access and role-based security groups for accessing SQL Server resources.

- Simplify deployment of database applications and increase manageability of database access with contained database authentication.

- When you are using Active Directory for role-based access, you cannot assign a default schema to the user accounts. Ensure that the security model accounts for this limitation.

- All database users belong to the public database role by default. Avoid using the public database role when assigning permissions unless absolutely necessary.

- The schema provides a way to manage security on groups of objects with a granular level of control. Use the schema to group related objects—that is, objects that can have the same permissions given to the same principals.

■ If possible, always use Windows Authentication mode to leverage Windows Server 2008 and above authentication protocols, such as Kerberos, along with domain-level password policies.

■ If you use SQL authentication, enable the options to enforce the local security policies and implement encrypted authentication.

■ Create database users without logins in SQL Server 2012. This approach can be used as an alternative to application roles in the database.

■ Endpoint permissions are associated with the actual name of the endpoint. This can be a problem when an endpoint is configured for dynamic ports because the name changes when the port changes. As a result, the security associated with the endpoint is lost. Avoid using endpoints with dynamic ports, specifically when endpoint permissions are used.

CHAPTER 9

Encrypting SQL Server 2012 Data and Communications

The data stored in Microsoft SQL Server 2012 can be both valuable and confidential. The sensitive information stored in databases in SQL Server could be medical records, Social Security numbers, salaries, income data, or company trade secrets. This information needs to be protected against unauthorized access. In many cases, government and industry regulations require that this sensitive data be stored in an encrypted format.

Many of the controls presented in this book have been *access* controls—that is, controls that determine who has authorization to access what. A determined hacker can circumvent these controls through various means, such as sniffing network traffic, going dumpster diving for backup tapes, or making inference attacks.

A more sophisticated approach to data protection is to use an in-depth defense strategy, where there are multiple layers of defense providing end-to-end protection. If a hacker breaches one layer, other layers underneath provide protection. In addition to the access-based controls, encryption provides another layer of protection.

Ultimately, there isn't just one encryption technology included with SQL Server 2012 or Windows Server that will provide end-to-end encryption of a SQL Server implementation from a holistic perspective. However, by combining the encryption technologies included with SQL Server 2012 and Windows Server, it is possible to achieve the goal of end-to-end encryption.

This chapter shows how to encrypt data in the database, at the disk level, and over the wire to prevent a hacker from obtaining valuable data. Furthermore, this chapter showcases how organizations can easily achieve heightened security, compliance, and data privacy by leveraging Hardware Security Modules (HSM) for enterprise key management and Windows BitLocker to encrypt the volumes in which SQL Server data resides.

What's New for Encryption with SQL Server 2012?

SQL Server 2012 introduces new features and functionality when it comes to encrypting SQL Server data. Moreover, when running SQL Server 2012 on Windows Server 2008 R2, organizations can also reap additional benefits. The new encryption elements associated with SQL Server 2012 consist of the following:

- **Hashing Algorithms**—SHA-2 is a set of cryptographic hash functions designed by the National Security Agency (NSA) and published by the National Institute of Standards and Technology (NIST) as a U.S. Federal Information Processing Standard. The HASHBYTES function now supports the latest SHA2_256 and SHA2_512 algorithms.

- **Certificate Key Length**—When creating certificates, the maximum length of private keys imported from an external source has been expanded from 3,456 to 4,096 bits.

- **3DES To AES**—SQL Server 2012 no longer uses 3DES for its Service Master Key (SMK) and Database Master Key (DMK) Encryption. The encryption algorithm AES has taken the place of 3DES. Note that SMK and DMK should be regenerated after an instance of the Database Engine is upgraded to SQL Server 2012. This is to ensure the master keys are upgraded to AES.

- **Certificates Can Be Created from Binary**—The "FROM BINARY" option is available in the CREATE CERTIFICATE (Transact-SQL), which enables you to indicate the binary description of an ASN encoded certificate. In addition, to extract a binary description of an existing certificate, two new functions may be used: CERTENCODED (Transact-SQL) and CERTPRIVATEKEY (Transact-SQL).

Encryption in SQL

The confidentiality of the data stored in your SQL Server system or transmitted between the server and the client application can be compromised. A hacker can eavesdrop on communications between the client and server, as shown in Figure 9.1. The hacker might also obtain a database file or a backup media of the database.

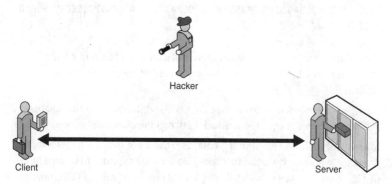

FIGURE 9.1
Unprotected client/server traffic.

To protect against these potential attacks, SQL Server 2012 allows you, as a DBA, to encrypt the data in the database, within a column, and in the network communications. Encryption allows you to protect the confidentiality of data during storage and transmission, as shown in Figure 9.2.

FIGURE 9.2
Encrypted client/server traffic.

Encryption does not prevent an attacker from capturing the data. Rather, it prevents the attacker from understanding what that data means. For example, if confidential salary information is stored in a database, it is open to potential discovery by a hacker. If the hacker can capture the value 100000, it is reasonably clear what the salary is. Suppose, instead, the hacker captures this value:

```
0x00057978740EBC4882D182DE0BC8943401000000B0D2747903102AD4696BC
980217970DAD5B4C38314DB45D065079C9B43F922D0A04517C38EC8CA9B5CD1
9702DEE0A042
```

This binary string makes it much more difficult to understand what the salary figure is. In this case, it is the encrypted version of the value 100000.

This chapter shows how to encrypt data both while stored in the database and while in transit over the network between the client and server.

In terms of the data stored in the database, there are two main methods to protect it with encryption: either using column encryption (first introduced in SQL Server 2005) or using Transparent Data Encryption (TDE, first introduced in SQL Server 2008). Those two features are independent of each other and quite different in the way they work. We will look into both of them, starting with column encryption.

Column Encryption

The column encryption feature was first introduced in SQL Server 2005. It is based on a simple principle: You create encryption keys and certificates within the database and use them, through special functions, to encrypt and decrypt your data as it is stored and read from a table column.

Encryption Hierarchy

SQL Server 2012 has an encryption hierarchy to protect the data and the encryption keys. The various levels are as follows:

- **Windows level**—The highest level of the hierarchy is the Windows operating system. This level uses Windows Data Protection (DP) API to encrypt and protect the next level.

- **SQL Server level**—This level contains the Service Master Key (SMK), which is protected by the Windows level. The SMK is used to protect the next level.

- **Database level**—This level contains the Database Master Key (DMK) and the remaining keys and certificates. The DMK encrypts and protects the certificates, symmetric keys, and asymmetric keys within the database.

The encryption hierarchy provides a scalable and granular mechanism for protecting the data within the server and databases. It allows for multiple database owners to coexist on the same server without compromising security of other databases.

Service Master Key

The Service Master Key is the root of all encryption within SQL Server 2012. This key is generated during the first time it is needed to encrypt a linked password, credential, or Database Master Key.

This key is accessible only by the Windows account used by the SQL Server service.

Database Master Key

The Database Master Key is used to secure the keys and certificates used to encrypt data. This key is manually created for each database.

If you don't want a DMK, you can encrypt the keys and certificates with a password rather than the DMK. This can be a useful alternative to prevent the owner of a database from gaining access to encrypted data in highly secure environments. However, when the key is encrypted with a password instead of the DMK, a weaker algorithm is used.

Keys and Certificates

Asymmetric and symmetric keys are used to encrypt keys, certificates, and data. Each has its own specific uses and pros and cons.

Symmetric keys are relatively straightforward. The keys are used to both encrypt and decrypt. The encryption is relatively fast, so symmetric keys are useful for encrypting large quantities of data. However, symmetric keys need to be shared, and this can make them difficult to use.

Asymmetric keys are composed of a public and private key pair. These pairs of keys are used to both encrypt and decrypt, but with a twist. Each key can decrypt what the other key encrypted, but not its own. Asymmetric encryption is resource intensive, so it is not suitable for encrypting large volumes of data. However, it is uniquely suited for encrypting symmetric keys for the purpose of sharing them.

Certificates are used to vouch for the identity of an entity presenting the public key contained in the certificate. In effect, a *certificate authority (CA)* issues a certificate that presents a public key and an identity that a third party can trust. Certificates can be issued by well-known third-party CAs such as VeriSign, by private CAs on Windows Server systems, or they can be self-signed certificates issued by instances of SQL Server.

Third-party certificates are typically expensive, private certificates require additional configuration, and self-signed certificates provide a lower level of protection.

Encryption Algorithms

SQL Server 2012 supports a variety of encryption algorithms. These algorithms are used to secure the data, keys, and certificates.

The algorithms supported by SQL Server 2012 are the following:

- Data Encryption Standard (DES)
- Triple DES
- Triple_DES_3Key
- Rivest Cipher (RC2)
- RC4
- 128-bit RC4
- DESX
- 128-bit Advanced Encryption Standard (AES)
- 192-bit AES
- 256-bit AES

Choosing an algorithm can be a complex undertaking because it requires balancing the strength of the algorithm, the resources required to use the algorithm, and the potential weaknesses of the algorithm.

Although these are all very valid considerations for choosing an algorithm, most organizations are, in reality, not encrypting data at all. Thus, using any of the preceding algorithms is a tremendous improvement in the level of security. Which particular algorithm is chosen matters less than the fact of using any of them.

In the examples in this chapter, we used the tried-and-true Triple DES algorithm. It provides a good balance between performance and security.

Securing the Data Storage

Unencrypted data residing in SQL Server is vulnerable to being read by a hacker who can elevate his privileges or gain access to backup tapes. To secure the data that is stored in the database, you can encrypt the values to provide an additional layer of security.

Creating a Database for Testing

To facilitate running these examples, these exercises use data from the SQL samples found on Microsoft's sample website. The customer.txt file can be downloaded at http://www.codeplex.com/MSFTISProdSamples/ under the Package Samples "Execute SQL Statements in a Loop Sample SS2008." Before starting, you need to create the customer database and import the customer data that is located in the customer.txt file.

> **Note**
>
> If the Customer database already exists from previous exercises, delete the database prior to completing the exercises in this chapter.

To create the database, first download the customers.txt file from http://www.codeplex.com/MSFTISProdSamples/ and follow these steps:

1. Choose Start, All Programs, Microsoft SQL Server 2012, SQL Server Management Studio, and then connect to an instance of SQL Server.

2. Expand the Databases folder in the Object Explorer.

3. In the SQL Server Management Studio, create a new database named Customer.

4. Right-click the Customer database and select Tasks, Import Data.

5. Click Next.

6. Select Flat File Source as the data source.

7. Click the Browse button and select the customers.txt file. The default directory is C:\Program Files\Microsoft SQL Server\100\ Samples\Integration Services\Package Samples\ExecuteSQL StatementsInLoop Sample\Data Files.

8. Click Open.

9. Check the Column names in the first data row check box.

10. Click Next.

11. Select the Customer database if not selected already and click Next.

12. Click Next to accept tables and views.

13. Click Next to execute immediately and not save the package.

14. Click Finish to run the import.

15. Click Close.

The basic database is now ready for the encryption exercises in this chapter.

Setting Up for Encryption

When the database is created, there is no Database Master Key initially. You need to create this key for each database.

To create a Database Master Key, open a query window and execute the following query:

```
USE Customer;
GO
CREATE MASTER KEY ENCRYPTION BY
    PASSWORD = 'MakeSureYouUseAStr0ngP@ssw0rd';
GO
```

This query prepares the database for encrypting the data. Clearly, the secret password could use some additional complexity.

> **Note**
>
> As stated earlier, the Service Master Key is created when the SQL Server instance is installed, so you do not need to create it manually.

Creating the Encryption Certificate

Now you need to create a certificate to protect the keys that will be used to encrypt the data itself.

To create the certificate, execute the following query:

```
USE Customer;
GO
CREATE CERTIFICATE Customer01
    WITH SUBJECT = 'Customer';
GO
```

After creating the certificate, you can create and protect the symmetric key. This key will be used to encrypt the data. Using a symmetric key allows the data to be encrypted rapidly, whereas encrypting it with a certificate provides strong protection.

To create the symmetric key, execute the following query:

```
USE Customer;
GO
CREATE SYMMETRIC KEY YearlyIncome_Key_01
    WITH ALGORITHM = TRIPLE_DES
    ENCRYPTION BY CERTIFICATE Customer01;
GO
```

We chose the Triple DES algorithm because of its security and compatibility.

Encrypting the Data

With the database now prepared, the next step is to encrypt a column of data. In this case, the data to be protected is the YearlyIncome column.

To encrypt the YearlyIncome column, execute the following query:

```
USE [Customer];
GO

ALTER TABLE dbo.Customers
    ADD EncryptedYearlyIncome varbinary(128);
GO

OPEN SYMMETRIC KEY YearlyIncome_Key_01
    DECRYPTION BY CERTIFICATE Customer01;
UPDATE dbo.Customers
SET EncryptedYearlyIncome = EncryptByKey
(Key_GUID('YearlyIncome_Key_01'), YearlyIncome);
CLOSE SYMMETRIC KEY YearlyIncome_Key_01;
GO
```

Note that the query adds a new column named EncryptedYearlyIncome of type varbinary to hold the encrypted values.

> **Note**
>
> The Customers table still retains the original column named YearlyIncome with the unencrypted data. In a real-world situation, you would need to drop the column to protect the data. The query to do this is ALTER TABLE Customer.dbo.Customers DROP COLUMN YearlyIncome;.
>
> We did not drop this column in the examples, to allow comparisons and to allow the column to be reencrypted.

Using Encrypted Data

The encrypted data is protected but can't be used directly. To select the data with no decryption, execute the following query:

```
SELECT EncryptedYearlyIncome
    FROM Customer.dbo.Customers;
GO
```

Rather than a nice set of Yearly Income numbers, the SELECT query returns a list of hexadecimal characters, as shown in Figure 9.3.

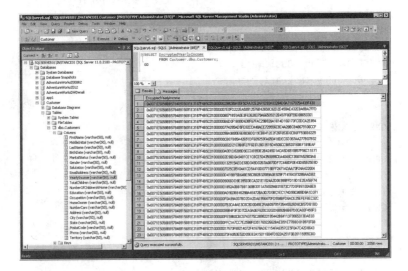

FIGURE 9.3
Encrypted data.

This result is good because it means that a hacker would not be able to discern the customer's yearly incomes. However, valid users need a way to see the actual values and cannot use the column of data directly. To use the data, you must decrypt it when selecting it.

To select the data with decryption, execute the following query:

```
OPEN SYMMETRIC KEY YearlyIncome_Key_01
    DECRYPTION BY CERTIFICATE Customer01;
GO
SELECT CONVERT(varchar, DecryptByKey(EncryptedYearlyIncome))
    AS 'Decrypted Yearly Income' FROM Customer.dbo.Customers;
CLOSE SYMMETRIC KEY YearlyIncome_Key_01;
GO
```

This query shows the actual values of the Yearly Income in unencrypted form, as shown in Figure 9.4.

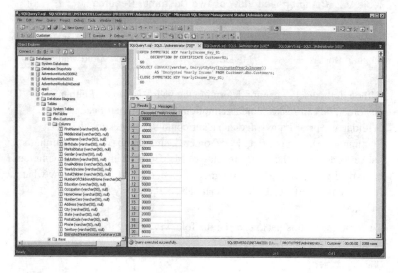

FIGURE 9.4
Decrypted data.

The data is now secured while stored in the database and would be protected in backups.

Attacking the Encryption

Although the data is protected against being viewed, a hacker might be able to subvert the control of the data. One way to accomplish this is to replace the encrypted value with another encrypted value. This is referred to as an *inference attack*.

Consider the two rows in the Customer database shown in Table 9.1.

Table 9.1 **View of Two Customer Records**

Name	Occupation	Yearly Income
Craig Dominguez	Management	100,000
Meghan Gomez	Manual	10,000

The Yearly Income values are encrypted, so a hacker who subverts the access controls might be able to gather the information about the rows shown in Table 9.2.

Table 9.2 **Compromised View of Two Customer Records**

Name	Occupation	Yearly Income
Craig Dominguez	Management	Encrypted Value 1
Meghan Gomez	Manual	Encrypted Value 2

Although the hacker cannot determine the yearly income of either customer, he can make some assumptions based on their occupations. Without any prior knowledge, a hacker could safely assume that Mr. Dominguez earns more than Ms. Gomez. Using that basic assumption, the hacker can elevate the yearly income of Ms. Gomez simply by moving the encrypted value from Mr. Dominguez without ever needing to know what the value is. In effect, the hacker can elevate the yearly income to $100,000.

To demonstrate this hack, execute the following query to hack the database:

```
USE Customer;
GO


UPDATE Customer.dbo.Customers
SET EncryptedYearlyIncome =
    (SELECT EncryptedYearlyIncome FROM Customer.dbo.Customers
    WHERE EmailAddress = 'cdominguez@fabrikam.com')
    WHERE EmailAddress = 'mgomez@fabrikam.com';
GO
```

This query copies the Encrypted Value 1 in Table 9.2 over Encrypted Value 2 in the table, in effect replacing Ms. Gomez's income with Mr. Dominguez's income. To verify that the hack was successful, execute the following query:

```
USE Customer;
Go
OPEN SYMMETRIC KEY YearlyIncome_Key_01
    DECRYPTION BY CERTIFICATE Customer01;
GO
SELECT CONVERT(varchar, DecryptByKey(EncryptedYearlyIncome))
    AS 'Decrypted Yearly Income'
    FROM dbo.Customers where EmailAddress =
    'mgomez@fabrikam.com';
CLOSE SYMMETRIC KEY YearlyIncome_Key_01;
GO
```

The result returned is 100000, indicating that the yearly income for Ms. Gomez was elevated to management-level pay. Good for Ms. Gomez, but bad for the company!

You can foil these types of attacks by using an authenticator when encrypting and decrypting the data.

Using an Authenticator

An *authenticator*, also known as a "salt value" in cryptography, is another column value that is unique to the row that is used in conjunction with the key to secure the data being encrypted. This prevents a hacker from moving an encrypted value between rows.

It is worth mentioning that the authenticator selected is one that is not likely to change, and if it ever does, you have lost your ability to decrypt the data.

To encrypt the YearlyIncome column with an authenticator (in this case, EmailAddress), execute the following query:

```
USE Customer;
GO
OPEN SYMMETRIC KEY YearlyIncome_Key_01
    DECRYPTION BY CERTIFICATE Customer01;
UPDATE dbo.Customers
    SET EncryptedYearlyIncome = EncryptByKey(Key_GUID
        ('YearlyIncome_Key_01'),
```

```
    YearlyIncome, 1, convert (varbinary, EmailAddress)));
CLOSE SYMMETRIC KEY YearlyIncome_Key_01;
GO
```

Note that the preceding query overwrites the data in the
EncryptedYearlyIncome column with freshly encrypted data from the
YearlyIncome column.

Verify that the EncryptedYearlyIncome column is still encrypted. To view
the results, execute the following query:

```
USE Customer;
GO
SELECT EncryptedYearlyIncome AS 'Encrypted Yearly Income'
    FROM dbo.Customers;
GO
```

The values should be displayed as long hexadecimal numbers, similar to
those shown in Figure 9.3. The next step is to see whether the hacker
substitution will succeed. Execute the hack again using the following
query:

```
USE Customer;
GO

UPDATE Customer.dbo.Customers
SET EncryptedYearlyIncome =
    (SELECT EncryptedYearlyIncome FROM Customer.dbo.Customers
    WHERE EmailAddress = 'cdominguez@fabrikam.com')
    WHERE EmailAddress = 'mgomez@fabrikam.com';
GO
```

The preceding query is the same query that was executed before and
successfully hacked the database. Note that the value is still replaced. The
question is whether the value will be accepted by the application or the
hack will be foiled.

To verify that the hacker was foiled, execute the following query:

```
USE Customer;
GO
OPEN SYMMETRIC KEY YearlyIncome_Key_01
    DECRYPTION BY CERTIFICATE Customer01;
GO
```

```
SELECT CONVERT(nvarchar, DecryptByKey(EncryptedYearlyIncome))
    AS 'Decrypted Yearly Income'
    FROM dbo.Customers where EmailAddress =
'mgomez@fabrikam.com';
CLOSE SYMMETRIC KEY YearlyIncome_Key_01;
GO
```

Now the decrypted Yearly Income value displays NULL, indicating that the decryption failed and the hacker was not successful in replacing Ms. Gomez's yearly income.

To verify that an authorized user can still access the data correctly, execute the following query:

```
USE Customer;
GO
OPEN SYMMETRIC KEY YearlyIncome_Key_01
    DECRYPTION BY CERTIFICATE Customer01;
GO
SELECT CONVERT(varchar, DecryptByKey(EncryptedYearlyIncome, 1,
    convert (varbinary, EmailAddress)))
    AS 'Decrypted Yearly Income'
    FROM dbo.Customers;
CLOSE SYMMETRIC KEY YearlyIncome_Key_01;
GO
```

The Yearly Income values should be displayed for all but Ms. Gomez.

Backing Up the Keys

The Service Master Keys and Database Keys are critical values that need to be preserved. Losing these keys can result in the loss of any data that is encrypted. Backing up the Service Master and Database Master Keys allows you to recover the data in case of problems.

To back up the Service Master Key, execute the following query:

```
BACKUP SERVICE MASTER KEY
TO FILE = 'c:\ServiceMasterKeyBackup.dat'
    ENCRYPTION BY PASSWORD = 'EnterComplexPassword';

GO
```

To back up the Database Master Key, execute the following query for the Customer database:

```
USE Customer;
GO
BACKUP MASTER KEY
TO FILE = 'c:\CustomerDatabaseMasterKeyBackup.dat'
    ENCRYPTION BY PASSWORD = 'EnterComplexPassword';

GO
```

Repeat this query for each Database Master Key that you need to back up.

You should store both key backup files offsite in case of server problems. In the event of a problem with the keys, the Service Master Key and Database Master Key can be restored from the files.

Extensible Key Management

SQL Server 2012 includes functionality called Extensible Key Management (EKM) that allows you to store your encryption keys outside of the Database Engine, using Hardware Security Modules (HSM). It allows you to store the encryption keys separately from the data being encrypted and provides an additional level of security. This functionality is available only in the Enterprise and Developer editions of SQL Server 2012.

EKM works by allowing integration of SQL Server data encryption with third-party solutions for key generation, key storage, key management, and hardware acceleration of the encryption process. The main part of this solution is the cryptographic provider DLL that allows access from SQL Server to the Hardware Security Module. This DLL is provided by the vendor of your HSM and is written using a common interface allowing SQL Server to access the key stored on the HSM. This DLL must be signed by a trusted source to be accepted by the SQL Server engine.

Enabling EKM

To use the EKM, you need to follow this procedure.

First, you must enable the use of EKM providers on the database instance level by changing the configuration option 'EKM provider enabled':

```
sp_configure 'show advanced', 1
GO
RECONFIGURE
GO
```

```
sp_configure 'EKM provider enabled', 1
GO
RECONFIGURE
GO
```

This will allow you to create and use the cryptographic providers in SQL Server.

Creating the Cryptographic Provider

Next, you need to create the cryptographic provider using the DLL obtained from your HSM vendor. This DLL provides SQL Server with access to the encryption keys stored on the HSM.

```
CREATE CRYPTOGRAPHIC PROVIDER MyHSM
FROM FILE='C:\MyHSM\HSMProvider.dll'
GO
```

Note that this example is fictional and assumes that you have the provider DLL file stored in file C:\MyHSM\HSMProvider.dll.

Creating the Credential to Access the HSM

Most of the HSMs require additional authentication to access the keys stored on them. Depending on your HSM and cryptographic provider, it may or may not support basic authentication using username and password. If the basic authentication is supported, you should create the credential for the login that will be using the key stored in the HSM. Otherwise, the authentication to the HSM must be performed independently of SQL Server.

To create a credential that allows access to the keys stored on the HSM created in the previous step and assign it to SQL Server login Bob, you would use the following code:

```
CREATE CREDENTIAL CredentialForMyHSM
WITH IDENTITY='HSMUser',
SECRET='StrongP@ssw0rd'
FOR CRYPTOGRAPHIC PROVIDER MyHSM;
GO
ALTER LOGIN Bob
ADD CREDENTIAL CredentialForMyHSM;
GO
```

Creating the Encryption Key with EKM

After the preceding steps are completed, you can use your HSM to create and store the encryption keys that you want to use to encrypt the data in the Database Engine.

To create a symmetric key based on the existing encryption key stored on your HSM, you can use the following syntax:

```
CREATE SYMMETRIC KEY MyEKMKey
AUTHORIZATION Bob
FROM PROVIDER MyHSM
WITH PROVIDER_KEY_NAME='MyHSMKey',
CREATION_DISPOSITION=OPEN_EXISTING;
GO
```

This would allow you to use the key for data encryption within SQL Server. After the key is created and mapped to a key stored on the HSM, the usage of the encryption functions is analogous to the one described in the previous section of this chapter.

Advantages of EKM

Storing of encryption keys outside of the Database Engine and on the HSM provides several security benefits, namely:

- Encryption keys stored independently of the Database Engine, which provides a higher level of security and protection
- Additional authorization checks for key retrieval
- Easier and more flexible key management for key generation, distribution, backup, recovery, and disposal
- Higher performance in case of the HSM supporting hardware encryption and decryption

> **Note**
>
> Configuring EKM is vendor specific; therefore, each HSM will have different setup instructions to follow when configuring.

Transparent Data Encryption

Transparent Data Encryption (TDE) is a new feature available in SQL Server 2012 Enterprise and Developer editions. It allows you to encrypt and protect the data in your database files, without having to change anything in your application and data access code (hence the name *transparent*). Using TDE will allow you to meet regulatory requirements of having your data encrypted "at rest" with a minimal administrative effort. It can also protect your data in case the media containing your database files or database backup is lost or stolen.

> **Note**
>
> When TDE is implemented, the entire database is encrypted; however, TDE does not provide encryption across communication channels. In addition, the backups associated with the database are also encrypted.

Mode of Operation

TDE works by encrypting data pages and log pages stored on disk. Encryption and decryption happens during I/O operations—data is encrypted as it is written to disk and decrypted as it is read from disk into memory. The performance overhead of TDE is relatively small because the data is encrypted only during I/O operations and remains decrypted while in memory. When you enable TDE, the entire database, including all data file and log files, is encrypted on disk. Such an encrypted database cannot be restored or attached to a different server without access to the server certificate from the original server.

> **Note**
>
> Data stored using FILESTREAM storage is not encrypted with TDE. If you use FILESTREAM data, you need to encrypt it separately—for instance, using NTFS or BitLocker encryption.

Encryption Hierarchy

As with column encryption, there is an encryption hierarchy that protects the keys used by TDE. The hierarchy is slightly different from the one used by the column encryption, but it serves the same purpose: to protect the key used for direct data encryption with some other, higher-level keys. In case of TDE, the levels are as follows:

- **Windows level**—The highest level of the hierarchy is the Windows operating system. This level uses the Windows DP API to encrypt and protect the next level.

- **SQL Server level**—This level contains the Service Master Key (SMK), which is protected by the Windows level. The Service Master Key is used to protect the next level.

- **Master database level**—This level contains the Database Master Key (DMK) in the master database, which is protected by the Service Master Key. It also contains a server certificate, or asymmetric key stored in the master database and encrypted with DMK. The server certificate or asymmetric key is used to protect the Database Encryption Key on the next level.

- **Database level**—This level contains the Database Encryption Key (DEK) used by the server to encrypt that particular database with TDE.

Enabling Transparent Data Encryption

The following example illustrates the steps required to enable TDE on the sample database AdventureWorks2012. To be able to use TDE, you need to create all the necessary encryption keys on all the appropriate levels before you enable TDE for your database.

Creating a Database Master Key in the Master Database

The first key we need to create is the Database Master Key in the master database. In some scenarios, you might have already created it (there can be only one DMK per database). Otherwise, you need to create it by running code similar to this:

```
USE master;
GO
CREATE MASTER KEY ENCRYPTION BY
  PASSWORD = 'MakeSureYouUseAStr0ngP@ssw0rd';
GO
```

> **Note**
>
> As indicated in this example, it is a best practice to select a strong password when creating the master key for encryption.

Creating Server Certificate in the Master Database

The next step is to create a server certificate or asymmetric key in the master database. From a TDE perspective, it does not matter if you choose to create a certificate or an asymmetric key—both are functionally equivalent, and their respective private keys are encrypted by the Database Master Key.

You can create a server certificate using the following code:

```
USE master;
GO
CREATE CERTIFICATE ServerCert WITH
  SUBJECT = 'Certificate for use with TDE';
GO
```

> **Note**
>
> After you create the server certificate or asymmetric key, you should immediately take a backup of it, containing the private key. This backup copy of the key will be necessary to restore the encrypted databases in cases when you are restoring to another server or when the original key is no longer available for any reason. Make sure to protect the backup file containing the private key by using a strong password and storing it on an offline media.

Creating a Database Encryption Key

Next step is to create the Database Encryption Key (DEK) in the database you plan to use TDE on. This key is protected by the server certificate or asymmetric key and cannot be opened without it. Under normal operation, this ensures that the database can be opened (and decrypted) only by the server instance that "owns" the database.

You can create the Database Encryption Key using the following code:

```
USE AdventureWorks2012;
GO
CREATE DATABASE ENCRYPTION KEY
WITH ALGORITHM = AES_256
ENCRYPTION BY SERVER CERTIFICATE ServerCert;
GO
```

While creating your Database Encryption Key, you should consider the choice of the encryption algorithm used. For performance and security reasons, only certain symmetric algorithms are available for use with TDE:

- Triple DES
- 128-bit AES
- 192-bit AES
- 256-bit AES

From those, the best choice in terms of protection provided is Advanced Encryption Standard (AES) in its 256-bit form, but it is also the one that requires most processing power during encryption.

Enabling Transparent Database Encryption for the Database

After you have created the necessary encryption key hierarchy, you are ready to enable TDE on your database. To enable it, just run the following code:

```
USE master;
GO
ALTER DATABASE AdventureWorks2012
SET ENCRYPTION ON;
GO
```

Enabling TDE is a metadata operation and happens very quickly. The actual encryption process takes place in the background and, depending on the size of your database and the load on the server, can take several hours to finish. You can check the status of TDE on your database by querying the sys.dm_database_encryption_keys DMV:

```
SELECT *
FROM sys.dm_database_encryption_keys
WHERE database_id = DB_ID('AdventureWorks2012');
GO
```

The encryption_state column of that DMV shows you the status of TDE for that particular database. Possible values are as follows:

    0—No Database Encryption Key present, no encryption

    1—Unencrypted

    2—Encryption in progress

    3—Encrypted

    4—Key change in progress

    5—Decryption in progress

Note

After you enable TDE for any database on the SQL Server instance, the tempdb database is encrypted as well, to protect data stored in any temporary objects. This can have a performance impact on other databases and applications running on the same instance.

After the backup thread finishes encrypting your database, both data files and log files are fully encrypted. Any database, file, or log backups you take from this point forward will contain encrypted data, and such backups can be restored only if you have access to the server certificate protecting the DEK.

Disabling Transparent Database Encryption for the Database

Should you ever decide that you no longer want your database to use TDE, disabling it is as simple as enabling:

```
USE master;
GO
ALTER DATABASE AdventureWorks2012
SET ENCRYPTION OFF;
GO
```

As with enabling, when you disable TDE, the decryption process takes place in the background and can take a considerable amount of time to finish. Again, you can check the status of this process by querying the sys.dm_database_encryption_keys DMV.

Notes from the Field: Column-Based Encryption or TDE in Production Environments

In earlier versions of SQL Server, the only thing DBAs could leverage out-of-the-box was column-based encryption. Although the solution worked, it did provide challenges for organizations where application changes were sometimes required to support the solution. This brought new problems because application changes were not possible for organizations using applications purchased by third-party vendors. With the release of TDE in SQL Server 2008, an increasing number of organizations shifted away from column-based encryption and leveraged TDE because it did not require application changes. Likewise, it was fairly straightforward to administer, and it protected the whole database by using four Transact-SQL statements. It is also worth noting that when TDE is implemented, it encrypts the TempDB system database. As a result, this can cause server and database performance degradation for other unencrypted databases within the instance of SQL Server using tempdb. For production customers, especially those doing massive database consolidation, it is a best practice to isolate and store all databases requiring TDE encryption on a dedicated instance; therefore, the unencrypted databases are not negatively impacted from a performance perspective.

Securing Connections

When you use column based or TDE encryption, the data is encrypted while in the database. However, when the client selects the data, it is unencrypted. The data needs to be protected while being transmitted as well as while being stored. SQL Server 2012 can use SSL certificate-based encryption to encrypt all communications between the client and server.

Hacking the Transmission

To understand the problem, you can use Network Monitor tools for this example to view the contents of the network traffic between the SQL Server and client. This tool is available for Windows Server 2008 R2 as an out-of-band download directly from Microsoft: http://www.microsoft.com/download/en/details.aspx?displaylang=en&id=4865. The examples in this section assume that the SQL Server Workstation Components are installed on the client.

Start the Network Monitor on the server, and then execute the following query from SQL Server Management Studio on the client:

```
USE Customer;
Go
OPEN SYMMETRIC KEY YearlyIncome_Key_01
    DECRYPTION BY CERTIFICATE Customer01;
GO
SELECT FirstName, LastName, BirthDate,
    CONVERT(nvarchar, DecryptByKey(EncryptedYearlyIncome, 1,
    convert (varbinary, EmailAddress)))
    AS 'Decrypted Yearly Income'
    FROM dbo.Customers where EmailAddress =
'cdominguez@fabrikam.com';
GO
```

The query returns the information shown in Table 9.3.

Table 9.3 **Query Results**

Decrypted FirstName	LastName	BirthDate	Yearly Income
Craig	Dominguez	7/20/1970	100000

This result is clearly confidential information that should be protected from the prying eyes of a hacker. It even includes the yearly income information that was encrypted in the Customer database to prevent unauthorized disclosure.

Figure 9.5 shows the results of the network capture of the preceding query. The highlighted frame in the figure contains the data sent from SQL Server (SQLServer01\Instance01) to the client (172.16.2.1). The circled section of the figure shows the information that a hacker was able to capture simply by listening in on the network transmission. The information includes the name, birth date, and yearly income. Although the information is not formatted in a pretty manner, it is all there for the hacker to see.

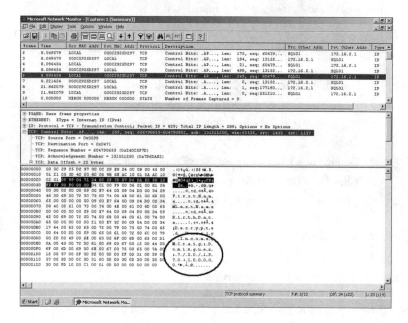

FIGURE 9.5
Hacked data transmission.

Most troubling is that the information that was encrypted in the database is transmitted unencrypted over the wire. The reason is that the query decrypts the information at the server side prior to transmission. The bottom line is that encrypting the columns in the database does nothing to protect the data while it is being transmitted over the network.

To protect data transmissions, you need to encrypt the connections.

Configuring Server-Initiated Encryption

SQL Server 2012 can be configured to require SSL-based encryption. Configuring the ForceEncryption setting of SQL Server to Yes forces all client/server communications to be encrypted. By default, the ForceEncryption setting is set to No, so SQL Server client/server communications are not protected.

> **Note**
>
> The SQL Server 2012 login process is always encrypted, regardless of the ForceEncryption setting of the server. This ensures that login and password combinations are not compromised.

To configure the server to require encrypted connections, follow these steps:

1. Launch the SQL Server Configuration Manager.
2. Expand the SQL Server Network Configuration.
3. Right-click Protocols for a SQL Server instance and select Properties.
4. On the Flags tab, change the ForceEncryption drop-down to Yes.
5. Click OK to save the setting.
6. Click OK on the dialog box indicating the service needs to be restarted.
7. Select the SQL Server Services folder.
8. Select the SQL Server (MSSQLSERVER) service.
9. Restart the SQL Server service.

The connections to your SQL Server 2012 server are now encrypted.

Hacking the Transmission: The Sequel

Now that the server has been configured to force encryption of the network transmissions, the hacker should not be able to see the contents of the network transmissions.

To verify that the transmissions are protected, start the Network Monitor on the server, and then execute the following query from the SQL Server Management Studio on the client:

```
USE Customer;
Go
OPEN SYMMETRIC KEY YearlyIncome_Key_01
    DECRYPTION BY CERTIFICATE Customer01;
GO
```

```
SELECT FirstName, LastName, BirthDate,
    CONVERT(nvarchar, DecryptByKey(EncryptedYearlyIncome, 1,
    convert (varbinary, EmailAddress)))
    AS 'Decrypted Yearly Income'
    FROM dbo.Customers where EmailAddress =
'cdominguez@fabrikam.com';
GO
```

Figure 9.6 shows the results of the network capture of the preceding query. The highlighted frame in the figure is the frame that contains the data sent from SQL Server (SQL01) to the client (172.16.2.1). The circled section of the figure shows the information that a hacker is able to capture. The information is now a jumble of strange characters and protected from the hacker's prying eyes.

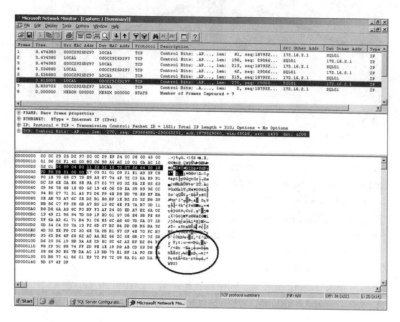

FIGURE 9.6
Encrypted data transmission.

Notice that the frames are a bit different. The encrypted frame length is 270 versus 249 for the unencrypted frame. Encryption carries some over-head both in the size of the frames and in the effort that the server and client have to make in processing the encryption.

Using Certificates

The encryption used until now in the chapter has been based on self-signed certificates. These certificates are generated when SQL Server does not have a certificate provisioned.

Self-signed certificates are vulnerable to certain attacks, most critically man-in-the-middle attacks. This means that without an independent verification of the identity of the SQL Server, there is no way to be sure that the communication is not really between a nefarious third party posing as the server to the client. Note that the communication is encrypted, as shown in Figure 9.7, but the encryption is between the hacker and the client and server.

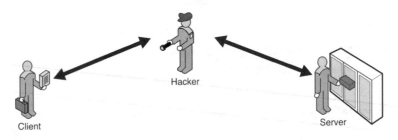

Hacker

Client

Server

FIGURE 9.7
Man-in-the-middle attack.

Neither the client nor the server detects the ruse because there is no independent third-party certificate authority to confirm that the certificate used to encrypt the transmission is trusted.

This attack is thwarted by using a third-party certificate to verify the identity of the SQL Server. When the hacker attempts to insert himself between the client and server, as shown in Figure 9.8, the attack is detected by both the client and server.

The following sections detail how to configure a certificate server and how to provision and configure certificates for SQL Server 2012.

Setting Up the Certificate Server

The first step when implementing certificates is to request a certificate from a trusted certificate authority. The certificate authority can be a third-party vendor such as VeriSign, or it can be an internal Active Directory or standalone CA residing on the corporate Windows infrastructure. For this example, the first step includes setting up a certificate server on a Windows

Server 2008 R2 system so that it can issue certificates for the SQL Server infrastructure. The example uses Microsoft Certificate Services, but a third-party CA and certificates could be used as well. If you already have a certificate or a certificate server within your infrastructure, proceed to the next section, "Provisioning a Server Certificate."

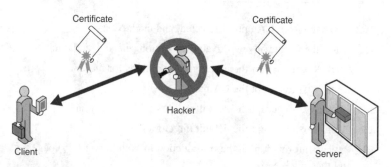

FIGURE 9.8
Third-party certificate protection.

The TOR-DC01.companyabc.com server was chosen for this example. The procedure assumes that the Windows 2008 R2 operating system has been installed and that the TOR-DC01 server is a domain controller for the companyabc.com domain.

Install the Certificate Services role on the TOR-SQL01 server using the following steps:

1. Launch Server Manager.
2. In the Roles Summary pane, select Add Roles to start the wizard.
3. Click Next.
4. Select Active Directory Certificate Services, and click Next.
5. Click Next.
6. Check the Certification Authority and Certification Authority Web Enrollment.
7. A window opens with an additional set of role services and features required to support web enrollment. Click Add Required Role Services to add these prerequisites.
8. Click Next.
9. Select Enterprise or Standalone option to create a standalone CA, and click Next. For this example, Enterprise was selected.

> **Note**
>
> The Enterprise option should be used if the server is part of a domain and there is need to leverage the Directory Services for issuing and managing certificates. The Standalone option is used when Directory Services will not issue and manage certificates.

10. Leave the Root CA option selected, and click Next.

11. Leave the Create a New Private Key option selected, and click Next.

12. Click Next to accept the cryptography options for the CA.

13. Click Next to accept the CA name.

14. Click Next to accept the default validity period of 5 years.

15. Click Next to accept the default directories.

16. Review information on the Introduction to Web Server (IIS) page, and then click Next.

17. Click Next to accept the default web server role services.

18. Click Install to install the roles.

19. When the installation finishes, click Close to close the wizard.

> **Note**
>
> To complete certificate enrollments, the website hosting the CA must be configured to use HTTPs authentication. This can be achieved on the default website in Internet Information Services by first adding HTTPs as a secure binding and then requiring SSL in the SSL settings. For this example, a brand certificate for IIS should be created.

This certificate server will be used on each of the components for the SQL Server infrastructure.

Provisioning a Server Certificate

The next step in protecting the data transmissions with a third-party certificate is to provision the certificate, which entails obtaining and installing a certificate from a third-party vendor or an internal Windows Certificate Authority that was created in the previous steps. The certificate requirements for SQL Server 2012 SSL encryption are as follows:

■ The certificate must be in the local computer certificate store or the current user certificate store.

- The current system time must be in the certificate valid range of dates.
- The certificate must be meant for server authentication; that is, the Enhanced Key Usage property of the certificate specifies Server Authentication (1.3.6.1.5.5.7.3.1).
- The common name (CN) must be the same as the fully qualified domain name (FQDN) of the server computer.

To provision (install) a certificate on the server from a Windows certificate authority, follow these steps:

1. Launch Microsoft Internet Explorer on the SQL Server system, in this sample TOR-SQL01.

2. Enter the uniform resource locator (URL) for the Certification Authority Web Enrollment, which in this example is `https://tor-dc01.companyabc.com/certsrv`.

3. Click Request a Certificate to request a new certificate.

4. Click Advanced Certificate Request to request a certificate.

5. Click Create and Submit a Request to This CA. You may be prompted with a dialog warning box indicating that the website is attempting to perform a digital certificate operation on your behalf. If so, click Yes to continue.

Note

You might need to add the site to the trusted sites in Internet Explorer to allow ActiveX controls to run.

---

6. In the Identifying Information for Offline Template section, enter the name, email, company, department, city, state, and country.

7. On the Advanced Certificate Request form, choose the Web Server certificate template and enter the FQDN of the computer in the Friendly Name field, which, in this example, is `SQLServer01.companyabc.com`.

Note

The name and friendly name must match the FQDN name of the computer exactly or the certificate will fail later on.

---

8. The request should look like the example shown in Figure 9.9. Click Submit to complete the request.

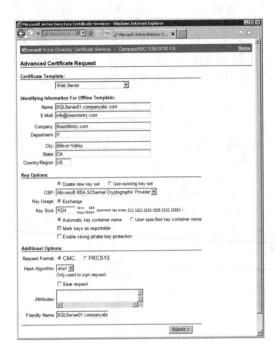

FIGURE 9.9
Certificate enrollment.

9. If prompted, click Yes to allow the website to request the certificate.

10. If you are using a certificate authority with an auto-enrollment feature, as we are in this example, the certificate will automatically be issued and you will be prompted to install the certificate. If so, click the link Install This Certificate. If not, the certificate request must be issued and installed manually.

If you are using a Windows Certificate Authority server, the steps include the following:

1. On the Certificate Authority server, launch the Certification Authority MMC from the Administrative Tools.

2. Expand the Certificate Authority name, and select the Pending Requests folder.

3. Locate the matching Request ID number in the Details pane.

4. Right-click the request and select All Tasks, Issue.

5. Go back to the Internet Explorer window.

6. Enter the URL for the Certification Authority Web Enrollment.

7. Select View the Status of a Pending Certificate Request.

8. Click the certificate request.

9. Click Install This Certificate to add the certificate to the local computer store.

10. Click Yes to allow the certificate to be installed.

> **Note**
>
> To enable Force Protocol Encryption between the server and client, you must have a certificate on the server, and the client must have the Trusted Root Authority updated to trust the server certificate.

SQL Server Certificate Configuration

After a certificate has been obtained and configured on the SQL Server system, you can configure SQL Server 2012 to use it. You do this with the SQL Server Configuration Manager tool.

The steps to configure SQL Server to use the certificate are as follows:

1. Launch the SQL Server Configuration Manager via Start, All Programs, Microsoft SQL Server 2012, Configuration Tools and then choose SQL Server Configuration Manager.

2. Expand the SQL Server Network Configuration.

3. Right-click Protocols for the SQL Server instance, such as SQLServer01\Instance01, and select Properties.

4. Select the Certificate tab.

5. Select the certificate from the drop-down list for the Certificate box.

6. On the Flags tab, in the ForceEncryption box, select Yes, and then click Apply to save the settings.

7. Click OK to acknowledge that the service needs to be restarted.

8. Restart the SQL Server service to use the certificate.

The SQL Server is now protected against man-in-the-middle attacks with the CA certificate. However, the clients need to be configured to use the server certificate and trust the CA if an internal CA was used.

Client Certificate Configuration

The certificate is stored in the SQL Server certificate store and needs to be exported so that it can be shared. To export the server certificate, follow these steps:

1. Click Start, Run, and in the Open box, type MMC; then click OK.

2. In the MMC, on the File menu, click Add/Remove Snap-in.

3. In the Add Standalone Snap-in dialog box, click Certificates, and then click Add.

4. In the Certificates Snap-in dialog box, click Computer Account, and then click Next.

5. On the next page, you will need to select the computer you want this snap-in to manage. Choose Local Computer, and then Finish.

6. In the Add/Remove Snap-in dialog box, click OK.

7. From the Certificates MMC snap-in, locate the certificate in the Certificates\Personal folder. It is worth noting that the certificate may also reside in the Remote Desktop folder.

8. Right-click the Certificate, select All Tasks, and click Export.

9. Complete the Certificate Export Wizard, saving the certificate file in a convenient location.

The certificate, stored in the file, is now ready to be used by the client. To import the certificate into the client computer store, follow these steps:

1. Copy the exported certificate file to the client computer.

2. In the Certificates snap-in on the client, expand Certificates.

3. Expand the Personal folder.

4. Right-click Personal, select All Tasks, and click Import.

5. Complete the Certificate Import Wizard.

The certificate is now ready to use. However, if you used a private CA to issue the certificate, you need to add the CA to the trusted CA list. For a Windows CA, use the following steps to do that:

1. On the client, launch Internet Explorer.

2. Enter the address `https://TOR-DC01.companyabc.com/certsrv` to access the Certificate Service Web Request site. This assumes that the certificate services were installed on the tor-dc01.companyabc.com server.

3. Click the Download CA Certificate link.

4. Click the Install Certificate, and complete the wizard to install the certificate.

5. Click the Download CA Certificate Chain link to configure the SQL Server to trust the CA.

6. Close the browser, and then continue. The Windows Certificate Authority is now trusted by the client.

Note

As an alternative methodology for trusting the root, it is possible to export the server certificate's Trusted Root Certificate Authority (CA). The following steps outline the strategy:

1. Open MMC, and then locate your certificate in the Personal folder.

2. Right-click the certificate name, and then click Open.

3. Review the Certification Path tab. Note the top-most item.

4. Navigate to the Trusted Root Certification Authorities folder, and then locate the Certificate Authority noted in the previous step.

5. Right-click CA, point to All Tasks, and then click Export.

6. Select all the defaults, and then save the exported file to your disk where the client computer can access the file.

Follow these steps to import the certificate on the client computer:

1. Navigate to the client computer by using the MMC snap-in, and then browse to the Trusted Root Certification Authorities folder.

2. Right-click the Trusted Root Certification Authorities folder, point to All Tasks, and then click Import.

Client-Initiated Encryption

In some cases, there might not be the need or the option to configure the server to force encryption for all clients. Perhaps only a few connections need to be encrypted, or there is no administrative control over the configuration of SQL Server.

To configure the client to request encrypted connections using the ODBC, follow these steps:

1. Select Start, Control Panel.
2. Double-click Administrative Tools to open the folder.
3. Double-click the Data Sources (ODBC) applet.
4. Select the System DSN tab.
5. Click Add to add a new data source.
6. Select either SQL Server or SQL Native Client.
7. Click Finish to launch the configuration of the data source.
8. Enter a name for the data source—in this case, **Customer Database**.
9. Enter the name of the SQL Server—in this case, **SQLServer01\ Instance01**.
10. Click Next.
11. Click Next to leave the default authentication.
12. Check the Change the Default Database box.
13. Select a database such as AdventureWorks2012 from the drop-down list.
14. Click Next.
15. Check the Use Strong Encryption for Data box to encrypt the client/server traffic.
16. Click Finish.
17. Click Test Data Source to verify the settings.
18. Click OK three times to close out the settings.

The connection now forces itself to use strong encryption regardless of the SQL Server setting. This option does require that a certificate issued by a trusted third party be used.

Encrypt a Connection from SQL Server Management Studio

In some cases, there may be a need to encrypt a connection from SQL Server Management Studio when connecting to an instance of SQL Server. Use the following steps to achieve this goal:

1. On the Object Explorer toolbar, click Connect, and then click Database Engine.

2. In the Connect to Server dialog box, complete the connection information, and then click Options.

3. On the Connection Properties tab, click Encrypt connection.

SQL Server Management Studio

The SQL Server Management Studio is a potential source of exploits itself. Given the level of communications with data, code, and passwords, a hacker can discover a ton of information from the traffic generated by the SQL Server Management Studio tool. This is the case when the tool is loaded on a client computer rather than the server itself.

Fortunately, the communications from the SQL Server Management Studio on a client to SQL Server can easily be encrypted. The steps to do this are as follows:

1. On the Object Explorer toolbar, click Connect.

2. Select a service—in this case, the Database Engine.

3. Select a server—in this case, SQLServer01\Instance01.

4. Click the Options button.

5. Check the Encrypt Connection box.

6. Click Connect to connect.

Now all communications between the SQL Server Management Studio and SQL Server are protected with encryption.

SQL Server and BitLocker Drive Encryption

Microsoft added Windows BitLocker Drive Encryption to Windows Server 2008 and later mostly as a result of organizations demanding protection not only for their operating systems, but also for the vital data stored on the system volume and data storage volumes housing both the SQL Server Database and Transaction Logs. BitLocker Drive Encryption, commonly referred to as BitLocker, is a hardware-enhanced, data-protection security feature included in all versions of the Windows Server 2008 and later family of operating systems. It is an optional component that you must install if you choose to use it.

BitLocker increases data protection for an operating system by merging two concepts: encrypting a volume and guaranteeing the integrity of the operating system's boot components. The first component, drive encryption, safeguards data residing on the system volume and configured data volumes by preventing unauthorized users from compromising Windows system files encrypted with BitLocker. Encryption at the volume level is achieved by leveraging the new features available with BitLocker, such as a Trusted Platform Module (TPM), which is discussed in the following section. The second component provides integrity verifications of the early boot components, which essentially refers to components used during the startup process, by validating that the hard disk has not been tampered with or removed from its original server. Equally important, when you use BitLocker, confidential data on a protected server cannot be viewed even if the hard disks are transferred to another operating system. If these two conditions are met, only then will data on a BitLocker volume be decrypted and the system allowed to boot.

If you have worked with previous versions of Windows Server, you will recognize immediately that BitLocker is a great addition to Windows Server 2008 and later; it protects all the data residing on a server's hard disks because everything written to the disk, including the operating system, is encrypted. In previous versions of Windows Server, encryption based on integration with TPM hardware was not supported, which meant personal information could be compromised. In addition, with BitLocker now on the map, branch offices concerned over the physical security and theft of their domain controllers stand to benefit the most from leveraging BitLocker because this feature further bolsters security and ensures that confidential data is not disclosed without authorization.

> **Note**
>
> Many professionals are posing questions as they wonder about the differences between BitLocker and Encrypting File System (EFS). Both technologies offer tools for encryption; however, BitLocker is intended to protect all personal and system files on a system and after it is enabled, it is transparent as well as automatic. EFS, on the other hand, encrypts individual files based on an administrator's judgment call.

Examining BitLocker's Drive Encryption Components

BitLocker was first introduced with the release of Windows Vista. Since entering the Windows 2008 family of operating systems, Microsoft has improved BitLocker by adding new features: data volumes; three-factor authentication that includes TPM, USB, and PIN; and Unified Extensible Firmware Interface (UEFI). Furthermore, BitLocker Drive Encryption is designed to offer a seamless user experience.

> **Note**
>
> UEFI is only supported when running 64-bit processor architecture in the system.

You will recognize when first attempting to use BitLocker that there are different ways to deploy it. To ensure that your installation receives the highest level of security and protection, you need to remember that the server requires the Trusted Platform Module (TPM) microchip and BIOS based on version 1.2 or later. Also required is the Static Root of Trust Measurement, which is defined by the Trusted Computing Group (TCG).

TPM is a component that provides enhanced protection of data and ensures boot integrity by validating the computer's boot manager integrity and boot files at startup. This hardware component confirms that the encrypted drive in a computer actually belongs to that computer.

TPM also runs a check of the hard disk to ensure it has not been subjected to unauthorized viewing while in an offline state by encrypting the entire Windows volume. This includes system and user files as well as swap files and hibernation files. In addition, BitLocker saves measurement details related to core operating system files in TPM, creating a sort of system fingerprint. The fingerprint remains the same unless someone tampers with the boot system.

BitLocker Drive Encryption provides seamless protection at system startup. Because this is transparent to the user, the user logon experience is unchanged. However, if the TPM is changed or missing, or if startup information has changed, BitLocker enters Recovery mode and the user must provide a recovery password to regain access to the data.

Two new major improvements to BitLocker introduced with Windows Server 2008 include data volumes and a new authenticator. Both of these are discussed in the following sections.

Data Volumes

BitLocker extends the functionality included in Windows Vista by supporting encryption beyond the functionality of the boot drive. All data volumes associated with a server can be encrypted by BitLocker, so SQL Server volumes associated with the database and transaction logs can be protected. A *data volume* is defined as any plug-and-play internal volume that does not contain the operating system files that are currently running. Typically, these could be volumes that store user data, such as Microsoft

Office files, music, or other downloads. To enable data volumes on an operating system volume, you must have BitLocker enabled.

New Authenticator

Like many other security products in the industry that handle authentication, the IT security community requested Microsoft to include a multifactor form of authentication built in to BitLocker. BitLocker on Windows Server 2008 and later supports three-factor authentication. For example, it is possible to configure BitLocker to use TPM, USB, and PIN to maximize security authentication.

Comprehending BitLocker's Drive Encryption Hardware Requirements

Configuring BitLocker Drive Encryption is not as simple as clicking through a few screens on a Windows Server wizard. A number of prerequisite steps must be fulfilled before BitLocker can be configured and implemented.

Before you implement BitLocker Drive Encryption, make certain the following hardware requirements and prerequisites are met and understood:

- The system should have a Trusted Platform Module (TPM) version 1.2 or higher.
- If the system does not have TPM, a removable USB memory device can be used to store the encryption key.
- There must be a minimum of at least two partitions on the system.
- One partition must be dedicated for the Windows operating system files.
- There must be an active system partition that is not encrypted. Therefore, the computer can be booted and/or started. The system volume must differ from the operating system volume and should be at least 1.5GB.
- All drives and partitions must be formatted with the NTFS file system.
- The system BIOS must support TPM and USB devices during startup.

Configuring BitLocker Drive Encryption on a SQL Server System

The following sections cover step-by-step procedures on how to implement BitLocker by first configuring the system partitions, installing the BitLocker feature, and then enabling BitLocker Drive Encryption. The enabling section includes steps for enabling BitLocker when using TPM hardware, when not using TPM hardware, and enabling BitLocker on additional volumes beyond the scope of the volume hosting the operating system. The final step-by-step procedures include how to use the BitLocker recovery password in the event of an issue and how to remove BitLocker after it has been installed and configured.

Configuring the System Partitions for BitLocker

As mentioned earlier, one of the prerequisite tasks when configuring an operating system for BitLocker is configuring a nonencrypted active partition also referred to as a system partition. Complete the following steps to configure this partition on a new server:

1. Insert the Windows Server 2008 or later media. The Install Windows screen should automatically launch; otherwise, click Setup.exe.

2. Input the appropriate Language, Time, Currency, and Keyboard preferences, and then click Next.

3. Click Repair Your Computer on the Install Now page.

4. Select Command Prompt on the System Recovery Options page.

5. Click Next on the System Recovery Options page.

6. In the Command Prompt window, type **Diskpart** to create prerequisite partitions.

7. Type **select Disk 0** and press Enter. A message stating that Disk 0 is now the selected disk should appear.

8. Type **Clean**, and then press Enter to erase the current partition table. A confirmation message stating that DiskPart succeeded in cleaning the disk message will be displayed.

9. Create the initial partition to boot the system by typing **create partition primary size=1500**.

Note

Allocate at least 1500MB for the system partition when creating the volume partitions.

---

10. Assign a drive letter to the partition by typing the following: **assign letter=z**. For this example, the letter Z was used to assign the drive letter to the partition. Another letter of your choice can be substituted.

11. Next, type **Active** to mark the newly created partition as an active partition for the system.

12. The next steps are used to create an additional partition for the Windows 2008 system files. This is accomplished by typing the words **create partition primary**.

13. Assign the new partition a drive letter such as C by typing the following: **assign letter=C**.

> **Note**
>
> It is possible to view the newly created volumes by typing the words *list volume* at the command prompt.

14. Now that the partitions have been created, type **Exit** to leave the DiskPart utility.

15. The final step requires both partitions to be formatted with NTFS. This can be done by typing **format X: /y /q /fs:NTFS**. Replace the letter *X* with the drive letters assigned in the previous steps. Repeat this step for both partitions created.

16. Type **Exit** to close the command prompt.

17. Close the System Recovery Options page by clicking the X icon in the upper-right corner or by pressing Alt+F4.

18. Now that the partitions have been created and formatted, click Install Now to proceed with the remainder of the Windows 2008 or later installation. Ensure that you install Windows on the larger partition, which was created in steps 12 and 13.

Installing BitLocker Drive Encryption

Now that the system partition has been configured, there are different ways to install BitLocker. Install it during the initial configuration through Server Manager or through a command prompt. The following sections illustrate how to execute both of these installations.

Installing BitLocker with Server Manager

To install the BitLocker server role using Server Manager, follow these steps:

1. Click Start, Administrative Tools, and Server Manager. The Server Manager tools appear.

2. Right-click Features in the left pane of Server Manager, and then select Add Features.

3. On the Select Features page, install BitLocker by selecting BitLocker Drive Encryption in the Features section, as shown in Figure 9.10, and then click Next.

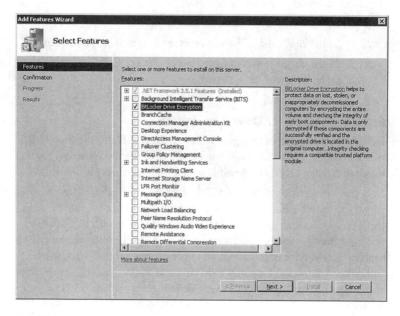

FIGURE 9.10
Selecting the BitLocker feature for installation.

4. On the Confirm Installation Selections page, review the roles, services, and features selected for installation, and then click Install to initiate the installation process.

5. Ensure the installation succeeded by reviewing the messages on the Installation Results page, and then click Close.

> **Note**
>
> Alternatively, the BitLocker Drive Encryption feature can be installed by selecting Add Features in the Initial Configuration Tasks Wizard.

Installing BitLocker via the Command Prompt

Another alternative to installing BitLocker is via the command prompt. This methodology should be reserved for branch office implementations using Windows 2008 Server Core installation because a graphical interface to manage the server does not exist. To install the BitLocker feature using the command prompt, follow these steps:

1. Click Start, Run, type **CMD**, and then click OK.

2. From the command prompt, type **start /w pkgmgr /iu:BitLocker**.

3. After the installation is complete, click Yes on the Windows Package Manager to restart the system.

Enabling BitLocker Drive Encryption

By default, BitLocker is configured to use a Trusted Platform Module. To recap, however, BitLocker's full functionality will not be witnessed unless the system being used is compatible with the TPM microchip and BIOS.

Now that the system partition and BitLocker are installed, it is time to look at ways to enable BitLocker. The next section looks at how to enable BitLocker Drive Encryption with TPM hardware. Microsoft recognizes that many laptops and computers do not have TPM chips (or are not "TPM enabled"). If you are in this situation, don't despair because you can use BitLocker without a compatible TPM chip and BIOS. As such, this section also covers information on how to enable BitLocker without TPM hardware.

Enabling BitLocker Drive Encryption with TPM Hardware

1. Click Start, Control Panel, and double-click BitLocker Drive Encryption.

2. Enable BitLocker Drive Encryption for the operating system volume by clicking Turn On BitLocker on the BitLocker Drive Encryption page. This will display the page shown in Figure 9.11.

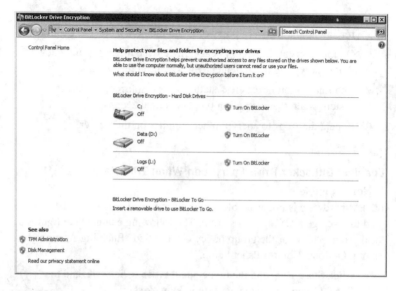

FIGURE 9.11
Turning on BitLocker via Control Panel.

Note

The Initialize TPM Security Hardware screen will be displayed if the TPM is not initialized. Launch the wizard to initialize the hardware, and then restart your computer. In addition, if the drive configuration is not suitable for BitLocker, repartition the hard disk based on the prerequisite tasks, and then start over from step 1.

---

3. Review the message on the BitLocker Drive Encryption Platform Check page, and then click Continue with BitLocker Drive Encryption to start the BitLocker process.

4. On the BitLocker Drive Encryption page, choose how you want to unlock this drive. The options include Use a Password to Unlock the Drive, Use My Smart Card to Unlock the Drive, or Automatically Unlock This Drive on the Computer. For this example, a password is used. Click Next to continue.

5. The Save the Recovery Password page is invoked. The administrator has the ability to save the BitLocker recovery password on a USB drive or to a folder on the system. In addition, the third option allows

for printing of the password. Choose the desired storage alternative for saving the recovery password, and then click Next to continue.

6. On the Encrypt the Volume page, review the messages and click Start Encrypting to implement BitLocker on this volume.

7. The Encryption in Progress status bar is displayed. Restart the system when the encryption process is finalized.

8. Repeat the steps to encrypt other volumes on this server.

Enabling BitLocker Drive Encryption When TPM Hardware Is Not Available

If TPM hardware is not available on the system, BitLocker must be configured to leverage a USB key at startup. The following example configures a local group policy for the group policy object titled "Enabling Advanced Startup Options: Control Panel Setup."

1. Click Start, Run, and then type gpedit.msc. Click OK, and the Local Group Policy Object Editor is invoked.

2. In the Local Group Policy Object Editor, expand Local Computer Policy, Computer Configuration, Administrative Templates, Windows Components, BitLocker Drive Encryption, and then select Operating System Drives.

3. In the right pane, double-click Require Additional Authentication at Startup.

4. Enable the BitLocker group policy settings by selecting the Enabled option, and then click OK.

5. Apply the new group policy settings by typing gpupdate.exe /force at the command prompt.

BitLocker Drive Encryption utilizing a USB device can now be configured by completing the following steps:

1. Click Start, Control Panel, and double-click BitLocker Drive Encryption.

2. Enable BitLocker Drive Encryption by clicking Turn On BitLocker on the BitLocker Drive Encryption page.

3. Review the message on the BitLocker Drive Encryption Platform Check page, and then click Continue with BitLocker Drive Encryption to start the BitLocker process.

4. Because a TPM does not exist in this example, select the option Require Startup USB Key at Every Startup, and then click Next. This option can be found on the Set BitLocker Startup Preferences page.

5. Ensure that a USB memory device has been inserted into the system. Then on the Save Your Startup Key page, specify the removable drive to which the startup key will be saved, and then click Save.

6. The Save the Recovery Password page is then invoked. The administrator has the ability to save the BitLocker recovery password on a USB drive or to a folder on the system. In addition, the third option allows for printing of the password. Choose the desired storage alternative for saving the recovery password, and then click Next to continue.

Note

It is a best practice to make additional copies of the recovery password and store them in a secure location such as a vault. For maximum security, the recovery password should not be stored on the local system, nor should the password be printed on paper. In addition, do not store the recovery password and the startup key on the same media.

---

7. On the Encrypt the Volume page, ensure that the Run BitLocker System Check option is enabled, and then click Continue. The system check guarantees BitLocker can access and read the recovery and encryption keys before encrypting the volume.

Note

Do not bypass the option to run a system check before encrypting the volume. Data loss can occur if there is an error reading the encryption or recovery key.

---

8. Insert the USB memory device containing the startup key into the system, and then click Restart Now. The Encryption in Progress status bar is displayed showing the completion status of the disk volume encryption.

> **Note**
>
> The USB device must be plugged into the system every time the system starts to boot and gain access to the encrypted volume. If the USB device containing the startup key is lost or damaged, you must use the Recovery mode and provide the recovery key to start the system.

Enabling BitLocker Drive Encryption on Additional Data Volumes

There might be situations when BitLocker Drive Encryption is warranted not only on the volume containing the operating system files, but also on the data volumes. This is especially common with domain controllers in branch offices where a lack of physical security and theft is a concern.

When encrypting data volumes with BitLocker, the keys generated for the operating system volume are independent of the drive volume. However, encryption of a data volume is similar to the encryption process of the operating system volume.

Follow these steps to enable BitLocker Drive Encryption for server data volumes:

1. Click Start, Run, and then type **Cmd**. Click OK to launch a command prompt.

2. From within the command prompt, type **manage-bde -on** **<volume>: -rp -rk <removable drive>:\.**

> **Note**
>
> Replace the *<volume>* argument with the desired volume drive letter that you want to encrypt. In addition, replace the *<removable drive>* argument with the drive letter of a USB device. The USB device is utilized to store the recovery key.

The data volume must be unlocked each time the server is rebooted. This can be accomplished through a manual or automatic process. The syntax to manually unlock a data volume after every restart consists of the following two options:

```
manage-bde -unlock <volume>: -rp <recovery password>
```

```
manage-bde -unlock <volume>: -rk U:\<recovery-key-file name>
```

The first option uses the recovery password, whereas the second option takes advantage of passing the recovery key to decrypt the data volume. As mentioned in the previous paragraph, it is possible to enable automatic unlocking of a data volume by utilizing the following syntax at the command prompt:

```
manage-bde -autounlock -enable <volume>:
```

This command creates a recovery key and stores it on the operating system volume. The data volume is automatically unlocked after each system reboot.

> **Note**
>
> After the Windows Server 2008 or later operating system has been successfully installed, the next step is to install SQL Server 2012. For more information on installing SQL Server 2012, see Chapter 1, "Installing or Upgrading the Database Engine to SQL Server 2012."

Utilizing the BitLocker Recovery Password

There might be situations when you need to leverage the recovery password to gain access to a volume that is encrypted with BitLocker. This situation might occur when there is an error related to the TPM hardware, one of the boot files becomes corrupt or modified, or TPM is unintentionally cleared or disabled. The following instructions outline the recovery steps:

1. Restart the system, and the BitLocker Drive Encryption console will come into view.
2. Insert the USB device containing the recovery password, and then press Esc. If the USB device is not available, bypass step 2 and proceed to step 3.
3. Press Enter. You will be prompted to enter the recovery password manually.
4. Type the recovery password, press Enter, and then restart the system.

Removing BitLocker Drive Encryption

The course of action for turning off BitLocker Drive Encryption is the same for both TPM-based hardware configurations and USB devices. When you're turning off BitLocker, two options exist. You can either remove BitLocker entirely and decrypt a volume, or you can temporarily disable BitLocker so that changes can still be made. The following steps depict the process for removing and disabling BitLocker:

1. Click Start, Control Panel, and double-click BitLocker Drive Encryption.

2. Turn off BitLocker Drive Encryption by clicking Turn Off BitLocker on the BitLocker Drive Encryption page.

3. The What Level of Decryption Do You Want dialog box will be invoked. Choose either Disable BitLocker Drive Encryption or Decrypt the Volume.

Summary

Confidential data is at risk if not protected by the appropriate measures. Access controls are not enough to secure confidential data, and an in-depth defense strategy is needed. A critical layer in this strategy is encryption.

Encryption is an effective method of protecting Microsoft SQL Server 2012 data, both while stored in the database and while on the wire. Encrypting data is an easy and straightforward process in SQL Server 2012, especially when you use Transparent Data Encryption.

The sections in this chapter illustrate how to encrypt data while in the database, on Windows Server volumes, and how to encrypt data during transmission. Given the ease with which data can be compromised by a determined hacker, it is important to protect the data with encryption using the methods outlined in this chapter.

Best Practices

Some important best practices from the chapter include the following:

- Encrypt client/server data transmissions.

- Use a third-party certificate to prevent man-in-the-middle attacks.

- Encrypt confidential data in the database to protect the data on disk and in backups.

- Encrypt entire databases by using Transparent Data Encryption for easy protection of data files and backups.

- Use an authenticator when encrypting data to protect against inference hacking.

- Force the clients to use strong encryption when SQL Server cannot be configured to always require encryption.
- Use self-signed certificates rather than nothing at all to secure data.
- Use the newer encryption AES algorithm to protect the Service Master Key and Database Master Key.
- Leverage EKM and store encryption keys in a HSM.
- Configure SQL Server Management Studio to use encryption when connecting to servers over the network.
- Leverage BitLocker to protect the operating system and data volumes associated with a SQL Server system.

PART III

SQL Server 2012 AlwaysOn High-Availability and Disaster Recovery Alternatives

IN THIS PART

CHAPTER 10   Implementing and Managing AlwaysOn Availability Groups

CHAPTER 11   Implementing and Managing AlwaysOn Failover Clustering Instances

CHAPTER 12   Implementing and Managing Database Mirroring

CHAPTER 13   Implementing and Managing Replication

CHAPTER 10

Implementing and Managing AlwaysOn Availability Groups

In SQL Server 2012, a majority of the investments made to high availability and disaster recovery are tailored toward AlwaysOn, specifically the new availability groups capability. As such, it makes sense to leverage availability groups. But let's not stop there. Availability groups are growing in popularity for a number of reasons: They offer multiple replicas—one primary replica and up to four secondary replicas—and provide a single virtual network name for clients and applications to connect with; they make it possible for multiple databases to fail over as a single unit, and organizations can increase hardware utilization by leveraging secondary replicas for read-only operations and maintenance tasks such as reporting and backups. Another benefit of availability groups is increased database availability and protection by providing and maintaining multiple replicas that can reside within the same datacenter or across different datacenters in different geographical locations.

To ensure organizations reap the full benefits that availability groups have to offer, this chapter helps DBAs understand the full potential of availability groups, how availability groups can be used to address different business scenarios, and how to implement, manage, monitor, and maintain it successfully. Specifically, the first section of the chapter takes readers through an overview of availability groups and ways to use it. The middle section of the chapter focuses on step-by-step implementation of availability groups, and the final section of the chapter shares information on how to manage and monitor availability groups.

> **Note**
>
> AlwaysOn Availability Groups is considered the principal high availability
> and disaster recovery feature for mission-critical databases. Expect it to
> replace the database mirroring technology over the next two releases.

SQL Server 2012 AlwaysOn Availability Groups Overview

AlwaysOn Availability Groups is a new SQL Server 2012 capability
enhancing both high availability and disaster recovery for enterprise-level,
mission-critical databases. For DBAs, availability groups are probably the
most highly anticipated feature in SQL Server 2012. It is especially exciting for those DBAs that have been working with this new feature since the
first SQL Server 2012 Community Technology Preview was released in
October 2011. In a nutshell, AlwaysOn availability groups provide a
failover environment for a group of user databases. The solution is similar
to database mirroring as synchronous or asynchronous commits move data
between replicas. What is new is that the solution uses the Windows
failover cluster feature for health and failover detection; it supports up to
five availability replicas, and within an availability group, databases fail
over as a single unit. In addition, to achieve superior hardware utilization,
databases residing on the secondary replicas can be used for read-only
access and limited operations such as backups and maintenance tasks at an
organization's discretion.

Before descending further into the chapter about AlwaysOn availability
groups, it is important to mitigate any confusion going forward in the book
and answer a question that plagues many DBAs. Many DBAs ask what the
difference is between AlwaysOn availability groups and AlwaysOn
failover cluster instances (FCIs). AlwaysOn availability groups provide
database level protection and do not require shared storage, whereas FCI
provide SQL Server instance-level protection and do require shared
storage. The two can be combined for maximum instances and database
protection. It is also worth noting that availability groups require the database to leverage the FULL recovery model, whereas FCIs do not.

The following picture illustrates an AlwaysOn availability groups implementation of three replicas providing high availability, disaster recovery,
and active secondary replicas for reporting in two different data centers.

Figure 10.1 depicts an AlwaysOn availability group implementation for an
organization with multiple data centers.

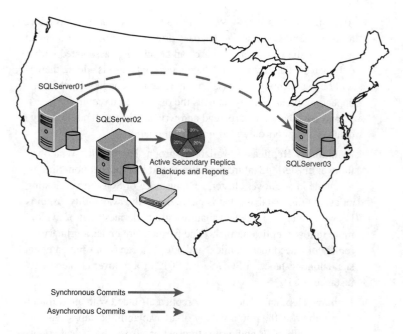

Synchronous Commits ⟶

Asynchronous Commits ⟶

FIGURE 10.1
AlwaysOn availability group implementation.

Availability Groups Concepts and Terminology

The anticipation of achieving greater uptime, improving productivity, and obtaining greater hardware utilization with AlwaysOn availability groups is igniting the fire under the feet of many DBAs and organizations. As a reminder, however, you should become educated about the new concepts and terminologies associated with this capability to ensure your installation is successful. Following are the fundamentals of AlwaysOn availability groups:

- **Availability Groups**—Availability groups offer increased protection for user databases by providing and maintaining copies of the database on up to five replicas. Within SQL Server Management Studio, an availability group is a logical container that hosts a set of availability databases. More than one availability group can be created within an instance of SQL Server. Availability databases within an availability group fail over as a single unit; however, if you are hosting more than one availability group on an instance, all of these availability groups can fail over independent of one another.

■ **Availability Databases**—When a traditional user database is added to an availability group for database protection, it becomes an availability database. A user database can be added or associated with only one availability group. When a user database is added, there will be one primary database and up to four secondary databases, depending on how many replicas the organization requires. The primary database supports read and writes, whereas the secondary databases support only read-only functionality.

■ **Availability Replicas**—Availability groups leverage the Windows failover clustering feature for failover and health detection. Similar to a node in a failover cluster, each instance of SQL Server hosting an availability database that is partaking in the availability group is known as a replica. Each availability group defines a set of two or more failover replica partners. The partners are either a primary replica or a secondary replica, and a replica can be hosted on either a standalone instance of SQL Server 2012 or a failover cluster instance (FCI).

■ **Primary Replica**—The primary replica affiliated with an availability group hosts the primary copy of an availability database and supports both reads and writes transactions from clients and applications. It is also used to send transaction logs from the primary database to all the secondary databases.

■ **Secondary Replica**—The secondary replica affiliated with an availability group hosts the secondary copy of an availability database and, if enabled, it also supports read-only transactions from clients and applications. Moreover, the secondary replica also serves as a failover target in the event the primary database or primary replica fails. Up to four secondary replicas can be configured within an availability group.

■ **Availability Modes**—Similar to database mirroring, availability groups use either a synchronous commit mode or an asynchronous commit mode for distributing data between replicas:

　　■ **Synchronous Commit Mode**—Similar to database mirroring, this commit mode is used to provide high availability with no data loss. A transaction needs to be hardened to the log disk of the secondary replica(s) before a client or application receives a transaction confirmation. When the primary and secondary replica(s) are in a synchronized state, automatic or manual failover is supported. Because transaction latency can be

introduced when using synchronous commits, it is recommended not to distribute the replicas over considerable
distances.

- **Asynchronous Commit Mode**—This mode is great for disaster recovery purposes or when there is a need to place the
  primary and secondary replica(s) in different data centers that
  are geographically dispersed. In this scenario, when a secondary replica is configured to use asynchronous-commit mode,
  the primary replica sends the transaction confirmation to the
  client or application immediately after writing the log record
  to the local log. Because the primary replica does not wait for
  the secondary replica(s) to harden the log, there is a potential
  chance for data loss. This mode supports only a manual
  failover.

- **Failover Alternatives**—When implementing or managing availability groups, a DBA can choose between two failover alternatives:
  automatic failover and manual failover. When a failover occurs, the
  primary and secondary roles interchange. The secondary replica
  target transitions to assume the primary role, and vice versa. After
  the secondary becomes the primary, clients and applications connect
  to the new primary. Up to two automatic failover replicas are
  supported.

- **Availability Groups Listener**—The availability group listener is a
  virtual network name that clients and applications use to connect to
  the availability database(s) partaking in an availability group. The
  listener directs incoming connections to a primary replica or to a
  read-only secondary replica. Each availability group within an
  instance of SQL Server has its own dedicated availability group
  listener; therefore, each set of applications can have a separate
  virtual network name for connectivity. For example, sales applications can connect to sales databases within a sales availability group
  using the sales virtual network name. Likewise, finance applications
  can connect to finance databases within a finance availability group
  using a finance virtual network name. Each availability group
  listener has a unique DNS name that serves as the virtual network
  name (VNN), one or more IP addresses, and a TCP port number,
  such as 1433.

- **Active Secondary Replicas**—One of the most compelling features of availability groups is their ability to use secondary replicas to provide read-only access to databases such as reporting, backups, and some maintenance tasks.

- **AlwaysOn Dashboard**—AlwaysOn Availability Groups ship with its own dashboard to improve availability group management and business productivity.

Additional Information on Availability Groups

Although SQL Server 2012 has evolved, it still has many familiar features to database mirroring, including encryption, compression, and automatic page repair. In SQL Server 2012, application performance and network throughput is enhanced over limited WAN connections because the transaction log data that's in transit from the primary replica to the secondary replica is extremely compressed. By having the transaction log data compressed by default, more data is sent from the primary replica to the secondary replicas improving performance. Equally important, the data in transit can be encrypted; this is a requirement for many organizations following regulatory compliance. Finally, automatic page repair and recovery for corrupted pages is a feature for availability groups. From a high level, the SQL Server hosting the secondary replicas will try to resolve specific types of errors and corruption that prevent a data page from being read. If an error is detected, the server will attempt to obtain a fresh copy of the data and replace the corrupted data page, thus increasing data consistency among the database between the primary and secondary replicas.

SQL Server Availability Groups Prerequisites

Configuring availability groups is almost as simple as clicking through a few pages of a SQL Server installation wizard. This is because the majority of the configurations are completed in SQL Server Management Studio and automatically propagate to the underlying Windows Server failover cluster. However, a number of prerequisite steps must be fulfilled before availability groups can be deployed. The prerequisites are detailed next:

- All instances of SQL Server partaking in an availability group must reside in the same Windows domain. This also applies to secondary replicas that could possibly reside in a datacenter that resides in a different geographic location.

- A Windows Server failover cluster (WSFC) must be created, and the appropriate quorum alternative should be selected based on how many nodes are within the solution.

- Ensure each server in the availability group has the latest Windows and SQL Server service packs and patches.

- An instance of SQL Server 2012 must be installed on each node expected to host an availability group replica. The Enterprise Edition of SQL Server 2012 must be used.

- Each instance of SQL Server hosting an availability group replica must use the same SQL Server collation settings.

- The AlwaysOn availability group feature must be enabled on every instance of SQL Server that hosts an availability replica.

- Anyone planning to use the contained database feature must ensure the contained database authentication server option is enabled on each instance of SQL Server.

- The recovery model on the availability database must be set to Full.

- A full backup of the availability database is required.

- Register each instance of SQL Server that will host an availability group in SQL Server Management Studio. This is an excellent way to ensure that you have connectivity and that the appropriate permissions are configured for each instance.

When to Leverage SQL Server 2012 AlwaysOn Availability Groups.

SQL Server 2012 with its new features, such as availability groups, gives organizations more options while enhancing their operations. Here are some of the key driving factors for implementing availability groups with SQL Server 2012:

- The organization wants a single integrated solution offering both high availability and disaster recovery for mission-critical database(s).

- From a performance optimization perspective, there is a need to offload read-only tasks such as reporting and backups from a primary database to a secondary database.

- The organization is interested in having multiple virtual network names for different sets of databases within an instance of SQL Server.

- There is a need for groups of databases to failover as a single unit.

- High availability is being sought after; however, the organization does not have identical servers and shared storage. These requirements may be expensive for an organization trying to deploy an AlwaysOn failover clustering instance (FCI).

- There is a need to fulfill the business continuity and disaster recovery requirements by placing and maintaining a redundant, up-to-date database(s) in a physical location different from the primary location.

- There is a need to remove the single point of failure intrinsic in failover clusters. The single point of failure is typically the shared storage because it maintains only one copy of the production data.

- There is the need to automatically redirect read-only traffic to secondary replicas.

- There is a need to reduce downtime during maintenance tasks by conducting a rolling upgrade of an instance of SQL Server participating in an availability group.

Implementing AlwaysOn Availability Groups

DBAs must adhere to a series of steps to implement AlwaysOn availability groups. Because the solution uses Windows Server failover clustering, the prerequisite tasks entail preparing and building a Windows Server failover cluster. After this build is complete, SQL Server should be installed on every node within the Windows Server failover cluster that will host an availability group replica. The final steps include enabling the AlwaysOn feature for each instance of SQL Server and then creating availability groups with the Availability Group Wizard. The following example simulates an availability group implementation that uses the three instances of SQL Server within a Windows Server failover cluster. The first two instances (SQLServer01\Instance01 and SQL Server02\Instance01) provide high availability within the primary data center. A third replica (SQLServer03\Instance01) resides in another datacenter providing disaster recovery protection. SQLServer01\Instance01 and SQL Server02\Instance01 are configured to use the synchronous commit availability mode with automatic failover, whereas SQLServer03\Instance01 is configured to use the asynchronous commit availability mode with manual failover.

SQLServer01\Instance01 is the primary replica, and SQLServer02\ Instance01 and SQLServer03\Instance01 are the secondary replicas and are configured to read-only access. Finally, the AdventureWorks2012 database is added to the availability group and a single virtual network name is used to provide client and application connectivity. Table 10.1 summarizes the information used for this example.

Without any more delays, the next section begins by building out the Windows Server failover cluster to support the availability groups. When preparing to deploy availability groups, the first step is creating a Windows Server failover cluster. Note that the steps for building the operating system that follow are based on the assumption that Windows Server 2008 R2 SP1 Enterprise Edition will be leveraged.

Preparing the Windows Server 2008 R2 Operating System for Each Node

The following section outlines prerequisite steps for preparing the operating system for each node that will partake in the availability group:

1. Install Windows Server 2008 R2 Enterprise Edition for each node in the Windows Server failover cluster that will host an availability group SQL Server replica. Use the traditional settings when setting up Windows Server 2008 R2.

2. Join the nodes to an Active Directory domain that will host the availability groups, such as CompanyABC.

3. Create a heartbeat network between the two nodes by addressing a network interface card (NIC) on a different IP space from the production network. Isolate the heartbeat NICs to an isolated VLAN or a separate network switch. This network is used by the cluster nodes to communicate with each other. Disable NetBIOS on the heartbeat adapters and ensure the public network card appears first in the network binding order.

4. Install the latest Windows service packs and hot fixes.

With the nodes prepared, initialized, and formatted, the Windows Server 2008 R2 SP1 failover cluster can be formed.

Table 10.1   Elements to Be Used for the Availability Group Example

AlwaysOn-01

10.10.50.80

AvailabilityGroup01

AG01-Listener

10.10.50.81

Physical Location Role	Availability Mode	Failover Mode	Connections Primary	Readable Secondary	Public IP	Heartbeat
Toronto	Primary Replica	Synchronous Commit	Automatic	Allow All Connections	No	10.10.50.75 192.168.10.1
Toronto	Secondary Replica	Synchronous Commit	Automatic	Allow All Connections	Read-Intent Only	10.10.50.76 192.168.10.2
New York	Secondary Replica	Asychronous Commit	Manual	Allow All Connections	Read-Intent Only	10.10.50.77 192.168.10.3

> **Note**
>
> For simplicity, this example assumes that all replicas across datacenters are using the same 10.10.50.x network/subnet. In a production scenario, most likely there will be more than one network and subnet between the two geographical data centers.

Preparing the Windows Server 2008 R2 Failover Cluster

Be sure to have these items ready for the cluster configuration: unique names for each node, a unique name for the cluster identity, and a unique IP address for the cluster identity. After everything is prepared, follow the steps in the next section. These steps should be conducted in the order they are presented.

Installing the Windows Server 2008 R2 Failover Cluster Feature on Each Node

With Windows Server 2008 R2, the failover cluster feature is no longer installed by default. Before a failover cluster can be deployed, it is necessary to install the failover cluster feature by performing these steps on each Windows Server 2008 R2 node:

1. Log on to the Windows Server 2008 R2 cluster node with an account that has administrator privileges.

2. Click Start, All Programs, Administrative Tools, and then select Server Manager.

3. When Server Manager opens, select the Features node in the tree pane.

4. In the Tasks pane, select the Add Features link.

5. In the Add Features window, select the failover clustering feature and click Install.

6. When the installation is completed, click the Close button to finalize the installation and return to Server Manager.

7. Close Server Manager and install the failover cluster feature on all remaining cluster nodes.

Running the Windows Server 2008 R2 Validate a Cluster Configuration Wizard

After the failover cluster feature is installed, it is time to run the Validate a Configuration Wizard from the Tasks pane of the Failover Cluster Management console. All nodes should be up and running before the wizard is initiated. To run the Validate a Configuration Wizard, perform the next steps:

1. Log on to one of the Windows Server 2008 R2 cluster nodes using an administrator account with privileges over all the nodes in the cluster.

2. Click Start, All Programs, Administrative Tools, and then select Failover Cluster Manager.

3. When the Failover Cluster Management console opens, click the Validate a Configuration link in the Actions pane.

4. When the Validate a Configuration Wizard opens, click Next on the Before You Begin page.

5. In the Select Servers or a Cluster page, enter the name of a cluster node and click the Add button. Repeat this process until all nodes are added to the list, such as SQLServer01\Instance01, SQLServer01\Instance02, and SQLServer01\Instance013. Click Next to continue.

6. In the Testing Options page, read the details explaining the requirements that must be met for all tests to pass to be supported by Microsoft. Select the Run All Tests (Recommended) option button. Click Next to continue.

7. In the Confirmation page, review the list of servers that will be tested and the list of tests that will be performed. Click Next to begin testing the servers.

8. When the tests are complete, the Summary window displays the test results. Click Finish to complete the Validate a Configuration Wizard. If a test failed, click the View Report button to review the details of a failed test.

Creating the Windows Server 2008 R2 Failover Cluster

When the Windows Server 2008 R2 failover cluster is created, all nodes in the cluster should be up and running. To create the failover cluster, perform the following steps:

1. Log on to one of the Windows Server 2008 R2 cluster nodes using an administrator account with privileges over all nodes in the cluster.

2. Click Start, All Programs, Administrative Tools, and then select Failover Cluster Manager.

3. When the Failover Cluster Management console opens, click the Create a Cluster link in the Actions pane.

4. When the Create Cluster Wizard opens, click Next on the Before You Begin page.

5. In the Select Servers page, enter the name of each cluster node and click Add. When all the nodes are listed, click the Next button to continue.

6. In the Access Point for Administering the Cluster page, type the name of the cluster and specify the IPv4 or IPv6 address. For this example, which is illustrated in Figure 10.2, the cluster name AlwaysOn-01 and the following IP address (10.10.50.80) were used.

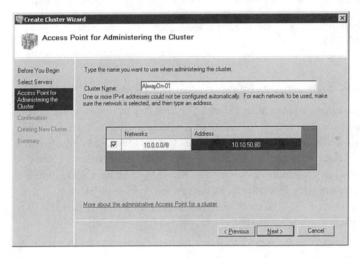

FIGURE 10.2
Specifying the cluster name and IP address for the Windows Server failover cluster.

7. On the Confirmation page, first review the settings and then click Next to create the cluster.

8. On the Summary page, review the results of the cluster creation process and then click Finish to return to the Failover Cluster Management console. If there are any errors, click the View Report button to see a detailed cluster creation report.

Installing an Instance of SQL Server 2012 on Each Node

After the Windows Server failover cluster is installed and fully operational, install an instance of SQL Server onto each node within the Windows Server failover cluster. Follow these steps to install an instance of SQL Server on each node:

1. Install a standalone installation of SQL Server 2012 onto each node in the Windows Server failover cluster that will host an availability

group replica. Use the Enterprise Edition and install the Database
Engine feature.

2. Install the latest SQL Server service packs and hot fixes.

> **Note**
>
> An availability group replica can be hosted on a standalone instance of
> SQL Server or on a failover cluster instance (FCI). In addition, verify that
> the instances of SQL Server that host availability replicas reside on a
> different Windows Server failover clustering (WSFC) node within the same
> WSFC failover cluster.

Enable AlwaysOn Availability Groups Feature

Stay on target. You are almost there! The final step in preparing the environment so that you can implement an availability group involves enabling
the AlwaysOn availability group feature. This task must be conducted on
each instance of SQL Server within the Windows Server failover cluster
that hosts an availability group replica. Either SQL Server Configuration
Manager utility or PowerShell can be used to accomplish this task. In the
following steps, SQL Server Configuration Manager is used to enable
AlwaysOn availability groups:

1. Connect to the Windows Server failover clustering (WSFC) node
   that hosts the SQL Server instance where AlwaysOn availability
   groups will be enabled.

2. Click Start, All Programs, Microsoft SQL Server 2012, Configuration
   Tools, and then click SQL Server Configuration Manager.

3. In SQL Server Configuration Manager, click the SQL Server
   Services node.

4. In the right pane, right-click a SQL Server Instance that you want to
   enable the availability groups feature on, such as SQL Server01\
   Instance01, and then click Properties.

5. On the AlwaysOn High Availability tab, first verify the Windows
   failover cluster name is correct; then select the Enable AlwaysOn
   Availability Groups check box and click OK, as shown in
   Figure 10.3.

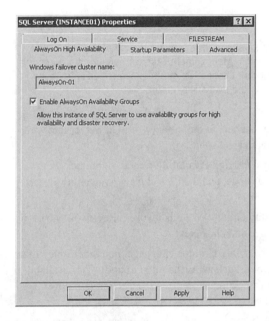

FIGURE 10.3
Enabling the AlwaysOn Availability Groups feature.

6. To complete the task, restart the instance of SQL Server.

7. Repeat these steps on each instance of SQL Server that will host an availability group replica within the Windows Server failover cluster.

Creating Availability Groups with the New Availability Group Wizard

Now that all the prerequisite steps are fulfilled, it is time to turn our attention to the task of installing and configuring availability groups to achieve greater business and service success with high availability, disaster recovery, and active secondary databases. Like the majority of the procedures in SQL Server, the next set of tasks can be completed using a wizard in SQL Server Management Studio or by using Transact-SQL code. Let's first start off by demonstrating how to use the wizard.

Tip

Although this is not a requirement, it is a best practice to register each instance of SQL Server within Management Studio to ensure the appropriate permissions and network connectivity are in place for each instance of SQL Server partaking in the availability group.

---

1. In Object Explorer, connect to the instance of SQL Server that will host the primary replica.

2. Expand the AlwaysOn High Availability node, right-click the Availability Groups node, and then select New Availability Group Wizard.

3. The New Availability Group Wizard is invoked. Review the notes in the Introduction page and click Next.

4. On the Specify Availability Group Name page, input the name of the new availability group, such as AvailabilityGroup01. This availability group name must be unique on the Windows Server failover cluster and cannot exceed 128 characters.

5. On the Select Databases page, select the user databases that will participate in the availability group, and then click Next to invoke the Specify Replicas page.

Note

Before you can add a database to an availability group, the wizard analyzes each database to ensure it meets the prerequisites. For example, the wizard will ensure the Full Recovery Model is enabled or that a full database backup was performed. If the prerequisites are not met, review the status message and correct the anomaly.

---

6. There are four tabs on the Specify Replicas page. First, click the Add Replica button on the Replicas tab to specify an instance(s) of SQL Server to host a secondary replica(s). By default, the server instance you are connected to and running the wizard from must host the primary replica. The Availability Replicas section is used to make a number of choices, including whether the replica will support automatic or manual failover, synchronous-commit availability mode or asynchronous-commit availability mode, and finally, whether or not the secondary replica will support read-only connections.

Figure 10.4 shows SQLServer01\Instance01 taking on the primary replica role and supporting a synchronous commit availability mode with automatic failover. This availability replica does not allow any connections. SQLServer02\Instance01 assumes the secondary replica role and supports a synchronous commit availability mode with automatic failover. This availability replica allows read-intent only connections. Finally, SQLServer03\Instance01 uses an asynchronous-commit availability mode and supports only a forced failover, which may lead to possible data loss. In addition, this availability replica allows only read-intent connections.

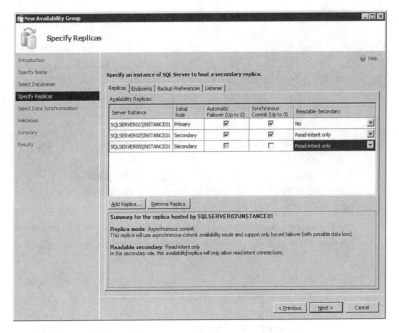

FIGURE 10.4
Specifying and configuring the primary and secondary replicas.

7. As shown in Figure 10.5, the next tab on the Specify Replicas page is called Endpoints. Use this tab to verify existing database mirroring endpoints. If none are found, endpoints will be created. In addition, DBAs have the ability to select whether data between endpoints should be encrypted.

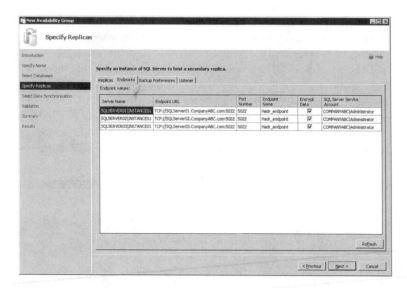

FIGURE 10.5
Configuring the AlwaysOn Availability Groups endpoints and encryption settings.

8. The third tab on the Specify Replicas page is the Backup
Preferences tab. Use this page to determine where backups should
occur. There are four options to choose from:

- **Prefer Secondary**—Automated backups occur on a secondary
replica and are conducted on a primary only if all secondary
replicas are unavailable.

- **Secondary Only**—All automated backups for this availability
group must occur on a secondary replica.

- **Primary**—All automated backups for this availability group
must occur on the current primary replica.

- **Any Replica**—Automated backups can occur on any replica
within the availability group.

9. The final section in the Backup Preferences tab, which is illustrated
in Figure 10.6 is the Replica Backup Priorities section. Priority is
rated from 1 to a 100, where 1 represents the lowest priority and 100
represents the highest priority. Also in this section is the option for
Excluding the Replica from Backups. In this example, backups
occur on the secondary replicas; however, SQLServer01\Instance01
is excluded from backups. In addition, backups will occur first on

SQLServer02\Instance01 followed by SQLServer03\Instance01 because SQLServer02/Instance01 has a higher priority.

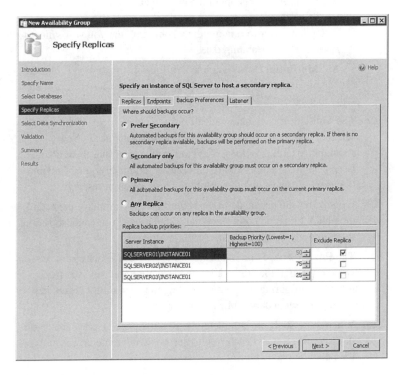

FIGURE 10.6
Configuring the AlwaysOn Availability Groups Backup Preferences.

10. The final tab, Listener, is found on the Specify Replicas page and is used to specify your preference for an availability group listener, which provides a client connection point. Specify your listener preference by providing the Listeners, DNS name, port, and network IP address. Alternatively, it is possible to create the listener using the Add Availability Group Listener dialog box.

11. On the Select Initial Data Synchronization page, select your data synchronization preference. The options include the following:

   ■ **Full**—Data synchronization begins by performing a full database and log backup for each selected database. These backups are restored on each secondary replica. If you plan to leverage this option, specify a network share that will be accessible by all replicas.

- **Join Only**—This option assumes that you have already manually restored and prepared the databases on all secondary replicas prior to running the wizard and that you will synchronize any outstanding data.

- **Skip Initial Data Synchronization**—If this option is chosen, you conduct your own backups and restores for each primary database.

12. The Validation page automatically runs a check to see if the options selected within the wizard meet the requirements of the New Availability Group Wizard. View the results to ensure there are no issues, and then click Next to proceed. Alternatively, click Previous to change settings, and then rerun the tests when necessary.

13. Review the choices made in the wizard on the Summary page, and then click Finish to commence the installations. You can also script these options by choosing the Script button.

14. The Progress page communicates your progress under each task you worked through toward creating the availability group. The tasks include configuring endpoints, creating the availability group, and joining the secondary replica to the group.

15. When these steps are complete, the Results page displays the result of each task. Review each step to ensure there are no errors, and then click Close to exit.

Validating and Viewing the Results of the New Availability Group Wizard

By expanding the availability groups folder in Object Explorer, it is possible to analyze the changes the wizard made to implement and configure the availability groups based on the example in the chapter. By expanding the availability group AvailabilityGroup01, it is possible to see all the replicas, including their roles, the availability databases partaking in the availability group, and the availability group listener name as illustrated in Figure 10.7. In addition, notice that the AdventureWorks2012 database has been automatically created on the secondary replicas and is in a restoring state.

FIGURE 10.7
Validating and viewing the New Availability Group in SQL Server Management Studio.

Back in the Failover Cluster Management console, take the opportunity to view the configuration changes made by the New Availability Group Wizard in SQL Server Management Studio. This can be achieved with the following steps:

1. Invoke Failover Cluster Manager by clicking Start, Administrative Tools, and Failover Cluster Manager.

2. In the Tree pane, select and expand the AlwaysOn availability group cluster created in previous steps; then expand the Services and Applications folder and the Nodes folder.

The availability group created in the previous steps called Availability Group01 shows up as a service and application in Failover Cluster Manager (see Figure10.8). In addition, the server name assumes the name

of the availability group listener (AG01-List) with the IP address
(10.10.50.81) provided during the installation wizard.

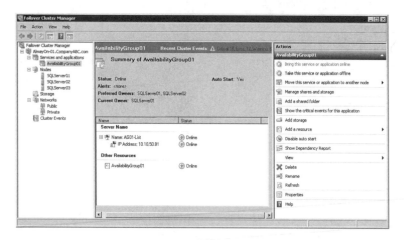

FIGURE 10.8
Validating and viewing the New Availability Group in Failover Cluster Manager.

Note

Notice how the steps that were executed with the New Availability Group
Wizard in SQL Server Management Studio are fully integrated with the
Windows Server, which makes it possible for the configurations to automatically propagate to Failover Cluster Manager. Therefore, when deploying availability groups, the DBA no longer has to be a failover cluster
expert.

Implementing an AlwaysOn Availability Group Using Transact-SQL

The following Transact-SQL syntax can be used to implement an availability group based on the examples illustrated in the previous sections.
Execute the script below in SQLCMD MODE:

```
---:Connect SQLServer01\Instance01

IF (SELECT state FROM sys.endpoints WHERE name =
N'Hadr_endpoint') <> 0
```

```
BEGIN
    ALTER ENDPOINT [Hadr_endpoint] STATE = STARTED
END
GO
use [master]
GRANT CONNECT ON ENDPOINT::[Hadr_endpoint] TO
[COMPANYABC\Administrator]
GO
:Connect SQLServer02\Instance01
IF (SELECT state FROM sys.endpoints WHERE name =
N'Hadr_endpoint') <> 0
BEGIN
    ALTER ENDPOINT [Hadr_endpoint] STATE = STARTED
END
GO
use [master]
GO
GRANT CONNECT ON ENDPOINT::[Hadr_endpoint] TO
[COMPANYABC\Administrator]
GO
:Connect SQLServer03\Instance01
IF (SELECT state FROM sys.endpoints WHERE name =
N'Hadr_endpoint') <> 0
BEGIN
    ALTER ENDPOINT [Hadr_endpoint] STATE = STARTED
END
GO
use [master]
GO
GRANT CONNECT ON ENDPOINT::[Hadr_endpoint] TO
[COMPANYABC\Administrator]
GO
:Connect SQLServer01\Instance01
IF EXISTS(SELECT * FROM sys.server_event_sessions WHERE
name='AlwaysOn_health')
BEGIN
 ALTER EVENT SESSION [AlwaysOn_health] ON SERVER WITH
(STARTUP_STATE=ON);
END
IF NOT EXISTS(SELECT * FROM sys.dm_xe_sessions WHERE
name='AlwaysOn_health')
```

```
BEGIN
 ALTER EVENT SESSION [AlwaysOn_health] ON SERVER STATE=START;
END
GO
:Connect SQLServer02\Instance01

IF EXISTS(SELECT * FROM sys.server_event_sessions WHERE
name='AlwaysOn_health')
BEGIN
 ALTER EVENT SESSION [AlwaysOn_health] ON SERVER WITH
(STARTUP_STATE=ON);
END
IF NOT EXISTS(SELECT * FROM sys.dm_xe_sessions WHERE
name='AlwaysOn_health')
BEGIN
 ALTER EVENT SESSION [AlwaysOn_health] ON SERVER STATE=START;
END
GO

:Connect SQLServer03\Instance01

IF EXISTS(SELECT * FROM sys.server_event_sessions WHERE
name='AlwaysOn_health')
BEGIN
 ALTER EVENT SESSION [AlwaysOn_health] ON SERVER WITH
(STARTUP_STATE=ON);
END
IF NOT EXISTS(SELECT * FROM sys.dm_xe_sessions WHERE
name='AlwaysOn_health')
BEGIN
 ALTER EVENT SESSION [AlwaysOn_health] ON SERVER STATE=START;
END
GO
:Connect SQLServer01\Instance01
USE [master]
GO

CREATE AVAILABILITY GROUP [AvailabilityGroup01]
WITH (AUTOMATED_BACKUP_PREFERENCE = SECONDARY)
FOR DATABASE [AdventureWorks2012]
```

```
REPLICA ON N'SQLServer01\Instance01' WITH (ENDPOINT_URL =
N'TCP://SQLServer01.CompanyABC.com:5022', FAILOVER_MODE =
AUTOMATIC, AVAILABILITY_MODE = SYNCHRONOUS_COMMIT,
BACKUP_PRIORITY = 50, SECONDARY_ROLE(ALLOW_CONNECTIONS = NO)),
    N'SQLServer02\Instance01' WITH (ENDPOINT_URL =
N'TCP://SQLServer02.CompanyABC.com:5022', FAILOVER_MODE =
AUTOMATIC, AVAILABILITY_MODE = SYNCHRONOUS_COMMIT,
BACKUP_PRIORITY = 50, SECONDARY_ROLE(ALLOW_CONNECTIONS =
READ_ONLY)),
    N'SQLServer03\Instance01' WITH (ENDPOINT_URL =
N'TCP://SQLServer03.CompanyABC.com:5022', FAILOVER_MODE =
MANUAL, AVAILABILITY_MODE = ASYNCHRONOUS_COMMIT,
BACKUP_PRIORITY = 50, SECONDARY_ROLE(ALLOW_CONNECTIONS =
READ_ONLY));
GO
:Connect SQLServer01\Instance01

USE [master]
GO
ALTER AVAILABILITY GROUP [AvailabilityGroup01]
ADD LISTENER N'AG01-Listner' (
WITH IP
((N'10.10.50.81', N'255.0.0.0')
)
, PORT=1433);

GO

:Connect SQLServer02\Instance01
ALTER AVAILABILITY GROUP [AvailabilityGroup01] JOIN;
GO
:Connect SQLServer03\Instance01
ALTER AVAILABILITY GROUP [AvailabilityGroup01] JOIN;
GO
:Connect SQLServer01\Instance01

BACKUP DATABASE [AdventureWorks2012] TO DISK = N'\\TOR-
DC01\AlwaysOn\AdventureWorks2012.bak' WITH COPY_ONLY, FORMAT,
INIT, SKIP, REWIND, NOUNLOAD, COMPRESSION, STATS = 5
GO
```

```
:Connect SQLServer02\Instance01

RESTORE DATABASE [AdventureWorks2012] FROM DISK = N'\\TOR-
DC01\AlwaysOn\AdventureWorks2012.bak' WITH NORECOVERY,
NOUNLOAD, STATS = 5
GO
:Connect SQLServer03\Instance01
RESTORE DATABASE [AdventureWorks2012] FROM DISK =
N'\\TOR-DC01\AlwaysOn\AdventureWorks2012.bak' WITH NORECOVERY,
NOUNLOAD, STATS = 5
GO
:Connect SQLServer01\Instance01
BACKUP LOG [AdventureWorks2012] TO DISK = N'\\TOR-
DC01\AlwaysOn\AdventureWorks2012_20120520174027.trn' WITH
NOFORMAT, NOINIT, NOSKIP, REWIND, NOUNLOAD, COMPRESSION, STATS
= 5
GO
:Connect SQLServer02\Instance01
RESTORE LOG [AdventureWorks2012] FROM DISK = N'\\TOR-
DC01\AlwaysOn\AdventureWorks2012_20120520174027.trn' WITH
NORECOVERY, NOUNLOAD, STATS = 5
GO
:Connect SQLServer03\Instance01
RESTORE LOG [AdventureWorks2012] FROM DISK = N'\\TOR-
DC01\AlwaysOn\AdventureWorks2012_20120520174027.trn' WITH
NORECOVERY, NOUNLOAD, STATS = 5
GO
GO
```

Notes from the Field: Quorum Selection and AlwaysOn Availability Groups

Selecting the correct quorum configuration for the Windows Server failover cluster hosting the SQL Server Availability Groups is one of the most important tasks when implementing availability groups. The quorum selection can significantly impact whether the Windows Server failover cluster will stop running, prematurely failover, and stop servicing client requests. This means that a significant SQL Server service outage can occur if the incorrect quorum configuration is selected. Before we discuss best practices from the field, let's first evaluate how the quorum and voting process works.

The quorum configuration in a Windows Server failover cluster determines the number of failures that a cluster can sustain while still remaining online. To achieve quorum, more than half of the voters must be operational and able to communicate with one another. If the number of voters drops below the majority, the cluster service will stop on the nodes in that group. Each node within the cluster, including a disk and file share (if configured), constitutes a vote when determining the overall health.

The following is a list of quorum configuration best practices when implementing availability groups on a Windows Server failover cluster:

- Commonly use the Node Majority quorum configuration alternative when there is an odd number of nodes in the Windows Server failover cluster.

- Commonly use the Node and File Share Majority quorum configuration alternative when there is an even number of nodes in the Windows Server failover cluster.

- If deploying availability groups to achieve high availability and disaster recovery by placing nodes in different datacenters, assign a vote to each node in the primary data center that will participate in automatic failover, and do not assign votes to all other nodes.

- Every node that hosts a primary replica or is the preferred owner of the AlwaysOn failover cluster instance should have a vote.

- Each node that could host a primary replica or FCI, as the result of an automatic failover, should have a vote.

- If using a file share witness, ensure it resides in the primary site.

- Reassess vote assignments post failover. You do not want to fail over into a cluster configuration that does not support a healthy quorum.

Managing AlwaysOn Availability Groups

Common management tasks associated with availability groups involve the following: adding or removing availability replicas, adding or removing databases, adding listeners, conducting failovers, suspending data movement, or modifying settings associated with an existing availability group. All these tasks can be conducted in SQL Server Management Studio using Transact-SQL or with PowerShell. The following sections articulate how to conduct these AlwaysOn availability groups management tasks.

Removing a Replica from an Availability Group

The following example shows how to remove a replica from an availability group by using SQL Server Management Studio:

1. Expand the Availability Groups folder in Object Explorer.

2. Expand the AlwaysOn High Availability Groups folder.

3. Expand the desired availability group you want to delete the replica from.

4. Expand the Availability Groups folder, right-click the desired availability replica you want to delete, and choose Remove from Availability Group.

5. The Remove Replica from Availability Group Wizard will be invoked.

6. Ensure you want to remove the selected replica and then click OK.

The replica is now removed from the availability group. Alternatively, the following Transact-SQL code can also be used to remove the secondary replica called SQLServer03\Instance01 from the availability group called AvailabilityGroup01 that was created in the earlier examples:

```
USE [master]
GO
ALTER AVAILABILITY GROUP [AvailabilityGroup01]
REMOVE REPLICA ON N'SQLServer03\Instance01';
GO
```

Adding a Replica to an Availability Group

Many situations can arise that require you to scale the availability group solution by adding replicas. You may, for example, start out by building a solution for high availability within the datacenter; however, you may decide later to add an additional replica for disaster recovery purposes. Use the following steps to add the replica we removed in the previous example back into the availability group:

1. Expand the Availability Groups folder in Object Explorer.

2. Expand the AlwaysOn High Availability Groups folder.

3. Expand a desired availability group you want to add a replica to.

4. Right-click the availability groups folder and click Add Replica.

5. Review the Introduction page in the Add Replica to Availability Group Wizard and then click Next.

6. Before proceeding, you must connect to all secondary replicas by clicking the Connect button. Once authenticated and connected, click Next.

7. On the Specify Replicas screen, click Add Replica, and connect to the replica you want to add to the availability group.

8. Choose the appropriate failover, commit, and readable secondary options, and then proceed to the Endpoint and Backup tab to finalize the configurations.

9. Click Next to continue.

10. On the Select Initial Data Synchronization page, choose your data synchronization preference and then click Next.

11. View the Validation page for any errors, and then click Next to proceed.

12. On the Summary page, review your choices and click Finish.

13. Review the Progress page and the Results page, and then click Close.

Adding a Database to an Availability Group

Again, just as you may need to scale the availability group solution, you will likely need to add additional databases to an availability group. For example, you may be consolidating mission-critical databases to a consolidation infrastructure, such as a private cloud, or you may need to add additional finance databases to a finance availability group. Whatever the case, follow these steps to add a database to an availability group:

1. Expand the Availability Groups folder in Object Explorer.

2. Expand the AlwaysOn High Availability Groups folder.

3. Expand a desired availability group you want to add a database to.

4. Right-click the Availability Databases folder and click Add database.

5. Review the Introduction screen in the Add Database to Availability Group Wizard screen, and then click Next.

6. On the Select Databases page, select the additional user databases for this availability group, and then click Next.

7. On the Select Initial Data Synchronization page, choose your data synchronization preference, and then click Next.

8. Before the wizard can configure existing endpoints to grant them appropriate permissions, you must connect to all the existing secondary replicas. After you do, click Next to continue.

9. Review the results for the availability group validation on the Validation page, and then click Next to continue.

10. On the Summary page, verify the choices made by the wizard and click Finish.

11. Review the Progress page and the Results page, and then click Close.

Use the following Transact-SQL code to add the MarketingDB01 database to an availability group called AvailabilityGroup01. This example assumes the Initial Data Synchronization Is Skipped option was selected and that the example is executed from SQLServer01\Instance01:

```
USE [master]
GO
ALTER AVAILABILITY GROUP [AvailabilityGroup01]
ADD DATABASE [MarketingDB01];
GO
```

Removing a Database from an Availability Group

Removing a database from an availability group is a straightforward task. Expand the Availability Groups folder and right-click the database that will be removed. Next, select Remove Database from Availability Group to invoke the wizard. The following Transact-SQL statement can also be used to remove a database named MarketingDB02 from an availability group called AvailabilityGroup01:

```
ALTER AVAILABILITY GROUP [AvailabilityGroup01]
REMOVE DATABASE [MarketingDB02];
GO
```

Changing Availability Group Properties

The great thing about availability groups is that configuration properties can change on-the-fly without the need to rebuild the availability group from scratch. For example, you may start off by using the Synchronous Commit Availability mode and then realize it is necessary to change to an Asynchronous Commit Availability mode because of network and application latency issues. On the other hand, you may want to change the failover mode, backup permissions, and connections for each of the replicas. All this can be done by right-clicking a desired availability group, selecting properties, and then making the appropriate changes. Have a look at Figure 10.9 to see all the configuration options.

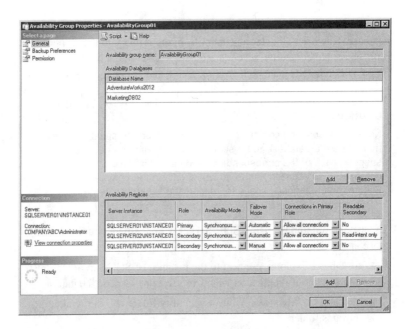

FIGURE 10.9
Validating and viewing the New Availability Group in Failover Cluster Manager.

Suspend Database Movement

From a management perspective, a DBA may need to temporarily or permanently suspend database synchronization between availability replicas. This may occur if an instance of SQL Server hosting the replica experiences issues, a datacenter is offline, or a need exists to conduct some form of routine maintenance. A DBA has the opportunity to suspend an availability database in AlwaysOn availability groups by using SQL Server Management Studio, Transact-SQL, or PowerShell. Note, however, that downtime and secondary connections can be impacted based on where you suspend the data.

If the database is suspended on the secondary database, only that specific secondary is impacted. As a result, the primary and all other secondary replicas are still online and fully operational. The secondary database that is suspended goes into a NON SYNCHRONIZING state and stops receiving and applying data. In addition, secondary connections are not permitted until data movement resumes.

The primary is still operational if the database is suspended on the primary database. However, all data movement from the primary to the secondary replicas are halted and the secondary database goes into a NON SYNCHRONIZING state and stops receiving and applying data.

Caution

Note that a suspend command must be issued on the server instance that hosts the database to be suspended or resumed. In addition, if you suspend each of the corresponding secondary databases, the primary database runs exposed and transaction logs on the primary can grow. Ensure there is enough space to support the log growth.

To suspend a database using SQL Server Management Studio, follow these steps:

1. In Object Explorer, connect to the instance of SQL Server that hosts the availability replica on which you want to suspend a database.
2. Expand the AlwaysOn High Availability folder and the Availability Groups folder.
3. Expand the availability group.
4. Expand the Availability Databases folder, right-click the database, and then select Suspend Data Movement.
5. In the Suspend Data Movement dialog box, click OK.

Note

After synchronization is suspended, the message next to the database will change to a pause indicator icon.

Alternatively, use Transact-SQL to suspend database movement. This is achieved by connecting to the instance of SQL Server that maintains the replica whose database you want to suspend. In this example, the AdventureWorks2012 database is suspended on the secondary replicas known as SQLServer02\Instance01:

```
ALTER DATABASE [AdventureWorks2012] SET HADR SUSPEND;
GO
```

Manually Failing Over an Availability Group

There are two types of strategies available when manually failing over availability groups from one replica to another. The first strategy consists of performing a manual failover without any data loss. This is often referred to as a *planned manual failover*. This strategy assumes the primary replica and the target secondary replica that will eventually transition to the new primary replica are using the synchronous-commit mode and that data between the two replicas are fully synchronized. The status of the secondary database will indicate SYNCHRONIZED. The second strategy assumes that the secondary replicas are in an UNSYNCHRONIZED or NOT UNSYNCHRONIZED state, which indicates there could be possible data loss in the event of a manual failover. This strategy is commonly referred to as a *forced manual failover with possible data loss*.

> **Note**
>
> Independent of the failover methodology chosen, the concept affiliated with a failover is similar. First, when a failover occurs, note that an availability group fails over at the level of an availability replica and not at the database level like database mirroring. In addition, the failover process will transition a secondary replica to a primary replica role while simultaneously transitioning the former primary replica to the secondary role.

Conducting an Availability Group Failover with SQL Server Management Studio

Follow these steps to swap the primary and secondary replica roles by manually failing over the availability group from a primary replica to a secondary replica. This example assumes the primary replica is SQLServer01\Instance01 and the secondary replica is SQLServer02\Instance01. Moreover, the two replicas are using the synchronous-commit mode, and data between the two replicas are fully synchronized:

1. In Object Explorer, connect to an instance of SQL Server that hosts a secondary replica of the availability group that needs to be failed over, such as SQLServer02\Instance01.

2. Expand the instance AlwaysOn High Availability Folder and then the Availability Groups folder.

3. To invoke the Failover Availability Group Wizard, right-click the availability group that will fail over, such as AvailabilityGroup01, and then select Failover.

4. Review the Introduction screen in the Failover to Availability Group Wizard screen, and then click Next.

5. On the Select New Primary Replica page, choose the new primary replica and review the failover readiness warnings; then click Next, as in Figure 10.10.

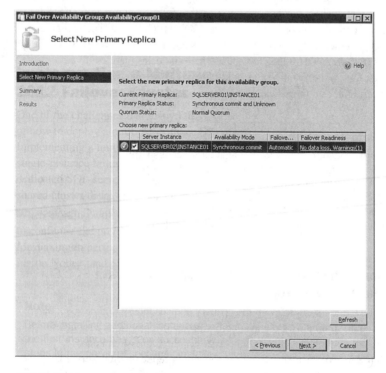

FIGURE 10.10
Specifying the primary replica during a planned failover.

6. On the Summary page, verify the choices that were made with the wizard and then click Finish.

7. Review the Progress page and then the Results page to ensure success.

8. Click Close to finalize.

If you plan to use Transact-SQL, the following statement can be used to conduct a planned failover from SQLServer01\Instance01 to SQLServer02\ Instance02:

```
---:Connect SQLServer02\Instance01
ALTER AVAILABILITY GROUP [AvailabilityGroup01] FAILOVER;
GO
```

Conducting a Forced Availability Group Failover with Possible Data Loss

If the primary replica is permanently offline or is in the process of failing over to a secondary replica that is not fully synchronized, this can result in data loss for those transactions that did not reach the secondary replica before failing over. This type of failover is known as a *forced failover*. If you manually force a failover and the former primary replica comes back online, it automatically transitions to a secondary; however, it is placed into a SUSPENDED state. At this time, you can attempt to retrieve data that did not make it to the secondary from the former primary.

Caution

Forcing service, which may involve some data loss, is strictly for disaster recovery. It is strongly recommend that you force a failover only if the primary replica is no longer running, no SYNCHRONIZED replica exists from which you can perform a manual failover, you are willing to risk losing some data, and you understand that service must be restored to the availability group immediately. Note that if you issue a forced failover command on a synchronized secondary replica, the secondary replica behaves the same as a manual failover.

The steps to conduct a forced failover with SQL Server Management Studio are similar to the steps described previously under "Conducting an Availability Group Failover with SQL Server Management Studio." However, a few minor differences exist. On the Select New Primary Replica screen, there is a data loss warning in the Failover Readiness section. The warning indicates the replica has one or more databases that were not synchronized, and failing over to this replica can result in data loss for any transactions that did not reach the secondary replica prior to failing over. You will have to confirm failover with potential data loss to proceed.

Note

After the forced failover is finalized, a DBA may have to reconfigure the Windows Server failover cluster quorum settings to ensure that clients and applications can connect to the secondary replica that is now the new primary replica.

If you are using Transact-SQL, here is an example of how to conduct a forced failover from SQLServer01\Instance01, which was the primary replica to SQLServer03\Instance01 to the secondary replica target called SQLServer03\Instance01. Note that you must execute the following script in SQLCMD MODE:

```
:Connect SQLServer03\Instance01
ALTER AVAILABILITY GROUP [AvailabilityGroup01]
FORCE_FAILOVER_ALLOW_DATA_LOSS;
GO
```

Connecting to an Availability Group Listener and Managing Read-Only Connectivity

The final management task looks at how to connect to an availability group and take advantage of the automatic failover capabilities provided by the virtual network name, including how to route read-only connections to a read-only secondary replica. The first step is ensuring you have created an availability group listener. Next, to support read-only routing, ensure the replica is configured to support read-only connections. This is typically done when configuring the replica via the Availability Group Wizard; however, changes can also be made after the fact by right-clicking a desired availability group, selecting Properties, and then making the change to a replica in the Readable Secondary section.

Follow these steps to configure connectivity and read-only access to a read-only secondary through an ODBC connection:

1. Choose Start, All Programs, Administrative Tools, Data Sources (ODBC).

2. On the ODBC Data Source Administrator page, select System DSN.

3. Click Add to create a new System DSN connection to the principal and mirror SQL Server instance.

4. In the Create New Data Source page, select SQL Native Client 11.0, and then click Finish.

5. In the Create a New Data Source to SQL Server page, enter the name, description, and the SQL Server that you want to connect to. For the SQL Server name, enter the name of the availability group listener that was previously created for the availability group, such as AG01-Listener, as illustrated in Figure 10.11. Click Next.

6. Select the Windows Authentication or SQL Server authentication mode and click Next.

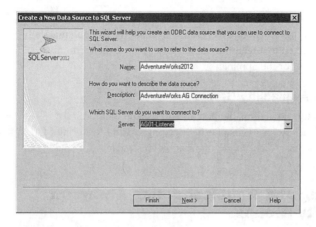

FIGURE 10.11
Specifying an availability group listener, aka a virtual network name.

7. Select the default database to specify the application intent. For this
   example, the database selected was AdventureWorks2012 and the
   application intent was Read-Only, as shown in Figure 10.12.
   Click Next.

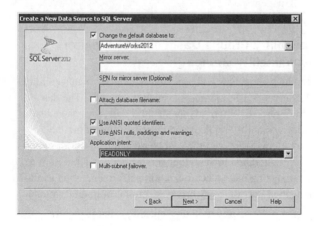

FIGURE 10.12
Creating a new SQL Server native client data source.

8. Click Finish and then click Test Data Source to finalize the connection settings.

Now when a client or application takes advantage of this connection string, all connections to the AdventureWorks2012 availability will automatically get routed or directed to a read-only secondary because the read-only option was chosen for the application intent.

Backing Up Availability Groups

Availability groups now allow the potential to backup data from the secondary replicas. Refer to Chapter 6, "Backing Up and Restoring SQL Server 2012 Databases," for more information on strategies for backing up availability groups.

Monitoring and Troubleshooting AlwaysOn Availability Groups

After implementing and configuring AlwaysOn availability groups, turn your attention to understanding the following tools for monitoring and troubleshooting availability groups:

- Availability Groups Dashboard
- System Performance
- System Views
- Operations Manager

Using the Availability Groups Dashboard to Monitor and Manage Availability Groups

Administrators can leverage a new and remarkably intuitive manageability dashboard in SQL Server 2012 to monitor availability groups. The dashboard, as shown in Figure 10.13, reports the health of an AlwaysOn availability group and its availability replicas and databases, including the health status of each item. Moreover, the dashboard can be used for choosing a replica when conducting a manual failover, estimating data loss if a failover is forced, analyzing data-synchronization performance, and evaluating the performance impact of a synchronous commit availability mode.

If an issue arises or if more information on a specific event is required, a DBA can click the availability group state, server instance name, or health status hyperlinks for additional information. The dashboard is launched by right-clicking the Availability Groups folder in the Object Explorer in SQL Server Management Studio and selecting Show Dashboard.

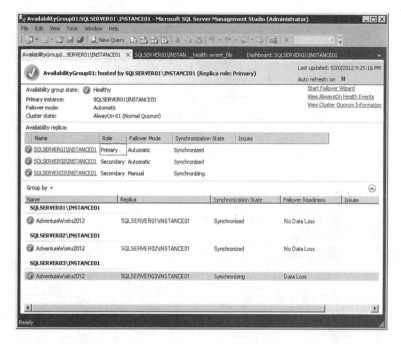

FIGURE 10.13
Using the Availability Groups Dashboard.

Monitoring Availability Groups Performance

The Availability Groups Monitoring tool is a great starting point for managing and analyzing availability groups. When additional metrics are needed for analysis troubleshooting, or creating a performance baseline, you can use the Performance Monitor tool included with Windows Server 2008 R2. To launch the tool, choose Start, All Programs, Administrative Tools, and Performance Monitor. Following are the specific counters that are included with the SQL Server Availability Groups Performance Object:

- Availability Replica Performance Object:
    - Bytes Received from Replica/sec
    - Bytes Sent to Replica/sec
    - Bytes Set to Transport/sec
    - Flow Control Time (ms/sec)

- Flow Control/sec
- Received from Replica/sec
- Resent Messages/sec
- Sends to Replica/sec
- Sends to Transport/sec
- Database Replica Performance Object:
  - File Bytes Received/sec
  - Log Bytes Received/sec
  - Log Remaining for Undo
  - Log Send Queue
  - Mirrored Write Transactions/sec
  - Recovery Queue
  - Redo Blocked/sec
  - Redo Bytes Remaining
  - Redone Bytes/sec
  - Total Log Requiring Undo
  - Transactions Delay
- Database Performance Object:
  - Log Flush Write Time (ms)
  - Log Flushes/sec
  - Log Pool Cache Misses/sec
  - Log Pool Disk Reads/sec
  - Log Pool Requests/sec

Collecting and analyzing the preceding metrics assists organizations with planning their availability groups implementations. Before availability groups are implemented in production, it is a best practice to simulate performance and scalability testing in a proof of concept lab and analyze the metrics collected. If possible, a bandwidth simulator tool should also be used to mimic the production network speed, especially if replicas will be placed in different geographic locations. This allows organizations to fully understand the availability groups, including bandwidth requirements when setting up availability groups in production over a private network. When analyzing bandwidth requirements, your organization should also assess the current bandwidth utilization. Therefore, if the link is already fully saturated, more bandwidth may be necessary to support the replicas. Alternatively, many organizations purchase dedicated network lines tailored specifically for availability groups replication.

Using the System Views to Monitor Availability Groups

The system views included with SQL Server are another great source of information when monitoring status and performance. The following system views should be used when monitoring availability groups on the Windows Server failover cluster, availability groups, and availability replicas.

Windows Server Failover Cluster

- **Sys.dm_hadr_cluster**—This system view returns data pertaining to the Windows Server failover cluster name and information settings associated with the quorum.

- **Sys.dm_hadr_cluster_members**—As the name suggests, this system view returns a row for each of the members who are forming quorum and indicates the status for them.

- **Sys.dm_hadr_cluster_networks**—Provides networking data such as member name, network subnet, and IP subnet for every member within the Windows Server failover cluster.

- **Sys.dm_hadr_instance_node_map**—Returns the name of the Windows Server failover cluster node that hosts the instance of SQL Server. This system view is beneficial for detecting whether multiple instances of SQL Server hosting replicas reside on the same node.

- **Sys.dm_name_id_map**—Displays availability group name, availability group ID, availability group resource ID, and availability group ID.

Monitoring Availability Groups

- **Sys.availability_groups**—Displays a row for each availability group found on the instance of SQL Server.

- **Sys.availability_groups_cluster**—Returns a row for each availability group in the Windows Server failover cluster.

- **Sys.dm_hadr_availability_groups_states**—Displays the health of each availability group found on the local instance of SQL Server.

Monitoring Availability Replicas

- **Sys.availability_replicas**—Displays all the availability group replicas for each availability group based on the instance of SQL Server.

- **Sys.availability_read_only_routing_lists**—Displays the read-only routing list for each availability group replica.

- **Sys.dm_hadr_availability_replica_cluster_nodes**—Returns the availability group name, replica server name, and the node name for each node within Windows Server failover cluster.

- **Sys.dm_hadr_availability_replica_cluster_states**—Provides the joined state of each availability group replica in the Windows Server failover cluster.

- **Sys.dm_hadr_availability_replica_states**—Provides a replica role description, operational state, connected state, connected state description, recovery health, synchronization health, and error states for each local availability replica.

- **Sys.fn_hadr_backup_is_preferred_replica**—Determines whether the current replica is the preferred backup replica.

Monitoring Availability Group Databases

- **Sys.availability_databases_cluster**—Illustrates all the availability databases associated with an availability group, independent of whether the local database has joined the availability group as of yet.

- **Sys.databases**—Displays generic information about all databases on an instance of SQL Server.

- **Sys.dm_hadr_auto_page_repair**—Returns a row for every automatic page-repair attempt on any availability database on an availability replica that is hosted for any availability group by the server instance.

- **Sys.dm_hadr_database_replica_states**—Indicates the state of the replica and includes a row for each database.

- **Sys.dm_hadr_database_replica_cluster_states**—Provides information into the health of the availability databases in each availability group on the Windows Server failover clustering.

Monitoring Availability Group Listeners

- **Sys.availability_group_listener_ip_addresses**—Displays the IP addresses associated with availability group listeners that are online.

- **Sys.availability_group_listeners**—Returns a row for every availability group listener that is associated with an availability group. Zero rows will be returned, indicating that no network name was found.

- **Sys.dm_tcp_listener_states**—Returns IP address and port information associated with the availability group listener.

Monitoring Availability Groups with Systems Center Operations Manager

Another great tool to proactively monitor AlwaysOn availability groups, including the health of the availability groups, availability replica, and availability databases is the Systems Center Operations Manager. It is also beneficial to leverage the latest SQL Server 2012 Management Pack that is included for free with Operations Manager 2012. The SQL Server 2012 Management Pack associated with Operations Manager 2012 provides tight alignment with availability groups and includes the following:

- Automatically discovers availability groups, availability replicas, and availability databases among every instance of SQL Server that is being proactively managed with Operations Manager.

- Anytime an issue occurs, an alert is fired to the Operations Manager centralized console, and a subsequent alert can be emailed to the DBA team managing the SQL Server infrastructure.

- Operations Manager includes a customer extension to monitor AlwaysOn health with Policy-Based Management.

- Custom tasks that Operations Manager Operators or DBAs have access to via the System Center Operations Manager console.

Summary

AlwaysOn Availability Group in SQL Server 2012 provides a set of capabilities that allow organizations to achieve both high availability and disaster recovery for mission-critical databases within a datacenter or across datacenters. The integrated solution is very straightforward to use and provides many options, such as automatic or manual failover, zero data loss protection, fast application failover, and support for up to four secondary replicas and two synchronous secondary replicas. Finally, secondary replicas can be used for read-only operations, and seamless application failover can be achieved when using an availability group listener.

Best Practices

The following are the best practices expressed in this chapter:

- Replace database mirroring and log shipping implementations with availability groups because database mirroring will eventually be deprecated.

- Leverage contained databases for encapsulating logins into the database for easier failover purposes.

- Always have an odd number of quorum votes in a Windows Server failover cluster. For the quorum model, selecting Node and Fileshare Majority is not uncharacteristic. However, follow the Windows Server failover cluster best practices because the number of nodes and placement of the replicas will dictate the right quorum model based on your organization's requirements.

- For the majority of cases dealing with replicas within the same datacenter, use Synchronous Commit Availability Mode and automatic failover for replicas.

- For replicas' indifferent data centers, the majority of cases use Asynchronous Commit Availability Mode and manual failover.

- For clients and applications, leverage the availability group listener for seamless application failover between replicas.

- For maximum instance and database protection, combine FCI with availability groups. Specifically, use FCI for local high availability within a datacenter and availability groups to provide the disaster recovery component.

- Leverage secondary replicas for read-only operations such as reporting and backups.

- For connection strings using an availability group listener, take advantage of the ApplicationIntent=ReadOnly setting for routing read-only requests to the secondary replicas and the MultiSubnet Failover=true setting for failovers between multi-subnets or different datacenters.

CHAPTER 11

Implementing and Managing AlwaysOn Failover Clustering Instances

AlwaysOn Failover Cluster Instances (FCI) is one of the SQL Server 2012 high-availability alternatives DBAs can choose from for achieving both high-availability and disaster recovery. Other SQL Server 2012 high-availability alternatives include AlwaysOn availability groups, database mirroring, log shipping, peer-to-peer replication, and Live-Migration if using Hyper-V.

This chapter first provides an overview of SQL Server 2012 AlwaysOn FCIs, including the new capabilities associated with the feature, and then the hardware and software prerequisites required for deploying FCI.

The chapter also includes step-by-step procedures for installing a SQL Server 2012 single FCI on a two-node Windows Server 2008 R2 SP1 failover cluster, how to deploy a SQL Server 2012 multi-instance FCI, and how to deploy a SQL Server 2012 multi-subnet FCI. The final portion of the chapter includes management tasks for managing an AlwaysOn FCI based on Windows Server 2008 R2 SP1.

SQL Server 2012 AlwaysOn Failover Cluster Instances Overview

AlwaysOn FCIs with SQL Server 2012 running on Windows Server 2008 R2 provides server-level redundancy by supporting the *shared-nothing cluster model*. In a shared-nothing cluster, two or more independent servers share resources; however, each computer, or *node*, owns and manages its local resources and provides nonsharing data services. In case of a node failure, the disks, resources, and services running on the failed node failover to a surviving node in the cluster. With SQL Server AlwaysOn FCIs, specifically, only one node manages one particular SQL Server instance, set of disks, and associated services at any given time.

> **Caution**
>
> SQL Server AlwaysOn FCIs provides high availability for mission-critical databases and server nodes. However, it does not replace the need for a comprehensive backup and recovery strategy for a SQL Server environment. Equally important, you should not rely on clustering as a replacement for disaster recovery and business continuity strategies.

What's New for SQL Server 2012 AlwaysOn Failover Cluster Instances?

SQL Server 2012 makes significant enhancements to AlwaysOn FCIs. The list of enhancements for SQL Server 2012 AlwaysOn FCIs includes the following:

- **Referencing failover clusters**—The terminology for this has changed to AlwaysOn FCIs or, simply, FCI.

- **Multisubnet failover capabilities**—These are available out-of-the-box with SQL Server 2012. As a result, each node associated within the FCI can reside in a different subnet or different set of subnets. This enhancement allows DBAs to easily create geographically dispersed clusters, also known as stretch clusters for disaster recovery purposes.

- **Support for tempdb on Local Disk**—Tempdb on a clustered disk is a thing of the past given that in SQL 2012, tempdb database file placement is supported on local disks. This enhancement brings about a number of benefits, including the ability for DBAs to offload tempdb I/O from shared-storage devices like a SAN and leverage fast SSD storage locally.

- **Flexible Failover Policy**—In SQL Server 2012, you have more flexibility when configuring a failover policy for a FCI. This is because of the introduction of failure condition-level properties.

- When combined with availability groups, AlwaysOn FCIs can offer maximum protection at a database level and at a SQL Server instance level.

- The marriage between SQL Server FCI and Windows Server Core results in improved availability and an impressive 50–60% reduction in OS patching.

- **Indirect checkpoints**—A new checkpointing algorithm has been introduced in the Database Engine to provide a more robust recovery in the event of crash or failover. This translates to faster recovery times.

Determining When to Implement a SQL Server 2012 Failover Cluster

Typically, organizations implement a SQL Server 2012 failover cluster to address the following situations:

- To increase server availability for mission-critical applications and network services.

- To provide high-availability support for an entire instance of SQL Server, not just a database.

- To provide a seamless failover that minimizes the impact to client applications and end users.

- To provide an automatic failover that does not require DBA intervention.

- To reduce downtime during routine maintenance or unplanned failures.

- To protect against hardware failures.

- To leverage flexible policies for granular trigger events for automatic failover.

- To have clients and applications connect to a single virtual network name.

- To minimize downtime when installing Windows Server and SQL Server 2012 critical fixes, patches, and service packs. This strategy is known as rolling upgrades.

Tip

With the release of the new AlwaysOn as a feature, many DBAs will contemplate whether they should use FCIs or availability groups. In a nutshell, FCIs should be used for instance-level protection, whereas availability groups should be used for database protection. In addition, availability groups also provide the ability to have up to four secondary replicas that can be used for read-only capabilities. It is possible to combine the two features for maximum protection. For example, if an organization had two data centers, you could implement one FCI in each datacenter for high availability and then use availability groups between the two FCIs for disaster recovery.

AlwaysOn Failover Cluster Instances Terminology

Before installing AlwaysOn FCIs, it is beneficial to understand the SQL Server and Windows Server terminology associated with FCIs. Let's examine the terminology in the following list:

■ **SQL Server virtual server**—A *SQL Server virtual server* is, in fact, a cluster-configured resource group that contains all resources necessary for SQL Server to operate on the cluster. This includes the NetBIOS name of the virtual server, a TCP/IP address for the virtual server and all disk drives, and vital SQL Server services required to operate in a clustered configuration. In a multiple instance, two or more node clusters and one or more SQL Server virtual servers are created per node, whereas there is a NetBIOS name and TCP/IP address for each SQL Server virtual instance. When failover occurs in this configuration, the entire SQL Server virtual instance fails over to the surviving node in the cluster dynamically.

■ **Heartbeat**—A single User Datagram Protocol (UDP) packet is sent every 500 milliseconds between nodes in the cluster across the internal private network. This packet relays health information about the cluster nodes as well as health information about the clustered application. If there is no response during a heartbeat to indicate that the node is alive, the cluster begins the failover process. In SQL Server 2012, this interval can be changed. This capability is useful when you are using a geographically dispersed cluster.

■ **Failover**—*Failover* is the process of one node in the cluster changing states from offline to online, resulting in the node taking over responsibility of the SQL Server virtual server. The Cluster Service fails over a group in the event that node becomes unavailable or one of the resources in the group fails.

- **Failback**—*Failback* is the process of moving a SQL Server virtual server that failed over in the cluster back to the original online node.

- **Quorum resource**—The *quorum* resource, also referred to as quorum configuration, determines the point at which too many cluster failures, such as nodes or, in some cases, a witness disk, will prevent the cluster from running.

- **Service and Applications**—Service and Applications, also referred to as resource groups, is a collection of cluster resources such as the SQL Server NetBIOS name, TCP/IP address, and the services belonging to the SQL Server cluster. A resource group also defines the items that fail over to the surviving nodes during failover. These items also include cluster resource items, such as a cluster disk. It is also worth noting that a resource group is owned by only one node in the cluster at a time.

- **Cluster resource**—*Cluster resources* contain vital information for the SQL Server virtual server and include its network TCP/IP addresses, NetBIOS name, disks, and SQL Server services, such as the System Attendant. These cluster resources are added to services or applications when the virtual server is created to form SQL Server virtual servers. With Windows Server 2008 R2, a clustered resource is known as an application and a service.

- **Dependency**—A *dependency* is specified when creating cluster resources. Similar to a dependency on SQL Server services, a cluster resource identified as a dependency indicates that a mandatory relationship exists between resources. Before a cluster resource is brought online, the resource defined as a dependent must be brought online first. For instance, the virtual server NetBIOS name is dependent on the TCP/IP address; therefore, the TCP/IP address of the virtual server must be brought online before the NetBIOS name is brought online.

- **Failover Cluster Management**—Failover Cluster Management in Windows Server 2008 R2 is a tool used by cluster and DBAs for accessing, creating, and administering Windows clusters. The Failover Cluster Administrator console is included in Windows Server 2008 R2 and can be launched from any active node within the cluster. Additional administration and management tasks include viewing, creating, and deleting services or applications, cluster resources, and nodes.

- **LUNs**—LUN stands for *Logical Unit Number*. It is used to identify a disk or a disk volume that is presented to a host server or multiple hosts by the shared storage device. Although there are shared storage controllers, firmware, drivers, and physical connections between the server and the shared storage, the concept is that the LUN or set of LUNs is presented to the server for use as a local disk. LUNs provided by shared storage must meet many requirements before they can be used with failover clusters, but when they do, all active nodes in the cluster must have exclusive access to these LUNs. More information on LUNs and shared storage is provided later in this chapter.

SQL Server AlwaysOn Failover Cluster Instances Prerequisites

SQL Server AlwaysOn FCIs is based on the Windows shared-nothing model. At least two or more nodes can control a single set of cluster resources that hold the application data. In the case of SQL Server 2012, this refers to a virtual instance where there is only a single copy of the database and logs residing on shared disks. Multiple nodes are available and can control these resources one at a time.

Before installing SQL Server clustering, ensure that the following prerequisites are met:

- A minimum of two servers running Windows Server 2008 R2 Enterprise or Datacenter Edition are required.

- At least two network interfaces are needed per server: one for the private heartbeat and the other for the public network. The public network should be the first network in the binding order.

- Shared disk storage is needed in order to deploy an FCI. This could be a storage area network (SAN), small computer system interface (SCSI), Serial Attached SCSI (SAS), or Internet SCSI (ISCSI) storage solution. All shared disks must be configured as basic because clustering does not support dynamic disks. In addition, all shared disks must be online, configured with NTFS, and be seen from all nodes.

- Distributed Transaction Coordinator (DTC) may need to be installed and configured prior to the installation of SQL Server. DTC is not required if only the Database Engine feature will be installed. However, it is required if the following components will be installed in conjunction with one another: Database Engine, Integration Services, and Shared components.

- Ensure that the shared disks have the same drive letter mappings or mountpoints on both nodes.

- If the Windows Server 2008 R2 Firewall is enabled, ensure that the SQL Server port, SQL Browser port, File and Printer Sharing (TCP 139/445 and UDP 137/138), and Remote Procedure Call (TCP port 135) have been allowed.

- The failover cluster feature of Windows Server 2008 R2 must be configured prior to the installation of SQL Server. The clustering groups and resources should be available, operational, and online.

- Separate service accounts should be used for both the Microsoft Failover Cluster Server and SQL Server services.

- All nodes should be identical and have the same service pack hot fixes and identical software. This includes the same processor version.

- NETBIOS must be disabled on all network adapters being used for the private heartbeat network.

- All hardware and software being used must be certified by Microsoft and be on its Windows Catalog and Hardware Compatibility List (HCL).

- Ensure that the network adapters are listed in the order in which they are accessed by network services. For example, the Public adapter should be listed first and then the Heartbeat adapter. This setting can be modified by going to Control Panel, Network Connections, Advanced, and Advanced Settings.

- Create a spreadsheet with the network names, IP addresses, and cluster disks that will be used for the administrative cluster and the High-Availability Services and Applications group or groups that will be deployed in the failover cluster. Each "Services and Application" group will require a separate network name and IPv4 or IPv6 address. The servers in the cluster must be using DNS for name resolution. All servers in the cluster must be in the same AD domain and should have the same domain role (recommended member server).

AlwaysOn Failover Cluster Instances Alternatives

The following list describes the types of clustering options available with SQL Server 2012:

- **Single FCI**—In a SQL Server 2012 single-instance failover configuration, the cluster runs a single virtual instance of SQL Server on all nodes in the cluster. Only one node in the cluster can service end users at any one time; this is known as the *active node*. The passive node, on the other hand, is on standby. If a failure occurs, the clustered resources are shifted to the passive node, which then begins to service clients. In this configuration, one virtual SQL Server instance is configured and shared by one or both nodes.

- **Multi-Instance Failover Cluster**—Each instance of SQL Server includes a separate installation of the full service and can be managed, upgraded, and stopped independently. If you want to apply a multiple-instance failover configuration, at least two instances of SQL Server need to be installed on the cluster, and each instance could be configured to run on a certain node as its primary server.

- **N+1**—This is a deviation of the multiple-instance AlwaysOn FCIs topology just discussed. In this scenario, more than two nodes are configured within the failover cluster solution and share the same failover node in the event of a failure. For example, in a four-node cluster, there may be three active nodes and one passive node. The passive node acts as a hot standby for any or all of the three active nodes. This solution reduces hardware costs because there isn't a one-to-one mapping between active and passive nodes. However, the major disadvantage is that the passive node must have enough hardware resources to take on the load of all three active nodes if they crash at the same time. The chances of three nodes crashing is highly unlikely; however, in the computer industry, we all know there is a first time for everything.

- **N+M**—Sometimes there is more than one active node in the cluster, so having a single dedicated failover node such as in the N+1 scenario is not sufficient enough to provide redundancy. Therefore, more than one standby node (M) is included in the cluster and available for failover. The number of standby servers is a trade-off between cost and reliability requirements.

- **Multi-subnet Failover Cluster**—A SQL Server multi-subnet failover cluster, also referred to as stretch clusters, is similar to a traditional SQL Server FCI. However, each node partaking in the FCI is connected to a different subnet or different set of subnets. These nodes can be in the same location or in geographically dispersed sites. A multi-subnet failover cluster supports either a single FCI or a multi-instance failover cluster.

- **Geographically dispersed (stretch) clusters**—SQL Server 2012 also offers geographically dispersed clusters. This scenario does not require a quorum drive to be configured on a shared disk, thus allowing active and passive nodes to be in separate physical locations. If you want to implement this solution, specific hardware is required from a vendor. This hardware must be certified from the vendor and Microsoft. This is a different list from the Microsoft Clustering HCL. Implementing geographically dispersed clusters is expensive. It is recommended to use database mirroring instead of building a geographical cluster because database mirroring is much cheaper and also provides high availability, seamless failover, and automatic client failover.

- **Guest Failover Cluster**—A guest failover cluster is similar to a traditional SQL Server FCI; however, each node partaking in the FCI resides on a virtualized guest operating system. Guest clustering supports either a single FCI or a multi-instance failover cluster.

Note

Server load and performance degradation should be analyzed when working with multiple instances within a single SQL Server failover cluster. You must ensure that the surviving node can handle the load if running more than one SQL Server instance on a single server. This can be achieved by manually tuning processor and memory settings within SQL Server Management Studio.

SQL Server 2012 AlwaysOn Failover Cluster Instances Scalability Metrics

A discussion on cluster basics is always essential because it can help organizations define a suitable operating system for their business. SQL Server 2012 Enterprise Edition on Windows Server 2008 R2 Enterprise or Windows Server 2008 R2 Datacenter Edition can support up to 16 nodes within a single cluster. SQL Server 2012 Standard Edition can support up to two nodes. AlwaysOn FCIs of SQL Server 2012 can be configured in two ways: a single-instance failover configuration or a multiple-instance failover configuration. SQL Server supports 25 instances on a failover cluster when using a shared cluster disk as the stored option and 50 instances if SMB file shares as the storage option is chosen.

> **Note**
>
> When implementing SQL Server multiple-instance AlwaysOn FCIs, you should be aware that each instance requires a separate virtual server, and each virtual server requires a separate clustered group with dedicated resources such as disks, network name, and IP address.

SQL Server 2012 Cluster-Aware Features

The SQL Server 2012 Database Engine Services, Analysis Services, and Full-Text Search features are cluster aware. This means that these features can be installed on a failover cluster, they have failover capabilities, and they show up as cluster resources in the Windows Server 2008 R2 Failover Cluster Management console. Unfortunately, Reporting Services and Integration Services are not cluster aware.

> **Notes from the Field: Combining AlwaysOn Failover Cluster Instances with Other SQL Server High-Availability Alternatives**
>
> Other SQL Server high-availability alternatives can be combined with AlwaysOn FCIs for maximum availability, business continuity, and disaster recovery. For example, CompanyABC may have a two-node FCI residing in its Toronto office. This cluster provides instance and database protection within the Toronto data center. Regulatory legislation such as the Sarbanes-Oxley Act may have a requirement that CompanyABC must maintain a disaster recovery site, and all production databases must be available in another location in the event of a disaster in the Toronto location. Therefore, CompanyABC can implement availability groups or database mirroring in conjunction with clustering and have replicas or mirror copies of the production databases from the Toronto location to its disaster recovery location in San Francisco. The production database would be available in San Francisco in the event of the total cluster failure (which is highly unlikely) or in the event that the Toronto site is unavailable. On a side note, availability groups or database mirroring is not the only other

high-availability alternative that works with AlwaysOn FCIs: Log shipping and replication can also be used.

Additional Elements of AlwaysOn Failover Cluster Instances

Some additional elements DBAs should be aware of include enhancements associated with the Quorum models on Windows Server 2008 R2 and the different types of shared storage available when configuring a failover cluster.

Windows Server 2008 R2 Failover Cluster Quorum Models

As previously stated, Windows Server 2008 R2 failover clusters support four different Cluster Quorum models. Each of these four models is best suited for specific configurations, but if all the nodes and shared storage are configured, specified, and available during the installation of the failover cluster, the best-suited Quorum model will be automatically selected.

Node Majority Quorum

The Node Majority Quorum model has been designed for failover cluster deployments that contain an odd number of cluster nodes. When determining the quorum state of the cluster, only the number of available nodes is counted. A cluster using the Node Majority Quorum is called a *Node Majority cluster*. A Node Majority cluster will remain up and running if the number of available nodes exceeds the number of failed nodes. As an example, in a five-node cluster, three nodes must be available for the cluster to remain online. If three nodes fail in a five-node Node Majority cluster, the entire cluster will be shut down. Node Majority clusters have been designed and are well suited for geographically or network dispersed cluster nodes, but for this configuration to be supported by Microsoft it will take serious effort, quality hardware, a third-party mechanism to replicate any back-end data, and a very reliable network. Again, this model works well for clusters with an odd number of nodes.

Node and Disk Majority

The Node and Disk Majority Quorum model determines whether a cluster can continue to function by counting the number of available nodes and the availability of the cluster witness disk. Using this model, the cluster quorum is stored on a cluster disk that is accessible and made available to all nodes in the cluster through a shared storage device using SAS, Fibre Channel (FC), or ISCSI connections. This model is the closest to the traditional single-quorum device cluster configuration model and is composed of two or more server nodes that are all connected to a shared storage device. In this model, only one copy of the quorum data is maintained on the witness disk. This model is well suited for failover clusters using shared storage, all connected on the same network with an even number of nodes. For example, on a two-, four-, six-, or eight-node cluster using this model, the cluster will continue to function as long as half of the total nodes are available and can contact the witness disk. In the case of a witness disk failure, a majority of the nodes will need to remain up and running. To calculate this, take half of the total nodes and add one; this will give you the lowest number of available nodes that are required to keep a cluster running. For example, on a six-node cluster using this model, if the witness disk fails, the cluster will remain up and running as long as four nodes are available.

Node and File Share Majority Quorum

The Node and File Share Majority Quorum model is similar to the Node and Disk Majority Quorum model, but instead of a witness disk, the quorum is stored on file share. The advantage of this model is that it can be deployed similarly to the Node Majority Quorum model, but as long as the witness file share is available, this model can tolerate the failure of half of the total nodes. This model is well suited for clusters with an even number of nodes that do not utilize shared storage.

No Majority: Disk Only Quorum

The No Majority: Disk Only Quorum model is best suited for testing the process and behavior of deploying built-in or custom services and/or applications on a Windows Server 2008 R2 failover cluster. In this model, the cluster can sustain the failover of all nodes except one, as long as the disk containing the quorum remains available. The limitation of this model is that the disk containing the quorum becomes a single point of failure, and that is why this model is not well suited for production deployments of failover clusters.

As a best practice, before deploying a failover cluster, determine whether shared storage will be used and verify that each node can communicate with each LUN presented by the shared storage device. When the cluster is created, add all nodes to the list. This will ensure that the correct recommended cluster quorum model is selected for the new failover cluster. When the recommended model utilizes shared storage and a witness disk, the smallest available LUN will be selected. This can be changed if necessary after the cluster is created.

Shared Storage for Failover Clusters

Shared disk storage is a requirement for SQL Server 2012 failover clusters when running on Windows Server 2008 R2 when using the Node and Disk Majority quorum and the Disk Only Quorum models. Shared storage devices can be a part of any cluster configuration, and when they are used, the disks, disk volumes, or LUNs presented to the Windows systems must be presented as basic Windows disks.

All storage drivers must be digitally signed and certified for use with Windows Server 2008 R2. One main reason for this is that all failover shared storage must comply with SCSI-3 Architecture Model SAM-2. This includes any and all legacy and serial attached SCSI controllers, Fibre Channel host bus adapters, and ISCSI hardware- and software-based initiators and targets. If the cluster attempts to perform an action on an LUN or shared disk and the attempt causes an interruption in communication to the other nodes in the cluster or any other system connected to the shared storage device, data corruption can occur, and the entire cluster and each SAN-connected system may lose connectivity to the storage.

When LUNS are presented to failover cluster nodes, each LUN must be presented to each node in the cluster. Also, when the shared storage is accessed by the cluster and other systems, the LUNs must be masked or presented only to the cluster nodes and the shared storage device controllers to ensure that no other systems can access or disrupt the cluster communication.

Shared Storage Requirements

There are strict requirements for shared storage support, especially with failover clusters. Storage Area Networks (SANs) or other types of shared storage must meet the following list of requirements:

- All Fibre Channel, SAS, and ISCSI host bus adapters (HBAs) and Ethernet cards used with ISCSI software initiators must have obtained the Designed for Microsoft Windows logo for Windows Server 2008 R2 and have suitable signed device drivers.

- SAS, Fibre Channel, and ISCSI HBAs must use Storport device drivers to provide targeted LUN resets and other functions inherent to the Storport driver specification. SCSIport drivers were at one point supported for two-node clusters, but if a Storport driver is available, it should be used to ensure support from the hardware vendors and Microsoft.

- All shared storage HBAs and back-end storage devices including ISCSI targets, Fibre Channel, and SAS storage arrays must support SCSI-3 standards and must also support persistent bindings or reservations of LUNs.

- All shared storage HBAs must be deployed with matching firmware and driver versions. Failover clusters using shared storage require a very stable infrastructure, and applying the latest storage controller driver to an outdated HBA firmware can cause a very undesirable situation and may disrupt access to data.

- All nodes in the cluster should contain the same HBAs and use the same version of drivers and firmware. Each cluster node should be an exact duplicate of each other's node when it comes to hardware selection, configuration, drivers, and firmware revisions. This allows for a more reliable configuration and simplifies management and standardization.

- When ISCSI software initiators are used to connect to ISCSI software- or hardware-based targets, the network adapter used for ISCSI communication must be connected to a dedicated switch, cannot be used for any cluster communication, and cannot be a teamed network adapter.

- For ISCSI shared storage, configure an additional, dedicated network adapter or hardware-based ISCSI HBA.

- Configure all necessary IPv4 and IPv6 addresses as static configurations. DHCP is supported but not recommended.

- Verify that any and all HBAs and other storage controllers are running the proper firmware and matched driver version suitable for Windows Server 2008 R2 failover clusters.

- If shared storage will be used, plan to utilize at least two separate LUNs: one to serve as the witness disk and the other to support DTC.

- Ensure that proper LUN masking and zoning has been configured at the FC or Ethernet switch level for FC or ISCSI shared storage communication, suitable for AlwaysOn FCIs. Each node in the failover cluster, along with the HBAs of the shared storage device, should have exclusive access to the LUNs presented to the failover cluster.

- If multiple HBAs will be used in each failover node or in the shared storage device, ensure that a suitable Multipath I/O driver has been installed. The Microsoft Windows Server 2008 R2 Multipath I/O feature can be used to provide this function if approved by the HBA, the switch and storage device vendors, and Microsoft.

- As required, test Multipath I/O for load balancing and/or failover using the appropriate diagnostic or monitoring tool to ensure proper operation on each node one at a time.

Types of Shared Storage

The final topic for storage that a DBA must fully understand is the different types of storage associated with Windows Server 2008 R2. The storage items consist of the following:

- SAS (Serial Attached SCSI) storage arrays
- Fibre Channel storage arrays
- ISCSI storage
- Multipath I/O

SAS Serial Attached SCSI Storage Arrays

SAS (Serial Attached SCSI) disks are one of the newest additions to the disk market. SAS storage arrays can provide organizations with affordable entry-level hardware-based Direct Attached Storage arrays suitable for Windows Server 2008 R2 clusters. SAS storage arrays commonly are limited to four hosts, but some models support extenders to add additional hosts as required. One of the major issues not with SAS but with Direct Attached Storage is that replication of the data within the storage is usually not achievable without involving one of the host systems and software.

Fibre Channel Storage Arrays

Using Fibre Channel (FC) HBAs, Windows Server 2008 R2 can access both shared and nonshared disks residing on a SAN connected to a common FC Switch. This allows both the shared storage and operating system volumes to be located on the SAN, if desired, to provide diskless servers. In many cases, however, diskless storage may not be desired if the operating system performs many paging actions because the cache on the storage controllers can be used up very fast and can cause delay in disk read-and-write operations for dedicated cluster storage. If this is desired, however, the SAN must support this option and be configured to present the operating system dedicated LUNs to only a single host exclusively. The LUNs defined for shared cluster storage must be zones and presented to every node in the cluster and no other systems. The LUN zoning or masking in many cases is configured on the Fibre Channel switch that connects the cluster nodes and the shared storage device. This is a distinct difference between Direct Access Storage and FC or ISCSI share storage. Both FC and ISCSI require a common Fibre Channel or Ethernet switch to establish and maintain connections between the hosts and the storage.

A properly configured FC zone for a cluster will include the World Wide Port Number (WWPN) of each cluster host's FC HBAs and the WWPN of the HBA controller(s) from the shared storage device. If either the server or the storage device utilize multiple HBAs to connect to a single or multiple FC switches to provide failover or load-balancing functionality, this is known as Multipath I/O, and a qualified driver for MPIO management and communication must be used. Also, the function of either MPIO failover and/or MPIO load balancing must be verified as approved for Windows Server 2008 R2. Consult the shared storage vendor, including the Fibre Channel switch vendor for documentation and supported configurations, and check the cluster HCL on the Microsoft website to find approved configurations.

ISCSI Storage

When organizations want to utilize ISCSI storage for Windows Server 2008 R2 failover clusters, security and network isolation is highly recommended. ISCSI utilizes an initiator or the host that requires access to the LUNs or ISCSI targets. Targets are located or hosted on ISCSI target portals. Using the Target Portal interface, the target must be configured to be accessed by multiple initiators in a cluster configuration. Both the ISCSI initiators and target portals come in software- and hardware-based models, but both models utilize IP networks for communication between the initiators and the targets. The targets will need to be presented to Windows as a basic disk. When standard network cards will be used for ISCSI communication on Windows Server 2008 R2 systems, the built-in Windows Server 2008 R2 ISCSI initiator can be used, provided that the ISCSI target can support the authentication and security options provided, if used.

Regardless of the choice of the Microsoft ISCSI initiator, software-based or hardware-based initiators or targets, ISCSI communication should be deployed on isolated network segments and preferably dedicated network switches. Furthermore, the LUNs presented to the failover cluster should be masked from any systems that are not nodes participating in the cluster by using authentication and IPsec communication as possible. Within the Windows Server 2008 R2 operating system, the ISCSI HBA or designated network card should not be used for any failover cluster configuration and cannot be deployed using network teaming software, or it will not be supported by Microsoft.

Hopefully by now it is very clear that Microsoft wants to support only organizations that deploy failover clusters on tested and approved entire systems, but in many cases, failover clusters can still be deployed and can function because the Create a Cluster Wizard will allow a cluster to be deployed that is not in a supported configuration.

> **Note**
>
> When deploying a failover cluster, pay close attention to the results of the Validate a Cluster Wizard to be sure that the system has passed all storage tests to ensure that a supported configuration is deployed.

Multipath I/O

Windows Server 2008 R2 supports Multipath I/O to external storage devices such as SANs and ISCSI targets when multiple HBAs are used in the local system or by the shared storage. Multipath I/O can be used to provide failover access to disk storage in case of a controller or HBA failure, but some drivers also support load balancing across HBAs in both standalone and failover cluster deployments. Windows Server 2008 R2 provides a built-in Multipath I/O driver that can be leveraged when the manufacturer conforms to the necessary specifications to allow for the use of this built-in driver.

> **Note**
>
> Support for parallel SCSI as a shared bus type has been deprecated in Windows Server 2008 R2 failover clusters. SAS is replacing parallel SCSI as a simple and low-cost cluster solution because Serial Attached SCSI (SAS) is the next evolution of parallel SCSI.

Implementing a Single-Instance SQL Server 2012 Failover Cluster

Based on the previous sections in this chapter, a number of prerequisites must be configured from a hardware and software perspective before we can start the implementation of a single-instance SQL Server 2012 failover cluster. When the prerequisite tasks are completed, the single-instance SQL Server 2012 failover cluster can be installed. SQL Server 2012 failover clusters are deployed using a series of high-level steps:

- Configure the shared storage for the failover cluster.
- Install the failover cluster feature.
- Run the Validate Cluster Configuration Wizard.
- Create the Windows Server 2008 R2 failover cluster.
- Implement DTC (optional depending on which SQL Server 2012 features will be installed).
- Install the first SQL Server 2012 failover cluster node.
- Add additional SQL Server 2012 failover cluster nodes.

The following example illustrates the implementation of a two-node SQL Server 2012 single FCI running on Windows Server 2008 R2 Enterprise Edition for a fictitious organization called CompanyABC.

> **Note**
>
> Tables 11.1 and 11.2 and Figure 11.1 depict the layout of the failover cluster, including settings that will be used for this example, Implementing a Single-Instance SQL Server 2012 Failover Cluster and the upcoming example, Implementing a Multiple-Instance SQL Server 2012 Failover Cluster.
>
> The values in the table include the cluster node names, drives, IP addresses, network card, and NetBIOS information used for this example in this chapter.

Table 11.1 **CompanyABC's SQL Server AlwaysOn Failover Cluster Instances Settings**

Item	Description
Cluster Nodes	
NODE 1 NETBIOS Name	TOR-CL01
NODE 2 NETBIOS Name	TOR-CL02
NODE 1 Public IP Address	10.10.50.3
NODE 2 Public IP Address	10.10.50.4
NODE 1 Private (Heartbeat) IP Address	192.168.0.1
NODE 2 Private (Heartbeat) IP Address	192.168.0.2
Windows Virtual Cluster Name	TOR-CLUS-SQL01
Cluster IP Address	10.10.50.15
SQL Server Virtual Instance01	
SQL Server Virtual Instance01 Name	TOR-CL01-SQL01\INSTANCE01
SQL Server Virtual IP Address	10.10.50.16
Instance01 Failover Components	Database Engine
SQL Server Virtual Instance02	
SQL Server Virtual Instance02 Name	TOR-CL01-SQL02\INSTANCE02
SQL Server Virtual IP Address	10.10.50.17
Instance02 Failover Components	Database Engine
Shared Storage Layout	
Quorum	Q Drive
Database Files - Instance01	E Drive
Database Logs - Instance01	L Drive
Database Files - Instance02	F Drive
Database Logs - Instance02	M Drive
DTC	Y Drive
Distributed Transaction Coordinator	
DTC Resource Name	TOR-CLUS-SQLDTC
DTC IP Address	10.10.50.18

Using the information in Table 11.1 and Figure 11.1, you can now turn your attention to preparing the operating system and configuring the Windows Server 2008 R2 failover cluster.

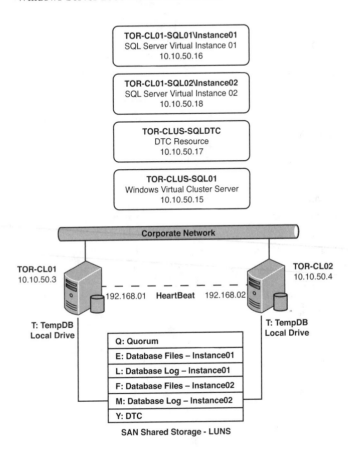

FIGURE 11.1
A multiple-instance failover cluster configuration including settings.

Preparing the Windows Server 2008 R2 Operating System for Each Node

For this example, creating a SQL Server 2012 single FCI starts out with a standard installation of Windows Server 2008 R2 Enterprise or Datacenter Edition. Follow these steps to build the operating system based on the assumption that Windows Server 2008 R2 Enterprise Edition will be leveraged:

1. For each node in the two-node cluster, install Windows Server 2008 R2 Enterprise Edition. Use the typical settings when setting up Windows Server 2008 R2.

2. Join the nodes to an Active Directory domain that will host the SQL Cluster, such as CompanyABC.

3. Create a heartbeat network between the two nodes by addressing a network interface card (NIC) on a different IP space from the production network. Isolate these heartbeat NICs to an isolated VLAN or a separate network switch, or use a crossover cable. This network will be used by the cluster nodes to communicate with each other. For this example, use the IP addresses based on the values in Table 11.1—192.168.0.1 for node 1 and 192.168.02 for node 2. Disable NetBIOS on the heartbeat adapters and ensure the public network card is the first in the network binding order.

4. Install the latest Windows service packs and hot fixes.

Configuring the Shared Storage for the Windows Server 2008 R2 Failover Cluster

The next step in the process is configuring the shared storage for the failover cluster. In the case of a two-node single-instance failover cluster, you need to configure several shared LUNs to be accessible by both nodes. These drives include the quorum drive, the DTC drive, 2x database drives, and 2x log drives, as shown in Table 11.2.

Table 11.2   **CompanyABC's Clustering Sample Storage Information**

Drive Description	Drive Letter	Location
Quorum	Q Drive	SAN
Database Files - Instance01	E Drive	SAN
Database Logs - Instance01	L Drive	SAN
Database Files - Instance02	F Drive	SAN
Database Logs - Instance02	M Drive	SAN
DTC	Y Drive	SAN
Tempdb	T Drive	LOCAL

> **Tip**
>
> When running Windows Server 2008 R2, it is possible to create a DTC resource for each cluster group within the failover cluster. This strategy prevents performance degradation and isolation for disparate applications within multiple cluster groups in the failover cluster. Independent of how many DTC resources you create, it is still recommended that the DTC resource should be placed on its own shared disk.

After the shared storage has been presented to the nodes in the failover cluster, it is necessary to initialize and format the disk using the Disk Management snap-in in Windows Server 2008 R2.

1. Open the Disk Management snap-in by choosing Start, All Programs, Administrator Tools, and Server Manager.

2. In Server Manager, expand the Storage icon and then select Disk Management.

3. Most likely the shared disks will be offline and are required to be in an online state to initialize them. Therefore, right-click each shared disk and select Online.

4. When the shared disks are online, right-click each shared disk and initialize them.

5. In the Initialize Disk dialog box, select the disks to initialize and select the partition style to use—either master boot record (MBR) or GUID partition table (GPT)—and then click OK.

> **Note**
>
> A GPT disk takes advantage of a GUID partition table disk partitioning system. GPT disks allow up to 128 partitions per disk, volume sizes of more than 2 terabytes, and in general are more reliable and scalable. MBR, which is the traditional partition style, has a limitation of four primary partitions and a maximum size of 2 terabytes.

6. The disks that are initialized as basic disks, however, show up as unallocated. On each shared disk, create a new simple volume, specify a volume size, assign a drive letter, and format the drive with NTFS. Be sure to create them as primary partitions and do not convert the disks to dynamic disks. For this example, the disk configuration is based on Table 11.2.

> **Note**
>
> Disks made available to a cluster must be configured as basic disks. A Windows 2008 R2 cluster can't access a dynamic disk.

Preparing the Windows Server 2008 R2 Failover Cluster

Now that the nodes are prepared and the shared storage is created, initialized, and formatted, the Windows Server 2008 R2 failover cluster can be formed. Be sure to have the following items ready for the cluster configuration: unique names for each node, unique name for the cluster identity, unique name for each SQL Server instance, and unique IP addresses for each of the names created previously. The following steps should be conducted in the order presented.

Installing the Windows Server 2008 R2 Failover Cluster Feature on Each Node

With Windows Server 2008 R2, the Failover Cluster feature is no longer installed by default. Before a failover cluster can be deployed, the necessary feature must be installed. To install the Failover Cluster feature, perform the following steps on a Windows Server 2008 R2 node:

1. Log on to the Windows Server 2008 R2 cluster node with an account with administrator privileges.

2. Click Start, All Programs, Administrative Tools, and then select Server Manager.

3. When Server Manager opens, in the Tree pane select the Features node.

4. In the Tasks pane, select the Add Features link.

5. In the Add Features window, select the Failover Clustering feature and click Install.

6. When the installation completes, click the Close button to complete the installation and return to Server Manager.

7. Close Server Manager and install the Failover Cluster feature on each of the remaining cluster nodes.

Running the Windows Server 2008 R2 Validate a Cluster Configuration Wizard

Failover Cluster Management is the new MMC Snap-in used to administer the Failover Cluster feature. After the feature is installed, the next step is to run the Validate a Configuration Wizard from the Tasks pane of the Failover Cluster Management console. All nodes should be up and running when the wizard is run. To run the Validate a Configuration wizard, perform the following steps:

1. Log on to one of the Windows Server 2008 R2 cluster nodes with an account with administrator privileges over all nodes in the cluster.

2. Click Start, All Programs, Administrative Tools, and then select Failover Cluster Manager.

3. When the Failover Cluster Management console opens, click the Validate a Configuration link in the Actions pane.

4. When the Validate a Configuration wizard opens, click Next on the Before You Begin page.

5. In the Select Servers or a Cluster page, enter the name of a cluster node and click the Add button. Repeat this process until all nodes are added to the list. For this example, TOR-CL01 and TOR-CL02 were specified. Click Next to continue.

6. In the Testing Options page, read the details that explain the requirements for all tests to pass in order to be supported by Microsoft. Select the Run All Tests (Recommended) option button and click Next to continue.

7. In the Confirmation page, review the list of servers that will be tested and the list of tests that will be performed and click Next to begin testing the servers.

8. When the tests complete, the Summary window will display the results and whether the tests passed. Click Finish to complete the Validate a Configuration wizard. If the test failed, click the View Report button to review the details of the results and determine which test failed and why.

> **Caution**
>
> You may stumble upon an error indicating that duplicate IP addresses were found on the Teredo Tunneling Pseudo-Interface network adapters among both nodes within the cluster. This error message is not accurate, but it will prevent you from going ahead and installing the failover cluster. The workaround is to disable the Teredo driver in Windows Server 2008 R2 Device Manager on all nodes within the cluster.

Creating the Windows Server 2008 R2 Failover Cluster

When the Windows Server 2008 R2 Failover Cluster is first created, all nodes in the cluster should be up and running. The exception to that rule is when failover clusters utilize direct attached storage, such as Serial Attached SCSI devices that require a process of creating the cluster on a single node and adding other nodes one at a time. For clusters that will not use shared storage or clusters that will connect to shared storage using ISCSI or Fibre Channel connections, all nodes should be powered on during cluster creation. To create the failover cluster, perform the following steps:

1. Log on to one of the Windows Server 2008 R2 cluster nodes with an account with administrator privileges over all nodes in the cluster.

2. Click Start, All Programs, Administrative Tools, and then select Failover Cluster Manager.

3. When the Failover Cluster Management console opens, click the Create a Cluster link in the Actions pane.

4. When the Create Cluster Wizard opens, click Next on the Before You Begin page.

5. In the Select Servers page, enter the name of each cluster node and click Add. When all the nodes are listed, click the Next button to continue.

6. In the Access Point for Administering the Cluster page, type the name of the cluster (**TOR-CLUS-SQL01**), specify the IPv4 address (**10.10.50.15**), and click Next, as shown in Figure 11.2.

7. On the Confirmation page, review the settings and click Next to create the cluster.

8. On the Summary page, review the results of the cluster creation process and click Finish to return to the Failover Cluster Management console. If there are any errors, click the View Report button to reveal the detailed cluster creation report.

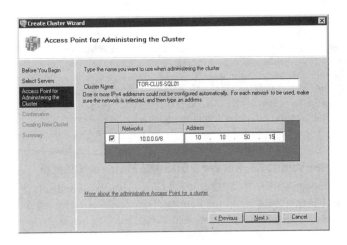

FIGURE 11.2
Defining the network name and IPv4 address for the failover cluster.

9. Back in the Failover Cluster Management console, select the cluster name in the Tree pane. In the Tasks pane, review the configuration of the cluster.

10. In the Tree pane, select and expand the Nodes folder to list all the cluster nodes.

11. Select Storage and review the cluster storage in the Tasks pane listed under Summary of Storage, as shown in Figure 11.3.

12. Expand Networks in the Tree pane to review the list of networks. Select each network and review the names of the adapters in each network. For example, public for the network that communicates to the public infrastructure and heartbeat for the private cluster network.

13. When you have completed reviewing the cluster, close the Failover Cluster Management console and log off the cluster node.

After the cluster is created, additional tasks should be performed before any Services and Application groups are created using the Failover Cluster Wizard. These tasks can include, but may not require, customizing the cluster networks, adding storage to the cluster, adding nodes to the cluster, changing the cluster Quorum model, and installing DTC.

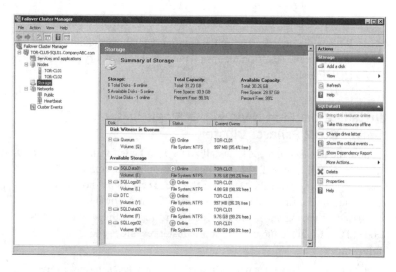

FIGURE 11.3
Displaying the dedicated cluster storage.

Installing DTC as a SQL Server AlwaysOn Failover Cluster Instances Prerequisite

As discussed earlier in the chapter, DTC is required as a prerequisite for installing SQL clustering. To create the DTC resource, follow these steps:

1. In Failover Cluster Management, expand the failover cluster created in the previous steps and then expand the Services and Applications node.

2. In the Actions pane, click Configure a Service or Application.

3. Read the information presented on the Before You Begin page and then click Next.

4. On the Select Service or Application page, select Distributed Transaction Coordinator (DTC) and then click Next.

5. On the Client Access Point page, specify a name for the DTC service and then a dedicated IP address. For this example, the DTC name is TOR-CLUS-SQLDTC, and the IP address is 10.10.50.17. Click Next to continue.

6. The next page is Select Storage. On this page, select the storage volume that you want to assign to the DTC clustered resource. For this example, use the DTC drive, which is the letter Y. Click Next to continue.

7. Review the settings on the confirmation page and then click Next.

8. Review the progress bar on the Configure High Availability page and then view the status on the installation on the Summary page and click Finish.

Installing the First Node in the Single-Instance SQL Server 2012 Failover Cluster

Follow the next set of steps to install AlwaysOn FCIs for the first virtual instance of SQL Server 2012. The features installed for this virtual instance are strictly for the Database Engine. These steps should be conducted on the first node of the Windows Cluster. The installation steps are based on the examples provided in Figure 11.1. Validate that the first node (TOR-CL01) is the owner for all cluster resources and then do the following:

1. Log in to the server with administrative privileges and insert the SQL Server 2012 media. Autorun should launch the SQL Server 2012 Installation Center landing page; otherwise, click Setup.exe.

2. To install a new SQL Server Failover Cluster installation, on the SQL Server Installation Center screen, first click the Installation link and then New SQL Server Failover Cluster Installation, as illustrated in Figure 11.4.

Note

If SQL Server's setup software prerequisites have not been met, the installation wizard will prompt and then install the prerequisites. After the prerequisites have been installed, the SQL Server installation process will resume. SQL Server 2012 software prerequisites may include hot fixes, .NET Framework, and the latest Windows Installer. In addition, system restarts may be required after SQL Server's setup software prerequisites are installed. If so, rerun setup after the reboot to continue with the SQL Server installation.

3. On the Setup Support Rules page, review the outcome of the System Configuration Checker. Ensure that all tests associated with the operation passed without any failures, warnings, or skipped elements. Alternatively, you can review a standard or comprehensive report by selecting the Show Details button or View Detailed Report. To continue with the installation, click OK.

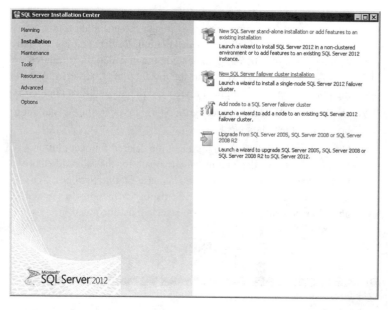

FIGURE 11.4
Selecting the option to install a new SQL Server failover cluster installation.

Note

During setup, the installation wizard will check to see if product updates are available to ensure that SQL Server is secure and performs optimally. If installation updates are found, click Install on the Install Setup Files page when prompted; if not, click Next to continue.

---

4. On the Product Key page, enter the SQL Server Product Key and click Next.

5. On the License Agreement page, accept the Licensing Terms. Alternatively, choose whether you want to participate in improving the product by sending feature usage to Microsoft and then click Next.

Note

The Install Setup Files page will be invoked, and the SQL Server installation wizard will scan for product updates. If updates are found, the wizard will download, extract, and install the setup files.

---

6. The Setup Support Rules page will be displayed again and will identify any outstanding items that may hinder the installation process
   associated with the SQL Server installation. Review and correct failures and warnings before commencing the installation. If failures are
   not displayed, click Next to start the installation. After any outstanding installations are complete, review the details and then click Next.

7. On the Setup Role page, specify the SQL Server Feature Installation
   option and then click Next.

8. On the Feature Selection page, select the desired failover cluster
   features to be installed and provide the path for the Shared Feature
   Directories. For this example, the Database Engine Services, SQL
   Server Replication, Full-Text and Semantic Extractions for Search,
   and Management Tools have been selected, as illustrated in
   Figure 11.5.

FIGURE 11.5

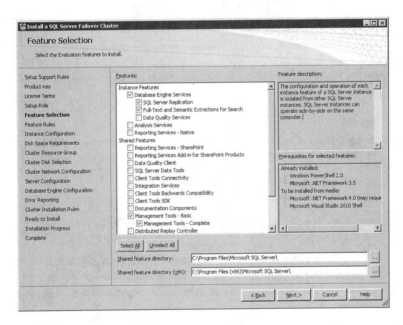

Specifying the SQL Server features to be installed.

9. On the Features Rules page, the installation wizard will attempt
   to find any final problems that could potentially block the setup
   operation. Review the report and then click Next to continue. If an

element failed, correct the issue and continue with the installation. Click the Show Details button or View Detailed Report if there is a need to review each rule checked and its correlating status.

10. On the Instance Configuration page, specify the SQL Server Failover Cluster Network Name, Instance Name, and Instance ID for the SQL Server FCI. In addition, provide the path for the Instance Root Directory and then click Next. For this example, the items specified in the Instance Configuration page are based on Table 11.3 and can be found in Figure 11.6.

Table 11.3 **CompanyABC's Instance Parameters**

Element Description	Element Value
SQL Server Failover Cluster Network Name	TOR-CL01-SQL01
Instance Name	Instance01
Instance ID	Instance01
Instance Root Directory	C:\Program Files\Microsoft SQL Server\

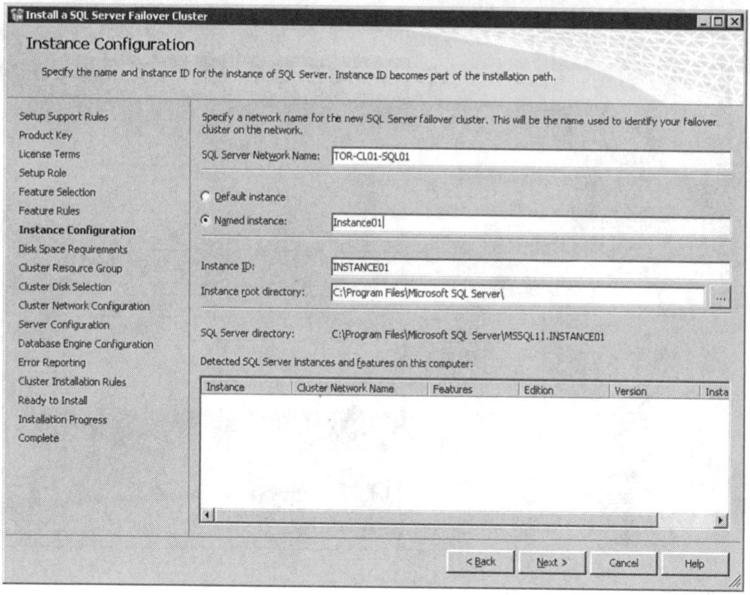

FIGURE 11.6
Configuring the SQL Server instance.

> **Note**
>
> Each instance name provided must be unique, and there can be only one default instance per SQL Server system.

11. The next page is the Disk Space Requirements. Review the disk space summary for the SQL Server components and features selected to be installed and then click Next.

12. On the Cluster Resource Group page, specify a name for the new SQL Server resource group, such as SQL Server Instance01, and then click Next. The resource group is where the new SQL Server virtual resources will be placed. This page also displays resource groups that are already in use.

13. Now you must specify the shared cluster disks that will be used with the new SQL Server failover cluster installation. For this example, the DatabaseFiles-Instance-01 and DatabaseLogs-Instance01 shared disks will be used. Click Next to continue, as shown in Figure 11.7.

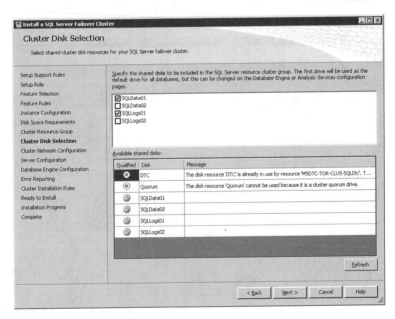

FIGURE 11.7
Specifying the cluster disk to be used for the failover cluster installation.

> **Note**
>
> By default, the first available disk located in the Available Shared Disks section will be selected for the installation. However, you can change this by specifying an alternative shared disk. Also, any disks already associated to another service or application, such as the quorum, will be unavailable.

14. A SQL Server 2012 failover cluster on Windows Server 2008 R2 supports both IPv4 and IPv6. On the Cluster Network Configuration page, first indicate which IP type will be utilized—IPv4 and/or IPv6—and enter a virtual IP address and subsequent subnet mask and then click Next. For this example, the IP address of 10.10.50.16 with a subnet mask of 255.0.0.0 was used.

> **Tip**
>
> When you're entering network configuration settings on a SQL Server 2012 cluster running Window Server 2008 R2, it is possible to obtain a dynamic IP address via DHCP for the virtual instance. Using DHCP addresses for mission-critical services is not an industry best practice; hence, it is not recommended.

15. The Server Configuration page includes configuration settings for both Service Accounts and Collation. On the Service Accounts tab, enter a valid low-privilege service account name and password for each service account. The Startup Type for each service account listed will be set to manual and cannot be changed. Before proceeding to the next step, click the Collation tab.

> **Tip**
>
> From a hardening perspective, Microsoft recommends entering a separate service account for each SQL Server component and feature being installed. In addition, the account specified should follow the principle of least privilege. For more information on selecting the desired service account and hardening a SQL Server implementation, see Chapter 7, "Hardening and Auditing a SQL Server 2012 Implementation."

16. On the Collation tab, enter the desired collation option for the Database Engine. It is possible to change default collation settings

used by the Database Engine and Analysis Services for language and sorting by selecting Customize. Click Next to continue.

17. The Database Engine Configuration page consists of three tabs. The tabs include Server Configuration, Data Directories, and FILESTREAM. On the first tab, in the Account Provisioning section, specify the Authentication mode, which consists of either Windows Authentication mode or mixed mode (SQL Server authentication and Windows authentication). If mixed mode is selected, enter and confirm the password for the Built-in SQL Server administrator account. The next step is to provision a SQL Server Administrator by either selecting the option Add Current User or by clicking Add and specifying a SQL Server administrator account.

18. The second tab, Data Directories, located still within the Database Engine Configuration page, is used for specifying the location of the default directories associated with the installation of this SQL Server instance. The directories include Data Root Directory, System Database Directory, User Database Directory, User Database Log Directory, Tempdb Directory, Tempdb Log Directory, and Backup Directory. Either maintain the default directories or specify a new directory for performance and availability. Either maintain the default directories or specify a new directory residing on the shared disks associated with the FCI.

Tip

During the installation, if you select to store the tempdb database on the local server, you will get a warning indicating that you have specified a local directory as the tempdb data or log directory for the FCI. To avoid possible failures during a failover, you must make sure that the same directory exists on each cluster node and ensure that the SQL Server service account has read/write permission on the folders.

---

19. The final tab on the Database Engine Configuration page is FILESTREAM. Here, decide whether you want to enable FILESTREAM. If FILESTREAM is enabled, additional parameters must be entered, such as Enable FILESTREAM for File I/O Streaming Access, Windows Share Name, and whether to allow remote clients to have streaming access to FILESTREAM data. Click Next to proceed.

20. On the Error and Usage Reporting page, help Microsoft improve SQL Server features and services by sending error reports and feature usage to Microsoft. Specify the level of participation and then click Next.

21. The final check will take place to ensure that the installation process will not be blocked. On the Cluster Installation Rules page, review for any outstanding errors or warnings and then click Next to continue.

22. Before commencing the SQL Server 2012 Installation, review the features to be installed on the Ready to Install page and then click Install. Take note of the Configuration File path location because the ConfigurationFile.ini file can be used to automate a similar installation.

23. When the installation process starts, you can monitor its progress accordingly. When the installation setup completes, review the success status based on each SQL Server feature and then click Next.

24. On the Complete page, review the location of the SQL Server summary upgrade log file and additional items that can be found in the supplemental information section. Click Close to finalize the installation. You may have to restart the computer after the setup process is complete, provided that one or more affected files have operations pending.

These steps conclude the installation of the first node associated with the single-instance failover cluster. As mentioned earlier, the SQL Server failover cluster installation is no longer a single-step process as the installation process since SQL Server 2008 is on a per-node basis. Therefore, in order to finalize the SQL Server failover cluster, the steps in the following section must be completed and repeated for every additional node(s) you plan on joining in the cluster.

Installing Additional Nodes in the Single-Instance SQL Server 2012 Failover Cluster

Based on conducting the steps in the previous section, we have successfully established the first node associated with the SQL Server 2012 failover cluster for TOR-CL01-SQL01\Instance01. As mentioned earlier, each node within the cluster is a peer and completely independent of one another. Therefore, we now have to conduct the following steps to add additional node(s) to the existing failover cluster configuration.

> **Note**
>
> The steps are very similar to adding the first node in the SQL Server 2012 failover cluster; however, the major difference is that you select the option Add Node to a SQL Server Failover Cluster instead of New SQL Server Failover Cluster Installation on SQL Server Installation Center.

1. Log in to the second node with administrative privileges and insert the SQL Server 2012 media. Autorun should launch the SQL Server 2012 Installation Center landing page; otherwise, click Setup.exe.

2. To install the additional node into the SQL Server failover cluster, on the SQL Server Installation Center page, first click the Installation link and then Add Node to a SQL Server Failover Cluster.

3. On the Setup Support Rules page, review the outcome of the System Configuration Checker. Ensure that all tests associated with the operation passed without any failures, warnings, or skipped elements. Alternatively, you can review a standard or comprehensive report by selecting the Show Details button or View Detailed Report. To continue with the installation, click OK.

4. On the Product Key page, enter the SQL Server Product Key and click Next.

5. On the License Agreement page, accept the Licensing Terms, and then click Next.

6. On the Install Setup Files page, the wizard will prompt if additional setup support files are required for the installation. If additional files are required, review the status of the files required and click Install.

7. The next page, Setup Support Rules, will identify any outstanding items that may hinder the installation process associated with the SQL Server cluster. Review and correct failures and click Next.

8. The Cluster Node Configuration page is now invoked. Use the drop-down box and select the name of the SQL Server instance name to join. The Name field of this node text box is prepopulated with the name of the associated node from which the installation is being conducted. For this example, use TOR-CL01-SQL01\Instance01. Click Next, as displayed in Figure 11.8.

9. The Cluster Network Name Configuration page is used to specify the IP type and IP address network settings for the failover cluster. For this example, the node being added is associated with the same subnet; therefore, additional IP addresses are not required, nor can they be added. After the network settings have been selected, click Next to Continue.

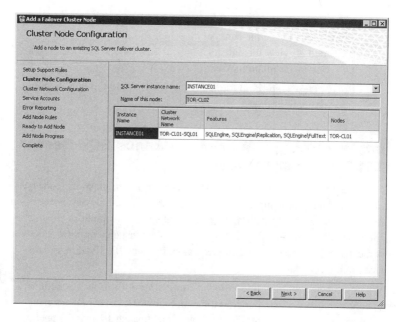

FIGURE 11.8
Specifying the name of the SQL Server instance to join.

10. On the Service Accounts page, specify the password for the accounts associated with each service and then click Next.

11. On the Error and Usage Reporting page, help Microsoft improve SQL Server features and services by sending error reports and feature usage to Microsoft. Specify the level of participation and then click Next.

12. Setup will run a final set of rules to ensure that the Add Node process will not be blocked. To continue, click Next on the Add Node Rules page.

13. Before adding the node to the existing failover cluster, in the Ready to Add Node page, review the components and features that will be installed and click Next.

14. Review the progress of the installation on the Add Node Progress page and then click Next to finalize the installation.

15. On the final page, complete information about the setup operation and the location of the summary log file, and the next steps are presented. Review this information and then click Close to exit the SQL Server Installation Wizard.

16. Repeat these steps if additional nodes exist within the SQL Server failover configuration.

Implementing a Multiple-Instance SQL Server 2012 Failover Cluster

One of the challenges that many DBAs face is trying to grasp the concept of how to deploy a multiple-instance SQL Server 2012 failover cluster. Implementing a multiple-instance failover cluster is as simple as creating a single-instance failover cluster; however, the new instance requires its own dedicated SQL server name, instance name, instance ID, IP address, and shared cluster disks.

When working with multiple-instance configurations, it is also beneficial to configure the preferred node settings in Failover Cluster Management for maximum performance. For example, SQL Instance01 may be operating on Node1, and SQL Instance02 would be operating on Node2.

> **Note**
>
> Before installing additional instances onto a failover cluster, ensure that the first instance has been successfully established by following the steps in the previous sections "Installing the First Node in the Single-Instance SQL Server 2012 Failover Cluster" and "Installing Additional Nodes in the Single-Instance SQL Server 2012 Failover Cluster."

The following example illustrates the implementation of a multiple-instance SQL Server 2012 failover cluster implementation using Windows Server 2008 R2 Enterprise Edition for CompanyABC. This example is based upon implementing the second instance, TOR-SQL02\Instance02, for the fictitious organization CompanyABC. Review Figure 11.1 to visualize this example. Moreover, this example is based on the data found in Table 11.1—specifically, items associated with the SQL Server Virtual Instance02.

Using the information in Figure 11.1 and Table 11.1, you can now turn your attention to the following steps to install the first node in the multiple-instance SQL Server 2012 failover cluster.

Installing the First Node in a Multiple-Instance SQL Server 2012 Failover Cluster

The first step is to use the New SQL Server Failover Cluster Installation Wizard to install the first node associated with the multiple-instance FCI. This can be achieved by following the steps in the "Installing the First Node in the Single-Instance SQL Server 2012 Failover Cluster" section earlier in the chapter. The steps within the wizard are very similar; however, the following steps are different:

1. When you get to the Instance Configuration page, specify the name and instance ID for the additional instance of SQL Server. The screen will also display detected SQL Server instances and features already found on the computer, such as TOR-CL01-SQL01, which was installed based on the previous steps. For this example, enter the following values as illustrated in Table 11.4 and Figure 11.9.

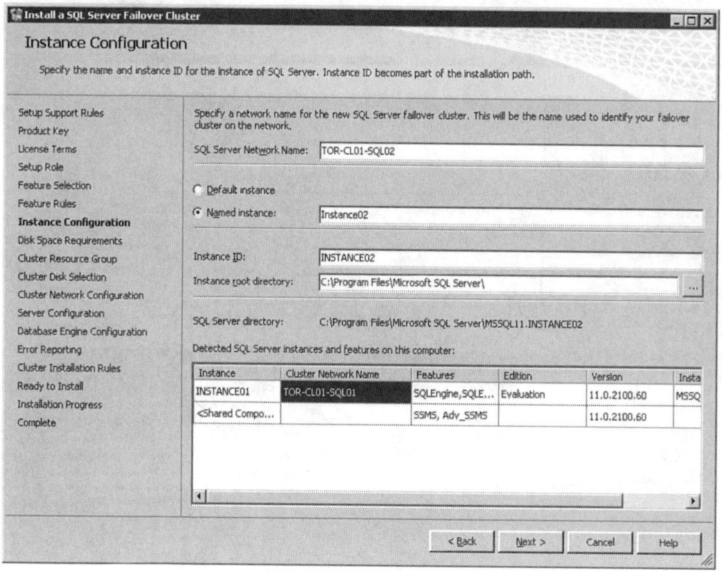

FIGURE 11.9
Specifying the name and instance ID for the instance of SQL Server.

Table 11.4 **Values for New Failover Cluster**

Element Description	Element Value
SQL Server Failover Cluster Network Name	TOR-CL01-SQL02
Instance Name	Instance02
Instance ID	Instance02
Instance Root Directory	C:\Program Files\Microsoft SQL Server\

2. On the Cluster Resource Group page, specify the new SQL Server cluster resource group name, such as SQL Server (Instance02).

3. On the Cluster Disk Selection, specify the shared disks to be used. Remember that each instance will require its own shared disk, such as SQLData02 and SQLLogs02 for this example, as illustrated in Figure 11.10.

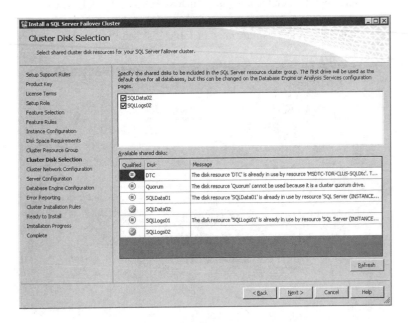

FIGURE 11.10
Specifying the shared cluster disk resources for the Instance of SQL Server.

4. On the Cluster Network Configuration page, you will need to specify an IP address for the new multi-instance failover cluster. For this example, 10.10.50.17 is used.

5. On the Data Directories tab on the Database Engine Configuration page, you will need to specify the directories for the new instance of SQL Server. Based on our example, the following directories are utilized, as illustrated in Figure 11.11.

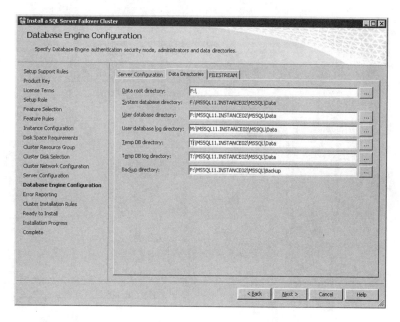

FIGURE 11.11
Specifying the data directories for the instance of SQL Server.

6. Now you must specify the shared cluster disks that will be used with the new SQL Server failover cluster installation. For this example, the DatabaseFiles-Instance-02 and DatabaseLogs-Instance02 shared disks are used. Click Next to finalize the steps in the remainder of the wizard.

Installing Subsequent Node(s) in a Multiple-Instance SQL Server 2012 Failover Cluster

Now that the first node affiliated with the multi-instance failover cluster has been established, the next step is to use the Add Node to a SQL Server Failover Cluster Wizard to add additional node(s). Again, the steps are very similar to installing additional nodes in the single-instance SQL Server 2012 failover cluster; however, on the Cluster Node Configuration page, use the drop-down box and select the name of the SQL Server instance to join, such as TOR-CL01-SQL02\Instance02, as displayed in Figure 11.12. As you can see from our example, the name of the node is automatically prepopulated in the Name of this Node text box.

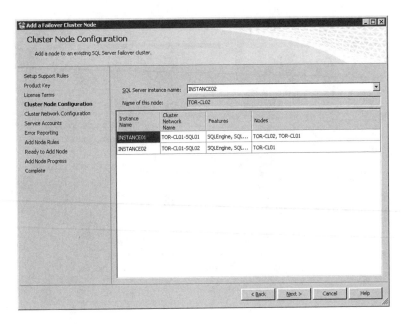

FIGURE 11.12
Adding a node to an existing SQL Server failover cluster.

Multi-subnet SQL Server 2012 Failover Cluster Overview

To recap, you no longer need to implement a stretch VLAN between subnets to deploy a multi-subnet FCI, given that SQL Server 2012 supports multi-subnet clustering out of the box. In SQL Server 2012, expect that each failover cluster node is either connected to a different subnet or a different set of subnets and that each failover cluster node either resides at the same location within the same site or each node resides in different sites residing in different graphical locations.

Anyone who has ever deployed a regular FCI will instantly recognize the process for deploying a multi-subnet SQL Server 2012 FCI is very similar. There is, however, an additional SQL Server network configuration step when using the wizard to deploy the first node and subsequent node(s) that are partaking in the multi-subnet failover cluster. Shared storage is not utilized when deploying a multi-subnet failover cluster. As a result, data between subnets or sites data must be replicated between the data storage solutions, such as a SAN.

Before we implement a multiple-instance failover cluster, review Figure 11.13; it shows a two-node multi-subnet FCI spanning two subnets. The first server resides in a Toronto datacenter on the 10.10.50.0/24 subnet, and the second node resides in a New York datacenter on the 10.10.60.0/24 subnet. Each node is connected to a local SAN, and SAN data is replicated between the two geographical locations. Because the cluster spans two subnets, two IP addresses are assigned to the Windows and SQL Server failover cluster. For example, the SQL Server virtual instance can have the following IP address: 10.10.50.20 from the 10.10.50.0/24 subnet, and another IP address, such as 10.10.60.20 from the 10.10.60.0/24 subnet. The failover cluster manager controls which IP address is online and offline, based on which node owns the resources. As a result, users, applications, and clients will connect to either 10.10.50.20 or 10.10.60.20, depending on the node controlling the failover cluster resources, which is depicted in Figure 11.14.

Note

Because multiple IP addresses are affiliated with the SQL Server FCIs virtual name, the online address changes automatically when there is a failover. In addition, Windows failover cluster issues a DNS update immediately after the network resource name comes online. The IP address change in DNS sometimes does not take immediate effect on clients because of DNS cache settings. If so, it is recommended to minimize the client downtime by configuring the HostRecordTTL in DNS to 60 seconds. Always consult with your DNS administrator before making any DNS changes because additional load requests can occur when tuning the TTL time with a host record.

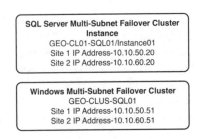

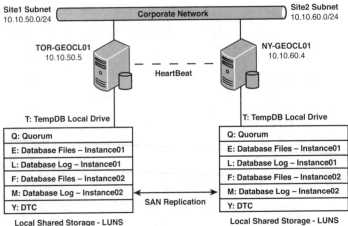

FIGURE 11.13
A SQL Server 2012 multi-subnet FCI.

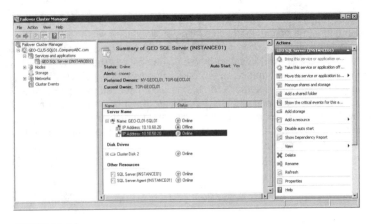

FIGURE 11.14
Failover Cluster Manager controlling which SQL Server virtual IP address is online and/or offline.

Implementing Multi-subnet SQL Server 2012 Failover Cluster

When implementing the multi-subnet cluster failover cluster, SQL Server Setup will detect the union of all subnets across all nodes associated with the multi-subnet failover cluster. Each node must be the possible owner of at least one IP address, and each IP address for the subnets will need to be entered during the installation process. Setup will set the IP address resource dependency for the virtual server name resource to OR.

Therefore, run the installation the same way you would set up a traditional cluster. However, when setting up the first node, on the Cluster Network Configuration page, you will have to specify the network settings associated with the subnet the first node is associated with. This is depicted in Figure 11.15. We have entered the address of 10.10.50.20 because this node is associated with 10.10.50.0/24 subnet. It is worth noting that it is not possible to configure the IP address for the other subnets at this time.

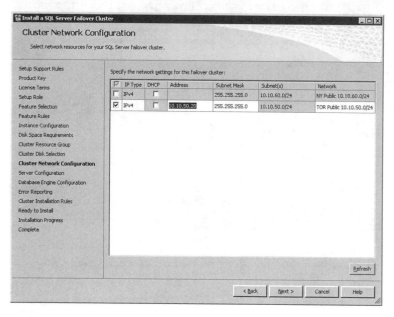

FIGURE 11.15
Configuring the network settings for the first node in a multi-subnet FCI.

After the installation associated with the first node in the multi-subnet FCI is complete, the next step is to install the additional node(s) associated with the multi-subnet FCI and specify the additional network settings based on the subnets of each additional node. When you run the Add Node to a SQL Server Failover Cluster Wizard in a multi-subnet FCI, you will need to specify the network settings for the additional node(s) when you get to the Cluster Configuration page. For this example, the 10.10.60 IP address was entered based on the 10.10.60.0/24 subnet, as illustrated in Figure 11.16. After the installation is complete, both IP addresses will be automatically provisioned and associated with the FCI in Failover Cluster Manager, as illustrated in Figure 11.17.

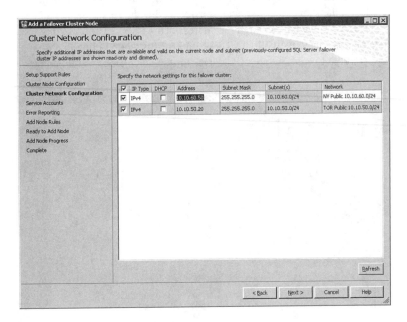

FIGURE 11.16
Configuring the network settings for the second node in a multi-subnet FCI.

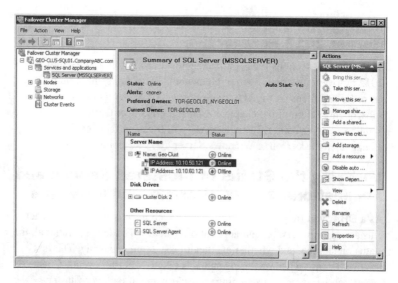

FIGURE 11.17
Viewing the two IP addresses associated with the SQL Server FCI in Failover
Cluster Manager.

Note

By default, a multi-subnet FCI uses the RegisterAllProvidersIP cluster
resource for its network name. In a multi-subnet configuration, both the
online and offline IP addresses of the network name are registered at the
DNS server. The client application retrieves all registered IP addresses
from the DNS server and attempts to connect to the addresses either in
order or in parallel. This means client recovery time in multi-subnet
failovers no longer depends on DNS update latencies. By default, the
client tries the IP addresses in order and, therefore, one at a time. When
the client uses the new optional MultiSubnetFailover=True parameter in
its connection string, it tries the IP addresses simultaneously and
connects to the first server that responds. This can help minimize the
client recovery latency when failovers occur. This optional parameter is
supported by the following data providers: SQL Native Client 11.0 and
Data Provider for SQL Server in .NET Framework 4.02 or later.

Managing Failover Clusters from a SQL Server 2012 Perspective

The following sections focus on management tasks after a SQL Server 2012 failover cluster has been implemented. These tasks are in no particular order and focus on the SQL Server aspect of AlwaysOn FCIs. The subsequent section of the chapter, "Managing Failover Clusters from a Windows Server 2008 R2 Perspective," will focus on failover cluster management tasks from a Windows Server 2008 R2 point of view.

Verifying the Status of Clustered Service and Applications, Nodes, Storage, and Networks

As a DBA, you frequently need to know which node is the owner of each clustered group, service, and application, whether a node is operational, the status on storage, and whether any health issues are occurring. The first level of defense when reviewing status is to check cluster events. Cluster events can be found by expanding a cluster name in Failover Cluster Management, and in the Tree pane selecting Cluster Events. Alternatively, the status of a failover cluster element can be determined by following these steps:

1. In Failover Cluster Management, select and expand the cluster name.

2. In the Tree pane, select either Services and Applications, Nodes, Storage, or Networks.

3. After the element has been selected, its status is displayed in the central pane.

Initiating Manual Service or Application Failovers

To manage service or application failovers, follow these steps:

1. In Failover Cluster Management, expand the desired failover cluster name.

2. Expand Services and Applications and then select a SQL Server Failover Service or Application, also formerly known as a cluster group.

3. From the Actions pane, select Move This Service or Application to Another Node and then specify the node to move to.

4. In the Please Confirm Action dialog box, read the warning message and select the option Move.

Managing SQL Server Failover Service Accounts

Sometimes a service account or a service account password needs to be changed for the FCI. Similar to a standalone SQL Server installation, all SQL Service account changes should be conducted with the SQL Server 2012 Configuration Manager tool. In addition, when you're working with clusters, all nodes must be online when a service account changes. Remember, when allocating service accounts, to follow the practice of least privilege and isolation; as a result, the SQL Cluster Service Account should be a different account from the service account running the Windows cluster.

Managing Preferred Owners of a Cluster Node and Group

For each service or application, you can assign a preferred owner. In the example, two instances of SQL Server are installed within the cluster. From a performance perspective, it is possible to configure node 1 to be the preferred owner of TOR-CL01-SQL/Instance01 and node 2 to be the preferred owner of TOR-CL01-SQL02/Instance02. Therefore, when the servers are brought online, the preferred owners maintain service operations of the desired service or application and SQL Server virtual instance. It is worth mentioning that preferred owners are necessary when you are running more than two nodes within a cluster. The preferred owners list dictates the failover behavior to the next available node based on the nodes in the list. For example, in an eight-node cluster, you may have dedicated passive standbys by having node 1 first fail over to node 3, then node 4, and then node 5.

> **Tip**
>
> When the cluster nodes are turned on, the cluster administrator tries to assign the SQL Server virtual server to the first node in the preferred owner's list. If this node is not available, the server is assigned to the next server name in the list. This behavior is similar to the failover process. If a failover occurs, the SQL Server cluster fails over to the available passive nodes based on the preferred owners list.

Follow the next set of steps to configure preferred owners for a SQL Server failover cluster. For example, based on our example, TOR-CL01-SQL01\INSTANCE01 should be homed in on node 1 (TOR-CL01), and TOR-CL01-SQL02\INSTANCE02 should be homed in on node 2 (TOR-CL02). Follow these steps to make preferred node changes on a failover cluster:

1. In Failover Cluster Management, expand the desired failover cluster name.

2. Expand Services and Applications, and then select a SQL Server failover service or application.

3. Right-click a SQL Server failover service or application and select Properties.

4. In the Service or Application Properties dialog box, specify the preferred owners of the service or application.

5. If more than one node is selected, use the Up and Down buttons to move the desired node owner to the top of the list.

6. To have the service or application automatically move to the particular node when the node becomes available, ensure that the Allow Failback option is selected on the Failover tab.

7. Click OK to finalize.

Managing AlwaysOn Failover Cluster Instances Failover Policies

There are a few ways to control how many failures will be allowed in a given period of time until the resource is left in a failed state. First, a global setting controls the threshold and period of a failover. This setting affects the whole service or application and dictates how many times a failover can occur during a period of time. Second, advanced parameters can be configured on each individual resource. Advanced parameters dictate whether the individual resource failure will affect the whole service or application and interval settings such as Looks Alive and Is Alive.

Follow these steps to configure failover settings for a service or application such as TOR-CL01-SQL01\INSTANCE01:

1. In Failover Cluster Management, expand the desired failover cluster name.

2. Expand Services and Applications, and then select a SQL Server Failover Service or Application you plan to modify.

3. Right-click the SQL Server failover service or application and select Properties.

4. In the Service or Application Properties box, select the Failover tab and specify the number of times the Cluster service will attempt to restart in a specified period.

5. Finally, in the Failback section, specify whether failback is allowed.

6. Click OK to finalize.

Managing AlwaysOn Failover Cluster Instances Failback Policies

When a primary node fails, you can control the behavior of the failback after the primary node becomes active again. The failback can be set to immediately, between a specific time of the day, or can be prevented. For mission-critical production clusters, it is a best practice to either prevent automatic failback or set the failback during hours of nonpeak usage. By using these settings, you can fail back the node manually or during nonpeak usage. As a result, the end-user community and application are not affected, resulting in downtime when the node fails back.

Follow these steps to configure failback settings for a service or application such as TOR-CL01-SQL01\INSTANCE01:

1. In Failover Cluster Management, expand the desired failover cluster name.

2. Expand Services and Applications and then select a SQL Server failover service or application.

3. Right-click a SQL Server failover service or application and select Properties.

4. In the Service or Application Properties box, select the Failover tab and specify whether failback is allowed.

5. If the Allow Failback option is selected, specify the option to fail back immediately or between a desired interval.

6. Click OK to finalize.

Managing AlwaysOn Failover Cluster Instances Failure Condition Property Settings

SQL Server 2012 introduces improved failure detection for the SQL Server FCI by introducing failure condition levels that allow you to configure a more flexible failover policy. The failure condition is rated on a level between 0 and 5:

- **Level 0: Condition No Automatic Failover or Restart**—This condition indicates that no failover will be triggered regardless of the failure. This level is recommended only for maintenance purposes.

- **Level 1: Condition Failover or Restart on Server Down—**
  A restart or failover will be triggered if the SQL Server service is
  unavailable.

- **Level 2: Condition Failover or Restart on Server Unresponsive—**
  A restart or failover will be triggered if the SQL Server service is
  unavailable or if the SQL Server instance is not responsive.

- **Level 3: Condition Failover or Restart on Critical Server
  Errors—**A restart or failover will be triggered if the SQL Server
  service is unavailable or if the SQL Server instance is not responsive
  or the system stored procedure returns a system error. This level is
  the default value.

- **Level 4: Condition Failover or Restart on Moderate Server
  Errors—**A restart or failover will be triggered if the SQL Server
  service is unavailable, if the SQL Server instance is not responsive,
  if the system stored procedure sp_server_diagnostics returns a
  system error, or if the system stored procedure returns a resource
  error.

- **Level 5: Failover or Restart on Any Qualified Failure
  Conditions—**A restart or failover will be triggered if the SQL
  Server service is unavailable or if the SQL Server instance is not
  responsive, if the system stored procedure returns a system error, if
  the system stored procedure returns a resource error, or if the
  systems stored procedure returns a query_processing_error.

Use Failover Cluster Manager to configure FailureConditionLevel property
settings:

1. Open the Failover Cluster Manager.
2. Expand the Services and Applications.
3. Select the desired Failover Cluster Instance.
4. Under the Other Resource section, right-click the SQL Server
   resource, and then select Properties from the menu.
5. Select the Properties tab, enter the desired value for the
   FailureConditionLevel property, and then click OK.

Removing SQL Server 2012 Nodes from an Existing SQL Server Failover Cluster

Because the SQL Server 2012 Enterprise Edition supports up to 16 nodes
in a cluster, sometimes you may need to remove a node from an existing

SQL Server 2012 clustered instance. Unfortunately, to achieve this goal, you must rerun Setup and from the SQL Server Installation Center, select the Maintenance link, and then double-click Remove Node from a SQL Server Failover Cluster. The good news is that the wizard for removing nodes is intuitive, and the removal process does not negatively affect surviving nodes in the cluster because each node is an independent peer. Run the following steps on the node or nodes you plan to evict from the SQL Server failover cluster:

1. On the SQL Server Installation Center screen, click the Maintenance link and then click Remove Node from a SQL Server failover cluster.

2. On the Setup Support Rules screen, review the outcome of the System Configuration Checker. Ensure that all tests associated with the operation passed without any failures, warnings, or skipped elements. Alternatively, you can review a standard or comprehensive report by selecting the Show Details button or View Detailed Report. Click OK to continue with the installation.

3. The Cluster Node Configuration page is now invoked. Use the drop-down box and specify an existing SQL Server failover cluster to modify. The Name field of this node text box is prepopulated with the name of the associated node from which the installation is being conducted. Therefore, you must conduct these steps from the node you plan to remove. Click Next.

4. On the Ready to Remove Node page, verify the SQL Server 2012 features to be removed as part of the removed node operation, and click Remove.

5. Review the remove node process on the Remove Node Progress page, and then click Next to finalize the removal process.

6. On the final page, complete information about the removal operation and the location of the summary log file, and the next steps are presented. Review this information, and then click Close to exit the SQL Server Installation Wizard.

Removing SQL Server AlwaysOn Failover Cluster Instances

There are multiple steps involved when removing SQL Server AlwaysOn FCI completely from a Windows Server 2008 R2 environment. First, use the Remove Node functionality found in the SQL Server Installation

Center, as depicted in the preceding section. Repeat this process on all SQL Server nodes within the cluster. Then, using Windows Server 2008 R2 Program and Features, remove each SQL Server element. Repeat steps for each node within the cluster. Windows Server 2008 R2 Programs and Features can be invoked by selecting Start, Control Panel, and then Programs and Features.

Managing Failover Clusters from a Windows Server 2008 R2 Perspective

The upcoming section includes step-by-step tasks for managing failover clusters from a Windows Server 2008 R2 perspective.

Administering Patch Management on a SQL Server 2012 Failover Cluster

Similar to a traditional nonclustered SQL Server, the operating system and SQL Server application require ongoing patch management to keep the servers up to date. Patch management includes installing service packs and critical hot fixes for both the operating system and SQL Server. When you're working in a clustered environment, each node within the cluster should have the same service pack and hot fixes to ensure consistency.

One of the main benefits of using failover clusters is your ability to install software, service packs, and critical updates on a node without interrupting service of the cluster. This process is known as a *rolling upgrade*. For example, when you install service packs and critical fixes for Windows Server 2008 R2, all the services or applications can be failed over to the second node, and the installation can then be conducted on the first node without affecting client operations. The node can be rolled back to node 1, and Windows Server 2008 R2 service packs and critical fixes can be applied to the second node. The rolling upgrade strategy has been reintroduced in SQL Server 2012.

Pausing and Resuming a SQL Server Cluster Node

When you're conducting maintenance or rolling upgrades, it is common to pause a node. When a node is paused, the existing services or applications and resources stay online; however, additional groups and resources cannot be brought online. Follow these steps to pause and resume a SQL Server cluster node:

1. In Failover Cluster Management, expand the desired failover cluster name.

2. Expand the Node tree.

3. Right-click the node you plan to modify and select Pause.

4. Repeat the steps, and choose Resume to recommence the node.

Adding Additional Windows Nodes to the Cluster

If additional Windows nodes need to be added to the cluster after the initial cluster creation process, perform the following steps:

1. In Failover Cluster Management, select and expand the cluster name.

2. Select and expand Nodes in the Tree pane.

3. Right-click Nodes and select Add Node.

4. When the Add Node Wizard opens, click Next on the Before You Begin page.

5. In the Select Server page, type the name of the cluster node and click the Add button. After the node has been added to the list, click Next to continue.

6. In the Confirmation page, review the names of the node or nodes that will be added, and click Next to continue.

7. When the process completes, review the results in the Summary page and click Finish to close the wizard.

Adding Storage to the Cluster

When shared storage is used with failover clusters, all of the LUNs or targets presented to the cluster hosts may not have been added to the cluster during the initial configuration. When this is the case, and additional storage needs to be added to the cluster, perform the following steps:

1. In Failover Cluster Management, select and expand the cluster name.

2. In the Tree pane, select Storage, right-click, and select Add a Disk.

3. If suitable storage is ready to be added to the cluster, it will be listed in the Add Disks to a Cluster window. If a disk is listed, check the box next to the desired disk or disks and click OK to add the disk(s) to the cluster.

4. When the process completes, if necessary change the drive letter of the new disk.

5. Close the Failover Cluster Management console.

6. Click the Start button and select Computer.

7. Review the list of disks on the cluster node and note that disks managed by the cluster are listed as clustered disks instead of local disks. This is a distinct change from server clusters in previous versions of Windows Server.

8. Close the Explorer windows and log off the server.

Managing Cluster Drive Dependencies

Unless otherwise specified, a SQL Server virtual instance uses only one shared hard drive during the installation of SQL Server AlwaysOn FCIs. Therefore, even though additional share drives are available in the cluster, such as the log and backup drives, a SQL Server instance cannot leverage those shared drives unless each additional shared drive is added as a resource dependency for the SQL Server Name clustered resource in Failover Cluster Management. These tasks should be configured prior to installing a SQL Server failover cluster. However, if they haven't been, these steps are a great way for adding additional shared disks to an existing cluster.

> **Note**
>
> In the past, you had to take the service or application offline when adding additional shared disk resources. However, when running AlwaysOn FCIs with Windows Server 2008 R2, this is no longer the case.

To add cluster drive dependencies, conduct the following steps in Failover Cluster Management:

1. In Failover Cluster Management, expand the desired failover cluster name.

2. Expand Services and Applications, and then select SQL Server Name resource, which is located in the central pane.

3. From the Actions pane, select Properties and then the Dependencies tab.

4. On the Dependencies tab, click Insert and select the desired shared disk, such as DatabaseLogs-Instance01.

5. Click Apply, and then Close to finalize this task.

6. Run the Show Dependency Report from the Action pane to verify that the newly added resource dependency drives are available to SQL Server.

Cluster Quorum Configuration

If all of the cluster nodes and shared storage was available during the creation of the cluster, the best-suited Quorum model was automatically selected during the cluster creation process. When the existing cluster quorum needs to be validated or changed, perform the following steps:

1. In Failover Cluster Management, select and expand the cluster name.

2. In the Tree pane, select the Cluster name, and in the Tasks pane, the current Quorum model will be listed.

3. Review the current Quorum model and if it is correct, close the Failover Cluster Management console.

4. If the current Quorum model is not the desired model, right-click the cluster name in the Tree pane, click More Actions, and select Configure Cluster Quorum Settings.

5. In the Select Quorum Configuration page, select the option button of the desired Quorum model or the recommended model, and then click Next to continue.

6. If a Quorum model contains a witness disk or file share, select the designated disk or specify the path to the file share and click Next.

7. In the confirmation page, review the settings and click Next to update the Cluster Quorum model for the Failover Cluster.

8. Review the results in the Summary page and click Finish to return to the Failover Cluster Management console.

Summary

AlwaysOn FCIs is a great high-availability alternative for maintaining maximum uptime for mission-critical databases and the whole SQL Server instance. Failover is seamless and transparent to end users and clients. The correct clustering topology must be selected based on Service Level Agreements, availability requirements, and budgets.

Best Practices

- Before installing SQL Server AlwaysOn FCIs, understand the prerequisites and verify that the clustering hardware is supported and certified by both the hardware vendor and Microsoft.

- Leverage the Cluster Validation Tool included with Windows Server 2008 R2 to ensure that all nodes within the cluster meet the prerequisites for deploying AlwaysOn FCIs.

- Use identical hardware for all nodes in the cluster. This includes processor, memory, and firmware.

- Configure AlwaysOn FCIs Feature from a Windows Server 2008 R2 perspective prior to SQL Server 2012 AlwaysOn FCIs.

- Ensure disk drive letters are identical on all nodes within the cluster.

- Avoid having the quorum resource and other cluster resources share the same disk.

- Ensure that the public network adapter is the first adapter in the network binding list.

- Disable NETBIOS on the private/heartbeat network adapters.

- Disable write-back caching on host controllers.

- Do *not* configure dynamic disks because clustering supports only basic disk configurations.

- Determine whether a single-instance or multiple-instance configuration will be implemented. Plan the disk layout accordingly while taking future growth into account.

- Identify which SQL Server features will be installed.

- Do *not* use the same service account for Windows and SQL Server AlwaysOn FCIs.

- Configure dependencies for shared disks so that they can be recognized and leveraged by SQL Server 2012.

- Before using multiple instances, understand the impact of multiple-instance configurations and performance degradation on the surviving node if a failover occurs.

- Change the service accounts only via SQL Server Configuration Manager.

- Do not configure DTC resources within the same service or application as the SQL Server virtual instances.

- Use the SQL Server Installation Center to modify a SQL Server failover cluster installation.

- Ensure that each virtual server name is unique on the Active Directory domain.

- Understand the benefit and impact associated with the different quorum models included in Windows Server 2008 R2.

- For advanced SQL Server 2012 AlwaysOn FCIs installations, use the planning and deployment tools included with the SQL Server Installation Center.

CHAPTER 12

Implementing and Managing Database Mirroring

This chapter takes a systematic look at database mirroring, one of the high-availability alternatives offered with SQL Server 2012. Database mirroring offers increased database availability and database protection by providing and maintaining a hot standby database on another instance of SQL Server. A key point to note is that the mirror database is an exact copy of the principal database. With database mirroring, continuous support is given to organizations, bolstering operations by decreasing downtime and reducing data loss.

To ensure that organizations can reap the full benefits of database mirroring, the topics in this chapter are geared toward giving you the knowledge necessary to understand the full potential of database mirroring and how it meets different business scenarios, as well as how to implement and maintain it successfully. Specifically, the chapter focuses on an overview of database mirroring, terminology, and ways to use database mirroring. The middle sections of the chapter focus on database mirroring configuration and administration. The final sections of the chapter discuss how to manage and monitor database mirroring.

Note

With SQL Server 2012, a majority of the high availability and disaster recovery investments have been tailored toward AlwaysOn, specifically the new availability group capability. Therefore, it is recommended to leverage availability groups over database mirroring because availability groups offer superior functionality such as multiple replicas, a single virtual network name for the availability group, the ability for multiple databases to failover as a single unit, and the capacity for active secondaries that support read operations.

Caution

AlwaysOn Availability Group is the primary high availability and disaster recovery feature for databases and will replace database mirroring technology over two releases.

SQL Server 2012 Database Mirroring Overview

As mentioned earlier, database mirroring offers increased database availability and database protection by providing and maintaining a hot standby database on another instance of SQL Server 2012. Its usefulness is best witnessed when a failure takes place on a primary database. In this situation, the standby database becomes active, and clients are redirected without the organization experiencing data loss or downtime.

Database mirroring is also commonly used to meet disaster recovery requirements and, therefore, should not be recognized only as an availability mechanism for a local site. When database mirroring becomes an integral part of an organization's disaster recovery plan, a hot or warm standby database is typically placed in a physical location other than the primary active database.

Note

The primary database is commonly referred to as the *principal* database, and the hot or warm standby is referred to as the *mirror* database.

The principal database handles client activity, whereas the mirror database receives continuous transaction log changes through a dedicated and secure TCP endpoint. This process keeps the mirror database up to date and ready to take on client operations in the event of a failure. Depending on the organization's requirements, database mirroring can be configured for either synchronous or asynchronous operations.

Figure 12.1 depicts the internals of a database mirroring session.

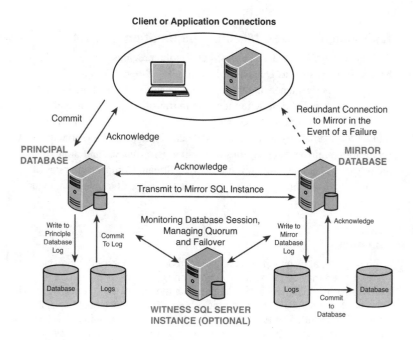

FIGURE 12.1
Overview of database mirroring.

Many DBAs find similarities between database mirroring and log shipping. They often refer to database mirroring as real-time log shipping or log shipping on steroids. However, in database mirroring, unlike log shipping, the primary server does not ship the logs to the standby server based on a time increment. Database mirroring transactions are continuously sent and committed between the principal and mirror; therefore, the databases are kept up to date and support automatic failover. However, log shipping offers the potential for multiple secondaries, whereas database mirroring is a one-to-one mapping. Again, as mentioned earlier, AlwaysOn Availability Groups is probably the best approach to take when deploying SQL Server 2012.

> **Note**
>
> It is not possible to configure a database mirroring session on the SQL Server system databases—that is, the master, msdb, tempdb, or model databases.

Additional Database Mirroring Information for DBAs

SQL Server 2012 includes features found in the previous versions of database mirroring, such as Database Mirroring Log Stream Compression. Application performance and throughput is enhanced over limited WAN connections because transaction log data in transit from the principal server to the mirrored server is extremely compressed. By compressing transaction log data by default, more data can be sent from the principal server to the mirrored server, thus increasing performance, and more log records can be shipped in a given time. Log Stream Compression rates of at least 13 percent or more have been achieved in specific lower-bandwidth networks.

> **Caution**
>
> The only caveat when using Database Mirroring Log Stream Compression is that there may be increased overhead on the processor because the processor must compress and decompress the logs, which translates to higher CPU usage. Depending on the workload, CPU usage could double compared to not using log compression. If WAN utilization and saturation is not an issue, Log Stream Compression can be disabled with Trace Flag 1463. The behavior returns to the same functionality as in SQL Server 2005.

Automatic page repair and recovery from corrupted pages is feature for database mirroring, which was introduced with SQL Server 2008. From a high level, the SQL Server hosting the mirrored database will try to resolve specific types of errors and corruption that prevent a data page from being read. If an error is detected, the server will attempt to obtain a fresh copy of the data and replace the corrupted data page, thus increasing data consistency among the principal and mirror databases and minimizing a database outage. It is typical to see an 823 or 824 error in the SQL Server logs, indicating that an error took place causing an automatic page repair attempt. These errors are subsequently followed by an event indicating that SQL Server 2012 successfully repaired the physical page by obtaining a copy from the partner. Error 823 represents a cyclic redundancy check due to failed data, and error 824 indicates logical errors.

Note

Automatic recovery from corrupted pages can only try to successfully resolve a failed data page when one or more of the following errors occur: page has been marked as restore pending, logical errors, or a cyclic redundancy check (CRC). These errors are also referred to by number: 823, 824, and 829.

Database Mirroring Terminology

Although you may be eager to install SQL Server 2012 database mirroring, you should take the time to fully understand all the new terminology and components that make up this new high-availability solution. By doing this, you and your organization can avoid running into roadblocks and will have an easier time with the installation. To prepare yourself for the installation, review the following terms regarding database mirroring:

- **Principal database**—The primary server in a database mirroring solution. This server maintains a live copy of the database that is accessed by clients and applications.

Note

The principal database must reside on a separate instance of SQL Server than the mirror database.

- **Mirror database**—The target database, which reflects all the changes of the principal database through a secure dedicated channel. The mirror database is a hot or warm standby and is continuously updated by transferring transaction logs from the principal database in chunks.

Note

The Mirror SQL Server instance does not require a SQL Server license if the server is strictly used as a standby.

- **Witness server**—An optional component in a database mirroring session. Typically, this component resides on a dedicated SQL

Server instance independent of both the principal database and the mirroring database servers. The witness facilitates the quorum role and monitors the database mirroring session. It initiates a failover from the principal to the mirror database in the event of a disaster. You can view the witness server as a requirement to support automatic failovers between the principal and mirror database instances. The Express Edition of SQL Server 2012 can host the Witness Server role.

- **Quorum**—The *quorum* monitors the state of a mirroring session. It controls the failover process based on communication among the principal, mirror, and witness databases. The principal server maintains the primary role of owning the database by maintaining quorum with either the mirror or witness. At least two servers are required to form a quorum; if the principal loses quorum with the mirror and/or the witness, a failover is initiated.

- **Synchronous/asynchronous**—A database mirroring session can transfer data between the principal database and mirror database by either a synchronous or an asynchronous commit operation. When you use the *synchronous* transfer mechanism, a transaction is successfully completed when it is committed on the principal and the principal receives an acknowledgment from the mirror that the same transaction has been written and committed. This process guarantees transactional consistency between the principal and mirror; however, transaction commits and client performance may be hindered based on the network speed, mirror location, and available bandwidth between the principal and mirror server instances.

- **Asynchronous transfer mechanism**—This commits transactions to the principal database much faster because it does not require an acknowledgment from the mirror. This process does not guarantee transactional consistency between the principal and mirror.

- **Automatic and manual failover**—Database mirroring supports both an automatic and manual failover process between the principal and mirrored databases. The type of failover is dictated by the type of database mirroring configuration mode selected, whether a witness server is present, and the type of client used.

- **Transparent client redirect**—In the event of a failure, clients and applications automatically redirect from the principal database to the mirror database, resulting in minimal downtime. Be aware that automatic failover requires SQL client based on the .NET and SQL Server Native Client (SNAC) providers/libraries. Basically, you should be in good shape if you are using SQL 2005 client libraries and later.

- **Database mirroring endpoint**—SQL Server 2012 uses endpoints to achieve secure server-to-server communication and authentication over the network. When you're configuring database mirroring, a dedicated endpoint is required exclusively for mirroring communications between both the principal and mirror database servers.

Database Mirroring Configuration/Operating Modes

Following are the database mirroring configuration and operating modes:

- **High Availability**—This database mirroring operating mode is also known as *High Safety with Automatic Failover* (synchronous with a witness). It provides maximum availability for a database mirroring session by using a synchronous form of mirroring. This operating mode requires a witness and supports automatic detection and automatic failover in the event the principal database is unavailable. Client performance is affected by the network speed and distance between the principal and mirror servers.

- **High Protection**—High protection is also referred to as *High Safety Without Automatic Failover* (synchronous without a witness). Like the high-availability operating mode, high protection uses a synchronous form of mirroring but does not require a witness. It does not require a witness SQL Server instance because failover is manual. With this mode, just as in the high-availability operating mode, principal performance is affected between the principal and mirror server based on network speed and distance.

- **High Performance**—High performance is the final operating mode and is also referred to as *High Performance Asynchronous*. High performance uses an asynchronous form of mirroring. In this situation, the principal server does not wait for confirmation that the transactions have been successfully committed to the mirror database instance. This increases performance because the network speed and distance are not factors. This solution does not require a witness. Therefore, there is no automatic detection or automatic failover as in high-availability mode.

Summary of Database Mirroring Configuration Modes

Table 12.1 provides an easy-to-read summary of the database mirroring configuration modes, detection levels, and failover process; it also indicates whether a witness server is required.

Table 12.1 **Database Mirroring Configuration Modes**

Database Transaction Mirroring Type	Automatic Detection	Automatic or Manual Failover	Synchronous or Asynchronous Modes	Requires Witness	Safety
High Availability	Yes	Automatic	Synchronous	Yes	Off
High Protection	No	Manual	Synchronous	No	Full
High Performance	No	Manual	Asynchronous	No	Full

> **Note**
>
> Asynchronous Database Mirroring (High-Performance Mode) is supported only by SQL Server 2012 Enterprise Edition.

When you use high-availability and high-protection modes, principal performance is affected by network speed, distance, and available bandwidth. Performance is not adversely affected when you use high performance. The mode you select ultimately determines how your organization wants to handle synchronization and failover processing.

SQL Server Database Mirroring Prerequisites

Configuring database mirroring is not as simple as clicking through a few pages of a SQL Server installation wizard. A number of prerequisite steps must be fulfilled before a database mirroring session can be configured and implemented. Following are the prerequisites:

- Register the principal, mirror, and witness SQL Server 2012 instances to ensure connectivity is present. The principal and mirror servers should be running the same edition of SQL Server 2012. Based on the features required, the Standard or Enterprise Edition can be used.
- The recovery model on the principal database must be set to Full.
- A full backup of the principal database is required.
- The mirror database needs to be initialized prior to implementing database mirroring by conducting a restore using the NORECOVERY

option. All transaction logs taken after the full backup must also be restored.

- The database names for both the principal and mirror database must be identical.

- The server hosting the mirrored database requires adequate disk space.

When SQL Server 2012 Database Mirroring Is Desirable

Some of the key driving factors for implementing database mirroring with SQL Server 2012 are as follows:

- There is a need to provide high-availability support for a specific database but not for an entire instance of SQL Server.

- A seamless failover that does not affect client applications and end users is required.

- An automatic failover that does not require intervention from a database administrator is favorable.

- High availability for a database in another physical location other than the principal is required. Note that there is no distance limitation with mirroring, but you must take available bandwidth and the amount of transactions into consideration.

- There is a need for high availability, and the organization does not have identical servers and shared storage, which is an expensive requirement for AlwaysOn Failover Clustering Instance (FCI).

- There is a need to fulfill the business continuity and disaster recovery requirements by placing and maintaining a redundant, up-to-date database in a different physical location than the principal.

- There is a need to remove the single point of failure intrinsic in failover clusters. The single point of failure is typically the shared storage because it maintains only one copy of the production data.

- Database mirroring can be used if there is a need to conduct a rolling upgrade of a SQL Server participating in a mirroring session without impacting database operations.

There are many other reasons organizations may turn to database mirroring. The first step your organization should take is to identify the gaps between the current and desired states of your business and then determine whether data mirroring fulfills your high-availability business goals.

Witness Server Placement

When an organization decides to use a witness server for high availability and automatic failure, it is often challenged with where to place the server. If the database mirroring session is configured over a wide area network (WAN), the witness can be placed either in the site with the principal or the site with the mirror. It is recommended to place the witness server in the same site as the mirror server. The reason is that if a site failure occurs where the principal resides, the witness server will still be operational and can initiate the failover with ease. On the other hand, some organizations place the witness server in the same site as the principal server because the network may not be reliable between the two sites. For these organizations, placing the principal and witness together minimizes unnecessary failovers due to network glitches.

Finally, if your organization is using database mirroring as a high-availability alternative, the witness server should be configured on a dedicated server that is not the principal or mirror. Placement on a dedicated server in this situation protects against hardware failure. It is important to mention that even if the witness is placed on a separate SQL Server instance, but the instance resides on the same server as the principal or mirror, you run into problems. If the physical hardware crashes, both instances fail, and the witness cannot conduct an automatic failover, resulting in a longer downtime. Finally, the witness server can be placed on the SQL Server 2012 Express Edition to reduce licensing and management costs.

To mitigate false failovers between two sites, some organizations place the witness in a third site or stick with the Microsoft recommendation of using high performance mode, also known as asynchronous database mirroring.

It is worth noting that a witness server can run on any reliable system that supports SQL Server 2012. However, it is recommended that the instance used to host the witness corresponds to the minimum configuration that is required for SQL Server 2012 Standard Edition.

Combining Database Mirroring with Other SQL Server 2012 Technologies

Other SQL Server high-availability alternatives and technologies can be combined with database mirroring for maximum availability, reporting, business continuity, and disaster recovery. The following sections explain how database mirroring interacts with other SQL Server 2012 technologies.

Database Mirroring and Other High-Availability Alternatives

Database mirroring has its advantages and disadvantages, and it does not solve every high-availability requirement. This is why database mirroring can be combined with other SQL Server high-availability alternatives such as AlwaysOn Failover Clustering Instance (FCI), log shipping, and replication.

Database Mirroring and AlwaysOn Failover Clustering Instance (FCI)

In many cases, database mirroring can be configured as a disaster recovery solution to a local SQL Server AlwaysOn Failover Cluster Instance by placing the principal database on the cluster and the hot standby mirror database in another physical location. If this combination is used, it is a best practice to use the high-protection or high-performance configuration mode because a cluster failover takes longer than the mirroring failover threshold. Therefore, if the high-availability configuration mode is being used, an automatic mirror failover takes place every time a cluster failover takes place between the two cluster nodes, making the cluster instance a mirrored database.

It is worth noting that the default threshold setting for controlling automatic failover with database mirroring is set to 10 seconds. When combined with AlwaysOn Failover Clustering Instance (FCI), a mirroring failover might take place when a node failover occurs within the cluster. Most likely this behavior is unwanted and occurs because a failover within a cluster takes more than 10 seconds. To address this concern, it is a best practice to increase the partner timeout value. The following example illustrates changing the mirroring failover threshold to two minutes:

```
ALTER DATABASE AdventureWorks2012
SET PARTNER TIMEOUT 120
```

> **Note**
>
> When combining these two technologies, a common high availability and disaster recovery solution includes a Failover Cluster Instance within the primary and disaster recovery data centers to achieve high availability within each site. Then asynchronous database mirroring is used in conjunction with Failover Cluster Instances to provide disaster recovery between the two sites.

Database Mirroring and Log Shipping

One of the limitations of database mirroring compared to log shipping is that database mirroring can have only one mirrored server associated with each principal, whereas log shipping can have multiple standby servers. The two technologies can be combined if there is a need to ship the principal database logs to a remote location other than the place where the mirror resides. In addition, log shipping databases can be used for reporting, whereas mirror databases cannot unless a snapshot is used.

> **Note**
>
> Log shipping needs to be reinitialized on the mirror SQL Server instance in the event of a failure or role change.

Database Mirroring and AlwaysOn Availability Groups

Database mirroring is still available as a feature in SQL Server 2012. However, AlwaysOn availability group is the primary high availability and disaster recovery feature for databases and will replace database mirroring technology over two releases. Therefore, there isn't a need to combine the technologies because database mirroring will eventually be deprecated, and availability groups offer far more superior features.

Database Mirroring and Replication

Finally, database mirroring can be used in conjunction with replication. The main focus is to provide availability for the publication database because the distribution and subscription databases are not supported with database mirroring. Because of the requirements and considerations, it is not a recommended practice to combine these two technologies; however, Microsoft includes a list of prerequisite tasks in SQL Server 2012 Books Online.

Database Mirroring and SQL Server 2012 Database Snapshots

Many organizations need to run reports against a production database for business purposes. To mitigate performance degradation and unnecessary locking due to sequential read and writes, it is a best practice to have a dedicated reporting server and not have reports run from the production database. Database mirroring offers this capability by allowing the mirror database to be used for reporting purposes. Unfortunately, the mirror database is in a constant recovering state, so it cannot be accessed directly.

You can create a point-in-time database snapshot from the mirror database, which can be used for reporting.

Tip

Again, although not discrediting database mirroring, AlwaysOn availability groups offer the potential to have active secondaries that provide read-only access to the secondary replicas for reporting purposes.

Note

For more information on creating database snapshots, see Chapter 6, "Backing Up and Restoring SQL Server 2012 Databases."

Implementing a Database Mirroring Session

To implement a database mirroring session, first follow the steps to configure database mirroring. The following example simulates a database mirroring implementation that uses the high-availability configuration mode (High Safety with Automatic Failover (Synchronous)), including a witness for CompanyABC's AdventureWorks2012 production database located in San Francisco. The mirroring and witness partner is also located in San Francisco. The server names that can be used in the example are shown in Table 12.2.

Table 12.2 Roles and Server Names for Database Mirroring Example

Role	SQL Server Instance	Location
Principal Server	SQLServer01\Instance01	San Francisco
Mirror Server	SQLServer02\Instance01	San Francisco
Witness Server	SQLServer03\Instance01	San Francisco

Configuring Database Mirroring Prerequisites

You must conduct the following steps to configure database mirroring on the AdventureWorks2012 database:

1. From the principal server (SQLServer01\Instance01), conduct a full backup of the AdventureWorks2012 database by using Transact-SQL code or SQL Server Management Studio (SSMS).

2. Conduct a transaction log backup of the AdventureWorks2012 database by using Transact-SQL code or SSMS.

Caution

Use independent files when creating the database and transaction log backups. Do *not* append both of these backups to the same file; otherwise, an erroneous error such as Error 1418 may occur when setting up the database mirroring session. Error 1418 typically represents network connectivity or issues when resolving server names in a mirroring session.

---

3. Copy the backup files from the principal server (SQLServer01\ Instance01) to the mirror server (SQLServer02\Instance01).

Tip

You need to create the AdventureWorks2012 database on the mirror server if it does not already exist. To simplify the backup and restore process, it is a best practice to maintain the same file path for the database and transaction log files that the principal database is using. Otherwise, the MOVE command is required when you're conducting the restore.

---

4. From the Mirror Server SQL Server instance (SQLServer02\ Instance01), conduct a restore of the AdventureWorks2012 database file and then the transaction log. Use the recovery state option RESTORE WITH –NORECOVERY for both restores. Therefore, the database is not in an operational state for end users and applications and ready to accept database mirroring transactions.

Note

For more information on backing up and restoring SQL Server with either SSMS or Transact-SQL, see Chapter 6.

---

5. In Object Explorer, on the principal server, register the principal, mirror, and witness SQL Server instances to ensure successful connectivity and authentication.

Configuring Database Mirroring with High Safety and Automatic Failover

Now that you've configured the prerequisites, follow these steps to configure database mirroring with high safety and automatic failover:

1. From the principal server (SQLServer01\Instance01), choose Start, All Programs, Microsoft SQL Server 2012, SQL Server Management Studio.

2. In Object Explorer, first connect to the Database Engine, expand the desired server (SQLServer01\Instance01), and then expand the Database folder.

3. Right-click the AdventureWorks2012 database, select Tasks, and then choose Mirror.

4. On the Database Properties page, select the Configure Security button located on the Mirroring page.

Note

Because database mirroring requires the transaction logs for synchronization, you receive a warning message if the database recovery level is not set to Full. If this occurs, switch the recovery model to Full and restart the Database Mirroring Wizard.

---

5. On the Configure Database Mirroring Security Wizard Starting page, select Next.

6. Specify whether to include a witness server in the configuration by selecting the option Yes on the Include Witness Server page. For this example, you use a witness server instance (SQLServer03\Instance01) to operate database mirroring in synchronous mode with automatic failure.

7. In the Choose Servers to Configure page, select the principal, mirror and witness server instances, as illustrated in Figure 12.2. Click Next.

8. On the Principal Server Instance page, specify the endpoint properties for the principal server instance, as shown in Figure 12.3. Ensure that the option Encrypt Data Sent Through This Endpoint is selected and then click Next to continue.

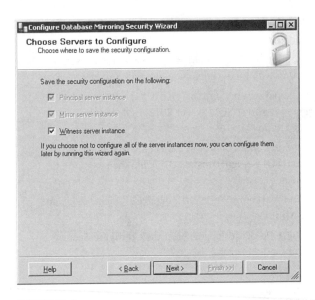

FIGURE 12.2
Configuring the database mirroring servers for security.

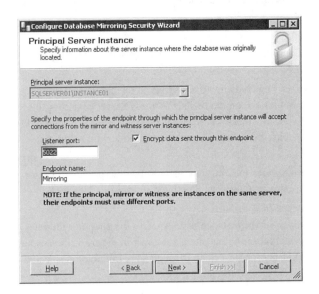

FIGURE 12.3
Entering the principal server instance information and settings.

Note

Typically, the default listener port for each endpoint is 5022. However, if the principal, mirror, or witness is configured on the same SQL Server instance, its endpoints must use different ports.

9. On the Mirror Server Instance page, specify the mirror server instance and the endpoint properties for the mirrored server instance, as shown in Figure 12.4. Click Next to continue.

Note

Before specifying options for this page, you may have to click the Connect button to first pass credentials for the desired mirror server instance.

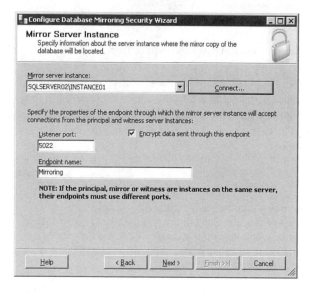

FIGURE 12.4
Entering the mirror server instance information and settings.

10. On the Witness Server Instance page, specify the witness server instance and the endpoint properties for the witness server instance, as shown in Figure 12.5. Click Next to continue.

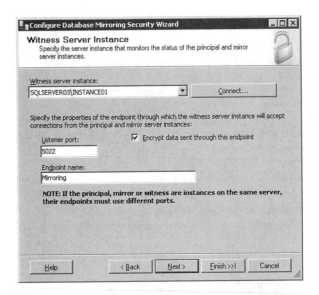

FIGURE 12.5
Entering the witness server instance information and settings.

11. On the Service Accounts page, enter the service account information for each instance partaking in the database mirroring session. If the service accounts are the same for each instance, as in this example, leave the text boxes blank, as illustrated in Figure 12.6, and click Next to continue.

Note

If the service accounts entered are different and the accounts do not already exist in the specific SQL Server instance, the wizard automatically creates the accounts, grants appropriate permissions, and associates the account credentials to the endpoints.

12. On the Complete the Wizard page, verify the configuration settings for each database mirroring instance, as shown in Figure 12.7, and then click Finish.

13. On the Configuring Endpoints page, verify the status of each endpoint to ensure it was successfully created, and click Close.

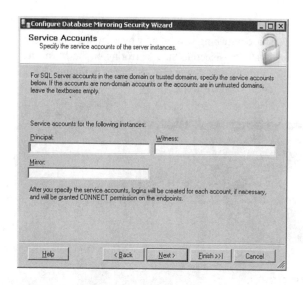

FIGURE 12.6
Specifying the database mirroring service accounts.

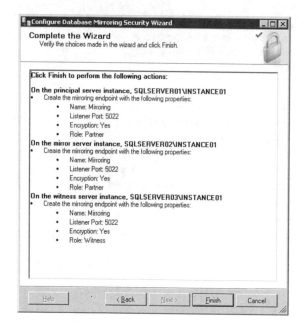

FIGURE 12.7
Verifying the database mirroring security settings.

14. When this Endpoint Security Wizard is closed, you are prompted to either start the database mirroring session now by selecting Start Mirroring or start it later by selecting Start Mirroring on the Mirroring page of the Database Properties dialog box, as shown in Figure 12.8. For this example, click Start Mirroring.

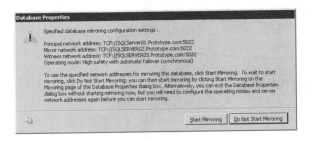

Database Properties

Specified database mirroring configuration settings :

Principal network address: TCP://SQLServer01.Prototype.com:5022
Mirror network address: TCP://SQLSERVER02.Prototype.com:5022
Witness network address: TCP://SQLSERVER03.Prototype.com:5022
Operating mode: High safety with automatic failover (synchronous)

To use the specified network addresses for mirroring this database, click Start Mirroring. To wait to start mirroring, click Do Not Start Mirroring; you can then start mirroring by clicking Start Mirroring on the Mirroring page of the Database Properties dialog box. Alternatively, you can exit the Database Properties dialog box without starting mirroring now, but you will need to configure the operating modes and server network addresses again before you can start mirroring.

[Start Mirroring]   [Do Not Start Mirroring]

FIGURE 12.8
Starting the database mirroring.

Note

The mirrored database must be present on the mirrored server; otherwise, an error occurs, stating that the mirrored database does not exist and must be created via a backup and restore prior to initializing the database mirroring session.

---

15. Verify that the initial synchronization was successful by viewing the Status section located in the Database Properties page, as shown in Figure 12.9, and then click OK.

When databases are configured in a database mirroring session, a status message appears next to the database and includes the server role. For example, on the SQLServer01\Instance01 server, the principal AdventureWorks2012 database status message indicates (Principal, Synchronized), and SQLServer02\Instance01 database status message indicates (Mirror, Synchronized/Restoring...).

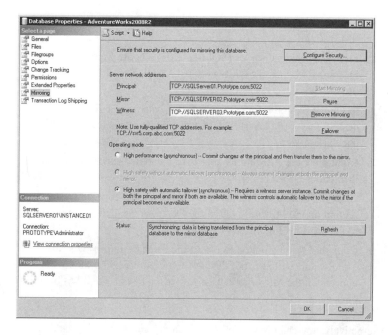

FIGURE 12.9
Viewing the database mirroring status in the Database Properties page.

Managing a Database Mirroring Session

The Mirroring page accessible from the Database Properties page allows
you to manage a database mirroring session. With this tool, you can pause,
remove, or failover a database mirroring session. In addition, it is possible
to change the database mirroring operation mode—for example, from high
performance (asynchronous) to high safety (synchronous). Finally, you can
use this page to initiate manual failovers and status verification. Alternatively,
any database mirroring tasks that can be conducted from the management
console can also be scripted with Transact-SQL.

Pausing and Resuming a Database Mirroring Session

Occasionally, you need to either pause or resume a database mirroring
session for administrative purposes. You can pause and resume a mirroring session by using SSMS or Transact-SQL.

608   CHAPTER 12   Implementing and Managing Database Mirroring

Follow these steps to either pause or resume a database mirroring session
with SSMS:

1. From the principal server (SQLServer01), choose Start, All
   Programs, Microsoft SQL Server 2012, SQL Server Management
   Studio.

2. In Object Explorer, first connect to the Database Engine, expand the
   desired server (SQLServer01\Instance01), and then expand the
   Database folder.

3. Right-click the AdventureWorks2012 database, select Tasks, and
   then choose Mirror.

4. Click the Pause button located in the Server Network Address
   section on the Mirroring tab of the Database Properties page (refer
   to the previous Figure 12.9).

5. Click the Resume button to restart the database mirroring session.
   The Resume button is not displayed in Figure 12.9 because it
   appears on the Mirroring tab only after the Pause button has been
   clicked.

Alternatively, you can use the following sample Transact-SQL syntax to
pause and resume a database mirroring session:

Pausing database mirroring:

```
Use Master
ALTER DATABASE <database_name> SET PARTNER SUSPEND
GO
```

Resuming database mirroring:

```
Use Master
ALTER DATABASE <database_name> SET PARTNER RESUME
Go
```

Manually Failing Over a Database Mirroring Session

Follow these steps to swap the principal and mirror roles by manually
failing over the database session from the principal server to the mirrored
server:

1. From the principal server (SQLServer01), choose Start, All
   Programs, Microsoft SQL Server 2012, SQL Server Management
   Studio.

2. In Object Explorer, first connect to the Database Engine, expand the desired server (SQLServer01\Instance01), and then expand the Database folder.

3. Right-click the AdventureWorks2012 database, select Tasks, and then choose Mirror.

4. Click the Failover button located in the Server Network Addresses section on the Mirroring tab of the Database Properties page.

5. Read the warning message and click Yes to finalize the role swap.

In SSMS, notice how the status messages have changed based on the role swap. On the SQLServer01\Instance01 server, the AdventureWorks2012 database status message indicates (`Mirror, Synchronized/In Recovery`), whereas the SQLServer02\Instance01 database instance status message indicates (`Principal, Synchronized`).

The following sample Transact-SQL syntax should be used to failover a database mirroring session:

```
Use Master
ALTER DATABASE database_name SET PARTNER FAILOVER
Go
```

Notes from the Field: When and How to Perform Forced Failover During Disaster Recovery

In some situations, the SQL Server instance hosting the principal database in a database mirroring session may fail or become permanently unavailable. In these rare circumstances, a DBA may have to perform a forced service failover to bring the SQL Server instance hosting the mirror database online. With forced failovers, the potential exists for possible data loss if transactions were not committed on the mirror before the principal went down. The following scenarios explain when to perform forced service failover depending upon the safety level and operating mode of database mirroring session:

- **High-safety mode with Automatic Failover (Synchronous)**—If your database mirroring environment is configured for High-Safety mode with Automatic Failover (Synchronous), you will have three servers or SQL Server Instances: Principal, Mirror, and a Witness. In this scenario, if the Mirror and Witness servers cannot communicate with the Principal server because the Principal server failed, you will need to perform forced service failover.

- **High-safety mode without Automatic Failover (Synchronous)**—If your database mirroring environment is configured in High-Safety mode without Automatic Failover, you will have two servers (Principal and Mirror). If the Principal server has failed, you will need to perform forced service failover from Principal to Mirror.

- **High-Performance: (Asynchronous)**—If your database mirroring environment is configured in High-Performance (Asynchronous) mode, you will have Principal, Mirror, and an optional Witness server. If the Principal server is unable to communicate with the mirror server because it has failed, you will need to perform forced service failover.

Use the following to perform a forced service failover:

```
Use Master;
Go
ALTER DATABASE <Database_Name> SET PARTNER
FORCE_SERVICE_ALLOW_DATA_LOSS;
Go
```

After the preceding statement is executed, the mirror server will transition its role to become the principal server, and database mirroring will be suspended. If the old principal server (the one that had failed) becomes available, it will attempt to become a mirror server after being recovered and will establish connection with the current principal server. However, the mirroring session will be suspended until you run the following statement:

You can use this statement on the mirror server to resume the database mirroring session:

```
Use Master;
Go
ALTER DATABASE <Database_Name> SET PARTNER RESUME;
Go
```

Changing the Database Mirroring Configuration/Operating Mode

In some situations, either you or your organization decides to change the operating mode. Reasons for changing the operating mode may include performance issues, the absence of a witness server, or even a need to manually control a failover instead of having SQL automatically conduct the role swap.

Follow these steps to change the database mirroring operating mode with SSMS:

1. From the principal server (SQLServer01), choose Start, All Programs, Microsoft SQL Server 2012, SQL Server Management Studio.

2. In Object Explorer, first connect to the Database Engine, expand the desired server (SQLServer01\Instance01), and then expand the Database folder.

3. Right-click the AdventureWorks2012 database, select Tasks, and then choose Mirror.

4. In the Operating Mode section, change the Operating Mode option to either High Performance, High Safety, or High Safety with Automatic Failover and click OK.

You can use the following basic Transact-SQL syntax to change the database mirroring operating mode:

Enable Transaction Safety:

```
Use Master
ALTER DATABASE <database> SET PARTNER SAFETY FULL
GO
```

Disable Transaction Safety:

```
Use Master
ALTER DATABASE <database> SET PARTNER SAFETY OFF
GO
```

Removing a Database Mirroring Session

Similar to the management steps you used previously, you can remove database mirroring sessions with either Transact-SQL or SSMS.

Follow these steps to swap roles by manually failing over the database session from the principal server to the mirrored server:

1. From the principal server (SQLServer01), choose Start, All Programs, Microsoft SQL Server 2012, SQL Server Management Studio.

2. In Object Explorer, first connect to the Database Engine, expand the desired server (SQLServer01\Instance01), and then expand the Database folder.

3. Right-click the AdventureWorks2012 database, select Tasks, and then choose Mirror.

4. Click the Remove Mirroring button located in the Server Network Addresses section on the Mirroring tab of the Database Properties page.

5. Read the warning message and click Yes to remove mirroring from the AdventureWorks2012 database.

6. In the Database Properties page, click OK to finalize the procedures.

The following Transact-SQL syntax can also be used to remove a database mirroring session:

```
Use Master
ALTER DATABASE <database_name> SET PARTNER OFF
Go
```

Managing Database Mirroring Client Connections and Redirect

In the event of a principal database failure, the principal database fails over to the mirror either manually or automatically. Therefore, all client connections need to be redirected from the principal server instance to the new mirror database instance. The latest ADO.NET or SQL Server clients have built-in redirect technologies that allow an application to automatically redirect its connection in the event of a database failure. Either you, as DBA, or an application developer must specify the principal and failover SQL Server instance in the connection string to make this happen.

Follow these steps to configure automatic client redirect by using the native SQL Server client:

1. Choose Start, All Programs, Administrative Tools, Data Sources (ODBC).

2. On the ODBC Data Source Administrator page, select System DSN.

3. Click Add to create a new System DSN connection to the principal and mirror SQL Server instance.

4. In the Create New Data Source page, select SQL Native Client 11.0 and then click Finish.

5. In the Create a New Data Source to SQL Server page, enter the name, description, and the principal database server instance, as

illustrated in Figure 12.10. For this example, use the principal SQL
Server instance SQLServer01\Instance01. Click Next.

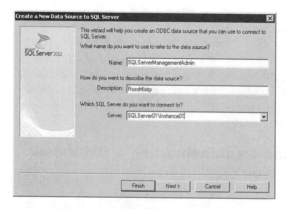

FIGURE 12.10
Creating a new SQL Server native client data source.

6. Select the SQL Server authentication mode for the SQL Server
   connection and click Next.

7. Select the default database to connect to and enter the name of the
   mirror server, as shown in Figure 12.11. For this example, select
   AdventureWorks2012 database and SQLServer02\Instance01 for the
   mirror server instance. Click Next.

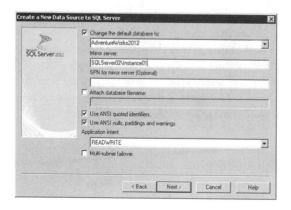

FIGURE 12.11
Specifying the mirror database settings.

8. Click Finish and then click Test Data Source to finalize the connection settings.

The new connection can be leveraged with a front-end SQL Server client such as Access, Visual Studio .NET, or Reporting Services. Use the newly created connection and display data from the AdventureWorks2012 database, such as the Employee table. When a connection is established and the data is presented, fail over the database mirroring session. The application should still be able to display the Employee table because it automatically redirects to the AdventureWorks2012 database residing on the mirror instance of SQL Server.

Monitoring and Troubleshooting a Database Mirroring Session

After you have configured database mirroring, you should turn your attention to understanding the following tools for monitoring and managing the mirroring session:

- Database Mirroring Monitoring tool
- System Performance
- System Catalogs
- Operations Manager

Using the Database Mirroring Monitoring Tool to Manage Database Mirroring

The Database Mirroring Monitoring tool is included with SSMS and should be used to monitor databases configured in a mirroring session. The tool can be launched by right-clicking the database partaking in a database mirroring session and then selecting Tasks, Launch Database Mirroring Monitor. You can use the tool to identify the status of the database mirroring session, identify the role of each partner, determine whether the mirroring session is behind schedule, and estimate the time it will take to catch up.

Use the following procedure to monitor the state of the database mirroring session configured in the earlier examples:

1. From the principal server (SQLServer01), choose Start, All Programs, Microsoft SQL Server 2012, SQL Server Management Studio.

2. In Object Explorer, first connect to the Database Engine, expand the desired server (SQLServer01\Instance01), and then expand the Database folder.

3. Right-click the AdventureWorks2012 database, select Tasks, and then choose Launch Database Mirroring Monitor.

4. To register a mirrored database, either click the Register Mirrored Database hyperlink in the right pane or select Action, Register Mirrored Database from the Tools menu.

5. In the Register Mirrored Database page, select the server instance by clicking the Connect button.

6. In the Connect to Server dialog box, select the Mirrored Database SQL Server Instance (SQLServer02\Instance01) and click OK.

7. In the Register Mirrored Database page, click the Register check box next to the database to register the mirrored database instance and then click OK.

8. The Database Mirroring Monitoring tool automatically connects to both the principal and mirror instances partaking in the database mirroring session. In the Manage Server Instance Connections, edit the credentials if necessary or click OK.

The Database Mirroring Monitoring Tool Status Tab

The Status tab includes a plethora of database mirroring status information for both the principal and mirror databases. The status information located on the Status tab is broken into four sections: Status, Principal Log, Mirror Log, and General Information.

The Status section indicates the server instance, current role, and mirrored state, and it validates that the witness is operational. The final command in the status window provides a history log file, as shown in Figure 12.12.

The Principal Log section includes metrics on the following:

- Unsent Log Information in KB
- Oldest Unsent Transaction
- Time to Send Log (Estimated)
- Current Send Rate in KB per Second
- Current Rate of New Transactions

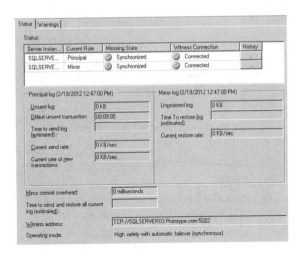

FIGURE 12.12
Displaying database mirroring history.

The General section located at the bottom of the Status tab page includes
additional status for troubleshooting and diagnostics:

■ Mirror Commit Overhead in Milliseconds

■ Time Estimates to Send and Restore All Current Logs

■ Witness Address

■ Operation Mode

The Database Mirroring Monitoring Tool Warnings Tab

The Warnings tab allows you to set database mirroring warning thresholds
for the principal and mirror SQL Server instances. The four warnings
included with this tool are as follows:

■ Warn If the Unsent Log Exceeds the Threshold

■ Warn If the Unrestored Log Exceeds the Threshold

■ Warn If the Age of the Oldest Unsent Transaction Exceeds the
Threshold

■ Warn If the Mirror Commit Overhead Exceeds the Threshold

The Set Warning Thresholds page should be used to enable/disable
warning per instance and set thresholds.

Monitoring Database Mirroring Performance

The Database Mirroring Monitoring tool is a great starting point for managing and analyzing a database mirroring session. When additional metrics are needed for analysis, or when troubleshooting or creating a performance baseline, you can use the Reliability and Performance Monitor tool included with Windows Server 2008 R2. To launch the tool, choose Start, All Programs, Administrative Tools, and Performance Monitor.

Following are the specific counters included with the SQL Server Database Mirroring Performance Object:

- Bytes Received/sec
- Bytes Sent/sec
- Log Bytes Received/sec
- Log Bytes Redone from Cache/sec
- Log Bytes Sent from Cache/sec
- Log Bytes Sent/sec
- Log Compressed Bytes Rcvd/sec
- Log Compressed Bytes Sent/sec
- Log Harden Time (ms)
- Log Remaining for Undo KB
- Log Scanned for Undo KB
- Log Send Flow Control Time (ms)
- Mirrored Write Transactions/sec
- Log Send Queue KB
- Pages Sent/sec
- Receives/sec
- Redo Bytes/sec
- Redo Queue KB
- Send/Receive Ack Time
- Sends/sec
- Transaction Delay

Collecting and analyzing the preceding metrics assists organizations with planning their database mirroring solution. Before database mirroring is implemented in production, it is a best practice to simulate mirroring in a prototype test lab and analyze the metrics collected. If possible, a bandwidth simulator tool should also be used to mimic the production network speed, especially if Log Stream Compression will be used. This allows an organization to fully understand the database mirroring and bandwidth requirements when setting up database mirroring in production over a private network. When analyzing bandwidth requirements, your organization should also assess the current bandwidth utilization. Therefore, if the link is already fully saturated, more bandwidth may be necessary to support the mirroring solution. Alternatively, many organizations purchase dedicated network lines tailored specifically for database mirroring replication.

Using the System Catalogs to Monitor Database Mirroring

The catalog view included with SQL Server is another great source of information when monitoring status and performance.

The following catalog views should be used:

- Sys.database_mirroring
- Sys.database_mirroring_witness
- Sys.database_mirroring_endpoints
- Sys.tcp_endpoints
- Sys.Server_principals
- Sys.Server_recovery_status
- Sys.dm_db_mirroring_auto_page_repair

The catalog view provides database mirroring metadata for a session, including witness, endpoint, principal, and recovery status.

Summary

Database mirroring is a SQL Server 2012 high-availability alternative that can be used for maintaining a redundant copy of the principal database on a standby server for increased availability and disaster recovery purposes. SQL Server 2012 allows organizations to implement database mirroring across physical sites with limited bandwidth, and automatic page repair protects the mirrored copy from corruption.

How well database mirroring performs is closely associated with the type of application, transaction safety level, and network performance between the principal and mirror servers. Understanding the application behavior in terms of the log generation rate, number of concurrent connections, and size of transactions is important in achieving the best performance.

In addition, the network plays a very important role in a database mirroring environment. When used with a high-bandwidth and low-latency network, database mirroring can provide a reliable high-availability solution against planned and unplanned downtime. With data centers in different geographical locations, database mirroring can provide the foundation for a solid, inexpensive disaster recovery solution.

Best Practices

The following are the best practices for this chapter:

- Replace database mirroring with AlwaysOn availability groups because database mirroring will eventually be deprecated.

- When performing Index maintenance in an OLTP environment, it is recommended that you change the operating mode of database mirroring to High Performance (Asynchronous) to minimize the effect on concurrent OLTP operations.

- Database mirroring using the high-availability configuration mode is a practical alternative when the principal and mirror server reside in the same physical location. The reason is that most organizations' production environments are running fast networks without network latency.

- Database mirroring using the high-performance configuration mode is a practical alternative when the principal and mirror server reside in different physical locations. The reason is that production performance is typically of higher importance than automatic failover and availability in these situations.

- For consistency, if you make any changes on the Principal Server such as SQL Server jobs, logins, or hardware modifications, ensure you make those same changes on the Mirror Server.

- Leverage database mirroring to reduce planned downtime, increase availability for mission-critical databases, and satisfy disaster recovery requirements.

- To increase performance, implement and leverage a dedicated high-bandwidth network for synchronization communications between the principal and mirror database servers when possible.

- Leverage Database Mirroring Log Compression in environments where there isn't enough available bandwidth between the principal database instance and the mirrored database instance.

- In the event of a failure, the mirror server needs to maintain the same workload as the principal. Both servers should be of similar class and have the same number of processors and the same amount of memory and storage. Unlike in AlwaysOn Failover Clustering Instance (FCI), the hardware does not have to be an exact match, but the mirror needs to support the same load as the principal.

- Use AlwaysOn Failover Clustering Instance (FCI) over database mirroring if there is a need to provide high availability on the whole SQL Server instance. This includes the master, model, msdb, and tempdb databases because these system databases cannot partake in a database mirroring session.

- To reduce the number of unforeseen issues with database mirroring, use the same edition of Windows and SQL Server for both the principal and mirror server. In addition, the service packs, hot fixes, drive letter layout, collation settings, and SQL Server configuration settings should be identical. Although this is not a requirement, it is a best practice.

- To reduce complications and troubleshooting, use a single mirror SQL Server instance if a principal instance is composed of multiple databases belonging to one application that needs to be mirrored.

- When using database mirroring, create items such as logins, scheduled jobs, and extended stored procedures that are identical on the mirrored database and instance.

- When configuring database mirroring, do *not* forget to initialize the mirror database by restoring the full backup and the last transaction log with the NORECOVERY option.

- If you configured the database mirroring session to use high-availability or high-protection mode and delays are experienced with client applications, switch to high-performance mode.

CHAPTER 13

Implementing and Managing Replication

Replication is a native SQL Server feature that allows a DBA to copy tables, views, indexed views, functions, stored procedures, and so on from one database to another and allows a DBA to control how synchronized the two copies are. In other words, you can replicate changes to both data and schema objects (that is, table, view, or stored procedure changes, and so on). Some replication types allow for bidirectional replication, where changes made on the destination database can be replicated back to the source database.

Replication is best used for the following purposes:

■ **To move data closer to clients**—For example, branch offices might need to access data in a central office, and the network hop involved makes the applications run very slowly. Having a local copy of the data will make their data access much faster.

■ **To offload reporting to another server**—Instead of having reporting clients accessing data from the production server, causing I/O and database user contention between the reporting users and the application users, data can be replicated to a reporting server, and the reporting clients can access their data there. The end result is greater scalability for both sets of users.

■ **To scale out performance**—Instead of having 1,000 users accessing a single server, 100 users can each access one of 10 servers with the end result being improved performance for all users.

- **Active-Active scale-out solutions**—In many cases, peer-to-peer replication is implemented for organizations to achieve a scaled-out implementation of a database across many SQL Server instances or data centers.

- **Moving only a subset of the data**—Even with great new investments in SQL Server 2012, such as AlwaysOn Availability Groups and Active Secondary Replicas, in some situations an organization may not want to duplicate the full database on all the secondary replicas. For example, perhaps the databases are 50 terabytes and they require only one table that is 5GB. In these scenarios, replications will still have play because you can replicate data at more of a granular level compared to using availability groups.

- **To fulfill application requirements**—This includes consolidating data from branch offices to a central location, replicating to tables with different schemas, replicating to different RDBMSs, replicating to handheld devices, and so on.

Replication is also frequently used as a disaster-recovery solution, but it is a poor choice for this for these reasons:

- There is no automatic failover of clients from the production server to the failover server.

- Latencies aren't predictable, and consequently exposure to data loss can be much greater than with other disaster recovery technologies.

- Not every object is replicated (for example, logins), and new objects require special handling.

- Replication requires licenses for both the production server and the failover server; the other Microsoft disaster recovery solutions for SQL Server do not.

The focus of this chapter is how to design, implement, and monitor replication topologies.

SQL Server 2012 Replication Essentials

To be able to implement SQL Server replication, you will need to understand the concepts behind it. Replication also has many components. This section introduces the main concepts and components of replication.

SQL Server 2012 Replication Roles

Replication uses metaphors from the world of publishing. The main components are as follows:

- **Publisher**—The source of the data and/or objects you are replicating. This could be a SQL Server or an Oracle Server; SQL Server Express is not supported as a publisher.

- **Subscriber**—The destination server; again this could be a database on the same server, another SQL Server Instance (2000, 2005, 2008, 2008 R2, or 2012), or an Oracle or DB2 RDBMS. SQL Server Express is supported as a subscriber.

- **Distributor**—Transactional and snapshot replication (these replication types are covered in the next section) use a store-and-forward metaphor. The distributor is a server that stores the replication commands before they are executed on the subscriber. In merge replication, the distributor holds only historical data. In most topologies, the distributor will be on the same server as the publisher; however, if you expect large workloads on your publisher, you might want to use a remote distributor.

  If you do not already have a distributor, connect to your SQL Server in SQL Server Management Studio and expand the Replication folder. If you do not see a folder labeled Local Publications, you are running SQL Server Express, which does not support the installation of a distributor. If you see a menu item Distributor Properties, your SQL Server is already configured with a distributor. If you do not have a distributor, right-click and select Configure Distribution. Click Next and accept the default to create a local distributor.

- **Publications**—Publications contain the objects you want to replicate. Group the objects you want to replicate into publications according to replication type, logical grouping (such as business unit), publications that have common properties, or common objects that need to go to a group of subscribers.

- **Articles**—Articles are objects you can replicate. They include schema-only objects (functions, views, and stored procedures) and schema and data objects (tables and indexed views). Tables and indexed views can be vertically or horizontally partitioned; in other words, a subset of the columns or rows or a subset of both can be replicated.

- **Bidirectional replication**—This metaphor is not from the world of publishing. In bidirectional replication, data modifications (DML) originating on the publisher are applied on the subscriber, and DML originating on the subscriber are applied on the publisher. The most common type of bidirectional replication used is merge replication. Please refer to the section "Configuring Merge Replication."

- **Push subscribers**—The publisher pushes the schema and data to the subscriber. This is normally used with a small number of subscribers on a Local Area Network (LAN).

- **Pull subscribers**—The subscriber pulls the schema and data from the publisher. This is normally used with large numbers of subscribers and most often over the Internet.

- **Publication Access List (PAL)** —A database group of subscriber SQL or Windows accounts that have rights to access the publication.

- **Conflict**—This metaphor is not from the world of publishing. In conflicts, a data modification occurs on one side of a replication topology that disagrees with a modification on another side of the replication topology. There are five basic types of conflicts:

  - **Primary key collision**—An insert originating on the publisher has the same primary key values as an insert on the subscriber, and the primary key constraint is violated when replication attempts to synchronize the two.

  - **Updating a deleted row**—This conflict occurs when a row is updated on one side of the replication topology (the publisher for instance) and deleted on the subscriber. The conflict occurs when replication attempts to synchronize the two.

  - **Lack of consistency**—One row is modified on the publisher, but when replication attempts to modify the same row on the subscriber, it does not exist, or there is more than one row with the same key values.

  - **Column-level tracking**—A tuple or cell is updated on one side of a replication topology and updated with a different value on the other side of the replication topology.

  - **Row-level tracking**—A row is updated on one side of a replication topology, and the same row is updated on the other side of the replication topology. Unlike column-level tracking, row-level tracking does not track to see if the change occurred in the same column.

Types of Replication Alternatives Available

There are three types of replication: snapshot, transactional, and merge, with some variants on the snapshot and transactional replication types such as peer-to-peer.

Snapshot Replication

■ **Snapshot replication**—This replication type generates an image of the data at a point in time (a *snapshot*) and distributes it to one or more subscribers. After the snapshot is deployed, no changes are replicated to the subscriber(s) until the next time the snapshot is generated and distributed. This replication type is best used when your data changes infrequently and the bulk of it changes at one time—for example, catalog updates. There are no schema modifications using this replication type.

■ **Snapshot replication with queued updating**—This replication type is a variation of snapshot replication; however, changes that occur on the subscriber are replicated back to the publisher on a continuous or scheduled basis. This replication type is best used in the following situations:

  ■ When the majority of the changes occur on the publisher.

  ■ When there are fewer than 10 subscribers.

  ■ This replication type is resilient to network interruptions; if a failure occurs, replication will pick up where it left off and replicate changes back to the publisher.

  ■ This replication type adds a GUID column and triggers to all tables that are replicated.

  ■ Adjustments must be made for constraints, triggers, and the identity property with this replication type.

  ■ Conflicts will be detected, but there are no facilities to roll them back. This variant is deprecated in SQL Server 2012, and peer-to-peer replication is recommended as an alternative.

■ **Snapshot replication with immediate updating**—This replication type is another variation of snapshot replication; however, changes that occur on the subscriber are applied as a two-phase commit via Distributed Transaction Coordinator (DTC) to the subscriber. Essentially, all transactions originating at the subscriber are applied in a transactional context on the publisher and then on the subscriber. In addition to the same caveats with queued updating, there are several important additional caveats to this replication type:

- Latency of transactions originating on the subscriber is increased. Now transactions have to make a network hop and be written on both sides. This latency can reduce scalability.

- If the link between the subscriber and the publisher goes down, transactions originating on the subscriber will hang until the transaction is rolled back. The transactions typically hang between 15 and 20 seconds before being rolled back.

■ **Snapshot replication with immediate updating and queued failover**—This variant of snapshot replication uses immediate updating by default; however, if your publisher goes offline, you have the option to manually switch to queued updating. The same caveats as queued updating apply here as well.

- The majority of the transactions originate at the publisher.

- There should be fewer than 10 subscribers.

- Conflict detection occurs but not conflict handling.

- A GUID column will be added to your tables being replicated.

- Conflicts will be detected, but there are no facilities to roll them back (more on conflict detection later). This variant is deprecated in SQL Server 2012. Microsoft recommends that you use peer-to-peer replication, although it is only supported in the Enterprise Edition of SQL Server.

Transactional Replication

■ **Transactional Replication**—This is the most common replication type. It is chosen because it tracks changes and replicates them to the subscriber. The latency with this replication type can be very low (typically slightly less than 3 seconds) even for large workloads that involve *singletons* (one-row inserts, updates, and deletes). However, latencies can be large for batch updates, inserts, and deletes. In transactional replication, transactions that occur on the publisher are read from the transaction log and stored in the distribution database on the distributor. They are then applied on the subscriber via stored procedures or SQL statements, within a transactional context. This replication type requires a primary key on every table you are replicating and is resilient to network interruptions. Transaction replication does not make any modifications to the tables it replicates.

■ **Transactional Replication with Queued Updating**—This replication type is very similar to snapshot replication with queued updating. Changes that originate on the publisher are replicated via a Distribution Agent. Changes that occur on the subscriber are replicated back to the publisher via a queue reader. The same caveats with snapshot replication with queued updating also apply here. This variant is deprecated in SQL Server. Microsoft recommends that you use peer-to-peer replication, although it is supported only in the Enterprise Edition of SQL Server.

■ **Transactional Replication with Immediate Updating**—This replication type is very similar to snapshot replication with immediate updating. Changes that originate on the publisher are replicated via a Distribution Agent (more on this later in the next section). Changes that occur on the subscriber are replicated back to the publisher using a two-phase commit via DTC. The same caveats with snapshot replication with immediate updating also apply here. Microsoft recommends that you use peer-to-peer replication, although it is supported only in the Enterprise Edition of SQL Server.

■ **Transactional Replication with Immediate Updating and Queued Failover**—This is a variant of snapshot replication with immediate updating and queued failover. Because the subscriber will roll back all transactions that originate on the subscriber when the publisher is offline, the topology is designed to be failed over to queued updating until the subscriber comes back online. The same caveats as in snapshot replication with immediate updating and queued failover hold here as well. Microsoft recommends that you use peer-to-peer replication, although it is supported only in the Enterprise Edition of SQL Server.

■ **Oracle Publishing**—In this type of replication, an Oracle RDBMs server replicates to SQL Server. This is supported on the Enterprise Edition of SQL Server. This is a variant of transactional replication.

■ **Bidirectional Transactional Replication**—This replication type is not available using the wizards and must be configured manually. Use transactional replication to replicate to the subscriber, and then the subscriber is configured as a publisher to replicate back to the original publisher. Set the `@loopback_detection` parameter to True in `sp_addsubscription` when configuring your subscribers. You must set the Not For Replication property on all constraints, triggers, and identity columns. You will also need to set the identity property to have different seeds on either side so that you don't get any primary key conflicts—configuring your primary keys or identity seeds to minimize primary key conflicts is called *partitioning*. This replication type does not require any schema modifications.

Although Microsoft recommends using peer-to-peer replication, which is an Enterprise Edition–only feature, bidirectional transactional replication is supported on the Standard Edition and higher and is faster than peer-to-peer replication but not scalable beyond a small number of nodes (two to three).

- **Peer-to-Peer Transactional Replication**—Peer-to-peer transactional replication is bidirectional replication extended to many more publisher/subscriber pairs called *nodes*. The practical limit is 10 nodes; however, this depends on available network bandwidth and workload. Peer-to-peer replication is popular because a node can drop off (for maintenance or if the link goes down), and the other nodes can continue to synchronize with each other. When the disconnected node comes back on, it will synchronize with the other partners. If the node is disconnected because of a failed wide-area network (WAN) link, for example, local users could access this node and do work, and when the WAN link comes back, the changes the users made when the node was disconnected from the WAN will be replicated to all other nodes. Peer-to-peer replication, like bidirectional transactional replication, does not require any schema changes. Peer-to-peer replication is available only in the Enterprise Editions of SQL Server 2005, SQL Server 2008, SQL Server 2008 R2, and SQL Server 2012.

- **Merge Replication**—Whereas all other bidirectional replication solutions are limited by the number of subscribers, merge replication is highly scalable. It has rich conflict detection and resolution features. Merge replication does tend to be slower than the other bidirectional replication options, but it is designed for low-bandwidth links. For example, it is an excellent fit where you have to replicate over phone lines.

So, which replication type should you use? If the bulk of your data changes infrequently but at regular intervals and you need one-way replication, use snapshot replication. If your data changes continuously, use transactional replication. If you need near-real-time bidirectional replication and have 2 to 3 subscribers and have partitioned your data to minimize conflicts, use bidirectional transactional replication. If you need near-real-time bidirectional replication and have between 2 and 10 subscribers, are running

Enterprise Edition, and have partitioned your data to minimize conflicts, use peer-to-peer replication. If you need bidirectional replication, have a large number of subscribers, and need rich conflict detection and resolution, use merge replication. Use Oracle Publishing if you are publishing from an Oracle RDBMs and your SQL Server is the Enterprise Edition.

Additional Replication Components

Replication uses agents to detect changes and migrate them to the subscriber and publishers. These agents are executables that you can find in C:\Program Files\Microsoft SQL Server\100\Com, and they function as described in the following list:

- **Log Reader Agent**—This agent is used by transactional replication. Changes that occur to published articles are written to the transaction log. The Log Reader Agent reads these changes, constructs replication commands, and writes these commands to the distribution database and also writes a marker in the distribution database indicating the last part of the log it read. The transaction log can be truncated to the last-read command. The distribution database is a repository on the distributor that stores replication commands (for transactional replication only) and history and metadata for all replication types. The Log Reader Agent then writes a marker in the transaction log stating that it has read these changes out of the transaction log. This way, if the Log Reader Agent fails, it will retrieve the record from the distribution database indicating the last command read from the log and then start reading from that point on.

- **Snapshot Agent**—The Snapshot Agent is used by all replication types to create a base image of the published articles and all replication data necessary for the replication processes; for example, replication stored procedures, tracking and conflict tables, and tracking triggers.

- **Queue Reader Agent**—This agent is used in queued replication. *Queued replication* uses tracking triggers to capture changes that originate by user activity on the Subscriber database and writes them to a queue. The queue reader reads this queue and writes the changes in the publication database.

- **Distribution Agent**—The Distribution Agent reads the changes that the Log Reader has written to the distribution database and writes them to the Subscriber. It places a marker in the Subscriber database indicating the last transaction applied there and also on the distribution database. This way, if the Distribution Agent fails, the next time it runs it will determine what the last command applied on the subscriber was and pick up where it left off.

- **Merge Agent**—The Merge Agent connects to the subscriber and publisher and determines the last time both synchronized. It then will determine what changes occurred on both sides since the last time it synchronized. It processes all deletes at one time and then processes all inserts and updates. While processing these changes, it determines whether any of the changes have occurred on the same row, or if you are using column-level tracking, it determines whether any of the changes have occurred on the same row and column. If so, the Merge Agent invokes the conflict detection mechanism specified for the article to which the row belongs. The Merge Agent also will write tracking metadata so that if the agent is interrupted, it will be able to pick up where it left off the next time the publisher and Subscriber synchronize.

- **Replication Monitor**—The central point for monitoring publishers and subscribers. You can administer most agents in Replication Monitor; however, you cannot modify the publishers, publications, subscribers, or subscriptions here. To access Replication Monitor, connect to your publisher in SQL Server Management Studio, right click the Replication folder, and select Launch Replication Monitor.

- **Conflict Viewer**—This allows you to see conflicts that have occurred in merge replication of one of the updatable subscriber variants of snapshot and transactional replication. It also lets you roll back and forth between conflicts if you are using merge replication. To use the Conflict Viewer, connect to your publisher in SQL Server Management Studio, expand the Replication folder, expand the Local Publishers folder, right-click your publication, and select View Conflicts.

- **Profiles**—Profiles are groups of settings that you can configure for your agents to use. For example, if your link between your publisher and subscriber is unstable, you can select the Slow Link Profiler for your Merge Agent. To select a profile, you need to launch Replication Monitor by right-clicking the Replication folder and selecting Launch Replication Monitor. Add your publisher if it is not already added by selecting Add Publisher. Expand the publisher, and in the right-hand pane, click the subscriber. Then right-click the subscriber and select Agent Profile. By default, the Default Agent Profile will be selected. At this point, choose another Profile or click the New button to create your own.

SQL Server 2012 Replication Topologies

There are basically five types of replication topologies:

- **Publisher-Distributor-Subscriber**—This is the most common replication topology and can be used by all replication types. This replication topology is illustrated in Figure 13.1. The publication originates at the publisher, and the schema, its data, and related metadata are replicated to the subscriber(s). Depending on your replication topology, data moves from the publisher to the subscriber (transactional and snapshot), and for all other replication types, it moves both ways.

Publisher / Multiple / Subscriber Replication Topology

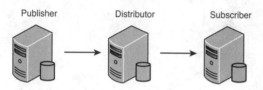

FIGURE 13.1
Publisher-Distributor-Subscriber topology.

- **Republishing**—Here a publisher replicates to the subscriber, which in turn publishes its schema, data, and related metadata to the downstream subscriber. The schema, data, and related metadata originate on the upstream publisher. Data moves from the main publisher downstream to the subscriber for transactional and snapshot replication. For all other replication types, it can move both ways. This replication topology is illustrated in Figure 13.2.

Republishing Replication Topology

FIGURE 13.2
Republishing topology.

- **Central Publisher**—In this replication topology, a central publisher publishes to multiple subscribers. In some cases, the subscribers may only get a subset of the data. This replication topology is illustrated in Figure 13.3.

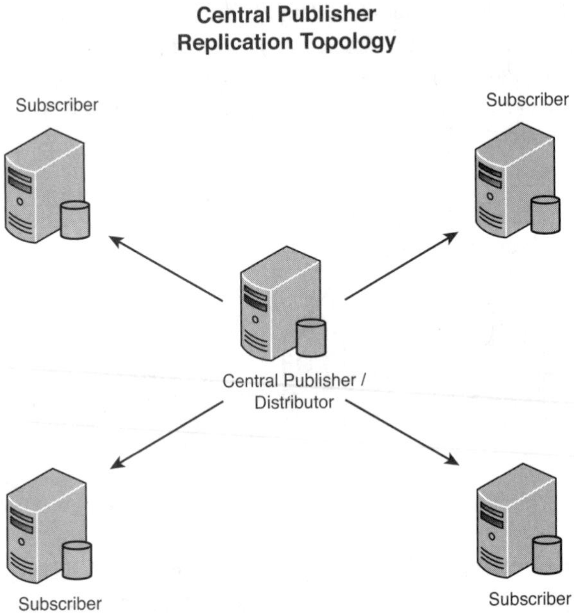

**Central Publisher
Replication Topology**

FIGURE 13.3
Central Publisher topology.

- **Central Subscriber**—In this topology, multiple publishers replicate to the same subscriber. This replication topology is illustrated in Figure 13.4.
- **Mesh**—This topology is used in peer-to-peer replication. The path taken by data from one subscriber to another is unpredictable, and one node can drop off the replication topology and return with no interruption to the other nodes in the mesh. This replication topology is illustrated in Figure 13.5.

**Central Subscriber / Multiple Publisher
Replication Topology**

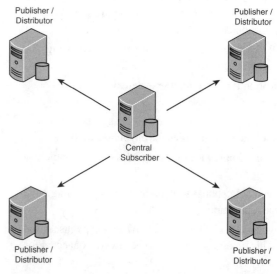

FIGURE 13.4
Central Subscriber topology.

**Peer-to-Peer
Replication Topology**

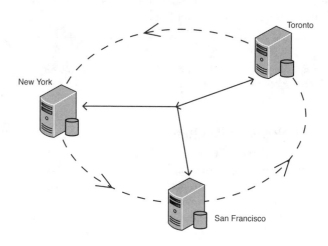

FIGURE 13.5
Mesh topology.

SQL Server 2012 Replication Prerequisites

Configuring replication is not as simple as clicking through a few screens of a SQL Server installation wizard. A number of prerequisite steps must be fulfilled before replication can be configured and implemented.

Before you install SQL Server replication, ensure that the following prerequisites are met or understood:

- All merge replication types require the installation of a local or remote distributor.

- A snapshot folder must be accessible by all the agents and be large enough to store all the snapshot files for the publications.

- Transactional replication requires primary keys on every table you replicate.

- You cannot have a table published in an immediate-updating publication and merge replication.

- You need to have a network connection between the publisher and the subscriber. This link does not need to be always connected for most replication types.

- You need to have at minimum an account that is in the dbo role on the subscriber for push replication, and an account that is in the dbo role on the distributor and in the PAL in the publication.

- If you are using web synchronization, you will need a certificate issued by a certificate authority (CA) from a trusted third party like VeriSign or an internal certificate server and have your IIS Server configured to use this certificate for SSL.

> **Note**
>
> To initialize a subscription from a backup in SQL Server 2012, a user must be a member of the dbcreator server role.

SQL Server 2012 Edition Limitations

There are several SQL Server edition-specific limitations to replication. SQL Server Express 2012 can be used only as a subscriber. SQL Server 2012 Enterprise, Standard, and the Business Intelligence editions support merge replication, transactional replication, snapshot replication, heterogeneous subscribers, and Oracle publishing. Peer-to-peer transactional replication is supported only on the Enterprise Edition of SQL Server 2012.

Knowing When to Implement SQL Server 2012 Replication

An organization can have many reasons for its implementation of SQL Server replication. Following are some of the situations organizations try to address by using SQL Server 2012 replication:

- **Distributing data**—This involves distributing data from one database to another database or from one server to another server. For example, an organization must make data such as pricing or sales data residing at corporate headquarters readily available to all field offices.

- **Consolidating data**—An organization may be interested in consolidating data from many servers to one server for centralized reporting, analysis, or business intelligence. Examples include consolidating data from field offices, manufacturing facilities, or data residing in mobile devices to a centralized SQL Server.

- **Ensuring high availability**—Replication is one of four SQL Server 2012 high-availability alternatives (five, if you count Live Migration). It can be used to maintain redundant copies of a database on multiple servers residing in different locations. Peer-to-peer transaction replication was introduced in SQL Server 2005 and is discussed later in this chapter. When replication is used for high availability, it does not provide automatic failover or automatic client redirect as AlwaysOn failover cluster instances, AlwaysOn availability groups, or database mirroring does.

- **Reporting**—If you want to minimize performance degradation on production databases/servers, it is advantageous to offload reporting from production database servers to dedicated reporting servers. Although there are a number of ways of achieving this goal, such as active secondary replicas with availability groups, transactional replication provides a means of replicating data to one or more reporting servers with minimal overhead on the production database. Unlike with database mirroring, the reporting database can be accessed for reporting purposes in real-time without the need for creating database snapshots.

- **Distributing or consolidating database subsets**—Unlike other high-availability alternatives or data distribution methods such as availability groups, log shipping, or database mirroring, replication offers a means to copy or replicate only a subset of the database if needed. For example, you can choose to replicate only a table, rows based on a filter, specific columns, or stored procedures.

■ **Ensuring scalability**—The goal is to scale the workload across multiple databases with replication. This provides increased performance and availability.

Replication is essentially copying or distributing data from one location to another. However, there are other technologies you can also use to accomplish this:

■ **SSIS**—SQL Server Integration Services (SSIS) does rich ETL (Extract Transform and Load); however, it does not easily track changes. SSIS is best for moving data from heterogeneous data sources. Transactional replication can be used to transform data but it is an involved task. Look up "Custom Sync Objects" in Books Online for more information on how to do this.

■ **BCP**—Bulk Copy Program (BCP) is used to copy data out of the file system and into another SQL Server. It does not track changes easily, but you can use it for high-performance data loads, which can perform much better than the other data load methods.

■ **Triggers**—Triggers can be used to replicate or transform data; however, they add latency to each transaction, do not scale well over a network, and there is an administrative burden with this method.

■ **Two-Phase Commit**—This technology involves writing to the source table and then writing to the destination table within a transaction. There is considerable latency associated with this; however, for some applications that have very high consistency requirements, two-phase commits are necessary.

■ **Backup and Restore**—Backup and restore can be used to replicate data; however, the source database is offline during the restore operation, and for large databases this can be unwieldy.

■ **Copy Database Wizard**—This wizard can be used to move or copy databases from a SQL Server 2000 or later instance to SQL Server 2005 or a later instance of SQL Server.

■ **Active Secondaries**—Availability groups can enable secondary instances to be utilized for reporting queries by using synchronous or asynchronous data movement from a primary replicas to one or more secondary replicas. As mentioned earlier, the full database is copied over, and it is not possible to move only a subset of the data.

- **Log shipping**—Log shipping is continuous backup and restore. The destination database is offline while the log is being applied. Microsoft does not require you to maintain a SQL Server license for the standby server because it is fulfilling only a standby role.

- **Database mirroring**—This can be considered to be contiguous log shipping. The destination database (called a mirror) is offline when participating in database mirroring. Database mirroring has two modes: high performance and high safety. With high performance, some data loss is possible, but performance is better than with high safety. With high safety, there will be no data loss. Microsoft does not require you to maintain a SQL Server license for the mirror server because it is fulfilling only a mirroring role. Database mirroring is the only technology that does client redirects on failover. So if clients are connected to your source server (called a *principal*), they will be automatically failed over to the mirror server when the principal goes down. Mirroring is most practical in high-performance mode, which is available only in Enterprise Edition. Note that database mirroring does not support FILESTREAM, whereas replication does.

For high-availability and disaster-recovery scenarios, failover clustering, AlwaysOn availability groups, database mirroring, log shipping, and in some cases backup and restore are a much better fit than replication, mainly because of the unpredictable latencies that replication offers and the lack of automatic and client failover. SSIS and BCP work best if there is some form of change tracking. Triggers are seldom a good solution. Two-phase commit fits best when your source and destination must be identical at all times. In all other scenarios, replication is a much better fit for copying data.

Combining Replication with Other SQL Server High-Availability Alternatives

Frequently, high-availability and disaster-recovery plans require a combination of technologies. For example, you may require implementing database mirroring in conjunction with replication. Such a topology would keep the publisher operational and redirect the clients to the mirror. Although clustering can achieve the same result, clustering has distance limitations, which mirroring can overcome. Finally, with SQL Server 2012, replication can also be combined with AlwaysOn availability groups. This section examines caveats associated with both technologies.

Combining Replication with Database Mirroring

You can mirror a published database or a subscriber database. The complications occur at failover.

If your publication database is mirrored and you are using a remote distributor, you can configure your log reader, distribution, queue reader, and merge agents to fail over to the mirror and pick up where they left off by configuring the PublisherFailoverParameter parameter with the mirror name in the agents. This ensures that if the principal is failed over to the mirror, the Log Reader, Snapshot, or Merge Agent will continue to work. You will need to enable trace flag 1448, and you may need to issue a sp_replrestart in your publication database to get the log reader to work again.

If your subscriber is mirrored and you need to fail over to the mirror, you will need to configure the Distribution Agent for the new subscriber (the former mirrored database). You will then need to configure the subscriber. To do this, you will need to clean up the old subscription in the principal database (use sp_subscription_cleanup) and then obtain the last Log Sequence Number (LSN) from the distribution database on the distributor. You will need to query the transaction_timestamp value from MSReplication_Subscriptions. Then add your subscription using the sp_addsubscription stored procedure and the subscriptionlsn parameter. The value you supply for the subscriptionlsn will be the value obtained in the transaction_timestamp column. After you have done this, your distribution database and new principal will be in sync, and you can start mirroring to the old principal.

Replication is a good fit with database mirroring because database mirroring is the only high-availability (HA) option that provides real-time synchronization with no data loss (in the high-safety mode). When replication is used with mirroring, the publisher's availability will be maximized.

Combining Replication with Log Shipping

If you have a remote distributor, you can configure the Publisher FailoverPartner parameter on the Log Reader Agent on your primary (the source database in your log shipping topology) with the name of your secondary (the destination database in your log-shipping topology). The PublisherFailoverPartner should be the secondary server name. On failover, the publisher will start to replicate to the remote distributor. Please refer to the section in Books Online titled "Strategies for Backing Up and Restoring Snapshot and Transactional Replication."

Combining Replication with Failover Clustering

Clustering is replication aware. You can create any type of publication on a clustered server. The only complication is that your snapshot folder must be on a clustered shared disk resource. If your snapshot folder is not shared, the active node may not be able to access the snapshot folder. This will be a problem only during snapshot generation and deployment.

Combining Replication with AlwaysOn Availability Groups

You can combine replication with AlwaysOn availability groups. Configuration is conducted in seven steps. First, a DBA must configure the database publications and subscriptions. Next, configure the AlwaysOn availability group for the published database. The following step requires the DBA to ensure that each secondary replica host has been configured to support replication, and then the secondary replicas must be configured as replication partners. Finally, a DBA must redirect the original publisher to use the listener name used for the availability group configured in the first step. For more information, review the following link for detailed steps: http://technet.microsoft.com/en-us/library/hh403414(v=SQL.110).aspx.

Implementing SQL Server Replication

Now that you've had the opportunity to understand SQL Server replication and familiarize yourself with the replication terminology, components, models, and prerequisites, it's time to implement replication. There are four parts involved in administering SQL Server replication:

- Creating the distributor
- Creating publications
- Creating subscriptions
- Administering and monitoring the publications and subscriptions

The upcoming sections include step-by-step procedures on how to implement and configure snapshot and peer-to-peer replication based on real-world examples.

Configuring Snapshot Replication

The following example illustrates the centralized publisher and multiple subscribers' replication model. Snapshot replication is used to distribute AdventureWorks2012 data from a centralized publisher residing in

CompanyABC's San Francisco headquarters to two sales offices residing in New York and Toronto.

To perform these tasks, ensure that you have three SQL servers in a domain such as the CompanyABC and each server can be successfully registered in SQL Server Management Studio. Table 13.1 summarizes CompanyABC's snapshot replication information based on items and descriptions for this example.

Table 13.1   **CompanyABC's Snapshot Replication Information for Upcoming Example**

Element	Description
SQLServer01\Instance01	PUBLISHER/DISTRIBUTOR (San Francisco Office)
SQLServer02\Instance01	SUBSCRIBER (New York)
SQLServer02\Instance01	SUBSCRIBER (Toronto)
Publication Name	AdventureWorks2012-Snapshot-Publication
Articles	AdventureWorks2012 Tables: Customer(Sales) and CustomerAddress(Sales)
Replication Type	Snapshot Replication

Using the information in Table 13.1, you can turn your attention to preparing the distributor for replication on SQLServer01\Instance01.

Configuring the Distributor for Replication

The first step to configuring snapshot replication in a centralized publisher/multiple subscriber topology is to configure the distributor for replication. Follow these steps to configure a SQL Server instance, such as SQLServer01\Instance01 as a distributor:

1. From the San Francisco server (SQLServer01\Instance01), choose Start, All Programs, Microsoft SQL Server 2012, and SQL Server Management Studio.

2. In Object Explorer, first connect to the Database Engine, expand the desired server (SQLServer01\Instance01), and then expand the Replication folder.

3. Right-click the Replication folder and select Configure Distribution.

4. On the Configure Distribution Welcome screen, select Next.

5. On the Distributor page, shown in Figure 13.6, you can configure the distributor on the local server or a remote server. For this example, select the first option, SQLServer01\Instance01\Principal, which acts as its own distributor, and then click Next.

Tip

For large workloads in a transactional replication topology, you should use a remote distributor on an AlwaysOn failover cluster instance. A remote distributor improves replication performance and scalability, whereas a failover cluster instance provides high availability for the distribution database. For merge replication, placement of the distribution database is not critical. Smaller transactional replication workloads can tolerate a local distributor without too much locking. If considerable locking occurs between Log Reader Agents and Distribution Agents, consider moving to a remote distributor. *Locking* occurs when two processes try to access the same resource (a table, index, page of a table, or index) simultaneously. A *remote distributor* is a SQL Server instance that hosts the distribution database and is neither the publisher nor a subscriber. After you have configured the remote distributor, you need to configure which publishers you want to publish to.

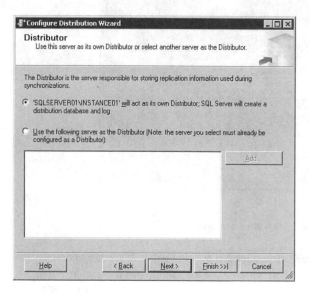

FIGURE 13.6
Selecting the SQL Server to host the distributor role.

Note

Prior to the next step, please ensure the SQL Server Agent service is running.

6. On the Snapshot Folder page, specify the physical location of the Snapshot folder and then click Next. It is recommended to use a network path so that distribution and merge agents can access the path of the snapshots over the network if they are used.

7. On the Distribution Database page, shown in Figure 13.7, specify the name and location of the distribution database and log files and then click Next. The drive letters you use must exist on the server that hosts the role of the distributor.

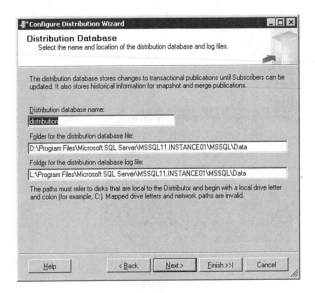

FIGURE 13.7
Specifying the distribution database options.

8. On the Publishers screen, shown in Figure 13.8, add additional publisher servers within the infrastructure that can use this server as a distributor. For this example, enter **SQLServer01\Instance01**. Click Next to continue.

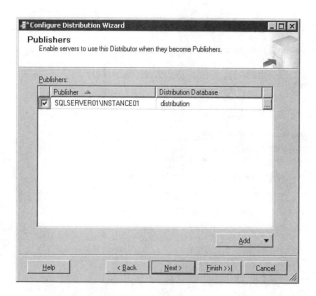

FIGURE 13.8
Enabling servers to use the distributor.

9. On the Wizard Actions page, select the option Configure Distribution, and if there is a need to generate a script file with steps to configure distribution, also choose the second option. Click Next to continue.

10. The Script File Properties page will be displayed if the option to save the script was selected in the preceding step. Specify the location of the file, whether to append or overwrite the existing file, and the final format, either International Text (Unicode) or Windows Text (ANSI). Then click Next to continue.

11. The final configuration step involves verifying the choices made in the Complete the Wizard page, as demonstrated in Figure 13.9. Click Finish to complete the distributor configuration.

12. Verify that the distributor is configured successfully and the publisher is enabled. Then click Close.

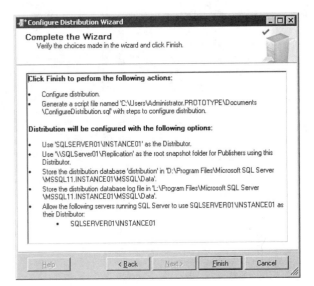

FIGURE 13.9
Configuring the distributor status.

As an alternative, Transact-SQL can also be used to configure the distributor. You can use the Transact-SQL script, `ConfigureDistribution.sql`, in Listing 13.1 to create a distributor based on the preceding example.

Listing 13.1 **ConfigureDistribution.sql—Configuring the Distributor with Transact-SQL**

```
/****** Scripting replication configuration. Script Date:
3/5/2012 6:57:53 PM ******/
/****** Please Note: For security reasons, all password
parameters were scripted with either NULL or an empty string.
******/

/****** Installing the server as a Distributor. Script Date:
3/5/2012 6:57:53 PM ******/
use master
exec sp_adddistributor @distributor =
N'SQLServer01\Instance01', @password = N''
GO
exec sp_adddistributiondb @database = N'distribution',
@data_folder = N'D:\Program Files\Microsoft SQL
Server\MSSQL11.INSTANCE01\MSSQL\Data', @log_folder =
```

```
N'L:\Program Files\Microsoft SQL
Server\MSSQL11.INSTANCE01\MSSQL\Data', @log_file_size = 2,
@min_distretention = 0, @max_distretention = 72,
@history_retention = 48, @security_mode = 1
GO

use [distribution]
if (not exists (select * from sysobjects where name =
'UIProperties' and type = 'U '))
        create table UIProperties(id int)
if (exists (select * from
::fn_listextendedproperty('SnapshotFolder', 'user', 'dbo',
'table', 'UIProperties', null, null)))
        EXEC sp_updateextendedproperty N'SnapshotFolder',
N'\\SQLServer01\Replication', 'user', dbo, 'table',
'UIProperties'
else
        EXEC sp_addextendedproperty N'SnapshotFolder',
N'\\SQLServer01\Replication', 'user', dbo, 'table',
'UIProperties'
GO

exec sp_adddistpublisher @publisher =
N'SQLServer01\Instance01', @distribution_db = N'distribution',
@security_mode = 1, @working_directory =
N'\\SQLServer01\Replication', @trusted = N'false',
@thirdparty_flag = 0, @publisher_type = N'MSSQLSERVER'
GO
```

Configuring Snapshot or Transactional Replication Publications

The second step when configuring snapshot replication in a centralized publisher/multiple subscriber topology involves configuring the publisher and selecting the articles that will be replicated. Follow these steps to define the articles for publication on SQLServer01\Instance01:

1. From the San Francisco server (SQLServer01\Instance01), choose Start, All Programs, Microsoft SQL Server 2012, and SQL Server Management Studio.

2. In Object Explorer, first connect to the Database Engine, expand the desired server (SQLServer01\Instance01), expand Replication folder, and then expand Local Publications.

3. Right-click the Local Publication folder and select New Publication.

4. On the New Publication Wizard screen, select Next.

5. Choose the AdventureWorks2012 database on the Publication Database screen because it contains the data that will be replicated. Then click Next.

6. On the Publication Type page, select the desired publication type that supports the replication model. For this example, choose Snapshot Publication and then click Next.

7. On the next page, Articles, you can choose the objects you want to publish, such as tables, stored procedures, views, indexed views, and user-defined functions. For this example, CompanyABC's business requirement is to publish the AdventureWorks2012 customer sales table. In the Objects to Publish section, select the Customer(Sales) Table, as shown in Figure 13.10, and then click Next.

Note

In general, you want to replicate all objects to support the requirements of the applications using the subscriber database. This can be all tables or a subset of them.

You can expand each object type—for example, the tables object to select individual tables, or check the check box to the left of the table icon to replicate all tables. In the Article Properties dialog box, you can select properties of the articles you want to replicate—for example, the choice to replicate nonclustered indexes or to replicate a table to a table with a different name or schema owner.

There are some differences in some of the Article Properties dialog settings between snapshot and transactional replication. For example, in transactional replication, the Statement Delivery option allows you to determine how incremental changes will be applied on the subscriber. This section does not appear in the snapshot publication creation dialogs. Statement Delivery refers to whether replication will use stored procedures or SQL statements to keep the two databases synchronized.

You also have the option to select which columns you want to replicate. Expand the Tables node and then expand the individual table you want to vertically partition (replicate only some of the columns): for example, vertically partitioning the Address table to not replicate the City column.

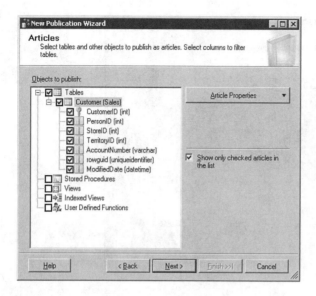

FIGURE 13.10
Choosing the articles for publication.

8. The Filter Table page allows you to create horizontal or vertical filters on the articles selected in your publication. For this example, do not leverage filters. Click Next to proceed.

9. On the Snapshot Agent screen, enable the two options Create a Snapshot Immediately and Keep the Snapshot Available to Initialize Subscriptions and Schedule the Snapshot Agent to Run every hour, as shown in Figure 13.11. These options control the frequency with which snapshots will be created. Then click Next.

10. On the next screen, Agent Security, you can specify accounts and security settings for all replication agents on this page. Click the Security Settings command button and enter a Windows account for the snapshot agent and publisher, as shown in Figure 13.12. Click OK to close the Snapshot Agent Security screen and then click Next.

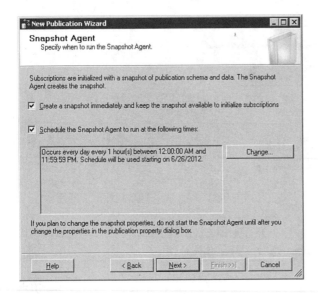

FIGURE 13.11
Specifying the snapshot initialization settings.

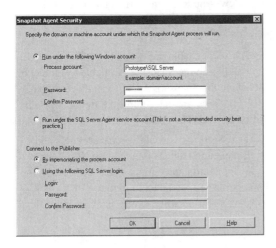

FIGURE 13.12
Entering the snapshot agent authentication credentials.

> **Note**
>
> You have two choices for the security context that the Snapshot Agent will run under: the SQL Server Agent account's security context or the context of a low-privilege Windows account. Microsoft has the following recommendations for the security context under which your agent will run:
>
> - Run each replication agent under a different Windows account and use Windows Authentication for all replication agent connections.
> - Grant only the required permissions to each agent.
> - Ensure that all Merge Agent and Distribution Agent accounts are in the publication access list (PAL).
> - Follow the principle of least privilege by allowing accounts in the PAL only the permissions they need to perform replication tasks. Do not add the logins to any fixed server roles that are not required for replication.
> - Configure the snapshot share to allow read access by all Merge Agents and Distribution Agents. In the case of snapshots for publications with parameterized filters, ensure that each folder is configured to allow access only to the appropriate Merge Agent accounts.
> - Configure the snapshot share to allow write access by the Snapshot Agent.
> - If you use pull subscriptions, use a network share rather than a local path for the snapshot folder.
>
> If you do not select the SQL Server Agent accounts security context, ensure that the Windows account you chose has rights to read and list files and folders on the snapshot folder or snapshot share. Microsoft recommends you do not use the SQL Server Agent account because it tends to run under an Administrator account, and if an exploit hijacks it, the exploit will have Administrator rights on your machine and possibly your domain. The Connect to Publisher dialog allows you to select how you want the Snapshot Agent executable to connect to the Publisher. You can use the account you specify the Snapshot Agent to run under or a SQL login.

11. On the Wizard Actions page, select the option Create the Publication and select the second option if you want to generate a Script File with Steps to Create the Publication and then click Next.

12. The Script File Properties page is displayed because the option to save the script was selected in the preceding step. Specify the location of the file, whether to append or overwrite the existing file, and the final format, either International Text (Unicode) or Windows Text (ANSI). Then click Next to continue.

13. On the Complete the Wizard screen, review the configuration
settings and then enter a name for the publication, as shown in
Figure 13.13. Click Finish to finalize the configuration.

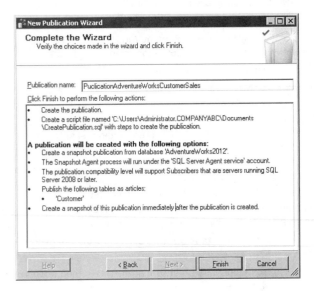

FIGURE 13.13
Finalizing the publication summary settings.

14. On the final screen titled Creating Publication, verify in detail the
status of each action in the publication, and then click Close to
finalize.

15. In Object Explorer, expand the Local Publication folder to view the
newly created publication for the AdventureWorks2012 database.

Note

When creating the publication, specify a domain account in order simplify
the authentication process between the servers by the Snapshot Agent.

Alternatively, you can use the following Transact-SQL syntax instead of
SQL Server Management Studio to configure the publication. The
Transact-SQL script, `CreatePublication.sql`, in Listing 13.2 is based on
the preceding example.

Listing 13.2   `CreatePublication.sql`—Creating a Publisher with Transact-SQL

```
use [AdventureWorks2012AdventureWorks20122012]
exec sp_replicationdboption @dbname =
N'AdventureWorks2012AdventureWorks20122012', @optname =
N'publish', @value = N'true'
GO
-- Adding the snapshot publication
use [AdventureWorks2012AdventureWorks20122012]
exec sp_addpublication @publication =
N'PublicationAdventureWorks2012CustomerSales', @description =
N'Snapshot publication of database
''AdventureWorks2012AdventureWorks20122012'' from Publisher
''SQLServer01\Instance01''.', @sync_method = N'native',
@retention = 0, @allow_push = N'true', @allow_pull = N'true',
@allow_anonymous = N'true', @enabled_for_internet = N'false',
@snapshot_in_defaultfolder = N'true', @compress_snapshot =
N'false', @ftp_port = 21, @ftp_login = N'anonymous',
@allow_subscription_copy = N'false', @add_to_active_directory =
N'false', @repl_freq = N'snapshot', @status = N'active',
@independent_agent = N'true', @immediate_sync = N'true',
@allow_sync_tran = N'false', @autogen_sync_procs = N'false',
@allow_queued_tran = N'false', @allow_dts = N'false',
@replicate_ddl = 1
GO
exec sp_addpublication_snapshot @publication =
N'PublicationAdventureWorks2012CustomerSales', @frequency_type
= 4, @frequency_interval = 1, @frequency_relative_interval = 1,
@frequency_recurrence_factor = 0, @frequency_subday = 8,
@frequency_subday_interval = 1, @active_start_time_of_day = 0,
@active_end_time_of_day = 235959, @active_start_date = 0,
@active_end_date = 0, @job_login = N'Prototype\SQL.Server',
@job_password = null, @publisher_security_mode = 1
```

Listing 13.2 **Continued**

```
use [AdventureWorks2012AdventureWorks20122012]
exec sp_addarticle @publication =
N'PublicationAdventureWorks2012CustomerSales', @article =
N'Customer', @source_owner = N'Sales', @source_object =
N'Customer', @type = N'logbased', @description = null,
@creation_script = null, @pre_creation_cmd = N'drop',
@schema_option = 0x0000000000803509D,
@identityrangemanagementoption = N'manual', @destination_table
= N'Customer', @destination_owner = N'Sales',
@vertical_partition = N'false'
GO
```

Configuring Subscriptions for the AdventureWorks2012 Database

Now that both the distributor and publication roles have been initialized
and configured, the final step is to subscribe to the publication created. You
carry out this task by creating a subscription on all servers that will receive
the published articles. For our example, we will create a subscription on
two subscribers. To create the subscription, first conduct the following
steps on SQLServer02\Instance01 and then repeat them on
SQLServer03\Instance01:

1. From the New York server (SQLServer02\Instance01), choose Start,
   All Programs, Microsoft SQL Server 2012, and then SQL Server
   Management Studio.

2. In Object Explorer, first connect to the Database Engine, expand the
   desired server (SQLServer02\Instance01), expand Replication folder,
   and then expand Local Subscriptions.

3. Right-click the Local Subscriptions folder and select New
   Subscriptions.

4. On the New Subscription Wizard screen, select Next.

5. On the Publication page, select the desired publisher SQL Server
   instance that is hosting the publication, such as SQLServer01\
   Instance01 for this example. Then from the Database and
   Publications section, choose the publication based on the publication
   created in the previous example (PublicationAdventureWorks2012
   CustomerSales), as shown in Figure 13.14. Then click Next.

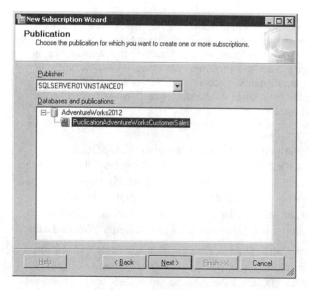

FIGURE 13.14
Subscribing to the publication already created.

Note

If the desired SQL Server publisher is not available, select Find SQL
Server Publisher from the Publisher drop-down list.

---

6. The next screen provides two options where the Distribution Agents
   can run. The default option on the Distribution Agent Location
   screen is Pull Subscription. The alternative is Push Subscription.
   Select the option Run Each Agent at Its Subscriber (Pull
   Subscriptions) and then click Next.

Tip

When configuring subscriptions, DBA's typically wonder if there should
leverage a push subscription or a pull subscription. The response is typically based on where do you want the processing of the load to occur—
on the subscriber or on the distributor. You should leverage a push
subscription strategy when the data will be synchronized continuously or
on a frequent basis, whenever you need near real-time data from the
publications, or when the higher processor usage on the distributor does
not affect the performance of Push subscription. On the flip side, use

Pull subscriptions when the data from publisher needs to be synchronized on demand or on schedule: whenever the publication on a Publisher server has a large number of subscribers that would make all agents on the distributor to be resource-intensive; or whenever the subscribers are autonomous, disconnected, and/or Mobile. It is worth noting that you cannot change subscription type (Push or Pull) once the subscription is created.

7. On the Subscribers screen, ensure the appropriate SQL Server subscriber (SQLServer02\Instance01) is selected and then select the Subscription database. Click Next to continue. For this example, the AdventureWorks database does not exist on SQLServer02\ Instance01; therefore, select New Database from the Subscription Database drop-down list and create a new AdventureWorks database.

8. On the New Database page, enter the database name (**Adventure Works**), select the appropriate path for the database and log files, and then click OK. Click Next on the Subscribers page to continue.

9. Enter the appropriate user account and password for both the distributor and subscriber connections by clicking the ellipses on the Distribution Agent Security page.

10. On this screen, specify the context for the Distribution Agent, distributor, and subscriber. Click OK to return to the Distribution Agent Security page and then click Next.

11. On the Synchronization Schedule page, set the agent schedule. The options available include Run Continuously, Run On Demand Only, and Define Schedule. For this example, select Run Continuously.

12. On the Initialize Subscriptions page, ensure that the Initialize check box is enabled and that Immediately is selected in the Initialize drop-down box. Click Next to continue.

13. On the Wizard Actions page, select the options Create the Subscription and Generate a Script File with Steps to Create the Subscriptions, and then click Next.

14. The Script File Properties page is displayed because the option to save the script was selected in the step 12. Specify the location of the file, whether to append or overwrite the existing file, and the final format, either International Text (Unicode) or Windows Text (ANSI).

15. On the Complete the Wizard screen, review the configuration settings and click Finish, as illustrated in Figure 13.15.

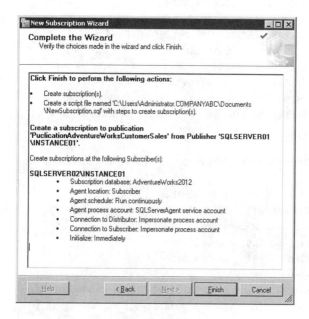

FIGURE 13.15
Completing the New Subscription Wizard.

16. On the final screen, Creating Subscription(s), verify the status details of each action in the subscription and click Close to finish.

17. To create an additional subscriber on the Toronto SQL Server instance, repeat steps 1 to 16 on the Toronto SQL Server instance or use the Create Subscription Transact-SQL script generated in these steps.

Just as with some of the earlier sets of instructions, you can use TSQL syntax instead of SQL Server Management Studio to create the subscription. The TSQL syntax, NewSubscription.sql, shown in Listing 13.3 configures the Subscription based on the preceding example depicted for SQLServer02\Instance01.

Listing 13.3   **NewSubscription.sql—Creating a Subscription with Transact-SQL**

```
--BEGIN: Script to be run at Publisher
'SQLServer01\Instance01'--
use [AdventureWorks2012AdventureWorks20122012]
exec sp_addsubscription @publication =
N'PublicationAdventureWorks2012CustomerSales', @subscriber =
N'SQLServer02\Instance01', @destination_db =
N'AdventureWorks2012AdventureWorks20122012', @sync_type =
N'Automatic', @subscription_type = N'pull', @update_mode =
N'read only'
GO
--END: Script to be run at Publisher 'SQLServer01\Instance01'--

--BEGIN: Script to be run at Subscriber
'SQLServer02\Instance01'--
use [AdventureWorks2012AdventureWorks20122012]
exec sp_addpullsubscription @publisher =
N'SQLServer01\Instance01', @publication =
N'PublicationAdventureWorks2012CustomerSales', @publisher_db =
N'AdventureWorks2012AdventureWorks20122012', @independent_agent
= N'True', @subscription_type = N'pull', @description = N'',
@update_mode = N'read only', @immediate_sync = 1

exec sp_addpullsubscription_agent @publisher =
N'SQLServer01\Instance01', @publisher_db =
N'AdventureWorks2012AdventureWorks20122012', @publication =
N'PublicationAdventureWorks2012CustomerSales', @distributor =
N'SQLServer01\Instance01', @distributor_security_mode = 1,
@distributor_login = N'', @distributor_password = null,
@enabled_for_syncmgr = N'False', @frequency_type = 64,
@frequency_interval = 0, @frequency_relative_interval = 0,
@frequency_recurrence_factor = 0, @frequency_subday = 0,
@frequency_subday_interval = 0, @active_start_time_of_day = 0,
@active_end_time_of_day = 235959, @active_start_date =
20120305, @active_end_date = 99991231, @alt_snapshot_folder =
N'', @working_directory = N'', @use_ftp = N'False', @job_login
= null, @job_password = null, @publication_type = 0
```

Listing 13.3 `NewSubscription.sql`—Creating a Subscription with Transact-SQL

```
GO
----------------END: Script to be run at Subscriber
'SQLServer02\Instance01'----------------
```

Testing Snapshot Replication

Any changes made to the data residing in the AdventureWorks2012 database on the publisher are propagated through replication to the subscribers based on the snapshot interval. To test the replication topology, make changes on the Customer(Sales) table located on the publisher. The changes should be replicated on the subscribers AdventureWorks2012 database.

Testing Your Publication

To verify that your publication is replicating successfully, do the following:

1. In SQL Server Management Studio, connect to your publisher.

2. Right-click the Replication folder and select Launch Replication Monitor.

3. After Replication Monitor has launched, click the Add Publisher hyperlink on the right pane to monitor your publisher.

4. When your publisher has been added, expand it in the left pane so that your publication shows up. If there are any errors, your publisher and publication will have a red circle with a white x on them.

5. After you have clicked your publication, all subscriptions to that publication will be displayed in the right pane. Click the Publications and Agents tabs to see if there are any red circles with a white x on them and observe any status messages that are displayed.

Typical errors you will see are connection errors; for example, the Distribution Agent is unable to connect to the subscriber. To fix these errors, right-click the agent with the error icon on it and select View Details. Read and evaluate the error message. Most errors can be solved by right-clicking the publication and changing the publication's properties, or in the case of a pull subscription, by right-clicking the subscription and selecting Properties.

Validations

You can also run a validation to verify that your publication and subscription are consistent (that is, have the same data):

1. In SQL Server Management Studio, connect to your publisher.

2. Right-click your publication in SQL Server Management Studio and select Validate Subscriptions.

3. You will be offered a choice to validate all subscriptions or individual subscriptions. Make the appropriate choice and click the Validation Options button. The options are a fast row count based on cached information, an actual row count, or a fast row count, and if differences are noted, an actual row count is done. You also have the option to perform a checksum and stop the Distribution Agent if a subscriber fails validation. Click OK.

You can view the results on the validation in Replication Monitor in the Publications tab:

1. Launch Replication Monitor by right-clicking on your publication in the Replication folder for your SQL Server.

2. Drill down on the publisher and expand your publication.

3. Right-click your subscription and select View Details.

4. Note the values in the Actions in the selected session; this appears as the lower half of the dialog.

Tracer Tokens

If you are concerned with latency issues or want to verify that replication is working, click the Tracer Tokens tab in Replication Monitor (you need to drill down on the Publisher, Publication, and Subscription and look in the right pane of Replication Monitor to see this). Click Insert Tracer and watch the tracer token being injected into the publication. Replication Monitor will track how long it takes for the tracer token to make its way from the publisher to the distributor and then from the distributor to the subscriber.

You'll see the breakdown of the time it took the token to go from the publisher to the distributor, the time from distributor to subscriber, and total latency. If latency is unacceptable, you may need to check network bandwidth or attempt to optimize your replication topology performance. Optimizing your network link is outside the scope of this book. Good values should be below a minute on a LAN (but can be as low as 2–4 seconds). WAN performance is highly variable and dependent on bandwidth and workloads. The tracer token can also be used to help determine the best QueryTimeout value. This can also be done by using Transact-SQL.

Replication Monitor can also be used to view undistributed commands. If you view the details of a subscription, you can see how many commands are waiting to be distributed and an estimate of how long the distribution will take.

Configuring Peer-to-Peer Transactional Replication

The following example illustrates the peer-to-peer transactional replication topology among three SQL Server instances or peer-to-peer nodes for CompanyABC. Each SQL Server instance is located in different geographical regions such as San Francisco, New York, and Toronto. This is summarized in Table 13.2.

As a prerequisite task, make sure that all three SQL Server nodes reside in a domain such as the CompanyABC and each server can be successfully registered in SQL Server Management Studio on the SQLServer01\Instance01 server to ensure proper connectivity. You may have to disable distributor and publications if they were created in the previous steps.

Table 13.2   **CompanyABC's Peer-to-Peer Replication Summary**

Item	Description
SQLServer01\Instance01	Peer-to-Peer Member (San Francisco)
SQLServer02\Instance01	Peer-to-Peer Member (New York)
SQLServer03\Instance01	Peer-to-Peer Member (Toronto)
Publication Name	AdventureWorks2012-Publication
Articles	Customer (Sales) Table
Replication Type	Transactional Replication

Configuring the Distributor for Replication

The first step in configuring peer-to-peer transactional replication topology is to configure all peer nodes as a distributor for replication. Conduct the following steps to configure SQLServer01\Instance01, SQLServer02\Instance01, and SQLServer03\Instance01 as distributors:

1. From the San Francisco server (SQLServer01\Instance01), choose Start, All Programs, Microsoft SQL Server 2012, and SQL Server Management Studio.

2. In Object Explorer, expand the desired server (SQLServer01\Instance01); then expand the Replication folder.

3. Right-click the Replication folder and select Configure Distribution.

4. On the Configure Distribution Welcome screen, select Next.

5. On the Distributor page, select the option Act as Its Own Distributor and click Next.

> **Note**
>
> When configuring peer-to-peer replication, you can use a remote distributor. If a remote distributor is used, it is not a best practice to have all peers use the remote distributor because it would be a single point of failure for the whole ring topology.

6. On the Snapshot Folder page, specify a network share location of the Snapshot folder and then click Next. It is recommended to use a network path so the replication peers can access the snapshots over the network.

> **Note**
>
> The network share used for the Snapshot folder should be secured with NTFS permissions.

7. On the Distribution Database page, specify the location of the distribution database and log files, and then click Next.

8. On the Publishers screen, add additional publisher servers within the infrastructure that can use this server as a distributor. For this example, enter only **SQLServer01\Instance01** and click Next.

9. On the Wizard Actions page, select the options Configure Distribution and Generate a Script File with Steps to Configure Distribution and click Next.

10. The Script File Properties page is displayed because the option to save the script was selected in the preceding step. Specify the location of the file, whether to append or overwrite the existing file, and the final format, either International Text (Unicode) or Windows Text (ANSI).

11. The final configuration step is to verify the choices made in the Complete the Wizard page. Click Finish to complete the distributor configuration.

12. Verify that the configuration of the distributor and enabling publisher were successful. Click Close.

13. To configure distribution on additional nodes in the peer-to-peer replication topology, repeat steps 1 to 12 on SQLServer02\ Instance01 and SQLServer03\Instance01. On each server, configure a secure shared Snapshot folder and configure a local distributor.

Configuring the Peer-to-Peer Publication on the First Node

After all three distributors have been configured, the next step in this procedure is to configure the publication on the first node. Follow these steps:

1. From the San Francisco server (SQLServer01\Instance01), choose Start, All Programs, Microsoft SQL Server 2012, and then SQL Server Management Studio.

2. In Object Explorer, first connect to the Database Engine, expand the desired server (SQLServer01\Instance01), and expand Replication folder and then Local Publications.

3. Right-click the Local Publication Folder and select New Publication.

4. On the New Publication Wizard screen, select Next.

5. Choose the AdventureWorks2012 database on the Publication Database screen because it contains the data that will be replicated and click Next.

6. On the Publication Type page, choose Transactional Publication and click Next.

7. On the next page, Articles, select the database objects to publish, such as the CreditCard(Sales) table, as shown in Figure 13.16. Then click Next.

8. Click Next on the Filter Table Rows page because peer-to-peer replication does not support filtering.

9. On the Snapshot Agent screen, clear the option to Create a Snapshot Immediately, and then click Next.

10. On the Agent Security page, enter credentials for the Snapshot Agent and Log Reader Agent and click Next.

FIGURE 13.16
Selecting articles for peer-to-peer replication.

11. On the Wizard Actions page, select the options Configure the Publication and Generate a Script File with Steps to Create the Publication and click Next.

12. The Script File Properties page is displayed because the option to save the script was selected in the preceding step. Specify the location of the file, whether to append or overwrite the existing file, and the final format, either International Text (Unicode) or Windows Text (ANSI).

13. On the Complete the Wizard screen, review the configuration settings, enter a peer-to-peer-publication as the publication name, and click Finish.

14. On the final screen, Creating Publication, verify the detail status of each action in the publication and click Close to finalize.

15. Expand the Local Publication folder to view the newly created publication for the AdventureWorks2012 database.

Enabling the Publication for Peer-to-Peer Replication

The next step is to enable the publication for peer-to-peer replication via the publication properties, as follows:

1. From the San Francisco server (SQLServer01\Instance01), expand the Replication folder and then Local Publications.

2. Right-click the publication you created in the previous steps and select Properties.

3. On the Subscriptions Options page of the Publication Properties dialog box, set the Allow Peer-to-Peer Subscriptions to True, as shown in Figure 13.17, and then click OK.

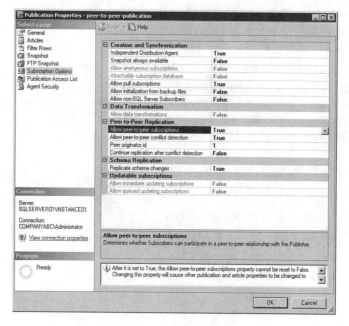

FIGURE 13.17
Enabling peer-to-peer replication settings.

Note

After the Peer-to-Peer Subscription setting has been enabled, the property cannot be disabled; therefore, you are forced to remove replication.

Configuring the Peer-to-Peer Topology

Before configuring the subscriptions on the nodes that will act as subscribers in the peer-to-peer replication topology, you must first initialize the peers with the source database schema and data. You can initialize the schema and database on the peers by creating a database package using SQL Server 2012 Integration Services (SSIS) or by backing up and restoring the source database. For more information on how to copy a database from one SQL Server instance to another, see Chapter 4, "Creating Packages and Transferring Data On-Premise and to the Cloud."

Follow these steps to configure the peer-to-peer topology:

1. From the San Francisco server (SQLServer01\Instance01), expand the Replication folder and then Local Publications.

2. Right-click the publication you created in the previous steps and select Configure Peer-to-Peer Topology.

3. On the Configure Peer-to-Peer Topology Wizard screen, click Next.

4. On the Publication screen, expand the AdventureWorks2012 database and select the peer-to-peer publication you created in the previous steps (peer-to-peer-publication), as illustrated in Figure 13.18. Click Next to continue.

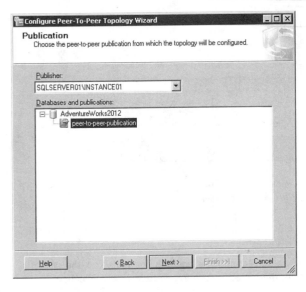

FIGURE 13.18
Configuring the peer-to-peer publication.

5. On the Configure Topology screen, right-click the design surface of the page, and then click Add a New Peer node.

6. In the Connect to Server dialog box, specify a server name, such as SQLServer02\Instance01, and click Connect.

7. In the Add a New Peer Node dialog box, select the publication database, such as AdventureWorks2012, and select Connect to All Displayed Nodes. If conflict detection is enabled, specify a unique value for each node in the Peer Originator ID box. Click OK, as illustrated in Figure 13.19, and then click OK.

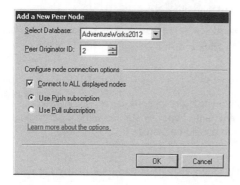

FIGURE 13.19
Adding a new peer node to the replication topology.

8. Repeat steps 5 to 8 for all other peers, such as SQLServer03\ Instance03, and then click Next.

Note

When choosing the server instances and database to be configured as peers, you cannot choose the original SQL Server instance hosting the peer database. In this example, the database would be SQLServer01\ Instance01. In addition, you must choose whether you want Pull or Push subscription.

9. On the Log Reader Agent Security screen, enter the appropriate Log Reader Agent user account and password for both the connections to the distributor and subscriber by clicking the ellipses on the Distribution Agent Security page. For this example, enable Use the First Peer's Security Settings for All Other Peers and click Next.

10. On the Distribution Agent Security screen, enter the appropriate Distribution Agent user account and password for both the connections to the distributor and subscriber by clicking the ellipses. For this example, enable Use the First Peer's Security Settings for All Other Peers option, and then click Next.

11. On the next screen, New Peer Initialization, select the option I Created the Peer Database Manually, or I Restored a Backup of the Original Publication Database Which Has Not Been Changed Since the Backup Was Taken, and then click Next.

12. On the Complete the Wizard screen, review the configuration settings selected, and then click Finish.

Note

An error may arise on the SQLServer01\Instance01 server stating that the publication or its log reader agent already exists and will not be modified. This error is erroneous and should be disregarded.

---

13. Review the status of each action; then click Close to finalize the building of the peer-to-peer topology.

14. To validate that the peer-to-peer replication topology has been created, expand both the Local Publication and Local Subscription folders on each SQL Server peer node. The appropriate publication and subscriptions should be created, as shown in Figure 13.20.

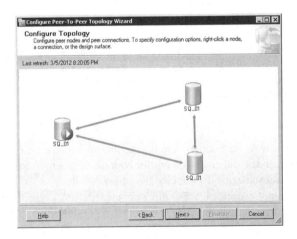

FIGURE 13.20
Viewing the peer-to-peer publications and subscriptions via SSMS.

Adding a Node to an Existing Peer-to-Peer Replication Topology

Sometimes you may need to add new peer nodes to the existing peer-to-peer replication topology after it has been created and initialized. If necessary, follow these high-level steps:

1. On the new server, first configure distribution based on the steps described previously.

2. Initialize the schema and data by either backing up and restoring the source database or by creating an SSIS package.

3. From a SQL Server instance, expand the Replication folder and then Local Publications.

4. Right-click the publication you created in the previous steps and select Configure Peer-to-Peer Topology.

5. On the Configure Peer-to-Peer Topology Wizard screen, click Next.

6. On the Publication screen, expand the AdventureWorks2012 database and select the peer-to-peer publication created in the previous steps.

7. On the Peers screen, click Add SQL Server. Connect to the new SQL Server instance to be added, and then select the new server as a peer. Click Next to continue.

8. On the Log Reader Agent Security screen, enter the appropriate Log Reader Agent user account and password for both the connections to the distributor and subscriber by clicking the ellipses on the Distribution Agent Security page. Click Next to continue.

9. On the Distribution Agent Security screen, enter the appropriate Distribution Agent user account and password for both the connections to the distributor and subscriber by clicking the ellipses on the Distribution Agent Security page, and then click Next.

10. On the New Peer Initialization screen, specify the option I Created the Peer Database Manually and then click Next.

11. On the Complete the Wizard screen, review the configuration settings you selected, and then click Finish.

12. Review the status of each action and click Close to finalize the building of the peer-to-peer topology.

Managing SQL Server 2012 Replication

The following sections focus on management tasks after SQL Server 2012 replication has been implemented. These tasks are in no particular

order and can be configured via SQL Server Management Studio or
Transact-SQL.

Managing the Distributor's Properties

There are several options for the distributor. Right-click the Replication
folder on your distributor and select Distributor Properties. In the General
tab, click the ellipsis button to the right of the distribution databases. There
are several text boxes of interest here:

- **Transaction Retention**—Transaction Retention has two options:

  - **Store Transactions: At Least**—This setting determines how
    long transactional replication commands remain in the distri-
    bution database after they are applied to all subscribers. In
    general, set this to 0, which means they are cleaned up the
    next time the distribution cleanup task runs. In some cases,
    you will want to set this to higher values, normally when
    replication is involved in some disaster recovery scenario.
    Limit this setting as low as possible because it can cause
    performance degradation if set to high.

  - **Store Transactions: But Not More Than**—This setting
    determines how long transactional replication commands can
    pool in the distribution database before the subscriber expires.
    Again, limit this setting as low as possible to cover any
    reasonable time periods your subscriber could be offline so
    that it does not cause performance problems.

- **History Retention**—Store replication performance history at least;
  history retention is frequently needed for debugging purposes. The
  more history you collect, the slower your agents will run. Accepting
  the defaults is the best choice here.

There is also an option to set default profiles on the General tab of the
Distributor Properties dialog box. You can set a default profile here for
each agent. For example, you could set the Continue on Data Consistency
Error Profile if you continually have problems with data collisions.

The Publishers tab of the Distributor properties dialog allows you to add
publishers and set an administrative link password.

Disabling Publishing and Distribution

If you need to disable replication on a server, connect to the server in SQL
Server Management Studio, right-click the Replication folder, and select

Disable Publishing and Distribution. Click Next at the splash screen. A dialog will ask if you want to disable publishing on the server, or continue using replication on this server. Make your selection and click Next. You will then be prompted to delete existing publications and subscriptions. Click Next, and you will be prompted to disable publishing and distribution and/or create a script to do so. Make the appropriate choice and click Next; then click Finish and Close.

Choose Disable Publishing if you no longer want to use this server as a publisher or distributor. If you still have active publications on this server or want to use it as a distributor, select No, Continue Using This Server as a Publisher.

Deleting Local Subscriptions

If you need to delete a subscription, connect to the Publisher in SQL Server Management Studio and expand the Local Publications folder, expand your publication, right-click your subscription, and select Delete. Select Yes at the confirmation prompt. You can also delete the subscription by connecting to the subscriber and expanding the Replication folder, expanding Local Subscriptions, right-clicking the subscription, and selecting Delete. Click Yes at the confirmation prompt.

Deleting Local Publications

To delete a publication, connect to the Publisher in SQL Server Management Studio, expand the Replication folder, expand the Local Publications folder, right-click the publication you want to delete, select Delete, and click Yes.

Managing Replication Passwords

To modify the Administrative Link Password to connect to a Remote Distributor, right-click the Replication folder and Select Update Replication Passwords. Enter the passwords and click OK.

Generating Replication Scripts

If you ever need to create a replication script, you can right-click the publication or subscription and select Generate Script. In SQL Server 2012, you can generate a script to a file (the default), to the clipboard, or to a new query window. The dialog allows you to generate scripts to create the publication or subscription or to delete it.

You can also right-click the Replication folder and generate scripts for selected databases or your entire server.

Notes from the Field: Avoid Losing Permissions When Subscription Is Reinitialized

Reinitializing a subscription involves applying a new snapshot of one or more articles to one or more Subscribers. Reinitialization of a subscription usually occurs when you perform a property change to an object or when you explicitly mark a subscription for reinitialization. Whenever a snapshot is reinitialized, all the objects in the subscription database are dropped and re-created. This operation causes the subscription database to lose all permissions that were granted on the objects or at the statement level. You can prevent losing permissions whenever subscription is reinitialized by following these recommendations:

■ Script out permissions at objects and statements level after replication has been set up along with any permissions or security applied on objects in your replication environment. This can be useful when you have to rebuild replication from scratch. For example, there could be a situation where the server hosting replication crashed. If you had not scripted out replication during the setup, you'll need to remember the list of articles, filters, and so on. Therefore, scripting out replication after it is set up could be helpful when you have to rebuild replication after server crash.

■ Another recommended option is to configure subscription in such a way that it does not drop any objects whenever you reinitialize subscription. This can be achieved by reapplying permissions after the reinitialization has been conducted. Keep in mind you would need to script out the permission beforehand. It is possible to script out the subscription so that is does not drop any objects by doing the following:

   ■ Use SP_CHANGEARTICLE system stored procedure to configure the value of PRE_CREATION_CMD for the parameter @PROPERTY and a value of 'NONE,' 'DELETE,' or 'TRUNCATE' for the parameter @Value.

   ■ In the Article Properties dialog box in the destination object section, select a value of "KEEP EXISTING OBJECT UNCHANGED, DELETE DATA," "IF ARTICLE HAS A ROW FILTER, DELETE ONLY THAT MATCHES THE FILTER," or "TRUNCATE ALL DATA IN THE EXISTING OBJECT."

Monitoring and Troubleshooting SQL Server Replication

The central point to monitor and troubleshoot replication is through Replication Monitor. To launch Replication Monitor, right-click the Replication folder. When Replication Monitor comes up, add your publisher by clicking the Add Publisher link. Then drill down on your publisher in the left pane and expand it to display all publications. As you click each publication, all subscriptions to it will be displayed in the right pane. Three to four tabs will be displayed, depending on your replication type. These tabs are for monitoring and managing subscriptions:

- **All Subscriptions**—This tab is similar to the Publications tab; however, this tab displays information on subscriptions, not publications. The information displayed based on the columns available includes the status of each subscription, the subscription name, performance, and latency. In addition, it is possible to filter subscriptions based on All Subscriptions, 25 Worst Performing Subscriptions, 50 Worst Performing Subscriptions, Errors and Warnings Only, Errors Only, Warning Only, Subscriptions Running, and Subscriptions Not Running.

- **Tracer Tokens**—The second tab is a great utility to test the replication topology, including performance, by placing an artificial synthetic transaction into the replication stream. By clicking the Insert Tracer command button, you can review and calculate performance metrics between the publisher to distributor, distributor to subscriber, and the total latency for the artificial transaction.

- **Agents**—This tab provides job information and status on all publications on the publisher. For each common job, the following information is displayed: Status, Job Name, Last Start Time, and Duration.

- **Warnings and Alerts**—When you're monitoring subscriptions, the final tab allows you to configure warnings, alerts, and notifications on subscriptions. The two warnings are Warn If a Subscription Will Expire Within Threshold and Warn If Latency Exceeds the Threshold. Click the Alerts button to display the alerts. Each of these predefined replication alerts can be configured and customized based on a SQL Server event, SQL Server performance condition alert, WMI event alert, error numbers, or severity. In addition, a response can be created for each alert. These responses can execute a specific job or notify an operator on each replication alert that has been customized. The predefined alerts include the following:
  - **Peer-to-peer conflict detection alert**
  - **Replication Warning**—Long merge over dialup connection (Threshold:Mergelowrunduration)
  - **Replication Warning**—Long merge over LAN connection (Threshold: mergefastrunduration)

- **Replication Warning**—Slow merge over dialup connection (Threshold: mereslowrunspeed)
- **Replication Warning**—Slow merge over LAN connection (Threshold: mergefastrunspeed)
- **Replication Warning**—Subscription expiration (Threshold: expiration)
- **Replication Warning**—Transactional replication latency (Threshold: latency)
- **Replication**—Agent custom shutdown
- **Replication**—Agent failure
- **Replication**—Agent retry
- **Replication**—Agent success
- **Replication**—Expired subscription dropped
- **Replication**—Subscriber has failed data validation
- **Replication**—Subscriber has passed data validation
- **Replication**—Subscription reinitialized after validation failure

Summary

Replication in SQL Server 2012 is a mature technology and a great utility to distribute data among SQL Server instances. For the most part, replication is predominantly used for distributing data between physical sites within an organization. However, it is also commonly used for creating redundant read-only copies of a database for reporting purposes and for consolidating data from many locations.

Although replication can be used as a form of high availability or for disaster recovery, failover clustering, log shipping, and database mirroring are preferred alternatives because they guarantee transaction safety in the event of a disaster.

Best Practices

Some of the best practices that apply to replication include the following:

- Create a backup and restore strategy after the replication topology has been implemented. Remember to include the distribution, MSDB, and master databases on the publisher, distributor, and all subscribers.
- Script all replication components from a disaster recovery perspective. Scripts are also useful for conducting repetitive tasks. Finally,

regenerate and/or update scripts whenever a replication component changes.

■ Use Replication Monitor to create baseline metrics for tuning replication and validate that the hardware and network infrastructure live up to the replication requirements and expectations.

■ Familiarize yourself with modifying database schema and publications after replication has been configured. Some replication items can be changed on-the-fly, whereas others require you to create a new snapshot.

■ When using transactional replication or merge replication, it is beneficial to perform data validation to ensure that data at the subscriber matches data at the publisher.

■ Place the Distribution system database on either a RAID 1 or RAID 1+0 volume other than the operating system. Finally, set the recovery model to Full to safeguard against database failures and set the size of the database to accommodate the replication data.

■ When configuring replication security, apply the principle of least privilege to ensure that replication is hardened and unwanted authorization is prevented.

■ To address performance degradation on the publisher, configure a distributor on its own server.

■ If data within the replication topology is sensitive, it is recommended that encryption should be used for securing data in transit and at rest.

■ The Service Master Key needs to be available to recover from some HA scenarios.

PART IV

Performance Tuning, Monitoring, Troubleshooting, and Maintenance

IN THIS PART

CHAPTER 14 Performance Tuning and Troubleshooting SQL Server 2012

CHAPTER 15 Monitoring SQL Server 2012

CHAPTER 16 SQL Server 2012 Maintenance Practices

CHAPTER 14

Performance Tuning and Troubleshooting SQL Server 2012

Speak with any DBA, and the conversation will eventually turn to performance issues and troubleshooting. This is because a large part of a DBA's time is spent on performance tuning and resolving issues that can ultimately affect a SQL Server system, database, or application. It is also worth mentioning that performance tuning and troubleshooting are such popular subjects because they are entwined with so many other tools and processes—making it one very large topic. Specifically, performance tuning and troubleshooting performance issues are iterative processes that include monitoring, troubleshooting, and adjusting. When troubleshooting SQL Server performance issues, it is helpful to have a baseline or a goal in mind, such as having a specific query execute in fewer than X milliseconds.

Performance tuning and troubleshooting can be viewed as a layered model. The layers consist of the hardware, operating system, SQL Server, database, and application. Each layer is dependent on the layers below it for its performance, as illustrated in Figure 14.1. For example, if the hardware layer is not performing due to a lack of resources, this affects the performance of the database layer. It makes little or no sense to optimize the upper layers if the lower layers have not been optimized. In some cases, the application and database may be on the same level.

This chapter augments other performance-tuning and troubleshooting techniques covered in other chapters, including such topics as Data Collector, Operations Manager, Resource Governor, and Dynamic Management Views in SQL Server 2012, and the Windows Performance and Reliability Monitor in Windows Server 2008 R2.

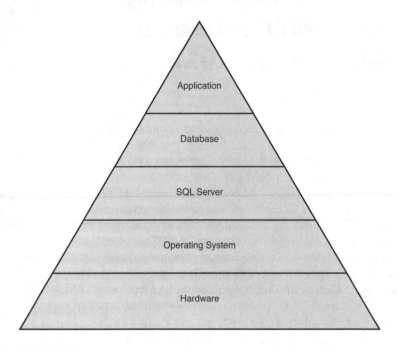

FIGURE 14.1
Optimization layers.

This chapter builds on the information already presented in the book, with new concepts in performance tuning and troubleshooting, such as which performance counters you should utilize when using Windows Performance Monitor, how to analyze workloads with SQL Server Profiler, how to leverage SQL Server Database Engine Tuning Advisor to make index recommendations, and how to use Dynamic Management Views (DMV) and Extended Events.

Note

Throughout the chapter are references to collecting performance counters and various logs, such as the SQL Server logs and Windows event logs. Although they are not covered in this chapter, Performance Studio and Operations Manager are great tools for collecting and keeping a long-term history of all the counters covered in this chapter. It is strongly recommended that you deploy and use either Data Collector in conjunction with Utility Control Point or Operations Manager to monitor the SQL Server 2012 infrastructure. Data Collector is covered in Chapter 15, "Monitoring SQL Server 2012."

Appropriately, this chapter starts with troubleshooting performance at the lowest level: the platform.

Notes from the Field: Performance Tuning 101

Many experienced data professionals have a difficult time with troubleshooting and performance tuning. They get anxious, sometimes even panicking. They are not sure where to begin. They worry that someone will get angry or that their phone will start to ring with frequent, angry calls from their internal customers. Yet successful performance tuning and troubleshooting follow a simple methodology:

- Check for errors in the Windows and SQL Server logs and, if found, remediate them. Refer to the SQL Server 2012 Books Online (BOL) for help resolving specific error numbers.

- If performance issues or troubles continue, examine the SQL Server 2012 wait statistics to determine the broad category of the root problem, such as I/O, locking, network connectivity, or memory issues, among many others. In some cases, the issue may appear to be external to SQL Server.

- Correlate the wait statistics analysis with Windows Performance Monitor (PerfMon) analysis and corroborate the initial wait statistics analysis. For example, high wait statistics in the latch categories should also exhibit high counter values for memory grants pending and, possibly, page life expectancy. Taken together, these findings constitute irrefutable evidence. If needed, use SQL Profiler (or server-side traces) to further corroborate the wait statistics analysis.

- Trace the troublesome wait statistic all the way down to the specific SPIDs, SQL transactions, and processes that are the root cause.

- Tune and/or rewrite the root cause problem, such as an individual query or stored procedure until it no longer exhibits the symptomatic behavior. If the root cause is a component of a third-party packaged application, send it back to the vendor under your support agreement and insist that they tune and/or rewrite the problematic object.

■ Fully test the new object and, when satisfied, put it into production. Monitor it closely until it proves itself to be error-free and a good performer.

Platform Troubleshooting and Optimization

At the root of almost all optimization efforts are the hardware and operating system that a SQL Server instance resides on, which is collectively referred to as the *platform*. The initial efforts should focus on investigating disk activity, processor utilization, and memory usage. Typically, one of these three elements will be the likely cause for performance degradation.

Windows Performance Monitor includes hundreds of performance objects and thousands of counters of sometimes dizzyingly minutia within the platform. This is where a short list of the most useful performance objects and counters becomes a necessary part of the optimization and troubleshooting process. The following section of the chapter discusses these objects and counters and how to leverage them when performance tuning and troubleshooting an instance of SQL Server 2012. In addition, this section focuses on how to interpret the counters against baseline thresholds.

This section should not be confused with Chapter 15, which also discusses the Performance and Reliability Monitoring tools included with Windows Server 2008 R2. Chapter 15, specifically the section titled "Adding Counters with Performance Monitor," focuses on how to use the Performance Monitoring tool to monitor a SQL Server system, whereas this chapter emphasizes the counters to use when tuning and troubleshooting.

Note

Both SQL Server 2012 and Windows Server 2008 R2 include a remarkable number of objects and counters to choose from when tuning and troubleshooting an instance of SQL Server 2012. Providing detailed information about what each counter does in this chapter would be great, but with so much other information to cover, it is unrealistic. Readers who are interested in finding out more about an individual performance counter, however, can get detailed information about counters by enabling the Show Description option in the Add Counters dialog box and highlighting a specific counter to obtain a detailed description.

Platform Performance Measures

If the hardware is not sufficient for the load placed on it by SQL Server, performance issues and failures will result. In cases like these, it is best to first turn your attention to performance objects and counters included with SQL Server. With the use of the Windows Performance Monitor tool and a set of the most important performance objects and counters, DBAs can learn whether the underlying platform is experiencing performance problems.

Note

When tuning SQL Server using performance counters, DBAs don't need to invoke Performance Monitor every time. Instead, they can query the DMV sys.dm_os_performance_counters anytime they want to interrogate SQL Server-specific counters. This is a great time saver and makes for easily building out a reusable toolkit of queries to investigate whenever SQL Server needs a little extra attention. For example, the following query finds out all the latest Perfmon counter data about SQL Server locks as applied to the entire server:

```
SELECT cntr_value, counter_name
FROM sys.dm_os_performance_counters
WHERE object_name = N'SQLServer:Locks'
    AND instance_name = N'_Total';
```

DBAs should capture the following counters at a minimum to understand how the hardware and operating system are performing. The common counters are broken down by memory, network, processor, and disk.

Memory Objects and Counters

- **Memory: Pages/sec**—The Pages/sec counter indicates the rate at which pages are read or written to disk during hard page faults. When memory pages are transferred to and from a relatively slow disk, the system will experience slow performance. The counter should be 20 or less on average, but the closer to 0 the better, although the number may spike. Add memory to the server if this number is continually high. If nothing is done, it is more than likely that SQL Server will experience memory pressure.

- **Memory: Available Bytes**—The Available Bytes counter illustrates the amount of physical memory available for allocation. There should be at least 100MB of free RAM. If there is less than 100MB, consider adding more RAM to the server.

When these two counters indicate memory pressure, DBAs should look more deeply into the situation by reviewing the following counters associated with SQL Server memory:

- **Process: Working Set**—This is the current size of the memory pages that the process is utilizing for the database and related applications. When memory is becoming scarce, the working sets of the applications will be trimmed. When memory is plentiful, the working sets are allowed to grow. Larger working sets mean more code and data in memory, making the overall performance of the applications increase. However, a large working set that does not shrink appropriately is usually an indication of a memory leak.

- **SQL Server: Buffer Manager: Page Life Expectancy**—Provides the average number of seconds SQL Server expects a data or index page to stay in the buffer pool. A general guideline for an OLTP system should be a value of 300 or more seconds.

- **SQL Server: Buffer Manager: Total Pages**—The total number of pages, including database, free, and stolen pages in the buffer pool.

- **SQL Server: Buffer Manager: Target Pages**—The ideal number of pages in the buffer pool according to the max memory setting for the instance.

- **SQL Server: Memory Manager: Total Server Memory (KB)**—The amount of memory that the SQL Server instance is currently using. The value for this counter should grow until it is equal to the value of the Target Server Memory (KB). If the value is less than the target value, the instance is not considered to be in a "steady-state." During this period, there may be more physical I/O reads than normal.

- **SQL Server: Memory Manager: Target Server Memory (KB)**—The amount of memory that the SQL Server instance should be using based on the maximum memory setting.

Network Objects and Counters

- **Network Interface: Bytes Total/sec**—The Network Interface: Bytes Total/sec counter identifies the rate in seconds at which data is passing though the network interface card (NIC). It is beneficial to track both input and output on all network cards installed on the SQL Server. For a 100Mbps network adapter, the value should be below 6 to 7Mbps, and for a 1000Mbps network adapter, it should

be below 60 to 70Mbps. In addition, when using 1Gbps, the value
should be below 0.06 Gbps, and if using 10Gbps, the value should
be below 0.6 Gbps.

■ **Network Interface: Packets Outbound Errors**—Indicates the
number of packages that should not be transmitted because of errors.
The expected value should be 0 at all times.

Page File Objects and Counters

■ **Paging File: %Usage**—This counter indicates the amount of page
file being used as a percentage. The value should be less than 70
percent.

■ **Paging File: %Usage Peak**—The Paging File: %Usage Peak
counter indicates the peak usage of the Page File instance based on a
percentage. This amount should be either less than 70 percent or
greater than the %usage value.

Physical Disk Objects and Counters

■ **Physical Disk: % Disk Time**—The % Disk Time counter illustrates
the amount of time the disk is busy as a percent. This should be less
than 55 percent over any sustained period of time, although that
number may spike occasionally. If this number is too high, consider
adding drives to the array to increase the spindles and spread the
load, adding additional channels, or changing the RAID version to a
higher performance version (for example, RAID 5 to RAID 1+0 or
moving to a Solid State Disks).

■ **Physical Disk: Avg. Disk Queue Length**—The Avg. Disk Queue
Length counter exposes the number of disk requests that are waiting
in the queue. According to queuing theory, this should be less than
two over any sustained period of time or the queue could become
backlogged. If this number is too high, consider using faster drives,
such as 15K RPM, and/or adding drives to the array to increase the
spindles and spread the load, adding additional channels, or changing the RAID version to a higher performance version (for example,
RAID 5 to RAID1+0 or moving to a Solid State Disks).

■ **Physical Disk: Reads/sec**—Indicates the rate of read operations on
the disk. Poor performance is indicated by a value greater than 20
milliseconds. Average performance is acceptable when the value is

between 12 and 20 milliseconds, and an optimal setting is less than 8 milliseconds.

■ **Physical Disk: Writes/sec**—Indicates the rate of write operations on the disk. If writes are high, it is possible that read latencies are also affected as of direct correlations with high write times. The average value should be below 100ms at all times.

If an organization is using a SAN as the storage device, the DBA should leverage the performance monitoring tools included with the SAN for accurately troubleshooting disk issues. This is especially important because the SAN administrator may have abstracted away many important details about the configuration of the disk subsystem when defining the logical units (LUN, that is, a drive letter) used by SQL Server. In addition, to isolate SQL Server I/O activity from all the other I/O activity on a system, use these SQL Server counters: SQL Server: Buffer Manager: Page reads/sec and SQL Server: Buffer Manager: Page writes/sec.

Note

When monitoring physical counters, it is recommended to not only include the total disk counters, but each individual disk counter should also be included based on the drives in the system. This will ensure that the results are not skewed and that it is possible to assess the exact disk causing the performance issue.

Processor Objects and Counters

■ **Processor: % Processor Time**—The % Processor Time counter exposes the time the processor is doing actual work. This value is arrived at in a backward fashion by measuring the percentage of time the processor is idle and subtracting that from 100 to get the time the processor is busy doing work. This should be less than 75 percent over any sustained period of time, although it will spike occasionally. If this number is too high, consider adding or upgrading the processors on the server.

■ **System: Processor Queue Length**—The Processor Queue Length counter displays the number of threads in the processor queue. There is a single queue for processor time even on computers with multiple processors. If this exceeds two per processor (that is, four on a two-processor server or eight on a four-processor server), consider adding or upgrading the processors on the server. It is common for queries without the proper indexes or with memory pressure occurring on a system to cause this spike.

- **System: Processor % Privileged Time**—This counter displays the percentage of time a process was running in privileged mode. The value should be less than 30 percent of the Total % Processor Time.

Tip

Keep in mind that SQL Server loves RAM. Sometimes, budget constraints force a choice between faster CPUs with a smaller L1-L3 cache or slower CPUs with larger L1-L3 cache. In most cases on SQL Server, performance is better using slightly slower CPUs with larger on-dye caches than on faster CPUs equipped with a smaller cache, especially when processing large amounts of data. The reason is that CPU cycles can be wasted while waiting for data fetches from RAM. Having a larger cache means that the CPU performs fewer round trips on data retrieval from the cache and speeds overall processing.

The example in Figure 14.2 shows a log for the recommended common performance counters. The nice part of this log is that the tool summarizes the average, minimum, and maximum for each counter.

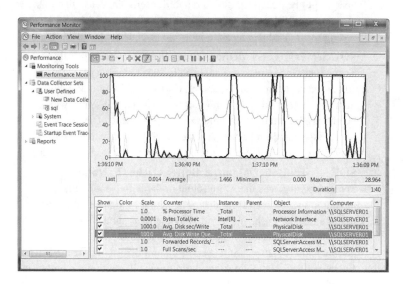

FIGURE 14.2
Performance log counters.

Database Engine and Integration Services Performance Measures

Over time, DBAs learn that they need to approach each troubleshooting and tuning issue methodically if they are to resolve them successfully and in a timely fashion. For instance, if bottlenecks were not found while troubleshooting the platform based on the common performance objects and counters recommended, the next step is dissecting the issue at a deeper level, like troubleshooting specific features of the SQL Server 2012, such as the Database Engine or Integration Services. It should be noted that each SQL Server 2012 Database Engine feature requires a slightly different approach and tools to troubleshoot performance issues.

The Database Engine

There are a number of counter objects and counters that SQL Server 2012 uses to monitor the SQL Server Database Engine. Following are the primary counters for performance troubleshooting of the Database Engine:

- **SQL Server: Access Methods Page Splits/sec**—This counter indicates the number of page splits per second that occur as the result of an overflow of index pages. The ideal threshold should be less than 20 per 100 Batch Requests/sec. If the value is very high, I/O overhead might be occurring due to random inserts. In a case like this, evaluate the fill factor system configuration setting (or the fill factor setting for individual clustered indexes) or consider reindexing.

- **SQL Server: Access Methods Index Searches/sec and Full Scans/sec**—Index searches are used to start range scans, perform single-index record fetches, and reposition within an index. Full Scans/sec represents the number of unrestricted full scans, which can be either a base table or full index scan. The value of Index Searches/sec and Full Scans/sec should be greater than 1000. Obviously, these values will not be presented if SQL Server is idle.

- **SQL Server: Buffer Manager Buffer Cache Hit Ratio**— Percentage of pages that were found in the buffer pool without having to incur a read from disk. The actual ratio is based on the total number of cache hits divided by the total number of cache lookups over the last few thousand page accesses. The counters start getting captured after a SQL Server system is restarted. If the Buffer Cache Hit Ratio is too low, you need to install additional memory in the SQL Server system. The value should be at least 90% and ideally at 99%. However, with large databases with extensive access, this number might be difficult to achieve. This ratio should be high, typically above 90% because you want SQL Server to read from cache instead of reading from disk. Potential problems could be based on memory pressure.

■ **SQL Server: Buffer Manager Page Life Expectancy**—Represents the number of seconds a page will stay in the SQL Server cache. If low page life occurs, it could be due to memory issues, missing indexes, or high page faults. The threshold should be greater than 300. If it is less than 300, SQL Server is experiencing memory pressure.

■ **SQL Server: General Statistics: User Connections**—Counts the number of users currently connected to SQL Server. Although there is no specific guideline on the number of users shown by the User Connections counter, the utilization of SQL Server is proportional to the number of users. The more users the server is supporting, the higher the load on the server.

■ **SQL Server: General Statistics Logins/sec**—Total number of logins occurring per second that are not already pooled. The preferred threshold should be < 2.

■ **SQL Server: General Statistics Logouts/sec**—Total number of logout operations started per second. The preferred threshold should be < 2.

■ **SQL Server: Latches Latch Waits/sec**—Indicates the number of latch requests that could not be granted immediately. The preferred threshold should be calculated with this formula: (Total Latch Wait Time) / (Latch Waits/Sec) < 10. If the value is high, it is likely there is an I/O or memory bottleneck, which can be relieved by adding more RAM and I/O throughput.

■ **SQL Server: Latches Total Latch Wait Time (ms)**—The Total Latch Wait Time identifies the latch requests that had to wait in the last second and presents them in milliseconds. The formula, which is (Total Latch Wait Time) / (Latch Waits/Sec) < 10, is similar to the formula for Latch Waits/sec and suggests that there are I/O or memory issues if the value is greater than 10.

■ **SQL Server: Locks Lock Waits/sec**—This counter shows the number of lock requests that could not be satisfied immediately and required the caller to wait before being granted the lock. Ideally, the counter's value should be very low; the closer to zero, the better.

Essentially, the lower the number, the shorter the transaction, which means the transaction is not causing a lock.

- **SQL Server: SQL Statistics: SQL Compilations/sec**—The number of SQL compilations per second is referenced by this counter, which indicates the number of times the compile code path is entered. Includes compiles caused by statement-level recompilations in SQL Server. After SQL Server user activity is stable, this value will reach a steady state. < 10 percent of the number of Batch Requests/sec. Batch Requests/sec represents the number of TSQL command batches received per second.

- **SQL Server: SQL Statistics:SQL Re-Compilations/sec**—This counter identifies the number of times statements recompiled per second. A low recompilation rate is ideal, such as < 10 percent of the number of SQL Compilations/sec. In later versions of SQL Server, recompilations are statement-scoped instead of batch-scoped as they are in Microsoft SQL Server 2000. Therefore, direct comparison of the counter values before SQL Server 2008 and later versions are not possible.

Integration Services

Integration Services fundamentally depends on the performance of queries; hence, optimizing queries and database access is critical to the performance of Integration Services.

When troubleshooting and performance tuning Integration Services, review the Progress tab information to see where the longest-running components are, and then optimize them. This information can also be captured in the package and data flow logs.

Integration Services also includes a number of performance counters in the SQL Server: SSIS Pipeline object that can be used to troubleshoot performance problems. These counters are listed in Table 14.1.

Table 14.1 **Integration Services Performance Counters**

Counter	Description
BLOB Bytes Read	The number of bytes of binary large object (BLOB) data that the data flow engine has read from all sources.
BLOB Bytes Written	The number of bytes of BLOB data that the data flow engine has written to all destinations.

Table 14.1 **Continued**

Counter	Description
BLOB Files in Use	The number of BLOB files that the data flow engine currently is using for spooling.
Buffer Memory	The amount of memory in use. This may include both physical and virtual memory. When this number is larger than the amount of physical memory, the Buffers Spooled count rises as an indication that memory swapping is increasing. Increased memory swapping slows performance of the data flow engine.
Buffers in Use	The number of buffer objects of all types that all data flow components and the data flow engine are currently using.
Buffers Spooled	The number of buffers currently written to the disk. If the data flow engine runs low on physical memory, buffers not currently used are written to disk and then reloaded when needed.
Flat Buffer Memory	The total amount of memory, in bytes, that all flat buffers use. Flat buffers are blocks of memory that a component uses to store data. A flat buffer is a large block of bytes that is accessed byte by byte.
Flat Buffers in Use	The number of flat buffers that the data flow engine uses. All flat buffers are private buffers.
Private Buffer Memory	The total amount of memory in use by all private buffers. A buffer is not private if the data flow engine creates it to support data flow. A private buffer is a buffer that a transformation uses for temporary work only. For example, the Aggregation transformation uses private buffers to do its work.
Private Buffers in Use	The number of buffers that transformations use.
Rows Read	The number of rows that a source produces. The number does not include rows read from reference tables by the Lookup transformation.
Rows Written	The number of rows offered to a destination. The number does not reflect rows written to the destination data store.

When you're troubleshooting a package executing within Integration Services, use event handlers to troubleshoot package execution problems. One of the most resource-intensive and performance-impacting operations is sorting within a package flow. This consumes large quantities of memory and processing resources. This is true if the package contains either the Sort transformation or a query within the data flow that includes the ORDER BY clause. The IsSorted hint property can be used to indicate to down-level components that the data is already sorted and bypass the sorting overhead of down-level components.

SQL Server Logs

There are other important areas to monitor when troubleshooting the SQL Server 2012 Database Engine, including the Windows application log and SQL Server error logs. The Windows application log contains application-level logs, including those from the SQL Server 2012 application. In addition, SQL Server and SQL Server Agent both log events to the SQL Server log. Because of all the information accessible through these logs, DBAs should make it a practice to review them when troubleshooting SQL Server 2012.

When more detailed information is warranted, DBAs should also inspect the SQL Server error log. In many ways, this log is also more important to the SQL Server application. The SQL Log File Viewer allows you to view various logs at the same time, interleaving the log entries for easy correlation, as shown in Figure 14.3. The figure shows the aggregation of the SQL Agent log, SQL Server log, Windows application log, and Windows security log. This presentation of data reduces the level of effort needed to troubleshoot problems because causative and related events can be analyzed in the same window.

You can access the SQL Server logs from the SQL Server Management Studio by selecting Management, and then selecting SQL Server Logs.

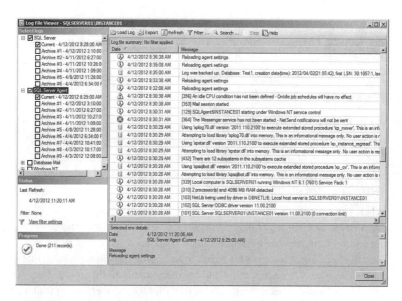

FIGURE 14.3
SQL Log File Viewer correlation.

Database Troubleshooting and Optimization

When thinking about database tuning, DBAs should have the mindset that database tuning will always be a work in process. Database tuning can result in a tremendous boost in performance and address the root cause of many troubleshooting issues. When you're setting up a database, it can be difficult to know exactly what indexes to create because it may not be completely clear how applications will use the database or which stored procedures will be created. DBAs rarely have insight into the types of queries and data access patterns an application will present to the database, especially if they have inherited a third-party database and application. On the other end, application developers rarely have any understanding about the inner workings of a database and may not know precisely what their application is doing from a data perspective. Given the complexity of the situation, developing a fully tuned database for any given application straight out of development is extremely difficult.

Fortunately, it is possible to cut the Gordian knot by capturing the application behavior during actual use and then using that captured data to make tuning recommendations. There are a number of specialized tools to do this, including SQL Server Profiler, Database Engine Tuning Advisor, and the new Extended Events interface.

The following sections conduct a basic optimization walkthrough to show how you can use these tools to optimize a database.

Wait Statistics Analysis

When troubleshooting, it is always important to first determine whether anything within SQL Server or the platform is *broken*. The only way to effectively do that is to check both the Windows Event Log and the SQL Server logs (described in Chapter 15).

When you are sure that there are no major failures of the system, as revealed in the error logs, there is no better place to begin the troubleshooting and performance tuning process than SQL Server *wait statistics*. Wait statistics are simply a means by which SQL Server classifies anything that inhibits a process from executing and are measured in milliseconds. For example, if user A is executing queries on SPID 99 and then has to wait for user B, executing an UPDATE statement on SPID 112, to release the locks, then user A's SPID will register the time spent waiting in one of the LCK wait statistics. Similarly, there are wait statistics for just about every comprehensible reason a process on SQL Server might be caused to wait. In fact, there are even wait statistics (often shortened to "wait stats") for things *outside* of SQL Server that might cause you to wait—the so-called PREEMPTIVE wait stats.

You can see the current wait statistics on a given SQL Server 2012 instance by querying the sys.dm_os_wait_stats DMV, as in the following:

```
SELECT *
FROM sys.dm_os_wait_stats
ORDER BY wait_type DESC;
```

A long and involved discussion of all of SQL Server 2012's wait statistics are beyond the scope of this book. However, when performing wait stat analysis, you can use a short list of wait stats to help you quickly categorize the type of problem that is causing poor performance on SQL Server. Consider these wait statistics as the "dirty dozen" that should warrant further investigation:

- **ASYNC_I/O_COMPLETION**—Generally, represents slowness in the I/O subsystem.

- **ASYNC_NETWORK_I/O**—Generally, the network is causing SQL Server to wait, possibly because of low bandwidth or an oversaturated NIC.

- **CXPACKET**—Specifically, CXPACKET (meaning "context exchange packet") represents wait caused by parallelized transactions. However, this wait stat generally appears when another subsystem of SQL Server, such as a slow I/O or a small buffer cache, causes one or more parts of a parallelized transaction to slow down. In other words, CXPACKET is usually a symptom of a deeper problem, not the problem in and of itself.

- **I/O_COMPLETION**—Generally, represents slowness in the I/O subsystem.

- **LATCH_X**—Meaning "latch exclusive," these wait stats usually indicate time spent waiting for a latch in regions of SQL Server memory outside of the data buffer—for example, excessive pressure on the plan cache.

- **LCK_xx**—LCK wait statistics indicate that SQL Server is waiting for locks to be released, especially for LCK_X, LCK_M_U, and LCK_M_X. (The _X suffix means "exclusive" locks; in contrast, the _SH suffix means "shared" locks.) High LCK waits usually indicates poor application design, problem indexes, and/or bad SQL queries and transactions.

- **LOGBUFFER and WRITELOG**—When either of these wait stats appear high on a SQL Server's list of wait statistics, the SQL Server is usually experiencing slowness in the transaction log I/O subsystem.

- **PAGEIOLATCH_X**—High pagiolatch waits are incurred whenever SQL Server has to transfer data from disk into the buffer cache. This wait stat might indicate a slow I/O subsystem, but it might also indicate very poorly written queries that push a lot of data into the cache (think of queries against big tables without a WHERE clause).

- **PAGELATCH_X**—A pagelatch wait occurs when SQL Server needs to latch an address in the buffer cache, so high pagelatch_x (as in "exclusive") waits usually indicate memory pressure, specifically in the buffer cache.

- **RESOURCE_SEMAPHORE**—High resource_semaphore waits usually indicate SQL Server is waiting for a memory grant from Windows.

- **RESOURCE_SEMAPHORE_QUERY_COMPILE**—This wait
  stat measures the time SQL Server spends compiling, and recompil-
  ing, execution plans. This is frequently an indicator of poorly written
  SQL and Transact-SQL code.

- **SLEEP_BPOOL_FLUSH**—The checkpoint process flushes dirty
  pages to disc, by default, every minute or so. If the SLEEP_
  BPOOL_FLUSH process is high on the list of waits for a given SQL
  Server, it means that the checkpoint process is probably hitting an
  I/O bottleneck.

- **SOS_SCHEDULER_YIELD**—When high SOS (as in SQLOS)
  scheduler yields are present, SQL Server is spending considerable
  time yielding access to CPU resources among the many SPIDs
  running on the server. Consequently, SOS_SCHEDULER_YIELD
  waits usually mean CPU pressure.

The preceding list of wait statistics is by no means complete. But it is a
very useful starting point when examining a SQL Server instance to determine what its biggest problems might be. It is possible to further trace wait
statistics not only to an instance-level view, but to specific sessions on the
SQL Server using the DMV sys.dm_os_waiting_tasks. For example, we
might have seen that LCK waits were at the top of the resultset in the
preceding example and now want to find which specific SPIDs are causing
10 or more sessions to wait on locks (perhaps due to blocking):

```
SELECT wait_type, COUNT(*)
FROM sys.dm_os_waiting_tasks
WHERE wait_type LIKE 'LCK%'
GROUP BY wait_type
HAVING COUNT (*) >= 10;
```

Having probed the SQL Server DMVs to find the specific sessions that are
causing a lot of other sessions to wait, we can now use a new DMV
sys.dm_exec_requests in a join with sys.dm_os_waiting_tasks to find out
the exact query plan used by the offending session(s):

```
SELECT a.session_id,
a.wait_duration_ms,
a.wait_type,
a.blocking_session_id,
a.resource_description,
b.statement_start_offset,
b.statement_end_offset,
```

```
c.objectid,
c.text,
d.query_plan
FROM sys.dm_os_waiting_tasks AS a
        LEFT JOIN sys.dm_exec_requests AS b ON
a.waiting_task_address = b.task_address
OUTER APPLY sys.dm_exec_sql_text (b.sql_handle) AS c
        OUTER APPLY sys.dm_exec_query_plan (b.plan_handle) AS d;
```

Finally, when discussing wait statistics, it is important to remember that SQL Server will register a large number of waits that are simply the natural and organic inner workings of SQL Server. Consequently, the following wait statistics may show up high on the list of a SQL Server's wait statistics, but they do not require remediation. In fact, the following wait statistics should usually be ignored in most troubleshooting and performance-tuning scenarios on SQL Server:

- **BROKER%**—Unless you have an application that uses Service Broker on the instance of SQL Server.

- **CLR%**—Unless you have an application that uses CLR on the instance of SQL Server.

- **FT%**—Unless you use the full-text engine within SQL Server.

- **%QUEUE%**—Generally, the QUEUE wait statistics, such as CHECKPOINT_QUEUE and LOGMGR_QUEUE, are normal background processes on SQL Server.

- **%SLEEP%**—Generally, all the SLEEP wait statistics, such as LAZYWRITER_SLEEP, are normal background processes on SQL Server.

- **XE%**—Unless you want to specifically monitor XEvents on your instance of SQL Server.

- **REQUEST_FOR_DEADLOCK_SEARCH**—A routine wait caused by the internal deadlock monitor.

- **SQLTRACE_BUFFER_FLUSH**—A routine wait caused by the default trace process.

- **WAITFOR**—This wait stat appears due to an explicitly coded WAITFOR Transact-SQL statement. Since it was intentionally coded, it may be safe to ignore.

Assuming that wait statistic analysis has revealed a serious performance issue on the instance of SQL Server, you should use the techniques shown in the next section to correlate and corroborate the findings of the wait stat analysis.

SQL Server Profiler

The SQL Server Profiler tool captures SQL Server events as they are generated on a SQL Server instance. (Profiler can be used to capture events in both the relational database engine and in the multidimensional database engine, called Analysis Services.) The captured information, referred to as a *workload*, can be reviewed in the graphical user interface or saved to a trace file. The workload can be used to analyze performance or replayed to conduct N+1 testing. In N+1 testing, the workload would be replayed and the results analyzed. Adjustments would be made to the application, and then the workload would be replayed and the results analyzed again. This is repeated N times until finally all issues are resolved in the final N+1 time.

You can use the tool to:

■ Step through queries to troubleshoot problems

■ Identify and optimize slow queries

■ Capture traces for replay or analysis

■ Conduct security audits of database activity

■ Provide input to the Database Engine Tuning Advisor for database optimization

■ Identify the worst performance queries

■ Identify the cause of a deadlock

■ Correlate a trace with data collected from Windows Performance Monitor

The SQL Server Profiler is invaluable for getting detailed insight into the internal workings of applications and databases from a real-world and real-time perspective.

Profiler Trace Templates

The Profiler tool can capture a wide variety of event classes and data columns in the trace. They are easily specified in the trace templates.

The different default trace templates are shown in Table 14.2. Additional templates can be created for specific needs.

Table 14.2   **Default Trace Templates in the Profiler Tool**

Template	Template Purpose	Event Classes
Standard	This is a generic starting point for creating a trace. Will capture all stored procedures and Transact-SQL batches that are run. Use to monitor general database server activity.	Audit Login Audit Logout ExistingConnection RPC:Completed SQL:BatchCompleted SQL:BatchStarting
SP_Counts	Captures stored procedure execution behavior over time.	SP:Starting
TSQL	Captures all Transact-SQL statements submitted to SQL Server by clients and the time issued. Use Transact-SQL to debug client applications.	Audit Login Audit Logout ExistingConnection RPC:Starting SQL:BatchStarting
TSQL_Duration	Captures all Transact-SQL statements submitted to SQL Server by clients, their execution time (in milliseconds), and groups them by duration. Use to identify slow queries.	RPC:Completed SQL:BatchCompleted
TSQL_Grouped	Captures all Transact-SQL statements submitted to SQL Server and the time they were issued. Groups information by user or client that submitted the statement. Use to investigate queries from a particular client or user.	Audit Login Audit Logout ExistingConnection RPC:Starting SQL:BatchStarting

Table 14.2 **Continued**

Template	Template Purpose	Event Classes
TSQL_Locks	Captures all the Transact-SQL that are submitted to SQL Server by clients along with exceptional lock events. Use this to troubleshoot deadlocks, lock timeout, and lock escalation events.	Blocked Process Report SP:StmtCompleted SP:StmtStarting SQL:StmtCompleted SQL:StmtStarting Deadlock Graph (Use against SQL Server 2005 and later.) Lock:Cancel Lock:Deadlock Lock:Deadlock Chain Lock:Escalation Lock:Timeout (Use against SQL Server 2000 instance.) Lock:Timeout (timeout>0) (Use against SQL Server 2005 and later.)
Transact-SQL_ Replay	Captures detailed information about Transact-SQL statements required in case trace will be replayed. Use to perform iterative tuning.	CursorClose CursorExecute CursorOpen CursorPrepare CursorUnprepare Attention Audit Login Audit Logout Existing Connection RPC Output Parameter RPC:Completed RPC:Starting Exec Prepared SQL Prepare SQL SQL:BatchCompleted SQL:BatchStarting
TSQL_SPs	Captures detailed information about all executing stored procedures. Use this to analyze the component steps of stored procedures.	Audit Login Audit Logout ExistingConnection RPC:Starting SP:Completed SP:Starting SP:StmtStarting SQL:BatchStarting

Table 14.2   **Continued**

Template	Template Purpose	Event Classes
Tuning	This template captures information about stored procedures as well as Transact-SQL batch execution. Use this to produce trace output for the Database Engine Tuning Advisor to use as a workload to tune databases.	RPC:Completed SP:StmtCompleted SQL:BatchCompleted

Although you do not need to use a template when creating a trace, when performance tuning, most often the Tuning template will be leveraged. It captures the events and columns that are used by the Database Engine Tuning Advisor. With SQL Server 2012, there are various ways to launch SQL Server Profiler. Any of these scenarios will do the trick and achieve the same result:

- Choose Start, All Programs, Microsoft SQL Server 2012, Performance Tools, and then choose SQL Server Profiler.

- Select SQL Server Profiler from the Database Engine Tuning Advisor Tools menu.

- From within SQL Server Management Studio, select SQL Server Profiler from the Tools menu.

First examine the Database Engine Tuning Advisor before creating a trace or analyzing a workload with SQL Server Profiler. The two tools go hand in hand when conducting performance tuning and troubleshooting.

Correlating Perfmon and Profiler Data

Although Profiler for the SQL Server Engine is marked for deprecation and Microsoft recommends that the Data Collector and/or Utility Control Point should be used over correlated Perfmon and Profiler data, Microsoft has not yet supplied a solution that gathers information across all components on all currently used versions of SQL Server. Consequently, correlating performance data from both Perfmon and Profiler is still a recommended best practice in troubleshooting and performance-tuning scenarios. To gain a valuable insight into the environment, it is possible to integrate the information from these two powerful tools. To accomplish this, follow these steps:

1. Choose Start, All Programs, Microsoft SQL Server 2012, Performance Tools, and then choose SQL Server Profiler.
2. Click File, select New Trace, and then choose the instance to monitor.
3. Figure 14.4 depicts the Trace Properties screen. Enter a name for the trace and a location to save the trace file.

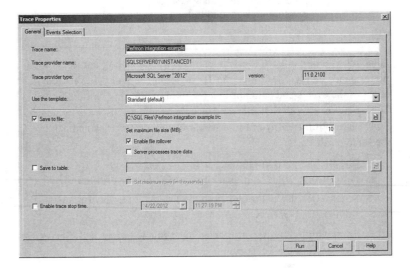

FIGURE 14.4
Profiler Profiler Trace Properties screen.

4. Select a base template; if required, select the Events Selection tab and amend the Events, Columns, and Filters as needed. Then click Run.
5. Open the Performance Monitor tool, via Start, All Programs, Administrator Tools, and then select Performance Monitor.
6. Expand the Data Collector Sets tree. Expand the User Defined tree.
7. Right-click the User Defined folder and choose New, Data Collector Set.
8. Name the collection and choose to create the collection manager as per Figure 14.5. Click Next.
9. Choose Create Data Logs, check the Performance Counter check box, and click Next.

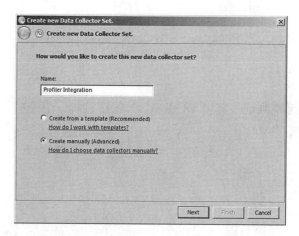

FIGURE 14.5
Create New PerfMon Data Collector Set.

10. Click Add and choose a selection of counters from those mentioned earlier in the chapter. Click Next to continue.

11. Select a directory for the collection set data to be stored, and click Next.

12. To create the collection, ensure Save and Close is selected; then click Finish.

13. Right-click the new collection set and choose Start.

14. Leave the Data Collector and Profiler session running until the required data has been captured.

15. Switch to the Profiler application, stop the trace, and then save and close it.

16. Switch to Perfmon and stop the Data Collector.

17. In Profiler, open the trace file that has just been created.

18. Click File, and then choose the new option Import Performance Data. Navigate to the Data Collector data file.

19. Select the Performance Counters to be displayed, and click OK.

After the data has been correlated, it is possible to scroll through the captured trace events and see what was captured in Perfmon at that point in time, as depicted in Figure 14.6. (Because the correlation is based on time, it means that the order cannot be sorted on another metric, such as query duration.) Conversely, when the user clicks a significant value in the bottom graph showing the PerfMon data, the GUI will immediately highlight the correlated transaction(s) executing at that time on the upper graph showing the Profiler data.

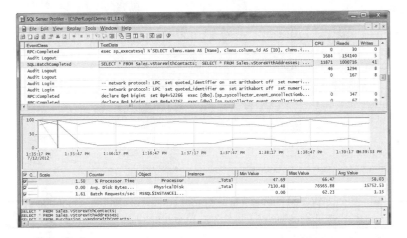

FIGURE 14.6
Profiler and Perfmon correlated view.

Database Engine Tuning Advisor

The Database Engine Tuning Advisor automates the process of selecting an optimized set of indexes, indexed views, statistics, and partitions and even provides the code to implement the recommendations it makes. It also provides recommendations on dropping existing indexes that do not make sense. To make your life even easier, you can use the tool to implement recommendations right from within the SQL Server Management Studio console.

The Database Engine Tuning Advisor can work with a specific query or can use a real-world workload as gathered by the SQL Server Profiler. The advantage of the latter approach is that the workload is generated based on actual usage, and the tuning recommendation reflects that.

The Database Engine Tuning Advisor is customizable and allows you to select the level of recommendation that the tool will recommend. This way, you can maintain the existing database design and make appropriate fine-tuning recommendations for indexes. Or you can make the existing design flexible and then have the tool recommend far-reaching changes to the structure, such as partitioning.

The following sections walk you through running the Database Engine Tuning Advisor, starting with capturing a workload.

Capturing a Workload

The first part of the process to run the SQL Server Profiler is to capture a workload. So far, we have been utilizing the AdventureWorks2012 database for all of our examples in this book. However, because the Adventure Works2012 database is already optimized, let's first create a new Customer database and import customer-related data we can use to create a workload.

Creating a Database in Order to Capture a Workload

The Customers.txt file can be downloaded from the Microsoft's sample Integration Services website at http://www.codeplex.com/MSFTISProd Samples. The package sample name is "Execute SQL Statements in a Loop Sample Package."

To create the database and import the customer data, follow these steps:

1. In SQL Server Management Studio, in the Object Explorer, expand a SQL Server instance.

2. Right-click the Database folder, and select New Database.

3. Create a new database called Customer.

4. To import data, right-click the Customer database, and select Tasks, Import Data.

5. Click Next on the Welcome screen.

6. Select Flat File Source as the data source.

7. Click the Browse button and provide the path to the Customers.txt file.

8. Check the Column names in the first data row check box, and then click Next.

9. In the Choose a Destination dialog box, select the Customer database if it is not already selected, and the click Next.

10. Click Next to accept tables and views.

11. Click Next to execute immediately and not save the package.

12. Click Finish to run the import.

13. Click Close.

Capturing a Workload with Database Engine Tuning Advisor

To capture a workload with SQL Server Profiler, follow these steps:

1. Choose Start, All Programs, Microsoft SQL Server 2012, Performance Tools, and then choose SQL Server Profiler.

2. In SQL Server Profiler, select File, and then select New Trace.

3. Connect to the Database Engine, which will capture the workload—in this case, SQLServer01\Instance01.

4. On the General tab of the Trace Properties window, enter **Customer Database Trace** for the Trace name.

5. Select the Tuning template from the Use the Template drop-down.

6. Check the Save to File box and select a location for the trace file.

7. Change the maximum file size to 100MB, although this example will not need this much space.

8. Select the Events Selection tab.

9. Review the events and columns that are preselected by the template you chose in this case, the Tuning template. Other templates select other events and columns.

10. Click Column Filters and limit the data returned to only the customer database by entering **Customer** in the Like attribute Database Name.

11. Click Run to start the trace.

The trace window shows the server activity. By selecting any line in the trace window, you can review the event class, the duration of the statement (in milliseconds), the name of the database, the login name of the executing process, and even the detailed statement itself in the details window.

Now that the SQL Server Profiler is tracing the events on the server, a workload needs to be generated. Usually, you would do this during normal operations, and the trace would gather a production workload seamlessly. However, in this example, there are no normal operations. A series of query statements need to be executed to simulate a workload.

Launch SQL Server Management Studio, and then execute the following series of queries.

The first statement selects all columns from the database:

```
USE Customer;
GO
SELECT *
```

```
FROM dbo.Customers;
GO
```

The first statement returns too many columns, so the following query narrows the data to only the columns needed:

```
USE Customer;
GO
SELECT FirstName, LastName, EmailAddress, Occupation, State
FROM dbo.Customers;
GO
```

This statement still returns too many rows, so the following query returns only the rows of management:

```
USE Customer;
GO
SELECT FirstName, LastName, EmailAddress, Occupation, State
FROM dbo.Customers
WHERE Occupation = 'Management'
GO
```

However, the rows needed are only for California rather than all states, so the following query returns exactly what is required:

```
USE Customer;
GO
SELECT FirstName, LastName, EmailAddress, Occupation,
State FROM dbo.Customers
WHERE Occupation = 'Management' and State = 'CA';
GO
```

This final query should return 192 rows. This is a simple workload, but effective for a demonstration of the process.

The workload has been generated, so the next step is to stop the Profiler tool and save the workload for analysis. Follow these steps:

1. Switch to the SQL Server Profiler tool.
2. Select File, Stop Trace to stop the trace.
3. Scroll through the events and locate each of the query statements that you just executed. Note the duration, database, login name for each statement, and query for each event.
4. Close the SQL Server Profiler.

Now the workload has been saved and is ready for analysis.

Analyzing the Workload

Run the Tuning Advisor to analyze the workload as follows:

1. Choose Start, All Programs, Microsoft SQL Server 2012, Performance Tools, Database Engine Tuning Advisor.

2. Connect to the Database Engine—in this case, SQLServer01\Instance01.

3. In the Workload section on the General tab, select the file that the trace was saved to—in this case, Customer Database Trace.trc.

4. Select the Customer database from the Database for Workload Analysis drop-down.

5. In the Select Databases and Tables to Tune section, check the Customer database. The configuration should look similar to that in Figure 14.7.

6. Select the Tuning Options tab. There are a number of tuning options for the advisor to use. By default, the advisor recommends index and statistical changes but can recommend changes to the physical design structures as well. Leave these at the default, which is to recommend index changes only.

7. Click the Advanced Options button, tick the Define Max Space for Recommendations (MB) and set the value to the specified maximum file size you prefer (a value of 32MB is a good place to start) and click OK.

8. Select Actions, Start Analysis to begin the analysis. In a real-world situation, the workload would be much longer, and an analysis would take a significant amount of time. In the case of this simple simulation, the analysis will take less than a minute.

> **Note**
>
> The Database Engine Tuning Advisor can make recommendations on clustered and nonclustered indexes, as well as indexed views and filtered indexes.

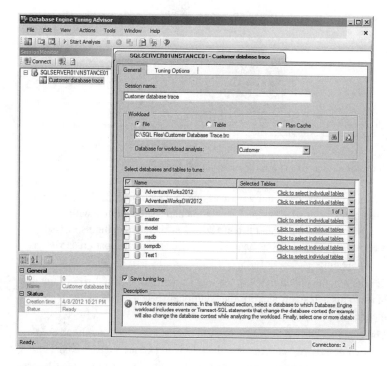

FIGURE 14.7
Database Engine Tuning Advisor settings.

Reviewing the Results

After the analysis, the Database Engine Tuning Advisor shows the Recommendations tab of the tool, which offers a set of recommendations for the Customers database based on the workload. This view is shown in Figure 14.8.

> **Note**
>
> The results, values, and recommendations included in the upcoming examples may deviate slightly from your results due to system variables.

The top line of the recommendations window shows an Estimated Improvement percentage. In the case of the Customer database analysis, the estimated improvement is 57 percent. Clearly, a gain of approximately 57 percent is a big gain in improvement, so the tool is doing something useful.

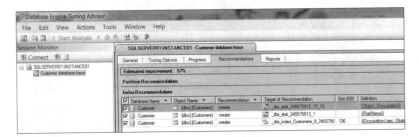

FIGURE 14.8
Database Engine Tuning Advisor recommendations.

Based on the database and workload, the tool recommends that a nonclus-tered index be created on the Occupation and State columns with FirstName, LastName, and EmailAddress as included columns. It also recommends that statistics be created for State and Occupation as well as for FirstName.

For the recommended indexes, the tool shows the estimated size of the new index. This helps you plan for the additional space needed by the recom-mended indexes.

You can view the existing structures in the database along with the recom-mended objects by selecting the Show Existing Objects check box. This shows the existing nonclustered indexes that already exist in the Customers database.

The last column in each recommendation, Definition, shows the definition for the object. These recommendation definitions are hyperlinks that show you the query needed to create the object. This information assists in the implementation of the recommendations.

Selecting the Reports tab shows the tuning summary and gives access to a collection of reports to interpret the recommendations. Table 14.3 shows the summary of the analysis.

Table 14.3 **Database Engine Tuning Advisor Tuning Summary**

Description	Value
Date	4/8/2012
Time	10:29:25 PM
Server	SQLServer01\Instance01

Table 14.3 **Continued**

Description	Value
Database(s) to tune	[Customer]
Workload file	C:\SQL Files\ Customer Database Trace.trc
Maximum tuning time	51 Minutes
Time taken for tuning	1 Minute
Expected percentage improvement	57.77
Maximum space for recommendation (MB)	50
Space used currently (MB)	2
Space used by recommendation (MB)	2
Number of events in workload	8
Number of events tuned	8
Number of statements tuned	4
Percent SELECT statements in the tuned set	100
Number of indexes recommended to be created	1
Number of statistics recommended to be created	2

In the Tuning Reports section, select the Statement Cost Report from the drop-down list. The report shows the four query statements in the simulated workload. More importantly, it shows the percent improvement that the recommendations will have on each statement. For the more complex statement, the recommendations will generate an impressive 90.26 percent improvement in the performance.

Select the Workload Analysis Report from the drop-down list. The report shows the number of query statements in the workload and the net impact of the tuning recommendation on the statements. In the case of this example, three statements would have a net decrease in cost and one would have no change in cost. Cost is measured in the time needed to execute the query. Depending on the recommendation, the cost might actually increase for some queries, as shown in the report.

Other reports show various aspects of the workload usage, such as which tables are used in the database and which columns are in each table. These are useful for understanding how the data is being used by the workload.

After reviewing the recommendations, you can apply the recommendations to the database.

Applying the Recommendations

The Database Engine Tuning Advisor tool provides several options for applying the recommendations:

- Cut/paste individual recommendations.
- Apply the recommendation from the tool.
- Save the recommendations to a file.

On the Recommendations tab, the Definition column of each recommendation is a hyperlink that pops up a window with the Transact-SQL query needed to implement that specific recommendation. The window shows the specific code and has a Copy to Clipboard button to copy the code. This code can be pasted directly into the SQL Server Management Studio query window or any other Transact-SQL query tool.

The tool allows the recommendations to be exported to a SQL file for execution at a later time or for editing of the query statements. Select Actions, Save Recommendations to save the query statements to a file.

The saved recommendations for the Customer Database Tuning session are as follows:

```
use [Customer]
go


SET ANSI_PADDING ON

go


CREATE NONCLUSTERED INDEX
[_dta_index_Customers_8_245575913__K13_K18_1_3_8] ON
[dbo].[Customers]
(
    [Occupation] ASC,
    [State] ASC
)
INCLUDE ( [FirstName],
    [LastName],
    [EmailAddress]) WITH (SORT_IN_TEMPDB = OFF, DROP_EXISTING =
OFF, ONLINE = OFF) ON [PRIMARY]
go
```

```
CREATE STATISTICS [_dta_stat_245575913_1] ON
[dbo].[Customers]([FirstName])
go


CREATE STATISTICS [_dta_stat_245575913_18_13] ON
[dbo].[Customers]([State], [Occupation])
go
```

The easiest method of applying the recommendations is to select Actions,
Apply Recommendations. This generates and runs the Transact-SQL statements on the database to implement the recommended changes. They can
be executed immediately or scheduled for a later date.

Note

Copies of all changes to production databases should be stored in a
source control system. Although deploying straight from DTA is the quickest option, these changes may need to be rolled back. Documentation
and change control is of paramount importance!

Monitoring Processes with the Activity Monitor

The Activity Monitor was introduced and discussed, from a monitoring
perspective, in Chapter 15. It is another tool that should be utilized not
only for monitoring a SQL Server system, but also for troubleshooting and
performance tuning. The Activity Monitor in SQL Server Management
Studio graphically displays information about these measures:

- Processes
- Resource Waits
- Data File I/O
- Recent Expensive Queries

Using this information, you can review activity, tune performance, and
troubleshoot a SQL Server instance in real-time. When troubleshooting
and tuning, DBAs will probably find the most value if they dive into the
Processes, Resource Waits, and Recent Expensive Queries sections. You
can launch the Activity Monitor by right-clicking a SQL Server instance
that you want to monitor within Management Studio and then selecting
Activity Monitor. Alternatively, you can invoke Activity Monitor by clicking the Activity Monitor icon on the SQL Server Management Studio
toolbar or pressing Ctrl+Alt+A.

For example, the Activity Monitor shows a list of the worst-performing queries based on the Recent Expensive Queries section. Therefore, as a DBA, if you are experiencing performance issues based on a resource-intensive query, this is one of the first places you should check to verify if a bottleneck occurs. Execution in minutes, CPU consumption, physical reads per second, logical writes per second, average duration in milliseconds, and the plan count are displayed for each recent expensive query residing in the SQL Server cache. Additional detail can be found to assist with the investigation by right-clicking any query and selecting either Edit Query Text or Show Execution Plan. By doing this, you can view the entire query or display the graphical execution plan of the query from within one utility.

DBAs should utilize the Processes section when there is a need to troubleshoot or terminate processes and user connections within a SQL Server instance. By right-clicking a Session ID, a DBA can obtain additional details, kill the process, or trace the process in SQL Server Profiler.

Leveraging Dynamic Management Views (DMVs)

It is also worth noting that the Activity Monitor is essentially a graphical user interface for queries against important SQL Server 2012 DMVs. As with the preceding sections on wait statistics and performance counters, the following list is by no means a comprehensive list of all SQL Server DMVs. (Also remember that the previous sections described how to extract wait statistics and performance counter information using DMVs.) However, this short list of DMVs provide a quick and reliable set of system information from which you can build. These DMVs should definitely be part of your toolkit as a data professional.

Configuration

SYS.DM_OS_SYS_INFO provides a host of details about the platform where the SQL Server instance resides. Ever wonder if the SQL Server is running on a server with hyperthreaded CPUs? This DMV will tell you.

Indexes

SYS.DM_DB_INDEX_USAGE_STATS returns details about a wide variety of types of index operations and the time each type of operation was last performed. Ever wondered when the last time an index was used? This DMV will tell you.

SYS.DM_DB_INDEX_PHYSICAL_STATS returns details about the size and fragmentation for the data and indexes of the given database, partition, table, or view. Ever wondered whether and how much fragmentation an index has experienced? This DMV will tell you.

SYS.DM_DB_INDEX_OPERATIONAL_STATS returns details about current low-level activity, such as the exact I/O, locking, latching, and access method activity (such as row-locks, page-locks, and table-locks) for a given index, table, partition, or database on the SQL Server instance. Ever wonder how many INSERT operations have occurred on a specific index? This DMV will tell you.

I/O Information

The DMV SYS.DM_IO_VIRTUAL_FILE_STATS provides an overview of I/O utilization on an instance of SQL Server, by database and file. Query this DMV to find out the number and amount of reads and writes occurring on each database (and on the files within the database), as well as the number of I/O stalls (the time in milliseconds that users had to wait for file access). It accepts database ID and file ID as parameters or, if no parameters are passed, returns I/O information for all databases and files on the instance of SQL Server.

Memory

The dynamic management view SYS.DM_OS_MEMORY_OBJECTS provides a list of all the memory objects currently allocated by SQL Server, allowing easy analysis of memory use and potential memory leaks.

SYS.DM_OS_MEMORY_CLERKS is useful to learn about all the various memory categories active on the SQL Server instance. It tells how memory pages are distributed across all of the various types of specific activities— for example, for compiling CLR procedures—on the instance of SQL Server.

Query Activity and Plan Cache

When troubleshooting SQL Server queries and other Transact-SQL objects like stored procedures, the DMV SYS.DM_EXEC_QUERY_STATS is essential. This DMV provides one row per SQL statement currently within a cached plan, aggregating its performance statistics for as long as the plan remains in the cache. (Note: That means anything that flushes query plans for the cache will prevent this information from being available. The plan must still be in the cache!) Ever wonder which query consumes the most resources on a given SQL Server? This DMV will tell you.

SYS.DM_EXEC_SQL_TEXT is a dynamic management function (DMF) that returns the text of the SQL batch identified by a given SQL_handle. Because this is a DMF, and not a DMV, it must be queried through a CROSS APPLY with another DMV possessing SQL_handle information, such as SYS.DM_EXEC_QUERY_STATS.

Transactions, Locking, and Blocking Information

The DMV SYS.DM_TRAN_LOCKS returns details about currently active transactions or transactions waiting to be granted locks. It provides columns with the data divided into two main groups: resource columns (the element of SQL Server where the lock request is targeted) and the request columns (the nature of the lock request itself, such as exclusive or intent update). Some of the columns, such as resource_description, have a lot of possible values, so consult the Books Online for further information.

Application Optimization and Troubleshooting

Application optimization and troubleshooting are typically beyond the scope of the DBA's duties. Application developers typically are responsible for the troubleshooting and optimization of applications, because they are fully aware of the database schema, stored procedures, and/or queries developed in the database.

However, you may find that certain query statements are consuming resources or taking a long time. This is typically discovered in database troubleshooting and optimization. Therefore, you can take key information and assist developers in their tasks.

Query Analysis with Execution Plan

The Query Editor in the SQL Server Management Studio allows you to analyze the execution plans of queries to determine their specific breakdown and costs for each step. Use the tool to ensure that your queries are executing at an optimal level or if remediation work is necessary.

For example, consider the following query that runs against the Customer database, which was configured in the previous examples:

```
USE Customer;
GO
SELECT FirstName, LastName, EmailAddress,
Occupation, YearlyIncome, City, State
```

```
FROM dbo.Customers
WHERE Gender = 'F' and MaritalStatus = 'S' and
        YearlyIncome = (SELECT MAX(YearlyIncome)
FROM dbo.Customers) ORDER BY City;
GO
```

This query essentially selects the data for the highest-income single females in California and displays it sorted by city. To analyze this query, follow these steps:

1. Launch SQL Server Management Studio and open the Query Editor by selecting New Query.

2. Enter the preceding Transact-SQL query into the editor.

3. Select Query, Display Estimated Execution Plan.

Figure 14.9 shows the resulting graphical view of the query. The table scans are clearly the highest-cost items at 41 pecent each. The sort is the next highest at 12 percent. Optimizing this query could significantly reduce the cost.

The following are some specific areas to look out for in the execution plan of a query:

- **Index or Table Scans**—They indicate that additional indexes are needed on the columns.

- **Sorts**—Sorting might be better done at the client or not at all.

- **Filters**—Filtering might require additional indexes, indicating that views are being used in Transact-SQL or that there are functions in the statement.

Adjusting the query to smooth out the high-cost areas that the execution plan exposes can improve the performance of the application immensely.

Figure 14.9 also shows how the query could be improved by adding an index. How to find missing indexes was covered in Chapter 5, "Managing and Optimizing SQL Server 2012 Indexes." To implement the suggested index, right-click the Missing Index Details and choose Missing Index Details from the list of options. This creates the DDL statement for the new index in a new query window, which can be tested on another server or run on a production instance. Just don't forget to change the name!

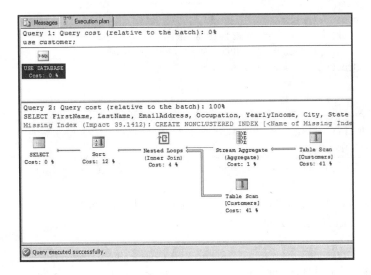

FIGURE 14.9
Estimated execution plan.

Cursors and the Lazy Developer

Another area to bring to the attention of application developers is the use of cursors. A SELECT statement normally returns a set of rows called a *resultset*, and the application has to work with the entire resultset. A cursor is a database object that lets applications work with single rows within the resultset. The cursor allows the following:

- Positioning within the resultset
- Retrieving a single row at the current position in the resultset
- Modifying the row at the cursor position in the resultset

Although this feature makes the developer's job easy, cursors are resource intensive. The use of cursors is normally associated with lazy development practices. Extensive use of cursors can affect the performance of the database, and their use is generally frowned on.

This information can all be passed on to the application developers for recommendations on how to optimize the application.

Locking and Deadlock Detection

Locking allows users and processes to synchronize access to data and objects. This allows users in a multiaccess environment to prevent data from being corrupted. For example, when process A begins a transaction to modify a chunk of data X, the SQL Server Database Engine locks that data. If process B attempts to modify data X before the first transaction finishes, process B is paused (that is, sleeping). After process A finishes, process B is awakened and gets its lock on data X.

This process is all well and good, except when deadlocks occur. A deadlock condition occurs when two processes are mutually waiting for each other to free up locks on data. For example, consider what happens if process A locks data Y and then requests a lock on data Z. At the same time, process B locks data Z and requests a lock on data Y. Both processes are paused and waiting for the other to free up the lock, which, in theory, will never happen, and the processes will sleep forever. That is, the processes are deadlocked.

Resources that can deadlock include the following:

- Locks
- Worker threads
- Memory
- Parallel queries
- Multiple active resultsets

Deadlocks can completely kill application performance and are often unavoidable in a multiuser application such as SQL Server 2012.

Luckily, SQL Server 2012 has a mechanism for dealing with this condition. The SQL Server Database Engine runs deadlock detection to find and resolve these deadlock conditions. The deadlock detection is somewhat atavistic, basically selecting a deadlock victim and then resolving the situation by:

- Terminating the ill-fated process's current batch command
- Rolling back the transaction, which frees all the locks it held
- Notifying the application with a 1205 error

The other, considerably luckier, process is then free to complete its transaction with the deadlock resolved. The deadlock victim is chosen on the basis of the least expensive transaction to roll back. This can be changed by setting the DEADLOCK_PRIORITY, which allows you or the application developer to force the selection.

The Database Engine executes deadlock detection on a periodic basis to locate deadlocks. The default interval is 5 seconds, but if a deadlock is encountered, the process triggers more often until it stops detecting dead-locks. Then it reverts to the 5-second interval.

Even though deadlocks are resolved, the delays that they cause affect performance. It is important to monitor SQL Server for errors and review the application code or logic if errors occur frequently.

Alternatively, the Dynamic Management View sys.dm_tran_locks returns information about active locks within a database. Each row represented in the resultset displays an active request to the lock manager for a lock that has been granted or is waiting to be established. The following example illustrates the active locks associated with the AdventureWorks2012 database:

```
Use AdventureWorks2012
Go
Select * from sys.dm_tran_locks
```

> **Note**
>
> Deadlocking should not be common on a properly designed SQL Server application. If you find that your application encounters lots of deadlocks, you should collect more information to determine which areas of the application are creating the deadlocks. To monitor deadlocks, enabling trace flag 1222 on the server will write deadlock information to the SQL Server Error Log, allowing easier resolution of deadlock issues. It is advisable to use this trace flag on systems that have an inordinately large number of deadlocks. After the cause of the deadlocking is resolved, the trace flag can be disabled. This information is also captured in the system_health Extended Event session, described in the following section.

Introducing Extended Events to Troubleshoot SQL Server

Extended Events, also referred to as XEvents, is a new, high-performing diagnostic mechanism available in SQL Server 2012 that, as its name suggests, handles system events as they occur. By leveraging the new event-based infrastructure, DBAs can define the events they want to monitor and further define how they want SQL Server to respond to those events. The numerous event concepts available allow this diagnostic mechanism to be highly customizable for pinpointing a problem. Using XEvents, DBAs can look forward to quickly diagnosing runtime issues by analyzing, filtering, and responding to events generated by the SQL Server system. In addition, XEvents are tightly integrated with the Windows Server 2008 R2 operating system. This means visibility is available at the OS-level for deeper diagnosis, troubleshooting, and obtaining event-based information beyond SQL Server.

Events can be processed in real-time (synchronous) or can be queued and processed later (asynchronous). Another characteristic of extended events is that a DBA can take action on events when they are executed. This provides flexibility if a deeper dive is required when diagnosing an issue. Finally, from a cost perspective, a single extended event is relatively cheap when compared to older techniques such as Profiler or Perfmon in terms of performance overhead because it does not consume a lot of system processes or resources.

DBAs should remember to exploit XEvents when there is a need to troubleshoot the following situations: excessive CPU usage is experienced, SQL Server is not responding quickly to memory pressure, investigation of deadlocks is warranted, transient performance issues are taking place that occur for a short period of time, and correlating request activity with Windows ETW logs is necessary.

Event-Related Components and Terminology

- **Events**—An event is a program that monitors a specific point of interest within a code. Events are defined against modules and deliver a specific payload. The `sys.dm_xe_objects` dynamic management view provides a list of all available events within SQL Server system as depicted in this query.

  ```
  SELECT * FROM sys.dm_xe_objects WHERE object_type =
  'event'
  ```

  SQL Server 2012 has more than 600 event objects to choose from. Some examples of events include Database Started, Checkpoint Has Begun, and SQL Statement Completed.

- **Actions**—Actions are programmatic responses that are bound to an event. Actions can capture and inspect data, store state information, aggregate event data, and write to event data. It is worth mentioning that the occurrence of an action takes place even before the event is available and can be consumed by a target. To become familiar with all the actions included with a SQL Server instance, query the `sys.dm_xe_objects` DMV. Some examples include Collect Database ID, Collect Transaction ID, Collect Current CPU ID, Run Time Statistics Calculation, and Collect the Current Task Execution Time. SQL Server 2012 has 50 actions preinstalled and ready to use.

- **Predicates**—Predicates are essentially used as filters, allowing a DBA to selectively capture event data based on specific criteria. Also, event costs are lowered with the use of predicates, whose filtering action takes place before events have an opportunity to get to their targets or prompt an action. Predicates can operate using local data or data from a global perspective. Predicates also leverage full Boolean expressions; therefore, they conform to True and False statements to filter events. Finally, predicates can store state data in local context. As such, it is possible to set a counter to publish the number of times an event fires every *n*th time. In this way, sample data is collected systematically for analysis, which beats recording data for every single event.

- **Targets**—Most of the time targets are referred to as event consumers; they are synonymous. Targets are responsible for processing events and can be set up to do quite a lot, including kicking off a task and targeting event data to a file. In addition, targets can be set up to process a single event or a buffer, which is full of events. Data can be processed either synchronously or asynchronously, and event data can be targeted to a file or can trigger a specific task, which is applicable to the event. Query the sys.dm_xe_objects DMV to obtain a list of all the targets available to a SQL Server system. For example:

```
Select *
From sys.dm_xe_objects
Where object_type = 'target'
```

SQL Server is shipped with 15 targets installed.

- **Types and Maps**—Types are found in packages and they define how events, targets, actions, and predicates will be interpreted. A map table maps an internal value to a string.

- **Packages**—A package is a logical container that maintains extended event information from a holistic perspective. A package consists of events, targets, actions, types, predicates, and maps. It can contain any or all of the objects. For identification purposes, each package must have a unique name and GUID. For a list of installed packages on a SQL Server instance, query the sys.dm_xe_packages DMV.

Creating an Extended Event with DDL Statements

The DDL Create Event Session allows you to add triggers, events, predicates, actions, and event session-level options all in one statement.

Based on SQL Server Books Online, the following syntax depicts how to create an Extended Event session:

```
CREATE EVENT SESSION event_session_name
ON SERVER
{
    <event_definition> [ ,...n]
    [ <event_target_definition> [ ,...n] ]
    [ WITH ( <event_session_options> [ ,...n] ) ]
}
;


<event_definition>::=
{
    ADD EVENT [event_module_guid].event_package_name.event_name
        [ ( {
                [ SET { event_customizable_
            attribute = <value> [ ,...n] } ]
                [ ACTION ( { [event_module_guid].event_
            package_name.action_name [ ,...n] } ) ]
                [ WHERE <predicate_expression> ]
        } ) ]
}


<predicate_expression> ::=
{
    [ NOT ] <predicate_factor> | {( <predicate_expression> ) }
    [ { AND | OR } [ NOT ] { <predicate_factor> |
        ( <predicate_expression> ) } ]
    [ ,...n ]
}


<predicate_factor>::=
{
    <predicate_leaf> | ( <predicate_expression> )
}
<predicate_leaf>::=
{
        <predicate_source_declaration>
    { = | < > | ! = | > | > = | < | < = } <value>
    | [event_module_guid].event_package_name.
```

```
    predicate_compare_name
    ( <predicate_source_declaration>, <value> )
}
<predicate_source_declaration>::=
{
        event_field_name | (
[event_module_guid].event_package_name.
    predicate_source_name )
}

<value>::=
{
        number | 'string'
}
<event_target_definition>::=
{
    ADD TARGET
[event_module_guid].event_package_name.target_name
        [ ( SET { target_parameter_name = <value> [ ,...n] } )
]
}
<event_session_options>::=
{
    [    MAX_MEMORY = size [ KB | MB ] ]
    [ [,] EVENT_RETENTION_MODE =
{ ALLOW_SINGLE_EVENT_LOSS | ALLOW_MULTIPLE_EVENT_LOSS |
 NO_EVENT_LOSS } ]
    [ [,] MAX_DISPATCH_LATENCY = { seconds SECONDS | INFINITE } ]
    [ [,] MAX_EVENT_SIZE = size [ KB | MB ] ]
    [ [,] MEMORY_PARTITION_MODE = { NONE | PER_NODE | PER_CPU } ]
    [ [,] TRACK_CAUSALITY = { ON | OFF } ]
    [ [,] STARTUP_STATE = { ON | OFF } ]
}
```

This Transact-SQL example illustrates how to create an XEvent session based on capturing two events:

```
CREATE EVENT SESSION Create_Extended_Event_Example
ON SERVER
    ADD EVENT sqlos.async_io_requested,
```

```
ADD EVENT sqlserver.lock_acquired
ADD TARGET package0.etw_classic_sync_target
    (SET default_etw_session_logfile_path =
    N'C:\Create_Extended_Event.etl' )
WITH (MAX_MEMORY=4MB, MAX_EVENT_SIZE=4MB);
GO
```

Leveraging the Extended Events Catalog Views

The following XEvents catalog views should be exploited to ascertain the metadata that is generated with an event session:

- **sys.server_event_sessions**—When this catalog view is executed, it displays all the event session definitions associated with a SQL Server instance.

- **sys.server_event_session_actions**—The sys.server_event_session_actions catalog view displays a row for each action on each event of an event session.

- **sys.server_event_session_events**—Returns information pertaining to each event in an event session.

- **sys.server_event_session_fields**—Displays information pertaining to each customizable column that was explicitly set on events and targets.

- **sys.server_event_session_targets**—Returns a row for each event target for an event session.

Leveraging the Extended Events Dynamic Management Views

The following Dynamic Management Views return XEvent information for a SQL Server instance:

- **sys.dm_xe_map_values**—Returns a mapping of internal numeric keys to human-readable text.

- **sys.dm_os_dispatcher_pools**—Returns information about session dispatcher pools.

- **sys.dm_xe_objects**—Returns a row for each object that is exposed by an event package.

- **sys.dm_xe_object_columns**—Returns the schema information for all the objects and relative columns.

- **sys.dm_xe_packages**—Displays all the packages registered with the extended events engine.

- **sys.dm_xe_sessions**—Returns information about an active extended events session.

- **sys.dm_xe_session_targets**—Returns information about session targets in real-time.

- **sys.dm_xe_session_events**—Returns information about session events.

- **sys.dm_xe_session_event_actions**—Returns information about event session actions.

- **sys.dm_xe_session_object_columns**—Shows the configuration values for objects that are bound to a session.

Leveraging the Extended Events User Interface

After two versions of SQL Server without a user interface, SQL Server 2012 finally ships with a UI to make creating extended events much easier for users.

The new interface can be used for both creating and viewing XEvent data. Follow these steps to create a new session and examine the captured data:

1. Open SQL Server Management Studio and connect to the required instance.

2. Expand the Object Explorer and expand the Management, Extended Events, and Sessions folders.

3. Right-click the Sessions folder, and choose the New Session Wizard option.

4. Click Next on the Introduction screen.

5. For this example, enter a session name of Errors, and click Next.

6. In this example, choose the option Do Not Use a Template; this option allows greater flexibility when setting up a session.

7. To capture information about errors, click the drop-down list next to the Category data grid label. Uncheck Select All, and check the error option.

8. Highlight one of the newly listed events in the event library, press Ctrl+A to highlight all the events, and click the single chevron to move the events into the selected events, as shown in Figure 14.10, and click Next.

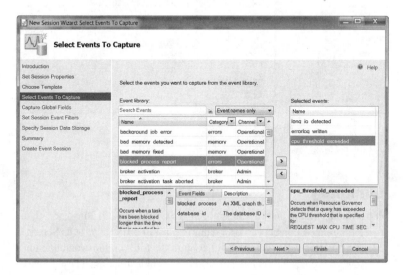

FIGURE 14.10
Select events to capture.

9. Check the boxes of the global fields to be collected in the event session and click Next.

10. For this example, choose to save the event data to a file, select a file location on the server, and click Next.

11. Review the Summary and click Finish.

12. Check the Start Event Session and Watch Live Data options, and then Click close.

13. Figure 14.11 depicts the live data that has been collated from the Errors session. Right-click a column header and choose the Choose Columns option to add additional columns to the display.

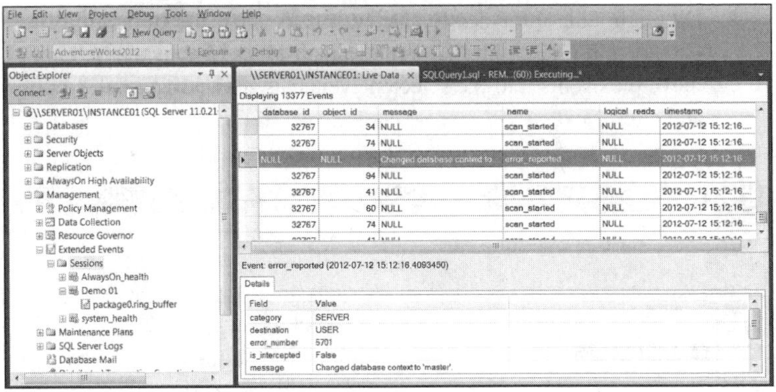

FIGURE 14.11
Viewing live data.

Summary

Performance tuning and troubleshooting a SQL Server 2012 instance, database, and related objects can be a daunting task. Fortunately, SQL Server 2012 and Windows Server 2008 R2 contain the tools and instrumentation to allow you to easily conduct performance troubleshooting. These tools include Activity Monitor, Windows Server Reliability and Performance Monitor, SQL Server Profiler, Database Engine Tuning Advisor, Dynamic Management Views, and Extended Events.

Best Practices

Here are some important best practices from the chapter:

- Use the Windows Reliability and Performance Monitoring tools to troubleshoot SQL Server objects and to capture performance baselines.

- Performance baselines should be captured on a regular basis so that when performance issues transpire, they can be correlated to the baseline to ensure that a SQL Server is running at a desired state.

- Use the SQL Server Profiler to gather workloads when troubleshooting SQL Server.

- Use the Database Engine Tuning Advisor to recommend indexes, statistics, and partitions based on the specific workloads.

- Use SQL Server Performance Studio, Utility Control Point, and Operations Manager to automate the collection of performance metrics and to maintain a historical record of the data.

- Review the logs when troubleshooting SQL Server.

- Augment performance tuning and troubleshooting capabilities by using Dynamic Management Views to return server state information.

- Leverage Activity Monitor to troubleshoot processes, resource waits, data file I/O, and recent expensive queries.

- Utilize built-in reports to quickly determine what areas should be looked at to improve performance.

- Extended Events should be exploited to correlate data from both SQL Server and the underlying operating system.

CHAPTER 15

Monitoring SQL Server 2012

The detection and resolution of anomalies within SQL Server will always be part of a DBA's duty. As such, DBAs should be aware that the effectiveness of the detection technique, and the first step to a resolution, lies in the department's commitment to monitoring. A strong commitment to monitoring is key for ensuring that any SQL Server system stays operational with as few unplanned interruptions as possible. When anomalies do occur, monitoring ensures that the issues are quickly identified and corrected. Without a strong commitment to monitoring, issues left unattended can quickly grow into major issues if not dealt with, eventually leading to a production outage.

For monitoring enthusiasts, there are many monitoring tools, new and old, to pique your interest in this chapter. For starters, the tools and utilities identified in this chapter are similar to those found in previous versions of SQL Server. As with most features associated with Microsoft, however, the features and functionality of the tools have been vastly improved and expanded upon in the latest edition. In this release, SQL Server 2012 provides new tools for monitoring in the form of a new Extended Events interface.

This chapter first covers the tools and utilities that allow a DBA to gain quick insight into a SQL Server system running on Windows Server 2008 R2. The latter part of the chapter covers data collection gathering with Data Collector, which now includes Utility Control Point, and explains how to conduct performance monitoring with the Windows Server 2008 R2 Reliability and Performance Monitor tools. The chapter ends with coverage of configuring SQL Server alerts, operators, and emails.

What's New for Monitoring in SQL Server 2012?

■ DBAs can easily achieve fiscal savings (and admiration of Financial Directors everywhere) by employing Utility Control Point, which was introduced in 2008 R2 to find underutilized servers and resources that can be used for further consolidation projects.

■ On systems that run Windows Server 2008 and later, DBAs can leverage the Task Manager, Resource Monitor, and Reliability and Performance Monitoring tools to monitor, diagnose, and troubleshoot a SQL Server system.

■ SQL Server 2012 also provides new and improved Dynamic Management Views (DMVs) for monitoring and troubleshooting SQL Server instances.

Tip

When an enterprise needs to monitor more than a handful of SQL Servers, it is advisable to invest in a specialized monitoring and alerting tool. Microsoft provides a very popular monitoring and alerting toolkit known as Operations Manager. (You will sometimes see this referred to as SCOM, for Systems Center and Operations Manager. But the Operations Manager is all that is needed for monitoring and alerting.) Operations Manager provides enterprises with the capability to monitor a large number of SQL Servers simultaneously and, when certain performance thresholds or preconfigured thresholds are crossed, to send alarms to operational staff so that they can remediate the problem. Operations Manager also includes a number of useful graphic dashboards that quickly inform the operational staff about the health of their SQL Servers and provides correlated hyperlinks to Microsoft knowledge bases to help staff understand and diagnose problem situations.

Operations Manager, by itself, offers a rudimentary set of monitoring capabilities. However, it can be vastly expanded for specific products in the Microsoft software stack, such as SQL Server, SharePoint, Exchange, and so on. The SQL Server management pack includes health checks and performance data collection for a variety of the most common problems encountered on SQL Server. Operations Manager, with the SQL Server Management Pack, is able to monitor and alert on all of the new features in SQL Server 2012, such as AlwaysOn. It also seamlessly integrates with policy-based management and other engines within SQL Server, such as Analysis Services, Integration Services, and Reporting Services.

Many other specialty management packs are available from third-party software vendors. For example, Operations Manager does not include a system to automatically create trouble tickets. But several third-party vendors provide management packs that can simply plug in to Operations Manager, adding that service to those provided natively by the tool. Look for Operations Manager plug-ins at http://systemcenter.pinpoint. microsoft.com.

Gaining Quick Insight into a SQL Server System

The preceding section is a testament to all the new monitoring tools introduced with SQL Server 2012. It is worth noting that even with these new tools, some DBAs will encounter situations when they need to gain insight into a SQL Server system quickly and effortlessly but don't have the cycles to implement features such as Management Data Warehouse, Data Collector, Profiler, or Extended Events. The following sections will illustrate SQL Server 2012 and Windows Server 2008 R2 tools and utilities that will ensure that a DBA's efforts are not impeded.

Leveraging Activity Monitor's New Performance Dashboard

The SQL Server Activity Monitor, as displayed in Figure 15.1, is one of the first tools a DBA should leverage when a quick overview of a SQL Server system's performance is needed. Activity Monitor was completely rewritten in SQL Server 2008 and, compared to its predecessors, is no longer limited to displaying processes, locks by object, and locks by process. Activity Monitor introduced a newly redesigned performance dashboard with intuitive graphs and performance indicators with drill-down and filtering capabilities. The new tool's look and feel is very similar to the Resource Monitoring tool found in Windows Server 2008; however, the information captured and presented is broken down into five major sections dedicated to SQL Server performance monitoring. The sections, as illustrated in Figure 15.1, are Overview, Processes, Resource Waits, Data File I/O, and Recent Expensive Queries. The tool can be invoked by right-clicking a SQL Server instance within Object Explorer and specifying Activity Monitor.

- **Overview**—The first section is called Overview. It provides a dashboard of intuitive graphs and charts that illustrate the SQL Server system's Process Time, Waiting Tasks, Database I/O and Batch Requests/sec in real-time.

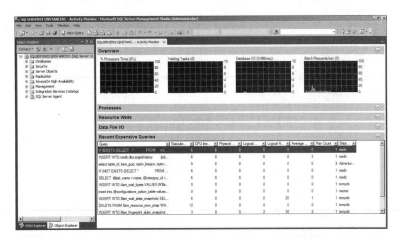

FIGURE 15.1
Viewing the Activity Monitor performance dashboard.

- **Processes**—The next section in the dashboard is Processes. When this section is expanded, a DBA can quickly monitor and assess the status of a given SQL Server process currently running on the system. Activity Monitor displays a list of current processes on the server, such as the session ID, the status of each process, who initiated it (by login ID), the database that the process is using, and the SQL command that the process is running. Moreover, metrics associated with each sessionID are also presented. A tremendous amount of data is presented in this section, but it is possible to filter data by rows within a specific column. By right-clicking a process, a DBA can obtain more details, kill a process, or trace the process directly in SQL Server Profiler.

- **Resource Waits**—This section displays resource waits vertically that are based on the following wait categories: CPU, SQLCLR, Network I/O, Latch, Lock, Logging, Memory, Buffer I/O, Buffer Latch, and Compilation. From a horizontal perspective, the Wait Time, Recent Wait Time, Average Waiter Counter, and Cumulative Wait Time metrics are published for each Wait Category. As in the

Processes section, data can be filtered based on items within a column.

- **Data File I/O**—The Data File I/O section displays I/O activity for relational database files within the Database Engine. It includes both the system and user databases. Information is broken down by database and database filename. In addition, MB/sec Read, MB/sec Written, and Response Time (ms) are presented.

- **Recent Expensive Queries**—The final section in Activity Monitor is Recent Expensive Queries, which provides DBAs the opportunity to capture the queries that are performing the worst and negatively impacting a SQL Server instance. Approximately 10 to 15 of the worst and most expensive queries are displayed in the performance dashboard. The actual query is displayed with augmenting metrics, such as Execution/Min, CPU ms/sec, Physical Reads/sec, Logical Write/sec, Logical Reads/sec, Average Duration in ms, Plan Count, and Database. It is also possible to right-click the most expensive query and edit the query text or show the execution plan.

Leveraging Windows Server 2008 R2 Task Manager

The Task Manager is a familiar monitoring tool found in Windows Server 2008 R2 and earlier versions of Windows. It still provides an instant view of system resources, such as processor activity, process activity, memory usage, networking activity, user information, and resource consumption. However, DBAs should be aware of some noticeable changes, including the addition of a Services tab and the ability to launch the Resource Monitor directly from within the Performance tab.

The Windows Server 2008 R2 Task Manager is very useful for an immediate view of key system operations. It comes in handy when a user notes slow response time, system problems, or other nondescript problems with the network. With a quick glance at the Task Manager, you can see whether a SQL Server system is using all available disk, processor, memory, or networking resources.

There are three methods to launch the Task Manager:

- Right-click the taskbar and select Task Manager.
- Press Ctrl+Shift+Esc.
- Press Ctrl+Alt+Del, and select Start Task Manager.

When the Task Manager loads, you will notice six tabs, as shown in Figure 15.2: Applications, Processes, Services, Performance, Networking, and Users.

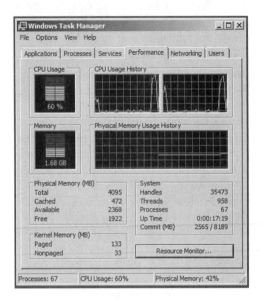

FIGURE 15.2
The Performance tab in Windows Task Manager.

The following sections provide a closer look at how helpful the Task Manager components can be.

Monitoring Applications

The first tab on the Task Manager is the Applications tab. The Applications view provides a list of tasks in the left column and the status of these applications in the right column. The status information enables you to determine whether an application like SQL Server Management Studio or SQL Server Configuration Manager is running and allows you to terminate an application that is not responding, in trouble, or causing problems for your server. To stop such an application, highlight the particular application and click End Task at the bottom of the Task Manager. You can also switch to another application if you have several applications running. To do so, highlight the program and click Switch To at the bottom of the Task

Manager. Finally, you can create a dump file that can be used when a point-in-time snapshot of every process running is needed for advanced troubleshooting. To create a dump file, right-click an application and select Create Dump File.

Monitoring Processes

The second Task Manager tab is the Processes tab. It provides a list of running processes on the server. It also measures the performance in simple data format. This information includes CPU percentage used, memory allocated to each process, and username used in initiating a process, which includes system, local, and network services.

If the initial analysis of the process on your server, such as SQL Server Integration Package or SQL Server instance, takes up too much CPU percentage or uses too many memory resources, thereby hindering server performance, you can sort the processes by clicking the CPU or Memory (Private Working Set) column header. The processes are then sorted in order of usage. This way, you can tell which one is slowing down performance on your server. You can terminate a process by selecting the process and clicking the End Process button.

Many other performance or process measures can be removed or added to the Processes view, including process identifier (PID), CPU time, session ID, and page faults. To add these measures, select View, Select Columns to open the Select Column property page. Here you can add process counters to the process list or remove them from the list.

Monitoring Services

When the Services tab is selected, you can quickly assess and troubleshoot a specific Windows or SQL Server service by viewing whether it has stopped or is still running. The Services tab also offers additional key details, including the service name, service description, and service group. It is also possible to launch the Services snap-in if you need to make changes to a specific service. For example, if you know a given service should be running and you don't see it running in the Process tab (common services include SQL Server Browser, SQL Server, or SQL Server Agent), you can go to the Services tab and attempt to start the service from there. It's very rudimentary, but in keeping with what Task Manager is typically used for, it does offer a quick overview of system status and preliminary problem resolution.

Monitoring Performance

The Performance tab allows you to view the CPU and pagefile usage in graphical form. This information is especially useful when you need a quick view of a performance bottleneck. The Performance tab makes it possible to graph a percentage of processor time in Kernel mode. To show this, select View, Show Kernel Times. The kernel time is represented by the red line in the graph. The kernel time is the measure of time that applications are using operating system services. The other processor time is known as User mode. User mode processor time is spent in threads that are spawned by applications on the system. If your server has multiple CPU processors installed, you can view multiple CPU graphs at a time by selecting View, CPU History. Also on the Performance tab, you will find a button labeled Resource Monitor. You can invoke Resource Monitor for additional analysis of the system. Resource Monitor is covered in the section "Using the Windows Server 2008 R2 Performance and Reliability Monitoring Tools."

> **Tip**
>
> Although Task Manager provides lots of useful information for monitoring system performance, experienced database administrators will tell you not to use Task Manager to troubleshoot memory problems. Why? In a nutshell, SQL Server will attempt to obtain as much memory as it is allowed to under the Max Memory configuration setting. Then, whenever Windows requests memory that is being held by SQL Server, it will give memory back to Windows for use by other processes. This natural and organic give and take works very well behind the scenes. However, SQL Server makes this memory grab regardless of whether it is using all the memory at any given moment to better enable caching of data and execution plans. That behavior, in turn, alarms many novice administrators who, when opening Task Manager, see that SQL Server is consuming the lion's share of memory on their server. But it's a false alarm because SQL Server is tuned to automatically give that memory back to Windows whenever requested. Instead, check in Chapter 14, "Performance Tuning and Troubleshooting SQL Server 2012," for other methods of monitoring SQL Server memory usage.

Monitoring Network Performance

The Networking tab provides a measurement of the network traffic for the connections on the local server in graphical form. This utility is a great way to monitor database mirroring traffic between two SQL Server systems. For multiple network connections—whether they are dial-up,

LAN connections, a WAN connection, a VPN connection, or the like—the Networking tab displays a graphical comparison of the traffic for each connection. It provides a quick overview of the adapter, network utilization, link speed, and state of your connection.

To show a visible line on the graph for network traffic on any interface, the view automatically scales to magnify the view of traffic versus available bandwidth. The graph scales from 0% to 100% if the Auto Scale option is not enabled. The greater the percentage shown on the graph, the less is the magnified view of the current traffic. To autoscale and capture network traffic, select Options, Auto Scale.

It is possible to break down traffic on the graph into Bytes Sent, Received, and Total Bytes by selecting View, Network Adapter History and checking the selections you'd like graphed. This can be useful if you determine the overall throughput is high and you need to quickly determine if inbound or outbound traffic is an issue. In this situation, the default setting is displayed in Total Bytes.

You can also add more column headings by selecting View, Select Columns. Various network measures can be added or removed; they include Bytes Throughput, Bytes Sent/Interval, Unicast Sent and Received, and so on.

> **Tip**
>
> If you suspect a possible network server problem, launch the Task Manager and quickly glance at the information on CPU utilization, memory available, process utilization, and network utilization. When the utilization of any or all of these items exceeds 80 to 90 percent, there may be a bottleneck or overutilization of the resource. However, if all the utilization information shows demand being less than 5 percent, the problem is probably not related to server operations.

Monitoring User Activity

The final tab on the Task Manager is the Users tab, which displays a list of the users who can access the server, session status, and names. The following five columns are available on the Users tab:

- **User**—Shows the users logged on the server. As long as the user is not connected by means of a console session, it is possible to control the session remotely or send a message. Remote Control can be initiated by right-clicking the user and selecting Remote Control. The level of control is dictated by the security settings associated with Remote Desktop.

- **ID**—Displays the numeric ID that identifies the session on the server.

- **Status**—Displays the current status of a session. Sessions can be either Active or Disconnected.

- **Client Name**—Specifies the name of the client computer using the session, if applicable.

- **Session**—Displays the ID numbers of active sessions on the server.

Obtaining Monitoring Metrics with Dynamic Management Views

Dynamic Management Views (DMVs) were first introduced in SQL Server 2005 to monitor performance and obtain state information on servers and databases without placing a heavy burden on the system from a performance perspective. Because DMVs are lightweight and less intrusive than other monitoring mechanisms, such as SQL Server Profiler and the Data Collector, they can be used to monitor, diagnose, and identify performance issues quickly. There is an extensive number of existing and new DMVs within SQL Server 2008 R2 and 2012. Some of them are tailored toward monitoring; however, others even provide server state information.

From the perspective of SQL Server internals, Dynamic Management Views and their associated functions are organized into the following self-explanatory categories:

- AlwaysOn Availability Group Dynamic Management Views and Functions

- Change Data Capture-Related Dynamic Management Views

- Change Tracking-Related Dynamic Management Views

- Common Language Runtime-Related Dynamic Management Views

- Database Mirroring-Related Dynamic Management Views

- Database-Related Dynamic Management Views

- Execution-Related Dynamic Management Views and Functions

- Extended Events Dynamic Management Views

- FILESTREAM and FileTable Dynamic Management Views (Transact-SQL)

- Full-Text Search and Semantic Search Dynamic Management Views

- Index-Related Dynamic Management Views and Functions
- I/O-Related Dynamic Management Views and Functions
- Object-Related Dynamic Management Views and Functions
- Query Notifications-Related Dynamic Management Views
- Replication-Related Dynamic Management Views
- Resource Governor Dynamic Management Views
- Security-Related Dynamic Management Views
- Service Broker-Related Dynamic Management Views
- SQL Server Operating System-Related Dynamic Management Views
- Transaction-Related Dynamic Management Views and Functions

To view a DMV, in Object Explorer, expand the Views folder in a given database, and then expand the Systems View folder. All DMVs reside in this folder and start with the prefix sys.dm_. The functions associated with a DMV can be found by expanding the master database, Programmability, Functions folder, System Functions, and Table Valued Functions. Unless you are a genius (and we aren't saying that you are not), it is challenging trying to remember all of the DMVs included in SQL Server. Use the following script to provide a listing of the hundreds of available DMVs:

```
SELECT * FROM sys.all_objects
  WHERE [name] LIKE '%dm_%'
        AND [type] IN ('V', 'TF', 'IF')
        AND [schema_id] = 4
ORDER BY [name]
```

Useful DMVs for Monitoring SQL Server 2012

As mentioned earlier, not only can DMVs assist you with performance tuning and monitoring, but they can also provide detailed information when you need to monitor a SQL Server system. For example, the sys.dm_os_sys_info DMV can be used to determine the number of logical CPUs in a system, the hyperthread ratio between the logical and physical processors, and the amount of physical memory available in the system. Here is the Transact-SQL code that illustrates this example, including the results:

```
SELECT cpu_count,
  hyperthread_ratio,
  physical_memory_in_bytes
```

```
FROM sys.dm_os_sys_info

Results
cpu_count |hyperthread_ratio |physical_memory_in_bytes
1 | 1 | 072447488
```

Another useful DMV that is applicable at the database scope level is
sys.dm_tran_locks. It allows a DBA to obtain information on currently
active Lock Manager resources. Locks that have been granted or waiting
are displayed. For a topical list of performance-tuning scenarios and the
DMVs best suited to help in those scenarios, refer to Chapter 14.

Using Predefined SQL Server 2012 Standard Reports for Monitoring

Reports were introduced in Chapter 2, "Administering and Configuring the
Database Engine Settings." The predefined standard reports included in
SQL Server 2012 are a great way for a DBA to monitor a SQL Server
system. These reports provide performance-monitoring statistics, resource
usage, and consumption at both the server-scope level and the database-
scope level.

The predefined standard reports can be displayed by right-clicking a SQL
Server instance in Management Studio, selecting Reports, and then
Standard Reports. The standard reports include the following:

- Server Dashboard
- Configuration Changes History
- Schema Changes History
- Scheduler Health
- Memory Consumption
- Activity—All Blocking Transactions
- Activity—All Cursors
- Activity—Top Cursors
- Activity—All Sessions
- Activity—Top Sessions
- Activity—Dormant Sessions
- Activity—Top Connections
- Top Transactions by Age

- Top Transactions by Blocked Transactions Count
- Top Transactions by Locks Count
- Performance—Batch Execution Statistics
- Performance—Object Execution Statistics
- Performance—Top Queries by Average CPU Time
- Performance—Top Queries by Average IO
- Performance—Top Queries by Total CPU Time
- Performance—Top Queries by Total I/O
- Server Broker Statistics
- Transaction Log Shipping Status

The standard report, titled Server Dashboard, is a great overall report that provides an overview of a SQL Server instance, including activity and configuration settings. All the reports provide strategic value for a DBA when monitoring a SQL Server system, specifically the ones associated with performance. From a monitoring perspective, give them a try and familiarize yourself with the content and output.

In addition, it is also possible to create reports associated to specific databases. This can be achieved by right-clicking a database, selecting Reports, Standard Reports, and then the specific report that you want displayed.

Monitoring Job Activity

The Job Activity Monitor allows the monitoring of all agent jobs for a specific SQL Server instance through the SQL Server Management Studio (SSMS). To view all jobs with the Job Activity Monitor:

1. In Object Explorer, expand SQL Server Agent, and then select Job Activity Monitor.
2. Right-click the Job Activity Monitor.
3. Select View Job Activity.

Within the Job Activity Monitor, each job hosted by the SQL Server instance is listed. The columns above the display fields can be used to sort the different jobs. Both the Filter link located in the status pane and the Filter button located at the top of the window can be used to filter the list of agent jobs. If the SQL Server Agent is configured as a Master based on the Multiserver Administration, you will be able to see job activity for other SQL Server instances that are using this SQL Server Agent as a target.

Filter settings can be applied to each of the agent job columns. This capability is helpful when many jobs are listed. To apply a filter to the list of jobs, follow these steps:

1. From within the Job Activity Monitor, click the Filter button or the View Filter Settings link.

2. To configure the filter to show only failed jobs, select Failed from the Last Run Outcome drop-down.

3. When the filter is configured, enable the Apply Filter option near the bottom of the window.

4. Click OK to accept the settings.

> **Note**
>
> The filter icon changes from blue to green when a filter is applied to the list. To remove the filter, click the Clear button from within the Filter Settings dialog box.

The Details pane does not update automatically; however, you can configure it by selecting View Refresh Settings from the Status pane. Note that the refresh interval and the filter settings are not persistent. When the Job Activity Monitor is closed, the settings revert to the defaults.

The jobs shown in the Details pane can also be managed. The context menu allows you to start, stop, enable, disable, delete, and view the job history. You also can access the properties of the job by right-clicking the job and selecting Properties.

Monitoring SQL Logs

SQL Server keeps several logs detailing the various processes that take place on the server. The most frequently used log files can be viewed through the Log File Viewer.

The SQL Server error logs are the primary logs kept for instances. By default, six archive logs and one active log are kept. A new log file is created each time an instance is started.

Follow these steps to access the SQL Server logs in SQL Server Management Studio:

1. In SQL Server Management Studio's Object Explorer, expand a SQL Server instance.

2. From within the Object Explorer pane, expand Management, and then expand the SQL Server Logs folder.

3. Double-click a log in order to view it.

You can change the number of SQL error logs kept by right-clicking the SQL Server Logs container in the Object Explorer and selecting Configure. In the Configure SQL Server Error Logs window, enable the option to limit the number of error log files and specify the number of error log files.

The SQL Server Agent error logs keep track of agent processes that take place on the SQL Server. If a problem with a SQL Server Agent process occurs, these logs should be checked to help determine the cause of the issue.

Nine Agent archive logs and one current log are kept. To access the Agent error logs from within the SSMS, expand the SQL Server Agent container, and then expand the Error Logs container. You can configure the Agent error-logging levels by right-clicking the Error Logs container and selecting Configure. By default, only error and warning messages are enabled. To enable informational logging messages, select the check box and click OK. Enabling informational logging may significantly increase the size of the log files.

By right-clicking either an Agent or SQL Server error log and selecting View Log, you can open the Log File Viewer. The Log File Viewer allows you to view each log file individually. A powerful feature of the Log File Viewer is to combine the log files, including the Windows event log, into a single view. You can accomplish this by enabling and disabling the logs from the menu pane on the left side of the window. Figure 15.3 shows the current SQL Server logs combined with the current Windows logs.

Note

It is a best practice to limit the size of the SQL Server and SQL Agent log files. To do this, Microsoft has provided two stored procedures in the form of sp_cycle_errorlog and sp_cycle_agent_errorlog, respectively. These should be scheduled as jobs on a regular basis to cycle the log and keep logs to a manageable size. For example, you might want to schedule a SQL Agent job to run sp_cycle_errorlog every three days because, based on the usual amount of log entries in a three-day period, the log files will normally be 3MB or less.

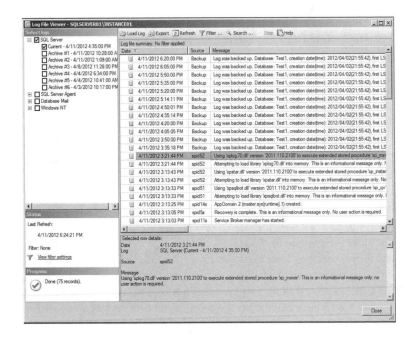

FIGURE 15.3
Viewing consolidated logs within the Log File Viewer screen.

The Data Collector and the Management Data Warehouse

SQL Server provides an integrated framework introduced in SQL Server 2008 for performance monitoring and troubleshooting capable of collecting performance and diagnostic data from one or more SQL Servers. The captured data is stored in a centralized management data warehouse (MDW). With the information yielded, DBAs are able to proactively analyze, troubleshoot, and monitor SQL Server as a result of the trends and historical knowledge they gain from just firing intuitive reports against a SQL Server system in question.

The Data Collector only captures performance and diagnostic data from the Database Engine of SQL Server 2008, SQL2008R2, and SQL2012 and later versions. Future releases are likely to focus on the other SQL Server components and features, such as Reporting Services and Analysis Services.

> **Note**
>
> So as not to get confused when reviewing other books or online materials, readers should remember that Performance Studio was used in older versions synonymously with Data Collector. They are the same tool.

Data Collection Components and Architecture

The Performance Studio infrastructure is based on a simple framework involving a few new components:

- **Data provider**—Sources of performance or diagnostic information.

- **Collector type**—A logical wrapper that recognizes how to leverage, obtain, and expose data from a specific data provider. Examples include Generic Transact-SQL Query Collector Type, Query Activity Collector Type, and Performance Counters Collector Types.

- **Collection item**—A collection item is an example of a collector type that defines the items to be collected in a collection set. When defining collection items, a name, collector type, and collection frequency must be established because a collection item cannot exist on its own.

- **Collection set**—A logical unit of data collection items associated with a SQL Server instance.

- **Collection mode**—Indicates how data will be collected, stored, and uploaded to the management data warehouse. The options include Non-Cached and Cached modes.

- **Management data warehouse**—A relational database that acts as a repository for maintaining all historical data captured via Performance Studio.

A data collector is installed by default on each SQL Server instance. After a collection set is established on a target, performance data and diagnostic information will upload on demand or based on a specified time interval to the management data warehouse as a result of a series of jobs executed by the SQL Server Agent. Also, depending on the collection set, some data may be cached on the SQL Server instance before it's uploaded. After the data is captured and consolidated within the management data warehouse, reports can be generated based on a specific collection set.

> **Note**
>
> Based on the schema design of the management data warehouse, the MDW must be hosted on an instance of SQL Server 2008 or later.

Configuring the Management Data Warehouse

The first step in conducting a Performance Studio implementation is creating and establishing the management data warehouse. Even though performance monitoring and diagnostic data is captured with minimal overhead, it is a best practice to implement the management data warehouse on a dedicated SQL Server system, especially if more than one SQL Server instance target is anticipated. In return, Performance Studio will not skew the performance numbers as a result of additional performance overhead from the data collector when data is being captured and analyzed from a SQL Server system.

By default, data from a target is uploaded to the MDW every 15 minutes. This event screams a potential performance bottleneck if there are hundreds of instances uploading data to the same MDW. To avoid this situation, it is a best practice to stagger the start time of the upload process when working with multiple instances; therefore, an MDW bottleneck will be alleviated because data is being uploaded at a distributed rate.

The space requirement for a system collection set is approximately 200 to 500 megabytes per day. Consider these numbers seriously when creating and allocating space for the MDW. It also makes sense to ensure that the recovery model is set to Simple to minimize excessive log growth. However, maintain the Full recovery model if there is a need to restore the database to the point of failure.

> **Tip**
>
> When creating customized collection sets, it is a best practice to test the amount of data captured in a dedicated prototype lab before going live in production. By simulating a production workload in the lab, the DBA will be able to accurately size the MDW and interpret the stress on the system. Performance may degrade and storage costs may increase when implementing a number of collection sets with a large number of services and performance counters being captured.

Follow these steps to implement the management data warehouse with SQL Server Management Studio:

1. In Object Explorer, connect to an instance of SQL Server that you plan to use as the management data warehouse.

2. In Object Explorer, expand a SQL Server instance, expand the Management Folder, and then select the Data Collection node.

3. Right-click the Data Collection node, and then select Configure Management Data Warehouse.

4. Click Next in the Welcome to the Configure Management Data Warehouse Wizard.

5. On the Select Configuration Task page, select the option Create or Upgrade a Management Data Warehouse, and then click Next.

6. On the next page, select a server and database to host the management data warehouse. If the database does not already exist, click New to manually generate a new management data warehouse database. Click Next to continue.

7. The next page, Map Logins and Users, is used for mapping logins and users to the predefined management data warehouse roles. If the desired login is not displayed, click New Login and add the account. The management data warehouse roles that need to be mapped to a login include `mdw_admin`, `mdw_reader`, and `mdw_writer`. After all logins are added and mapped to the management data warehouse roles, click Next, as displayed in Figure 15.4.

   ■ `mdw_admin`—Ultimately this role is the superuser role associated with management data warehouse because members of this role have read, write, and delete access to the MDW. Members can also modify the schema and run maintenance jobs.

   ■ `mdw_writer`—Similar to write permissions with a database, members of this role can upload and write data to the MDW; however, they cannot read the data.

   ■ `mdw_reader`—This group can only read data in the MDW and that's it.

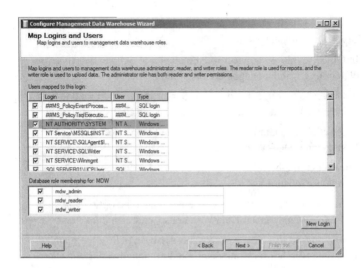

FIGURE 15.4
Mapping logins and users to the MDW roles.

8. Review the management data warehouse configuration settings in the Complete the Wizard page, and then click Finish.

9. The final page will indicate the status of the installation. Verify that all actions were successful, and then click Close.

10. When the wizard is complete, connect to the same SQL Server instance and ensure that the new management data warehouse database exists in Object Explorer. In addition, ensure that the database recovery model is set to Simple.

A simple review of the MDW database will show that the database objects are grouped together based on a number of schemas. The Core schema represents objects associated with collected data. The Snapshot schema is used for storing system-collected data sets, which are included with SQL Server and the Custom Snapshot schema is used when adding new data types for out-of-the-box data collector types or for third-party collector types for user-defined collector sets. When installing on an instance of SQL Server 2008 R2 or SQL Server 2012, you will also see three added schemas starting with sysutility_ucp.

Set Up a Data Collection

Now that the management data warehouse is created and initialized, the next step is to set up a data collection on one or more SQL Server instances:

1. In Object Explorer, connect to an instance of SQL Server that you plan to collect data from.

2. In Object Explorer, expand the instance of SQL Server, expand the Management Folder, and then select the Data Collection node.

3. Right-click the Data Collection node, and then select Configure Management Data Warehouse.

4. Click Next in the Welcome to the Configure Management Data Warehouse Wizard.

5. On the Select Configuration Task page, select the option Set Up Data Collection to configure this SQL Server instance, which will start collecting data for an existing management data warehouse. Click Next to continue.

6. Ensure that the names of the SQL Server instance and management data warehouse hosting the management data warehouse are accurate. Then specify the cache directory that will store collected data before it is updated to the management data warehouse. The TEMP directory of the collector process will be used automatically if these settings are left blank. Click Next, as displayed in Figure 15.5.

7. Review the management data warehouse configuration settings on the Complete the Wizard page, and then click Finish.

8. The final page should communicate the following: the appropriate management data warehouse is selected, the collection sets are started, and the data collection is enabled. Click Close when all actions are completed successfully.

9. Expand the System Data Collection Sets folder under the Data Collection node in Object Explorer to see the newly created system data collection sets.

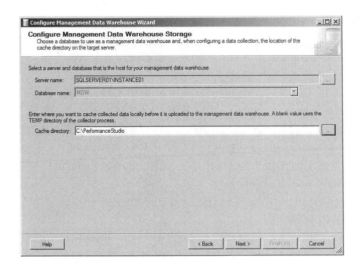

FIGURE 15.5
Configuring a data collection.

Examining the System Data Collection Sets Included with Data Collector

Starting with SQL Server 2008, Microsoft included three built-in system data collection sets, which were installed when a data collection was set up on a SQL Server instance. Each of these built-in collection sets also included Collection Set Reports, which can be found in the data collection folder.

Each data collection set included with SQL Server is explained in the following sections:

■ **Disk Usage System Data collection set**—The Disk Usage System Data collection set, as illustrated in Figure 15.6, captures data files and log files of disk usage performance data associated with SQL Server relational databases via the Generic T-SQL Query Collection collector type. Also, the disk usage data uploads to the MDW every 6 hours, where it is then retained for 90 days. After the data is collected, it is stored in MDW tables under the snapshot schemas `Snapshots.disk_usage` and `Snapshots.log_usage`. Performance counters for free drive space are also captured. Additional performance data associated with a database can be obtained if you click a database. This is presented in Figure 15.7.

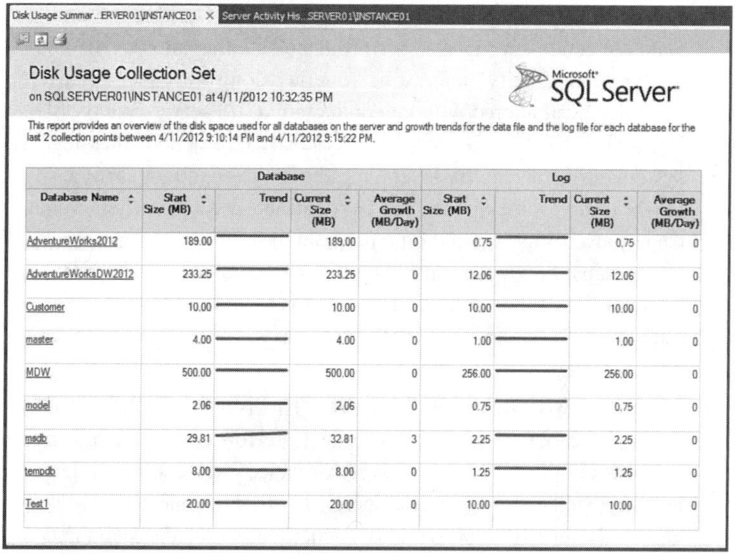

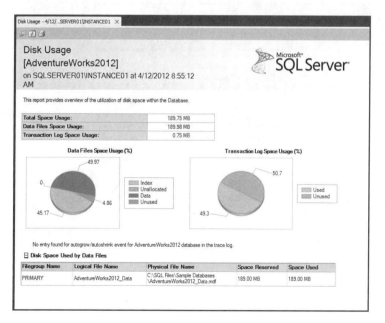

FIGURE 15.6
Viewing the Disk Usage Summary Data Collection report.

FIGURE 15.7
Viewing the Disk Usage Data Collection report for a specific database.

- **Query Statistics System Data collection set**—The Query Statistics
  Data collection set captures performance data that allows DBAs to
  analyze and identify "interesting" queries along with query plans
  that have been altered without conducting a full server-side profiler
  trace. Server-side traces are typically costly transactions that degrade
  system performance. By leveraging the dm_exec_query_stats
  DMV, troublesome queries can be identified because snapshot plan
  caches are being captured on a periodic basis. By comparing query
  stats against previous snapshots, the topmost interesting queries can
  be identified. When data is captured, it is stored in the snapshots.
  query_stats, snapshots.notable_query_text, and snapshots.
  notable_query_plan tables.

- **Server Activity Data collection set**—This is another data collection
  set included out-of-the-box that collects performance data on active
  sessions and requests, memory, performance counters, schedules,
  and wait statistics. The data associated with this collection is
  captured every 10 to 60 seconds, cached on the local system, and
  uploaded every 15 minutes. The Server History Data Collection
  report can be seen in Figure 15.8.

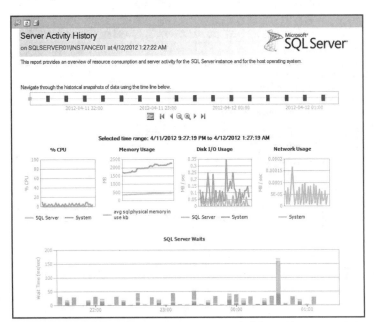

FIGURE 15.8
Viewing the Server History Data Collection report.

Managing Data Collection Set Properties

It is possible to manage the properties associated with a data collection set by right-clicking a data collection set in Object Explorer and then selecting Properties. Examples of built-in system data collection sets in SQL Server include Disk Usage Collection Set, Query Activity Collection Set, and Server Activity Collection Set. Each of these collection sets can be managed.

The Data Collection Set Properties dialog box has a total of three pages. The settings in many sections on these pages are customizable. Become familiar with these pages by reading the next section.

The Data Collection Set General Page

The General page is broken down into the following sections, as depicted in Figure 15.9.

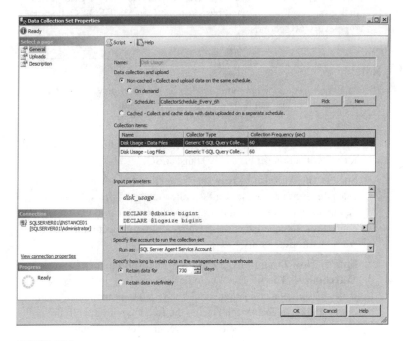

FIGURE 15.9

Viewing the General page associated with the properties of a data collection set.

- **Name**—This text box is self-explanatory; it displays the name of the data collection set.

- **Data Collection and Upload**—The two options available in this section include Non-Cached and Cached mode. These options dictate how data is collected and uploaded to the management data warehouse. The Non-Cached mode is the default option involved in collecting performance data based on a scheduled interval. Alternatively, noncached data is collected and uploaded on demand. The second option, known as Cached mode, collects performance data at collection frequencies and then uploads the data based on a separate schedule.

- **Collection Items**—The next section located on the general page is Collection Items. A DBA can review the collected items including names, category type, and collection frequency in seconds. For example, performance data associated with Disk Files or Log Files disk usage can be collected based on the Generic T-SQL Collector type every 60 seconds.

> **Note**
>
> The Collection frequency time interval can be modified only if the Data Collection and Upload setting is configured as Cached.

- **Input Parameters**—This section presents the input parameters used for the collection set based on Transact-SQL.

- **Specify the Account to Run the Collection Set**—This setting indicates the account used to run the collection set. The SQL Server Agent account is the default account; however, if proxy accounts are configured and available, there is the option to select an account from the drop-down list.

- **Specify How Long to Retain Data in the Management Warehouse**—The final setting indicates how long performance data that is based on a collection should be retained in the management data warehouse. DBAs can change the frequency by specifying a new value or selecting the option to retain data indefinitely.

The Data Collection Set Uploads Page

The Data Collection Set Uploads page is used for viewing or setting upload schedules for collected data. Settings are displayed only and cannot be changed unless the Cached option is configured on the General tab for Data Collection and Uploaded. The settings and information include the server hosting the management data warehouse, the MDW name being written to, the time associated with the last upload, and the upload schedule.

The Data Collection Set Description Page

The final page in the Data Collection Set Properties dialog box is the Description Page. Here you can view detailed description for the data collection set. For example, the detailed description for the Server Activity Data Collection Set gathers top-level performance indicators for the computer and the Database Engine. DBAs can benefit from this page by conducting an analysis on resource use, resource bottlenecks, and Database Engine activity.

Viewing Collection Set Logs

When viewing collection set logs, a DBA has two choices: Either review logs associated with all the collection sets, or drill down on a specific collection set and view just one log file. Follow these steps to review the logs associated with all the collection sets:

1. In Object Explorer, connect to an instance of SQL Server that you plan to view the collection set's logs.

2. In Object Explorer, expand an instance of SQL Server, expand the Management folder, and then select the Data Collection node.

3. Right-click the Data Collection node, and then select View Logs.

Capturing Performance Counters from Multiple SQL Server Instances

If you need to capture performance data from one or more SQL Server instances, the best practice is to use one MDW within the SQL Server infrastructure. Again, ensure that the MDW can support the workload based on the number of instances recording performance data to the MDW.

Follow these steps to implement a data collection on a SQL Server instance that is not hosting the MDW. For this example, our MDW is residing on SQLServer01\Instance01, and a data collection will be configured on SQLServer01\Instance02 to record performance data to the MDW residing on SQLServer01\Instance01:

1. In Object Explorer, connect to an instance of SQL on which you plan to set up a data collection (SQLServer01\Instance02).

2. In Object Explorer, expand a SQL Server instance (SQLServer01\ Instance02), expand the Management folder, and then select the Data Collection node. This SQL Server instance should not be hosting the MDW database.

3. Right-click the Data Collection node, and then select Configure Management Data Warehouse.

4. Click Next in the Welcome to the Configure Management Data Warehouse Wizard.

5. On the Select Configuration Task page, select the option Set Up Data Collection, and then click Next.

6. On the subsequent page, specify a SQL Server instance that is already hosting the MDW, such as SQLServer01\Instance01. Next, specify the database name of the MDW and the Cache directory, and then click Next, as shown in Figure 15.10.

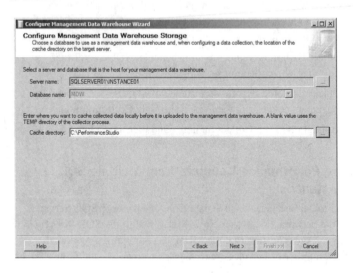

FIGURE 15.10
Configure a data collection to use a MDW on another SQL Server instance.

7. Verify the configuration on the Complete the Wizard page, and then click Finish.

8. The final page will indicate the status of the installation. Verify that all actions were successful, and then click Close.

9. Repeat steps 1 through 8 on all SQL Server instances for which you want to capture performance monitoring data.

Running Data Collection Reports

Each built-in data collection set includes intuitive reports that should be leveraged for analyzing trends and diagnostics. To generate a report, conduct the following steps:

1. In Object Explorer, expand a SQL Server instance, expand the Management folder, and then select the Data Collection node.

2. Right-click the Data Collection node, select Reports, Management Data Warehouse, and then select a report to preview like Disk Usage Summary, which was displayed in Figure 15.6.

SQL Server Utilities

SQL Server 2008 R2 shipped with an exciting set of features called utilities. The idea behind these utilities was to enable DBAs to have a holistic view of resource utilization across their SQL Server infrastructure. As with every new feature, there are caveats and a number of new terms to learn.

The first term is Utility Control Point, a SQL Server instance that is used as a central repository in which data about other instances is stored. Microsoft has reused the data collection technology introduced in Data Collector and expanded it to collect more data.

The second and third terms are Utility Explorer and System Utility Viewpoints, both of which are built in to SQL Server Management Studio and allow Microsoft to provide a reporting portal for the end user. Each report can either be at the enterprise (that is, reporting on multiple SQL Server instances at one time) or the instance level, and configurable thresholds allow the user to decide if specific instances are over- or underutilized.

Utility Control Point Caveats

- The repository must be installed on an instance of SQL Server 2008 R2 or 2012.

- Instances being monitored must be SQL Server 2008 SP2 or later.

- Enterprise Edition in SQL Server 2008 R2 and SQL Server 2012 is licensed to report against 25 instances of SQL Server. Datacenter Edition in SQL Server 2008 R2 is licensed to report against an unlimited number of licenses, hardware permitting.

- The database repository name and collection periods are nonconfigurable.

- You must use the SQL Server Utility for all collection sets on a managed instance of SQL Server; it cannot sit alongside Data Collector. All existing collections must be disabled, the instance enrolled, and the collections pointed at the new repository.

Installing the Utility Control Point

To install a Utility Control Point repository on a SQL Server 2008 R2 or SQL Server 2012 instance, follow these steps:

1. In Object Explorer, connect to a SQL Server Database Engine instance that you plan to use as the Utility Control Point.

2. Click the View Menu option and choose the Utility Explorer option.

3. Click the Create Utility Control Point button in the Utility Explorer or click the link Create a Utility Control Point (UCP) in Utility Explorer Details pane. This launches a new wizard.

4. Click Next on the Introduction screen.

5. On the Specify the Instance of SQL Server screen, click the Connect button to choose the host for the Utility Control Point repository and assign a name for the Utility Control Point. This name is not the name of the repository; in the current incarnation, this cannot be changed. In this demo scenario, choose the name Development Utility.

6. Figure 15.11 depicts the Specify Account screen. The account specified could be either a Windows Domain Account or the SQL Server Agent Service account. Click Next to continue.

7. Click Next on the Instance Validation screen to run the validation report. Should an action fail, read the error message, act on it, and press the Rerun Validation button. After all errors have been fixed, click Next.

8. Review the information on the Summary page and click Next.

9. Click Finish on the UCP Creation screen to complete the process, as shown in Figure 15.12.

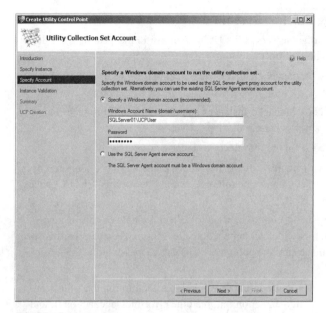

FIGURE 15.11
Specify account.

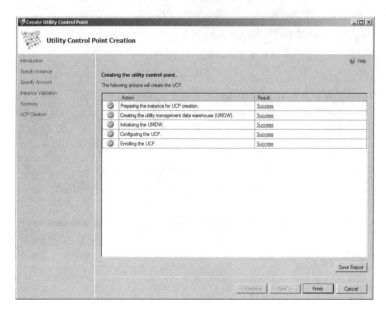

FIGURE 15.12
Utility Point Creation.

Monitoring Further Servers

To monitor further servers in the Utility Control Point, you must enroll them. To do this, follow these steps:

1. Expand the newly created DevelopmentUtility UCP in the Utility Explorer.

2. Right-click Managed Instances and choose Enroll Instance. This will spawn a new wizard.

3. Click Next on the Introduction screen.

4. Specify the name of the first instance that should be monitored by clicking the Connect button and entering the details. Click Connect and then Next.

5. Specify an account to be used to collect the data on this instance. Again, this will need to be a domain account. As a password is specified, make sure the chosen account has its password set to never expire.

6. Click Next on the Instance Validation screen to run the validation report. Should an action fail, read the error message, act on it, and press the rerun validation button. After all errors have been fixed, click Next.

7. Review the information on the Summary page and click Next.

8. Click Finish on the Instance Enrollment screen.

9. Repeat steps 2 to 8 as necessary for other instances.

Viewing Utility Information

To view the Utility Explorer Content as shown in Figure 15.13, complete the following steps:

1. Launch SQL Server Management Studio.

2. Click View and choose Utility Explorer. This will open two new tabs in the main development window—Getting Started and Utility Explorer Content.

3. To populate the Utility Explorer Content tab, click the Connect to Utility button, enter the details for the Utility Control Point, and click Connect.

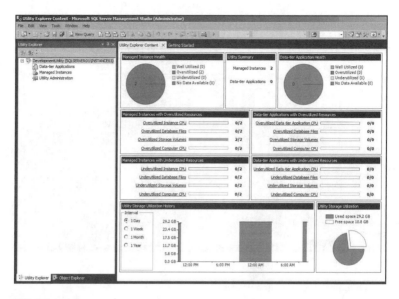

FIGURE 15.13
Utility Explorer content.

In the case of the lab environment created for this book, the reader can see that the storage has been overutilized. Clicking the hyperlink changes the display to include only the servers that meet this condition, as shown in Figure 15.14. From this screen, information regarding the utilization of CPU and storage can be viewed on a per SQL Server instance basis. One of the nice touches here is the ability to look at the data over a number of time frames from 1 day to 1 year to see potential trends in data.

Clicking the Policy Details tab allows for customization of the policies that the utilization levels are based on for the scope of the chosen instance. Details outlining how to change the global policies will be explained later in this chapter. To override a policy, click the Override the Global Policy option button for the appropriate policy and increase or decrease the overutilized and/or underutilized percentage values to meet the business needs of the SQL Server instance.

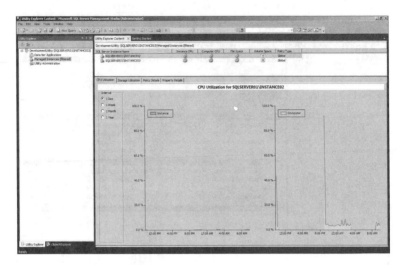

FIGURE 15.14
Utility Content Explorer filtered view.

Clicking Utility Administration in the Utility Explorer window changes the scope of the Utility Explorer tab. The Utility Explorer tab showcases three tabs labeled Policy, Security, and Data Warehouse. The Policy tab enables the end user to define or revert changes to each of the global policies used to define resource usage of the monitored instances. In a similar manner, Data-tier Application global policies can be changed. The Volatile Resource Policy Evaluation page allows for configuration changes to the frequency of polling and the establishment of thresholds for overutilized or underutilized system resources. A resource is considered underutilized when its percentage of utilization drops below a specified value and as overutilized when it rises above a specified value. The following are some examples of potential global policies for managed instances in SQL Server 2012:

- **CPU**—The default policies for a managed instance of SQL Server 2012 are underutilized = 0% CPU activity (or below) and over-utilized = 70% (or above).

- **File Space**—The default policies for both data and log files are underutilized = 0% and overutilized = 70%.

- **Computer CPU**—The same as the instance CPU, except that it applies to the entire physical or virtual machine where the SQL Server 2012 instance is running.

- **Storage Volume**—The same as File Space, except that it applies to the individual storage volumes for a given instance of SQL Server 2012.

The security tab controls account-level privileges to the utility dashboards. The Data Warehouse tab allows configuration of the data retention period for the Utility Control Point repository. Note that it is not possible to change either the repository database name or the collection frequency.

Creating Operators and Sending Email Alerts

Being proactive by obtaining alerts via email is another form of monitoring within SQL Server. To send and receive alerts, a DBA must first configure the Database Mail feature, define an operator, and then create an alert and bind it to an operator. The upcoming sections will depict this process.

Configuring Database Mail

The mail delivery architecture in SQL Server 2012 is known as Database Mail. Database Mail in SQL Server 2012 uses the industry standard Simple Mail Transfer Protocol (SMTP). This means that one or more available SMTP servers in the organization can be used to relay mail, which could include an existing Exchange Server running either the Hub Transport or Edge role.

To use the new Database Mail feature, the user must be part of the DatabaseMailUserRole role in the MSDB database. This role allows the execution of the `sp_send_dbmail` stored procedure.

Implementing Database Mail

After installing and configuring the SMTP server, follow these steps to configure Database Mail for a SQL Server instance:

1. In Object Explorer, expand a SQL Server instance and then the Management folder. Database Mail should be listed.
2. Right-click Database Mail and select Configure Database Mail.
3. On the Welcome page, click Next.
4. Select the Set Up Database Mail option and click Next.
5. If prompted, click Yes to enable Database Mail.
6. Type **Email Notification** into the Profile Name field.

Note

If the Database Mail feature is not available, a message will be displayed. Click Yes to enable the Database Mail feature.

The next step is to establish a Database Mail account, which is simply a list of SMTP servers used to send the email.

Multiple Database Mail accounts can be used. When email is sent, each mail account is tried in order until one of them is successful. When the email is successfully sent through an account, that account is used for subsequent email delivery until it becomes unavailable.

Each account can be configured with a different authentication, depending on the requirements of the environment. Follow these steps to add the Database Mail account:

1. Still on the New Profile page, click the Add button to open the New Database Mail Account page.

2. Type **Local SMTP** into the Account Name field.

3. Type an email address such as **dbSupport@companyabc.com** for the Email Address field.

4. Type a display name such as **Email Notification** into the Display Name field.

5. The Server Name field must be populated with the name of your SMTP server. For this example, type **Exchange01.companyabc.com** into the Server Name field.

6. Select the type of SMTP authentication to use, such as Windows Authentication using Database Engine Service Credentials, Basic Authentication, or Anonymous Authentication. The setting selected will be based on the relay security associated with the SMTP server.

7. Click OK, and then click Next.

Figure 15.15 shows how the New Database Mail Account page should look. You can add additional accounts using the same procedure.

On the Manage Profile Security page, you can configure the profile as public or private. Public profiles can be used by any user in the DatabaseMailUserRole role, whereas private profiles can be used only by specific database users. The profile can also be configured as the default profile.

FIGURE 15.15
New Database Mail account.

8. To continue using the wizard, enable the Email Notification Profile by checking the Public check box, and then click Next.

9. On the Configure System Parameters page, you can configure the setting that controls how Database Mail operates. For example, to configure the system to retry delivery if an error is experienced, set the Account Retry Attempts and Account Retry Delay (Seconds) options.

10. To continue the wizard, accept the default values and click Next. Click Finish to complete the wizard and execute the defined configuration.

Tip

From a security perspective, it is a best practice to use a dedicated SMTP server within the infrastructure and not the SQL Server system. Adding the IIS and SMTP roles on a SQL Server system increases the surface area of attack. On systems that are running Exchange Server, relaying can be achieved on an Exchange Server system running the Hub Transport or Edge Transport role.

Validating the Database Mail Configuration

To test the email delivery and validate that email is working correctly, follow these steps from within SSMS:

1. Right-click Database Mail.
2. Select Send Test Email.
3. Select Email Notification as the profile.
4. Enter an email address in the To field.
5. Click Send Test Email, and then click OK.

The Database Mail log can be used to validate that the email was sent from the SQL Server to the SMTP server. To view the log, right-click the Database Mail container and select View Database Mail Log from the menu.

The following stored procedures can be used to configure Database Mail using the data definition language (DDL):

- sysmail_add_account_sp
- sysmail_add_profile_sp
- sysmail_add_profileaccount_sp
- sysmail_add_principalprofile_sp
- sp_send_dbmail

For example, you can now use the following code to send an email notification:

```
EXEC msdb.dbo.sp_send_dbmail @recipients='user@companyabc.com',
    @profile_name = 'Email Notification',
    @subject = 'Test Email Notification',
    @body = 'Email message from SQLServer01\INSTANCE01',
    @body_format = 'HTML';
```

> **Tip**
>
> The first port of call for troubleshooting unsent emails is to query the MSDB view sysmail_event_log. To access this view, the user must be a member of either the sysadmin server role or the MSDB database role DatabaseMailUserRole. If users are not a member of the sysadmin role, they will be able to see events only for their submitted emails.

Adding Operators

An *operator* is a user or a group that receives notifications. Notifications can include email, pagers, and net send. The schedule of the operator can also be configured; for example, an operator can be defined to receive notification during business hours, and a different operator can be defined to use notifications during nonbusiness hours or on the weekend.

From within SSMS, you can define new operators. To add a new operator to the SQL Server instance, follow these steps:

1. In Object Explorer, expand SQL Server Agent.
2. Right-click Operators and select New Operator.
3. Enter the name of the operator in the field provided.
4. Enter the email address in the Email Name field.
5. Enable a suitable schedule for the operator; for example, from 8 a.m. to 9 p.m. Monday through Friday.
6. Click OK.

You can use the Notification section of the New Operator page to enable notifications for existing alerts on the server.

Adding Failsafe Operators

A FailsafeOperator is used when all pager notifications have failed. To set up anFailsafeOperator, follow these steps:

1. In Object Explorer, right-click SQL Server Agent and choose Properties.
2. Click the Alert System page.
3. Ensure the correct Mail Profile for the SQL Server Agent has been chosen.
4. Choose the appropriate Failsafe Operator.

Note that both net-send and pager operations have been marked for deprecation and will be removed from a future version of SQL Server.

Defining Alerts

Alerts can be defined for a wide range of SQL Server events. You can receive alerts on the following types of events:

- SQL Server events
- SQL Server performance conditions
- WMI events

Follow these steps to generate an alert when the used log file space falls below 100MB in the AdventureWorks2012 database:

1. Expand the SQL Server Agent in Object Explorer.

2. Right-click Alerts and select New Alert.

3. In the Name field, type `AW Log Files Used Size`.

4. Select SQL Server Performance Condition Alert from the Type drop-down.

5. Select Databases for the object. The first part of the object corresponds to the instance name; if the SQL Server was installed as the default instance, the object name is Databases.

6. Select Log File(s) Used Size (KB) for the counter.

7. Select AdventureWorks2012 for the instance.

8. Select Falls Below for the alert condition.

9. Enter `102400` for the value.

You can also define a response to an alert. Responses can include executing a job or notifying an operator. The following steps demonstrate how to add an operator to the previously created alert:

1. In the New Alert window, select the Response option page.

2. Enable the Notify Operators option.

3. Enable the Email column for the operator created earlier.

4. Click OK to finish creating the alert.

You can use the Options page of the new alert to specify whether the error text is included in the different types of alerts.

Notes From the Field: SQL Agent Alerting

The quickest and easiest way to enable lightweight and low-overhead monitoring of SQL Server 2012 is to enable SQL Agent alerting. Under SQL Agent alerting, you can create an alert for each error severity level from severity level 18 to level 25. It is important to monitor level 18 and greater because level 18 errors are the point at which SQL Server processes are beginning to encounter problems and errors, not just informational tidbits from the system.

It is also quick and easy to use SQL Agent monitoring to watch for SQL Server performance conditions—for example, when CPU utilization rises above 90% or file I/O latency is greater than 100ms in duration. For each

> error severity level or performance condition, be sure to specify an operator who should be notified of the problem. (Adding SQL Agent alert, operators, and notification details is described toward the end of this chapter.) The entire process of adding several operators, defining one or more notification conditions, and adding the error severity alerts described earlier only takes a few minutes.
>
> With SQL Agent alerting in place, DBAs can be assured that they will be proactively emailed whenever a significant performance problem or important error situation arises on their SQL Server.

Using the Windows Server 2008 R2 Performance Monitoring Tools

Windows Server 2008 R2 provides tools to measure and monitor both performance metrics and reliability metrics. Performance is a basis for measuring how fast application and system tasks are completed on a computer, and reliability is a basis for measuring system operation. How reliable a system is will be based on whether it regularly operates at the level at which it was designed to perform. Based on these descriptions, it should be easy to recognize that performance and reliability monitoring are crucial aspects in the overall availability and health of a SQL Server system running on Windows Server 2008 R2. To ensure maximum uptime, a well-thought-through process needs to be put in place to monitor, identify, diagnose, and analyze system performance. This process should invariably provide a means for quickly comparing system performances at varying instances in time and detecting and potentially preventing a catastrophic incident before it causes system downtime.

Microsoft provides two tools in Windows Server 2008 R2, the Performance Monitor and the Reliability Monitor, so that administrators and DBAs can conduct real-time SQL Server system monitoring, examine system resources, collect performance data, and create performance reports from a single console. The tool is combination of three legacy Windows server monitoring tools: System Monitor, Performance Monitor, and Server Performance Advisor. However, extra features and functionalities were introduced including data collector sets, Resource Overview, scheduling, diagnosis reporting, and wizards and templates for creating logs. To launch the Reliability and Performance Monitor in Windows Server 2008 and later versions of Windows, select Start, All Programs, Administive Tools, Performance Monitor, or type `perfmon.msc` at a command prompt.

The Reliability and Performance Monitor is made up of the following elements:

- Resource Monitor
- Performance Monitor
- Reliability Monitor
- Data Collector Sets
- Report Generation

Windows Server 2008 R2 has split the Performance Monitoring and Reliability monitoring into separate components. Performance Monitor can still be called via perfmon.msc, but Reliability Monitor is now found via Control Panel, System and Security, Action Center, Maintenance.

Resource Monitor

The first area of interest in the Reliability and Performance Monitoring toolkit is the Resource Overview screen, also known as the Resource Monitor. Resource Monitor can be launched from within the Performance tab in the Windows Task Manager or by running "perfmon.exe /res" from the run prompt.

The Resource Monitor screen presents a holistic real-time graphical illustration of a SQL Server system's CPU usage, disk usage, network usage, and memory usage. Other tabs on the Resource Monitor provide drill-down information on systemwide CPU, memory, disk, and network utilization. Figure 15.16 provides an example of Resource Monitor Network information:

You can view additional process-level detail to better understand your system's current resource usage by expanding subsections beneath the graphs. For example, when expanded, the CPU subsection includes CPU consumption by application, such as SQL Server, and the Disk subsection displays disk activity based on read and write operations. For example, you can view disk activity associated with SQLServer.exe. In addition, the Network subsection exhibits bytes being sent and received based on an application. This comes in handy when measuring Network Utilization monitoring SQL Server database mirroring between two systems. Finally, the Memory subsection reveals information about the memory use of SQL Server.

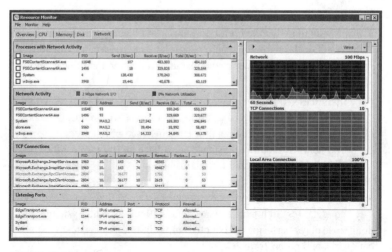

FIGURE 15.16
Viewing the Resource Overview home page in Reliability and Performance Monitor.

The Resource Monitor Overview screen is the first level of defense when you need to get a quick overview of a SQL Server system's resources. If quick diagnosis of an issue cannot be achieved, an administrator should leverage the additional tools within the Reliability and Performance Monitor. These are covered in the upcoming sections.

Performance Monitor

Windows Server 2008 R2 comes with two tools for performance monitoring: Performance Monitor and Reliability Monitor. These tools together provide performance analysis and information that can be used for bottleneck, performance, and troubleshooting analysis of a SQL Server system.

First, defining some terms used in performance monitoring will help clarify the function of Performance Monitor and how it ties in to software and system functionality. The three components noted in the Performance Monitor, Data Collector Sets, and Reports are as follows:

- **Object**—Components contained in a system are grouped into objects. Objects are grouped according to system functionality or by association within the system. Objects can represent logical entities, such as memory, or a physical mechanism, such as a hard disk drive. The number of objects available in a system depends on the configuration. For example, if Microsoft SQL server is installed on a server, some objects pertaining to Microsoft SQL would be available.

- **Counter**—Counters are subsets of objects. Counters typically provide more detailed information for an object, such as queue length or throughput for an object. The System Monitor can collect data through the counters and display it in either a graphical format or a text log format.

- **Instances**—If a server has more than one similar object, each one is considered an instance. For example, a server with multiple processors has individual counters for each instance of the processor. Counters with multiple instances also have an instance for the combined data collected for the instances.

The Performance Monitor provides an interface that allows for the analysis of system data, research performance, and bottlenecks. The System Monitor displays performance counter output in line graphs, histogram (bar chart), and report format.

The histogram and line graphs can be used to view multiple counters at the same time. However, each data point displays only a single value that is independent of its object. The report view is better for displaying multiple values.

Launching the Performance Monitor is accomplished by entering `perfmon.msc` in the command prompt. When a new Performance console is started, it loads a blank system monitor graph into the console with % Processor Time as the only counter defined.

Adding Counters with Performance Monitor

Before counters can be displayed, they have to be added, which can be done by using the menu bar. The Counter button on the button bar includes Add, Delete, and Highlight. You can use the Add Counter button to display new counters. On the other hand, use the Delete Counter button to remove unwanted counters from the display. The Highlight button is helpful for highlighting a particular counter of interest; a counter can be highlighted with either a white or black color around the counter.

The following step-by-step procedures depict how to add counters to the Performance Monitor after it is opened:

1. In the navigation tree, first expand Monitoring Tools, and then Performance Monitor.

2. Either click the Add icon in the menu bar or right-click anywhere on the graph and select Add Counters.

Note

Typical baseline counters consist of Memory—Pages/Sec, Physical Disk—Avg. Disk Queue Length, and Processor—% Processor time.

3. The Add Counters dialog box is invoked, as shown in Figure 15.17. In the Available Counters section, select the desired counters and click Add.

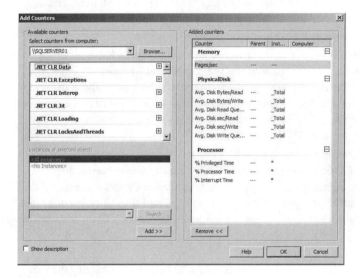

FIGURE 15.17
Adding counters to Performance Monitor.

4. Review the selected counters in the Added Counters section, and then click OK.

Note

This chapter focuses on monitoring. Chapter 14 illustrates the useful SQL Server counters that should be utilized when performance tuning and troubleshooting SQL Server 2012.

Managing Performance Monitor Settings

In the Performance Monitor display, update displays by clicking the Clear button. Clicking the Freeze Display button or pressing Ctrl+F freezes displays, which suspends data collection. Data collection can be resumed by pressing Ctrl+F or by clicking the Freeze Display button again. Click the Update Data button to display an updated data analysis.

It is also possible to export and import a display by using the Cut and Paste buttons. For example, a display can be saved to the Clipboard and then imported into another instance of the Performance Monitor. This is commonly used to view or analyze system information on a different system, such as information from a production server.

The Properties page of Performance Monitor has five additional tabs of configuration: General, Source, Data, Graph, and Appearance. Generally, the Properties page provides access to settings that control the graph grid, color, style of display data, and so on. Data can be saved from the monitor in different ways. The easiest way to retain the display features is to save the control as an HTML file.

The Performance Monitor enables you to also save log files in comma-separated (CSV) or tab-separated (TSV) format, which you can then analyze by using third-party tools such as Seagate Crystal Reports. Alternatively, a comma-separated or tab-separated file can be imported into a spreadsheet or database application, such as Microsoft Excel or Access.

Reliability Monitor

Use the Reliability Monitor when you need help troubleshooting the root cause associated with reduced reliability of a SQL Server system running on Windows Server 2008 R2. Reliability Monitor provides event details through system stability charts and reports that help diagnose items that may be negatively impacting the reliability of a system.

The tool uses a System Stability Index to rate the stability of a system each day over its lifetime by means of an index scorecard that identifies any reduction in reliability. An index rating of 1 represents a system in its least stable stage, whereas an index rating of 10 indicates a system in its most stable stage. Each day's index rating is displayed in a System Stability Chart graph. This graph typically helps administrators to identify dates when stability issues with the Windows Server 2008 system occurred. Additional itemized system stability information can be found in an accompanying System Stability Report section of the Reliability Monitor screen. The additional stability information further assists by identifying the root cause of the reliability issues. This information is grouped into the following categories: Software Installs and Uninstalls, Application Failures, Hardware Failures, Windows Failures, and Miscellaneous Failures.

Reliability Monitor is an essential tool for identifying problems with Windows Server 2008 and 2008 R2. With Reliability Monitoring, an administrator can quickly identify changes in a system that caused a negative trend with system reliability. As such, this tool can also help administrators anticipate other problems, which all ultimately leads to solving issues efficiently and effectively.

Data Collector Sets

The Data Collector Set is a vital new feature available as a subfolder within the Performance Monitor snap-in. The purpose of a data collector set is to review or log system performance data. This is achievable through a single component that encompasses organized multiple data collection points. This information can then be analyzed to diagnose problems, correct system performance issues, or create baselines.

Performance counters, event trace data, and system configuration information are all data collector elements that can be captured and contained in a data collector set. Data collector sets can be based on a predefined template, created from a data collector set that already exists, created manually or with a wizard, or can be user defined. Data collector sets can be exported and used for multiple systems easing the administrative load involving the configuration of new systems producing more effective monitoring. Wizards facilitate the creation of data collector sets and enable an administrator to quickly create collections based on server roles or the type of information that is required.

> **Note**
>
> When capturing and consolidating SQL Server performance Metrics, DBAs should leverage Performance Studio as a data-collecting mechanism over the Data Collector Sets feature in Windows Server 2008 and 2008 R2.

Reports

The final folder in the Performance Monitor console is Reports. The Reports folder provides diagnostic reports to support administrators in troubleshooting and diagnosing system performance problems, including reliability. Reports are viewed in the central details pane of the Reliability and Performance Monitor snap-in.

The Reporting folder is broken into two main subfolders: User Defined Reports and System Reports. The default System Reports subfolder typically includes reports relating to LAN diagnostics, system diagnostics, and system performance. Additional system reports are automatically generated depending on the server role installed on the Windows Server 2008 system. For example, an Active Directory diagnostics system report is automatically included in the console when the Active Directory Domain Services server role is installed on the Windows Server 2008 R2 system.

Tip

Although not a native tool, there is a solution on Codeplex, called PAL, that can be used to aggregate and report on data collector sets. These reports can be of real help when trying to identify bottlenecks because they contain guideline counter thresholds that you can measure your environment against. Codeplex is a project hosting website for open source software. The website is http://www.codeplex.com/.

Additional Tools to Monitor SQL Server 2012

SQL Server 2012 provides several additional built-in tools that assist in your ongoing monitoring efforts. DBAs commonly use these tools to verify that the different SQL Server components are running correctly and to troubleshoot problems as they are encountered. These tools will be introduced here; however, they are covered in greater detail in the other chapters of the book.

Using the SQL Server Profiler

The SQL Server Profiler tool captures SQL Server 2012 events as they are generated on a SQL Server. The captured information, referred to as a *workload*, can be reviewed in the UI or saved to a trace file or database table. The workload can be used to analyze performance or can be replayed to conduct N+1 testing. The SQL Server Profiler tool is invaluable for getting detailed insight into the internal workings of applications and databases from a real-world and real-time perspective.

SQL Server Profiler has been placed on the deprecation list for a future version of SQL Server. It will be available in the next version. However, you are advised to move to the newer more efficient way of capturing event information via Extended Events.

For additional information on using the SQL Server Profiler and Extended Events, see Chapter 14.

Using the Database Engine Tuning Advisor

The Database Engine Tuning Advisor automates the process of selecting an optimized set of indexes, indexed views, statistics, and partitions and even provides the code to implement the recommendations it makes. The Database Engine Tuning Advisor can work with a specific query or can use a real-world workload as gathered by the SQL Server Profiler tool. The advantage of the latter approach is that the workload is generated based on actual usage, and the tuning recommendations reflect that.

The Database Engine Tuning Advisor is customizable and allows you to select the level of recommendation that the tool recommends. This feature allows you to maintain the existing database design and make appropriate fine-tuning recommendations for indexes. Or you can make the existing design flexible and then have the tool recommend far-reaching changes to the structure, such as partitioning.

For additional information on using the Database Engine Tuning Advisor, see Chapter 14.

Summary

The built-in monitoring tools in SQL Server 2012 provide a tremendous amount of proactive monitoring by allowing you to audit events, create alerts, collect performance data, send email notification, and review monitoring metrics via the established performance dashboards. In addition, when monitoring a SQL Server system, do not forget the tools in Windows Server 2008 R2, such as Task Manager, Performance Monitor, and Reliability Monitor, which together bolster a DBA's monitoring capability.

Best Practices

- Leverage the SSMS Activity Monitor as the first line of defense when there is a need to gain quick and effortless insight into a SQL Server system.

- Use the predefined standard reports included with SSMS Server, available via right-clicking on a specific database, for monitoring performance and utilization information.

- Leverage the existing and new DMVs when gathering performance, state, and monitoring metrics.

- Don't forget to view both Windows and SQL Server logs regularly for trends, irregularities, and issues.

- Leverage the Data Collector to capture and store performance data from one or more SQL Server instances.

- When using the Data Collector, take advantage of the Windows Server Log as a target, because it is the least likely log to be tampered with.

- Review the reports associated with the built-in Windows Performance and Reliability collections for monitoring state and historical information.

- Use the SQL Server Profiler to create a trace file capable of replaying workloads and testing database performance. Also, remember that SQL Server Profiler is capable of providing detailed information about the internal behavior of SQL Server Analysis Services.

- Use the Database Engine Tuning Advisor to assist in the creation of indexes, indexed views, statistics, and partitions for the database and to test the results of the changes.

- Examine the use of System Center Operations Manager (SCOM) for monitoring SQL Server at enterprise scale.

CHAPTER 16

SQL Server 2012 Maintenance Practices

For SQL Server databases to perform at optimal levels, a database administrator (DBA) should conduct routine maintenance on each database. Some of these routine database tasks involve rebuilding indexes, checking database integrity, updating index statistics, and performing internal consistency checks and backups. These routine database maintenance tasks are often overlooked because they are redundant, tedious, and often time consuming. Moreover, today's DBAs are overwhelmed with many other tasks throughout the day. In recognition of these issues, SQL Server provides a way to automate or manually create these routine tasks that many DBAs find to be boring and tedious with a maintenance plan. After the maintenance tasks are identified and created, routine maintenance should commence daily, weekly, monthly, or quarterly, depending on the task. Ultimately, these tasks will put organizations on the path to having healthier, consistent, and more trustworthy databases.

What's New for Maintenance with SQL Server 2012?

SQL Server 2012 doesn't necessarily introduce any new compelling features and functionality associated with creating maintenance plans; however, the rich features delivered in the previous releases are still present. The following list describes some of these features:

- The Define Rebuild Index Task includes new options for handling exceptions for index types that do not support online index rebuilds. You can now choose to exclude indexes that do not support online indexing, or you can choose to rebuild the indexes offline.

- The Full, Differential, and Transaction Log Backup Tasks provide the option to ignore Replica Priority for Backup and Backup on Primary Settings when databases are partaking in an AlwaysOn Availability Group.

Establishing a SQL Server Maintenance Plan

A maintenance plan performs a comprehensive set of SQL Server jobs that run at scheduled intervals. The maintenance plan conducts scheduled SQL Server maintenance tasks to ensure that relational databases within the database engine are performing optimally, conducting regular backups, and checking for anomalies. The Database Maintenance Plan, a feature included within the SQL Server Database Engine, can be used to automatically create and schedule these daily tasks. In addition, a Maintenance Plan provides a workflow creation with conceptual hierarchies and supports multiserver environments. A comprehensive maintenance plan includes these primary administrative tasks:

- Running database integrity checks
- Updating database statistics
- Reorganizing database indexes
- Performing database backups
- Cleaning up database historical operational data
- Shrinking a database
- Cleaning up leftover files from the maintenance plan
- Executing SQL Server jobs
- Notify operator tasks
- Execute Transact-SQL statements
- Cleaning up maintenance tasks

Check Database Integrity Task

The Check Database Integrity Task verifies the health and structural integrity of both user and system tables within relational databases selected in the SQL Server Database Engine. When running this task, you have the option to also check the integrity of all index pages. This specific task can be created in the Maintenance Plan Wizard, which will manually create a maintenance task. On the other hand, you can use Transact-SQL to create this task. When you create the Database Integrity Task, the database options available include all system databases, all user databases, or specific databases.

Although the following example shows basic syntax, it supplies the information you need to assess the health and integrity of the database on the AdventureWorks2012 database:

```
USE [AdventureWorks2012]
GO
DBCC CHECKDB(N'AdventureWorks2012') WITH NO_INFOMSGS
```

Shrink Database Task

The Shrink Database Task, as illustrated in Figure 16.1, reduces the physical database and log files to a specific size, similar to the Automatic Shrink Task available in SSMS. When creating a maintenance task, you can shrink all databases, all system databases, all user databases, or specific databases within a single task. This operation removes excess space in the database based on a percentage value you enter in MB. In addition, thresholds must be entered, indicating the amount of shrinkage that needs to take place after the database reaches a certain size and the amount of free space that must remain after the excess space is removed.

Finally, free space can be retained in the database or released back to the operating system. For example, if you believe that the database will grow again after a shrink operation, it is a best practice to retain freed space in database files. This will condense the database based on contiguous pages. However, the pages are not deallocated, and the database files will not physically shrink. On the other hand, if you anticipate that the files will not regrow after a shrink operation, the second option will physically shrink the files and release the free space back to the operating system.

This Transact-SQL syntax shrinks the AdventureWorks2012 database, returns freed space to the operating system, and allows for 15 percent of free space to remain after the shrink:

```
USE [AdventureWorks2012]
GO
DBCC SHRINKDATABASE(N'AdventureWorks2012', 15, TRUNCATEONLY)
GO
```

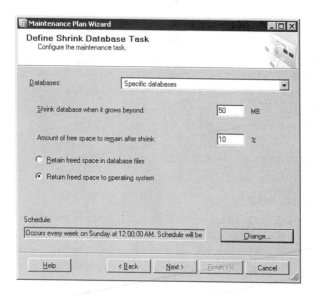

FIGURE 16.1
Using the Shrink Database Task to shrink a database.

Tip

When you create maintenance plans, it is a best practice not to select the option to shrink the database. First, when shrinking the database, SQL Server moves pages toward the beginning of the file, allowing the tail end of the files to be shrunk. This process can increase the transaction log size because all moves are logged. Second, if the database is heavily used and there are many inserts, the database files will have to grow again. Since SQL Server 2005, Microsoft has addressed slow autogrowth with instant data file initialization; therefore, the growth process is not as slow as it was in the past. It should be noted that instant file initialization occurs only on the data file and not the log file. If the log file must grow, it still must "zero" out the new space to ensure consistency, which will cause performance issues. However, at times autogrow does not catch up with the space requirements, causing performance degradation.

Third, constant shrinking and growing of the database leads to excessive fragmentation. Therefore, if you need to shrink the database size, it should be done manually when the server is not being heavily utilized.

Reorganize Index Task

When there is a need to improve index scanning performance, look to the Reorganize Index Task.

This task defragments and compacts clustered and nonclustered indexes on all tables or views or a particular table or view. The Reorganize Index Task can also be applied to all databases, system databases, user databases, or individually targeted databases. By also selecting an additional option, large object (LOB) data types such as images, text, and FILESTREAM data will also be included in the compacting process.

To gain better insight into the operation of this task, use the Transact-SQL syntax that follows to reorganize indexes for the AdventureWorks2012 [Sales].[SalesOrderDetail] table. This example also includes the option to compact large objects:

```
USE [AdventureWorks2012]
GO
ALTER INDEX [AK_SalesOrderDetail_rowguid]
ON [Sales].[SalesOrderDetail]
REORGANIZE WITH ( LOB_COMPACTION = ON )
GO
USE [AdventureWorks2012]
GO
ALTER INDEX [IX_SalesOrderDetail_ProductID]
ON [Sales].[SalesOrderDetail]
REORGANIZE WITH ( LOB_COMPACTION = ON )
GO
USE [AdventureWorks2012]
GO
ALTER INDEX
[PK_SalesOrderDetail_SalesOrderID_SalesOrderDetailID]
ON [Sales].[SalesOrderDetail]
REORGANIZE WITH ( LOB_COMPACTION = ON )
```

Rebuild Index Task

The Rebuild Index Task aims to eliminate fragmentation by reorganizing all the table indexes in the database. This task is particularly good for ensuring that query performance and application response do not degrade. Therefore, when SQL is called on to conduct index scans and seeks, it operates at its full potential. In addition, this task optimizes the distribution of data and free space on the index pages, which allows for growth to take place faster.

The two Rebuild Index Task free space options consist of the following:

- **Reorganize Pages with the Default Amount of Free Space**—Drop the indexes on the tables in the database and re-create them with the fill factor that was specified when the indexes were created.

- **Change Free Space per Page Percentage To**—Drop the indexes on the tables in the database and re-create them with a new, automatically calculated fill factor, thereby reserving the specified amount of free space on the index pages. The higher the percentage, the more free space is reserved on the index pages, and the larger the index grows. Valid values are from 0 through 100.

The Rebuild Index Task advanced options consist of the following:

- **Sort Results in tempdb**—The Sort Results in tempdb option is the first advanced option available in the Rebuild Index Task. This option is comparable to the SORT_IN_TEMPDB option for the index. When this option is enabled, the intermediate results are stored in tempdb during the rebuild of an index.

- **Keep Index Online While Reindexing**—The second advanced option allows users to access the underlying table, clustered index data, and the associated indexes during the index rebuild operation. It is worth mentioning that the online index option requires a significant amount of free space on the hard disk. For example, if the indexes on the table take up 3GB of space, an additional 3GB of disk space is required for this process because the old indexes get swapped out after the new ones have been created. For index types that do not support online index rebuilds, you have the option to specify two options: Do Not Rebuild Indexes or Rebuild Indexes Offline. Remember the online index functionality is a feature available only in the Enterprise edition of SQL Server 2012.

Armed with the knowledge of what the Rebuild Index Task can do, use the following information to gain some hands-on experience. Use the Rebuild Index syntax that follows to rebuild indexes for the AdventureWorks2012 [Sales]. [SalesOrderDetail] table. The option to Reorganize pages using the default amount of free space has been selected. This example will also sort results in tempdb and keep the index online while reindexing.

```
USE [AdventureWorks2012]
GO
ALTER INDEX [AK_SalesOrderDetail_rowguid]
ON [Sales].[SalesOrderDetail]
REBUILD PARTITION = ALL WITH ( PAD_INDEX   = OFF,
STATISTICS_NORECOMPUTE  = OFF, ALLOW_ROW_LOCKS  = ON,
ALLOW_PAGE_LOCKS  = ON, IGNORE_DUP_KEY  = OFF,
ONLINE = ON, SORT_IN_TEMPDB = ON, DATA_COMPRESSION = NONE )
GO

USE [AdventureWorks2012]
GO
ALTER INDEX [IX_SalesOrderDetail_ProductID]
ON [Sales].[SalesOrderDetail]
REBUILD PARTITION = ALL WITH ( PAD_INDEX   = OFF,
STATISTICS_NORECOMPUTE  = OFF, ALLOW_ROW_LOCKS  = ON,
ALLOW_PAGE_LOCKS  = ON, ONLINE = ON,
SORT_IN_TEMPDB = ON, DATA_COMPRESSION = NONE )
GO

USE [AdventureWorks2012]
GO
ALTER INDEX
[PK_SalesOrderDetail_SalesOrderID_SalesOrderDetailID]
ON [Sales].[SalesOrderDetail]
REBUILD PARTITION = ALL WITH ( PAD_INDEX   = OFF,
STATISTICS_NORECOMPUTE  = OFF,
ALLOW_ROW_LOCKS  = ON, ALLOW_PAGE_LOCKS  = ON,
ONLINE = ON, SORT_IN_TEMPDB = ON, DATA_COMPRESSION = NONE )
```

Notes from the Field: When Should Indexes Be Rebuilt or Reorganized?

One of the most common questions we get from customers is, "When should indexes be rebuilt or reorganized?" This note from the field provides guidance on when DBAs should rebuild an index and when to reorganize an index.

SQL Server automatically maintains indexes when there are insert, update, or delete operations on a table or a view. However, over a period of time, these operations can cause the information in the index to become scattered or fragmented, affecting the performance of the queries and potentially causing the application to perform slowly.

Address this issue by either reorganizing or rebuilding an index to remove fragmentation. The best practice is to first identify the percentage of index fragmentation based on the percent value from a table. It is important to identify the % fragmentation value to be able to determine which operation you can perform. Use the following query to reveal the average percent fragmentation of an index:

```
SELECT a.index_id, name, avg_fragmentation_in_percent
    FROM sys.dm_db_index_physical_stats
(DB_ID(N'database_name'),
        OBJECT_ID(N'table_name'), NULL, NULL, NULL) AS a
    JOIN sys.indexes AS b ON a.object_id = b.object_id AND
a.index_id = b.index_id;
    GO
```

This query identifies the average fragmentation value of an index for all the indexes associated with 'table_name'. After the average percentage fragmentation value of an index is obtained, determine the best operation—rebuild or reorganize. If an index has an average fragmentation that is >5% and <=30%, reorganize an index. Likewise, if an index has an average fragmentation of > 30%, rebuild an index.

Update Statistics Task

The Update Statistics Task ensures the data in the tables and indexes on one or more SQL Server databases are up to date by resampling the distribution statistics of each index on user tables. These statistics are used by SQL Server to optimize the navigation through tables, specifically for queries.

Numerous choices are available to customize this task. Each of the options is explained next:

- **Databases**—First select the databases that will be impacted by this task. The choices are All Databases, System Databases, User Databases, and These Databases.

- **Object**—After the databases are selected, decide in the Objects box whether to display both tables and views or only one of these options.

- **Selection**—Choose the tables or indexes that will be impacted. If the Tables and Views option was selected in the Objects box, this box will be unavailable.

- **Update**—The Update box offers three choices. Select All Existing Statistics if you need to update both columns and indexes. Select Column Statistics if you need to update only column statistics, and select Index Statistics if you need to update only index statistics.

- **Scan Type**—The Scan Type section allows you to update statistics based on a Full Scan or by entering a Sample By value. The Sample By values can be either a percentage or a specific number of rows.

The syntax to update statistics on the AdventureWorks2012 [Sales].[Sales OrderDetail] table with the advanced options to update all existing statistics and conduct a full scan is as follows:

```
use [AdventureWorks2012]
GO
UPDATE STATISTICS [Sales].[SalesOrderDetail]
WITH FULLSCAN
```

Notes from the Field: Best Practices on When to Create and/or Update Statistics

DBAs often find themselves deliberating over the best time to create or update statistics. Although SQL Server 2012 query optimizer automatically creates query plans using statistics to help improve the performance of most of the queries, in some instances DBAs still need to create or update statistics or modify the query design for achieving optimum performance from a query.

To assist DBAs, the next section discusses the best practices for creating statistics.

- When the query indicates it has missing statistics, create statistics. The best way to identify missing statistics is by looking for warning signs in the execution plan of a query. The table name in the execution plan of a query is shown in red text. Additionally, you can also monitor the Missing Column Statistics event class when using SQL Server Profiler.

- Create statistics when the WHERE clause of the query contains multiple columns that have cross-column relationships or dependencies that do not already appear in the same index. Creating statistics on multiple columns may improve the cardinality estimates, which greatly help improve the query plan.

- When queries return a subset of a dataset from tables, filtered statistics should be created. Filtered statistics can improve query plans, which can help impact the performance of a query. You can use the CREATE STATISTICS statement with the WHERE clause to create the filter predicate expression.

■ Create Statistics whenever the Database Engine Tuning Advisor recommends. Database Engine Tuning Advisor has been greatly improved in SQL Server 2012 and can be found under Performance Tools of SQL Server 2012 program folder.

This next section describes best practices on when to update statistics:

■ Update statistics whenever the query response times are slow or unpredictable. In situations like this, DBAs must make sure the queries contain up-to-date statistics by using the STATS_DATE function to determine when the statistics were last updated.

■ Update statistics when an Insert operation occurs on the ascending or descending key columns, such as the IDENTITY or timestamp columns. Insert operations such as these can prevent Update statistics from firing automatically if the number of rows inserted in the key columns are too small.

■ Update statistics when performing maintenance on a table that changes the distribution of data. Operations such as truncating a table or performing a bulk insert on a large dataset can change the distribution of data impacting the performance of queries.

History Cleanup Task

The History Cleanup Task offers organizations the perfect opportunity to remove historical data in a few simple steps. You can delete several types of history data using this task. The following two options are associated with this task:

■ **Historical Data to Be Deleted**—Use the Maintenance Plan Wizard to purge several types of data, including Backup and Restore history, SQL Server Agent Job history, and Maintenance Plan history.

■ **Remove Historical Data Older Than**—Use the wizard also to select the age of the data you want to delete. For example, you can choose to periodically remove older data based on daily, weekly, monthly, and yearly increments.

When the History Cleanup Task is complete, you can save a report to a text file or email the report to an operator by clicking Next. The Select Report Options page is invoked, and you must enable the check box. Write a Report to a Text File and then indicate the storage location of the report by specifying the file and folder location.

The following Transact-SQL example removes historical data older than four weeks for the following items: Backup and Restore history, SQL Server Agent Job history, and Maintenance Plan history:

```
declare @dt datetime
select @dt = dateadd(wk,-4,getdate())
exec msdb.dbo.sp_delete_backuphistory @dt
EXEC msdb.dbo.sp_purge_jobhistory @oldest_date=@dt
EXECUTE msdb..sp_maintplan_delete_log null,null,@dt
```

Execute SQL Server Agent Job

The Execute SQL Server Agent Job Task allows you to run SQL Server Agent jobs that already exist as well as SSIS packages as part of the maintenance plan. This is done by selecting the job in the Available SQL Server Agent Jobs section in the Define Execute SQL Server Agent Job Task page. Alternatively, Transact-SQL syntax can be used to execute a job by entering the appropriate Job ID of a specific job that already exists.

The syntax to execute a SQL Server Agent job is as follows:

```
EXEC msdb.dbo.sp_start_job @job_
id=N'35eca119-28a6-4a29-994b-0680ce73f1f3'
```

Back Up Database Task

The Back Up Database Task is an excellent way to automate and schedule full, differential, or transaction log backups.

You can choose from an expanded set of options when creating full, differential, or transaction log backups with maintenance plans. With these expanded options, you can choose to back up a database or an individual component, set expiration dates, verify integrity, compress data, and even determine whether to use disk or tape. Each of the backup options is described in more detail in the following list:

- **Specify the Database**—A maintenance plan can be generated to perform a variety of backups, including backing up a single database, all databases, system databases, or all user databases.

- **Backup Component**—The Backup Component section offers the option of either backing up the entire database or individual files or filegroups.

- **Backup Set Will Expire**—To stipulate when a backup set will expire and can be overwritten by another backup, you need only to specify the number of days or enter a hard date, such as September 5, 1974, for the set to expire.

- **Back Up To**—This option allows the backup to be written to a file or a tape. A tape drive must be present on the system to back up to tape. The other option is having a backup written to a file residing on a network share.

- **Back Up Databases Across One or More Files**—When selecting the backup destination, you can either add or remove one or more disk or tape locations. In addition, you can view the contents of a file and append to the backup file if it already exists.

- **Create a Backup File for Every Database**—Instead of selecting the preceding option, Back Up Databases Across One or More Files, you can let SQL Server automatically create a backup file for every database selected. In addition, you can automatically create a subdirectory for each database selected.

> **Note**
>
> If the Automatically Create a Subdirectory option is selected, the new subdirectory created will inherit permissions from the parent directory. NTFS permissions should be used to secure the root folder to restrict unauthorized access.

- **Verify Backup Integrity**—This option verifies the integrity of the backup when it is completed by firing a Transact-SQL command that determines whether the backup was successful and is accessible.

- **Set Backup Compression**—When using the Enterprise Edition of SQL Server 2012, the options available include Leverage Backup Compression Based on the Server Default Settings, Compress the Backup Regardless of the Server-Level Default, and finally, Do Not Compress Backup.

> **Note**
>
> For a more thorough and detailed discussion of full, differential, and transaction log backups, see Chapter 6, "Backing Up and Restoring SQL Server 2012 Databases."

You can choose to back up a database in one of three ways when you create a maintenance plan. Using the wizard, you select the Define Back Up Database (Full) Task when it is necessary to capture the full database. Similarly, select Define Back Up Database (Differential) Task if it is important to record only data that has changed since the last full backup, or select the Define Back Up Database (Transaction Log) Task, which will back up only entries that are recorded to logs. The backup file extension for the Full and Differential Task is *.bak, whereas the Transaction Log Task is *.trn. Other than these noted differences, the options for each task are the same. If the Maintenance Plan Wizard will not be used, a DBA must choose the Back Up Database Task and specify the backup type. Backup types include Full, Differential, and Transaction Log.

Caution

It is probably abundantly clear by now that maintenance plans are regularly used by DBAs to back up databases, including the transaction logs. A problem may occur during the restore process if you create a transaction log backup with the maintenance plan on a database that has already been configured for log shipping or is already part of another backup set. Ultimately, two sets of transaction log backups are created: one from the maintenance task and the other from the log shipping task or other backup job. Therefore, if a restore is needed, a combination of the transaction log backups is required to conduct the restore; otherwise, it is not possible to restore the database to the point of failure. If transaction log backups already exist based on log shipping, it is a best practice not to create additional transaction log backups with the maintenance plan. This will eliminate confusion and the potential of a botched restore resulting in lost data.

Tip

If you want to perform an out-of sequence database backup, you can use the COPY_ONLY backup type, which will not affect the log shipping backup sequence or the sequence of any scheduled full or log backups. For more information on COPY_ONLY backups, visit Chapter 6.

Maintenance Cleanup Task

The Maintenance Cleanup Task is used to delete files such as backups and reports that reside on the database after the maintenance plan is completed. There are many options for deleting data using this task:

- **Delete Files of the Following Type**—You can choose to delete database backup files or maintenance plan text reports.

- **File Location**—You can also choose to delete a specific file using the File Name box.

- **Search Folder and Delete Files Based on an Extension**—You can delete numerous files with the same extension within a specified folder using this option; for example, all files with the extension *.txt. You can also select to delete all first-level subfolders within the folder identified with this option.

- **File Age**—Files can be deleted by age. You will need to indicate the age of the files to be deleted. For example, you may choose to delete files older than two years. The unit of time also includes hours, days, weeks, and months.

Creating a Maintenance Plan

You can use several methods for creating a maintenance plan. You can use the Database Maintenance Plan Wizard from SQL Server Management Studio (SSMS), or you can manually create a maintenance plan using the design surface and the maintenance tasks associated with the Maintenance Plan Tasks Toolbox. Review the following sections to appreciate how easy and straightforward it is to create a maintenance plan manually and with the wizard.

Creating a Maintenance Plan with the Wizard

Maintaining SQL Server databases is a vital activity for DBAs everywhere. A well-maintained system requires the use of a maintenance plan that automates administrative tasks according to each organization's needs. This section demonstrates using the Maintenance Plan Wizard to create a customized maintenance plan of all system and user databases.

For this example, the steps include the following maintenance tasks: Check Database Integrity, Reorganize Index, Rebuild Index, Update Statistics, and Clean Up History. In a production environment, you should not include both the Reorganize Index and Rebuild Index task in the same plan. These tasks would be considered redundant because one task rebuilds the indexes from scratch and the other reorganizes the indexes. They have been included only for explanation purposes. In production environments, it is a best practice to create separate maintenance plans for system and user databases and allocate separate schedules based on your requirements and maintenance windows.

> **Note**
>
> How to create database and transaction log backups with the Maintenance Plan Wizard is discussed in Chapter 6 in the section titled "Automating Backups with a Maintenance Plan."

1. Choose Start, All Programs, Microsoft SQL Server 2012, SQL Server Management Studio.

2. In Object Explorer, first connect to the Database Engine and then expand the desired server, the Management folder, and then the Maintenance Plans folder.

3. Right-click Maintenance Plans and choose Maintenance Plan Wizard.

4. In the Welcome to the Database Maintenance Plan Wizard page, read the message and then click Next.

5. In the Select Plan Properties page, enter a name and description for the maintenance plan.

6. Choose either the first option (Separate Schedules for Each Task) or the second option (Single Schedule for the Entire Plan or No Schedule). For this example, a single schedule will be created for the backup plan. Click Next, as shown in Figure 16.2.

FIGURE 16.2
Scheduling and selecting the Maintenance Plan properties.

Note

Creating separate independent schedules for each subtask within a
single maintenance plan is possible when working with SQL Server 2012.
A scenario when this can be done includes a weekly schedule for a full
backup and an hourly schedule for a transaction log backup.

7. On the Select Maintenance Tasks page, as shown in Figure 16.3,
   place a check next to the following maintenance tasks: Check
   Database Integrity, Reorganize Index, Rebuild Index, Update
   Statistics, and Clean Up History, and then click Next.

FIGURE 16.3
Selecting database maintenance tasks.

8. On the Select Maintenance Task Order page, select the order in
   which the tasks should be executed and then click Next.

Tip

Many maintenance tasks, including reindexing or updating statistics, alter
the database when they run. In recognition of this situation, it is a best
practice to make the full database backup maintenance task the first
order of operation when prioritizing maintenance tasks. This ensures that
the database can be rolled back if the maintenance plan tasks that
change the database fail.

9. The first option in the maintenance plan is checking the database integrity. In the Define Database Check Integrity Task page, select All Databases from the drop-down list. The next item is to accept the defaults. Do this by validating that the Include Indexes Check option is enabled, which will ensure that all index pages and table databases have an integrity check run against them. Proceed to change the schedule by clicking Change and then set this task so it reoccurs every week starting during nonpeak times, such as Sunday at midnight. Click Next to proceed, as in Figure 16.4.

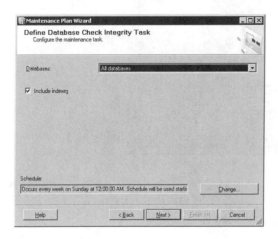

FIGURE 16.4
The Define Database Check Integrity Task page.

10. The second option selected is Reorganize Index. From the drop-down box on the Define Reorganize Index Task page, select All Databases. Ensure that the option for Compact Large Objects is enabled. Schedule this task to occur once a week on Sunday at 1 a.m. Click Next to proceed, as in Figure 16.5.

11. The Rebuild Index is the third task selected in the maintenance plan. On the Define Rebuild Index Task page, first select All Databases and then proceed to schedule this task to occur once a week on Sunday at 2 a.m. Verify in the Free Space Options area that the Reorganize Pages with the Default Amount of Free Space option is selected. In the Advanced Options section, enable Sort Results in tempdb and Keep Index Online While Reindexing. Finally, for index types that do not support online index rebuilds, select the

option to Rebuild Indexes Offline, as shown in Figure 16.6. Schedule this task to occur once a week on Sunday at 2 a.m. Click Next to proceed.

FIGURE 16.5
The Define Reorganize Index Task page.

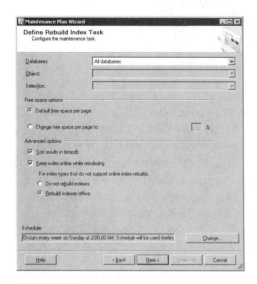

FIGURE 16.6
The Define Rebuild Index Task page.

12. For the fourth task, on the Define Update Statistics Task page, select All Databases from the Databases drop-down list. Ensure that the default Update settings, All Existing Statistics and Scan Type, Full Scan, are selected. Set this task to occur weekly on Sundays at 3 a.m. Click Next to proceed, as shown in Figure 16.7.

FIGURE 16.7
Specifying options on the Define Update Statistics Task page.

13. In the Define History Cleanup Task page, select the options to delete historical data, such as Backup and Restore History, SQL Server Agent Job History, and Maintenance Plan History. For the Remove Historical Data Older Than option, you can use the default of 4 Weeks. This value should be based on the organization's retention requirements, as shown in Figure 16.8. Schedule the task to reoccur on a weekly basis on Sundays at 5 a.m. and then click Next.

14. In the Select Report Options page, set the option to either write a report to a text file and enter a folder location or to email the report. To email the report, Database Mail must be enabled, configured, and an Agent Operation with a valid email address must already exist. Click Next to continue.

15. The Complete the Wizard page summarizes the options selected in the Maintenance Plan Wizard. It is possible to drill down on a task to view advanced settings. Review the options selected and click Finish to close the Summary page.

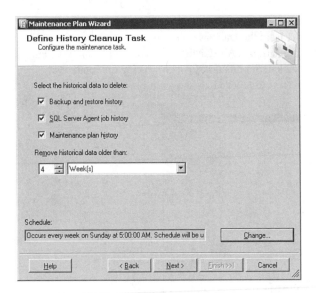

FIGURE 16.8
Specifying options on the Define History Cleanup Task page.

16. On the Maintenance Plan Wizard Progress page, review the creation status as shown in Figure 16.9 and click Close to end the Maintenance Plan Wizard.

Creating a Maintenance Plan Manually

Maintenance plans can also be created manually with the aid of the Maintenance Plan (Design tab). You can create a much more flexible maintenance plan with an enhanced workflow using the Maintenance Plan Design tab compared to the Maintenance Plan Wizard because it is equipped with better tools and superior functionality, including workflow engines and subplans.

Since the release of Service Pack 2 for SQL Server 2005, maintenance plan history can still be logged to a remote server when you're creating a manual plan. This is a great feature when managing many SQL Servers within an infrastructure because all data that is logged can be rolled up to a single server for centralized management.

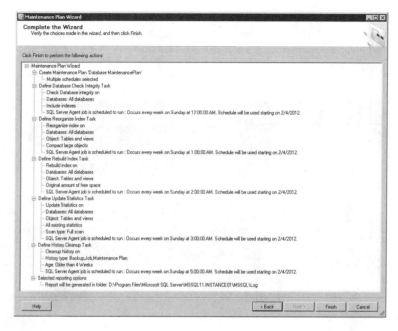

FIGURE 16.9
Verifying the Choices Made with the Maintenance Plan Wizard Progress page.

Note

Creating manual maintenance plans with the Maintenance Plan (Design tab) is very similar to the design surface available when creating packages with SSIS.

The Maintenance Plan design surface, as shown in Figure 16.10, can be launched by right-clicking the Maintenance Plans folder and selecting New Maintenance Plan.

You will find the Maintenance Tasks toolbox in the left pane of the Maintenance Plan (Design tab). You can drag maintenance tasks from this toolbox to the design surface in the center pane. If more than one task is dragged to the designer, it is possible to create a workflow process between the two objects by establishing relationships between the tasks. The workflow process can consist of precedence links. As such, the second task will only execute based on a constraint, which is defined in the first task such as "on success, failure or completion." For example, you can choose to create a workflow that will first back up the AdventureWorks2012 database and then, on completion, rebuild all the AdventureWorks2012 indexes, as illustrated in Figure 16.11.

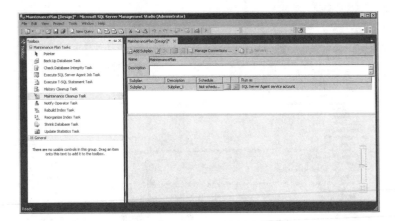

FIGURE 16.10
Viewing the Maintenance Plan design surface and toolbar screen.

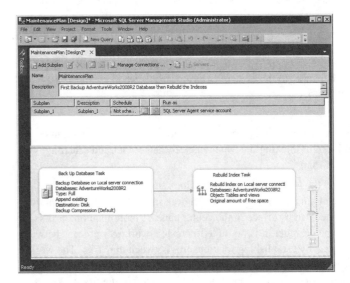

FIGURE 16.11
Implementing a Precedence Constraint between two maintenance plan tasks.

The Precedence Constraint link between two objects can control the workflow if there is a statement to execute the second rebuild index task when the first backup task is successful. In this situation, when a backup task fails, the second task will not fire. As for creating a Precedence Constraint, you should first highlight both of the maintenance tasks in the designer, right-click, and then choose Add Precedence Constraint. After the Precedence Constraint is created, either double-click the connector arrow or right-click it and select Edit. This will bring up the Precedence Constraint Editor, where you can define the constraint options, as shown in Figure 16.12.

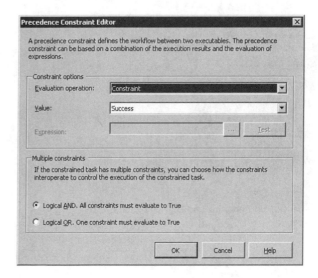

FIGURE 16.12
Setting the Precedence Constraints on the Maintenance Plan Tasks page.

In addition to creating precedence links, you also can execute tasks simultaneously. This is known as *task parallelism* and is commonly used when executing the same type of maintenance tasks on different SQL Servers. For example, you can execute a full backup of the master database on all the SQL Servers from a central master SQL Server starting on Sunday at 9 p.m.

The final item worth mentioning is the reporting capabilities. After the maintenance plan is completed, you can create a report. To do this, locate the Reporting and Logging icon in the Maintenance Plan designer. The

Reporting and Logging dialog box, as shown in Figure 16.13, displays options such as Generate a Text File Report and Send Reports to an Email Recipient. Additional logging functionality exists, such as logging extended information and log maintenance plan history to a remote server.

FIGURE 16.13
Configuring Maintenance Plan Reporting and Logging options.

Tip

When working with maintenance plan tasks, you can use the View Transact-SQL Command button to convert the options selected for the task into Transact-SQL syntax. This is a great feature for DBAs who do not have an extensive background in programming and can also be helpful if DBAs need to rebuild the maintenance task after server restore or if the maintenance task needs to be deployed on multiple servers, which would prevent them from having to remember all the options they had selected during the initial setup of maintenance plans.

Viewing Maintenance Plans

All maintenance plans can be viewed under the Maintenance Plan folder in SSMS and stored in SQL Server as jobs. They require the SQL Server Agent to be running to launch the job at the scheduled interval. If the SQL

Server Agent is stopped, the jobs will not commence. In addition, all jobs can be edited or changed for ongoing support or maintenance.

Follow these steps to view the maintenance plan jobs in SQL Server Management Studio:

1. Choose Start, All Programs, Microsoft SQL Server 2012, SQL Server Management Studio.

2. In Object Explorer, first connect to the Database Engine, expand the desired server, expand the Maintenance Plan folder, and you should be able to review the maintenance plans that already exist.

3. Next, expand SQL Server Agent, and then expand the jobs folder.

4. Click Jobs to see a list of jobs created by the Maintenance Plan Wizard. The jobs are displayed in the Object Explorer Details tab located in the right pane; otherwise, the jobs are displayed under the Jobs folder in Object Explorer. This is shown in Figure 16.14.

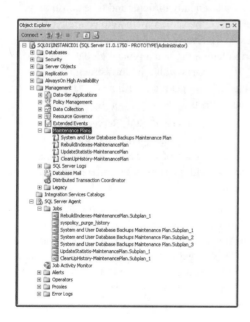

FIGURE 16.14
Viewing Maintenance Plan scheduled jobs.

If the SQL Server Agent is not running, a dialog box may appear, stating that the SQL Server Agent on the target server is not running. The SQL

Server Agent must be started for SQL Server jobs to commence. Follow these steps to start the SQL Server Agent:

1. Choose Start, All Programs, Microsoft SQL Server 2012, SQL Server Management Studio.

2. In Object Explorer, first connect to the Database Engine, and then expand the desired server.

3. Right-click SQL Server Agent and then click Start.

Creating Multiserver Maintenance Plans

In the past, DBAs encountered numerous challenges when managing more than one maintenance plan within their pre-SQL Server 2005 Service Pack 2 infrastructures. The task of creating maintenance plans in a multi-server environment was exceedingly tedious because a maintenance plan had to be created on each and every server. Moreover, the task of verifying success, failure, and job history was equally difficult and time consuming; it had to be conducted on each server because a method to centrally manage these plans did not exist. To clearly illustrate just how difficult life could get for DBAs, it is worth mentioning that a typical global organization may have well over 100 SQL Servers within its infrastructure; therefore, imagine the heartache and lack of operational efficiency that came along with managing maintenance plans.

Today, these nuisances continue to be alleviated. SQL Server 2012 continues to offer support for multiserver maintenance plans. Specifically, you can now create maintenance plans for each of your SQL servers from a single central master server. This provides a significant difference in operational efficiency and administration.

To take full advantage of this new feature in SQL Server 2012, a multi-server environment containing one master server and one or more target servers must be constructed before a multiserver maintenance plan can be created. It should be mentioned that target servers can be used only to view the maintenance plans. As a result, multiserver maintenance plans must be created and maintained on the master server so that you can provide regular maintenance.

> **Note**
>
> To create or manage multiserver maintenance plans, you must be a member of the sysadmin fixed server role on each of the SQL Servers.

Multiserver maintenance plans can be created with either the Maintenance Plan Wizard or by manually using the Maintenance Plan (Design tab).

Establishing Maintenance Schedules for SQL Server

With each new release, SQL Server has become more self-maintaining. However, even with self-maintenance and automated maintenance plans, DBAs must conduct additional maintenance. Some maintenance procedures require daily attention, whereas others may require only yearly checkups. The maintenance processes and procedures that an organization follows depend strictly on the organization's individual environment.

The categories described in the following sections and their corresponding procedures are best practices for organizations of all sizes and with varying IT infrastructures. The following sections will help organizations establish sound maintenance practices to help them ensure the health of their SQL Server Database Engines. The suggested maintenance tasks that follow are based on daily, weekly, monthly, and quarterly schedules.

Daily Routine Maintenance Tasks

Maintenance tasks requiring close and regular attention are commonly checked each day. DBAs who take on these tasks daily ensure system reliability, availability, performance, and security. Following are some of the daily routine maintenance tasks:

- Check that all required SQL Server services are running.
- Check Daily Backup logs for success, warnings, or failures.
- Check the Windows Event logs for errors.
- Check the SQL Server logs for security concerns such as invalid logins.
- Conduct full or differential backups.
- Conduct Transaction Log backups on databases configured with the Full or Bulk-Logged recovery model.
- Verify that SQL Server jobs did not fail.
- Check that adequate disk space exists for all database files and transaction logs.
- At least monitor processor, memory, or disk counters for bottlenecks.

Weekly Routine Maintenance Tasks

Maintenance procedures that require slightly less attention than daily checking are categorized in a weekly routine. The following list details these weekly tasks:

- Conduct full or differential backups.
- Review Maintenance Plan reports.
- Check database integrity.
- Shrink the database if needed.
- Compact clustered and nonclustered tables and views by reorganizing indexes.
- Reorganize data on the data and index pages by rebuilding indexes.
- Update statistics on all user and system tables.
- Delete historical data created by backups, restores, SQL Server agent, and maintenance plan operations.
- Manually grow database or transaction log files if needed. Adjust automatic growth values if needed.
- Remove files left over from executing maintenance plans.

Monthly or Quarterly Maintenance Tasks

Some maintenance tasks are managed more infrequently, such as on a monthly or quarterly basis. Do not interpret these tasks as unimportant because they don't require daily maintenance. These tasks also require maintenance to ensure the health of their environment, but on a less regular basis because they are more self-sufficient and self-sustaining. Although the following tasks may appear mundane or simple, they should not be overlooked during maintenance.

- Conduct a restore of the backups in a test environment.
- Archive historical data if needed.
- Analyze collected performance statistics and compare them to baselines.
- Review and update maintenance documentation.
- Review and install SQL Server patches and service packs (if available).
- Test failover if running a cluster, database mirroring, or log shipping.

- Validate that the backup and restore process adheres to the Service Level Agreement defined.
- Update SQL Server build guides.
- Update SQL Server disaster recovery documentation.
- Update maintenance plan checklists.
- Change Administrator passwords.
- Change SQL Server service account passwords.

Summary

The maintenance plan feature alone should be one of the key selling points for SQL Server 2012. The ability to use an uncomplicated wizard to automate administrative tasks that SQL Server will perform against a single database or multiple databases has decreased the amount of manual work DBAs must do and ensures that tasks do not get overlooked. To take advantage of running tasks concurrently, or using precedence constraints to run tasks sequentially, you should create plans manually. This is the best way to develop maintenance plans for those looking for a lot of flexibility on advanced workflow.

SQL Server 2012 continues to allow organizations to extend their use of maintenance plans. The following are just some of the features SQL Server 2012 has brought to the table. SQL Server 2012 offers support for multi-server maintenance plans. SQL Server 2012 does not require SSIS to be installed, and it supports the potential for remote logging.

In the end, the most important thing to take away from this chapter is the importance of having a maintenance plan in place early and ensuring that maintenance is scheduled accordingly to preserve the health of each database.

Best Practices

Some important best practices from the chapter are the following:

- DBAs should fully understand all maintenance activities required and implemented within the SQL Server environment.
- Use the Maintenance Plan Wizard to automate and schedule routine maintenance operations.
- When creating maintenance plans with the wizard, leverage the features included in SQL Server 2012 and create independent schedules for subtasks.

- Maintenance tasks should be scripted, automated, and fully documented.

- Maintenance tasks should be conducted during nonpeak times or after hours, such as on weekends and after midnight.

- When you configure the order of the maintenance tasks, backups should be executed first and then other tasks that change the database.

- Do not include the Shrink Task when creating maintenance plans. Manually shrink the database if needed during nonpeak hours.

- Maintenance tasks should be grouped into daily, weekly, and monthly schedules.

- Schedule and conduct routine maintenance tasks on a daily, weekly, and monthly basis.

- For a large enterprise environment running many SQL Servers, take advantage of subplans and the multiserver maintenance plan.

PART V

Multi-Instance Management, Consolidation, and Private Clouds

IN THIS PART

CHAPTER 17 Implementing and Managing Policy-Based Management

CHAPTER 18 Managing Workloads with Resource Governor

CHAPTER 19 Consolidation, Virtualization, and Private Clouds

CHAPTER 17

Implementing and Managing Policy-Based Management

Policy-Based Management is one of the most sought after multi-instance management capabilities in SQL Server 2012. It gives an organization the potential to create policies for managing one or more instances of SQL Server, databases, or some other objects within the Database Engine. Policies can be evaluated against target systems to ensure that the standard configuration settings for an instance of SQL Server are not out of compliance. Policy-Based Management was developed in response to the following industry trends:

- Increasing amounts of data being stored
- Data center consolidation and virtualization
- Growing product capabilities
- Proliferation of SQL Server instances within organizations
- Need for a way to manage SQL Server settings from a holistic perspective
- Regulatory compliance demanding secure and standardized settings

Introduction to Policy-Based Management

DBAs are frequently being asked to do more with less. When you combine this challenge with the volume of data in the workplace increasing exponentially and the increase in the deployment of instances of SQL Server, it is easy to see that

DBAs require tools to help manage their multi-instance SQL Server environment. Policy-Based Management provides DBAs some relief through automation, which helps reduce administrative burden. As a result, DBAs are free to focus on efficient, scalable management and standardization.

A well-managed SQL Server enterprise that follows best practices offers the following advantages:

- **Standardization**—Every SQL Server will have a common disk layout and settings. As a result, DBAs moving from one SQL Server to another will not be surprised by different disk layouts or unusual settings that could account for a performance problem.

- **Adherence to best practices**—Microsoft internal studies have shown that 80 percent of the support calls to their Customer Service and Support (CSS) could have been avoided if the customer had been following best practices. Best practices not only offer performance advantages but also lead to fewer failure events caused by poorly configured SQL Servers, and security breaches due to SQL Servers that have not been hardened (security holes not locked down).

- **Ease of deployment**—A well-managed data center will have automated procedures for building SQL Servers (that is, unattended installations using the template.ini file) that require less time to build and minimal administrative interaction, resulting in fewer mistakes in a build and a reduction in administrative tasks.

- **Compliance**—By maintaining controlled and standardized settings, organizations can easily adhere to the demanding requirements of compliance and regulations such as Sarbanes-Oxley, HIPPA, and PCI.

The intent of Policy-Based Management is to provide a management framework that allows DBAs to automate management in their enterprise according to their own set of predefined standards. By implementing Policy-Based Management within a SQL Server infrastructure, organizations will reap the following benefits: Total cost of ownership associated with managing SQL Server systems will be reduced, configuration changes to the SQL Server system can be monitored, unwanted system configuration changes can be prevented, and policies will ensure compliance.

The stated goals of Policy-Based Management fall into the following categories:

- **Management by intent**—Allows DBAs to enforce standards and best practices from the start rather than in response to a performance problem or failure event.

- **Intelligent monitoring**—Allows DBAs to detect changes that have been made to their SQL Server environments that deviate from the desired configuration.

- **Virtualized management**—Provides a scalable framework that allows for establishment management across the enterprise.

- **Explicit administration**—Allows DBAs to explicitly validate that instances of SQL Server adhere to a specific policy.

Note

The Microsoft SQL Server Product Group has a blog dedicated entirely to Policy-Based Management. Visit http://blogs.msdn.com/sqlpbm/ to discover a wealth of information, including sample scripts and best practices.

Policy-Based Management Concepts

Before we start learning about enforcing Policy-Based Management, DBAs must understand a few key concepts, including the following:

- Facets
- Conditions
- Policies
- Categories
- Targets
- Execution mode
- Central Management Servers

Policy-Based Management Facets

A *facet* is a logical grouping of predefined SQL Server configuration settings. When a facet is coupled with a condition, a policy is formed and can be applied to one or more instances of SQL Server, including the host. Common facets include Surface Area Configuration, Server Audit, Database File, and Database. SQL Server 2012 also includes new facets tailored toward managing AlwaysOn capabilities, such as Availability Database, Availability Group, Availability Group State, and Availability Replica.

The complete list of predefined facets can be viewed in SQL Server 2012 Management Studio by expanding the Management folder, the Policy-Based Management node, and then the Facets folder. Alternatively, to view facets applied to a specific database, right-click the database and select Facets.

Policy-Based Management Conditions

A *condition* is a Boolean expression that dictates an outcome or desired state of a specific management condition, also known as a facet. Condition settings are based on properties, comparative operators, and values such as String, EQUAL, NOT EQUAL, LIKE, NOT LIKE, IN, or NOT IN. For example, a check condition could verify that data and log files reside on separate drives, that the state of the database recovery model is set to Full Recovery, that database file sizes are not larger than a predefined value, and that database mail is disabled.

Policy-Based Management Policies

A *policy* is a standard for a single setting of an object. It ultimately acts as a verification mechanism of one or more conditions of the required state of SQL Server targets. Typical scenarios for creating policies include imposing Surface Area Configuration settings, enforcing naming conventions on database objects, enforcing database and transaction log placement, and controlling recovery models. As mentioned earlier, a tremendous number of policies can be created against SQL Server 2012 systems. Surface Area Configurations are a very common policy, especially because the SQL Server 2005 Surface Area Configuration tool has been deprecated in SQL Server 2012. In addition, a DBA may implement a policy that prohibits Database Mail from being enabled or a policy that requires all databases to start with the letters RKM.

Note

A policy can contain only one condition and can be either enabled or disabled.

Policy-Based Management Categories

Microsoft recognized that although you may want to implement a set of rigid standards for your internal SQL Server development or deployments, your enterprise may have to host third-party software that does not follow your standards. Although your internally developed user databases will subscribe to your own policies, the third-party user applications will subscribe to their own categories. To provide flexibility, you can select which policies you want a table, database, or server to subscribe to, group them into groups called *categories*, and then have a database subscribe to a category and unsubscribe from a group of other policies.

Policy-Based Management Targets

A *target* is one or more instances of SQL Server, databases, or database objects that you want to apply your categories or policies to. Full functionality of Policy-Based Management is for targets that are running SQL Server 2008 and later. Some facets may apply with limited functionality on SQL Server 2005 or earlier. If necessary, it is still possible to create system configuration policies with the Security Configuration Wizard, which is included with Windows Server 2008.

Note

The use of the Security Configuration Wizard is covered in Chapter 7, "Hardening and Auditing a SQL Server 2012 Implementation."

Policy-Based Management Execution Modes

When implementing policies, there are three types of execution modes: On Demand, On Schedule, and On Change. The On Change mode has two variations: Prevent and Log Only:

- **On Demand**—The On Demand policy ensures that a target or targets are in compliance. This task is invoked manually by right-clicking the policy in the Management folder, Policy Management folder, Policy folder, and selecting Evaluate. The policy will not be enforced and will be verified only against all targets that have been subscribed to that policy. You can evaluate a policy also by right-clicking the database and selecting Policies and Evaluate.

- **On Schedule**—Policies can be evaluated on a schedule. For example, a policy can be scheduled to check all SQL Server 2012 systems once a day. If any anomalies arise, these out-of-compliance policies will be logged to a file. This file should be reviewed on a periodic basis. In addition, whenever a policy fails, the complete tree in SQL Server Management Studio would display a red downward-pointing arrow next to the policy, as illustrated in Figure 17.1.

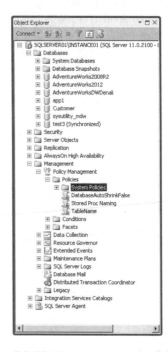

FIGURE 17.1
SQL Server management tree illustrating failed policies for table name.

- **On Change Prevent**—The On Change Prevent execution mode prevents changes to server, server object, database, or database objects that would make them out of compliance. For example, if you select a policy that restricts table names to begin with the prefix tbl, and you attempt to create a table called MyTable, you will get the following error message, and your table will not be created:

```
Policy 'table name' has been violated by
'/Server/(local)/Database/iFTS/Table/dbo.mytable'.
This transaction will be rolled back.
Policy description: ''
Additional help: '' : ''.
```

```
Msg 3609, Level 16, State 1, Procedure sp_syspolicy_
dispatch_event, Line 50
The transaction ended in the trigger.
The batch has been aborted.
```

- **On Change Log Only**—If you select On Change Log Only, a policy condition that is evaluated as failed will be logged in the SQL Server Error log. The change does not prevent out-of-compliance changes.

Central Management Servers

Large enterprises typically have more than one instance of SQL Server they need to manage to ensure they meet compliance. DBAs needing to implement these policies to multiple instances or servers have two options: exporting the policy and then importing it into different instances of SQL Server or creating one or more Central Management Servers.

If there are more than 1,000 instances of SQL Server within your environment, and you are using the import and export methodology, imagine how time consuming this option can be for your organization. Therefore, the Central Management Server may be a better option.

This option involves creating one or more Central Management Servers. DBAs who register one or more SQL Servers with a Central Management Server can deploy multiserver policies and handle administration from a central system. For example, a DBA can create two Central Management Servers: OLAP and OLTP. Next, the DBA registers servers into each Central Management Server, imports the different policies into each Central Management Server, and then evaluates policies on each Central Management Server. After these steps are completed, the servers OLTP1, OLTP2, and OLTP3 registered in the OLTP Central Management Server will have the OLTP policies evaluated on them.

Creating a Central Management Server

Follow these steps to register a Central Management Server:

1. In SQL Server Management Studio, from the View menu, click Registered Servers.

2. In Registered Servers, expand the Database Engine, right-click Central Management Servers, and then select Register Central Management Server.

3. In the New Server Registration dialog box, specify the name of the desired Central Management Server.

4. If needed, specify additional connection properties on the Connection Properties tab or click Save.

Registering SQL Server Instances in a Central Management Server

The next step registers SQL Server instances to be associated with a Central Management Server. The following procedures outline these tasks:

1. Right-click the Central Management Server you want to associate your SQL Server instance with.

2. Select New Server Registration.

3. In the New Server Registration dialog box, specify the name of the desired Central Management Server.

4. Repeat these steps for all SQL Server instances that you want to register with this Central Management Server.

Figure 17.2 illustrates a Central Management Server with one Server Group and two SQL Server instances registered.

FIGURE 17.2
Central Management Server.

Importing and Evaluating Policies to the Central Management Server

After the Central Management Server has been established, the Server Group has been created, and the desired SQL Server instances registered, it is time to import and evaluate policies. Importing policies for multiple instances can be done by right-clicking the Central Management Server or Server Group and selecting Import Policies. After the policies have been imported, the next step is to evaluate the policies by right-clicking the Central Management Server or Server Group and selecting Evaluate. The output will indicate the status of policies associated with all the SQL Server instances associated with the Central Management Server or Server Group.

Note

Importing, exporting, and evaluating policies are covered later throughout the chapter.

Implementing Policy-Based Management

Now that you understand the basic purpose and concepts behind Policy-Based Management and Centralized Management Servers, let's look at how to administer Policy-Based Management and how to apply it to an instance of SQL Server, and then to a group of servers.

There are essentially six steps to implementing and administering Policy-Based Management:

1. Creating a condition based on a facet
2. Creating a policy based on that condition
3. Creating a category
4. Creating a Central Management Server (optional task)
5. Subscribing to a category
6. Exporting or importing a policy

Let's look at each of these in turn. The upcoming sections explain each step in its entirety.

Creating a Condition Based on a Facet

When you create conditions, the general principle includes three elements: selecting a property, an operator, and then a value. Follow the steps to create a condition based on a facet. This example will enforce a naming standard on a table.

1. To create a condition, connect to an instance of SQL Server 2012 on which you want to create a policy.

2. In Object Explorer, expand the Management folder, expand the Policy Management Folder, and then expand the Facets folder.

3. Within the Facets folder, browse to the desired facet on which you want to create the policy.

4. To invoke the Create New Condition window, right-click the facet, such as Table, and select New Condition.

5. In the Create New Condition dialog box, type a name for the condition and ensure that the facet selected is correct.

6. In the Expression section, perform the following tasks to construct an expression:

    a. Select the property on which you want to create your condition. For this example, the Name field will be used.

    b. In the Operator drop-down box, select the NOT LIKE operator.

    c. In the value text box, enter 'tbl%'.

7. Repeat step 6 for any additional expressions. For this example, the following expressions were entered, as displayed in Figure 17.3.

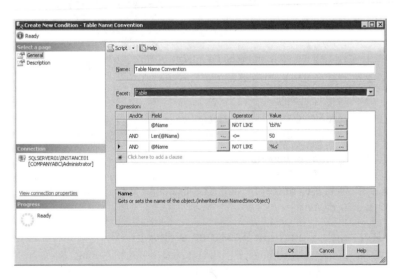

FIGURE 17.3
Creating a condition based on a facet.

AndOr	Field	Operator	Value
@Name	NOT LIKE	'tbl%'	
AND	Len(@Name)	<=	50
AND	@Name	NOT LIIKE	'%s'

> **Note**
>
> You can create conditions that query Windows Management Instrumentation (WMI) (using the `ExecuteWSQL` function) or SQL Server (using the `ExecuteSQL` function). For example, you can do this to check on available disk space or the number of processors on the server. WMI allows you to issue SQL-like queries against Management Objects, which can return information on the physical machine hosting SQL Server, and configuration and performance information, which is not accessible from within SQL Server itself.

7. Click OK to finalize the creation of the condition. You may have to click the Field text box again for the OK button to be enabled.

Creating a Policy

After the condition or conditions have been created, it is necessary to create the policy. The *policy* is a standard that can be enforced on one or more instances of SQL Server, systems, server objects, databases, or database objects. This procedure includes the step-by-step instructions for creating a policy with SQL Server Management Studio:

1. In Object Explorer, expand the Management folder, expand the Policy Management Folder, and then click Policies.

2. Right-click the Policies folder and select New Policy.

3. On the General tab in the Create New Policy dialog box, enter a name for the new policy, such as Stored Proc Naming.

4. In the Check Condition drop-down box, select a condition, such as the one created in the previous example, or select New to generate a new condition from scratch. Since the previous condition created was based on a Table facet, it would be practical to create a new condition for this example.

5. The Against Targets section indicates which objects the policy should be evaluated against. For example, you could create a new condition that applies to a specific database, all databases, a specific

table, all tables, or to databases created after a specific date. In the
Action Targets section, indicate which targets this condition should
apply to.

6. Specify the Evaluation Mode by selecting one of the options in the
drop-down menu. The options include On Demand, On Schedule,
On Change Log Only, and On Change Prevent.

Note

If On Schedule is selected, specify a schedule from the predefined list or
enter a new schedule.

---

7. The final drop-down box is Server Restrictions. You can restrict
which servers you do not want the policy to be evaluated against or
enforced on by creating a server condition. Create a server restriction or leave the default setting, None. The policy settings are
displayed in Figure 17.4.

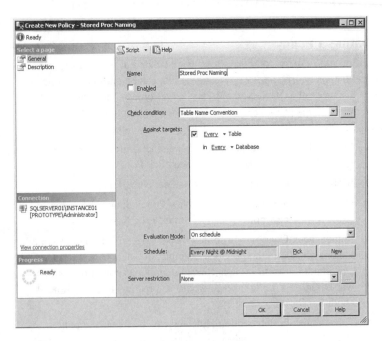

FIGURE 17.4
The Create New Policy dialog box.

8. Before you close the Create New Policy dialog, ensure that the policy is Enabled, and then click the Description page. The description page allows you to categorize your policy, but it also allows you to display a custom text message when a policy is violated and a hyperlink where the DBA/developer can go for more information about the policy.

9. Click OK to finalize the creation of the new policy.

An Alternative to Creating Policies

As you can imagine, for complex policies you may need to create many conditions. In some cases, it may be easier to create a table, database, or server that is configured to conform to the policy you want to create, and then right-click the specific object, select Facets, and then click the New Policy from Facets button.

This will export a policy and a single condition to which the existing object will conform. Figure 17.5 illustrates the dialog that prompts you for a name for your policy and dialog as well as where you want to store the policy. You can store it in the file system and then import it to a Central Management Server or other servers where you want the policy to be evaluated, or you can import it directly to a server. Note that this policy will contain conditions specific to the object you use as a template; for example, if you use the AdventureWorks2012 database, the policy will test for the condition where the database name is equal to AdventureWorks. For this to be useful, you will likely need to edit the conditions to ensure that they are generic and will evaluate exceptions correctly.

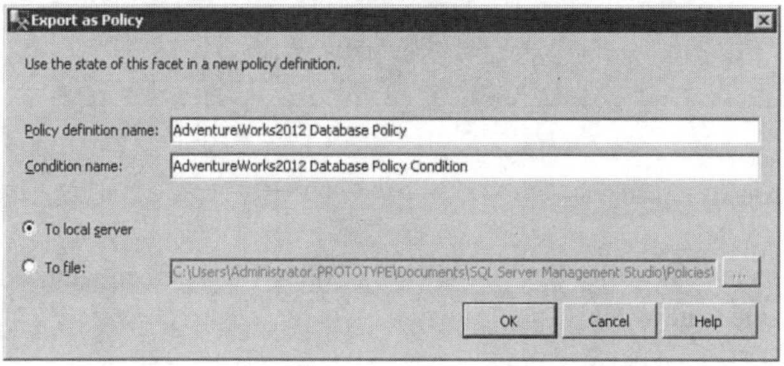

FIGURE 17.5
Exporting a policy based on an existing object.

Creating a Category

After you have created a policy, it should be categorized. Categorization allows you to group policies into administrative or logical units, and then allow database objects to subscribe to specific categories. It is worth mentioning that server objects can't subscribe to policies.

To create a category, click the Description page in the Create New Policy Dialog box. Policies can be placed in the default category or a specific category, or you can create a new category. Specifying a category is illustrated in Figure 17.6.

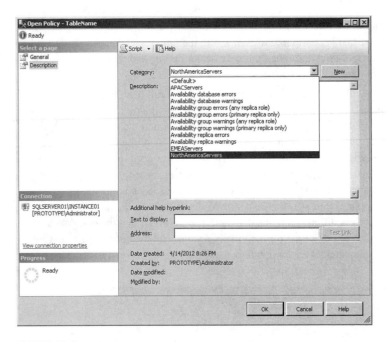

FIGURE 17.6
The Category Selection dialog.

You can also create categories by right-clicking Policy Management and selecting Manage Categories.

If you choose to create a new category, click the New button. This will present a dialog that allows you to name the category. By default, this policy will be parked in the new category.

You can also select which category you want policies to belong to by selecting a specific category in the drop-down box. After you have categorized your policies, you can select which categories you want your database to subscribe to. Right-click the Policy Management folder and select Manage Categories. The Manage Policy Categories dialog box (illustrated in Figure 17.7) will appear. Check the categories to which you want all databases on your server to subscribe, and deselect the ones that you do not want your server database to be subscribed to by default.

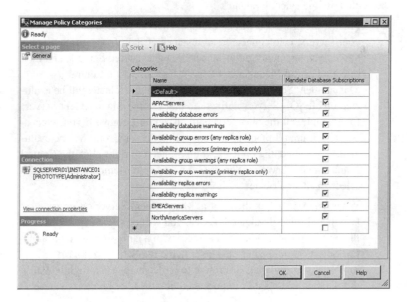

FIGURE 17.7
The Manage Policy Categories dialog box.

Other than the default category, DBAs can select which category (and policies belonging to that category) they want their databases to subscribe to. For example, if you have third-party software that does not follow your naming standards, you should ensure that the policies that enforce your naming standards are not in the default category. Then selectively have each of your user databases on your server subscribe to these database.

Evaluating Policies

After you have created an organization's policies and categories, you will want to evaluate them to determine which of your servers and databases are out of compliance. You can leverage three management points to evaluate policies:

■ For the first alternative, right-click an instance of SQL Server, server object, database, or database object in SQL Server Management Studio, select Policies, and then Evaluate.

■ For the second alternative, expand the Management Folder, expand Policy Management, right-click Policies, and select Evaluate. It is also possible to select an individual policy in the Policy folder, right-click it, and select Evaluate.

■ Finally, the preferred way to evaluate all your servers, or a group of your servers, is to connect to an instance of SQL Server in SQL Server Management Studio, select View Registered Servers, and then select a Central Management Server. If you select a Central Management Server, the policies you select to evaluate will be evaluated on all SQL Servers defined on that Central Management Server; for example, all member servers in all Server Groups. If you select a Server Group, all member servers in that Server Group will be evaluated. To evaluate the policies, you will need to right-click the Central Management Server, or Server Group, or even Member Server, and select Evaluate Policies.

When you right-click the Central Management Server or Server Group and select Evaluate Policies, you will be presented with a dialog that prompts you for a source, with a Choose Source prompt. For Select Source, enter the server name into which you have imported your policies, or browse to a file share. Then highlight all the policies you want to import and click the Close button to close the dialog.

After the policies are imported, you can select the individual policies you want to run and click Evaluate. The policies will be evaluated on the member servers, and the results will be displayed in the Evaluation Results pane, as illustrated in Figure 17.8.

The Evaluation Results pane displays servers where a policy has failed. Notice in the target details that there is a View hyperlink, which will allow you to browse to get more details on why the individual target server failed compliance to the policy you evaluated.

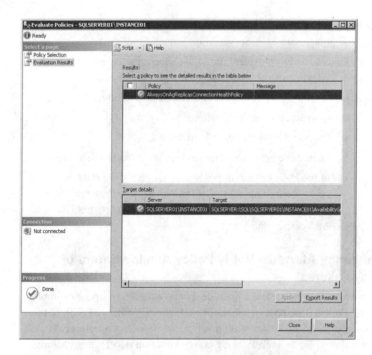

FIGURE 17.8
The Evaluation Results pane.

Importing and Exporting Policies

There may be situations when a DBA wants to export one or many policies
with their conditions from one or many instances of SQL Server and
import them to another instance or system. Fortunately, this can be done
easily with an export and import wizard because the policies fully integrate
with XML files.

Follow these steps to export a policy with SQL Server Management
Studio:

1. In Object Explorer, expand the Management folder, expand the
   Policy Management Folder, and then click Policies.

2. Right-click a desired policy to export, and then click Export Policy.

3. In the Export Policy dialog box, specify a name and path for the
   policy, and click Save.

Importing a policy from an XML file is just as simple. Follow these steps to import a policy with SQL Server Management Studio:

1. In Object Explorer, expand the Management folder, expand the Policy Management Folder, and then select Policies.

2. Right-click the Policies folder and click Import Policy.

3. The import screen has three options:

    a. Provide the path to the file to import.

    b. Enable the option to Replace Duplicate Items When Imported.

    c. In the Policy State drop-down box, specify the state of the policy being imported. The options include Preserve Policy State on Import, Enable All Policies on Import, and Disable All Policies on Import.

Configuring Alerts to Notify Policy Administrators of Policy Failures

The question that gets asked a great deal is: What is the purpose of implementing Policy-Based Management or evaluating instances of SQL Server against best practices if there isn't a way to notify policy administrators of policy failures? Fortunately, when a policy violation occurs, it is captured in an event log. Therefore, it is also possible to create an alert that monitors the event log and automatically notifies an operator if a policy violation is detected. Table 17.1 points out the types of policy violations that are written to the event log based on the execution mode and its correlated message number.

Table 17.1. **Policy Errors Written to the Event Log**

Execution Mode	Error Message Number
On change: prevent (if automatic)	34050
On change: prevent (if On demand)	34051
On schedule	34052
On change	34053

Three steps must be performed to ensure an operator responds to a Policy-Based Management error message. First, create an operator, as described in Chapter 15, "Monitoring SQL Server 2012." Next, create an alert using an error number from the preceding table. Finally, assign an alert to an operator created in the first step.

Creating an Alert Using an Error Number

Follow these steps to create an alert using an error number:

1. In Object Explorer, connect to an instance of SQL Server where you want to create an alert using an error number.

2. Expand the SQL Server Agent folder.

3. Right-click the Alerts folder and select New Alert.

4. In the New Alert dialog box, enter a name for this new alert, as shown in Figure 17.9.

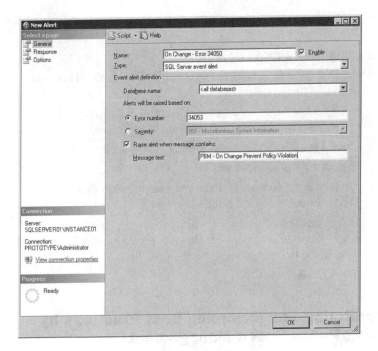

FIGURE 17.9
Creating an alert to notify an operator of a policy violation.

5. Ensure the Enable check box is set to True. This is the default setting and is required to ensure the alert will run.

6. Select SQL Server Event Alert in the Type drop-down list.

7. Under Event Alert Definition, in the Database name list, select a database to restrict the alert to a specific database. You can choose a single database, such as AdventureWorks2012, or you can choose all databases.

8. Under Alerts Will Be Raised Based On, click Error Number, and then type a valid error number for the alert. Remember to reference Table 17.1 for the execution mode and their correlating error message numbers. Alternatively, click Severity, and then select the specific severity that will raise the alert.

9. Check the box corresponding to Raise Alert When Message Contains check box to restrict the alert to a particular character sequence, and then enter a keyword or character string for the Message text. The maximum number of characters is 100.

10. Click OK.

Assigning Alerts to an Operator

Follow these steps to assign alerts to an operator that was already created based on steps found in Chapter 15:

1. In Object Explorer, connect to an instance of SQL Server that contains the operator to which you want to assign an alert.

2. Expand the SQL Server Agent folder.

3. Expand the Operators folder.

4. Right-click the operator to which you want to assign an alert, select Properties, and select the Notifications page.

5. In the Alert list section on the Notifications page, specify how you would like to be notified if this alert is triggered by selecting one or more of the following: Email, Pager, or Net Sent.

6. When finished, click OK.

Monitoring and Enforcing Best Practices by Using Policy-Based Management

The remaining sections show policy-based best practices and the policy templates included with SQL Server 2012. These sections offer real-world examples for using Policy-Based Management and can be imported into a SQL Server 2012 system. Leverage them to evaluate instances of SQL Server against best practices.

Enforcing Best Practices with Templates

The best practice policies available for import are located in the default installation drive at C:\Program Files (x86)\Microsoft SQL Server\110\ Tools\Policies\DatabaseEngine\1033. As mentioned earlier, you can import a policy by right-clicking the Policies node and selecting Import. It is evident from the following list that the sample templates are categorized by a SQL Server feature such as Database Engine, Reporting Services, and Analysis Services:

- **Asymmetric Key Encryption Algorithm**—This rule checks whether asymmetric keys were created by using 1024-bit or stronger encryption.

- **Backup and Data File Location**—This rule checks to see if database files and backup files reside on different devices. As a best practice, database and backup files should be kept on separate devices to decrease the risk of the database and backup failing together.

- **Data and Log File Location**—This rule checks to see if data and log files appear on different logical drives. Data and log files should be placed on different drives when you create a new database to ensure maximum uptime. The database must be placed in a offline state if there is a need to move files after the fact.

- **Database Auto Close**—This rule determines whether the AUTO_CLOSE option is turned off. If a database is regularly accessed, the AUTO_CLOSE should be set to off.

- **Database Auto Shrink**—This rule determines if the AUTO_SHRINK option is OFF. Physical fragmentation can occur if a database is regularly allowed to shrink and expand. In the event you need to reclaim unused space, manually shrink the database.

- **Database Collation**—To reduce collation conflict, this rule checks to see if collations of the user-defined database and the master or model database should be the same.

- **Database Page Verification**—This rule checks whether the PAGE_VERIFY database option is set to CHECKSUM. The policy will ultimately provide a high level of data-file integrity.

- **Database Page Status**—This policy looks for 824 logical consistency errors that represent that the database status is set to suspect.

- **Guest Permissions**—This rule will verify every user and system database to validate if permission was given for a guest user to gain access to a database. This is a great policy to use to verify that security, compliance, and back doors weren't left open.

- **Last Successful Backup Date**—This rule decreases the chances of data loss by checking to see if a database has recent backups.

- **Public Not Granted Server Permissions**—This is another great rule to ensure security and compliance because this rule determines whether the public server role has server permissions. If this condition is met, every login on the server will have server permissions.

- **SQL Server Affinity Mask Overlap 32 Bit and 64 Bit**—This rule will verify and report a violation if a SQL Server instance has processers designated to be used with both the affinity mask and affinity I/O mask options enabled. The goal of this rule is to ensure that a single processor is not assigned to both the affinity mask and the affinity I/O mask because it causes performance degradation. Two different rules are affiliated with this policy. One verifies conditions for 32-bit processors and the other for 64-bit.

- **SQL Server Affinity Mask**—This policy verifies if the affinity mask setting that controls CPU affinity is set to 0. Typically, this setting was used to move process threads among different processors to carry out multitasking when using the Windows 2000 and Windows Server 2003 family of operating systems.

- **SQL Server Blocked Process Threshold**—This Blocked Process setting is enabled and typically is used only to troubleshoot deadlocks on an instance of SQL Server. Therefore, it should be disabled by default or set to a value higher than 5 seconds. Values 1 to 4 should be used only when troubleshooting deadlocks, because it could cause performance degradation. This policy will verify that the blocked process threshold options are configured to values of 0 or higher than 5 seconds.

- **SQL Server Default Trace**—This policy is used to verify if the default trace log file setting is enabled. Typically, this setting should be enabled only when troubleshooting issues associated with the Database Engine. When enabled, information about configuration and DDL changes are logged.

- **SQL Server Dynamic Locks**—This rule checks the value of the locks configuration option. The locks configuration option is responsible for limiting how much memory the instance of SQL Server uses for locks.

- **SQL Server Lightweight Pooling**—This rule checks that the lightweight pooling option on each instance of SQL Server is disabled. As a best practice, the lightweight pooling option should be disabled by default and turned on only when context switching is a known issue within your environment.

- **SQL Server Login Mode**—This rule returns which instance of SQL Server within your infrastructure is configured to use the SQL Server Authentication mode. As a reminder, it is a best practice to leverage the Windows Authentication mode when possible.

- **SQL Server Max Degree of Parallelism**—This option can be leveraged to limit the number of processors to use in parallel plan executions. SQL Server detects the best degree of parallelism when a server has more than one CPU. This rule determines whether the max degree of parallelism (MAXDOP) option is configured for a value greater than 8.

- **SQL Server Max Worker Threads for 32-Bit SQL Server 2000**—This rule is very important because if incorrectly configured, an instance of SQL Server could experience thread starvation or address space could be wasted. The rule will check for incorrect settings affiliated with the Max Worker Thread option. It is worth noting that there are three variations for this rule: 32-bit SQL Server 2000, 64-bit SQL Server 2000, and SQL Server 2005 and later. As a best practice, the setting should be configured to its default, which is zero; therefore, SQL Server automatically determines the correct number of threads per request.

- **SQL Server Network Packet Size**—To prevent performance degradation on an instance of SQL Server, this rule will evaluate the network packet size configuration to ensure the value is not greater than 8060 bytes.

- **SQL Server Password Expiration**—To prevent hackers from exposing or compromising an instance of SQL Server, a DBA must ensure that the password expiration for SQL Server logins is enabled. This rule will verify whether the Password Expiration of each SQL Server login is enabled; therefore, an attacker cannot repeatedly exploit a known SQL Server login password.

- **SQL Server Password Policy**—This rule checks whether the Enforce Password Policy setting for each SQL Server login is enabled. This is another great rule for ensuring security, compliance, and preventing hackers from obtaining access to a database.

- **Symmetric Key Encryption for Databases**—This rule checks whether encryption keys have a length of less than 128 bytes. Moreover, the rule also checks for the use of RC2 or RC4 encryption algorithm. As a best practice, it is recommended to use AES 128 bit or larger to create symmetric keys for data encryption.

There are three variations of this rule: Symmetric Key Encryption for User Databases, Symmetric Key for Master Database, and Symmetric Key for System Databases.

- **Trustworthy Database**—This rule determines whether the dbo role for a database is assigned to the sysadmin fixed server role and the database has its trustworthy bit set to ON. If these conditions are met, a privileged database user can elevate privileges to the sysadmin role. In this role, the user can create and run unsafe assemblies that compromise the system.

- **Windows Event Log Cluster Disk Resource Corruption Error**— This rule is great for those who are leveraging AlwaysOn Failover Clustering to provide high availability for mission-critical databases. The rule checks the system event log for EventID 1066. EventID 1066 represents configuration issues and corruption for a volume used for failover clustering.

- **Windows Event Log Device Driver Control Error**—This rule checks for system event log EventID 11 to protect against corrupt device drivers, faulty cabling, or possible connectivity issues.

- **Windows Event Log Device Not Ready Error**—This rule checks the system event log for EventID 15, which represents issues with SCSI host adapters.

- **Windows Event Log Failed I/O Request Error**—This rule checks the system event log for EventID 50, which represents a failed I/O request.

- **Windows Event Log I/O Delay Warning**—It is important to know if an instance of SQL Server experiences a wait time of more than 15 seconds when reading or writing from disk, because it represents a problem with the disk I/O subsystem. Use this policy to eradicate this issue because it will check the event log for error message 833.

- **Windows Event Log I/O Error During Hard Page Fault Error**— This rule will check and report on EventID 51, which represents an issue caused by an error during a hard page fault.

- **Windows Event Log Read Retry Error**—Use this rule to identify issues that could lead to data loss or database corruption because SQL Server was unable to read data from the disk. This rule checks the event log for SQL Server error message 825.

- **Windows Event Log Storage System I/O Timeout Error**—This is another rule that focuses on ensuring the storage system is healthy by checking the system event log for EventID 9. EventID 9 represents I/O timeouts.

■ **Windows Event Log System Failure Error**—This rule verifies that SQL Server did not inadvertently shut down by checking the event logs for EventID 6008.

Additional Policy-Based Management Use Cases

The next section outlines additional policy-based management use cases to achieve best practices.

Recovery Models

Recovery models determine how SQL Server uses the transaction log. On OLTP systems, the most appropriate recovery model is generally the Full Recovery model. For OLAP systems, the most appropriate recovery model is generally the simple recovery model. For most development environments, the most appropriate recovery model is also the simple recovery model.

For mission-critical databases, or databases where point-in-time recovery is important, having a transaction logged back up every 5 minutes may be required. Policy-Based Management can be used to determine if the appropriate recovery model is in place for each user database for each server type. Central Management Servers could be created for each server type, and a policy can be created to ensure that the appropriate recovery model is in place.

Surface Area Configuration

SQL Server 2005 shipped with the SQL Server Surface Area Configuration tool (SAC). This tool allowed you to enable or disable various components and services on individual SQL 2005 Servers. This feature was deprecated in SQL Server 2012, because the Microsoft team felt that the better way to handle these configuration tasks was through Policy-Based Management.

If you want to implement the Surface Area Configuration feature in SQL Server 2012 to configure components and services, import the following policies:

■ Surface Area Configuration for Database Engine Features.xml

■ Surface Area Configuration for Service Broker Endpoints.xml

■ Surface Area Configuration for SOAP Endpoints.xml

SQL Server Health Checks

One of the SQL Server Support Engineers has blogged on how to do server health checks using PBM. You can access his blog using this URL: http://blogs.msdn.com/bartd/archive/2008/09/11/defining-complex-server-health-policies-in-sql-2008.aspx.

The main part of the SQL Server health check revolves around ensuring that the disk response times are less than 100ms. The policy uses ExecuteSQL to query the DMV sys.dm_io_virtual_file_stats to ensure that the disk response time is within this limit. You can extend this policy to query other DMVs for other health checks; for example, the use of excessive parallelism, or checking to ensure that cumulative wait stats have not exceeded predefined boundaries.

Object-Naming Conventions

Your company may have standards for naming objects. For example, stored procedures must start with the prefix usp, tables must start with the prefix tbl, and functions must start with the prefix ufnc. Policy-Based Management can be used to ensure that all objects are compliant with this policy. This policy can be implemented on change, which will prevent the creation of such noncompliant objects.

Summary

Policy-Based Management in SQL Server 2012 allows you to manage your instances of SQL Server by creating policies that can be used to enforce compliance to best practices or to report on out-of-compliance servers. It provides a highly granular, flexible, and extensible toolset that allows you to manage all aspects of your SQL Server. Properly used, it is a great tool to enforce standardization in your environment and to ease the management burden.

Best Practices

- When deploying Policy-Based Management in your environment, be very careful about using On Change Prevent. For example, a policy that prevents stored procedure creation with the sp_ prefix will prevent the enabling of replication on a SQL Server.

■ When you create a policy that you want enforced on all user data-bases, place this policy in the default category, and it will be subscribed to all databases. Otherwise, you will need to manually subscribe all databases to the categories that contain the policies you want enforced.

■ Make use of multiple Configuration Servers or Server Groups to group your SQL Servers according to logical groupings on which you want to group your policies.

■ Importing policies into centralized SQL Server 2012 servers makes it easier to deploy groups of policies against groups of servers using Central Management Servers; for example, to store data warehouse policies on Server A. Use this server as a source when selecting policies to evaluate against your data warehouse servers registered in the Data Warehousing Central Management Server.

■ Enforce best practices by levering the best practices policy templates.

■ You may find that your environment contains third-party user applications/databases that are not in compliance with the policies you have created for your enterprise. Policy-Based Management uses the opt-in metaphor where all policies are enforced by default. For servers you do not want the policy to be enforced on, you will need to tag the database, perhaps with an extended property or a specially named table that the server exception category or the target will detect and exempt that server or database from the policy.

■ Use the ExecuteWSQL task to issue WMI queries to extend condi-tions and policies beyond the SQL Server environment; for example, to check what other services may be running on a server hosting SQL Server.

CHAPTER 18

Managing Workloads with Resource Governor

Resource Governor was a new management feature introduced in SQL Server 2008. It bolstered SQL Server performance by allowing DBAs to manage SQL Server workloads and system resource consumption by establishing resource limits and priorities on processor and memory-related workloads and resource pools. By defining resource limits on resource consumption, it was possible to prioritize multiple workloads to ensure consistent performance, maximize the experience of clients and applications, and improve the efficiency of the applications without performance degradation.

It is important for every DBA to know that Resource Governor throttles processes only if SQL Server is experiencing CPU or memory pressure, and that it throttles only incoming requests. For example, a process that consumes high CPU will not be throttled, but the next process may be throttled. It is also worth noting that Resource Governor is unable to throttle high I/O consumers, which are processes that read and write excessively from disk.

Some highlights of Resource Governor that are expected to excite DBAs are its ability to control the following:

- **Runaway processes**—These are processes that can degrade overall SQL Server performance. For example, a badly written cursor will be able to consume all of the CPU resources. Likewise, a query without the appropriate indexes cannot cause a CPU spike, or a long-running query that returns a large rowset cannot consume large amounts of memory in the process.

- **Login priorities**—DBAs can selectively assign different priorities to different groups of logins. For example, reporting users may have a lower priority assigned than logins associated with order entry applications.

- **Unpredictable responses**—By throttling high-resource consumers, SQL Server can deliver predictable response times because the high-resource consumers do not degrade SQL Server performance as an ungoverned SQL Server infrastructure.

> **Note**
>
> Resource Governor resource management applies only to the SQL Server Database Engine; it cannot be used in conjunction with Reporting Services, Analysis Services, or Integration Services. Also, it is not instance aware. In other words, many instances of SQL Server are installed on the same server; performance issues experienced on one instance could severely and negatively affect another instance.

What's New for Resource Governor in SQL Server 2012

Customers familiar with Resource Governor requested improvements to the product. Specifically, they were seeking improvements to increase the maximum number of resource pools and the capability to support large-scale multi-tenant database solutions with a higher level of isolation between workloads. Customers also wanted predictable chargeback and vertical isolation of machine resources. The outcome of their appeals for Resource Governor in SQL Server 2012 follows:

- Resource Governor now natively supports up to 64 resource pools. This means a single instance of SQL Server can support larger scale multi-tenant environments.

- A maximum cap for CPU usage has been introduced to enable predictable chargeback and isolation on the CPU.

- Resource pools can be affinitized to an individual schedule or a group of schedules for vertical isolation of machine resources.

- A new Dynamic Management View (DMV) called sys.dm_resource_governor_resource_pool_affinity improves DBAs' success in tracking resource pool affinity.

Overview of Resource Governor Concepts, Workflow, and Scenarios

The following sections will provide you with an overview of the Resource Governor concepts, the workflow process and several scenarios use cases.

Resource Governor Concepts

This section introduces readers to the components that are fundamental to understanding Resource Governor. The three components of Resource Governor are resource pools, workload groups, and classification, which are discussed next.

Resource Pool

A resource pool or pools represent the physical resources of an instance of SQL Server. Resource Governor parcels out CPU and RAM into groups called pools so it can share resources among the different pools, similar to how a SQL Server shares resources among other instances running on a single physical machine.

Workload Groups

By default, two resource pools are created for Resource Governor: a default and an internal resource pool. All internal database engine processes run in the internal resource pool. A DBA can neither modify the properties of the internal resource pool nor create workload groups to run inside it. All workloads run in the default resource pool unless another resource pool is defined, and the classifier function identifies workloads to run in workload groups in other resource pools. Note that you can create your own user resource pools and modify their properties on-the-fly. Changes made to user resource pools are applied to newly logged-on workloads and not to current workloads.

Classifications

A resource pool has a minimum set of resources assigned to it, which are non-overlapping. Other pools cannot use these resources. In addition, the minimum settings for all pools combined cannot exceed 100 percent. A resource pool will also have a maximum set of resources that are shared with other pools. Although the maximum resource setting for a pool can be 100 percent, the effective maximum is likely to be less. Take a moment to reflect on the range of pools in Table 18.1, which consists of the internal pool, default pool, and two user-defined pools. In addition, it is important to understand the formulas used for calculating the effective Max percentage and the Shared percentage.

Table 18.1   Minimum and Maximum Pool Values

Name	Minimum %	Maximum %	Effective Max%	Shared %
Internal	0	100	100	100
Default	0	100	100-30-20=50	0
Resource Pool A	20	50	50-30-0=20	20 (50-20)
Resource Pool B	30	70	70-20-0=50	20 (70-50)

Consider Resource Pool A in the table. It has a minimum value of 20 for CPU and an effective max of 20. The effective maximum percentage is calculated by taking the maximum for Pool A subtracted by the minimum for Pool B. The minimum of Pool B and the minimum of the default pool is subtracted because these are dedicated to these pools and are not overlapping with the other pools. The calculated shared percentage is the effective maximum percentage value minus the minimum percentage value.

Workload Groups

A workload group serves as a logical collection for session requests that are similar, according to the classification criteria that is applied to incoming requests. Policies associated with workload group will dictate the behavior of the session. A workload group has properties associated with it including, but not limited to, Max CPU and degree of parallelism. You can monitor the resource consumption of workload groups inside a resource pool. This is valuable as it allows you to move a workload from one workload group to another, or a newly created workload group. As with resource pools, by default there are two workload groups: the internal workload group and the default workload group. Although you cannot modify the internal workload group, you can monitor it. As for the default group, it handles all unclassified workloads. Workload groups can be created with either Resource Governor Properties page in SQL Server Management Studio or with Transact-SQL.

Classification

Classifications are internal rules that classify incoming requests and route the request to the appropriate workload group. In addition, it is a Transact-SQL function invoked at login that determines the workload group a session executes in during the process. Resource Governor can use only a single classifier function at one time. However, you can dynamically change the classifier function Resource Governor uses. Workloads are classified by the classifier function after the login is authenticated and logon triggers are executed.

Resource Governor Workflow

The Resource Governor concepts discussed previously all have an intricate relationship with one another in the SQL Server Database Engine. This relationship is clearly recognized as it follows the process of a workflow. First, there is an incoming connection for a session. The incoming session is classified, and the session workload is routed to a workload group. The workload group uses the resource pool it is associated with, and then the resource pool provides and limits the resources required by an application.

Resource Governor Scenarios

Most DBAs will want to understand how Resource Governor applies to their SQL Server infrastructure and the benefits they can gain from it. This section walks you through four potential scenarios to assist you in understanding Resource Governor. For starters, Resource Governor ensures predictable performance by allowing DBAs to "bucket" their workloads into resource pools, which have preset limits on the amount of CPU and RAM they can consume.

Consider a case where the DBA is using backup compression, which is a high-CPU consumer. While the backups are occurring, the backups will consume CPU resources that would otherwise be available to other workloads within the instance of SQL Server. The net result is that all workloads using SQL Server could experience degraded performance while the backup process is running. If a DBA implements a resource pool with a max CPU usage of 25 percent, the backup process would be throttled, and the impact to the CPU while the backup is running is considerably lower because Resource Governor was used. In the end, the backup process will take longer, but the other workloads that are running while the backup is running will be protected and will not experience performance degradation.

In this next scenario, consider that a cursor or WHILE loop is missing a FETCH NEXT or increment step. In this case, the cursor or WHILE loop would execute the same portion of code and never exit the cursor or WHILE loop. Such a process, called a runaway process, would preempt other processes and consume all the CPU resources. With Resource Governor, the impact of runaway processes is lowered by limiting their priority.

The third scenario identifies Resource Governor's ability to classify workloads and place them in workload groups, thereby isolating these workloads from other processes. By placing a reporting workload in its own workload group, limits can be set on the workload group, which minimizes the adverse effect the workloads in other workload groups can have on the reporting workload while ensuring the performance is predictable.

The last scenario in this section shows how isolating workloads into their own groups allows you to monitor them and tune the resources they consume. Resource Governor allows you to closely monitor CPU and memory consumption of workloads in workload groups so you can correctly allocate resources to a workload to improve the overall performance of all workloads on your instance of SQL Server.

While monitoring workloads with Resource Governor, you can selectively prioritize workloads as Low, Medium, or High, and then create workload groups for prioritized workloads. This ensures the processes with a high priority are completed faster than processes with a lower priority. Prior to Resource Governor, it was impossible to monitor or prioritize your workloads.

Tip

As you will see later in the chapter, the best way to deploy Resource Governor is to place all workloads in the default resource pool, observe their resource requirements, and then create resource pools that are appropriate for their resource demands and resource pools that limit the impact of these workloads on the entire SQL Server. After these resource pools are created, these workloads can be moved into these resource pools, and SQL Server dynamically throttles new workloads as they exceed their resource limits.

Notes from the Field: Leveraging Resource Governor in Consolidated Multitenant Environments

Many organizations are consolidating instances of SQL Servers and databases to reduce the total cost of ownership affiliated with their data platform environment. Consolidation may take place in the form of migrating many databases onto fewer instances, virtualization with Hyper-V, or implementing a private cloud to host Instance of SQL Servers and databases. Consolidation provides a tremendous set of benefits; however, it also raises concerns for DBAs in a multi-tenant environment because a single runaway query could negatively impact the performance of all

databases residing within the instance of SQL Server. This type of negative performance could lead to downtime, which would defeat an organization's purpose of consolidation. Resource Governor can help in this
scenario because it allows a DBA to manage SQL Server workloads and
resources within the consolidated instance by specifying limits on
resource consumption by incoming requests. Therefore, even though
there are many databases within a single instance of SQL Server, a
single runaway query would not negatively impact all the other databases
within the multi-tenant environment. Typically, when I conduct Consolidation, Virtualization, and Private Cloud Architecture Design Sessions for
my customers, I recommend Resource Governor to manage workloads.

Implementing and Configuring Resource Governor

The following sections will articulate how to enable Resource Governor,
including configuration tasks such as creating a classifier function, creating
a resource pool, creating a workload group, and using SQL Server
templates. We will start by first enabling Resource Governor.

Enabling Resource Governor

Resource Governor is disabled by default and must be enabled for each
instance of SQL Server you plan to use it for. Review the following steps
to enable Resource Governor. It is worth noting that your login must have
sys_admin privileges to enable and manage Resource Governor. The
following steps should be used to enable Resource Governor via SQL
Server Management Studio:

1. Choose Start, All Programs, Microsoft SQL Server 2012, SQL
   Server Management Studio, and then connect to an instance of SQL
   Server.

2. In Object Explorer, expand a desired SQL Server, and then expand
   the Management folder.

3. Right-click Resource Governor and select Enable.

To enable Resource Governor using Transact-SQL, issue the following
command:

```
ALTER RESOURCE GOVERNOR RECONFIGURE
GO
```

Similarly, you can disable Resource Governor by using the following steps in SQL Server Management Studio:

1. In Object Explorer, expand the Management folder.

2. Right-click Resource Governor and select Disable.

Disabling Resource Governor will not drop classifier functions, workload groups, or resource pools. Essentially, disabling Resource Governor places all workloads in the default resource pool and workload group. The next time you enable Resource Governor, it will govern newly logged-on workloads.

Use the following Transact-SQL command to disable Resource Governor:

```
ALTER RESOURCE GOVERNOR DISABLE
RECONFIGURE
GO
```

Note

You cannot place the ALTER RESOURCE GOVERNOR statements within a transaction. Moreover, issuing repeat calls to disable or enable Resource Governor will not raise an error message. Finally, if you disable Resource Governor, existing workloads will continue to be throttled based on their current resource pool/workload group settings. Only new incoming requests will be assigned to the default resource pool and workload group.

Creating a Classifier Function

A *classifier function* is a Transact-SQL function created in the master database. It evaluates the properties of a workload at login and places the workload in the appropriate workload group based on defined policies. The classifier function works by detecting properties of the login and then returning the name of the workload group into which the workload is to be placed by Resource Governor.

The available properties that the classifier function can use are as follows:

```
HOST_NAME()
APP_NAME()
SUSER_NAME()
SUSER_SNAME()
IS_SRVROLEMEMBER()
IS_MEMBER()
```

```
LOGINPROPERTY(suser_name(),'DefaultDatabase')
LOGINPROPERTY('MyAccount,' DefaultLanguage')
```

However, you are free to use any function, or even a lookup table, to classify your workloads. Be careful when writing your classification function, because a poorly written classification function will be applied to all login sessions and can cause performance problems. The Dedicated Admin Connection (DAC) will not be classified and can be used to troubleshoot problems with the classification function.

Creating a Classifier Function Example

The following Transact-SQL example can be used to create a classifier function:

```
CREATE FUNCTION [dbo].[MyClassifier] ()
   RETURNS sysname WITH SCHEMABINDING
AS
BEGIN
DECLARE @grp_name AS sysname
IF (SUSER_NAME() = 'Backup')
BEGIN
SET @grp_name = 'BackupGroup'
END
ELSE
BEGIN
IF (APP_NAME() LIKE '%MANAGEMENT STUDIO%')

OR (APP_NAME() LIKE '%QUERY ANALYZER%')
BEGIN
SET @grp_name = 'DevGroup'
END
ELSE
IF (APP_NAME() LIKE '%REPORT SERVER%')
BEGIN
SET @grp_name = 'ReportingGroup'
END
ELSE
SET @grp_name = 'WorkLoadGroup1'
END
RETURN @grp_name
END
GO
```

This function starts by determining whether the login is the Backup login. If it is, it returns the name BackupGroup, and Resource Governor places this login in the BackupGroup workload group.

It then checks to see if the application name is in the instance of SQL Server. If so, the classifier function returns the name DevGroup, and Resource Governor places this login in the DevGroup workload group.

Finally, the classifier function checks to see if the application name is Report Server. If so, it returns the name ReportingGroup to Resource Governor, and the workload will be placed in the ReportingGroup workload group. All other workloads will be placed in the workload group WorkLoadGroup1.

After you have written your classification function, you need to configure Resource Governor to use it. Here is an example of how to accomplish this task:

```
ALTER RESOURCE GOVERNOR WITH
(CLASSIFIER_FUNCTION = dbo.MyClassifier);
GO
```

> **Note**
>
> You will need Control Server permission to make any changes to Resource Governor configuration, including changing the classifier function, which Resource Governor uses.

There are some considerations when writing the classifier function. The classifier function must return the workgroup name using the data type sysname or nvarchar(128). Group names returned are case-sensitive comparisons. For example, Default (referring to the default workload group) might not resolve to the default workload group. The default resource pool and workload group are lowercased.

Troubleshooting Your Classifier Function

If your classifier function causes performance problems on your instance of SQL Server, you have two options for logging on to your server and bypassing the classifier function to troubleshoot it.

Option 1:

Start SQL Server with the -m switch from the console. Following is an example of how to do this:

At a command prompt, navigate to the location of your SQL Server binaries. They are likely to be at C:\Program Files\Microsoft SQL Server\
MSSQL11.INSTANCE01\MSSQL\Binn. Then issue the following command:

```
sqlservr -con -m
```

This will put SQL Server into single-user mode. Using the DAC (explained
next) is preferable.

Option 2:

Alternatively, use the Dedicated Admin Connection (DAC). Log on to SQL
Server using the DAC. The DAC will not be subject to the classifier function. The DAC is disabled by default on SQL Server; to enable the DAC,
you will need to issue the following command in a Database Engine query
window:

```
sp_configure 'show advanced options',1
reconfigure with override
go
sp_configure 'remote admin connections',1
reconfigure with override
GO
```

After you have done this, you can use the DAC. There are two ways to log
on using the DAC:

1. In SQLCMD, log on using the -A parameter. Here is an example:

```
sqlcmd -S SQLSERVER01SQLServer01\Instance01 -U sa -P
(ComplexPassword) -A
```

   Where SQLServer01\Instance01 is the name of your SQL Server, sa
   is the sa account, and sapassword is the sa password.

2. To log on to SQL Server using the DAC in SQL Server Management
   Studio, take the following steps:

   a. In SQL Server 2012 Management Studio, connect to an
      instance of SQL Server with no other DACs open, and on the
      toolbar, click Database Engine Query.

   b. In the Connect to Database Engine dialog box, in the Server
      name box, type **ADMIN:** followed by the name of the server
      instance. For example, to connect to a server instance named
      SQLServer01\Instance01, type **ADMIN: SQLServer01**
      Instance01. `

    c. Complete the Authentication section, providing credentials for a member of the sysadmin group, and then click Connect.

Creating a Resource Pool

To create a resource pool, follow these steps:

1. Choose Start, All Programs, Microsoft SQL Server 2012, SQL Server Management Studio, and then connect to an instance of SQL Server.

2. In Object Explorer, expand a desired SQL Server, and then expand the Management folder.

3. Right-click the Resource Governor icon, and select New Resource Pool.

4. Enter the name of your resource pool (ResourcePoolName), the Minimum and Maximum CPU%, and the Minimum and Maximum Memory%, as illustrated in Figure 18.1. For this example, enter **20** for the minimum and **50** for the maximum CPU, and for memory enter the same values.

5. Click the OK button.

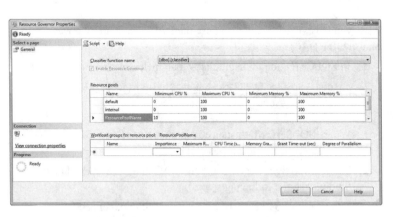

FIGURE 18.1
Dialog for creating a resource pool.

Your resource pool is now created. You will need to create some workload groups in it to make it useful.

To create a resource pool using Transact-SQL commands, use the following syntax:

```
CREATE RESOURCE POOL ResourcePoolName
 WITH
(
MIN_CPU_PERCENT = 20,
MAX_CPU_PERCENT = 50,
MIN_MEMORY_PERCENT = 20,
MAX_MEMORY_PERCENT = 50
)
GO
ALTER RESOURCE GOVERNOR RECONFIGURE
GO
```

The value for MIN_CPU_PERCENT is the minimum CPU you want to dedicate to workloads in this resource pool. This value will not be shared among other resource pools. The value will be between 0 and 100 and must be less than the MAX_CPU_PERCENT. If you attempt to set the minimum larger than the maximum, you will get the following error message:

```
Msg 10908, Level 15, State 4, Line 5
Attribute 'max_cpu_percent' with value of 50 is less than
attribute 'min_cpu_percent' with value of 60.
```

The value for MAX_CPU_PERCENT is the maximum value of CPU you want to share among workloads using this resource pool. Note that this will not be the effective maximum CPU percent; the effective maximum will be the MAX_CPU_PERCENT less the minimum CPU percent values for all other resource pools.

When deriving values for max and min CPU, you will need to measure the CPU taken by these workloads using Profiler for a single execution, and then multiply this value by the expected number of executions per second.

MIN_MEMORY_PERCENT is the minimum memory dedicated to this resource pool. The range is between 0 and 100 and must be less than the value assigned for the MAX_MEMORY_PERCENT. Estimating representative values for minimum and maximum memory is difficult. The best way to do this is to create workload groups that run in the default resource pool and measure the total and average memory taken by individual workloads over several days. Use these results for your minimum and maximum memory percentages. Use the performance monitor counter SQL Server:Resource Pool Stats:Default to get these values.

MAX_MEMORY_PERCENT is the maximum memory to dedicate to your resource pool. As with MAX_CPU_PERCENT, the effective maximum memory is the MAX_MEMORY_PERCENT less the MIN_MEMORY_PERCENT settings of all the other resource pools.

After you have configured your resource pool settings, you will need to apply them to Resource Governor by running the following command:

```
ALTER RESOURCE GOVERNOR RECONFIGURE
GO
```

Creating a Workload Group

To create a workload group, follow these steps:

1. Choose Start, All Programs, Microsoft SQL Server 2012, SQL Server Management Studio, and then connect to an instance of SQL Server.

2. Expand the Management folder, expand the Resource Governor node, and expand the Resource Pools folder.

3. Expand the resource pool in which you want to create your workload group, right-click the Workload Groups folder, and select New Workload Group, as illustrated in Figure 18.2.

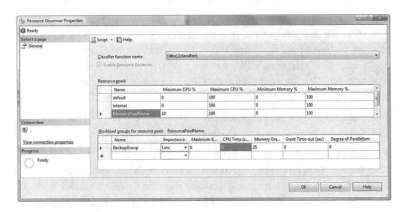

FIGURE 18.2
Creating a new workload group.

4. In the Resource Pools section, highlight your resource pool (in this case, the resource pool named ResourcePoolName), and then in the bottom part of the dialog titled Workload Groups for Resource Pool: ResourcePoolName, enter the name of your workload group. Enter

BackupGroup. For the rest of the settings in this area, enter the following values, as shown in Figure 18.2:

- For Importance, select Low.
- For Maximum Requests, select 0.
- For CPU Time, select 0.
- For Memory Grant %, select 25.
- For Grant Timeout, select 0.
- For Degree of Parallelism, select 0.

   5. Click OK, to save the workload group.

The following list gives additional details about the meaning of these settings:

- **Importance**—The Importance setting is the relative importance of a request in the workload group. Available settings are Low, Medium, and High.

   For Resource Governor, Importance is a simple weighting schema among active workers for the pool. SQL Server will at any one time be simultaneously executing several tasks. Tasks that are ready to run will be in a runable task queue. When a worker is added to the runable queue, the Importance is used as a factor for position in the list against other workers in the same pool on the same scheduler. The Importance does not carry across multiple schedulers, nor does it carry across multiple pools on the same scheduler. It applies only to active workers of groups assigned to the same pool.

- **Maximum Requests**—Specifies the maximum number of simultaneous requests that are allowed to execute in the workload group. A setting of 0 indicates unlimited requests.

- **CPU Time (sec)**—Determines how much CPU time a request can use. 0 indicates unlimited time. The values are in seconds.

- **Memory Grant %**—The maximum amount of memory a single request can take from the resource pool.

- **Grant Time-Out (sec)**—Refers to the maximum time a query will wait for resources to become available before timing out. Values are in seconds and can range from 0 and higher.

- **Degree of Parallelism**—This setting controls the degree of parallelism; 0 means all processors may be used to return or manipulated large results sets. You can select a value between 0 and the maximum number of processors you have on your server. The maximum value is 64, which corresponds to the number of processors on the Wintel platform. Although parallelism can result in faster generations of resultsets, it typically means high CPU consumption, which may degrade overall performance. Select a value that is best for your system.

To create a workload group using Transact-SQL, use a command similar to the following:

```
CREATE WORKLOAD GROUP BackupGroup1
WITH(group_max_requests=0,
    importance=Medium,
    request_max_cpu_time_sec=0,
    request_max_memory_grant_percent=25,
    request_memory_grant_timeout_sec=0,
    max_dop=0)
USING [ResourcePoolName]
GO
ALTER RESOURCE GOVERNOR RECONFIGURE
GO
```

In the preceding example, we are creating a workload group called Backup Group and placing it in the resource pool ResourcePoolName.

Leveraging Resource Governor Using a Template

SQL Server 2012 provides a variety of out-of-the-box templates. Templates are beneficial for DBAs because they provide a boilerplate file containing sample SQL scripts that help a DBA create objects in a database. A myriad of templates are available in Template Explorer.

As you can imagine, there is a Resource Governor template that allows you to generate a resource pool and a workload group for the pool. In addition, this template enables you to create a classifier user-defined function that routes new connections to either the default group or the workload group that you create.

The following steps demonstrate how to use the Resource Governor template in SQL Server Management Studio:

1. Click Template Explorer on the View menu in SQL Server Management Studio.

2. In Template Browser, expand the Resource Governor folder, and then double-click Configure Resource Governor template.

3. The Resource Governor sample template should be used to create and configure a resource pool, a workload group, and a classifier function based on your requirements.

> **Note**
>
> To change the values in the template, it is worth noting that a DBA can press Ctrl+Shift+M to invoke the Specify Values for Template Parameters dialog box, as illustrated in Figure 18.3.

4. Click OK to save the changes that were made in the template.

5. Click Execute to run the query .

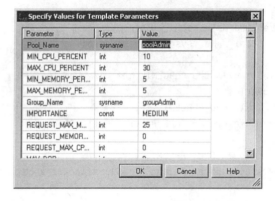

FIGURE 18.3
Specify values for template parameters associated with configuring Resource Governor.

Leveraging the Resource Governor SQL Server Template

The following Transact-SQL syntax illustrates the SQL Server Resource Governor SQL Server Template:

```
-- =================================================
-- Template generated from Template Explorer using:
-- Configure Resource Governor.sql
--
-- Use the Specify Values for Template Parameters
-- command (Ctrl-Shift-M) to fill in the parameter
```

```
-- values below.
--
-- This template creates "admin" workload group
-- which uses "admin" resource pool and creates
-- corresponding classifier function which puts
-- sysadmins in such group
-- =================================================
-- Classifier functions for the Resource Governor must
-- reside within the master database.
USE [master]
GO
SET ANSI_NULLS ON
GO
SET QUOTED_IDENTIFIER ON
GO

-- Create resource pool to be used
CREATE RESOURCE POOL <Pool_Name, sysname, poolAdmin>
WITH (
    -- allocate at least <MIN_CPU_PERCENT, int, 10>% of the CPU
bandwidth for admin queries
    MIN_CPU_PERCENT = <MIN_CPU_PERCENT, int, 10>
    -- do not let them exceed <MAX_CPU_PERCENT, int, 30>%
either
    , MAX_CPU_PERCENT = <MAX_CPU_PERCENT, int, 30>
    -- admin queries should be small and we will allocate about
<MIN_MEMORY_PERCENT, int, 5>%
    -- of the server memory for them
    , MIN_MEMORY_PERCENT = <MIN_MEMORY_PERCENT, int, 5>
    , MAX_MEMORY_PERCENT = <MAX_MEMORY_PERCENT, int, 5>
)
GO

-- TODO
-- Create additional resource pools here

-- Create admin workload group
CREATE WORKLOAD GROUP <Group_Name, sysname, groupAdmin>
WITH (
    -- use all defaults
    IMPORTANCE = <IMPORTANCE, const, MEDIUM>
```

```
        , REQUEST_MAX_MEMORY_GRANT_PERCENT =
<REQUEST_MAX_MEMORY_GRANT_PERCENT, int, 25>
        , REQUEST_MEMORY_GRANT_TIMEOUT_SEC =
<REQUEST_MEMORY_GRANT_TIMEOUT_SEC, int, 0>
        , REQUEST_MAX_CPU_TIME_SEC = <REQUEST_MAX_CPU_TIME_SEC,
int, 0>
        , MAX_DOP = <MAX_DOP, int, 0>
        , GROUP_MAX_REQUESTS = <GROUP_MAX_REQUESTS, int, 0>
)
USING
        <Pool_Name, sysname, poolAdmin>
GO


-- TODO
-- Create additional workload groups here

CREATE FUNCTION <Classifier_UDF_Name, sysname,
[dbo].[rgClassifier]>()
RETURNS sysname
WITH SCHEMABINDING
AS
BEGIN
    -- Define the return sysname variable for the function
    DECLARE @grp_name AS sysname;
    SET @grp_name = 'default';

    -- Specify the T-SQL statements for mapping session
information
    -- with Workload Groups defined for the Resource Governor.
    IF (IS_SRVROLEMEMBER ('sysadmin') = 1)
       SET @grp_name = '<Group_Name, sysname, groupAdmin>';

       -- TODO
       -- Put additional classification logic here
    RETURN @grp_name;
END
GO


-- Set the classifier function for Resource Governor
ALTER RESOURCE GOVERNOR
```

```
WITH (
    CLASSIFIER_FUNCTION = <Classifier_UDF_Name, sysname,
[dbo].[rgClassifier]>
)
GO


-- Make changes effective
ALTER RESOURCE GOVERNOR RECONFIGURE
GO
```

Understanding Default Transact-SQL Syntax with Resource Governor

To leverage Resource Governor to manage SQL Server workloads and system resource consumption, it is beneficial to understand the default Transact-SQL syntax affiliated with creating resource pools, creating workload groups, and creating functions. The following sections articulate the default Transact-SQL syntax that should be used.

Creating Resource Pool

As mentioned earlier, a resource pool represents a subset of the physical resources of an instance of SQL Server; up to a maximum of 64 pools can be created. You can use the following Transact-SQL syntax to create a resource pool:

```
CREATE RESOURCE POOL pool_name
[ WITH
  ( [ MIN_CPU_PERCENT = value ]
  [ [ , ] MAX_CPU_PERCENT = value ]
   [ [ , ] CAP_CPU_PERCENT = value ]
   [ [ , ] AFFINITY {SCHEDULER = AUTO | (Scheduler_range_spec) |
NUMANODE = (NUMA_node_range_spec)} ]
  [ [ , ] MIN_MEMORY_PERCENT = value ]
  [ [ , ] MAX_MEMORY_PERCENT = value ])
]
[;]
```

The arguments and values affiliated with creating a resource pool are self-explanatory; however, it is worth mentioning the new functionality introduced with SQL Server 2012. First, the CAP_CPU_PERCENT specifies a hard limit on the CPU bandwidth that all requests in the resource pool will

receive. The value entered needs to be an integer ranging between
1 through 100, with the default setting of 100. Next, the AFFINITY
{SCHEDULER = AUTO | (Scheduler_range_spec) | NUMANODE =
(<NUMA_node_range_spec>)} attaches the resource pool to specific
schedulers. The default setting is Auto. Finally, to create a resource pool,
the DBA requires the CONTROL SERVER permission.

The following Transact-SQL syntax illustrates the new SQL Server 2012
Resource Governor create resource pool features in action. The CAP_
CPU_PERCENT sets the hard limit to 80 percent and the AFFINITITY
SCHEDULER is set to range of 8 and 12 to 16. This example assumes
there are 16 cores in the system as the statement is trying to affinitize the
pool to schedulers as high as 16:

```
ALTER RESOURCE POOL Pool100
WITH(
    MIN_CPU_PERCENT = 5,
    MAX_CPU_PERCENT = 40,
    CAP_CPU_PERCENT = 80,
    AFFINITY SCHEDULER = (8, 12 TO 16),
    MIN_MEMORY_PERCENT = 5,
    MAX_MEMORY_PERCENT = 15,
);
```

Creating Workload Group

After the Resource Governor resource pool has been generated, it's time to
create a workgroup group and associate the workload group to the resource
pool. The following Transact-SQL syntax can be used to create a workload
group:

```
CREATE WORKLOAD GROUP group_name
[ WITH
  ( [ IMPORTANCE = { LOW | MEDIUM | HIGH } ]
    [ [ , ] REQUEST_MAX_MEMORY_GRANT_PERCENT = value ]
    [ [ , ] REQUEST_MAX_CPU_TIME_SEC = value ]
    [ [ , ] REQUEST_MEMORY_GRANT_TIMEOUT_SEC = value ]
    [ [ , ] MAX_DOP = value ]
    [ [ , ] GROUP_MAX_REQUESTS = value ] )
  ]
[ USING { pool_name | "default" } ]
[ ; ]
```

Creating Function

Finally, the default Transact-SQL syntax to create a function is as follows:

```
--Transact-SQL Scalar Function Syntax
CREATE FUNCTION [ schema_name. ] function_name
( [ { @parameter_name [ AS ][ type_schema_name. ]
parameter_data_type
  [ = default ] [ READONLY ] }
  [ ,...n ]
 ]
)
RETURNS return_data_type
  [ WITH <function_option> [ ,...n ] ]
  [ AS ]
  BEGIN
    function_body
    RETURN scalar_expression
  END
[ ; ]
```

Managing Resource Governor

While using Resource Governor, you will find it necessary to modify your classifier function to move workloads in and out of workload groups as your workload changes to consume more or fewer resources. Initially you will need to place some workloads in the default workload group, until you understand that workload's memory consumption, and then move it to another more appropriate workload group—sometimes in a different resource pool.

To make these changes, you can use SQL Server Management Studio or use Transact-SQL commands.

Here is an example of how to do this using SQL Server 2012 Management Studio:

1. In Object Explorer, connect to a instance of SQL Server.

2. Expand the Management folder, expand Resource Governor, expand the Resource Pools folder, right-click your resource pool (called ResourcePoolName), and select Properties.

3. A dialog similar to the one you saw in Figure 18.1 appears. You can make changes to the ResourcePoolName resource pool. For example, increase the minimum CPU to 25 percent.

4. Click OK to reconfigure your resource pool to use this new minimum for CPU.

In Transact-SQL you would issue the following command:

```
ALTER RESOURCE POOL [ResourcePoolName] WITH
(min_cpu_percent=25)
GO
ALTER RESOURCE GOVERNOR RECONFIGURE
GO
```

To make changes to your classifier function, you can use the ALTER FUNCTION command, and then issue a call to ALTER RESOURCE GOVERNOR RECONFIGURE. This must be done in the query pane; you can't make any modifications through the Resource Governor menu items that show up in SQL Server 2012 Management Studio.

You should modify your classifier function when you need to change the workload group in which workloads will run.

To make changes to your workload groups, follow these steps:

1. Using SQL Server 2012 Management Studio, connect to a instance of SQL Server.

2. Expand the Management folder, expand Resource Governor, expand the Resource Pools folder, expand your resource pool ResourcePoolName, expand the Workload Groups folder, and then right-click your workload group (BackupGroup) and select Properties.

3. A dialog similar to the one you saw in Figure 18.2 appears. You can make changes to the test workload group. For example, decrease the Importance to Low.

4. Click OK to reconfigure your workload group to use this new Importance setting.

To make this change using Transact-SQL, use the following commands:

```
ALTER WORKLOAD GROUP [BackupGroup] WITH (group_max_requests=0,
    importance=Low,
    request_max_cpu_time_sec=0,
    request_max_memory_grant_percent=25,
    request_memory_grant_timeout_sec=0,
    max_dop=0)
GO
```

In addition, it is possible to script configuration settings associated with Resource Governor. This can be achieved by right-clicking the Resource Governor folder in SQL Server Management Studio and selecting the appropriate statement.

Monitoring Resource Governor

Resource Governor needs to be closely monitored to get maximum benefit from it.

The three tools you can use to do this are the following

■ Performance Monitor

■ Profiler

■ Dynamic Management Views (DMVs)

Monitoring Resource Governor with Performance Monitor

In Performance Monitor, use the counters SQLServer:WorkloadGroup Stats and SQLServer:Resource Pool Stats to monitor the active workloads in a workload group or resource pool. If one workload group consumes a significant portion of the resources in the default resource pool, you will need to migrate it to its own resource pool to minimize the impact on the other workloads in this workload group or resource pool.

Of the counters in the SQLServer:WorkloadGroup Stats object, the following will be most useful:

■ **Active Parallel Threads**—Number of threads used by parallel queries in the workload group.

■ **Active Requests**—Number of currently running requests in the workload group.

■ **Blocked Tasks**—Number of blocked tasks in the workload group.

■ **CPU Usage**—System CPU usage by all requests in this workload group.

■ **Max Request CPU Time (ms)**—Maximum CPU time in milliseconds used by a request in the workload group.

■ **Max Request Memory Grant (KB)**—Maximum value of memory grant in kilobytes used by a query in the workload group.

■ **Queued Requests**—Number of requests waiting in the queue due to resource governor limits in the workload group.

■ **Query Optimizations/sec**—Number of query optimizations per second within the workload group.

- **Reduced Memory Grants/sec**—Number of queries per second getting a less than ideal amount of memory in the workload group.

- **Suboptimal Plans/sec**—Number of suboptimal query plans generated per second in the workload group.

- **Requests Completed/sec**—Number of completed requests per second in the workload group.

Of the counters in the SQLServer:Resource Pool Stats object, the following will be most useful:

- **Active Memory Grant Amount (KB)**—Total amount of granted memory in kilobytes in the resource pool.

- **Active Memory Grant Count**—Number of query memory grants in the resource pool.

- **Cache Memory Target (Kb)**—Represents the memory target for cache memory in KB.

- **Compile Memory Target (KB)**—Current memory target for query complied in KB.

- **CPU Usage %**—System CPU usage by all requests in the specified instance of the performance object.

- **CPU Usage Target %**—Target value of "CPU usage %" for the resource pool based on the configuration settings and the system load.

- **Max Memory**—Maximum amount of memory in kilobytes that the resource pool can have based on the settings and server state.

- **Memory Grant Timeouts/sec**—Number of query memory grant timeouts per second occurring in the resource pool.

- **Memory Grant/sec**—Number of query memory grants per second occurring in the resource pool.

- **Pending Memory Grants Count**—Number of queries waiting for memory grants in the resource pool.

- **Query Exec Memory Target**—Current memory target for query execution memory grant in kilobytes.

- **Target Memory**—Target amount of memory in kilobytes that the resource pool is trying to attain based on the settings and server state.

- **Used Memory**—Amount of memory used in the resource pool in kilobytes.

Figure 18.4 illustrates the CPU Usage % counter for the SQLServer: Resource Pool Stats objects. This figure shows three resource pools. The first pool uses maximum CPU, until a workload in the second pool requires CPU resources and Resource Governor throttles the first workload to give the second resource pool its maximum. Then the third resource pool requires resources, and both other resource pools are throttled.

FIGURE 18.4

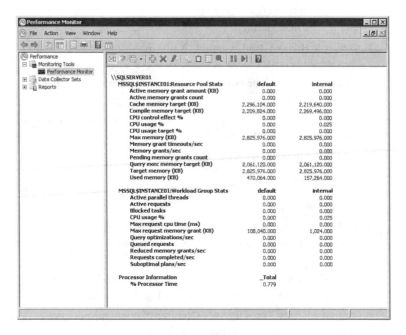

Each resource pool throttles workloads to the maximums for each pool.

Monitoring Resource Governor with Profiler

In Profiler, use the events CPU Threshold Exceeded, PreConnect: Starting, and PreConnect:Completed. CPU Threshold Exceeded tells you when the Request_Max_CPU_TIME_SEC thresholds are exceeded for workloads. The PreConnect counters tells you when the classifier function is operating. Launch Profiler by choosing, Start, All Programs, Microsoft SQL Server 2012, Performance Tools and SQL Server Profiler. You can use a standard template and the following events can be selected by clicking on the Events Selection tab and enabling the option to show all events.

Monitoring Resource Governor with DMVs

The following DMVs give you a window into Resource Governor, the resource pools, and the workload groups:

- **Sys.dm_resource_governor_workload_groups**—Returns workload group statistics and the current in-memory configuration of the workload group. The most significant columns that are returned by this DMV are the following:

  - **Name**—The name of the workload group.

  - **pool_id**—The ID of the pool in which the workload group is located.

  - **total_request_count**—The total number of requests for this workload group.

  - **total_queued_request_count**—The total number of requests queued in this workload group. This is an indication that some workloads in this workload group are being throttled.

  - **active_request_count**—The number of active requests in this workload group.

  - **queued_request_count**—The number of queued requests in this workload group.

  - **total_cpu_limit_violation_count**—The number of requests exceeds the maximum CPU limit.

  - **total_cpu_usage_ms**—The total CPU usage by workloads in this workload group.

  - **max_request_cpu_time_ms**—The maximum CPU usage for a single request in milliseconds.

  - **blocked_task_count**—The number of blocked tasks.

  - **total_lock_wait_count**—Cumulative number of lock waits.

  - **total_lock_wait_time_ms**—Total time spent waiting for locks.

  - **total_reduced_memgrant_count**—Cumulative count of memory grants that reached the maximum query size limit.

  - **max_request_grant_memory_kb**—Maximum memory grant size, in kilobytes, of a single request since the statistics were reset.

  - **active_parallel_thread_count**—Current count of parallel thread usage.

- **importance**—Current configuration value for the relative importance of a request in this workload group.

- **request_max_memory_grant_percent**—Current setting for the maximum memory grant, as a percentage, for a single request.

- **request_max_cpu_time_sec**—Current setting for maximum CPU use limit, in seconds, for a single request.

- **request_memory_grant_timeout_sec**—Current setting for memory grant timeout, in seconds, for a single request.

- **group_max_requests**—Current setting for the maximum number of concurrent requests.

- **max_dop**—Maximum degree of parallelism.

- This DMV will return a wealth of information about requests in each group. The following query returns a list of requests in each workload group:

```
SELECT r.group_id, g.name, r.status, r.session_id,
r.request_id, r.start_time, r.command, t.text
FROM sys.dm_exec_requests r
INNER JOIN sys.dm_resource_governor_workload_groups g
ON g.group_id = r.group_id
CROSS APPLY sys.dm_exec_sql_text(r.sql_handle) AS t
ORDER BY g.name
GO
```

- **Sys.dm_resource_governor_resource_pools**—Returns information about the current resource pool state, the current configuration of the resource pools, and the resource pool statistics.

- **Sys.dm_resource_governor_resource_pool_affinity**—This is a new DMV released with SQL Server 2012 that tracks resource pool affinity.

- **Sys.dm_resource_governor_configuration**—Returns a row that contains the current in-memory configuration state of Resource Governor.

- This DMV will return two columns: classifier_function_id and is_ reconfiguration_pending. The classifier_function_id matches with the object_id column in sys.objects. A value of 0 for is_reconfiguration_pending confirms that there is no pending reconfiguration of the Resource Governor due to changes in configuration, and the

Resource Governor configuration metadata matches its in-memory configuration.

- Following is a query example illustrating usage of `sys.dm_resource_governor_configuration`, returning the name of the classifier function:

```
select object_schema_name(classifier_function_id) +'.'+
OBJECT_NAME(classifier_function_id) AS
ClassifierFunction, is_reconfiguration_pending
```

The following query will tell you how the classifier function is classifying workloads:

```
select Sessions.session_id, Sessions.group_id,
CONVERT(NCHAR(20), Groups.name)
as group_name from sys.dm_exec_sessions as Sessions
join sys.dm_resource_governor_workload_groups as Groups
on Sessions.group_id = Groups.group_id where session_id > 50
```

This query will display which CPU/scheduler each workload/session is running on:

```
select Requests.session_id,
CONVERT(NCHAR(20), WorkLoadGroup.name) as group_name,
Tasks.scheduler_id,
Requests.status
from sys.dm_exec_requests Requests
join sys.dm_os_tasks Tasks on Requests.task_address =
Tasks.task_address
join sys.dm_resource_governor_workload_groups WorkLoadGroup on
Requests.group_id = WorkLoadGroup.group_id
where
Requests.session_id > 50
GO
```

Summary

Resource Governor allows DBAs to selectively throttle workloads so that resource-hungry workloads will not negatively affect the performance of other processes on the box. Take care creating resource pools and workload groups so that you can get optimal performance out of your Resource Governor solution.

Best Practices

- Try to estimate the CPU and memory resources that workloads will consume and place them in a workload group that approximates this load. Monitor the resource consumption in using the DMVs and adjust the workload group settings if appropriate. Create a new resource pool if necessary.

- For workloads whose characteristics are unknown, place them in the default workload group for the default resource pool and monitor its resource consumption there. Create a new resource pool or Workload group if necessary and move it there if required.

- Ensure that your classifier function performs well, and if you need to use a large lookup table, ensure that there are covering indexes in place on it.

- Ensure that any application using Resource Governor has retry/recovery logic built into it, so that if a grant request should fail, there will be no data loss.

- Test and ensure the Dedicated Administrator Connection (DAC) is enabled before associating a classifier function with the Resource Governor. Remember DAC is a backdoor into the SQL Server and bypasses the function; therefore, if the server activity is blocked, DAC can be used to get into the server and correct the anomaly.

- Do not leverage lookup tables in a classifier function because it could lead to performance degradation.

- When workloads are competing with one another, it is easier for the scheduler to fairly divide and cap similar workloads. If you are governing resources for very variable workloads—for example a mixture of high CPU versus high I/O—it is recommended that you favor the MAX_CPU_PERCENT option over the CAP_CPU_PERCENT option and consider partitioning those workloads using scheduler affinity rather than setting maximums.

CHAPTER 19

Consolidation, Virtualization, and Private Clouds

Many organizations are making the move to SQL Server both because of an increase in the number of Microsoft applications and line-of-business applications that call for SQL Server as the back-end database platform. Currently, DBAs install an instance of SQL Server every time their organization requires a SQL Server database, resulting in a proliferation of SQL Server installations and servers within the infrastructure.

Take, for example, a DBA who installs a dedicated SQL Server installation to support databases associated with applications such as SharePoint, Systems Center Operations Manager, Systems Center Virtual Machine Manager, and an antivirus application. Most likely, four independent SQL Server installations are not required, especially if each application is being underutilized. This action gets the job done, but it also translates into higher costs for organizations in many areas, including hardware, licensing, power, cooling, management, and maintenance.

In an effort to help organizations reduce costs and even simplify their infrastructure while managing even larger workloads on their systems, Microsoft invites organizations to consolidate and/or virtualize on fewer systems using Hyper-V, an integral feature associated with Windows Server 2008 and later. It is worth noting that a proliferation of SQL Server within an organization's infrastructure is known as SQL Server *sprawl*.

This chapter focuses on consolidation, virtualization, and private cloud strategies. In addition, the chapter outlines how to deploy Hyper-V to support SQL Server 2012, including optimizing SQL Server for private cloud strategies.

> **Note**
>
> Virtualization and private cloud are large topics and include many
> Microsoft technologies that go above and beyond SQL Server. Therefore,
> many of the topics in this chapter do not focus on step-by-steps but on
> concepts and best practices to get you familiar with the strategies.

Understanding Consolidation, Virtualization, and Private Cloud Strategies

The following sections provide an overview and outline the different strategies DBAs should be aware of when trying to consolidate, virtualize, and optimize SQL Server for private cloud. Let's first start off by reviewing the different consolidation strategies available.

Understanding SQL Server 2012 Consolidation Strategies

The main objective of SQL Server consolidation is to discover underutilized instances of SQL Server, including hardware, and improve utilization by choosing an appropriate consolidation strategy. Some compelling reasons for organizations to consolidate instances and databases are to reduce capital expenses such as hardware and software costs, improve efficiency, provide business continuity, address lack of physical space in the data center, create more effective service levels, standardize platform modernization, and centralize management. Strategies associated with SQL Server consolidation include database consolidation, instance consolidation, and virtualization.

Database Consolidation

This common strategy, as depicted in Figure 19.1, consists of consolidating many databases onto a single instance of SQL Server running on either a physical or virtual server. This approach offers organizations improved operations through centralized management, standardization, and improved performance. Databases are consolidated from a source instance to a target instance using a backup and restore strategy, attach or detach strategy, or with the Copy Database Wizard. It is worth mentioning that many organizations will leverage a Failover Cluster Instance for their target environment to achieve high availability for all their consolidated databases. Some limitations exist with this type of consolidation strategy. For example, consolidating too many databases onto a single instance can bring about issues such as performance degradation and resource contention—specifically with the tempdb database. In addition, other issues may arise because every database must adhere to the same service level agreement and maintain the same global settings and service pack levels. Additional instances within a consolidated infrastructure may be deployed to alleviate these issues. Also, you can use Resource Governor to manage SQL Server workloads and system resource consumption for databases within an instance.

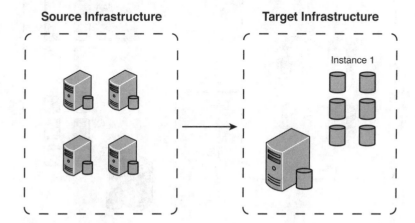

FIGURE 19.1
Conducting database consolidation.

Instance Consolidation

Some organizations might be prevented from consolidating all their databases onto a single SQL Server instance because of the issues stated in the previous section. Therefore, with instance level consolidation, multiple databases are moved to a physical or virtual server that is running more than one instance of SQL Server. This is illustrated in Figure 19.2. Databases are strategically spread out between instances to support security, compliance and administration isolation, alleviate tempdb resource contention, and each database can run on different patch levels and maintain different global and collation settings. Potential problems or resource contention can occur because all instances share resources, such as CPU, memory, network, and disk I/O. The following tools and settings—Resource Governor, CPU affinity mask, and max server memory—can be used to provide resource isolation. It is worth noting that Resource Governor can isolate workloads only within an instance of SQL Server.

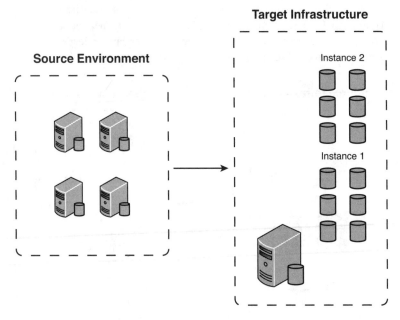

FIGURE 19.2
Conducting instance consolidation.

Virtualization

The latest theme in SQL Server consolidation is to leverage virtualization to consolidate many physical servers running instances of SQL Server (see Figure 19.3). Virtualization offers several benefits for organizations. It can significantly reduce total cost of ownership (TCO) and the number of physical servers within the infrastructure, and with fewer physical servers, organizations require fewer licenses. Through virtualization, organizations can also achieve complete operating system isolation and gain the potential to host multiple editions of SQL Server, including running both 32- and 64-bit versions within a physical host. In addition, physical SQL Servers experiencing the end of their hardware life can easily be virtualized by using a physical-to-virtual migration tool. Virtualization is Microsoft's primary recommendation for SQL Server consolidation because organizations reap the benefits of virtualization and private cloud. The benefits of virtualization and private cloud are discussed throughout this chapter.

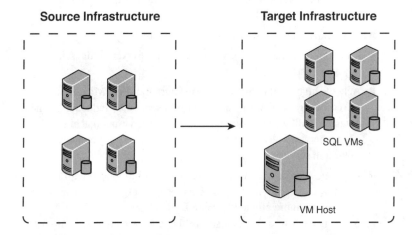

FIGURE 19.3
Conducting SQL Server virtualization.

Understanding Microsoft's Virtualization Strategy

Server virtualization uses a single or multiple Hyper-V systems to host one or more guest operating-system sessions by effectively taking advantage of the computing capabilities of a very powerful server(s). With most servers in datacenters utilizing only 5 to 10 percent of their processing power, a large amount of unused capacity exists on servers. By combining the capabilities of multiple servers through virtualization, organizations can better exploit the processing and computing power available in their virtualized datacenter or private cloud infrastructure.

Take, for example, the metrics gathered by SQL Server virtualization studies: The typical SQL Server installation runs on two physical cores with 4GB of RAM. Based on this configuration, the average SQL Server workload consumes less than 10 percent of the CPU, only 60 percent of the memory installed is being utilized, and the average network traffic for each system is 400 kilobytes per second. As you can see, this type of SQL Server system is heavily underutilized, which makes this type of system a great candidate to virtualize.

By virtualizing servers such as SQL Server 2012, organizations can completely isolate the operating system and gain numerous benefits:

- Reduce TCO associated with procuring and managing physical hardware.

- Drastically reduce power consumption costs.

- Run both 64-bit and 32-bit versions of SQL Server on the same physical host.

- Achieve high availability with Live Migration. Live Migration increases high availability and improves service by reducing planned outages. It allows DBAs to move SQL Server virtual machines (VMs) between physical Hyper-V hosts without any perceived interruption in service.

- Dynamic Memory is a Hyper-V feature first introduced with Windows Server 2008 R2 SP1. This feature helps a DBA use physical memory more efficiently. With Dynamic Memory, Hyper-V treats memory as a shared resource that can be reallocated automatically among running virtual machines. Dynamic Memory adjusts the amount of memory available to a virtual machine, based on changes in memory demand and values that are specified.

- Consolidate many databases within the infrastructure into one or more virtual SQL Server implementations.

- Consolidate many underutilized SQL Server servers and instances into one or more virtual guest operating systems.

- Scale up by installing more than one instance on a virtual guest operating system.

- Reduce SQL Server license costs because SQL Server licenses can be obtained for organizations to achieve unlimited virtualization of SQL Server.

- Isolate database workloads such as OLTP and OLAP.

- Isolate SQL Server features such as the Database Engine, Analysis Services, and so on.

- An organization can support up to 1,024 virtual machines when using Windows Server 2008 R2 SP1 Hyper-V configured in a 16-node failover cluster with Cluster Shared Volumes. This provides massive scalability for the most demanding data center. In addition, these numbers will drastically increase with the release of Windows Server 2012 because up to 64 nodes can be configured in a Hyper-V cluster.

Note

Although Hyper-V provides the capability to host guest operating systems for Windows servers, client systems, and non-Windows systems, many of the tools enterprises use in virtual server environments require the addition of the System Center Virtual Machine Manager (SCVMM) tool.

VMM provides a more centralized view and administration of multiple virtual guest sessions; the tools to do physical-to-virtual image creation, virtual-to-virtual image copying, and load balancing of virtual images across VMM servers; and the capability to do quick migration of guest sessions for disaster recovery between virtual host systems. VMM adds the administrative tools that take the basic virtual server sessions and enables administrators to better manage the guest sessions.

Understanding Microsoft's Private Cloud Strategy

With SQL Server virtualization on the rise, the latest trend is how to optimize SQL Server in a private cloud. Microsoft private cloud is a new model for IT delivery built on Windows Server and System Center. It turns an organization's datacenter infrastructure resources into a single compute "cloud" and enables the key benefits of cloud-based computing. Unlike a public cloud, an organization is the sole tenant and is in full control of the resources. The four fundamental attributes of Microsoft Private Cloud solution are the following:

- **Pooled resources**—A cloud solution runs on a shared virtualized infrastructure and ensures the resources affiliated with the shared virtualized infrastructure are fully optimized, standardized, and highly available. The key resources that typically make up a private cloud solution include the compute, storage, and networking resources. The cloud is multi-tenant capable with the ability to host multiple applications and services while meeting security and privacy concerns.

- **Scalable and elastic**—The cloud infrastructure is able to dynamically grow and contract through automation and workflow based on the business requirements of the application, service, or organization.

- **Self-service based**—The cloud solution offers a self-service experience so application and service owners can perform real-time deployments of applications or services, such as an instance of SQL Server, in a rapid fashion.

- **Usage based**—The cloud is metered so that the organization can implement a charge-back system to charge consumers or business owners for resource consumption. If the organization doesn't charge customers or business owners for usage, the organization can use the information provided to monitor usage.

Microsoft Private Clouds are built with familiar technologies, such as Windows Server for the virtualization layer and Systems Center for management, orchestration, workflow, and self-service. The following items describe the private cloud components:

- **Windows Server Hyper-V**—Hyper-V, on Windows Server 2008 R2 with SP1, provides the virtualization platform that enables organizations to deploy a Microsoft Private Cloud and eventually transition workloads to a public cloud if desired. Hyper-V includes many capabilities, such as multi-tenant support, increased scalability, and support for up to 64 logical processors and 1TB of RAM on each host. In addition, as mentioned earlier, the Live Migration and Dynamic Memory features are beneficial for Microsoft Private Cloud deployments for SQL Server.

- **System Center Virtual Machine Manager**—SC VMM is a centralized solution for managing VMs and Hyper-V hosts. It enables increased server utilization and the intelligent placement of VMs. VMM includes tools for rapid provisioning and a library for storing VM templates and software for Microsoft Private Cloud deployments. VMM also includes migration tools to convert physical servers to virtual servers, which is a common task when migrating physical machines running SQL Server to the Microsoft Private Cloud.

- **System Center Virtual Machine Manager Self-Service Portal**— This portal provides self-service and rapid-provisioning capabilities for the Microsoft Private Cloud solution. This means an organization can consume SQL Server by means of Infrastructure as a Service (IaaS).

- **System Center Operations Manager**—Ops Manager provides end-to-end service management that can be customized and extended for improved service levels across all VMs or the Hyper-V hosts within the Microsoft Private Cloud. Administrators can use it to identify and resolve problems affecting the health of the private cloud and the distributed IT services (for example, SQL Server) within the private cloud. Ops Manager includes a SQL Server Management Pack that proactively monitors SQL Server and provides alerts. When an alert is detected, Ops Manager sends out an email notification or runs a script to address the alert. Ops Manager can also be used to manage physical servers and applications within an organization's data center.

- **System Center Configuration Manager**—SCCM provides unified device management and many other capabilities for private cloud implementations. First, SCCM can be used for asset management by conducting an inventory of all the private cloud resources, such as VMs, Hyper-V hosts, services, and applications. Alternatively, you can use SCCM to inventory all the SQL Server instances in a physical infrastructure that you plan to migrate to the Microsoft Private Cloud. Secondly, SCCM can be used to rapidly deploy services and applications. For example, you can use it to deploy Windows Server 2008 R2 and the SQL Server 2012 or SQL Server 2008 R2 database platform to VMs. Finally, SCCM can be used to achieve security and compliance by automatically updating VMs and applications with the latest critical updates and service packs. This is advantageous for organizations with a very large private cloud implementation, because it can be a long and tedious process to ensure that all VMs running SQL Server are updated with the latest patches and service packs.

- **System Center Data Protection Manager**—DPM offers infrastructure management by providing continuous data protection for VMs hosted on servers running within the Microsoft Private Cloud. This protection includes online backups of supported guest VMs hosted on clustered or standalone systems, protection of VMs during the Live Migration process, and item-level recovery from host-level backups. DPM 2010 also has a component that provides protection for SQL Server databases. All these features help ensure that the private cloud solution is protected and always available.

- **System Center Orchestrator**—Service and delivery is the one of the most important requirements in a private cloud. Orchestrator allows organizations to define and standardize best practices and improve operational efficiency within their private cloud solution. For example, an organization might use Orchestrator to automate a workflow process that conducts a rolling service pack upgrade on a SQL Server failover cluster instance. The workflow process could apply service packs to the appropriate passive nodes, run tests to validate that the installation on each passive node was successful, conduct a failover, and eventually conduct the installation on the active node.

Planning Your Implementation of Hyper-V

For the organization that chooses to leverage the capabilities of Windows Server 2008 R2 SP1 Hyper-V virtualization, a few moments should be spent to determine the proper size, capacity, and capabilities of the host server that would be used as the virtual server that will host the SQL Server guest operating systems. Many server system applications get installed with little assessment of the resource requirements of the application itself because most servers in a datacenter are running at less than 10 percent server utilization, so there is plenty of excess server capacity to handle server workload capabilities.

However, with Hyper-V, because each guest session is a completely running operating system, the installation of many high-performance SQL Server guest sessions could quickly bring a server to 50 or 60 percent of the server performance limits from a capacity perspective. So the planning phase is an important step in a Hyper-V deployment.

Sizing Your Windows Server 2008 R2 SP1 Systems to Support SQL Server 2012 Virtualization

To take advantage of the latest Hyper-V features, the physical host that will be utilized for the underlying Private Cloud infrastructure should be Windows Server 2008 R2 SP1 and later. In addition, because server virtualization is the focus of this host, the minimum Windows Server 2008 R2 SP1 server requirements are insufficient to run Hyper-V. There needs to be enough computing power—CPU, memory, disk, and network—to run the Hyper-V host and all the guest operating systems you plan to deploy within the private cloud.

Tip

To maximize resource pooling and SQL Server efficiency, configure guests to utilize only the resources needed to achieve the desired performance and maximum consolidation ratio.

RAM for the Host Server(s)

For Hyper-V, one of the most important memory architecture choices is the quantity of RAM placed within a host. The general rule for memory of a Windows Server 2008 R2 host running Hyper-V is to have at least 2GB of RAM for the host server, plus enough memory for each guest session. Therefore, if a guest SQL Server session needs to have 2GB of RAM and there are three such guest sessions running on the host system, the host system should be configured with at least 8GB of RAM. If a guest session requires 8GB of memory and three of those systems are running on the system, the server should be configured with 24GB of memory to support the three guest sessions, plus at least 2GB of memory for the host system itself. When establishing the amount of RAM required for the system hosting the SQL Server guest operating systems, it is a best practice to calculate and total the memory utilization required of each physical SQL Server instance you plan to virtualize. Don't forget to include the amount of RAM required to support each SQL Server instance and factor in a minimum of least 512MB of RAM for the guest operating system itself. The majority of the commodity servers in the market today can cost effectively support between 32 and 128GB of RAM, which is the limiting factor in host server capacity. Large SMP servers in the market can support up to 2TB of RAM; however, these types of servers may not be as cost effective compared to commodity servers.

> **Tip**
>
> When purchasing RAM for Hyper-V hosts, it is recommended to purchase the maximum amount of RAM as possible, provided it fits within your budget.

Processors for the Host Server

The Hyper-V host itself has very low processor I/O requirements. In the virtualized environment, the processor demands of each guest session dictate how much processing capacity is needed for the server. If a guest session requires two cores to support the processing requirements of an instance of SQL Server, and eight guest sessions are running on the system, the server should have at least 16 cores available in the system. With quad-core processors, the system would need four processors. With dual-core processors, the system would need at least eight processors.

With Windows Server 2008 R2 SP1, each guest operating system can have up to four cores dedicated to the session, or processing capacity can be distributed either equally or as necessary to meet the SQL Server performance demands of the organization. This will obviously change with the long-awaited release of Windows Server 2012. By sharing cores among several virtual machines that have low processing needs, an organization can make more use of its investment in hardware systems.

When deciding on the number of processors needed for the system hosting the SQL Server guest operating system, it is a best practice to calculate and total the processor utilization of each physical SQL Server instance you plan to virtualize. It is also a good idea to ensure that there are enough CPUs and cores to handle all the SQL Server workloads.

> **Tip**
>
> For new servers, Microsoft recommends selecting the maximum number of cores per processor available and choosing the fastest clock speed available.

Disk Storage for the Host Server

A host server would typically have the base Windows Server 2008 R2 SP1 operating system running on the host system itself with additional guest sessions either sharing the same disk as the host session, or the guest sessions being linked to a storage area network (SAN) or some form of external storage for the virtualized guest session images. From a SQL Server perspective, it is a best practice to leverage a SAN for maximum I/O performance.

For guest sessions running databases or other storage-intensive configurations, the guest image can exceed 10GB, 20GB, or more. When planning disk storage for the virtual server system, plan to have enough disk space to support the host operating system files (typically about 20GB of actual files plus space for the pagefile when running Windows Server) and disk space to support the SQL Server guest sessions.

Designing the back-end storage for a virtualized SQL Server implementation is similar to designing a solution for a physical SQL Server. It is a best practice to isolate the I/O workload by dedicating spindles for database files, transaction logs, and tempdb and then isolating the workloads on each spindle. Additional spindles should be leveraged for isolation of additional databases, database filegroups, and SQL Server instances.

SQL Server Virtualization Considerations

When consolidating and virtualizing SQL Server, a DBA should first take an inventory of all the SQL Server instances within the infrastructure. The next step is to determine potential virtualized candidates by analyzing SQL Server workloads and performance metrics during peak hours over a period of time, such as one to two months for each database and instance. After a baseline is established for each potential candidate, a DBA can decide whether to consolidate this SQL Server instance. In addition, understanding the performance baseline of each SQL Server instance will ensure that the host server selected has the correct amount of processor, memory, and disk space to support all virtualized candidates. The following are some considerations for virtualizing SQL Server 2012:

- A single guest SQL Server session should be selected if there is a need to completely isolate the operating system and/or SQL Server installation from others.

- Multiple virtual operating systems can be installed on one physical host. Each virtual operating system can handle the installation of one or more SQL Server instances. For example, many organizations may conduct a Physical to Virtual migration; therefore, they will need to host different versions of the operating system and instances of SQL Server until they can migrate and standardize on a single platform, such as SQL Server 2012.

- If a virtual host cannot handle any more SQL Server guest sessions because of resource constraints, another virtual host can be implemented within the infrastructure. They should be configured in a failover cluster to achieve high availability and guest operation system portability with Live Migration.

- Multiple databases can be hosted on a single instance of SQL Server running on a guest operating system.

- If databases have different security, collation, and management requirements, these databases can be placed on different SQL Server instances. Each SQL Server instance can reside on one or more SQL Server guest sessions.

Notes from the Field: SQL Server Consolidation and Virtualization Planning

It is recommended to use the Microsoft Assessment and Planning (MAP) Toolkit to accelerate the SQL Server consolidation planning and deployment to a private cloud infrastructure. The MAP toolkit is a free solution accelerator provided by Microsoft and can be downloaded at the following link: http://www.microsoft.com/en-us/download/details.aspx?&id=7826. The tool provides a complete network-wide inventory of SQL Server and other database competitors such as MySQL, Oracle, and Sybase instances. The instance information and performance data captured in conjunction with the intuitive reports on workloads can be utilized for consolidating databases and moving them to a private cloud. I leverage the tool on all my consolidation and virtualization engagements. In working with one large financial services customer, the tool identified more than 4,000 databases on 550 instances of SQL Server running on physical hardware. The mix of SQL Server solutions consisted of 45% on SQL Server 2005, 40% on SQL Server 2008, and 5% on SQL Server 2008 R2. The majority of the physical systems had approximately 12 cores and were running under 10% CPU utilization. In addition, the average memory usage per instance of SQL Server was 4GB of RAM and 5TB of total storage. Based on our consolidation, virtualization, and private cloud design, we ended up virtualizing 100 instances on five phys- ical servers configured in a Hyper-V cluster. Each physical server had 40 cores and 192GB of RAM. Standardization on SQL Server 2012 was chosen because of the AlwaysOn Availability Groups capability of provid- ing both high availability and disaster recovery across the virtual machines.

Running Other Services on the Hyper-V System

On a system running Hyper-V, typically an organization would not run other roles or services on the actual host, such as making the virtual server dedicated for the SQL Server guest operating systems also a file and print server, or making the host server a domain controller, and so on. Typically, a server running virtualization is already going to be a system that will maximize the memory, processor, and disk storage capabilities of the system. So, rather than impacting the performance of all the guest sessions by having a system-intensive application like SharePoint running on the host system, organizations choose to make servers running virtualization dedicated solely to the operation of virtualized guest sessions.

Tip

To reduce surface attack and increase availability during planned outages, many organizations choose to leverage the Server Core operat- ing system for Hyper-V hosts.

Planning for the Use of Snapshots on the Hyper-V System

A technology built into Hyper-V is the concept of a snapshot. A *snapshot* uses the Microsoft Volume Shadow Copy Service (VSS) to make a dupli- cate copy of a file; however, in the case of virtualization, the file is the entire virtual SQL Server guest image. The first time a snapshot is taken, it contains a compressed copy of the contents of RAM on the system along with a bitmap of the virtual disk image of the guest session. If the original guest image is 8GB in size, the snapshot will be significantly smaller in size; however, the server storage system still needs to have additional disk space to support both the original disk image, plus the amount of disk space needed for the contents of the snapshot image.

Subsequent snapshots can be taken of the same guest session; however, the way VSS works, each additional snapshot identifies the bits that are different from the original snapshot, thus limiting the required disk space for those additional snapshots to be the same as needed for the incremental difference from the original snapshot to the current snapshot. This difference might be only megabytes in size.

The use of snapshots in a Windows virtualization environment is covered in more detail later in this chapter in the section titled "Using Snapshots of Guest Operating System Sessions."

Caution

Snapshots are not a replacement for restoring a database to the point of failure. Remember, a snapshot brings the database back to the state of when the snapshot was taken; therefore, use this feature wisely. Maintain the full recovery mode and conduct a transaction log backup if there is a need to restore the database to the point of failure.

Installation of the Microsoft Hyper-V Server Role

With the basic concepts of Windows virtualization and private cloud covered so far in this chapter, and the background on sizing and planning for server capacity and storage, this section now focuses on the installation of the Microsoft Hyper-V Server role on a host running Windows Server 2008 R2 SP1.

Installing Windows Server 2008 R2 SP1 as the Host Operating System

The first step is to install an x64 version of Windows Server 2008 R2 SP1 with Hyper-V as the host operating system. Step-by-step guidance for the installation of the Windows operating system can be found on Microsoft's website.

Running Server Manager to Add the Hyper-V Role

After the base image of Windows Server 2008 R2 SP1 has been installed, some basic initial tasks should be completed. The basic tasks are as follows:

1. Change the server name to the name that you want the virtual server to be.

2. Configure the server to have a static IP address.

3. Join the server to an Active Directory domain (assuming the server will be part of a managed Active Directory environment with centralized administration).

4. Run Windows Update to confirm that all patches and updates have been installed and applied to the server.

After these basic tasks have been completed, the next step is to install the server virtualization software on the server by adding the Hyper-V role to the server system.

Do the following to add the Hyper-V server role to the system:

1. Make sure that you are logged on to the server with local Administrator or Domain Admin privileges.

2. Click Start and then click Run.

3. In the Run dialog box, type `ServerManager.msc` and click OK. This will start the Server Manager console if it is not already running on the system.

4. Right-click Roles in the left pane of the console and select Add Roles.

5. After the Add Roles Wizard loads, click Next to continue past the Welcome screen.

6. On the Select Server Roles page, select the Hyper-V Server role and click Next as shown in Figure 19.4.

> **Note**
>
> Hyper-V requires a supported version of hardware-assisted virtualization. Both Intel VT or AMD-V chipsets are supported by Hyper-V. In addition, virtualization must be enabled in the BIOS. Please check your server documentation for details on how to enable this setting.

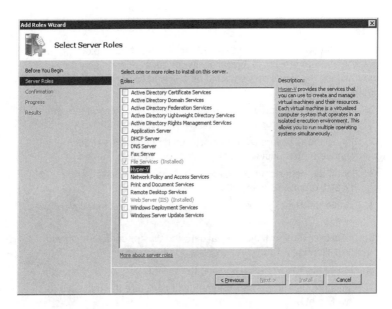

FIGURE 19.4
Adding the Hyper-V role to the Server Manager console.

7. On the Hyper-V page, read the notes and information about the role, and then click Next.

8. On the Create Virtual Networks page, select the LAN adapters you want to have shared with guest sessions. Click Next to continue.

9. On the Confirm Installation Selections page, review the selections made, and then click Install.

10. On the Installation Results page, review the results and click Close.

11. When prompted to restart the server, click Yes.

12. After the server restarts, log on to the server with local Administrator or Domain Admin privileges.

13. After you've logged on, the installation and configuration will continue for a few more moments. When complete, the Installation Results page will be displayed. Review the results in the page and confirm that the Windows Hyper-V role has been installed successfully. Click Close.

> **Note**
>
> A Hyper-V failover cluster using shared storage must be deployed to use Live Migration to provide high availability for guest operating systems. The following high-level steps should be followed to deploy a Hyper-V cluster:
>
> 1. Ensure that the hardware, software, drivers, and components are supported by Microsoft and Windows Server 2008 R2.
>
> 2. Set up the hardware, shared storage, and networks as recommended in the failover cluster deployment guides.
>
> 3. For all the nodes that you plan to use, install Windows Server 2008 R2 SP1 or later (Server with GUI or Server Core).
>
> 4. Enable the Hyper-V role on each node partaking in the failover cluster.
>
> 5. In Failover Cluster Manager, validate the cluster configuration with the Validating a Configuration Wizard tool.
>
> 6. Deploy the Failover Cluster using the wizard.
>
> 7. Configure Cluster Shared Volumes and configure the networks for Live Migration.

Becoming Familiar with the Hyper-V Administrative Console

After Hyper-V has been installed, the next step is to install guest operating systems to support workloads such as SQL Server 2012. However, before jumping into the installation of guest images, here is a quick guide on navigating through the Hyper-V Administrative console and the virtual server settings that apply to all guest sessions on the server.

Launching the Hyper-V Administrative Console

You can use two ways to open the Hyper-V Administrative console and access the configuration options. One way is to use the Server Manager tool and administer the host server through Server Manager; the other option is to launch the freestanding Microsoft Management Console (MMC) to perform administrative tasks for the host system.

Using the Server Manager Tool to Manage Hyper-V Systems

For administrators who want to manage their Hyper-V systems from a centralized console, the Server Manager tool provides a common administrative interface for all the server roles installed on a particular system. To start the Server Manager tool to view and edit Hyper-V settings, do the following:

1. Click Start and then click Run.

2. In the Run dialog box, type **ServerManager.msc**, and click OK. This will start the Server Manager application if it is not already running on the system.

3. Expand the Roles section of the tree by clicking the plus sign (+).

4. Expand the Hyper-V branch of the tree and expand the Virtualization Services branch of the tree.

Using the Hyper-V MMC Tool to Manage Hyper-V Systems

For administrators who want to manage their Hyper-V systems from a dedicated console just for Hyper-V administration, the Hyper-V tool should be used. To start the Hyper-V administration tool, do the following:

1. Click Start, All Programs, Administrative Tools, and then choose Hyper-V Manager for the tool to launch.

2. Click Virtualization Services to see the virtual servers to which you are connected.

3. Click the name of one of the virtual servers listed to see the virtual machines and actions available for the confirmation of the server system. By default, the Hyper-V MMC will have the local virtual server system listed, as shown in Figure 19.5.

Connecting to a Different Virtual Server System

If you want to administer or manage a different virtual server system, you need to log on and connect to another server. To connect to a different virtual server, do the following:

1. From within the Hyper-V Manager Console, click the Virtualization Services option in the left pane.

2. Select Action, Connect to Server.

3. Select Another Computer and either enter the name of the server and click OK or click Browse to search Active Directory for the name of the server you want to remotely monitor and administer.

4. When the server appears in the Hyper-V Management Console, click to select the server to see the actions available for administering and managing that server.

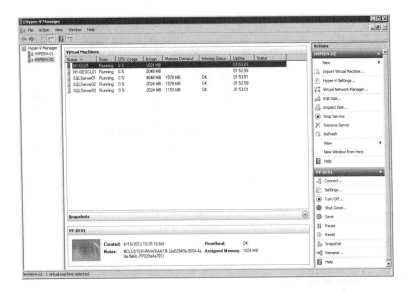

FIGURE 19.5
Hyper-V Virtualization Management Console.

Navigating and Configuring Host Server Settings

Regardless of whether you have chosen to use Server Manager or the
MMC tool, the configuration options and settings are the same. When you
click the virtual server system you want to administer, action settings
become available. These action settings allow you to configure the host
server settings for the system you have chosen to administer.

Hyper-V Settings

When you select the Hyper-V Settings action item, you have access to
configure server and user settings, such as default paths and remote control
keyboard settings. Specifics on these settings are as follows: default folder
to store virtual hard disk files, default folder location to store virtual
machines, the ability for virtual machines to span NUMA nodes, and user
settings such as keyboard and mouse behaviors, accept default credentials,
delete saved credentials, and reset check boxes.

Virtual Network Manager

By selecting the Virtual Network Manager action item, you have access to
configure, manage, or create virtual networks. Many virtual networks can

be created on the server running Hyper-V. At a minimum, it is for best practice to have one network for management traffic, Live Migration, one network for cluster interconnect, and multiple networks for SQL Server virtual machine traffic. In addition, Hyper-V also supports the use of VLAN and VLAN IDs with the virtual network switch. Click the Add button to create external, internal, and private Networks.

Tip

For large virtualized datacenter or private cloud implementations, organizations typically leverage System Center—Virtual Machine Manager (SC VMM). As mentioned earlier, VMM 2012 is the latest version of the management solution used to centrally view and manage physical and virtual resources within a virtualized datacenter or private cloud. SC VMM also includes tools to manage the private cloud and optimize SQL Server, such as service templates that contain configuration settings for applications such as SQL Server, a library to store file based resources such as SQL Server guest operating templates, which can be used for rapid deployment, and a self-service portal, which is a website that users are assigned to. Therefore, they can deploy and manage their own virtual machines to the private clouds.

Installing a SQL Server 2012 Guest Operating System Session

One of the key tasks noted in the previous section is to begin the installation of a new guest operating system session. The guest operating system installation is wizard-driven and provides the administrator with the ability to configure settings for the guest session and to begin the installation of the guest operating system software itself. When working with SQL Server 2012, a guest operating system recommended is Windows Server 2008 R2 SP1 or later. In addition, the Windows Server Core is the operating system of choice if there is a need to reduce surface attach and operating system patches.

Gathering the Components Needed for a Guest Session

When creating a guest operating system, DBAs need to make sure they have all the components needed to begin the installation, as follows:

- **Operating system media**—A copy of the operating system is required for the installation of the guest image. The media could be either a DVD or an ISO image of the media disc itself.

- **License key**—During the installation of the operating system software, if you are normally prompted to enter the license key for the operating system, you should have a copy of the license key available.

Following are some other things you should do before starting to install a guest operating system on the virtual server system:

- **Guest session configuration settings**—You will be prompted to answer several core guest session configuration setting options, such as how much RAM you want to allocate for the guest session hosting SQL Server, how much disk space you want to allocate for the guest image, and so on. Either jump ahead to the next section, "Beginning the Installation of the SQL Server 2012 Guest Session," so that you can gather up the information you'll need to answer the questions you'll be asked, or be prepared to answer the questions during the installation process.

- **Host server readiness**—If you are preplanning the answers to the questions that will be asked, ensure that the host system has everything it needs, including RAM and disk space to support the addition of a guest session on the virtual server system. If your requirements exceed the physical capacity of the server, stop and add more resources (memory, disk space, and so on) to the server before beginning the installation of the guest operating system.

- **SQL Server 2012 installation media**—A copy of the SQL Server 2012 media is required when the installation of the guest image is complete. The media could be either a DVD or an ISO image of the media disc itself.

Beginning the Installation of the SQL Server 2012 Guest Session

When you are ready to begin the installation of the guest operating system, launch the guest operating system installation wizard, as follows:

1. From the Actions pane, choose New, Virtual Machine.
2. Click Next to continue past the initial Welcome screen.
3. Give your virtual machine a name that will be descriptive of the virtual guest session you are creating, such as **SQLServer01**, **SQLOLTP01**, or **SQLVirtual01**, and so on.

4. If you had set the default virtual machine folder location where guest images are stored, the new image for this virtual machine will be placed in that default folder. However, if you need to select a different location where the image files should be stored, click Create a New Folder for the Virtual Machine Files and select Browse to choose an existing disk directory or to create a new directory where the image file for this guest session should be stored. Click Next to continue.

5. Enter the amount of RAM you want allocated to this guest image (in megabytes), and then click Next.

6. Choose the network segment to which you want this guest image to be initially connected. This would be an internal or external segment created in the section "Virtual Network Manager" earlier in this chapter. Click Next.

Note

You can choose Not Connected during this virtual machine creation process and change the network segment option at a later date.

---

7. The next option allows you to create a new virtual hard disk or use an existing virtual hard disk for the guest image file. Creating a new virtual hard disk creates a VHD disk image in the directory you choose. By default, a dynamic virtual disk image size setting is set to 127GB. The actual file itself will be only the size needed to run the image (potentially 20GB for the OS to start) and will dynamically grow up to the size noted in this setting. Alternatively, you can choose an existing hard disk image you might have already, or you can choose to select a hard disk image later. The options for this configuration are shown in Figure 19.6. Click Next to continue.

8. The next option allows for the installation of an operating system on the disk image you created in the previous step. You can choose to install an operating system at a later time, install an operating system from a bootable CD/DVD or ISO image file, install an operating system from a floppy disk image, or install an operating system from a network-based installation server (such as Windows Deployment Service). Typically, operating system source discs are on either a physical disk or ISO image file, and choosing a CD or DVD or an associated ISO image file will allow for the operating system to be installed on the guest image. Select your option, and then click Next to continue.

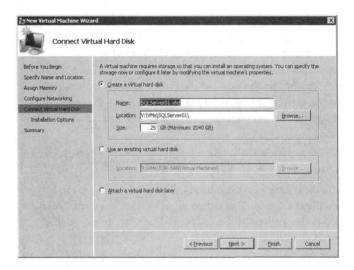

FIGURE 19.6
Virtual Hard Disk creation or selection option.

9. Review the summary of the options you have selected and either click Previous to go back and make changes or click Finish if the settings you've chosen are fine. Choosing the Start the Virtual Machine Once This Wizard Is Finished check box will launch the guest session and begin the guest session installation process. If you need to make changes to the settings, you would not want to select this option yet—just click Finish so that you can make configuration setting changes and start the installation process after that.

Completing the Installation of the Guest Session

The guest operating system installation will proceed to install just like the process of installing the operating system on a physical system. Typically, at the end of an operating system installation, the guest session will restart and bring the session to a logon prompt. Log on to the guest operating system and configure the guest operating system as you would any other server system. This typically requires you to do things such as the following:

- Change the system name to the name that you want for the virtual server. For many versions of operating systems, you will be prompted to enter the name of the system during the installation process.

- Configure the guest session with an appropriate IP address. This might be issued by DHCP; however, if you are building a server system, a static IP address is typically recommended.

- Provision the storage for the SQL Server system.

- Join the system to an Active Directory domain (assuming the system will be part of a managed Active Directory Domain Services environment with centralized administration).

- Download and apply the latest patches and updates on the guest session to confirm that all patches and updates have been installed and applied to the system.

The installation of the guest operating system typically requires yet another reboot, and the operating system will be installed and operational.

Installing SQL Server 2012 on the Guest Session

With the guest session's operating system successfully installed, the next step is to install SQL Server 2012. The steps for performing the SQL Server 2012 installation are the same steps for performing an installation on a physical server. Therefore, leverage the steps included in Chapter 1, "Installing or Upgrading the Database Engine to SQL Server 2012," to perform the installation of SQL Server 2012 on the guest session.

Modifying SQL Server 2012 Guest Session Configuration Settings

After a guest session has been installed, the SQL Server 2012 host configuration settings for the guest session can be changed. Common changes to a SQL Server 2012 guest session include things such as the following:

- Adding or limiting the memory and processors of the guest session

- Changing network settings of the guest session

- Mounting a CD/DVD image or mounting a physical CD/DVD disc

Adding or Limiting the Memory and Processors of the Guest Session

Two common configuration changes made to a SQL Server guest session involves increasing or decreasing the amount of memory or processors allocated to the guest session. The default memory and processors allocated to the system typically is fine for a basic SQL Server system configuration; however, depending on the components being installed and the expected workload, there may be a need to increase the memory leverage the dynamic memory feature or change the processor count. As long as the host server system has enough memory and processors to allocate to the guest session, adding memory or processors to a guest session is a very simple task.

Note

You cannot change the allocated RAM or processor on a running virtual guest session. The guest session must be shut down first, memory re-allocated to the image, and then the guest image booted for the new memory allocation to take effect. In addition, ensure that you revisit the Max Memory setting in SQL Server if you have hard-coded the memory based on a specific threshold.

To add memory and processors to the guest session, carry out the following steps:

1. From the Server Manager console or from the Virtualization MMC snap-in, click to select the guest session for which you want to change the allocated memory.

2. Right-click the guest session name and choose Settings.

3. To configure memory, click Memory and enter the amount of RAM you want allocated for this guest session (in megabytes), as illustrated in Figure 19.7. The configuration options include static or dynamic memory. For dynamic memory, review the upcoming note.

4. To configure the processor, click Processor. If multiple processors are supported by the guest operating system, specify the number of processors to assign to the virtual machine. Then click OK.

5. Click OK when you are finished.

Note

To leverage Dynamic Memory, follow these steps:

1. On the Memory page, under Memory Management, click Dynamic.

2. Set the amount of memory for Startup RAM and Maximum RAM. For Startup RAM or for Maximum RAM, use a value that allows for additional memory as needed but not more than what you would want the virtual machine to consume.

3. If you want to adjust the memory buffer for the virtual machine, use the slider to set the percentage of memory.

4. If you want to give this virtual machine a higher or lower priority for memory allocation compared to other virtual machines running on this server, use the slider to set the relative weight.

FIGURE 19.7
Configuring Dynamic Memory for a SQL Server guest operating system.

Changing Disk Settings for the Guest Session

Another common configuration change made to a guest session is to change the disk settings or create additional disks for the guest session. Creating disks can be achieved by adding a hard drive, either SCSI or IDE in the guest settings. As illustrated in Figure 19.8, the options for creating a new disk include the following:

■ **Fixed Size**—The .vhd file is created using the size of the fixed virtual hard disk. This disk provides better performance and is recommended for virtual machines running workloads such as SQL Server.

- **Dynamically Expanding**—This .vhd file is small when created and dynamically grows as data is written to the disk. Again, it's not the greatest idea for SQL Server because there will be a performance penalty when the disk grows. However, it does offer better use of physical storage space for workloads that are not disk intensive.

- **Differencing**—This type of disk is associated in a parent-child relationship with another disk. Changes to the parent virtual hard disk can be made without altering that disk.

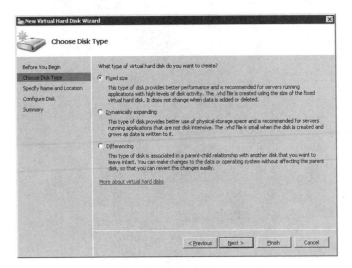

FIGURE 19.8
Creating a new virtual hard disk.

Tip

Another strategy to achieve optimal performance from a disk perspective is to leverage dedicated pass-through disks. Pass-through disk configuration offers the shortest code path from host to I/O subsystem, and in repeated tests it offers the best disk performance, which is excellent for SQL Server workloads.

Mounting a Physical CD/DVD Image or Mounting a CD/DVD Image File

When installing software on a guest session of a virtual server system, the administrator either inserts a CD or DVD into the drive of the physical server and accesses the disc from the guest session, or mounts an ISO image file of the disc media.

To access a physical CD or DVD disc or to mount an image of a CD or DVD, such as the SQL Server media, do the following:

1. From the Server Manager console or from the Hyper-V MMC snap-in, click to select the guest session for which you want to change the allocated memory.

2. Right-click the guest session name, and choose Settings.

3. Click DVD Drive and choose Physical CD/DVD Drive if you want to mount a disc in the physical drive of the host system or click Image File and browse for the ISO image file you want to mount as a disc image.

4. Click OK when you are finished.

Other Settings to Modify for a Guest Session Configuration

Other settings can be changed for a guest session. These options can be modified by going into the Settings option of the guest session and making changes. These other settings include the following:

■ **BIOS**—This setting allows for the selection of boot order on the guest machine: The boot order can include floppy, CD, IDE (disk), or network boot.

■ **Processor**—Hyper-V provides the capability to allocate core processors to the guest image, so a guest image can have up to four core processors allocated for each session. Additionally, resource control can be weighted between guest sessions by allocating system resource priority to key guest server sessions versus other guest sessions.

■ **IDE Controller**—The guest session initially has a single virtual hard drive associated with it. Additional virtual hard drives can be added to a virtual guest session.

■ **SCSI Controller**—A virtual SCSI controller can be associated with a virtual guest session and provide different drive configuration options.

■ **COM Ports**—Virtual communication ports such as COM1 or COM2 can be associated with specific named pipes for input and output of information.

Launching a Hyper-V Guest Session

After a Hyper-V guest session has been created and the settings have been properly modified to meet the expected needs of the organization, the virtual guest session can be launched and run. You need to make decisions about whether you want the guest session to launch automatically as soon as the server is booted, or whether you want to manually launch a guest session. Additionally, you should decide on the sequence in which guest sessions should be launched so that systems that are prerequisites to other sessions come up first.

Automatically Launching a Guest Session

One option for launching and loading guest sessions is to have the guest session boot right after the physical server completes the boot cycle. This is typically the preferred option if a guest session is core to the network infrastructure of a network (such as a domain controller or host server system) so that in the event of a physical server reboot, the virtual guest sessions boot automatically as well. It would not be convenient to have to manually boot each virtual server session every time the physical server is rebooted.

The option for setting the boot option for a virtual session is in the configuration settings for each guest session.

To change the boot action, perform the following steps:

1. From the Server Manager console or from the Hyper-V MMC snap-in, right-click the virtual machine for which you want to change the setup option, and select Settings.

2. In the Management section of the settings, click Automatic Start Action.

3. Three options are provided, as shown in Figure 19.9, of what to do with this virtual guest session upon boot of the physical server. Either click Nothing (which would require a manual boot of the guest session), or click Automatically Start If It Was Running When the Service Stopped, or click Always Start This Virtual Machine Automatically. To set the virtual session to automatically start after the physical server comes up, choose the Always Start This Virtual Machine Automatically option.

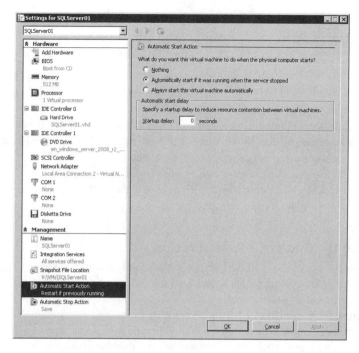

FIGURE 19.9
Automatic start actions.

4. Also on this Settings page is the choice of an *Automatic Start Delay*.
This allows you to sequence the boot of image files by having some
images take longer to automatically start than others. Click OK to
save these settings.

Manually Launching a Guest Session

Another option for guest session boot is to not have a guest session automatically start after a physical server boots up. This is typically the
preferred option if a guest session will be part of a demonstration or test
server where the administrator of the system wants to control which guest
sessions are automatically launched and which need to be manually
launched. It would not be convenient to have a series of demo or test
sessions automatically boot every time the system is booted. The administrator of the system would typically want to choose to boot guest sessions.

To set the boot action to manually launch a guest session, do the following:

1. From the Server Manager console or from the Hyper-V MMC snap-in, right-click the virtual machine for which you want to change the setup option and select Settings.

2. In the Management section of the settings, click Automatic Start Action.

3. In the three options of what to do with this virtual guest session upon boot of the physical server, either click Nothing (which would require a manual boot of the guest session), click Automatically Start If It Was Running When the Service Stopped or click Always Start This Virtual Machine Automatically. If you choose the Nothing option, the session will need to be manually started.

Saving the State of a Guest Session

In Windows Server 2008 R2 SP1 Hyper-V, there are two concepts for saving guest images: snapshots and a saved state. At any time, an administrator can select a guest session and choose Action, Save State. This Save State function is similar to a Hibernate mode on a desktop client system. It saves the image into a file with the option of bringing the saved state image file back to the state the image was in prior to being saved.

Using Snapshots of Guest Operating System Sessions

A highly versatile function in Windows Server 2008 R2 SP1 Hyper-V is the option to create a snapshot of a guest session. A snapshot in Windows Hyper-V uses Microsoft Volume Shadow Copy Service (VSS) technology that captures an image of a file on a server—in this case, the file is the VHD image of the virtual server itself. At any future point in time, the snapshot can be used for recovery. Many DBAs use snapshots to roll back changes after a test is complete and to maintain a pristine test environment for training end users and other DBAs.

Snapshots for Image Rollback

One common use of a guest image snapshot is to roll back an image to a previous state. This is frequently done with guest images used for demonstration purposes, for test labs where a scenario is tested to see the results and compare them with identical tests of other scenarios, or for the purpose of preparing for a software upgrade or migration.

For the case of a guest image used for demonstration purposes, users might run through a demo of a software program where they add information, delete information, make software changes, or otherwise modify information in the software on the guest image. With a snapshot, rather than having to go back and delete the changes, or rebuild the image from scratch to do the demo again, a user can roll the image back to the snapshot that was available before the changes were made to the image.

Image rollback has been successfully used for training purposes where an employee runs through a process and then rolls back the image to run through the same process again, repeating the process on the same base image but without previous installations or configurations.

In network infrastructures, a snapshot is helpful when an organization applies a patch or update to a server, or a software upgrade is performed and problems occur; the administrator can roll the image back to the point prior to the start of the upgrade or migration.

Snapshots for Guest Session Server Fault Tolerance

Snapshots are commonly used in business environments for the purpose of fault tolerance or disaster recovery. A well-timed snapshot right before a system failure can help an organization roll the server back to the point right before the server failed or a problem occurred. Rather than waiting hours to restore a server from tape, the activation of a snapshot image is nothing more than choosing the snapshot and selecting to start the guest image. When the guest image starts up, it is in the state that the image was in at the time the snapshot was created.

Creating a Snapshot of a Guest Image

Snapshots are very easy to create. To create a snapshot, do the following:

1. From the Server Manager console or from the Hyper-V MMC snap-in, click to select the guest session for which you want to create a snapshot.

2. Right-click the guest session name and choose Snapshot. A snapshot of the image will immediately be taken of the guest image, and the snapshot will show up in the Snapshots pane, as shown in Figure 19.10.

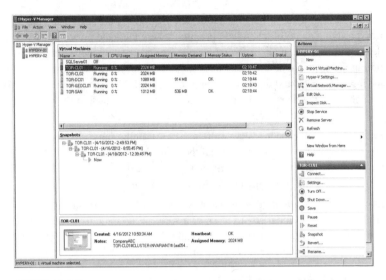

FIGURE 19.10
Viewing snapshots of a guest server.

Rolling Back a Guest Image to a Previous Snapshot Image

The term used in Windows Server 2008 R2 SP1 Hyper-V to roll back an image is called *applying* a snapshot to an existing image. When an image is rolled back, the image that is currently running has the snapshot information applied to the image, thus bringing the image back to an earlier configuration state. To apply a snapshot, do the following:

1. From the Server Manager console or from the Hyper-V MMC snap-in, click the snapshot to which you want to revert the running guest image.

2. Right-click the snapshot image and choose Apply. The configuration state of the image will immediately be reverted to the state of the image when the snapshot was taken.

> **Note**
>
> By default, the name of the snapshot image takes on the date and time the image was created. For example, if the image was called "Windows Server 2008 R2 SP1 IIS," an image taken on April 26, 2012 at 6:19 a.m. would show up as "Windows Server 2008 R2 SP1 IIS-20080426-061900."

Reverting a Snapshot Session

When working with snapshots, if you create a snapshot of a session and then apply an older session snapshot to the current session, to effectively undo the rollback, choose Action, Revert to bring the server back to the state it was in before the rollback occurred.

Optimizing SQL Server 2012 for Private Cloud

As mentioned earlier, one of the main goals affiliated with deploying private clouds is a reduction in the total cost of ownership (TCO) affiliated with an organization's capital and operational investments, while simultaneously ensuring that the organization's compute model such as computers, processors, memory, network, and storage resources are fully utilized and optimized. Here's how you can optimize a Microsoft Private Cloud for SQL Server.

Resource Pooling

Pooling resources in the private cloud can reduce hardware costs and data center space. The key steps affiliated with pooling SQL Server resources are discovering all the SQL Server instances and databases within the physical infrastructure, conducting capacity planning, and moving the appropriate SQL Server instances and databases to the private cloud. As mentioned earlier, use the Microsoft Assessment and Planning (MAP) Toolkit to identify the SQL Server instances and databases within your physical infrastructure.

After you determine which SQL Server instances and databases to move to the private cloud, you can use SC VMM's tools to convert SQL Server physical servers to virtual servers that will reside in the private cloud. Alternatively, you can use native tools within SQL Server such as Copy Database Wizard or Attach and Detach or Backup and Restore to migrate the databases from the physical servers to the private cloud.

Elasticity and Scalability

Deploying SQL Server in a private cloud can improve an organization's agility and scalability because more databases can be efficiently hosted on a single solution. The strategies for achieving elasticity and scalability for SQL Server databases in a Microsoft Private Cloud include the following:

- Load balancing SQL Server VMs among Hyper-V hosts with VMM.
- Scaling out private cloud resources by adding up to 16 Hyper-V hosts within a single private cloud cluster deployment; the 16-host

limit within a cluster is based on Windows Server 2008 R2. This will change with Windows Server 2012.

■ Scaling up by first installing the maximum amount of processors and memory within each Hyper-V host and then using Hyper-V's Dynamic Memory to increase SQL Server VM density.

High Availability

The private cloud offers high availability for mission-critical SQL Server workloads by offering Live Migration and guest failover clustering capabilities. Live Migration can be used to move running SQL Server VMs from one Hyper-V host to another without service disruption or downtime. You can use guest failover clustering if additional protection is required from unplanned downtime. A guest failover cluster is simply a SQL Server failover cluster. However, each node affiliated with the SQL Server failover cluster is virtualized within the private cloud.

With SQL Server 2012, many organizations are using AlwaysOn Availability Groups to provide both high availability and disaster recovery for databases running on instances of SQL Server 2012 within the Microsoft Private Cloud. You can also leverage AlwaysOn Failover Clustering to create a multi-subnet guest cluster between two data centers.

Self-Service Provisioning and Rapid Deployments

Windows Server 2008 R2, SQL Server 2012, and SQL Server 2008 R2 offer support for the Sysprep tool. You can use Sysprep to create SQL Server VM templates and store them in the VMM library.

Alternatively, you use the Self-Service Portal workflow interface to rapidly provision VMs. For example, suppose you need to deploy a new SQL Server instance that will support a new application. By placing a self-service request on the portal, you can choose a SQL Server instance that meets your needs from a predefined list of configurations. The SQL Server VM is deployed in the Microsoft Private Cloud within minutes after the request is approved by the person who manages the cloud. Moreover, you can include how long the VM will be needed in the self-service request. The Microsoft Private Cloud solution will then automatically decommission the VM after it's no longer needed and reclaim the private cloud resources.

Metering and Usage Reports

By using the metering and usage reports associated with System Center, you can track resource usage and charge-back costs. You can even use the information in the reports to assign a cost for the consumption of SQL Server VMs within the Microsoft Private Cloud.

Private Cloud Appliances for SQL Server

The next evolution in private cloud solutions for SQL Server is Private Cloud Appliances. Some organizations might not want to build their own private cloud solution using the Microsoft Private Cloud reference architecture because they don't have the appropriate hardware or in-house technical experience. These organizations can purchase a preconfigured Microsoft Private Cloud Appliance from a Microsoft vendor. For example, the SQL Server Database and Consolidation Appliance from HP is available in half rack, full rack, and multi rack configurations. The full rack configuration has 192 processor cores, 2TB RAM, 396 disk drives, 57TB raw disk space, 25TB formatted disk space, and 60,000 random 8KB IOPS at 60% read, 40% write. The full rack is able to run up to 1,000 workloads.

Summary

As you can see, there are tremendous benefits for consolidating SQL Server on physical hardware or by means of virtualization. In addition, as the trend continues in the industry, private cloud deployments are a great way to consolidate SQL Server because they not only provide the virtualization layer, they also offer application management, service delivery, automation, and infrastructure management.

Many DBAs and organizations believe that SQL Server is not a good candidate to virtualize because the workload is typically I/O intensive. However, with Windows Server and the hardware associated with today's servers, it is possible to virtualize even the heaviest SQL Server workload.

When consolidating and virtualizing SQL Server instances, it is possible to place all databases on one guest operating system, or one guest session can host many SQL Server instances. Again, the number of sessions and instances supported is based on the hardware selected for the host system and workloads associated with each SQL Server database and instance to be virtualized.

Best Practices

The following are best practices from this chapter:

- Consolidate and virtualize SQL Server systems to centralize data management and to reduce hardware costs.

■ Plan for the number of virtual SQL Server guest sessions you will have on a server to properly size the host system with respect to memory, processor, and disk space requirements. Leverage the MAP solution accelerator to assist in the planning efforts.

■ Do *not* virtualize for the sake of virtualizing. For example, if you are planning to virtualize a SQL Server system that may consume all the host system's resources, and no other guest sessions can be created, this type of server is not an ideal candidate to virtualize.

■ Deploy SQL Server within a private cloud and leverage the private cloud benefits, such as pooled resources, self-service, elasticity, and usage-based reports.

■ Use Virtual Machine Manager, Operations Manager, Configuration Manager, and Data Protection Manager for private cloud infrastructure management.

■ Leverage Orchestrator and Service Manager for service delivery and automation.

■ Leverage service templates and sysprep for SQL Server rapid deployment.

■ Save on SQL Server licensing by leveraging the SQL Server Enterprise Edition and virtualizing as many SQL Server systems on one physical host as possible.

■ Leverage Resource Governor to manage SQL Server performance, resources, workloads, and priorities among virtualized SQL Server sessions.

■ Virtualize SQL Server components that are not resource intensive, such as Integration Services and Reporting Services.

■ Leverage a SAN and spread SQL Server sessions and resources across multiple spindles for maximum I/O performance.

■ For Microsoft Windows guest sessions, install the Windows add-in components to improve the use and operation of the guest session.

■ Leverage the Hyper-V performance counters to monitor resource utilization.

■ After installing the guest session and its associated applications, confirm whether the memory of the guest session is enough and adjust the memory of the guest session accordingly to optimize the performance of the guest session. Otherwise, use the Dynamic Memory feature in Hyper-V.

- Achieve high availability with the Live Migration feature in Hyper-V or use native AlwaysOn technologies such as FCI or Availability Groups in conjunction with the guest operating system.

- Allocate enough disk space to perform snapshots of images so that the disk subsystem can handle both the required guest image and the associated snapshots of the guest session.

- Leverage pass-through disks or fixed VHDs for best performance for storage.

- Consider using snapshots before applying major patches, updates, or upgrades to an image session to allow for a rollback to the original image.

- Have the installation media and license keys needed for the installation of the guest operating system handy when you are about to install the guest operating system session.

- Apply all patches and updates on guest sessions soon after installing the guest operating system, just as you would for the installation of updates on physical systems.

Index

Number

3DES, 430

A

access credentials for HSM, 445

account lockout policies, 397

actions, defined, 719

Active Directory, role-based access, 391

Active Secondaries, 636

active secondary replicas, 488

Activity Monitor

    performance dashboard, 731-733

    process monitoring, 711-712

adding

    configurations, enhancing packages, 208-211

    counters with Performance Monitor, 772-773

    databases from availability groups, 511-512

    error handling, enhancing packages, 207-208

    failsafe operators, 767

    features to SQL Server 2012 installations, 62

    logging enhancing packages, 204-205

    maintenance tasks, enhancing packages, 211

memory to guest sessions,
893-897

nodes to existing peer-to-peer
replication topology, 667

operators, 767

processors to guest sessions,
893-897

replicas from availability groups,
510-511

storage to clusters (Windows
Server 2008 R2), 581

administering

database files, 152-153

Database Properties dialog box,
98-99

Change Tracking page, 113

Compatibility Level, 107

Containment, 108

containment type, 108

Extended Permissions
page, 113

Filegroups page, 103-104

Files page, 100-103

FILESTREAM, 109

General page, 99

Mirroring page, 114

miscellaneous options,
110-111

Options page, 104

Permissions page, 113

recovery models, 105-106

recovery options, 111

Service Broker options, 111

state options, 112

Transaction Log Shipping
page, 114

Database Properties Files
page, 153

indexes, 247

clustered indexes, creating,
259-262

columnstore indexes, creating,
263-264

nonclustered indexes, creating, 263

SSMS, 255-256

SSMS, Extended Properties
page, 259

SSMS, Filter page, 259

SSMS, Options page, 257-258

SSMS, Storage page, 258

Transact-SQL, 247-251

Transact-SQL. See Transact-
SQL

partitions, 164-165

Create Partition wizard,
165-167

enhancements, 167-168

partition switching, 168-170

sliding window partitions,
170-172

properties, 68-70

SQL Server Properties dialog
box. See SQL Server
Properties dialog box

Replication folder, 96

Security folder, 92

Server Objects folder, 92-95

SQL Server Agent, 119

Alerts and Operators
folder, 123

Error Logs folder, 123

Jobs folder, 121-122

properties, 119-120

Proxies folder, 123

SQL Server Database Engine
folders, 87

AlwaysOn High Availability, 96

Databases folder, 88-91

Integration Services Catalogs folder, 98

Management folder, 96-98

Replication folder, 96

Security folder, 92

Sever Objects folder, 92-95

SQL Server security, 404

application roles, 417-418

database role administration, 413-414

database user administration, 411-413

security schema administration, 416-417

server endpoint administration, 418-421

server login administration, 405-411

server role administration, 414-416

storage, 140-141

data file initialization, 150

database files. See database files

filegroups, 155-158

shrinking databases, files, and I/O performance, 150-154

Administrative console, Hyper-V, 886

launching, 886-888

ADO.NET destinations, 185

ADO.NET sources, 185

Advanced page

SQL Server Agent, 120

SQL Server Properties dialog box, 83-86

AES, 15, 430

Aggregate transform, 186

Alert System page, SQL Server Agent, 120

alerts

assigning to operators, 830

configuring for policy failures, 828-830

defining, 767-768

SQL Agent alerting, 768

Alerts and Operators folder, SQL Server Agent, 123

algorithms (encryption), 434

Allow Remote Connections to This Server, 80

Allow Triggers to Fire Others, 84

ALTER DATABASE command, 53

ALTER INDEX, 270

ALTER LOGIN statement, 399

ALTER SCHEMA statement, 403

ALTER TABLE...SWITCH statement, 169

alternatives, AlwaysOn Failover Cluster instances, 534-535

AlwaysOn versus standalone installation, 26

AlwaysOn Availability Groups, 68, 588

backing up, 520

backups from multiple secondaries, 284

combining with replication, 639

conducting failovers with SSMS, 515-516

conducting forced failovers with SSMS, 517-518

connecting availability group listeners and managing read-only connectivity, 518-519

database mirroring, 598

implementing, 490-491

enabling Groups feature, 496-497

installing instances on each node, 495-496

New Availability Group Wizard,
497-504

Transact-SQL, 504-508

Windows Server 2008
R2, 491

Windows Server 2008 R2
failover cluster, 493-495

leveraging, 489-490

managing, 509

adding databases, 511-512

adding replicas, 510-511

changing properties, 512

manually failing, 514-515

removing databases, 512

removing replicas, 509-510

suspending movement,
513-514

monitoring

Dashboard, 520

performance, 521-523

system views, 523-525

Systems Center Operations
Manager, 525

overview, 484

quorum selection, 508-509

AlwaysOn Backup Preference
page, 326

AlwaysOn Dashboard, 488

AlwaysOn Failover Cluster Instances
(FCI), 68

alternatives, 534-535

cluster aware, 536

combining with other high-availability alternatives, 536-537

determining when to
implement, 529

managing

failback policies, 577

failover policies, 576-577

failure condition property
settings, 578

new features, 528-529

Node Majority Quorum model,
537-540

overview, 527-528

prerequisites, 532-533

scalability metrics, 535

shared storage, 541-542

Fiber Channel storage
arrays, 541

ISCSI storage, 542-543

Multipath I/O, 543

SAS serial attached SCSI
storage arrays, 541

terminology, 530-532

Windows Server 2008 R2 Failover
Cluster Quorum models, 537

AlwaysOn High Availability, 96

AlwaysOn Replica Priority, 284

AlwaysOn Replica Priority for
backups, 324-325

Analysis Services, 28

analyzing

query execution, 714-716

workloads, 706-707

application failovers, initiating, 574

application roles, managing, 417-418

applications

monitoring, Task Manager
(Windows Server 008 R2), 734

troubleshooting and
optimization, 714

cursor usage, 716

deadlock detection, 716-717

Query Editor, 714-716

Applications tab, Task Manager, 734

applying

recommendations from Database
Engine Tuning Advisor, 710-711

Resource Governor templates, 854-855

articles, 623

asymmetric keys, 433

asynchronous, 592

asynchronous commit mode, 487

attack surfaces, hardening and reducing on SQL Server instances, 350

attacks

inference attacks, 439-441

man-in-the-middle attacks, 456

Audit components, 360-361

audit destinations, 360

audit files, viewing security events (Transact-SQL), 372

audit logs, viewing, 364

audit specifications, dropping, 372

auditing SQL Server 202 implementation, new features, 336-337

auditing strategies, leveraging, 357

configuring security logs, 357

enhanced auditing functionality, 358

security logs, 357

audits

dropping, 372

managing Windows Server 2008 R2 security logs as audit targets, 370-371

authentication, 337

configuring SQL Server 2012 authentication modes, 339

contained database authentication, 421

connecting to databases with contained users, 425

creating contained users, 424-425

enabling, 421-422

enabling partial containment within databases, 423-424

enforcing or changing strong passwords, 341

hardened authentication, 338-339

mixed mode authentication, 338

SA accounts, disabling and renaming, 342-343

server authentication, 77

server login, 390

SQL Server Authentication mode, 340-341

Windows Authentication mode, 337-338

authenticators, 441-443

BitLocker, 468

authorization, new features, 383-385

Autogrowth, 102

configuring for database files, 149

data files, 148-149

automatic failover, 592

high safety, 609

automatic failovers, configuring database mirroring, 601-606

Automatically Create a Subdirectory option, 790

automating

backups with maintenance plans, 308, 311-314

installation of SQL Server 2012 using configuration files, 38

availability databases, 486

availability group databases, monitoring, 524

availability group listeners, 487

connecting, 518-519

monitoring, 525

availability groups, 483-485, 488

  monitoring, 523

  prerequisites, 488-489

Availability Groups Dashboard, monitoring, 520

Availability Groups Monitoring tool, 521

availability modes, 486-488

availability replicas, 486

  monitoring, 524

avoiding losing permissions, subscriptions, 670

B

Back Up Database Task, 789-791

backing up

  availability groups, 520

  encryption keys, 443-444

  full-text catalogs, 326

  large mission-critical databases, 315-316

  servers, upgrading to SQL Server 2012, 41

backing up and recovering (Database Engine), 289

  backing up examples with SQL Server Management Studio, 301-314

  database files, 289

  FILESTREAM files, 290

  full database recovery, 316-324

  recovery models, 291-293

  SQL Server backup methods, 294-301

  storage architecture, 289

  transaction log files, 290

backup and recovery plans, considerations when creating, 286-287

Backup and Restore

  Database Settings page, 82

  replication, 636

backup compression, 287-288

backup devices, Server Objects folder, 93

backups

  AlwaysOn Availability Groups, 284

  AlwaysOn Replica Priority, 284, 324-325

  automating with maintenance plans, 308, 311-314

  copy-only backup, 299

  database backup encryption, 289

  differential backups, 295

    SSMS, 306

  differential partial backup, 299

  file and filegroup backup, 297

  full backups, 295

    SSMS, 302-305

  importance of, 285

  mirrored backup, 300-301

  partial backup, 298

  transaction log backups, 296-297

    SSMS, 307-308

batch mode processing, indexes, 237

BCP (Bulk Copy Program), 636

Best Practice Analyzer (BPA) tool, 349

best practices

  encryption, 478-479

  performance tuning and troubleshooting, 726-727

  Policy-Based Management, 836-837

  for Resource Governor, 868

bidirectional replication, 624

bidirectional transactional replication, 627

binary, creating certificates from, 430

BitLocker Drive Encryption, 465-466

   components, 466-467

     authenticators, 468

     data volumes, 467

     configuring system partitions, 469-470

     disabling, 477

     EFS versus, 466

     enabling, 472-477

     hardware requirements, 468

     installing, 470-472

     recovery password, 477

BLOB storage, designing for, 158-159

   FILESTREAM data, 159-163

Blocked Process Threshold, 84

blocking DMVs, 714

BPA (Best Practice Analyzer) tool, 349

broadcasting information, hiding SQL Server instances from, 346-347

BUILTIN\Administrators Windows group, removing (Transact-SQL), 373

Bulk Copy Program (BCP), 636

Bulk Copy utility, 224

Bulk Insert Task, 223

bulk-logged recovery models, 105, 291

Business Intelligence, 14

Business Intelligence Studio, 14

C

CA (certificate authority), 434

cache, DMVs, 713

calculating disk space requirements, indexes, 245-247

capacity planning, 148

capturing

   performance counters from multiple SQL Server instances, 755-756

   workloads, 703-706

catalog views, Extended Events, 723

categories

   creating, 824-825

   explained, 815

Category Selection dialog, 824

CD/DVD image files, mounting, 896

Central Management Servers

   creating, 817-818

   explained, 817

   importing and evaluating policies to, 818

   registering SQL Server instances in, 818

Central Publisher topology, 632

Central Subscriber topology, 632

certificate authority (CA), 434

certificate servers, setting up, 456-458

certificates, 434

   creating, 436-437

   creating from binary, 430

   key length, 430

   self-signed certificates, 456

   server certificates, creating, 448

   third-party certificates, 456-457

     client-based encryption, 463-464

     configuring client for, 462-463

     configuring SQL Server for, 461-462

     provisioning, 458-461

     setting up certificate server, 456-458

Change Tracking page, Database Properties dialog box, 113

changing

database mirroring configuration/operating mode, 610-611

disk settings for guest sessions, 895

properties, availability groups, 512

service accounts with SQL Server Configuration Manager, 354

characteristics of indexes, 238

clustered indexes, 239

column constraints, 238

computed columns, 238-239

filtered indexes, 241

nonclustered columnstore indexes, 240-241

nonclustered indexes, 239-240

spatial indexes, 242

XML indexes, 241

Check Database Integrity Task, 780

choosing

new installation, upgrade, or transition, 23-25

SQL Server editions, 18-20

Windows operating system versions and editions, 20-25

classifications, explained, 842

classifier functions

creating, 846-848

troubleshooting, 848-850

client authentication, 390

client connections, database mirroring, 612-614

Client Tools Backward Compatibility, 30

Client Tools Connectivity, 30

Client Tools SDK, 30

client-based encryption, 463-464

clients, configuring for third-party certificates, 462-463

clouds, moving data to, 224

Windows Azure SQL Database, 224-227

cluster aware, AlwaysOn Failover Cluster Instances, 536

cluster drive dependencies, Windows Server 2008 R2, 582

Cluster Network Configuration page, 566

cluster nodes

managing preferred owners, 575-576

pausing and resuming, 580

cluster quorum configuration, Windows Server 2008 R2, 583

Cluster Resource Group page, 566

cluster resources, 531

clustered indexes, 231-232

characteristics of, 239

choosing, 262

creating, 259-262

design and strategies, 242-243

primary keys, 233

clusters

AlwaysOn Failover Cluster. See AlwaysOn Failover Cluster Instances

failover clusters, managing from a SQL Server 2012 perspective, 574

Hyper-V failover cluster, 886

multi-subnet SQL Server 2012 failover clusters. See multi-subnet SQL Server 2012 failover cluster

Node Majority clusters, 537

shared storage for failover clusters, 539

single-instance SQL Server 2012 failover clusters. See single-instance SQL Server 2012 failover clusters

Collation setting, Database Properties Options page, 104

collection set logs, 755

column constraints, indexes, 238

column encryption, 432, 437
    algorithms, 434
    asymmetric keys, 433
    certificates, 434
    Database Master Key, 433
    encryption hierarchy, 432
    Service Master Key, 433
    symmetric keys, 433
    TDE (Transparent Data Encryption) versus, 451

column-level tracking, conflicts, 624

columns
    computed columns, indexes, 238-239
    constraints, indexes, 238
    include columns, nonclustered indexes, 240

columnstore indexes, 235-237
    creating, 263-264
    creating with Transact-SQL, 252
    design and strategies, 244

combining
    AlwaysOn Failover Cluster instances with other high-availability alternatives, 536-537
    replication
        with AlwaysOn Availability Groups, 639
        with database mirroring, 638
        with failover clustering, 639
        with log shipping, 638

command prompt, installing
    SQL Server 2012 in Windows Server Core, 58
    BitLocker, 472

common sources, data flow, 185

communication
    endpoints and, 387-389
    network communications. See network communications

Compatibility Level, Database Properties dialog box, 107

compatibility tests, SQL Server Upgrade Advisor, 43-46

Complete the Wizard page, 313

components
    of guest sessions, 889
    replication, 630

Compress Backup, 82

computed columns, indexes, 238-239

Computer Management, SQL Server Configuration Manager settings, 60-62

Conditional Split item, 202

conditions
    creating, 819-821
    explained, 814

configuration files, automating installation, 38

configuration mode, database mirroring, 610-611

configuration settings, changing, 114-115

configurations, adding (enhancing packages), 208-211

Configure Resource Governor template, 855

configuring
    alerts for policy failures, 828-830
    autogrowth on database files, 149
    clients for third-party certificates, 462-463
    Database Mail, 763-765
    database mirroring, 593-594
        with high safety and automatic failovers, 601-606

database mirroring prerequisites, 599-600

distributors for replication, 640-645, 659

DMVs, 712

indexes

Database Engine Tuning Advisor, 273-275

determining when to rebuild or reorganize indexes, 271-272

fill factor, 269-271

finding unused indexes with Database Engine, 276-278

fragmentation considerations, 268-269

index statistics, 268

recommending indexes with system information, 276

sorting indexes in tempdb, 272

MDW, 746-748

peer-to-peer publication on first node, 661-662

peer-to-peer topology, 663-666

peer-to-peer transactional replication, 659-661

security logs, 357

server-based encryption, 453-454

snapshot or transactional replication publications, 645-652

snapshot replication, 639-640

SQL Server 2012

Authentication modes, 339

for third-party certificates, 461-462

subscriptions for AdventureWorks 2012 database, 652-656

system partitions for BitLocker Drive Encryption, 469-470

tempdb databases, 89-91

Windows Server Core installation, 55-57

Windows Server Core with SCONFIG, 56

Conflict Viewer, 630

conflicts, 624

connecting

availability group listeners, 518-519

to databases with contained users, 425

virtual server systems, 887

connection managers, walkthrough, 196-197

connection types, 188

connections

Connections page, 80

network connections. See network communications

packages, 187-188

Connections page

SQL Server Agent, 121

SQL Server Properties dialog box, 79-80

CONNECT permission, 389

consolidated multitenant environments, Resource Governor in, 844

consolidation, 870

database consolidation, 870-871

instance consolidation, 871

virtualization. See virtualization

contained database authentication, 421

connecting to databases with contained users, 425

creating contained users, 424-425

enabling, 421-422

partial containment within databases, 423-424

contained users
  connecting to databases, 425
  creating, 424-425
Containment Database, Advanced
  page, 84
Containment, Database Properties
  dialog box, 108
containment type, Database
  Properties dialog box, 108
control flow
  packages, 184
  walkthrough, 192-194
control flow tasks, 185
Copy Database Wizard, 181,
  221-223, 636
copy-only backup, 299
counters, adding with Performance
  Monitor, 772-773. See also
  performance counters
CPU speed, RAM versus, 685
CREATE INDEX, 247, 249
CREATE LOGIN statement, 399
Create New Condition dialog
  box, 820
Create New Policy dialog box,
  821-823
Create Partition wizard, 165-167
credentials for HSM access, 445
cryptographic providers, creating, 445
cryptography. See encryption
Cursor Threshold, 84
cursors
  application troubleshooting and
    optimization, 716
  Database Properties Options
    page, 109

D

DAC (Dedicated Administrator
  Connection), 96, 387-388
daily routine maintenance tasks, 805
data
  moving to clouds, 224
    Windows Azure SQL Database,
      224-227
  transferring (SSIS), 221
    Bulk Insert Task, 223
    Copy Database Wizard,
      221-223
  transforming, enhancing pack-
    ages, 199-204
Data Collection, 97
data collection
  configuring MDW, 746-748
  Performance studio, 745
  reports, running, 757
  setting up, 749
data collection set properties,
  managing, 753
  Description page, 755
  General page, 753-754
  Uploads page, 754
data collection sets, viewing
  logs, 755
Data Collector, 744
  managing data collection set
    properties, 753-755
  system data collection sets,
    750-752
Data Collector Set, Reliability and
  Performance Monitor, 775
data collectors, 745
data compression, 172-173
  Data Compression Wizard,
    173-174
  Transact-SQL, 174-175

Data Compression Wizard, 173-174

data definition language. *See* DDL (data definition language)

data explosion, 283

data files

autogrowth and I/O performance, 148-149

Database Properties Filegroups page, 158

filegroups, 157-158

initializing, 150

placing onto disks, 142-145

sizing multiple, 146-147

utilizing multiple, 145-146

data flow

packages, 185-187

transformation components, 187

walkthrough, 194-196

data flow path, 185

Data Flow Task, 221

Data Protection Manager (DPM), 877

Data Quality Client, 30

Data Quality Services (DQS), 14, 28

Data Recovery Advisor, 283-284

data volumes, 467

enabling BitLocker, 476-477

Data-tier Applications (DAC), 96

database administrator. *See* DBA (database administrator)

Database Audit Specification object, 361

database audit specifications, creating with Transact-SQL, 369-370

database backup encryption, 289

database compatibility levels, choosing after upgrades, 52

database consolidation, 870-871

Database Default Locations, 83

Database Encryption Key, creating, 449-450

Database Engine, 13

AlwaysOn Replica Priority for backups, 324-325

backing up and recovering, 289

backing up examples with SQL Server Management Studio, 301-314

database files, 289

FILESTREAM files, 290

full database recovery, 316-324

recovery models, 291-293

SQL Server backup methods, 294-301

storage architecture, 289

transaction log files, 290

backing up and recovering full-text catalogs, 326

database snapshots, 327-328

dropping, 329

SSMS, 328

Transact-SQL, 328

deprecated elements, 15

finding unused indexes, 276-278

management tasks

changing SQL Server configuration settings, 114-115

informational reports, 115-116

PowerShell, 117

renaming databases, 119

scripting database objects, 117

taking SQL Server databases offline, 118

transferring SQL Server data, 118

new features, 68

subfeatures, installing, 31

upgrading to SQL Server 2012, 40

  backing up servers, 41

  considerations for, 46-47

  creating SQL Server Feature discovery report, 41

  installing SQL Server Upgrade Advisor, 43

  Microsoft Assessment and Planning (MAP) Toolkit for SQL Server, 41

  running SQL Server Upgrade Advisor, 42-46

  verifying system compatibility, 42

Database Engine Configuration page, 37, 560

Database Engine Services, 28

database engine troubleshooting and optimization, 686-688

Database Engine Tuning Advisor, 702-703, 777

  analyzing workloads, 706-707

  applying recommendations, 710-711

  capturing workloads, 703-706

  indexes, 273-275

  reviewing results, 707-709

database files

  administering, 152-153

  configuring autogrowth, 149

  Database Engine, 289

  designing and administering, 141-147

    autogrowth and I/O performance, 148-149

    configuring autogrowth, 149

  increasing size of, 154

  managing, 100

Database Mail, 98

  configuring, 763-765

  validating configuration, 766

Database Maintenance Plan Wizard, creating maintenance plans, 792-798

Database Master Key, 433

  backing up, 444

  creating, 436, 448

database mirroring, 587

  client connections and redirect, 612-614

  combining with replication, 638

  configuration/operating modes, 593-594, 610-611

  database snapshots, 598-599

  DBAs, 590

  high performance, 610

  high safety, 610

  high-availability alternatives, 597

    AlwaysOn Availability Groups, 598

    FCI (Failover Cluster Instances), 597

    log shipping, 598

    replication, 598

  monitoring system catalogs, 618

  overview, 588-589

  performance, monitoring, 617-618

  prerequisites, 594

  replication, 637

  terminology, 591-592

  when to use, 595

  witness server placement, 596

database mirroring endpoint, 593

Database Mirroring Log Stream Compression, 590

Database Mirroring Monitoring tool, 614-615

  Status tab, 615-616

  Warnings tab, 616

Database Mirroring Performance Object, 617

database mirroring sessions
  implementing, 599
    configuring prerequisites, 599-600
    configuring with high safety and automatic failover, 601-606
  managing, 607
    manually failing over database mirroring sessions, 608-609
    pausing and resuming, 607-608
  removing, 611-612

database objects, scripting Database Engine, 117

Database Properties, Filegroups page, 158

Database Properties dialog box, administering, 98-99
  Change Tracking page, 113
  Compatibility Level, 107
  Containment, 108
  containment type, 108
  Extended Permissions page, 113
  Filegroups page, 103-104
  Files page, 100, 102-103
  FILESTREAM, 109
  General page, 99
  Mirroring page, 114
  miscellaneous options, 110-111
  Options page, 104
  Permissions page, 113
  recovery models, 105-106
  recovery options, 111
  Service Broker options, 111
  state options, 112
  Transaction Log Shipping page, 114

Database Properties Files page, administering, 153

Database Properties Option page, enabling FILESTREAM, 160

Database Properties Options page, 108
  cursor, 109
  miscellaneous, 110

Database Recovery Advisor, 318

Database Recovery Model, switching
  with SSMS, 293
  with Transact-SQL, 107, 293

database recovery options, 317

database role administration, 413-414

database schemas, 394

Database Settings page, SQL Server Properties dialog box, 81-83

database snapshots, 327-328
  database mirroring, 598-599
  dropping, 329
  SSMS, 328
  Transact-SQL, reverting to, 328

Database Snapshots subfolder, administering, 91

Database subfolder, administering, 91

database user administration, 411-413

database users, 389-391

databases
  adding to availability groups, 511-512
  backing up
    Database Engine, 118
    large mission-critical databases, 315-316
  connecting to with contained users, 425

encryption of data, 435
  authenticators, 441-443
  backing up keys, 443-444
  column encryption, 437
  creating certificate, 436-437
  creating Database Master
    Key, 436
  creating test database,
    435-436
  decrypting data, 438-439
  inference attacks, 439-441
master databases, 301
model databases, 301
msdb databases, 302
removing from availability
  groups, 512
renaming, 119
restoring Database Engine, 118
shrinking, 150-154
suspending movement, availability
  groups, 513-514
tempdb databases, 302
troubleshooting and optimization,
  691-692
  Activity Monitor, 711-712
  correlating Perfmon and
    Profiler data, 699-702
  Database Engine Tuning
    Advisor, 702-711
  DMVs, 712-714
  SQL Server Profiler, 696
  SQL Server Profiler trace
    templates, 697-699
  wait statistics analysis,
    692-696
Databases folder, 88
  administering
    Database Snapshots
      subfolder, 91
    Database subfolder, 91

    System Databases
      subfolder, 89
DBAs (database administrator), 68
  database mirroring, 590
DDL (data definition language), 398
  managing
    logins, 399-400
    permissions, 403-404
    roles, 401-402
    schemas, 402-403
    users, 400-401
DDL statements, creating Extended
  Events, 720-723
deadlock detection, 716-717
debugging packages, 198
decrypting database data, 438-439
Dedicated Administrator Connection.
  See DAC
Default Backup Media Retention (In
  Days), 82
Default Full-Text Language, 85
Default Index Fill Factor, Database
  Settings page, 81
default system endpoints, 387
Define Rebuild Index Task, 779
deleting
  indexes, 264-265
  local publications, 669
  local subscriptions, 669
DENY statement, 403
dependency, 531
deploying packages, 212-213
  DontSaveSensitive, 217-218
  DTUTIL, 216
  EncryptAllWithUserKey, 218
  EncryptSensitiveWithUserKey,
    218
  manual deployment, 213-214
  package deployment utility,
    214-216

security, 216-217

storing packages, 212-213

deprecated elements, 15

Description page, data collection set, 755

design and strategies, indexes, 242

calculating disk space requirements, 245-247

clustered indexes, 242-243

columnstore indexes, 244

nonclustered indexes, 243

unique indexes, 244

designing

BLOB storage, 158-159

FILESTREAM data, 159-163

partitions, 164-165

Create Partition wizard, 165-167

enhancements, 167-168

partition switching, 168-170

sliding window partitions, 170-172

storage, 140-141

data file initialization, 150

database files. See database files

filegroups, 155-158

shrinking databases, files, and I/O performance, 150-154

destinations

data flow, 185

setting up, 202

Details pane, Job Activity Monitor, 742

determinism, 239

differential backup, 295

SSMS, 306

Differential Backup Tasks, 780

differential partial backup, 299

disabling

BitLocker Drive Encryption, 477

indexes, 264-265

publishing and distribution, 668

SA accounts, 342-343

TDE (Transparent Data Encryption), 451

disaster recovery, forced failovers, 609-610

disk controllers, 136-137

disk requirements for installation, 17

disk settings, changing for guest sessions, 895

disk space requirements, calculating for indexes, 245-247

disk storage for host servers, Hyper-V, 880

Disk Usage System Data collection set, 750

disks, 129

performance counters, 683-684

placing data files onto, 142-145

Distributed Replay Controller, 30

Distributed Transaction Coordinator (DTC), 98

distribution, disabling, 668

Distribution Agent, 629

Distributor Properties, managing, 668

distributors, 623

configuring for replication, 640-645, 659

DMV sys.dm_os_performance_counters, querying, 681

DMVs (dynamic management views), 712-714, 738

Extended Events, 723-724

monitoring, 738-740

monitoring Resource Governor with, 865-867

viewing in Object Explorer, 739

Domain User Account, 352

DontSaveSensitive, 217-218

downloading updates, 51

DPM (Data Protection Manager), 877

DQS (Data Quality Services), 14, 28

DQS Cleansing transformation, 180

DRAM, 138

drive encryption. See BitLocker Drive Encryption

dropping

audit specifications, 372

audits, 372

database snapshots, 329

DROPUSER statement, 401

DTC (Distributed Transaction Coordinator), 98, 532

installing as a SQL Server AlwaysOn failover cluster instances prerequisite, 553

DTEXEC, running packages, 220

DTUTIL, 216

dynamic management views. See DMVs (dynamic management views)

Dynamic Memory, 894

E

EFS (Encrypting File System), BitLocker versus, 466

EKM (Extensible Key Management), 444

advantages of, 446

creating cryptographic provider, 445

creating encryption keys, 446

creating HSM access credentials, 445

enabling, 444

elasticity, optimizing SQL Server 2012 for private clouds, 903

email, sending (enhancing packages), 206-207

email alerts

Database Mail, validating, 766

sending with Database Mail, 763-765

enabling

BitLocker Drive Encryption, 472-477

EKM (Extensible Key Management), 444

Resource Governor, 845-846

TDE (Transparent Data Encryption), 448-451

EncryptAllWithUserKey, 218

Encrypting File System (EFS), BitLocker versus, 466

encryption

best practices, 478-479

BitLocker Drive Encryption, 465-466

authenticators, 468

components, 466-467

configuring system partitions, 469-470

data volumes, 467

disabling, 477

EFS versus, 466

enabling, 472-477

hardware requirements, 468

installing, 470-472

recovery password, 477

column encryption, 432

algorithms, 434

asymmetric keys, 433

certificates, 434

Database Master Key, 433

encryption hierarchy, 432

Service Master Key, 433

symmetric keys, 433

of database data, 435
  authenticators, 441-443
  backing up keys, 443-444
  column encryption, 437
  creating certificate, 436-437
  creating Database Master
    Key, 436
  creating test database,
    435-436
  decrypting data, 438-439
  inference attacks, 439-441
EKM (Extensible Key
  Management), 444
  advantages of, 446
  creating cryptographic
    provider, 445
  creating encryption keys, 446
  creating HSM access
    credentials, 445
  enabling, 444
of network communications, 452
  configuring server-based
    encryption, 453-454
  reasons for needing, 452-453
  verifying server-based encryp-
    tion, 454-455
  new features, 430
  purpose of, 431-432
  self-signed certificates, 456
  SQL Server Management Studio,
    464-465
  TDE (Transparent Data
    Encryption), 446-447
  column encryption
    versus, 451
  creating Database Encryption
    Key, 449-450
  creating Database Master
    Key, 448
  creating server
    certificates, 448

disabling, 451
  enabling, 448-451
  encryption hierarchy, 447-448
third-party certificates, 456-457
  client-based encryption,
    463-464
  configuring client for, 462-463
  configuring SQL Server for,
    461-462
  provisioning, 458-461
  setting up certificate server,
    456-458
encryption hierarchy, 432
EncryptSensitiveWithUserKey, 218
Endpoint Security Wizard, 606
endpoints
  communication and, 387-389
  default system endpoints, 387
  server endpoint
    administration, 421
  Server Objects folder, 93
enhanced auditing functionality, 358
enhancements
  to FILESTREAM, 162-163
  partitions, 167-168
enhancing packages, 199
  adding
    configurations, 208-211
    error handling, 207-208
    logging, 204-205
    maintenance tasks, 211
  expressions, 205-206
  sending email, 206-207
  transforming data, 199-204
Enterprise Edition of SQL Server
  2012, indexing features, 278-279
error handling, adding (enhancing
  packages), 207-208
error logs, monitoring, 742-743

Error Logs folder, SQL Server Agent, 123

error numbers, creating alerts with, 829-830

establishing maintenance plans, 780

Back Up Database Task, 789-791

Check Database Integrity Task, 780

Execute SQL Server Agent Job Task, 789

History Cleanup Task, 788-789

Maintenance Cleanup Task, 791-792

Rebuild Index Task, 783-786

Reorganize Index Task, 783

Shrink Database Task, 781-782

Update Statistics Task, 786-788

ETL (Extraction, Transformation, Loading), 179

evaluating policies, 825-826

event handlers, packages, 188

events

defined, 719

Extended Events, 718-719

catalog views, 723

creating with DDL statements, 720-723

DMVs, 723-724

terminology, 719-720

user interface, 724-726

monitoring with SQL Server Audit, 359-360

Audit components, 360-361

SQL Server Audit Failed Logon Attempt example, 362-364

Execute Package Utility, 219

Execute SQL Server Agent Job Task, 789

ExecuteSQL function, 821

execution modes

On Change Log Only, 817

On Change Prevent, 816

On Demand, 815

On Schedule, 815

exporting policies, 827-828

expressions, enhancing packages, 205-206

Extended Events, 97, 718-719

catalog views, 723

creating with DDL statements, 720-723

DMVs, 723-724

terminology, 719-720

user interface, 724-726

Extended Permissions page, Database Properties dialog box, 113

Extended Properties page, SSMS (creating indexes), 259

Extensible Key Management (EKM), 444

advantages of, 446

creating cryptographic provider, 445

creating encryption keys, 446

creating HSM access credentials, 445

enabling, 444

F

facets, explained, 813-814

failback, 531

failback policies, managing, 577

failing manually, availability groups, 514-515

failover, 530

failover alternative, 487

Failover Cluster Instances (FCI). See AlwaysOn Failover Cluster Instances

Failover Cluster Management, 531, 574

failover clustering, combining with replication, 639

failover clusters

   managing from a SQL Server 2012 perspective, 574

   Windows Server 2008 R2

     adding additional nodes, 581

     adding storage, 581

     cluster drive dependencies, 582

     cluster quorum configuration, 583

     patch management, 580

     pausing and resuming cluster nodes, 580

failover policies, managing, 576-577

failovers

   conducting availability group failovers with SSMS, 515-516

   conducting forced availability group failovers with SSMS, 517-518

   forced failovers, disaster recovery, 609-610

failsafe operators, adding, 767

failure condition property settings, managing, 578

FC (Fibre Channel), 541

FCI (Failover Cluster Instances). See AlwaysOn Failover Cluster Instances

features, adding to existing SQL Server 2012 installation, 62

Fiber Channel storage arrays, 541

file and filegroup backup, 297

file system packages, 213

filegroups, 102, 155-157

   data files, 157-158

   Database Properties Filegroups page, 158

Filegroups page, Database Properties dialog box, 103-104

files, shrinking, 150-154

Files page, Database Properties dialog box, 100-103

FILESTREAM, 68, 109

   Advanced page, 84

   Database Properties dialog box, 109

   managing, 103

FILESTREAM data

   BLOB storage, 159-160

     enabling with Database Properties Option page, 160

     enabling with Server Properties Dialog Advanced page, 161

     enhancements, 162-163

   encryption, 447

   instance-level, 159

FILESTREAM Directory Name, 109

FILESTREAM files, Database Engine, 290

FILESTREAM Non-Transacted Access, 109

fill factor, indexes, 269-271

fill factor index option, 246

Filter page, SSMS (creating indexes), 259

filtered indexes, 234-235

   characteristics of, 241

   creating with Transact-SQL, 255

filtering unwanted traffic with firewalls, 374-379

firewalls

   filtering out unwanted traffic, 374-379

   Integrated Windows Firewall, 379

first node in single-instance SQL Server 2012 failover cluster, installing, 554-561

first nodes

configuring peer-to-peer publication, 661-662

installing in multiple-instance SQL Server 2012 failover clusters, 565-567

fixed database-level roles, 392

fixes, installing, 355-356

updating and patching SQL Server and the operating system, 356

forced failovers, disaster recovery, 609-610

fragmentation considerations, indexes, 268-269

full backup, 295

SSMS, 302-305

Full Backup Task, 780

full database recovery, 316-324

full edition with graphical user interface versus Server Core, 26

Full recovery models, 105, 291

full-text indexes, partition switching, 169

Full-Text and Semantic Extractions for Search, 28

full-text catalogs, backing up and recovering, 326

functions

classifier functions

creating, 846-848

troubleshooting, 848-850

ExecuteSQL, 821

G

General page

data collection set, 753-754

Database Properties dialog box, 99

SQL Server Agent, 120

SQL Server Properties dialog box, 70

generating

.INI files by launching setup.exe, 39

replication scripts, 669

geographically dispersed clusters, 535

GPT (GUID partition table) disk, 548

GRANT statements, 403

groups

managing preferred owners, 575-576

workload groups

creating, 852-854, 859-860

explained, 841-842

Groups feature, AlwaysOn Availability Groups, 496-497

guest failover cluster, 535

guest operating system sessions

installing, 889-893

snapshots, 900

creating snapshots of guest images, 901

image rollback, 900

reverting, 903

server fault tolerance, 901

guest sessions

adding or limiting memory and processors, 893-897

changing disk settings, 895

components, 889

configuration settings, modifying, 893-895

Hyper-V, launching, 898-900

modifying configurations, 897

saving, 900

H

hard disks, **129-131**

hardened authentication, **338-339**

hardening

attack surfaces on SQL Server instances, 350

recommendations for, 373

removing BUILTIN\ Administrators Windows group, 373

using firewalls to filter out unwanted traffic, 374-379

servers with Security Configuration Wizard in Windows Server 2008 R2, 348-349

service accounts, 350-351

isolation, 352

principle of least privilege, 351

SQL Server Services, 352-353

types of accounts, 352

SQL Server 2012 implementation, new features for, 336-337

SQL Server installation, 52

hardening techniques

Best Practice Analyzer (BPA) tool, 349

reducing SQL Server 2012 surface area, 343

SQL Server Configuration Manager tool, 344-345, 348

Windows Server Core, 348

hardware, platform troubleshooting and optimization, **680-681**

memory objects and counters, 681-682

network objects and counters, 682

page file objects and counters, 683

physical disk objects and counters, 683-684

processor objects and counters, 684-685

hardware requirements

BitLocker Drive Encryption, 468

verifying, 16

Hardware Security Modules (HSM), **444**

creating access credentials, 445

hashing algorithms, **430**

HBAs (host bus adapters), **136-137**

health checks (SQL Server), Policy-Based Management, **836**

heap structures, indexes, **231**

heartbeats, **530**

hiding SQL Server instances from broadcasting information, **346-347**

hierarchy, encryption hierarchy

column encryption, 432

TDE (Transparent Data Encryption), 447-448

high availability

database mirroring, 593

optimizing SQL Server 2012 for private clouds, 904

high performance, database mirroring, **593, 610**

high protection, database mirroring, **593**

high safety

automatic failover, 609

database mirroring, 610

configuring, 601-606

high-availability alternatives, database mirroring, **597**

AlwaysOn Availability Groups, 598

FCI (Failover Cluster Instances), 597

log shipping, 598

replication, 598

History Cleanup Task, 788-789

History page, SQL Server Agent, 121

history retention, 668

host bus adapters (HBAs), 136-137

host server settings, Hyper-V, 888

HSM (Hardware Security
Modules), 444

creating access credentials, 445

Hyper-V, 875, 878

Administrative console, 886

launching, 886-888

guest sessions, launching,
898-900

managing with Server Manager
tool, 886

MMC tool, 887

running other services on, 882

sizing Windows Server 2008 R2
SP1 Systems to support
virtualization, 878-880

snapshots, 882-883

virtualization considerations,
880-882

Hyper-V failover cluster, 886

Hyper-V server role, installing, 883

running server manager to add
the Hyper-V role, 884-886

Hyper-V Settings, 888

I

I/O

DMVs, 713

performance, data files, 148-149

segregating, 139-140

I/O performance

options, 154-155

shrinking, 150-154

image rollback, snapshots (guest
operating sessions), 900

implementing

AlwaysOn Availability Groups,
490-491

enabling Groups feature,
496-497

installing instances on each
node, 495-496

New Availability Group Wizard,
497-504

Transact-SQL, 504-508

Windows Server 2008
R2, 491

Windows Server 2008 R2
failover cluster, 493-495

database mirroring sessions, 599

configuring prerequisites,
599-600

configuring with high safety
and automatic failovers,
601-606

multiple-instance SQL Server
2012 failover clusters, 564-565

installing the first node,
565-567

installing the subsequent
nodes, 567

multi-subnet SQL Server 2012
failover cluster, 571-573

replication, 639

configuring distributors for
replication, 640-645

configuring peer-to-peer transactional replication, 659-661

configuring snapshot or transactional replication publications, 645-652

configuring snapshot replication, 639-640

tracer tokens, 658-659

single-instance SQL Server 2012
failover clusters, 544-545

creating Windows Server 2008
R2 failover cluster, 551-552

installing additional nodes, 561-564

installing the first node, 554-561

installing Windows Server 2008 R2 failover cluster, 549

preparing Windows Server 2008 R2 operating system for each node, 546

Import and Export Wizard, 181

importing

packages, SSMS, 214

policies, 827-828

to Change Management Servers, 818

include columns, nonclustered indexes, 240

increasing size of database files, 154

Index Creation Memory, 72

index maintenance, implementing, 266-267

index partitions, 165, 167

index statistics, 268

indexed views, 233-234

partition switching, 169

indexes

administering, 247

clustered indexes, creating, 259-262

columnstore indexes, creating, 263-264

nonclustered indexes, creating, 263

with SSMS, 255-256

with SSMS, Extended Properties page, 259

with SSMS, Filter page, 259

with SSMS, Options page, 257-258

with SSMS, Storage page, 258

Transact-SQL. *See* Transact-SQL

batch mode processing, 237

characteristics of, 238

clustered indexes, 239

column constraints, 238

computed columns, 238-239

filtered indexes, 241

nonclustered columnstore indexes, 240-241

nonclustered indexes, 239

nonclustered indexes, include columns, 240

spatial indexes, 242

XML indexes, 241

clustered indexes, 231-232

choosing, 262

columnstore indexes, 235-237

creating with Transact-SQL, 252

configuring

Database Engine Tuning Advisor, 273-275

determining when to rebuild or reorganize, 271-272

fill factor, 269-271

finding unused indexes with Database Engine, 276-278

fragmentation considerations, 268-269

index statistics, 268

recommending indexes with system information, 276

sorting indexes in tempdb, 272

deleting, 264-265

design and strategies, 242

calculating disk space requirements, 245-247

clustered indexes, 242-243

columnstore indexes, 244

nonclustered indexes, 243

unique indexes, 244

disabling, 264-265

DMVs, 712

enabling, 265-266

Enterprise Edition, 278-279

filtered indexes, 234-235

creating with
Transact-SQL, 255

how they work, 230-231

heap structures, 231

implementing index maintenance
and maintenance plans,
266-267

importance of, 230

indexed views, 233-234

new features, 229-230

non-clustered indexes, 233

partition switching, 169

rebuilding, 265-266, 271-272

recommending with system information, 276

relational indexes

creating with Transact-SQL,
247-249

modifying with Transact-SQL,
249-251

removing with
Transact-SQL, 251

reorganizing, 271-272

sorting in tempdb, 272

spatial indexes, 237

creating with Transact-SQL,
252-255

unused indexes, finding with
Database Engine, 276-278

XML indexes, 237

inference attacks, 439-441

informational reports, Database
Engine, 115-116

.INI files

generating by launching
setup.exe, 39

for use with setup.exe, 39-40

initializing data files, 150

Install Setup Files page, 555

installation wizard, 555

installations, managing, 62-63

installing

additional nodes in single-
instance SQL Server 2012
failover cluster, 561-564

BitLocker Drive Encryption,
470-472

with configuration files, automating, 38

Database Engine,
subfeatures, 31

determining which features to
install, 28-29

DTC as a SQL Server AlwaysOn
failover cluster instances
prerequisite, 553

first node in single-instance SQL
Server 2012 failover cluster,
554-561

first nodes in multiple-instance
SQL Server 2012 failover
clusters, 565-567

full edition with graphical user
interface or Server Core, 26

guest operating system sessions,
889-893

hardening SQL Server
installation, 52

Hyper-V server role, 883

running server manager to add
Hyper-V role, 884-886

instances on each node,
AlwaysOn Availability Groups,
495-496

minimum disk requirements, 17

new installation of SQL Server 2012, 31-38

nodes in multiple-instance SQL Server 2012 failover clusters, 567

physical versus virtual installation, 26

processor and memory system requirements, 16

service packs, 355-356

updating and patching SQL Server and the operating system, 356

side-by-side installations with previous versions, 27-28

single-instance versus multiple-instance installation, 27

software prerequisites, 18

SQL Server 2012, new installation features, 14-15

SQL Server 2012 on Windows Server Core, 57-59

via command prompt, 58

SQL Server Upgrade Advisor, 43

standalone installation versus AlwaysOn, 26

third-party certificates, 458-461

updates, 51

Utility Control Point, 758

Windows Server 2008 R2 failover cluster, 549

Windows Server 2008 R2 Server Core, 54-55

Windows Server 2008 R2 SP1 as the host operating system, 883

on Windows Server Core, 53

instance consolidation, 871

instance IDs, 377

instance-level, FILESTREAM data, 159

instances

AlwaysOn Failover Cluster. See AlwaysOn Failover Cluster Instances

installing on each node, AlwaysOn Availability Groups, 495-496

Integrated Windows Firewall, 379

Integration Services, 29

troubleshooting and optimization, 688-690

Integration Services Catalogs folder, 98

Integration Services. See SSIS

ISCSI (Internet SCSI), 532

ISCSI storage, 542-543

isolation, service accounts, 352

J

job activity, monitoring, 741-742

Job Activity Monitor, 741-742

Job System page, SQL Server Agent, 121

Jobs folder, SQL Server Agent, 121-122

K

key columns, indexes, 238

key length (certificates), 430

keys

asymmetric, 433

backing up, 443-444

EKM (Extensible Key Management), 444

advantages of, 446

creating cryptographic provider, 445

creating encryption keys, 446

creating HSM access credentials, 445

enabling, 444

symmetric, 433

keywords, TOP, 15

L

lack of consistency, conflicts, 624

latency, 130

launching

   command prompt in Windows Server Core installation, 56

   Hyper-V Administrative console, 886-888

   Hyper-V guest sessions, 898-900

layered model, performance tuning and troubleshooting, 677-678

Legacy, 98

leveraging

   AlwaysOn Availability Groups, 489-490

   partially contained databases, 426

   rolling upgrade strategies, 356

   SQL Server auditing strategies, 357-358

limitations of replication, 634

limiting

   memory of guest sessions, 893-897

   processors of guest sessions, 893-897

linked servers, Server Objects folder, 94

local publications, deleting, 669

Local Service Account, 352

local subscriptions, deleting, 669

Local System Account, 352

Local TembDB support with Failover Clustering, 15

locking

   deadlock detection, 716-717

   DMVs, 714

log providers, packages, 189

Log Reader Agent, 629

log shipping

   combining with replication, 638

   database mirroring, 598

   replication, 637

logging

   adding, enhancing packages, 204-205

   packages, 189

   performance counters, 679

logical units (LUN), 137-138, 532

Login Auditing, Security page, 78

logins, 386

   managing with DDL, 399-400

logon triggers, 397-398

logs

   collection set logs, viewing, 755

   monitoring, 742-743

   reviewing, 51

   SQL Server logs, 690-691

LUNs (logical unit number), 137-138, 532

M

Maintenance Cleanup Task, 791-792

Maintenance Plan design surface, 799

Maintenance Plan Wizard, 267, 287, 805

maintenance plans, 97

   automating backups, 308, 311-314

   creating

      manually, 798-802

      multiserver maintenance plans, 804-805

      with Database Maintenance Plan Wizard, 792-798

establishing, 780
Back Up Database Task, 789-791
Check Database Integrity Task, 780
Execute SQL Server Agent Job Task, 789
History Cleanup Task, 788-789
Maintenance Cleanup Task, 791-792
Rebuild Index Task, 783-786
Reorganize Index Task, 783
Shrink Database Task, 781-782
Update Statistics Task, 786-788
indexes, 266-267
viewing, 802-804
maintenance schedules, 805-806
maintenance tasks, adding (enhancing packages), 211
man-in-the-middle attacks, 456
Manage Policy Categories dialog box, 825
management data warehouse. See MDW (management data warehouse)
Management folder, 96-98
management tasks, Database Engine
changing SQL Server configuration settings, 114-115
informational reports, 115-116
PowerShell, 117
renaming databases, 119
scripting database objects, 117
taking SQL Server databases offline, 118
transferring SQL Server data, 118
Management Tools Basic, Shared Features, 30

Management Tools Complete, 30
managing
AlwaysOn Availability Groups, 509
adding databases, 511-512
adding replicas, 510-511
backing up, 520
changing properties, 512
conducting failovers with SSMS, 515-516
conducting forced failovers with SSMS, 517-518
connecting availability group listeners and read-only connectivity, 518-519
manually failing, 514-515
removing databases, 512
removing replicas, 509-510
suspending database movements, 513-514
AlwaysOn Failover Cluster Instances, failure condition property settings, 578
AlwaysOn failover cluster instances failback policies, 577
AlwaysOn failover cluster instances failover policies, 576-577
Audits, Windows Server 2008 R2 security logs as audit targets, 370-371
data collection set properties, 753
Description page, 755
General page, 753-754
Uploads page, 754
database files, 100
database mirroring client connections and redirect, 612-614
database mirroring sessions, 607
manually failing over database mirroring sessions, 608-609

pausing and resuming, 607-608

failover clusters from a SQL Server 2012 perspective, 574

FILESTREAM, 103

preferred owners of a cluster node and group, 575-576

replication, 667

Distributor Properties, 668

passwords, 669

Resource Governor, 860-862

SQL Server 2012 installations, 62-63

SQL Server failover service accounts, 575

manual failover, 592

manually failing, availability groups, 514-515

manually failing over database mirroring sessions, 608-609

MAP (Microsoft Assessment and Planning), 881

MAP (Microsoft Assessment and Planning) Toolkit for SQL Server, 41

maps, defined, 720

Master Data Services. See MDS, 29

master database, 89, 301

MDS (Master Data Services), 29

MDW (management data warehouse), 744

configuring, 746-748

mdw_admin, 747

mdw_reader, 747

mdw_writer, 747

memory

adding/limiting guest sessions, 893-897

DMVs, 713

performance counters, 681-682

Memory page, SQL Server Properties dialog box, 71-73

memory requirements, 16

merge replication, 628

Merge Agent, 630

metering and usage reports, optimizing SQL Server 2012 for private clouds, 904

Microsoft Assessment and Planning (MAP), 881

Microsoft Assessment and Planning (MAP) Toolkit for SQL Server, 41

Microsoft Private Clouds, 876

Microsoft Trustworthy Computing Initiative, 335

migrating to Windows Azure SQL Database, 225-227

Minimum Memory per Query, 72

mirror database, 591

mirrored backup, 300-301

mirrored media sets, 300

mirroring, 132-133

Mirroring page, 607

Database Properties dialog box, 114

Miscellaneous, Advanced page, 84

miscellaneous options, Database Properties dialog box, 110-111

mixed mode authentication, 338

server login administration, 405

MMC tool, Hyper-V, 887

model databases, 89, 301

modifying guest session configuration, 897

settings, 893-895

monitoring

Activity Monitor. See Activity Monitor

availability group databases, 524

availability group listeners, 525

availability groups, 523

system views, 523-525

Systems Center Operations Manager, 525

Availability Groups
Dashboard, 520

availability groups performance,
521-523

availability replicas, 524

database mirroring, 614-615

　　system catalogs, 618

database mirroring performance,
617-618

DMVs, 738-740

events with SQL Server Audit,
359-364

job activity, 741-742

new features for, 730

processes with Activity Monitor,
711-712

replication, 670-672

Resource Governor

　　with DMVs, 865-867

　　with Performance Monitor,
　　862-864

　　with Profiler, 864

servers, Utility Control Point, 760

SQL logs, 742-743

Standard Reports, 740-741

Task Manager. See Task Manager
(Windows Server 2008 R2),
733-734

monthly routine maintenance
tasks, 806

mounting CD/DVD image files, 896

moving data to clouds, 224

　　Windows Azure SQL Database,
　　224-227

msdb databases, 89, 302

Multi-Instance Failover Cluster, 534

Multipath I/O, 543

multiple data files

　　sizing, 146-147

　　utilizing, 145-146

multiple SQL Server instances,
capturing performance counters,
755-756

multiple-instance installation versus
single-instance installation, 27

multiple-instance SQL Server 2012
failover cluster, 564-565

　　installing the first node, 565-567

　　installing the subsequent
　　nodes, 567

multiserver maintenance plans,
creating, 804-805

multi-subnet failover cluster, 535

multi-subnet SQL Server 2012
failover cluster

　　implementing, 571-573

　　overview, 568-570

N

N+1, 534

N+M, 534

NAS (network attached storage),
137-138

navigating host server settings,
Hyper-V, 888

network, performance counters, 682

network attached storage (NAS),
137-138

network communications,
encryption, 452

　　configuring server-based encryp-
　　tion, 453-454

　　reasons for needing, 452-453

　　verifying server-based encryption,
　　454-455

network performance, monitoring
with Task Manager (Windows
Server 2008 R2), 736-737

Network Service Account, 352

Network settings, Advanced page, 85

Networking tab, Task Manager, 736

New Availability Group Wizard,
497-502

validating and viewing results,
502-504

new features

AlwaysOn Failover Cluster
instances, 528-529

Database Engine, 68

encryption, 430

for hardening and auditing,
336-337

for monitoring, 730

indexes, 229-230

maintenance, 779-780

security and authorization,
383-385

SSIS, 180

storage, 128

new installation, 31-38

choosing, 23-25

versus in-place upgrade, 25

new installation features, 14-15

New Server Registration dialog
box, 818

No Majority: Disk Only Quorum
model, 538

Node and Disk Majority Quorum
model, 537

Node and File Share Majority
Quorum model, 538

Node Majority cluster, 537

Node Majority Quorum models,
AlwaysOn Failover Cluster
Instances, 537-540

nodes

adding to clusters, Windows
Server 2008 R2, 581

adding to existing peer-to-peer
replication topology, 667

installing in multiple-instance
SQL Server 2012 failover
clusters, 567

nodes in single-instance SQL Server
2012 failover cluster, installing,
561-564

non-clustered indexes, 233

nonclustered columnstore indexes,
characteristics of, 240-241

nonclustered indexes

characteristics of, 239

include columns, 240

creating, 263

design and strategies, 243

notifications

alerts, defining, 767-768

failsafe operators, adding, 767

operators, adding, 767

O

Object Explorer, viewing DMVs, 739

object-naming conventions

Policy-Based Management, 836

On Change Log Only execution
mode, 817

On Change Prevent execution
mode, 816

On Demand execution mode, 815

On Schedule execution mode, 815

online indexing, Enterprise Edition of
SQL Server 2012, 279

operating modes, database mirroring,
593-594, 610-611

operating systems, updating and
patching, 356

Operations Manager, 730

operators

adding, 767

assigning alerts to, 830

failsafe operators, adding, 767

optimization. See performance tuning

optimizing SQL Server 2012 for private clouds, 903

    elasticity and scalability, 903

    high availability, 904

    metering and usage reports, 904

    private cloud appliances, 905

    resource pooling, 903

    self-service provisioning and rapid deployments, 904

Options page

    Database Properties dialog box, 104

    SSMS, creating indexes, 257-258

Oracle Publishing, transactional replication, 627

Other Memory Options, 72

    Transact-SQL statements, 73

P

package deployment utility, building, 214-216

Package Store, 212

packages, 182-183

    connections, 187-188

    control flow, 184

    creating, 190-191

    data flow, 185-187

    debugging, 198

    defined, 720

    deploying, 213

        DTUTIL, 216

        manual deployment, 213-214

        package deployment utility, 214-216

    deploying and running, 212

        storing packages, 212-213

    developing, 189

        creating packages, 190-191

        creating projects, 190

    running, 197-199

    walkthrough of connection managers, 196-197

    walkthrough of control flow, 192-194

    walkthrough of data flow, 194-196

    walkthrough of packages, 191-192

  enhancing, 199

    adding configurations, 208-211

    adding error handling, 207-208

    adding logging, 204-205

    adding maintenance tasks, 211

    expressions, 205-206

    sending email, 206-207

    transforming data, 199-204

  event handlers, 188

  importing SSMS, 214

  log providers and logging, 189

  options for creating, 181-182

  projects, 183

  running, 197-199

    with DTEXEC, 220

    scheduling, 220-221

    with SSMS, 218-220

  securing, 216-217

    DontSaveSensitive, 217-218

    EncryptAllWithUserKey, 218

    EncryptSensitiveWithUserKey, 218

  solutions, 183

  storing, 212-213

  tasks, 184

  variables, 188

  walkthrough, 191-192

    of connection managers, 196-197

of control flow, 192-194

of data flow, 194-196

Pad Index option, 270

page file, performance counters, 683

Page Verify, 111

PAL (Publication Access List), 624

Parallelism, Advanced page, 86

parallel indexing, Enterprise Edition of SQL Server 2012, 279

partial backup, 298

partial containment within a database, enabling, 423-424

partially contained databases, leveraging, 426

partition switching, 168-170

partitioning indexes, Enterprise Edition, 278

partitions

    designing, 164-165

        Create Partition wizard, 165-167

        enhancements, 167-168

        partition switching, 168-170

        sliding window partitions, 170-172

    system partitions, configuring for BitLocker, 469-470

password policies, 394-397

passwords

    replication, 669

    strong passwords, 341

patch management, failover clusters (SQL Server 2012), 580

patching SQL Server and operating systems, 356

pausing

    cluster nodes, 580

    database mirroring sessions, 607-608

peer-to-peer publication, configuring on first node, 661-662

peer-to-peer replication, 626

    enabling publications, 662

peer-to-peer replication topology, adding nodes to, 667

peer-to-peer topology, configuring, 663-666

peer-to-peer transactional replication, 628

    configuring, 659-661

Perfmon. See Performance Monitor

performance, 769

    database mirroring, monitoring, 617-618

    monitoring

        AlwaysOn Availability Groups, 521-523

        Task Manager (Windows Server 2008 R2), 736

    segregating I/O, 139-140

performance counters

    capturing from multiple SQL Server instances, 755-756

    database engine, 686-688

    detailed information about, 680

    Integration Services, 688-690

    logging, 679

    memory, 681-682

    network, 682

    page file, 683

    physical disk, 683-684

    processor, 684-685

    querying, 681

performance dashboard, 731-733

Performance Monitor

    correlating with SQL Server Profiler, 699-702

    counters, adding, 772-773

    monitoring Resource Governor with, 862-864

Reliability and Performance
Monitor, 771-772

settings, 774

Performance Studio, 745

Performance tab, Task Manager, 736

performance tuning

application troubleshooting and
optimization, 714

cursor usage, 716

deadlock detection, 716-717

Query Editor, 714-716

basic steps in, 679-680

best practices, 726-727

database engine troubleshooting
and optimization, 686-688

database troubleshooting and
optimization, 691-692

Activity Monitor, 711-712

correlating Perfmon and
Profiler data, 699-702

Database Engine Tuning
Advisor, 702-711

DMVs, 712-714

SQL Server Profiler, 696

SQL Server Profiler trace
templates, 697-699

wait statistics analysis,
692-696

Integration Services troubleshooting and optimization, 688-690

layered model, 677-678

platform troubleshooting and
optimization, 680-681

memory objects and counters,
681-682

network objects and
counters, 682

page file objects and counters, 683

physical disk objects and
counters, 683-684

processor objects and
counters, 684-685

SQL Server logs, 690-691

**performing SQL Server 2012
upgrade, 47-50**

permissions, 384, 387

CONNECT, 389

managing with DDL, 403-404

Permissions page

Database Properties dialog
box, 113

SQL Server Properties dialog
box, 86

**physical CD/DVD images,
mounting, 896**

**physical disk, performance counters,
683-684**

**physical installation versus virtual
installation, 26**

pipelines, 185

**platform troubleshooting and opti-
mization, 680-681**

memory objects and counters,
681-682

network objects and
counters, 682

page file objects and
counters, 683

physical disk objects and counters, 683-684

processor objects and counters,
684-685

policies

configuring alerts for, 828-830

creating, 821-823

evaluating, 825-826

explained, 814

importing/exporting, 827-828

policies available for import,
830-835

**Policy-Based Management Surface
Area Configuration, 343**

Policy Management, 97

Policy-Based Management

alerts

assigning to operators, 830

configuring for policy failures, 828-830

best practices, 836-837

categories

creating, 824-825

explained, 815

Central Management Servers, 817-818

conditions

creating, 819-821

explained, 814

execution modes, 815-817

explained, 811-813

facets, explained, 813-814

Microsoft SQL Server Product Group blog, 813

policies

configuring alerts for, 828-830

creating, 821-823

evaluating, 825-826

explained, 814

importing/exporting, 827-828

policies available for import, 830-835

targets, explained, 815

use cases

object-naming conventions, 836

recovery models, 835

SQL Server health checks, 836

Surface Area Configuration (SAC), 835

pooled resources, private clouds, 875

PowerShell, Database Engine, 117

predicates, defined, 720

preferred owners, managing (cluster nodes and groups), 575-576

preparing Windows Server 2008 R2 failover cluster, 549

prerequisites

AlwaysOn Failover Cluster instances, 532-533

database mirroring, 594

configuring, 599-600

for availability groups, 488-489

replication, 634

primary key collision, conflicts, 624

primary keys, 233

Primary Replica, 486

principal database, 591

principle of least privilege, 351, 385

private cloud appliances, optimizing SQL Server 2012 for private clouds, 905

private clouds, 875-877

optimizing SQL Server 2012, 903

elasticity and scalability, 903

high availability, 904

metering and usage reports, 904

private cloud appliances, 905

resource pooling, 903

self-service provisioning and rapid deployments, 904

processes, monitoring

with Activity Monitor, 711-712

Task Manager (Windows Server 2008 R2), 735

Processes tab, Task Manager, 735

processor requirements, 16

processors

adding/limiting guest sessions, 893-897

for host servers, Hyper-V, 879

performance counters, 684-685

Processors page, 74

Processors page, SQL Server
  Properties dialog box, 73-79
product update, 14
Profilers. See SQL Server Profiler
Profiles, replication, 630
projects
  creating, 190
  packages, 183
properties
  administering, 68-70
    SQL Server Properties dialog
    box. See SQL Server
    Properties dialog box
  changing in availability
    groups, 512
  SQL Server Agent, 119-120
protection levels, securing
  packages, 217
provisioning third-party certificates,
  458-461
Proxies folder, SQL Server Agent, 123
Publication Access List (PAL), 624
publications, 623
  configuring snapshot or transac-
    tional replication publications,
    645-652
  deleting local subscriptions, 669
  peer-to-peer replication,
    enabling, 662
  testing, 657
Publisher-Distributor-Subscriber, 631
publishers, 623
publishing, disabling, 668
pull subscribers, 624
push subscribers, 624

Q

quarterly routine maintenance
  tasks, 806
queries, DMVs, 713
Query Editor, 714-716
Query Optimizer, 268
Query Statistics System Data
  collection set, 752
querying performance counters, 681
Queue Reader Agent, 629
queued replication, 629
quorum resources, 531
quorum selection, AlwaysOn
  Availability Groups, 508-509
quorums, 592

R

RAID (redundant arrays of inexpen-
  sive disks), 131
  RAID0, 131-132
  RAID1, 132-133
  RAID10, 135-136
  RAID5, 133-135
RAID0, 131-132
RAID1, 132-133
RAID5, 133-135
RAID10, 135-136
RAM (random access memory)
  CPU speed versus, 685
  for host servers, Hyper-V, 878
rapid deployment, optimizing SQL
  Server 2012 for private clouds, 904
RBS (Remote BLOB Store), 163
read-only connectivity, managing,
  518-519
Rebuild Index Task, 783-786
rebuilding indexes, 265-266,
  271-272

recommendations from Database
Engine Tuning Advisor
  applying, 710-711
  reviewing, 707-709
recommending indexes with system
information, 276
recovering full-text catalogs, 326
recovery
  BitLocker Drive Encryption, 477
  Database Settings page, 83
Recovery Interval (Minutes), 83
Recovery Model, Database Properties
Options page, 105
recovery models
  Database Engine, 291-293
  Database Properties dialog box,
  105-106
  Policy-Based Management, 835
  selecting, 106, 292
  switching with SQL Server
  Management Studio, 107
recovery options, Database
Properties dialog box, 111
recovery password, BitLocker Drive
Encryption, 477
recovery plans
  full database recovery, 316-324
  SSMS, 319-323
  Transact-SQL, 324
redirect, database mirroring, 612-614
reducing
  attack surfaces on SQL Server
  instances, 350
  SQL Server 2012 surface
  area, 343
referential integrity, partition switching, 169
registering SQL Server instances in
Change Management Servers, 818

relational indexes
  creating with Transact-SQL,
  247-249
  modifying with Transact-SQL,
  249-251
  removing with Transact-SQL, 251
Reliability and Performance Monitor
(Windows 2008 R2), 769
  Data Collector Set, 775
  Performance Monitor, 771-772
    settings, 774
  Reliability Monitor, 774
  Reports, 775
  Resource Monitor, 770-771
Reliability Monitor, Reliability and
Performance Monitor, 774
Remote BLOB Store (RBS), 163
remote management, Server Core
(SCONFIG), 59
Remote Query Timeout, 80
remote server connections,
Connections page, 80
removing
  BitLocker Drive Encryption, 477
  BUILTIN\Administrators Windows
  group with Transact-SQL, 373
  database mirroring sessions,
  611-612
  databases from availability
  groups, 512
  indexes with Transact-SQL, 251
  replicas from availability groups,
  509-510
  SQL Server 2012 nodes from
  existing SQL Server failover
  clusters, 578-579
renaming
  databases, 119
  SA accounts, 342-343
Reorganize Index Task, 783
reorganizing indexes, 271-272

replicas

adding to availability groups, 510-511

removing from availability groups, 509-510

replication, 621-622

bidirectional replication, 624

bidirectional transactional replication, 627

combining

with AlwaysOn Availability Groups, 639

with database mirroring, 638

with failover clustering, 639

with log shipping mirroring, 638

components, 630

database mirroring, 598

distributors, configuring, 659

implementing, 639

configuring distributors for replication, 640-645

configuring snapshot or transactional replication publications, 645-652

configuring snapshot replication, 639-640

peer-to-peer transactional replication, 659-661

tracer tokens, 658-659

knowing when to implement, 635-637

managing, 667

Distributor Properties, 668

passwords, 669

merge replication, 628

monitoring, 670-672

peer-to-peer replication, 626

peer-to-peer transactional replication, 628

prerequisites, 634

publications, testing, 657

queued replication, 629

roles, 623-624

snapshots, testing, 657

troubleshooting, 670-672

types of, 625

snapshot replication, 625-626

transactional replication, 626-629

validations, 658

Replication folder, administering, 96

Replication Monitor, 630, 670-672

replication scripts, generating, 669

replication topologies, 631-632

replications, limitations of, 634

Reporting Services, 29

Reporting Services Add-in for SharePoint Products, 30

Reporting Services - SharePoint, 30

reports

data collection reports, running, 757

informational reports, Database Engine, 115-116

metering and usage reports, 904

Reliability and Performance Monitor, 775

SQL Server Feature discovery report, 41

Republishing topology, 631

Require Distributed Transactions for Server-to-Server Communication, 80

requirements, hardware requirements (BitLocker Drive Encryption), 468

Resource Governor, 97

best practices, 868

classifications, explained, 842

classifier functions

creating, 846-848

troubleshooting, 848-850

in consolidated multitenant environments, 844

enabling, 845-846

explained, 839-840

managing, 860-862

monitoring

with DMVs, 865-867

with Performance Monitor, 862-864

with Profiler, 864

new features, 840

resource pools

creating, 850-852, 858-859

explained, 841-842

scenarios, 843-844

templates

applying, 854-855

Configure Resource Governor template, 855

SQL Server Resource Governor SQL Server Template, 855-858

workflow, 843

workload groups

creating, 852-854, 859-860

explained, 841-842

resource groups, 531

Resource Monitor, Reliability and Performance Monitor, 770-771

resource pooling, optimizing SQL Server 2012 for private clouds, 903

resource pools

creating, 850-852, 858-859

explained, 841-842

resources, 839. See also Resource Governor

restoring databases, Database Engine, 118

resuming

cluster nodes, 580

database mirroring sessions, 607-608

reverting

to database snapshots, Transact-SQL, 328

snapshot sessions, 903

reviewing SQL Server 2012 logs, 51

REVOKE statement, 404

role-based access, 391-393

fixed database-level roles, 392

server-level roles, 392

roles

managing with DDL, 401-402

replication, 623-624

rolling back guest images to previous snapshot images, 902

rolling upgrade strategy, leveraging, 356

row set transformations, 186

row transformations, 186

row-level tracking, conflicts, 624

running

data collection reports, 757

packages, 197-199, 212

with DTEXEC, 220

scheduling packages, 220-221

with SSMS, 218-220

storing packages, 212-213

server manager to add Hyper-V role, 884-886

SQL Server Management Studio, 52

SQL Server Upgrade Advisor, 42

S

SA accounts
  disabling, 342-343
  renaming, 342-343
  security ramifications, 340-341
SAC (Surface Area Configuration), Policy-Based Management, 835
SAN (storage area networks), 137-138, 532-539
SAS (Serial Attached SCSI), 532
SAS Serial Attached SCSI storage arrays, 541
SATA, 136
saving guest sessions, 900
scalability, optimizing SQL Server 2012 for private clouds, 903
scalability metrics, AlwaysOn Failover Cluster Instances, 535
SCCM (System Center Configuration Manager), 877
scenarios for Resource Governor, 843-844
  in consolidated multitenant environments, 844
scheduling packages, 220-221
schemas, managing with DDL, 402-403
SCONFIG, 56
SCONFIG Server Core, remote management, 59
scripting database objects, Database Engine, 117
securing packages, 216-217
  DontSaveSensitive, 217-218
  EncryptAllWithUserKey, 218
  EncryptSensitiveWithUserKey, 218

security, 385
  account lockout policies, 397
  administering, 404
    application roles, 417-418
    database role administration, 413-414
    database user administration, 411-413
    security schema administration, 416-417
    server endpoint administration, 418-421
    server login administration, 405-411
    server role administration, 414-416
  authentication. See authentication
  database schemas, 394
  database users, 389-391
  encryption. See encryption
  endpoints and communication, 387-389
  logins, 386
  logon triggers, 397-398
  new features, 383-385
  password policies, 394-397
  permissions, 387
  role-based access, 391-393
  SA accounts, 340-341
  server logins, 389-391
Security page, SQL Server Properties dialog box, 76
Security Configuration Wizard, hardening servers, 348-349
security events, viewing from audit files (Transact-SQL), 372
Security folder, administering, 92
security logs, 357

security management, DDL, 398

managing

logins, 399-400

permissions, 403-404

roles, 401-402

schemas, 402-403

users, 400-401

security schema administration, 416-417

segregating I/O, 139-140

selecting recovery models, 106, 292

self-service provisioning, optimizing SQL Server 2012 for private clouds, 904

self-signed certificates, 456

sending

email, enhancing packages, 206-207

email alerts, configuring Database Mail, 763-765

sequential operations, 130

Serial Attached SCSI (SAS), 532

Server Activity Data collection set, 752

server audit specification, creating with SSMS, 367-368

Server Audit Specification object, 361

server authentication, Security page, 76

server certificates, creating, 448

Server Configuration page, 35, 559

Server Core, 14

versus full edition with graphical user interface, 26

managing with Server Manager, 60

Server Core remote management, SCONFIG, 59

server endpoint administration, 418-421

server fault tolerance, snapshots for guest sessions, 901

server login administration, 405

mixed-mode authentication, 405

SQL authentication logins, 405-409

Windows authentication logins, 409-411

server logins, 389, 391

Server Manager

installing BitLocker, 471

managing Server Core, 60

Server Manager tool, managing Hyper-V systems, 886

Server Memory Options, 71

Server Objects folder, administering, 92-93, 95

Server Properties dialog Advanced page FILESTREAM, 161

Server Properties dialog box, 69

server proxy account, Security page, 78

server role administration, 414-416

Server Roles Wizard, 375

server-based encryption

configuring, 453-454

verifying, 454-455

server-level roles, 392

servers

Central Management Servers

creating, 817-818

explained, 817

importing and evaluating policies to, 818

registering SQL Server instances in, 818

certificate servers, setting up, 456-458

service accounts

changing with SQL Server Configuration Manager, 354

hardening, 350-351

    isolation, 352

    principle of least
      privilege, 351

    SQL Server Services, 352-353

    types of accounts, 352

Service and Applications, 531

**Service Broker options, Database
Properties dialog box, 111**

service failovers, initiating, 574

Service Master Key, backing up, 443

service packs, installing, 355-356

    updating and patching SQL
      Server and the operating
      system, 356

**services, monitoring with Task
Manager (Windows Server 2008
R2), 735**

Services tab, Task Manager, 735

Setup Support Rules page, 47

setup.exe

    creating .INI files, 39-40

    generating .INI files, 39

SHA-2 hashing algorithms, 430

Shared Features, 29

    Client Tools Backward
      Compatibility, 30

Shared Features

    Client Tools Connectivity, 30

    Client Tools SDK, 30

    Data Quality Client, 30

    Distributed Replay Controller, 30

    Integration Services, 29

    Management Tools Basic, 30

    Management Tools Complete, 30

    MDS (Master Data Services), 29

    Reporting Services Add-in for
      SharePoint Products, 30

    Reporting Services -
      SharePoint, 30

SQL Client Connectivity SDK, 30

SQL Server Books Online, 30

SQL Server Data Tools, 29

**shared storage, AlwaysOn Failover
Cluster instances, 541-542**

    Fibre Channel storage arrays, 541

    ISCSI storage, 542-543

    Multipath I/O, 543

    SAS Serial Attached SCSI storage
      arrays, 541

**shared storage for failover
clusters, 539**

**shared storage requirements, Node
Majority Quorum models, 539**

shared-nothing cluster model, 527

SharePoint, 30

**Shrink Database task, 150-154,
781-782**

shrinking

    databases, 150-154

    files, 150-154

    I/O performance, 150-154

**side-by-side installations with
previous versions, 27-28**

Simple recovery models, 105, 291

Single Failover Cluster Instance, 534

**single-instance installation versus
multiple-instance installation, 27**

**single-instance SQL Server 2012
failover cluster, 544-545**

    configuring shared storage for
      Windows Server 2008 R2
      failover cluster, 547-548

    creating Windows Server 2008
      R2 failover cluster, 551-552

    installing

      additional nodes, 561-564

      DTC as a SQL Server
        AlwaysOn Failover Cluster
        Instances prerequisite, 553

      the first node, 554-561

Windows Server 2008 R2 failover cluster, 549

preparing Windows Server 2008 R2 operating system for each node, 546

sizing multiple data files, 146-147

sliding window partitions, 170-172

SMB support, 15

SMTP, 765

Snapshot Agent, 629

Snapshot Folder page, 642

snapshot replication, 625-626

    configuring, 639-640

    testing, 657

snapshots, 91

    guest operating system sessions, 900

        creating snapshots of guest images, 901

        image rollback, 900

        reverting, 903

        server fault tolerance, 901

    Hyper-V, 882-883

SNI (SQL Server Network Interface), 387

software prerequisites for installation, 18

solid state disks (SSD), 138-139

Solution Explorer, 191

solutions, packages, 183

Sort transforms, 186

sorting indexes in tempdb, 272

spatial indexes

    characteristics of, 242

    creating with Transact-SQL, 252-255

Specify How Long SQL Server Will Wait for a New Tape, 82

spindles, 129

sp_addrolemember statement, 402

sp_addsrvrolemember statement, 402

sp_droprolemember statement, 402

sp_dropsrvrolemember statement, 402

SQL Agent alerting, 768

SQL authentication, 404

SQL authentication logins, 405-409

SQL Client Connectivity SDK, 30

SQL Native Client Configuration, 344

SQL Server 2012

    configuring for third-party certificates, 461-462

    health checks, Policy-Based Management, 836

    optimizing for private clouds, 903

        elasticity and scalability, 903

        high availability, 904

        metering and usage reports, 904

        private cloud appliances, 905

        resource pooling, 903

        self-service provisioning and rapid deployments, 904

SQL Server 2012 Business Intelligence Edition, 19

SQL Server 2012 Developer Edition, 20

SQL Server 2012 editions, changing, 63

SQL Server 2012 Enterprise Edition, 19

SQL Server 2012 Express Edition, 20

SQL Server 2012 Installation Media, 890

SQL Server 2012 Integration Services. See SSIS

SQL Server 2012 nodes, removing from existing SQL Server failover clusters, 578-579

SQL Server 2012 Standard
Edition, 19

SQL Server 2012 surface area,
reducing, 343

SQL Server 2012 Web Edition, 20

SQL Server Active Directory
Helper, 351

SQL Server Agent, administering, 119

Alerts and Operators folder, 123

Error Logs folder, 123

Jobs folder, 121-122

properties, 119-120

Proxies folder, 123

SQL Server Agent Account, 372

SQL Server Agent job, 122

SQL Server Agent job history,
viewing, 122

SQL Server Agent Service, 350

SQL Server Analysis Services
Service, 351

SQL Server Audit

enabling with SSMS, 367

monitoring events, 359-360

Audit components, 360-361

SQL Server Audit Failed Logon
Attempt example, 362-364

SQL Server Audit Failed Logon
Attempt example, 362-364

SQL Server Audit objects, 360

creating with Transact-SQL, 362

SQL Server Audit Specification object,
creating with Transact-SQL, 363

SQL Server auditing strategies, leveraging, 357-358

SQL Server audits, creating with
SSMS, 364-367

SQL Server Authentication mode,
385

SQL Server backup methods, 294

copy-only backup, 299

differential backup, 295

differential partial backup, 299

file and filegroup backup, 297

full backup, 295

mirrored backup, 300-301

partial backup, 298

transaction log backup, 296-297

SQL Server Books Online, 30

SQL Server Browser, 351

SQL Server Configuration Manager

Computer Management, 60-62

changing service accounts, 354

SQL Server ports, 345

SQL Server Configuration Manager
tool, hardening installations,
344-345, 348

SQL Server data, transferring
(Database Engine), 118

SQL Server Data Tools, 14, 29, 182

SQL Server Database Engine folders,
administering, 87

AlwaysOn High Availability, 96

Databases folder, 88-91

Integration Services Catalogs
folder, 98

Management folder, 96-98

Replication folder, 96

Security folder, 92

Server Objects folder, 92-95

SQL Server Database Engineer
Service, 350

SQL Server database mirroring. See
database mirroring

SQL Server Extended Events, 97

SQL Server failover cluster, removing
(SQL Server 2012 nodes), 578-579

SQL Server failover service accounts,
managing, 575

SQL Server Feature discovery
report, 41

SQL Server Full-Text Filter Daemon
Launcher, 351

SQL Server instances

capturing performance counters, 755-756

hardening and reducing attack surfaces, 350

hiding from broadcasting information, 346-347

registering in Change Management Servers, 818

SQL Server Integration Services. *See* **SSIS**

SQL Server Integration Services Service, 351

SQL Server login, 386

SQL Server logs, 98, 690-691

SQL Server Management Studio

backing up examples, 301-314

encryption, 464-465

new features, 68

running, 52

switching with Database Recovery Model, 107

SQL Server Multi-subnet Clustering, 14

SQL Server Network Configuration, 344

SQL Server Network Interface (SNI), 387

SQL Server ports, SQL Configuration Manager, 345

SQL Server principals, 390

SQL Server Profiler, 696, 704, 776. *See also* **Database Engine Tuning Advisor**

correlating with Performance Monitor, 699-702

trace templates, 697-699

SQL Server Properties dialog box, 68

Advanced page, 83-86

Connections page, 79-80

Database Settings page, 81-83

General page, 70

Memory page, 71-73

Permissions page, 86

Processors page, 73-79

Security page, 76

SQL Server Replication, 28

SQL Server Reporting Services, 351

SQL Server Resource Governor SQL Server Template, 855-858

SQL Server Services, 344

hardening service accounts, 352-353

SQL Server Upgrade Advisor

installing, 43

compatibility tests, 43-46

running, 42

SQL Server utilities, 757

monitoring further servers, 760

Utility Control Point, 757

installing, 758

viewing utility information, 760-763

SQL Server virtual server, 530

SQL Server VSS Writer, 351

SSD (solid state disks), 138-139

SSIS (SQL Server Integration Services), 179, 636

deploying and running packages, 212-213

DTUTIL, 216

manual deployment, 213-214

package deployment utility, 214-216

storing packages, 212-213

enhancing packages, 199

adding configurations, 208-211

adding error handling, 207-208

adding logging, 204-205

adding maintenance tasks, 211

expressions, 205-206

sending email, 206-207

transforming data, 199-204

ETL, 179

new features, 180

options for creating packages, 181

Copy Database Wizard, 181

Import and Export Wizard, 181

SQL Server Data Tools, 182

packages, 182-183, 189

connections, 187-188

control flow, 184

creating, 190-191

creating projects, 190

data flow, 185-187

event handlers, 188

log providers and logging, 189

projects, 183

running, 197-199

solutions, 183

tasks, 184

variables, 188

walkthrough, 191-192

walkthrough of connection managers, 196-197

walkthrough of control flow, 192-194

walkthrough of data flow, 194-196

running packages

DTEXEC, 220

scheduling packages, 220-221

SSMS, 218-220

securing packages, 216-217

DontSaveSensitive, 217-218

EncryptAllWithUserKey, 218

EncryptSensitiveWithUserKey, 218

transferring data, 221

Bulk Insert Task, 223

Copy Database Wizard, 221-223

SSIS Designer

packages, 189

creating, 190-191

running, 197-199

walkthrough, 191-192

walkthrough of connection managers, 196-197

walkthrough of control flow, 192-194

walkthrough of data flow, 194-196

projects, creating, 190

SSMS (SQL Server Management Studio), 364-367

conducting a recovery, 319-323

conducting availability failovers, 515-516

conducting forced availability failovers, 517-518

creating indexes, 255-256

Extended Properties page, 259

Filter page, 259

Options page, 257-258

Storage page, 258

creating server audit specification, 367-368

creating SQL Server audits, 364, 366-367

database snapshots, 328

differential backups, 306

enabling SQL Server Audit, 367

full backups, 302-305

importing packages, 214

packages, running, 218-220

switching Database Recovery Model with, 293

transaction log backups, 307-308

standalone installation versus AlwaysOn, 26

Standard Reports, monitoring, 740-741

state options, Database Properties dialog box, 112

status of clustered service and applications, verifying, 574

Status tab, Database Mirroring Monitoring tool, 615-616

storage

adding to clusters (Windows Server 2008 R2), 581

BLOB storage, 158

designing and administering, 140-141

data file initialization, 150

database files, 141-148

filegroups, 155-158

shrinking databases, files, and I/O performance, 150-154

new features, 128

storage architecture, Database Engine, 289

storage area networks (SAN), 137-138, 532-539

storage hardware, 129

disk controllers, 136-137

hard disks, 129-131

HBAs (host bus adapters), 136-137

LUN (logical units), 137-138

NAS (network attached storage), 137-138

RAID (redundant arrays of inexpensive disks), 131

RAID0, 131-132

RAID1, 132-133

RAID10, 135-136

RAID5, 133-135

SAN (storage area networks), 137-138

SSD (solid state disks), 138-139

Storage page, SSMS (creating indexes), 258

storing packages, 212-213

striping, 131-132

strong passwords, 341

subfeatures, installing Database Engine, 31

subscribers, 623-624

subscriptions

avoiding losing permissions, 670

configuring for AdventureWorks 2012 database, 652-656

deleting local subscriptions, 669

Surface Area Configuration (SAC), Policy-Based Management, 835

suspending database movement, availability groups, 513-514

switching

database recovery model with SSMS, 293

Database Recovery Model

with SQL Server Management Studio, 107

with Transact-SQL, 107, 293

symmetric keys, 433

synchronous, 592

synchronous commit mode, 486

sys.availability_groups, 523

sys.availability_groups_cluster, 523

SYS.DM_DB_INDEX_OPERATIONAL_STATS, 713

SYS.DM_DB_INDEX_PHYSICAL_
STATS, 712

SYS.DM_DB_INDEX_USAGE_
STATS, 712

SYS.DM_EXEC_QUERY_STATS, 713

SYS.DM_EXEC_SQL_TEXT, 714

sys.dm_hadr_availability_groups_stat
es, 523

sys.dm_hadr_cluster, 523

sys.dm_hadr_cluster_members, 523

sys.dm_hadr_cluster_networks, 523

sys.dm_hadr_instance_node_
map, 523

SYS.DM_IO_VIRTUAL_FILE_
STATS, 713

sys.dm_name_id_map, 523

SYS.DM_OS_MEMORY_CLERKS, 713

SYS.DM_OS_MEMORY_OBJECTS, 713

SYS.DM_OS_SYS_INFO, 712

Sys.dm_resource_governor_
configuration, 866

Sys.dm_resource_governor_resource_
pools, 866

Sys.dm_resource_governor_resource_
pool_affinity, 866

Sys.dm_resource_governor_work-
load_groups, 865-866

SYS.DM_TRAN_LOCKS, 714

sys.endpoints catalog view, 388

sys.server_permissions catalog
view, 388

sys.server_principals catalog
view, 388

system catalogs, monitoring database mirroring, 618

System Center Configuration
Manager (SCCM), 877

System Center Data Protection
Manager (DPM), 877

System Center Operations
Manager, 876

System Center Orchestrator, 877

System Center Virtual Machine
Manager (VMM), 876

System Center Virtual Machine
Manager Self-Service Portal, 876

System Configuration Checker, 42

system data collection sets, Data
Collector, 750-752

system databases, understanding
need for backing up, 301

System Databases subfolder,
administering, 89

system partitions, configuring for
BitLocker Drive Encryption, 469-470

system views, monitoring (AlwaysOn
Availability Groups), 523-525

Systems Center Operations Manager,
monitoring (AlwaysOn Availability
Groups), 525

T

tables

    partition switching, 169

    partitions, 165-167

Tabular Data Stream (TDS), 387

targets

    defined, 720

    explained, 815

Task Editor window, 193

Task Manager (Windows Server 2008
R2), 733-736

    monitoring

        apps, 734

        network performance,
        736-737

        performance, 736

        processes, 735

        services, 735

        user activity, 737

TaskHost, 184

tasks
> Bulk Insert Task, 223
> packages, 184
> Transfer Database Task, 221

TCP Dynamic Ports, 346

TCP Port, 346

TDE (Transparent Data Encryption), 289, 446-447
> column encryption versus, 451
> creating
>> Database Encryption Key, 449-450
>> Database Master Key, 448
>> server certificates, 448
> disabling, 451
> enabling, 448-451
> encryption hierarchy, 447-448

TDS (Tabular Data Stream), 387

tempdb, sorting indexes, 272

tempdb databases, 89, 302
> configuring, 89-91

templates
> Resource Governor templates
>> applying, 854-855
>> Configure Resource Governor Template, 855
>> SQL Server Resource Governor SQL Server Template, 855-858
> trace templates, 697-699

terminology
> AlwaysOn Failover Cluster instances, 530-532
> database mirroring, 591-592

test databases, creating, 435-436

testing
> publications, 657
> snapshot replication, 657

third-party certificates, 456-457
> client-based encryption, 463-464
> configuring client for, 462-463
> configuring SQL Server for, 461-462
> provisioning, 458-461
> setting up certificate server, 456-458

threads, Processors page, 74

tools
> Database Engine Tuning, 777
> Database Mirroring Monitoring tool, 614-615
>> Status tab, 615-616
>> Warnings tab, 616
> SQL Server Profiler, 776
> VMM (Virtual Machine Manager), 875

TOP, 15

TPM (Trusted Platform Module), 467
> enabling BitLocker, 472-474

trace templates, 697-699

tracer tokens, replication, 658-659

Transact-SQL
> AlwaysOn Availability Group, 504-508
> conducting a recovery, 324
> configuring distributors, 644
> creating SQL Server Audit objects, 362
> data compression, 174-175
> database audit specifications, 369-370
> database role administration, 414
> database snapshots, reverting to, 328
> enabling Audit objects, 363
> failing over database mirroring, 609

index syntax, 247

columnstore indexes, creating, 252

filtered indexes, creating, 255

relational indexes, 247-251

relational indexes, 251

spatial indexes, creating, 252-255

removing

BUILTIN\Administrators Windows group, 373

database mirroring sessions, 612

SQL Server Audit Specification object, 363

switching with Database Recovery Model, 107, 293

viewing security events from audit files, 372

Transact-SQL statements, Other Memory Options, 73

transaction log backup, 296-297

SSMS, 307-308

Transaction Log Backup Tasks, 780

transaction log files, Database Engine, 290

Transaction Log Shipping page, Database Properties dialog box, 114

Transaction Retention, 668

transaction safety, 611

transactional replication, 626-629

transactions

deadlock detection, 716-717

DMVs, 714

Transfer Database Task, 221

transferring

data (SSIS), 221

Bulk Insert Task, 223

Copy Database Wizard, 221-223

SQL Server data, Database Engine, 118

transformations, 186

data flow transformation components, 187

row set transformations, 186

row transformations, 186

transforming data, enhancing packages, 199-204

transitioning, 23-25

transparent client redirect, 592

Transparent Data Encryption (TDE), 289, 446-447

column encryption versus, 451

creating Database Encryption Key, 449-450

creating Database Master Key, 448

creating server certificates, 448

disabling, 451

enabling, 448-451

encryption hierarchy, 447-448

triggers, 636

Server Objects folder, 95

troubleshooting

classifier functions, 848-850

with Extended Events, 718-719

catalog views, 723

creating with DDL statements, 720-723

DMVs, 723-724

terminology, 719-720

user interface, 724-726

performance issues

application troubleshooting and optimization, 714-717

basic steps in, 679-680

best practices, 726-727

database engine troubleshooting and optimization, 686-688

database troubleshooting and optimization, 691-714

Integration Services troubleshooting and optimization, 688-690

layered model, 677-678

platform troubleshooting and optimization, 680-685

SQL Server logs, 690-691

replication, 670-672

Trusted Platform Module (TPM), 467

enabling BitLocker, 472-474

tuning. See performance tuning

two-phase commit, 636

types

defined, 720

of replication, 625

snapshot replication, 625-626

transactional replication, 626-629

U

unique indexes, design and strategies, 244

uniqueifier column, unique indexes, 244

unused indexes, finding with Database Engine, 276-278

Update Statistics Task, 786-788

updates, 51

updating

deleted rows, conflicts, 624

SQL Server and operating systems, 356

upgrading

Database Engine to SQL Server 2012, 40

backing up servers, 41

considerations for, 46-47

creating SQL Server Feature discovery report, 41

installing SQL Server Upgrade Advisor, 43

Microsoft Assessment and Planning (MAP) Toolkit for SQL Server, 41

running SQL Server Upgrade Advisor, 42-46

verifying system compatibility, 42

deciding to, 23-25

items to consider after, 52-53

SQL Server 2012

performing, 47-50

versus new installation, 25

Uploads page, data collection set, 754

USB keys, enabling BitLocker, 474-475

user activity, monitoring with Task Manager (Windows Server 2008 R2), 737

user interface, Extended Events, 724-726

users, managing with DDL, 400-401

Users tab, Task Manager, 737

utilities, 757

Bulk Copy, 224

DTUTIL, 216

monitoring further servers, 760

package deployment utility, 214-216

Utility Control Point, 757

installing, 758

viewing utility information, 760-763

Utility Control Point, 757

installing, 758

Utility Explorer Content, 760-763

V

Validate a Cluster Configuration
  Wizard, 493-494, 550
validating
    Database Mail configuration, 766
    results, New Availability Group
      Wizard, 502-504
validations, replication, 658
variables, packages, 188
verifying
    minimum hardware
      requirements, 16
    server-based encryption, 454-455
    status of cluster service and
      applications, nodes, storage,
      and networks, 574
    system compatibility, upgrading to
      SQL Server 2012, 42
viewing
    audit logs, 364
    collection set logs, 755
    maintenance plans, 802-804
    results, New Availability Group
      Wizard, 502-504
    security events from an audit file
      via Transact-SQL, 372
    SQL Server Agent job history, 122
    utility information, 760-763
virtual installation versus physical
  installation, 26
Virtual Machine Manager (VMM),
  875-876
Virtual Network Manager, 888
virtual server systems,
  connecting to, 887
virtualization, 872-874
    considerations for, 880-882
    Hyper-V. See Hyper-V
VMM (Virtual Machine Manager),
  875-876

VSS (Volume Shadow Copy
  Service), 882

W

wait statistics analysis, 692-696
walkthrough
    of connection managers, 196-197
    of control flow, 192-194
    of data flow, 194-196
    of packages, 191-192
Warnings tab, Database Mirroring
  Monitoring tool, 616
weekly routine maintenance
  tasks, 806
Windows 2008 R2
    security logs as audit targets,
      370-371
    Validate a Cluster Configuration
      Wizard, 550
Windows authentication logins,
  409-411
Windows Authentication Mode, 77,
  337-338, 385, 390, 405
    password policies, 395
Windows Azure SQL Database,
  224-227
Windows BitLocker Drive Encryption.
  See BitLocker Drive Encryption
Windows Server 2008 R2
    AlwaysOn Availability Groups, 491
    benefits of using, 21-22
    failover clusters
        adding additional nodes, 581
        adding storage, 581
        cluster drive
          dependencies, 582
        cluster quorum
          configuration, 583
        patch management, 580

pausing and resuming cluster nodes, 580

family of operating systems, 22-23

firewalls

with advanced security, 375

creating rules, 376

hardening servers with Security Configuration Wizard, 348-349

preparing for nodes, 546

Reliability and Performance Monitor, 769

Data Collector Set, 775

Performance Monitor, 771-772

Performance Monitor settings, 774

Reliability Monitor, 774

Reports, 775

Resource Monitor, 770-771

Task Manager, 733-734

monitoring apps, 734

monitoring network performance, 736-737

monitoring performance, 736

monitoring processes, 735

monitoring services, 735

monitoring user activity, 737

Validate a Cluster Configuration Wizard, 493-494

virtualization, Hyper-V, 878-880

Windows Server 2008 R2 failover cluster, AlwaysOn Availability Groups, 493-495

Windows Server 2008 R2 Failover Cluster Quorum models, AlwaysOn Failover Cluster instances, 537

Windows Server 2008 R2 Server Core, installing, 54-55

Windows Server 2008 R2 SP1, installing as host operating system, 883

Windows Server Core

configuring

installation, 55-57

with SCONFIG, 56

hardening SQL Server installation, 348

installing SQL Server 2012, 53, 57-59

via command prompt, 58

launching command prompt, 56

Windows Server failover cluster, system views, 523

Windows Server Hyper-V, 876

Windows Update, 355

WITH GRANT option, 403

witness server, 592

witness server placement, database mirroring, 596

Wizard Actions page, 643

wizards

Copy Database Wizard, 181, 221-223, 636

Create Partition wizard, 165-167

Data Compression Wizard, 173-174

Database Maintenance Plan Wizard, creating maintenance plans, 792-798

Endpoint Security Wizard, 606

Import and Export Wizard, 181

Maintenance Plan Wizard, 267, 287, 805

New Availability Group Wizard, 497-502

validating and viewing results, 502-504

Security Configuration Wizard, hardening servers with, 348-349

Server Roles Wizard, 375

Validate a Cluster Configuration Wizard, 493-494, 550

workflow for Resource Governor, 843

workload groups

creating, 852-854, 859-860

explained, 841-842

workloads, 696

analyzing, 706-707

capturing, 703-706

X-Y-Z

XEvents, 718-719

catalog views, 723

creating with DDL statements, 720-723

DMVs, 723-724

terminology, 719-720

user interface, 724-726

XML indexes, 237

characteristics of, 241

XML Source, 185